Carolina Academic Press Context and Practice Series

Michael Hunter Schwartz
Series Editor

Administrative Law
Richard Henry Seamon

Advanced Torts
Alex B. Long and Meredith J. Duncan

Animal Law—New Perspectives on Teaching Traditional Law
Kathy Hessler, Joyce Tischler, Pamela Hart, and Sonia S. Waisman

Antitrust Law
Steven Semeraro

Civil Procedure
Gerald F. Hess, Theresa M. Beiner, and Scott R. Bauries

Civil Procedure for All States
Benjamin V. Madison, III

Complex Litigation
James M. Underwood

Constitutional Law, Second Edition
David Schwartz and Lori Ringhand

A Context and Practice Global Case File:
An Intersex Athlete's Constitutional Challenge,
Hastings v. USATF, IAAF, and IOC
Olivia M. Farrar

A Context and Practice Global Case File:
***v. Bryce*, An International Embryo and Surrogacy Dispute**
Olivia M. Farrar

A Context and Practice Global Case File:
***v. Lightfoot*, A Mother's International Hague Petition**
for the Return of Her Child
Olivia M. Farrar

Contracts, Second Edition
chael Hunter Schwartz and Adrian Walters

Property Law

Criminal Law
Steven I. Friedland, Catherine Carpenter,
Kami Chavis, and Catherine Arcabsacio

Current Issues in Constitutional Litigation, Second Edition
Sarah E. Ricks, with co-author Evelyn M. Tenenbaum

Employment Discrimination, Second Edition
Susan Grover, Sandra F. Sperino, and Jarod S. Gonzalez

Energy Law
Joshua P. Fershee

Evidence, Second Edition
Pavel Wonsowicz

International Business Transactions
Amy Deen Westbrook

International Women's Rights, Equality, and Justice
Christine M. Venter

The Lawyer's Practice
Kris Franklin

Professional Responsibility
Barbara Glesner Fines

Property Law
Alicia B. Kelly and Nancy J. Knauer

Sales, Second Edition
Edith R. Warkentine

Secured Transactions
Edith R. Warkentine and Jerome A. Grossman

Torts
Paula J. Manning

Workers' Compensation Law, Second Edition
Michael C. Duff

Your Brain and Law School
Marybeth Herald

Property Law

A Context and Practice Casebook

Alicia B. Kelly
Professor of Law,
Delaware Law School of Widener University

Nancy J. Knauer
Professor of Law,
Beasley School of Law, Temple University

Carolina Academic Press
Durham, North Carolina

ISBN 978-1-59460-499-7
Ebook ISBN 978-1-5310-0863-5
LCCN 2017950120

Carolina Academic Press, LLC
700 Kent Street
Durham, NC 27701
Telephone (919) 489-7486
Fax (919) 493-5668
www.caplaw.com

Printed in the United States of America

Contents

PART FOUR
Public Land Use Law

PART FIVE

Private Land Use Law: Servitudes

Table of Principal Cases

Series Editor's Preface

Welcome to a new type of casebook. Designed by leading experts in law school teaching and learning, Context and Practice casebooks assist law professors and their students to work together to learn, minimize stress, and prepare for the rigors and joys of practicing law. **Student learning and preparation for law practice are the guiding ethics of these books.**

Why would we depart from the tried and true? Why have we abandoned the legal education model by which we were trained? Because legal education can and must improve.

In Spring 2007, the Carnegie Foundation published *Educating Lawyers: Preparation for the Practice of Law* and the Clinical Legal Education Association published *Best Practices for Legal Education*. Both works reflect in-depth efforts to assess the effectiveness of modern legal education, and both conclude that legal education, as presently practiced, falls quite short of what it can and should be. Both works criticize law professors' rigid adherence to a single teaching technique, the inadequacies of law school assessment mechanisms, and the dearth of law school instruction aimed at teaching law practice skills and inculcating professional values. Finally, the authors of both books express concern that legal education may be harming law students. Recent studies show that law students, in comparison to all other graduate students, have the highest levels of depression, anxiety and substance abuse.

The problems with traditional law school instruction begin with the textbooks law teachers use. Law professors cannot implement *Educating Lawyers* and *Best Practices* using texts designed for the traditional model of legal education. Moreover, even though our understanding of how people learn has grown exponentially in the past 100 years, no law school text to date even purports to have been designed with educational research in mind.

The Context and Practice Series is an effort to offer a genuine alternative. Grounded in learning theory and instructional design and written with *Educating Lawyers* and *Best Practices* in mind, Context and Practice casebooks make it easy for law professors to change.

I welcome reactions, criticisms, and suggestions; my e-mail address is mschwartz@pacific.edu. Knowing the author(s) of these books, I know they, too, would appreciate your input; we share a common commitment to student learning. In fact, students, if your professor cares enough about your learning to have adopted this book, I bet s/he would welcome your input, too!

Michael Hunter Schwartz, Series Designer and Editor
Consultant, Institute for Law Teaching and Learning
Dean and Professor of Law, University of the Pacific,
McGeorge School of Law

PART ONE
Introduction to Property Law

Chapter 1

Introduction

Property law is influential in everyday life—impacting individuals, relationships, businesses, the economy and society. It mediates disputes and conflicts over the control of valued resources. It establishes the rights and responsibilities of owners, non-owners, and neighbors. In this course, you will explore what constitutes property and how one acquires property. You will also learn about different ways to structure property, including ways to share property and divide ownership or possession of property over time. A significant part of the casebook deals with land use restrictions that limit what an owner or a possessor can do with land. Some of these restrictions are in the form of laws that apply equally to all similarly situated landowners. These laws include nuisance laws, zoning laws, and the takings doctrine. The power of eminent domain authorizes the state to take property for a public use, subject to the constitutional requirement of "just compensation." Private land use restrictions, called servitudes, are agreements between and among landowners regarding the use of property that can bind future owners. This casebook also covers the special rules governing real estate transactions, including conveyancing and real estate finance. The following chart illustrates the organization of the casebook and the field of Property law.

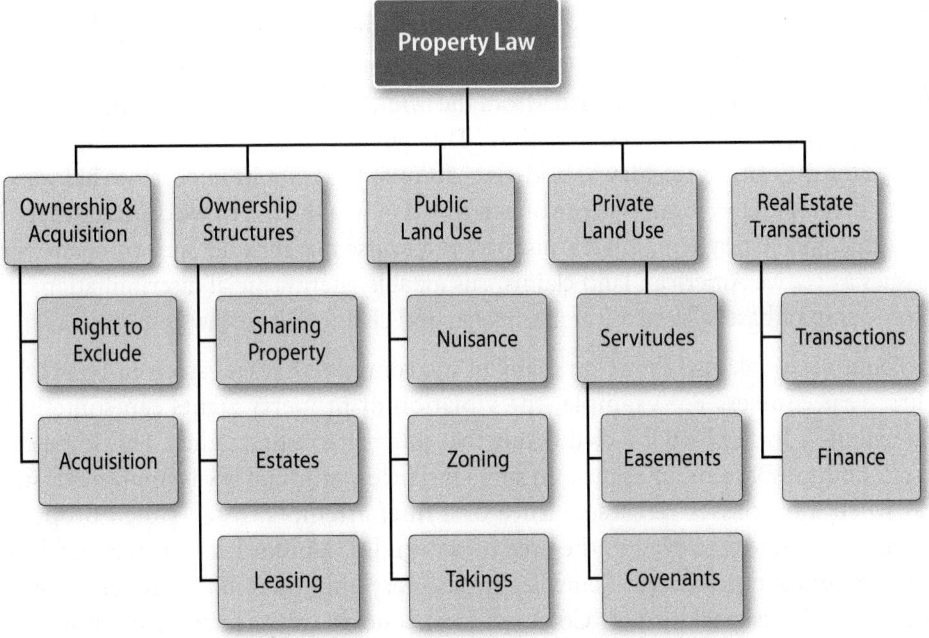

The Casebook

Property is a foundational course that has been a core part of the law school curriculum since the late 19th century when Dean Christopher Columbus Langdell of Harvard Law School popularized a required first-year curriculum that consisted of Civil Procedure, Contracts, Criminal Law, Torts—and Property. Today, Property remains part of the required first-year curriculum in practically all law schools in the United States, although schools differ with respect to the number of credit hours they allocate to the basic Property course. Some law schools have retained the traditional six-credit year-long course, whereas others offer Property as a three- or four-credit course usually in the Spring semester. The number of credit hours naturally affects the extent of the coverage of topics. This book is designed to accommodate a six-credit year-long course that typically will include a section on real estate transactions. It can also be used for a three- or four-credit course.

Even though Property has long been a staple of the law school curriculum, this textbook is likely to be different from others you will encounter. It has a lawyering practice orientation and in addition draws on best practices for student learning. The text continually places you in the role of a practitioner where you apply your learning by evaluating real world practice based problems and documents and also engage in professional identiy development. The book is structured to make learning easier and more effective by implementing proven instructional strategies, including explicit organization with clear explanation of law. Then, against this backdrop you dive into cases and statutes with framing questions up front, multiple methods of instruction, graphic organizers and illustrations, active learning exercises, and plentiful opportunities for practice, recursion and synthesis.

In addition, this casebook presents Property law and doctrine in contemporary terms and with real life applications. For example, traditional Property courses emphasized the estates in land system that dates from the Middle Ages and prescribes the ways that ownership can be structured over time. This system was of paramount importance when the majority of wealth was held in the form of land, but its importance has waned with statutory reforms and the rise of new forms of wealth. Today, we continue to teach the estates in land system, but it is just part of a course that includes such contemporary issues as Native American land claims, sustainable energy, racial discrimination, the ownership of baseballs, medical marijuana, and civil forfeiture laws.

Your casebook also draws on many of the concepts that you study in your other first-year courses. For example, the violation of property rights can sometimes constitute a tort, which is a civil wrong that causes harm to another. This is the case with both trespass and nuisance. In some instances, criminal law is implicated, such as when a trespasser refuses to leave or a thief attempts to sell stolen property. Contracts come into play in the area of servitudes, landlord-tenant relationships, and real estate transactions. Remedies are also very important in the property context and often have special rules. Constitutional concerns arise in connection with all zoning matters and, of course, with respect to the exercise of eminent domain. In addition, you will learn about procedural issues and the hierarchy of authority, including the distinction between common law and statutory law, the relative weight of federal, state, and local statutory authority, and the difference between state constitutions and the federal Constitution. The casebook also focuses on planning issues, problems, and professional development questions.

As a broad survey course, there is something for everyone in the first-year Property course. Whether you enjoy learning about the rules governing marital property or stolen artwork, the basic Property course will introduce you to many new topics and provide an important foundation for many upper level courses. These courses include: Environmental Law, Intellectual Property, Land Use Planning, Real Estate Transactions, Trusts & Estates, Estate Planning, Family Law, and even Political & Civil Rights.

Overview of Property Law

Property rights determine who controls valued resources and under what terms. In order to understand property law, it is important to unpack the different components of that sentence and consider each one: 1) the nature of property or "valued resources," 2) the extent of property rights, 3) the concept ownership or "control" of property, and 4) how we resolve competing claims to property.

Types of Property

Traditionally, property doctrine separated property into categories, which were subject to different rules. The first and most important distinction was between real property and personal property. Real property includes land and any improvement on the land, such as a building, that is also immovable. Personal property is everything that is not real property, meaning that it is movable. Within the category of personal property, there is a further distinction made between tangible and intangible property.

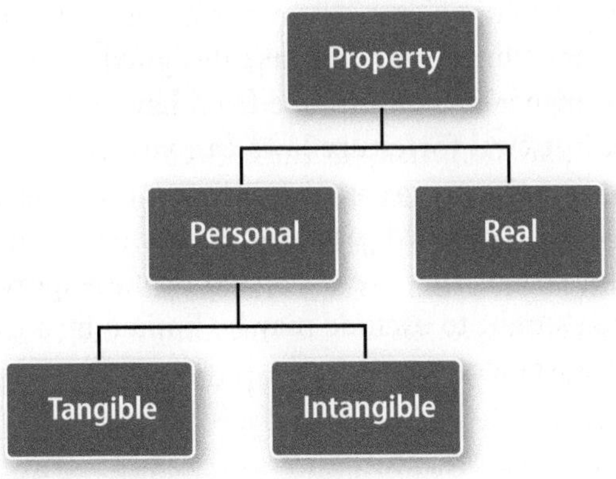

In this hierarchy of types of property, the room where you are sitting is considered real property, but if you look around the room, you will see many items of personal property, such as your computer, your book, a desk, a window, a water bottle. These items are all examples of tangible property—property that you can touch and feel. There are also many examples of intangible property: the software on your computer, the copyright for this book, the trademark for the brand of water. Intangible property is subject to being owned just like any other type of property, but it also subject to additional rules governing intellectual property.

Property Rights

Rights are sources of authority that are enforceable at law. Property rights can arise from private ordering through contract and agreement, such as the right of a tenant to sublet an apartment. They can also arise under public law, such as the right of a landowner to enjoin his neighbor if the neighbor interferes with his "quiet enjoyment." A key feature of property rights is that they are enforceable in a court of law, whether they are common law, statutory, or constitutional rights. Accordingly, rights differ from norms or customs that individuals may choose to follow, but may not be enforceable at law. For example, "space savers" are used in many cities after a large snow storm. After drivers shovel out their cars, they place a trash can or traffic cone in the spot to signal that it is taken. It is customary for other drivers to not park in a "saved" space, but a driver who has shoveled out a spot has no legally enforceable right to stop other drivers from parking in the spot.

When talking about property, we often focus on who owns the property, but the concept of ownership is really shorthand for a collection of property rights. These rights are: 1) the right to exclude, 2) the right to use, 3) the right to transfer, and 4) the right to be free from damage or takings. To illustrate these different rights, property is often described as a "bundle of sticks" with each right representing a separate stick. Throughout this course, you will explore the scope and limitations of the various property rights.

It is very important to remember that property rights are not absolute. For example, a property owner may have the right to use her property, but her neighbor also has the right to quiet enjoyment. An owner generally has the right to transfer property, but there are limitations that are designed to protect spouses from impoverishment. An owner is typically free from having his property confiscated by the government, but civil forfeiture laws can vest title in the state when the property is used for certain enumerated crimes, and eminent domain can take property for a public use, provided just compensation is paid. Accordingly, each right is subject to limitations that are expressed by corresponding rights held by others. Even an owner's right to exclude may be limited by a non-owner's right to access in certain circumstances.

Ownership

As noted above, when we say that you "own" something, it means that you possess a bunch or bundle of rights, each one of which is subject to certain limitations. There are a variety of ways that an individual can become an owner. One of the most common methods is when an owner transfers property by either purchase or gift. It goes without saying that an owner cannot transfer more than he owns. However, an owner can transfer less than he owns. A common example of this is when an owner leases his property to a tenant. An individual can also become an owner by creating or inventing property. Sometimes an individual may find property that is lost or unowned, and different rules apply to determine when a "finder" is actually a "keeper." A thief will generally not be considered an owner, and the true owner will typically be entitled to recoup stolen property. True owners must remain vigilant, because if they allow another to use their property for an extended period of time, they may lose their rights to property under the doctrine of adverse possession. Finally, a sovereign country may sometimes claim property through discovery or conquest.

Short of absolute ownership, there are many other ways that an individual can exert control over property. For example, if you rent your apartment, you have a right to possess and use the property, but you do not own it. The same would be true if you lease your car. A neighbor can require you to turn down your music or stop raising hogs if either activity impermissibly interferes with your neighbor's right to quiet enjoyment. When a non-owner acquires a right-of-way over the land of another, the owner of the land cannot obstruct or interfere with the non-owner's ingress or egress. Other servitudes, known as covenants and equitable servitudes, can empower neighbors to enforce land use restrictions. Local zoning laws mandate land use restrictions and prescribe what owners can and cannot do with their land. Ownership may also be shared, which is a common way for spouses and other family members to hold property.

Context Matters

Property disputes are necessarily relational, because in order to have a dispute, there must be at least two parties. In many instances, the context of the dispute will determine both the rules that are applied and the outcome. Sometimes the dispute is over who owns the property. Often the dispute involves an attempt to exert control over property, but not complete ownership. This would be the case in a trespass or nuisance action. The relationship between the parties is also important. For example, a neighbor who "came to the nuisance" may be barred in some states from asserting a nuisance claim. A spouse has certain property rights in the case of divorce or death, and family members are entitled to a decedent's property in the absence of a will. If you entrust property to certain merchants, you could lose title to the property. If you hold your property open to the general public, you could lose your right to exclude. The importance of context means that you must always pay careful attention to the facts and the relationships between and among the parties.

Property rights are constantly evolving to address new and previously unforeseen situations and challenges. The push for sustainable energy has led to conflicts and claims of nuisance between neighbors over solar panels and wind turbines. The prevalence of nonmarital partnerships has led to a re-evaluation of shared property rules. Home owner associations and condominiums have changed our residential living patterns. The frontiers of biotechnology and animal rights have made us question the very meaning of property. Laws serve human values. Accordingly, it is appropriate that they change and evolve with us.

PART TWO
Introduction to Ownership and Acquisition of Property

Chapter 2

Ownership and Acquisition

Introduction

This Chapter explores the original acquisition of property. It answers the question of how one becomes an owner and how the law mediates disputes over ownership. As discussed in the Introduction, the concept of ownership is shorthand for a collection of rights that are enforceable at law: 1) the right to exclude, 2) the right to use, 3) the right to transfer, 4) the right to be free from damage or takings. To illustrate these different rights, property is often described as a "bundle of sticks" with each right representing a separate stick. Throughout this course we will examine both the scope and limitations of the various rights because, as we will see, no property right is absolute. For example, Chapter 3 focuses on the right to exclude and the law of trespass, but it also considers the right of access of some non-owners to private property.

There are a variety of ways that an individual can become an owner. One of the most common methods is when an owner transfers property by either purchase or gift. It goes without saying that an owner cannot transfer more than he owns. However, you will learn in later chapters that it is possible to customize a transfer of property to enable an owner to transfer less than he owns. A common example of this is when an owner leases his property to a tenant. An individual can also become an owner by creating or inventing property. Sometimes an individual may find property that is lost or unowned, and different rules apply to determine when a "finder" is actually a "keeper." A thief will generally not be considered an owner, and the true owner will typically be entitled to recoup stolen property. True owners must remain vigilant, because if they allow another to use their property for an extended period of time, they may lose their rights to property under the doctrine of adverse possession. Finally, a sovereign country may sometimes claim property through discovery or conquest. This Chapter begins with a discussion of the property law governing the European colonization of North America.

Chapter Problem: Exercise 2-1

Whenever a snowstorm hits an urban area, the residents who park their cars on the streets share a special dread because they will have to shovel out their cars once the snow stops. Depending on the amount of snowfall, shoveling out a car can be a back-breaking all-day affair. Municipal snow plows often push snow into the newly cleared spots as they work to remove the snow from the streets.

Understandably, when it is time for residents to move their cars, they are often reluctant to relinquish the cleared spot. When they return, not only may someone else have parked in "their" spot, but they might not be able to find another spot that is both cleared and empty. To avoid this eventuality, it is common practice in some cities for residents to put "space savers" in the spot when they move their cars. Space savers are frequently lawn chairs or construction cones, although just about anything will work in a pinch.

The purpose of the space saver is to claim the spot and signal that no one else should park there. Of course, a parking space on a city street is public property, and individual residents cannot legally own a parking space on a public street. Still, most people respect "space savers" and will not park in a spot that has been so claimed. Individuals who violate a space saver have been known to experience retaliation and vandalism. Every year brings new stories of violence erupting over space savers.

Boston has long grappled with the question of space savers, which makes sense given that its average annual snowfall is 43.8 inches. The current policy allows residents to use space savers to hold a parking spot for up to 48 hours after the end of a snow emergency. After that time, city crews will remove any and all items used to save spots. After a record snowfall in 2015, however, the Mayor suspended the 48-hour policy and banned the use of space savers entirely. Some neighborhoods in Boston have also banned space savers.

As you read through this Chapter, think about why residents feel entitled to claim a parking spot after they shovel it out. What does a space saver signify? Why are they so widely respected? Do you think space savers should be banned or allowed? What do you think of Boston's 48-hour policy?

Overview of Chapter 2

In this Chapter, you will learn how courts determine competing claims of ownership and establish the chain of title. You will see that different rules apply to different types of owners and different rules also apply to different types of property. In order to sort through these various rules, it will be helpful to organize your reading around three basic questions: 1) What is the property? 2) Who claims ownership of the property? and 3) What is the basis of the ownership claim? If you remember to answer these questions for each of the cases, you will be prepared to engage the court's reasoning. For some cases, it will be a good idea to draw a map of the property in question in order to see the scope of the conflicting claims. In other instances, you may want to chart the chain of title or develop a time line in order to sort through the conflicting claims. A central concern in many of the cases is the passage of time and the related concept of reliance. How does the passage of time complicate ownership claims? As you work through the cases, be sure to identify the values underlying the ownership claim. What values are protected and advanced by property law? What values should be advanced by property law?

The Chapter is divided into five subunits:

1. Conquest and Discovery
2. Government Grant of Land
3. Possession, Labor, and Investment
4. Abandoned, Lost, and Mislaid Property
5. Adverse Possession and Related Concepts

Conquest and Discovery

It is fitting to begin the Chapter on Ownership with a discussion of the role of conquest and discovery in the allocation of property rights. Although everyone is familiar with the story of the "discovery" of the Western Hemisphere by the European colonial powers, this section examines the legal justifications provided by the common law that facilitated the colonization of the Americas. The legal doctrine known as Discovery affirmed the right of European sovereigns to appropriate land that had been used by native peoples for thousands of years. The doctrine of Discovery continues to have application in contemporary Native American land claims, many of which date back to the colonial period.

The general outlines of the story of discovery are well known. Seeking a western route to Asia and the spice trade, Christopher Columbus, who was acting as an agent of Spain, instead landed in 1492 in what is now The Bahamas. His successful voyage prompted other European sovereigns to follow suit as they raced to establish colonies in the Americas. The notion that Columbus "discovered" what became known as the "New World" is difficult to reconcile with the fact that the Americas were inhabited by indigenous peoples with diverse cultures, languages, and customs. Estimates of the pre-Columbian population of the land mass that is now the United States range from between 5 and 10 million. European colonization and immigration caused a precipitous decline in the native populations. Through the introduction of disease, war, and forced relocation, the number of Native Americans in the United States declined to only 200,000 by 1910.

The doctrine of Discovery provided a way to settle claims of ownership between and among competing nations. A claim of Discovery gave title to the government by whose subjects, or by whose authority, the claim was made. The title to the land was good against all other European governments. The title granted by Discovery was subject to the native peoples' right of occupancy that could be extinguished by the European sovereign by either purchase or conquest.

As a result of the American Revolution, the land owned by the British crown in the thirteen original colonies was ceded to the thirteen individual states. Much of that property was then ceded by the states to the United States government. As discussed later in this Chapter, the United States eventually distributed much of that land to individuals through a program of land sales. Accordingly, title to all property can be traced to a colonial power.

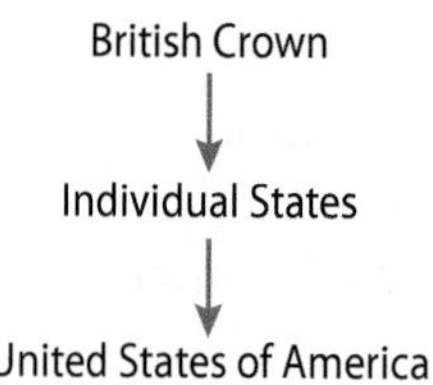

This simple chain of title that starts with a European colonial power, however, does not take into account the rights of Native Americans that were recognized by the doctrine of Discovery. Discovery did not simply eradicate the property rights of Native Americans. Instead, it created a "right to occupy," which only the government could extinguish through either purchase or conquest. This right was considerably less than full ownership and was designed to preserve what the European colonial powers considered to be the traditional land use patterns of Native Americans. In other words, Discovery did not divest the Native Americans of ownership, because the European colonial powers did not believe that the Native Americans had a valid claim of ownership over the land. This belief was justified by prevailing theories of property where ownership resulted from a particular type of land use and cultivation that the European powers believed were absent in Native American cultures.

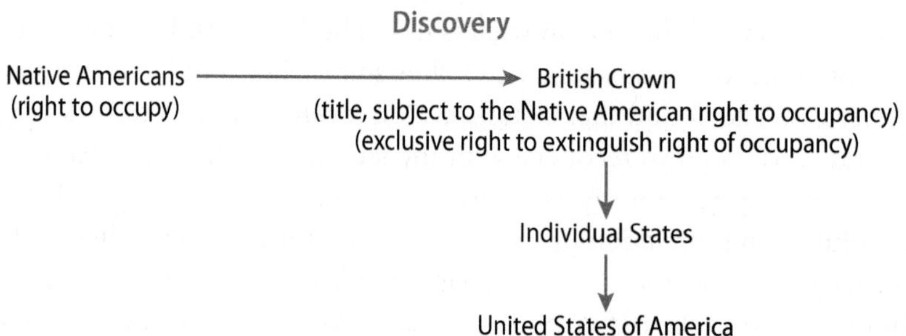

Article I, section 8 of the U.S. Constitution grants Congress the authority to regulate commerce with the "Indian Tribes." Beginning with the Non-Intercourse Act of 1790, Congress passed laws that restricted the ability of the states or individuals to purchase land directly from Native American tribes. The British had imposed similar laws. Despite these laws, individuals and states continued to enter into land transactions with Native American Tribes. In this section, we will see how courts viewed these transactions by examining two cases that are separated by over 180 years.

Exercise 2-2. *Johnson v. M'Intosh*—The "Courts of the Conqueror"

Johnson v. M'Intosh is one of the most famous cases involving Native American land rights. It is the first of three U.S. Supreme Court decisions authored by Chief Justice Marshall that established the legal and political status of Native American Tribes: *Johnson v. M'Intosh* (1823); *Cherokee Nation v. Georgia* (1831); *Worcester v. Georgia* (1832). The cases are known as the Marshall Trilogy.

Johnson v. M'Intosh is a challenging case to read because the facts are complicated and the language is archaic. As you read the case, be sure to answer our three basic questions:

1. What is the Property in Question?
2. Who claims ownership of the Property?
3. What is the basis of their claims?

It will also be helpful to jot down a time line. What is the chain of events that led the parties to seek relief through the courts? You will want to pay attention to the chain of title. Both Johnson and M'Intosh claim ownership of the property. Follow their individual claims back to the beginning using the chart set forth in the preceding section.

It is a basic tenet of property law that you can't sell what you don't own—just ask all those out-of-town tourists who thought they were buying the Brooklyn Bridge. For example, it goes without saying that if you are renting a house, you may be able to sublet or assign your lease, but you can't sell the house. If an investor pays you a handsome sum for the house and later records a deed purporting to transfer ownership, the investor is still not the owner, because he can only acquire what you can sell. You can't pass good title to the house because you can't sell more than you own. Moreover, you may be guilty of fraud. If you are the buyer or represent a buyer, it is important to do your due diligence and check the chain of title before entering into a transaction to make sure that the seller has clear title to the property that is not in any way encumbered or subject to competing claims. Think about these concerns as you consider the arguments presented in *Johnson v. M'Intosh.*

Johnson v. M'Intosh

21 U.S. 543 (1823)

Mr. Chief Justice MARSHALL delivered the opinion of the Court. The plaintiffs in this cause claim the land, in their declaration mentioned, under two grants, purporting to be made, the first in 1773, and the last in 1775, by the chiefs of certain Indian tribes, constituting the Illinois and the Piankeshaw nations; and the question is, whether this title can be recognised in the Courts of the United States?

The facts, as stated in the case agreed, show the authority of the chiefs who executed this conveyance, so far as it could be given by their own people; and likewise show, that the particular tribes for whom these chiefs acted were in rightful possession of the land they sold. The inquiry, therefore, is, in a great measure, confined to the power of Indians to give, and of private individuals to receive, a title which can be sustained in the Courts of this country.

As the right of society, to prescribe those rules by which property may be acquired and preserved is not, and cannot be drawn into question; as the title to lands, especially, is and must be admitted to depend entirely on the law of the nation in which they lie; it will be necessary, in pursuing this inquiry, to examine, not singly those principles of abstract justice, which the Creator of all things has impressed on the mind of his creature man, and which are admitted to regulate, in a great degree, the rights of civilized nations, whose perfect independence is acknowledged; but those principles also which our own government has adopted in the particular case, and given us as the rule for our decision.

On the discovery of this immense continent, the great nations of Europe were eager to appropriate to themselves so much of it as they could respectively acquire. Its vast extent offered an ample field to the ambition and enterprise of all; and the character and religion of its inhabitants afforded an apology for considering them as a people over whom the superior genius of Europe might claim an ascendency. The potentates of the old world found no difficulty in convincing themselves that they made ample compensation to the inhabitants of the new, by bestowing on them civilization and Christianity, in exchange for unlimited independence. But, as they were all in pursuit of nearly the same object, it was necessary, in order to avoid conflicting settlements, and consequent war with each other, to establish a principle, which all should acknowledge as the law by which the right of acquisition, which they all asserted, should be regulated as between themselves. This principle was, that discovery gave title to the government by whose subjects, or by whose authority, it was made, against all other European governments, which title might be consummated by possession.

The exclusion of all other Europeans, necessarily gave to the nation making the discovery the sole right of acquiring the soil from the natives, and establishing settlements upon it. It was a right with which no Europeans could interfere. It was a right which all asserted for themselves, and to the assertion of which, by others, all assented. Those relations which were to exist between the discoverer and the natives, were to be regulated by themselves. The rights thus acquired being exclusive, no other power could interpose between them. In the establishment of these relations, the rights of the original inhabitants were, in no instance, entirely disregarded; but were necessarily, to a considerable extent, impaired. They were admitted to be the rightful occupants of the soil, with a legal as well as just claim to retain possession of it, and to use it according to their own discretion; but their rights to complete sovereignty, as independent nations, were necessarily diminished, and their power to dispose of the soil at their own will, to whomsoever they pleased, was denied by the original fundamental principle, that discovery gave exclusive title to those who made it.

While the different nations of Europe respected the right of the natives, as occupants, they asserted the ultimate dominion to be in themselves; and claimed and exercised, as a consequence of this ultimate dominion, a power to grant the soil, while yet in possession of the natives. These grants have been understood by all, to convey a title to the grantees, subject only to the Indian right of occupancy. Thus, all the nations of Europe, who have acquired territory on this continent, have asserted in themselves, and have recognised in others, the exclusive right of the discoverer to appropriate the lands occupied by the Indians.

Have the American States rejected or adopted this principle?

By the treaty which concluded the war of our revolution, Great Britain relinquished all claim, not only to the government, but to the "propriety and territorial rights of the United States," whose boundaries were fixed in the second article. By this treaty, the powers of government, and the right to soil, which had previously been in Great Britain, passed definitively to these States. We had before taken possession of them, by declaring independence; but neither the declaration of independence, nor the treaty confirming it, could give us more than that which we before possessed, or to which Great Britain was before entitled. It has never been doubted, that either the United States, or the several States, had a clear title to all the lands within the boundary lines described in the treaty, subject only to the Indian right of occupancy, and that the exclusive power to extinguish that right, was vested in that government which might constitutionally exercise it.

The States, having within their chartered limits different portions of territory covered by Indians, ceded that territory, generally, to the United States, on conditions expressed in their deeds of cession, which demonstrate the opinion, that they ceded the soil as well as jurisdiction, and that in doing so, they granted a productive fund to the government of the Union. The lands in controversy lay within the chartered limits of Virginia, and were ceded with the whole country northwest of the river Ohio. This grant contained reservations and stipulations, which could only be made by the owners of the soil; and concluded with a stipulation, that "all the lands in the ceded territory, not reserved, should be considered as a common fund, for the use and benefit of such of the United States."

The ceded territory was occupied by numerous and warlike tribes of Indians; but the exclusive right of the United States to extinguish their title, and to grant the soil, has never, we believe, been doubted.

The United States, then, have unequivocally acceded to that great and broad rule by which its civilized inhabitants now hold this country. They hold, and assert in themselves, the title by which it was acquired. They maintain, as all others have maintained, that discovery gave an exclusive right to extinguish the Indian title of occupancy, either by purchase or by conquest; and gave also a right to such a degree of sovereignty, as the circumstances of the people would allow them to exercise.

We will not enter into the controversy, whether agriculturists, merchants, and manufacturers, have a right, on abstract principles, to expel hunters from the territory they possess, or to contract their limits. Conquest gives a title which the Courts of the conqueror cannot deny, whatever the private and speculative opinions of individuals may be, respecting the original justice of the claim which has been successfully asserted. The British government, which was then our government, and whose rights have passed to the United States, asserted a title to all the lands occupied by Indians, within the chartered limits of the British colonies. It asserted also a limited sovereignty over them, and the exclusive right of extinguishing the title which occupancy gave to them. These claims have been maintained and established as far west as the river Mississippi, by the sword. The title to a vast portion of the lands we now hold, originates in them. It is not for the Courts of this country to question the validity of this title, or to sustain one which is incompatible with it.

Although we do not mean to engage in the defence of those principles which Europeans have applied to Indian title, they may, we think, find some excuse, if not justification, in the character and habits of the people whose rights have been wrested from them.

The title by conquest is acquired and maintained by force. The conqueror prescribes its limits. Humanity, however, acting on public opinion, has established, as a general rule, that the conquered shall not be wantonly oppressed, and that their condition shall remain as eligible as is compatible with the objects of the conquest. Most usually, they are incorporated with the victorious nation, and become subjects or citizens of the government with which they are connected. The new and old members of the society mingle with each other; the distinction between them is gradually lost, and they make one people. Where this incorporation is practicable, humanity demands, and a wise policy requires, that the rights of the conquered to property should remain unimpaired; that the new subjects should be governed as equitably as the old, and that confidence in their security should gradually banish the painful sense of being separated from their ancient connexions, and united by force to strangers.

When the conquest is complete, and the conquered inhabitants can be blended with the conquerors, or safely governed as a distinct people, public opinion, which not even the conqueror can disregard, imposes these restraints upon him; and he cannot neglect them without injury to his fame, and hazard to his power. But the tribes of Indians inhabiting this country were fierce savages, whose occupation was war, and whose subsistence was drawn chiefly from the forest. To leave them in possession of their country, was to leave the country a wilderness; to govern them as a distinct people, was impossible, because they were as brave and as high spirited as they were fierce, and were ready to repel by arms every attempt on their independence.

What was the inevitable consequence of this state of things? The Europeans were under the necessity either of abandoning the country, and relinquishing their pompous claims to it, or of enforcing those claims by the sword, and by the adoption of principles adapted to the condition of a people with whom it was impossible to mix, and who could not be governed as a distinct society, or of remaining in their neighbourhood, and exposing themselves and their families to the perpetual hazard of being massacred.

Frequent and bloody wars, in which the whites were not always the aggressors, unavoidably ensued. European policy, numbers, and skill, prevailed. As the white population advanced, that of the Indians necessarily receded. The country in the immediate neighbourhood of agriculturists became unfit for them. The game fled into thicker and more unbroken forests, and the Indians followed. The soil, to which the crown originally claimed title, being no longer occupied by its ancient inhabitants, was parcelled out according to the will of the sovereign power, and taken possession of by persons who claimed immediately from the crown, or mediately, through its grantees or deputies.

That law which regulates, and ought to regulate in general, the relations between the conqueror and conquered, was incapable of application to a people under such circumstances. The resort to some new and different rule, better adapted to the actual state of things, was unavoidable.

However extravagant the pretension of converting the discovery of an inhabited country into conquest may appear; if the principle has been asserted in the first instance, and afterwards sustained; if a country has been acquired and held under it; if the property of the great mass of the community originates in it, it becomes the law of the land, and cannot be questioned. So, too, with respect to the concomitant principle, that the Indian inhabitants are to be considered merely as occupants, to be protected, indeed, while in peace, in the possession of their lands, but to be deemed incapable of transferring the absolute title to others. However this restriction may be opposed to natural right, and to the usages of civilized nations, yet, if it be indispensable to that system under which the country has been settled, and be adapted to the actual condition of the two people, it may, perhaps, be supported by reason, and certainly cannot be rejected by Courts of justice.

This opinion conforms precisely to the principle which has been supposed to be recognised by all European governments, from the first settlement of America. The absolute ultimate title has been considered as acquired by discovery, subject only to the Indian title of occupancy, which title the discoverers possessed the exclusive right of acquiring.

Another view has been taken of this question, which deserves to be considered. The title of the crown, whatever it might be, could be acquired only by a conveyance from the crown. If an individual might extinguish the Indian title for his own benefit, or, in other words, might purchase it, still he could acquire only that title. The person who purchases lands from the Indians, within their territory, incorporates himself with them, so far as respects the property purchased; holds their title under their protection, and subject to their laws. If they annul the grant, we know of no tribunal which can revise and set aside the proceeding. We know of no principle which can distinguish this case from a grant made to a native Indian, authorizing him to hold a particular tract of land in severalty.

As such a grant could not separate the Indian from his nation, nor give a title which our Courts could distinguish from the title of his tribe, as it might still be conquered from, or ceded by his tribe, we can perceive no legal principle which will authorize a Court to say, that different consequences are attached to this purchase, because it was made by a stranger. By the treaties concluded between the United States and the Indian nations, whose title the plaintiffs claim, the country comprehending the lands in controversy has been ceded to the United States, without any reservation of their title.

The Court is decidedly of opinion, that the plaintiffs do not exhibit a title which can be sustained in the Courts of the United States.

Judgment affirmed, with costs.

Exercise 2-3. *Johnson v. M'Intosh* Revisited

1. According to Chief Justice Marshall, what property rights did the Native Americans retain? Could an individual purchase Indian title?
2. Johnson, as the heir of a grantee, traces his claim of ownership back to 1775. Johnson's ancestor paid a hefty sum for the property in question. M'Intosh, on the other hand, paid the statutory minimum for the land and received a land grant from the federal government in 1818. If Johnson's ancestor was first in time and paid valuable consideration for the property, why does M'Intosh prevail? Did Johnson have any rights?
3. To add one more wrinkle to your chain of title chart, the British originally acquired the property in question from France as a consequence of the French and Indian War (1754–1763). By the 1763 Treaty of Paris, France ceded its North American possessions east of the Mississippi. Here's an updated chart. See if you can fill in 1) the dates, 2) how each of the transfers occurred (e.g., direct purchase, inheritance, land grant), and 3) the nature of the property interest (e.g., right to occupy, ownership, ownership subject to right to occupy).

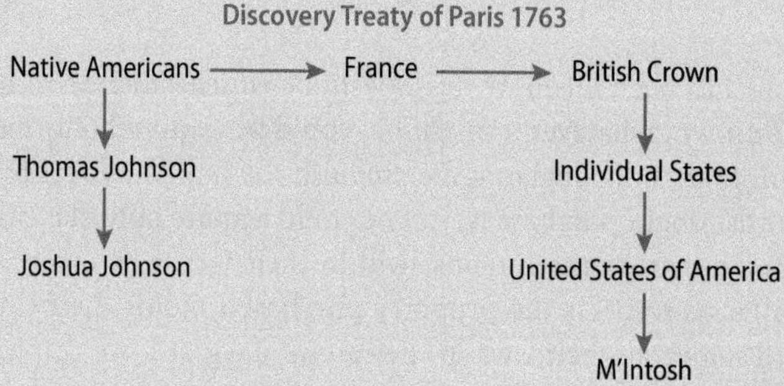

4. The Court offers several rationales for the doctrine of Discovery. The political philosopher John Locke advanced a natural law theory of property that informed the development of Anglo-American property law. In his *Second*

Treatise on Government published 1689, Locke presented a theory of private property that is referred to as the labor theory of property or the theory of first possession. Locke theorized that individual ownership was justified when a person took property out of a "state of nature" by mixing his labor with the soil. It is easy to see how this theory could be used to justify homesteading and the colonial settlement of North America. Simply put, an individual should have a right to the fruit of his labors. Can you point to instances in the decision where the Court seems to rely on this theory? Also, does it have implications for the space saver debate set forth in the Chapter Problem?

5. Did the conception of Native Americans as "fierce savages" who were unable to be "blended with the conquerors or safely governed as a separate people" also serve as a rationale for the doctrine of Discovery? Consider the following description of Native Americans as:

> fierce savages, whose occupation was war, and whose subsistence was drawn chiefly from the forest. To leave them in possession of their country, was to leave the country a wilderness; to govern them as a distinct people, was impossible, because they were as brave and as high spirited as they were fierce, and were ready to repel by arms every attempt on their independence.

Among other things, this description inaccurately portrays all Native Americans as "hunter-gatherers," whereas many Native American tribes had highly complex agricultural systems. Does this factual error undermine the doctrine of Discovery?

6. Chief Justice Marshall also introduces a healthy dose of pragmatism when he declares that "Conquest gives a title which the Courts of the conqueror cannot deny." He states that the Court "will not enter into the controversy" about theories of property and the effect of such "abstract principles" on ownership rights. He seems to be saying that the doctrine of Discovery exists because of the actions of the sovereign—not because of real or imagined land use patterns. Is Chief Justice Marshall asserting that "might makes right" or acknowledging the limits of the courts to determine political questions? Throughout the course, we will consider the effect of the passage of time on property rights. Are you persuaded by Chief Justice Marshall's argument?

> If the principle has been asserted in the first instance, and afterwards sustained; if a country has been acquired and held under it, if the property of the great mass of the community originates in it, it becomes the law of the land and cannot be questioned ... if it be indispensable to that system under which the country has been settled ... it certainly cannot be rejected by the courts.

Contemporary Native American Land Claims

The history of Native American land rights in the United States has been marred by cultural misunderstandings, profiteering, and exploitation. The common law doctrine of Discovery recognized that Native America tribes possessed a right to occupy that could be extinguished by the federal government by purchase or conquest. Until 1871, the federal government entered into treaties with Native American tribes that established property rights. Since then, the federal government has recognized Native American property rights through executive order and statute. As noted earlier, states and individuals are forbidden from dealing directly with Native American tribes.

In many instances, the agreements between the federal government and Native American tribes were not respected. Moreover, the various non-intercourse acts were often disregarded, as both individuals and states continued to engage in transactions with Native American tribes. Native Americans were denied access to the courts to address these shortcoming until 1966 when Congress passed a statute granting federal courts jurisdiction over civil actions brought by Native American tribes. Even then, further litigation was required to establish the right of Native American tribes to sue on their own behalf. As a result, the first contemporary Native American land claim suit asserting title to their ancestral lands was not filed in federal court until 1970.

Some of these contemporary land claims related to events that had occurred more than two hundred years ago. They raise an important question as to the effect of the passage of time on property rights. The length of time that had elapsed also gave rise to two defenses: the statute of limitations and the equitable claim of laches. A statute of limitation is a law that prescribes a certain amount of time within which a claim must be brought. It functions as a bright line rule. Failure to bring the claim within the allotted time will forever bar the action. The equitable doctrine of laches is governed by case law. It does not establish a set time limit, but rather asks what is fair. Under the doctrine of laches, an action may be barred if the plaintiff engaged in an unreasonable delay, which is usually expressed as a delay that caused a detriment to the defendant.

Exercise 2-4. *Cayuga v. Pataki*

In 1795 and 1809, the Cayuga Nation entered into treaties with the State of New York under which the State acquired the certain tribal land in exchange for money. The treaties were in clear violation of the Non-Intercourse Act of 1790, and they were never ratified by the federal government. The Cayuga filed suit in 1980, requesting that the Court "declare that plaintiffs are the owners of and have the legal and equitable title and the right of possession" to all of the land covered by the treaties. As explained above, Native American tribes did not begin to file land claims in federal court until 1970 because such claims had be barred by various jurisdictional hurdles.

As you read the following case, pay particular attention to the timeline. How long is too long when dealing with land claims? If the agreements between the Cayuga Nation and the State of New York are void, then what should be the result? In this case, the claim would disrupt the longstanding investment backed expectations of generations of residents who claim title through the State of New York. It would also disrupt a longstanding community. On the other hand, the wrong experienced by the Cayuga Nation is arguably compounded by the delay. How should the court balance these important and competing interests? Is this a case where two wrongs won't make a right?

Cayuga Indian Nation v. Pataki

413 F.3d 266 (2d Cir. 2005)

Cabranes, J. We are here confronted by land claims of historic vintage—the wrongs alleged occurred over two hundred years ago, and this action is itself twenty-five years old—which we must adjudicate against a legal backdrop that has evolved since the District Court's rulings. The United States District Court for the Northern District of New York determined (1) that treaties between the Cayuga Nation and the State of New York in 1795 and 1807 were not properly ratified by the federal government and were thus invalid under the Nonintercourse Act, 25 U.S.C. § 177; and (2) that none of defendants' other arguments barred plaintiffs' suit. After ruling in plaintiffs' favor on liability, the District Court conducted a jury trial on damages, which resulted in a verdict for plaintiffs of approximately $36.9 million, representing the current fair market value of the land as well as fair rental value damages for 204 years. The District Court then concluded, following a month-long hearing, that plaintiffs were entitled to about $211 million in prejudgment interest, resulting in a total award of $247,911,999.42.

In another case raising land claims stemming from late-eighteenth-century treaties between Indian tribes and the State of New York, the Supreme Court recently ruled that equitable doctrines—such as laches, acquiescence, and impossibility—can be applied to Indian land claims in appropriate circumstances. *See City of Sherrill v. Oneida Indian Nation,* 544 U.S. 197 (2005). Based on *Sherrill,* we conclude that the possessory land claim alleged here is the type of claim to which a laches defense can be applied. [W]e further conclude that plaintiffs' claim is barred by laches. Accordingly, we reverse the judgment of the District Court and enter judgment for defendants.

Because of the disposition we reach here, we need not describe in great detail the long history of relations between the Cayuga Nation and the State of New York. We set forth below a concise description of the events underlying this lawsuit, as well as a more extended recounting of the case's procedural history.

Plaintiffs allege that from time immemorial until the late eighteenth century the Cayuga Nation owned and occupied approximately three million acres of land in what is now New York State, a swath of land approximately fifty miles wide that runs from Lake Ontario to the Pennsylvania border. This action involves 64,015 acres of that land, encompassing the Cayuga's "Original Reservation," as set forth in a treaty with the State of New York, concluded on February 25, 1789 ("1789 Treaty"). In the 1789 Treaty, the Cayugas ceded all of their lands to New York, except the lands designated as the "Original Reservation," which consists of lands on the eastern and western shores of the northern end of Cayuga Lake.

Congress passed the first Indian Trade and Intercourse Act, known as the "Nonintercourse Act," in 1790, pursuant to Congress's power under Article I, Section 8, clause 3 of the Constitution. As the Supreme Court described it, "the Act bars sales of tribal land without the acquiescence of the Federal Government." *Sherrill, supra.* Successive versions of the Act have been continuously in force from that time to the present day. On November 11, 1794, the Six Iroquois Nations entered the Treaty of Canandaigua with the United States. This treaty acknowledged the Original Reservation the Cayugas retained in the 1789 Treaty with New York, and promised the Cayugas that the land would remain theirs until they "chose to sell the same to the people of the United States who have the right to purchase." On June 16, 1795, William Bradford, then Attorney General of the United States, issued an opinion concluding that, under the 1793 version of the Nonintercourse Act, no Indian land sale was valid, nor could the land claims of the Six Iroquois Nations be extinguished, except pursuant to a treaty entered into by the Federal Government.

On July 27, 1795, the Cayuga entered into a treaty with the State of New York in which the State acquired the entire Original Reservation of the Cayugas (except for a three-square-mile-area on the eastern shore of Cayuga Lake) in exchange for a promise that the State pay the Cayuga Nation $1,800 annually in perpetuity. Although there is some debate about whether a federal official who signed the treaty as a witness was acting in a personal or official capacity, it is undisputed that this treaty was never explicitly ratified by a treaty of the Federal Government. In 1807, the State of New York purchased the Cayugas' remaining three-square-mile-parcel for $4,800. Again, the Federal Government never explicitly ratified this treaty.

Many years later, on November 19, 1980, the Tribe filed its complaint in this action, alleging these facts and requesting that the Court "declare that plaintiffs are the owners of and have the legal and equitable title and the right of possession" to all of the land in the Original Reservation and that the Court "restore plaintiffs to immediate possession of all portions of the subject land claimed by any defendant or member of the defendant class and eject any defendant claiming their chain of title through the 1795 and 1807 New York State 'treaties.'"

In separate opinions in 1991, the District Court rejected defendants' remaining defenses of abandonment and laches. *Cayuga Indian Nation v. Cuomo*, 758 F. Supp. 107 (N.D.N.Y. 1991) ("*Cayuga IV*"); *Cayuga Indian Nation v. Cuomo*, 771 F. Supp. 19 (N.D.N.Y. 1991) ("*Cayuga V*"). [In *Cayuga VI*], [t]he Court determined that the "1794 Treaty of Canandaigua conferred recognized title to the Cayugas concerning the land at issue" and that "proof of the plaintiffs' physical abandonment of the property at issue is irrelevant in a claim for land based upon reserved title to Indian land, for such title can only be extinguished by an act of Congress." With regard to laches, the District Court concluded [in *Cayuga V*] that Second Circuit precedent was clear that "claims brought by Indian tribes in general, including the plaintiffs herein, should be held by courts to be timely, and therefore not barred by laches, if, at the very least, such a suit would have been timely if the same had been brought by the United States." The Court thus found plaintiffs' action timely.

The Supreme Court's recent decision in *City of Sherrill v. Oneida Indian Nation*, has dramatically altered the legal landscape against which we consider plaintiffs' claims. *Sherrill* concerned claims by the Oneida Indian Nation, another of the Six Iroquois Nations, that its "acquisition of fee title to discrete parcels of historic reservation land revived the Oneidas' ancient sovereignty piecemeal over each parcel" and that, consequently, the Tribe need not pay property taxes to the City of Sherrill. The Supreme Court rejected this claim, concluding that "the Tribe cannot unilaterally revive its ancient sovereignty, in whole or in part, over the parcels at issue."

We understand *Sherrill* to hold that equitable doctrines, such as laches, acquiescence, and impossibility, can, in appropriate circumstances, be applied to Indian land claims, even when such a claim is legally viable and within the statute of limitations. "The distance from 1805 to the present day, the Oneidas' long delay in seeking equitable relief against New York or its local units, and developments in the city of Sherrill spanning several generations, evoke the doctrines of laches, acquiescence, and impossibility, and render inequitable the piecemeal shift in governance this suit seeks unilaterally to initiate."

The Court's characterizations of the Oneidas' attempt to regain sovereignty over their land indicate that what concerned the Court was the disruptive nature of the claim itself. "We decline to project redress for the Tribe into the present and future, thereby disrupting the governance of central New York's counties and towns." ..."This long lapse of time, during which the Oneidas did not seek to revive their sovereign control through equitable relief in court, and the attendant dramatic changes in the character of the properties, preclude [the Tribe] from gaining the disruptive remedy it now seeks." ..."[The Oneidas'] claim concerns grave, but ancient, wrongs, and the relief available must be commensurate with that historical reality." Although we recognize that the Supreme Court did not identify a formal standard for assessing when these equitable defenses apply, the broadness of the Supreme Court's statements indicates to us that *Sherrill*'s holding is not narrowly limited to claims identical to that brought by the Oneidas, seeking a revival of sovereignty, but rather, that these equitable defenses apply to "disruptive" Indian land claims more generally. While the equitable remedy sought in *Sherrill*—a reinstatement of Tribal sovereignty—is not at issue here, this case involves comparably disruptive claims, and other, comparable remedies *are* in fact at issue.

Despite the eventual award by the District Court of monetary damages, we emphasize that plaintiffs' claim is and has always been one sounding in ejectment; plaintiffs have asserted a continuing right to immediate possession as the basis of all of their claims, and have always sought ejectment of the current landowners as their preferred form of relief. As noted above, in their complaint in this case the Cayugas seek "immediate possession" of the land in question and ejectment of the current residents. Indeed, the District Court noted early in the litigation that it was "clear" that the complaint "presents a possessory claim, basically in ejectment." Plaintiffs continue to maintain, on appeal in this Court, that ejectment is their preferred remedy. It was not until 1999, nineteen years after the complaint was filed, and eight years after the District Court's decision on liability, that the District Court determined that the ejectment remedy sought by the Cayugas was, "to put it mildly, ... not an appropriate remedy in this case." The District Court thus effectively "monetized" the ejectment remedy in concluding that "monetary damages will produce results which are as satisfactory to the Cayugas as those which they could properly derive from ejectment."

The nature of the claim as a "possessory claim," as characterized by the District Court, underscores our decision to treat this claim like the tribal sovereignty claims in *Sherrill*. Under the *Sherrill* formulation, this type of possessory land claim—seeking possession of a large swath of central New York State and the ejectment of tens of thousands of landowners—is indisputably disruptive. Indeed, this disruptiveness is inherent in the claim itself—which asks this Court to overturn years of settled land ownership—rather than an element of any particular remedy which would flow from the possessory land claim. Accordingly, we conclude that possessory land claims of this type are subject to the equitable considerations discussed in *Sherrill*.

Inasmuch as the instant claim, a possessory land claim, is subject to the doctrine of laches, we conclude that the present case must be dismissed because the same considerations that doomed the Oneidas' claim in *Sherrill* apply with equal force here. These considerations include the following: "generations have passed during which non-Indians have owned and developed the area that once composed the Tribe's historic reservation," *Sherrill, supra*; "at least since the middle years of the 19th century, most of the [Tribe] have resided elsewhere," *id.*; "the longstanding, distinctly non-Indian character of the area and its inhabitants," *id.*; "the distance from 1805 to the present day," *id.* at 1494; "the [Tribe's] long delay in seeking equitable relief against New York or its local units," *id.*; and "developments in [the area] spanning several generations." *Id.* "[T]his Court has recognized the impracticability of returning to Indian control land that generations earlier passed into numerous private hands." *Id.* "It is impossible ... to rescind the cession and restore the Indians to their former rights because the lands have been opened to settlement and large portions of them are now in the possession of innumerable innocent purchasers...." We thus hold that the doctrine of laches bars the possessory land claim presented by the Cayugas here. "Thus, even though some delay on the part of the Cayugas is explainable, in the context of determining whether ejectment is an appropriate remedy, ... the delay factor tips decidedly in favor of the defendants." *Id.*

To summarize: the import of *Sherrill* is that "disruptive," forward-looking claims, a category exemplified by possessory land claims, are subject to equitable defenses, including laches. Insofar as the Cayugas' claim in the instant case is unquestionably a possessory land claim, it is subject to laches.

Although we conclude that plaintiffs' ejectment claim is barred by laches, we must also consider whether their other claims, especially their request for trespass damages in the amount of the fair rental value of the land for the entire period of plaintiffs' dispossession, are likewise subject to dismissal. In assessing these claims, we must recognize that the trespass claim, like all of plaintiffs' claims in this action, is predicated entirely upon plaintiffs' possessory land claim, for the simple reason that there can be no trespass unless the Cayugas possessed the land in question. Inasmuch as plaintiffs' trespass claim is based on a violation of their constructive possession, it follows that plaintiffs' inability to secure relief on their ejectment claim alleging constructive possession forecloses plaintiffs' trespass claim. In other words, because plaintiffs are barred by laches from obtaining an order conferring possession in ejectment, no basis remains for finding such constructive possession or immediate right of possession as could support the damages claimed. Because the trespass claim, like plaintiffs' other requests for relief, depends on the possessory land claim, a claim we have found subject to laches, we dismiss plaintiffs' trespass claim, and plaintiffs' other remaining claims, along with the plaintiffs' action in ejectment.

The judgment of the District Court is REVERSED and judgment is entered for defendants.

Exercise 2-5. *Cayuga v. Pataki* Revisited

1. The court ruled the plaintiffs' claims were barred by the equitable doctrine of laches. Unlike a statute of limitations, laches does not set a bright line rule regarding when a claim must be filed. Instead, the length of time that is too long will depend on the circumstances and the equities of the situation. A statute of limitations provides an element of certainty, whereas laches is designed to promote fairness. How well do you think the court did in promoting fairness?
2. Were you persuaded by the court's finding that the claim would be "disruptive"? Aren't all legal claims disruptive, especially when they involve claims for ejectment? Are money damages disruptive?
3. Once the court determined that the possessory claim was barred by laches, it dismissed all related claims for trespass and for back rent. Do you agree with the court's all-or-nothing reasoning? Could you fashion a remedy that would address the wrong asserted by the Cayuga Nation?
4. Why does the court analyze the claim as one of possession when the District Court had decided that ejectment was not an appropriate remedy?

5. Do you agree when the court states "the broadness of the Supreme Court's statements indicates to us that *Sherrill*'s holding is not narrowly limited to claims identical to that brought by the Oneidas, seeking a revival of sovereignty, but rather, that these equitable defenses apply to 'disruptive' Indian land claims more generally."

Reparations and Restitution

Reparations are a political remedy to address property claims and civil rights abuses. Internationally, they have been used as a form of post-conflict transitional justice. Domestically, the United States has awarded reparations to the Japanese Americans who were interned and lost property during World War II. Canada has paid reparations to aboriginal Canadian children who were forcibly removed from their homes and sent to church-run Indian residential schools. There has also been a renewed interest in reparations for the Atlantic slave trade.

Restitution is an equitable remedy that courts employ to avoid unjust enrichment when there is no remedy at law. It is primarily used in the area of contracts, but has also been applied in criminal law where a defendant may be ordered to make restitution to the victim or to society. In the case of contracts, restitution could be ordered where the plaintiff cannot recover under the contract, but the defendant has committed a wrong and unjustly benefitted from that wrong. Restitution is designed to make the plaintiff whole for his loss and divest the defendant of his unjust gain.

In *Johnson v. M'Intosh*, Chief Justice Marshall acknowledged that there were limits to what the courts could accomplish when he wrote "Conquest gives a title which the Courts of the conqueror cannot deny." Similarly, the court in *Cayuga v. Pataki* dismissed the claim brought by the Cayuga Nation not on its merits, but because it would be too disruptive. Reparations are a political solution that can address longstanding and systemic wrongs that may otherwise be beyond the power of courts to remedy. Land claims brought in court involve issues of ownership, trespass, back rent, and other claims related to possession. Reparations, however, represent an official acknowledgement of responsibility and a commitment to redress and repair the harm. Reparations may include restitution for lost property, as well as compensation, rehabilitation, and guarantees that future harm will not occur.

Some of the most well-known reparation schemes relate to World War II-era atrocities and property seizures. For example, Germany is still paying annual restitution for the Jewish slave labor and property confiscated in the Holocaust. As of 2015, it had paid over $89 billion in claims. Other Western European countries also implemented reparations through legislation. During the Cold War, however, such relief was generally not forthcoming from the former Soviet Union or its satellite countries. The situation changed with the fall of communism in 1989. Many countries in Central and Eastern Europe have since enacted legislation to deal with World War

II property claims. Some descendants of Russian aristocracy have even argued for restitution for property confiscated during the Russian Revolution of 1917.

If you think that the Russian Revolution seems too long ago, it bears mentioning that in 2010, a member of the Canadian parliament half-jokingly instigated legislation that called for the return of property confiscated at the end of the American Revolution from loyalists, consisting of great swaths of the U.S. Eastern seaboard. More recently, the Cuban revolution of 1959 has also spurred claims for property confiscated by the state. With the normalization of diplomatic relations between the U.S. and Cuba, the U.S. has made the resolution of property claims by U.S. citizens and companies a priority. Cuban exiles who were not American citizens when their property was confiscated will have to negotiate directly with the Cuban government.

Government Grant of Land

The United States acquired vast tracts of land from European colonial powers that had claimed titled through Discovery. The 1803 Louisiana Purchase doubled the size of the young nation. By 1850, the United States held title to 1.2 billion acres. As a matter of policy, the United States chose to distribute the public land to individual landowners. The vision of the yeoman farmer was central to Jeffersonian democracy and republican values. A nation of small landowners was thought to provide an important check on the power of the central government. Over the years, the United States experimented with a variety of methods to distribute the land and encourage western expansion, including land sales and outright gifts.

Prior to the ratification of the Constitution, the Land Ordinance of 1785 established the systematic process by which the United States would distribute its public lands to individual owners. The Ordinance called for an official survey that would be completed prior to settlement. The land was to be divided into townships that were six miles square, and each township was further divided into 36 one mile square sections of 640 acres each that would be sold at public auction. A central section was reserved for public education. The Northwest Ordinance of 1787 set forth the guidelines for local governance.

In some instances, settlers did not wait for the formal survey before staking their claims and working the land. These settlers did not have legal title to the land and were considered "squatters." The squatters disrupted the orderly settlement of the western lands and often interfered with the official land sales. They organized more than 100 land claim societies that were extra-legal organizations designed to protect their interests. Congress recognized the rights of squatters in 1841 with the passage of the Preemption Act. It gave squatters the right to purchase up to 160 acres of land at a reduced rate prior to the public sale, provided they met certain requirements.

The Homestead Act of 1862 represented a shift in policy. It gave settlers who had lived on the land for five years or more the right to obtain up to 160 acres of public land for free. In order to qualify, an individual had to be twenty-one years of age or the head of a household. The homesteader had to be a citizen or have declared an intention to become a citizen. Women were eligible. African Americans were also eligible after the passage of the Fifteenth Amendment to the U.S. Constitution in 1868 invalidated the infamous U.S. Supreme Court decision of *Dred Scot v. Sanford*, 60 U.S. 393 (1857), that declared African Americans were not citizens regardless of whether they were enslaved. The federal government granted 1.6 million homesteads between 1862 and 1934 and transferred 270,000,000 acres of public land to private ownership. The land distributed through the homestead program represented 10% of all land in the United States. The Federal Land Policy and Management Act of 1976 repealed the Homestead Act in the 48 contiguous states, but it granted a ten-year extension on claims in Alaska. Accordingly, homesteading officially ended in the United States in 1986.

In 1862 Congress also passed the first of the Pacific Railroad Acts. The legislation provided both land and loan subsidies for the completion of the intercontinental railroad that would link California to the East. The 1862 Act provided that the railroads would receive 6,400 acres of public land for each mile of track completed. It is estimated that the railroads received a total of 170,000,000 acres of public land. The railroads then sold the land to private settlers at a profit in order to finance the construction of the railroad.

That same year Congress approved another land giveaway that was designed to subsidize an important civic improvement. The Morrill Act of 1862 used public land to fund a system of higher education, known as land-grant colleges. Under the Act, the federal government transferred to each state 30,000 acres of public land for each member of its Congressional delegation. The land was then sold by the states to fund the creation of public colleges. Over seventy institutions of higher education were created from the funds generated by the Morrill Act of 1862 and subsequent legislation. The majority of the land-grant colleges are public colleges and universities such as Clemson University, the University of Wisconsin at Madison, Penn State University, and Ohio State. However, some private institutions, such as Cornell University and the Massachusetts Institute of Technology, also began as land-grant colleges.

Possession, Labor, and Investment

The prior section discussed the role of the government in the distribution and recognition to property rights. Under the doctrine of Discovery, a government was able to claim title to property, but the same right was not afforded to individuals. This section asks when individuals can claim ownership to property. According to the Lockean theories of property, ownership rights arise when an individual mixes his or her labor with the land. This view was reflected in the 19th century legislation recognizing the rights of squatters and the Homestead Acts, both of which rewarded individuals who improved the land and took it out of "the state of nature."

This section shifts the focus from land to consider ownership of other types of property. Land is referred to a "real property," perhaps recognizing the historical importance of land as both a resource and a form of wealth. Property, however, can take many forms other than land. In the following readings, we will study the ownership of wild animals, baseballs, natural resources, and intellectual property. Property other than land is referred to as personal property. It can be divided into tangible personal property and intangible personal property. Tangible personal property is generally things that you can touch or move. Both the wild animal and the baseball qualify as tangible property. Intangible personal property, as its name suggests, is incorporeal. It includes copyrights, patents, and trademarks. It also includes money, and other investments, even though they might have a physical representation in the form of a stock certificate or a dollar bill.

In this section, we will examine when the law will reward labor and investment. Under what circumstances will the law recognize ownership rights in personal property? Is it sufficient to have possession of an item or is something more required? What level of labor is sufficient? When does the law seek to protect reasonable investment backed expectations? In addition to legal doctrine, we will also consider the institutional role of the courts. Are there some matters that are best left to the legislature? We will also consider the different ways that courts fashion legal rules. Some judges will impose a bright line rule, whereas other prefer a flexible standard. As you read through the materials, consider which judicial approach you prefer.

Capture and Wild Animals

Exercise 2-6. *Pierson v. Post*—"Beware the Saucy Intruder"

Pierson v. Post is a classic case that has been entertaining first-year law students for generations. Although it is ostensibly about a squabble over who owns the carcass of a deceased fox, the case reveals just as much about judicial temperament and the nature of legal rules as it does about the law of wild animals.

When approaching a complicated case like this, be sure to answer our three central questions:

1. What is the Property in question?
2. Who claims ownership of the Property?
3. What is the basis of their claims?

This case presents both a majority and a dissenting opinion. Accordingly, it gives you the opportunity to see two very different ways of resolving the conflict. Pay attention to the differences between the two opinions and ask yourself which opinion more closely aligns with your view of justice and fairness.

Both judges liberally incorporate Latin phrases and maxims in their opinions, such as *ferae naturae* and *mortuis nil nisi bonum.* The Latin words and phrases are in italics so you won't miss them. Be sure to look them up as you read the case. Also, both judges refer to ancient legal commentators, although one judge relies on them more than the other. You should also look up the commentators and familiarize yourself with the authority relied on (or not) in the opinions. Are you surprised these commentators exerted such a strong influence over the development of American law?

Pierson v. Post

3 Caines Reporter 175 (N.Y. 1805)

THIS was an action of trespass on the case commenced in a justice's court, by the present defendant against the now plaintiff.

The declaration stated that Post, being in possession of certain dogs and hounds under his command, did, "upon a certain wild and uninhabited, unpossessed and waste land, called the beach, find and start one of those noxious beasts called a fox," and whilst there hunting, chasing and pursuing the same with his dogs and hounds, and when in view thereof, Pierson, well knowing the fox was so hunted and pursued, did, in the sight of Post, to prevent his catching the same, kill and carry it off. A verdict having been rendered for the plaintiff below, the defendant there sued out a certiorari, and now assigned for error, that the declaration and the matters therein contained were not sufficient in law to maintain an action.

Tompkins, J. This cause comes before us on a return to a certiorari directed to one of the justices of Queens County.

The question submitted by the counsel in this cause for our determination is, whether Lodowick Post, by the pursuit with his hounds in the manner alleged in his declaration, acquired such a right to, or property in, the fox as will sustain an action against Pierson for killing and taking him away?

The cause was argued with much ability by the counsel on both sides, and presents for our decision a novel and nice question. It is admitted that a fox is an animal *ferae naturae*, and that property in such animals is acquired by occupancy only. These admissions narrow the discussion to the simple question of what acts amount to occupancy, applied to acquiring right to wild animals.

If we have recourse to the ancient writers upon general principles of law, the judgment below is obviously erroneous. Justinian's Institutes, and Fleta, adopt the principle, that pursuit alone vests no property or right in the huntsman; and that even pursuit, accompanied with wounding, is equally ineffectual for that purpose, unless the animal be actually taken. The same principle is recognized by Breton.

Puffendorf defines occupancy of beasts *ferae naturae*, to be the actual corporeal possession of them, and Bynkershock is cited as coinciding in this definition. It is indeed with hesitation that Puffendorf affirms that a wild beast mortally wounded or greatly maimed, cannot be fairly intercepted by another, whilst the pursuit of the person inflicting the wound continues. The foregoing authorities are decisive to show that mere pursuit gave Post no legal right to the fox, but that he became the property of Pierson, who intercepted and killed him.

It, therefore, only remains to inquire whether there are any contrary principles or authorities, to be found in other books, which ought to induce a different decision. Most of the cases which have occurred in England, relating to property in wild animals, have either been discussed and decided upon the principles of their positive statute regulations, or have arisen between the huntsman and the owner of the land upon which beasts *ferae naturae* have been apprehended; the former claiming them by title of occupancy, and the latter *ratione soli*. Little satisfactory aid can, therefore, be derived from the English reporters.

Barbeyrac, in his notes on Puffendorf, does not accede to the definition of occupancy by the latter, but, on the contrary, affirms that actual bodily seizure is not, in all cases, necessary to constitute possession of wild animals. He does not, however, describe the acts which, according to his ideas, will amount to an appropriation of such animals to private use, so as to exclude the claims of all other persons, by title of occupancy, to the same animals; and he is far from averring that pursuit alone is sufficient for that purpose. To a certain extent, and as far as Barbeyrac appears to me to go, his objections to Puffendorf's definition of occupancy are reasonable and correct.

That is to say, that actual bodily seizure is not indispensable to acquire right to, or possession of, wild beasts; but that, on the contrary, the mortal wounding of such beasts, by one not abandoning his pursuit, may, with the utmost propriety, be deemed possession of him; since thereby the pursuer manifests an unequivocal intention of appropriating the animal to his individual use, has deprived him of his natural liberty, and brought him within his certain control. So, also, encompassing and securing such animals with nets and toils, or otherwise intercepting them in such a manner as to deprive them of their natural liberty, and render escape impossible, may justly be deemed to give possession of them to those persons who, by their industry and labor, have used such means of apprehending them. Barbeyrac seems to have adopted and had in view in his notes, the more accurate opinion of Grotius, with respect to occupancy. That celebrated author, speaking of occupancy, proceeds thus: "*Requiritur autem corporalis quoedam possessio ad dominium adipiscendum; atque ideo, vulnerasse non sufficit.*" But in the following section he explains and qualifies this definition of occupancy: "*Sed possessio illa potest non solis manibus, sed instrumentis, ut decipulis, ratibus, laqueis dum duo adsint; primum ut ipsa instrumenta sint in nostra potestate, deinde ut fera, ita inclusa sit, ut exire inde nequeat.*" This qualification embraces the full extent of Barbeyrac's objection to

Puffendorf's definition, and allows as great a latitude to acquiring property by occupancy, as can reasonably be inferred from the words or ideas expressed by Barbeyrac in his notes. The case now under consideration is one of mere pursuit, and presents no circumstances or acts which can bring it within the definition of occupancy by Puffendorf, or Grotius, or the ideas of Barbeyrac upon that subject.

[Other cases are] clearly distinguishable from the present; inasmuch as there the action was for maliciously hindering and disturbing the plaintiff in the exercise and enjoyment of a private franchise; and in the report of the same case [the judge] states, that the ducks were in the plaintiff's decoy pond, and so in his possession, from which it is obvious the court laid much stress in their opinion upon the plaintiff's possession of the ducks, *ratione soli.*

We are the more readily inclined to confine possession or occupancy of beasts *ferae naturae*, within the limits prescribed by the learned authors above cited, for the sake of certainty, and preserving peace and order in society. If the first seeing, starting or pursuing such animals, without having so wounded, circumvented or ensnared them, so as to deprive them of their natural liberty, and subject them to the control of their pursuer, should afford the basis of actions against others for intercepting and killing them, it would prove a fertile source of quarrels and litigation.

However uncourteous or unkind the conduct of Pierson towards Post, in this instance, may have been, yet this act was productive of no injury or damage for which a legal remedy can be applied. We are of opinion the judgment below was erroneous, and ought to be reversed.

Livingston, J. My opinion differs from that of the court. The controversy [involves] a single question.

Whether a person who, with his own hounds, starts and hunts a fox on waste and uninhabited ground, and is on the point of seizing his prey, acquires such an interest in the animal as to have a right of action against another, who in view of the huntsman and his dogs in full pursuit, and with knowledge of the chase, shall kill and carry him away.

This is a knotty point, and should have been submitted to the arbitration of sportsmen, without poring over Justinian, Fleta, Bracton, Puffendorf, Locke, Barbeyrac, or Blackstone, all of whom have been cited: they would have had no difficulty in coming to a prompt and correct conclusion. In a court thus constituted, the skin and carcass of poor Reynard would have been properly disposed of, and a precedent set, interfering with no usage or custom which the experience of ages has sanctioned, and which must be so well known to every votary of Diana. But the parties have referred the question to our judgment, and we must dispose of it as well as we can, from the partial lights we possess, leaving to a higher tribunal the correction of any mistake which we may be so unfortunate as to make. By the pleadings it is admitted that a fox is a "wild and noxious beast." Both parties have regarded him, as the law of nations does a pirate, *hostem humani generis*, and although *de mortuis nil nisi bonum* be a maxim of our profession, the memory of the deceased has not been spared. His depredations on farmers and on barnyards, have not been forgotten; and to put him to death wherever found, is allowed to be meritorious, and of public benefit. Hence it follows, that our decision should have in view the greatest possible encouragement to the destruction of an animal, so cunning and ruthless in his career. But who would keep a pack of hounds; or what gentleman, at the sound of the horn, and at peep of day, would mount his steed, and for hours together, *sub jove frigido*, or a vertical sun, pursue the windings of this wily quadruped, if, just as night came on, and his stratagems and strength were nearly exhausted, a saucy intruder, who had not shared in the honors or labors of the chase, were permitted to come in at the death, and bear away in triumph the object of pursuit? Whatever Justinian may have thought of the matter, it must be recollected that his code was compiled many hundred years ago, and it would be very hard indeed, at the distance of so many centuries, not to have a right to establish a rule for ourselves. In his day, we read of no order of men who made it a business, in the language of the declaration in this cause, "with hounds and dogs to find, start, pursue, hunt, and chase," these animals, and that, too, without any other motive than the preservation of Roman poultry; if this diversion had been then in fashion, the lawyers who composed his institutes, would have taken care not to pass it by, without suitable encouragement. If anything, therefore, in the digests or pandects shall appear to militate against the defendant in error, who, on this occasion, was the fox hunter, we have only to say *tempora mutantur*; and if men themselves change with the times, why should not laws also undergo an alteration?

It may be expected, however, by the learned counsel, that more particular notice be taken of their authorities. I have examined them all, and feel great difficulty in determining, whether to acquire dominion over a thing, before in common, it be sufficient that we barely see it, or know where it is, or wish for it, or make a declaration of our will respecting it; or whether, in the case of wild beasts, setting a trap, or lying in wait, or starting, or pursuing, be enough; or if an actual wounding, or killing, or bodily tact and occupation be necessary. Writers on general law, who have favored us with their speculations on these points, differ on them all; but, great as is the diversity of sentiment among them, some conclusion must be adopted on the question immediately before us. After mature deliberation, I embrace that of Barbeyrac as the most rational and least liable to objection. If at liberty, we might imitate the courtesy of a certain emperor, who, to avoid giving offense to the advocates of any of these different doctrines, adopted a middle course, and by ingenious distinctions, rendered it difficult to say (as often happens after a fierce and angry contest) to whom the palm of victory belonged. He ordained, that if a beast be followed with large dogs and hounds, he shall belong to the hunter, not to the chance occupant; and in like manner, if he be killed or wounded with a lance or sword; but if chased with beagles only, then he passed to the captor, not to the first pursuer. If slain with a dart, a sling, or a bow, he fell to the hunter, if still in chase, and not to him who might afterwards find and seize him.

Now, as we are without any municipal regulations of our own, and the pursuit here, for aught that appears on the case, being with dogs and hounds of imperial stature, we are at liberty to adopt one of the provisions just cited, which comports also with the learned conclusion of Barbeyrac, that property in animals *ferae naturae* may be acquired without bodily touch or manucaption, provided the pursuer be within reach, or have a reasonable prospect (which certainly existed here) of taking what he has thus discovered an intention of converting to his own use.

When we reflect also that the interest of our husbandmen, the most useful of men in any community, will be advanced by the destruction of a beast so pernicious and incorrigible, we cannot greatly err in saying that a pursuit like the present, through waste and unoccupied lands, and which must inevitably and speedily have terminated in corporeal possession, or bodily seisin, confers such a right to the object of it, as to make any one a wrong-doer who shall interfere and shoulder the spoil. The justice's judgment ought, therefore, in my opinion, to be affirmed.

Exercise 2-7. *Pierson v. Post* Revisited

1. We have all heard the expression that "possession is nine-tenths of the law." Post had possession of the deceased fox, but Pierson still thought that he was the rightful owner because he had with "his own hounds, start[ed] and hunt[ed] a fox on waste and uninhabited ground, and [was] on the point of seizing his prey." For those of you with siblings, this might remind you of when you or one of your brothers or sisters would try to "call the front seat" or "call shotgun" whenever you were going for a family drive. Should the law respect an informal system of "calling dibs"?
2. Judge Tompkins mentions that "nets and toils" can deprive a wild animal of its natural liberty. Lobster traps provide a contemporary example of an instance where wild animals are considered owned once they are trapped—even though the owner of the trap does not have the lobsters in his or her possession. Each commercial lobster trap is licensed to its owner and identified by a number on a buoy attached to the trap. It is a crime to remove lobsters from a commercial lobster trap. You might recall that Cosmo Kramer ran afoul of this rule in season 5 of the television sitcom *Seinfeld.* In the episode entitled *The Hamptons,* Kramer and the gang travel to see their friends' new baby at their house in the Hamptons. Kramer treats everyone to a lobster dinner when he finds a commercial lobster trap filled with lobster. The episode ends with Kramer's arrest for lobster poaching.
3. The practice of commercial whaling also gave rise to disputes regarding ownership. As a matter of tradition and practice, if a deceased whale washed ashore with a harpoon, the owner of the harpoon could claim the whale subject to a finder's fee. In the 1881 case of *Ghen v. Rich,* the U.S. District Court for the District of Massachusetts addressed the ownership of a finback whale that had washed ashore and been sold to the defendant Rich by the person who found the whale. *Ghen v. Rich,* 8 F. Supp. 159 (1881). The whale

was killed by the plaintiff's bomb lance, which was an exploding harpoon. Just like the commercial lobster traps, the bomb lance had a distinctive marking that identified it as belonging to Ghen. When whales were killed in this way, they sank and then would wash up on shore days later. After taking into account the customs of the industry, the court held that the whale belonged to Ghen and ordered Rich to compensate Ghen for the whale.

4. Returning to the question of the fox, would the result have been different if Pierson had tripped Post just as Post was about to swoop down and carry off the fox?
5. Judge Tompkins and Judge Livingston both set forth a rule to address the "novel" situation presented by the dispute between Pierson and Post. A close reading of their opinions will reveal some fundamental differences in their approaches. Prepare a side-by-side comparison that begins by stating the two different rules. Then answer the following questions:
   a. Where did each judge look for authority?
   b. What are the pros and cons of each rule?
   c. What values does each rule protect?
   d. What behaviors does each rule encourage or discourage?
   e. How does each judge view the role of the judiciary?

Natural Resources

Although *Pierson v. Post* may seem to have little relevance today, the rule of capture has been applied to natural resources more generally and has played an important role in the development of the contemporary field of oil and gas law. It also has been applied in disputes over groundwater and water rights.

The common law doctrine *ratione soli* provided landowners constructive possession of natural resources on their land, but it also granted rights to the natural resources that were both over and under the surface of their land. This doctrine is often expressed by the Latin maxim, *cujus est solum, ejus est usque ad coelum ad infernos*, meaning: "whoever's is the soil, it is theirs all the way to Heaven and all the way to hell." In *Pierson v. Post*, the fox was hunted on land that was not owned, which is why both Pierson and Post were able to claim the fox. Had the "wily quadruped" been on land owned by Post, Pierson would not have been permitted to hunt and carry away the fox because title to the fox would have been vested in Post as the landowner.

Oil and Gas

In the latter part of the 19th century, technological advancements made it possible to tap oil and gas deposits by drilling. The first oil well was placed into service in

Pennsylvania in 1859. These oil and gas deposits represented a valuable new form of property, and their boundaries did not always conform to the ownership of the surface land. It was possible for an oil or gas reserve to exist beneath the surface of multiple landowners, leading to disputes over ownership. Take for example the adjoining landowners in the figure below. The oil reserve is located below the surface of both of their properties. Who owns the right to the oil? Owner A? Owner B? Do they share ownership to the oil?

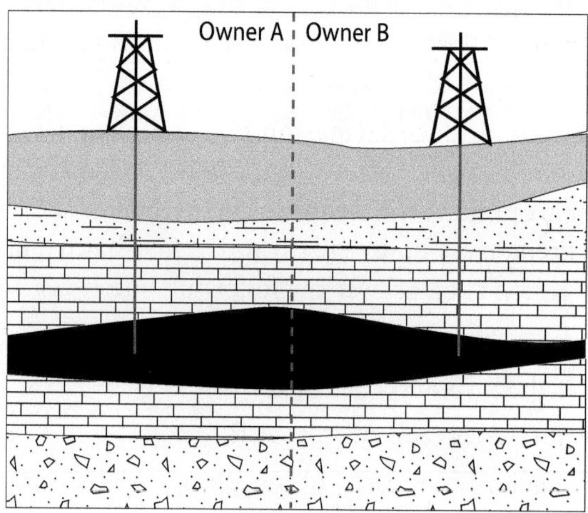

Reasoning by analogy, courts initially maintained that oil and gas reserves were akin to wild animals. Oil and gas deposits migrated under the surface of the land; in constant motion. Applying the rule of capture, the surface owner who deprives the oil or gas of its natural liberty is considered the owner. If Owner A drills an oil well on his property, he is entitled to remove as much oil as he can, even though it may have migrated from reserves under the surface of the property of Owner B. Likewise, Owner B is entitled to drill for oil on her property and remove oil from the common pool. Owner A, however, is not entitled to drill from his property on an angle to reach an oil reservoir located under the property of Owner B.

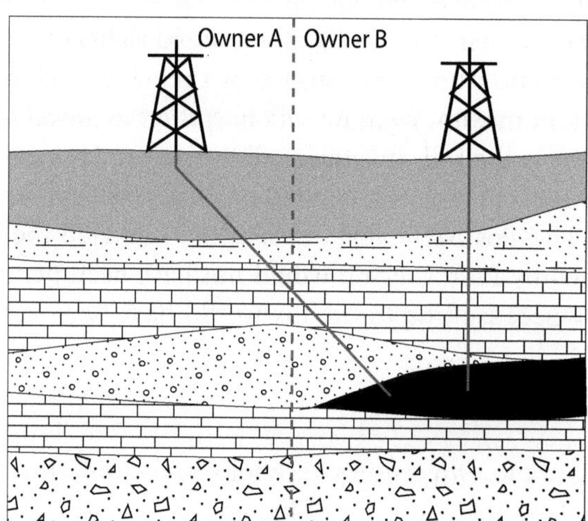

The rule of capture created an incentive for property owners to remove as much oil or gas as possible, as quickly as possible. This incentive led to practices that were both unsafe and wasteful. In order to avoid waste, courts developed an equitable doctrine of "reasonable use,"Ó holding that adjoining owners had to exercise due care in drilling and could be held liable for losses suffered by their neighbors.

Today, oil and gas are strictly regulated by state and local environmental laws. In a number of states, it is common to split the title to property between surface rights and mineral rights. (We will address the topic of air rights in Chapter 7 when we talk about Nuisance). Mineral rights can include the right to remove coal and oil and gas from beneath the surface of a property. In the majority of countries, the state owns the mineral rights under all property. The United States is among a handful of countries where individuals can own the mineral rights to their property. The importance of mineral rights has received renewed interest with the widespread and increasingly controversial use of hydraulic fracturing as a method to remove natural gas deposits.

Water

The rule of capture has also been applied in varying degrees to both groundwater and surface water. Groundwater refers to water that has accumulated in underground aquifers comprised of permeable rock, sand, and gravel. Surface water refers bodies of water, such as streams and lakes, that may be located on a landowner's property.

Groundwater

Groundwater supplies water for drinking, agriculture, and industrial use. Groundwater aquifers can extend under the property of many landowners. When water is withdrawn from the aquifer by one landowner, it depletes the remaining reservoir of water and thereby implicates the rights of the other landowners who rely on the aquifer. Diminishing aquifers in some of the Western states have been an increasing cause of concern, especially for agriculture.

The traditional rule applied the doctrine of free use to groundwater. Under this rule, any surface owner was free to extract an unlimited amount of water regardless of the impact it might have on neighboring landowners. Only a small minority of states follow that rule today, although those states also prohibit the use of water that constitutes waste. The majority of states take the interests of the other landowners into account. Some states impose a reasonable use rule that sets limits on the use of the water. The *Second Restatement of Torts* § 858 imposes liability when a surface owner withdraws an amount of water that unreasonably harms other owners or exceeds the surface owner's "reasonable share" of groundwater.

A minority of states follow the doctrine of prior appropriation. The rule of prior appropriation rewards the landowner who first begins withdrawing water and is sometimes referred to "first in time, first in right." Under the rule, the first person to start withdrawing water can continue to do so for the original purpose. Additional landowners may withdraw water, but only to the extent that it does not interfere with the rights of the original user. The states that apply the rule of prior appropriation tend to be states where water is a scare resource. In cases of declining aquifers, the rule of prior appropriation can have a severe impact on neighboring landowners. It also applies to surface water, as explained below.

Surface Water

Surface water can be used for drinking, agriculture, industrial uses, energy production, and recreation. In the United States, there are two distinct legal regimes: riparian rights and the prior appropriation doctrine. The doctrine of riparian rights is the older doctrine, and it is recognized by the states east of Mississippi River. The Western states follow the rule of prior appropriation, reflecting the fact that water in those states is a limited resource. All states also regulate the use of surface water for both health and safety and environmental reasons.

In riparian jurisdictions, an owner whose land borders a body of water is entitled to riparian rights. These rights convey with the land to future owners. To resolve disputes between and among riparian owners, the states apply a reasonable use rule that will take into account the social utility of competing uses and the potential for harm. In some instances, use may be apportioned in a manner to guarantee all riparian owners reasonable access.

In the Western states, the rule of prior appropriation provides very different results and rejects the notion that rights to surface water should be shared. As in the case of groundwater, prior appropriation is based on a system of temporal priority or "first in time, first in right." The doctrine originated in California during the time of the California Gold Rush when mining operations were eager to secure sources of water. Unlike riparian rights, water rights under the rule of prior appropriation do not attach to land and can be bought and sold independently of the land. Water rights attach to the first person who uses surface water for a beneficial use. That person then has the right to continue to use the same quantity of water for the same purpose. Subsequent users are permitted to use any remaining water, provided they do not impair the rights of prior users. These rights can then be bought or sold. They can also be lost for nonuse.

Exercise 2-8. *Popov v. Hayashi*—America's Pastime

Have you ever attended a major league baseball game? If so, you have no doubt seen people in the crowd with their baseball gloves hoping to catch an errant fly ball. As a matter of property law, a spectator who catches a baseball that is out of play is entitled to keep the baseball. The baseball is the property of the team until it is hit by the bat. At that point, the baseball becomes what is referred to as abandoned property, and the next person who takes the baseball into his or her possession becomes the owner.

Today there is a thriving market in sports memorabilia. As a result, historically significant baseballs can be very valuable. For example, the baseball that Mark McGwire hit for his 70th homerun sold at auction in 1998 for $3 million. The following case involves a baseball that was estimated for the purposes of trial to be worth approximately $1.5 million.

Popov v. Hayashi

2002 WL 31833731 (California Superior Court 2002)

McCarthy, J. In 1927, Babe Ruth hit sixty home runs. That record stood for thirty-four years until Roger Maris broke it in 1961 with sixty one home runs. Mark McGwire hit seventy in 1998. On October 7, 2001, at PacBell Park in San Francisco, Barry Bonds hit number seventy-three. That accomplishment set a record which, in all probability, will remain unbroken for years into the future.

The event was widely anticipated and received a great deal of attention.

The ball that found itself at the receiving end of Mr. Bond's bat garnered some of that attention. Baseball fans in general, and especially people at the game, understood the importance of the ball. It was worth a great deal of money and whoever caught it would bask, for a brief period of time, in the reflected fame of Mr. Bonds.

With that in mind, many people who attended the game came prepared for the possibility that a record setting ball would be hit in their direction. Among this group were plaintiff Alex Popov and defendant Patrick Hayashi. They were unacquainted at the time. Both men brought baseball gloves, which they anticipated using if the ball came within their reach. They, along with a number of others, positioned themselves in the arcade section of the ballpark. This is a standing room only area located near right field. It is in this general area that Barry Bonds hits the greatest number of home runs. The area was crowded with people on October 7, 2001 and access was restricted to those who held tickets for that section.

Barry Bonds came to bat in the first inning. With nobody on base and a full count, Bonds swung at a slow knuckleball. He connected. The ball sailed over the right-field fence and into the arcade. Josh Keppel, a cameraman who was positioned in the arcade, captured the event on videotape. Keppel filmed much of what occurred from the time Bonds hit the ball until the commotion in the arcade had subsided. He was standing very near the spot where the ball landed and he recorded a significant amount of information critical to the disposition of this case.

When the seventy-third home run ball went into the arcade, it landed in the upper portion of the webbing of a softball glove worn by Alex Popov. While the glove stopped the trajectory of the ball, it is not at all clear that the ball was secure.

Popov had to reach for the ball and in doing so, may have lost his balance. Even as the ball was going into his glove, a crowd of people began to engulf Mr. Popov. He was tackled and thrown to the ground while still in the process of attempting to complete the catch. Some people intentionally descended on him for the purpose of taking the ball away, while others were involuntarily forced to the ground by the momentum of the crowd. Eventually, Mr. Popov was buried face down on the ground under several layers of people. At one point he had trouble breathing. Mr. Popov was grabbed, hit and kicked. People reached underneath him in the area of his glove. Neither the tape nor the testimony is sufficient to establish which individual members of the crowd were responsible for the assaults on Mr. Popov. The videotape clearly establishes that this was an out of control mob, engaged in violent, illegal behavior.

Mr. Popov intended at all times to establish and maintain possession of the ball. At some point the ball left his glove and ended up on the ground. It is impossible to establish the exact point in time that this occurred or what caused it to occur. Mr. Hayashi was standing near Mr. Popov when the ball came into the stands. He, like Mr. Popov, was involuntarily forced to the ground. He committed no wrongful act. While on the ground he saw the loose ball. He picked it up, rose to his feet and put it in his pocket.

It is important to point out what the evidence did not and could not show. Neither the camera nor the percipient witnesses were able to establish whether Mr. Popov retained control of the ball as he descended into the crowd. Mr. Popov's testimony on this question is inconsistent on several important points, ambiguous on others and, on the whole, unconvincing. We do not know when or how Mr. Popov lost the ball. Perhaps the most critical factual finding of all is one that cannot be made. We will never know if Mr. Popov would have been able to retain control of the ball had the crowd not interfered with his efforts to do so. Resolution of that question is the work of a psychic, not a judge.

Plaintiff has pled causes of actions for conversion, injunctive relief and constructive trust. Conversion is the wrongful exercise of dominion over the personal property of another. There must be actual interference with the plaintiff's dominion. Wrongful withholding of property can constitute actual interference even where the defendant lawfully acquired the property. If a person entitled to possession of personal property demands its return, the unjustified refusal to give the property back is conversion.

The act constituting conversion must be intentionally done. There is no requirement, however, that the defendant know that the property belongs to another or that the defendant intends to dispossess the true owner of its use and enjoyment. Wrongful purpose is not a component of conversion. The injured party may elect to seek either specific recovery of the property or monetary damages. Conversion does not exist, however, unless the baseball rightfully belongs to Mr. Popov. One who has neither title nor possession, nor any right to possession, cannot sue for conversion. The deciding question in this case then, is whether Mr. Popov achieved possession or the right to possession as he attempted to catch and hold on to the ball.

The parties have agreed to a starting point for the legal analysis. Prior to the time the ball was hit, it was possessed and owned by Major League Baseball. At the time it was hit it became intentionally abandoned property. The first person who came in possession of the ball became its new owner. In order to assist the court in resolving this disagreement, four distinguished law professors participated in a forum to discuss the legal definition of possession. The professors also disagreed.

We start with the observation that possession is a process which culminates in an event. The event is the moment in time that possession is achieved. The process includes the acts and thoughts of the would-be possessor which lead up to the moment of possession.

The focus of the analysis in this case is not on the thoughts or intent of the actor. Mr. Popov has clearly evidenced an intent to possess the baseball and has communicated that intent to the world. The question is whether he did enough to reduce the ball to his exclusive dominion and control. Were his acts sufficient to create a legally cognizable interest in the ball?

Mr. Hayashi argues that possession does not occur until the fan has complete control of the ball. Professor Brian Gray, suggests the following definition "A person who catches a baseball that enters the stands is its owner. A ball is caught if the person has achieved complete control of the ball at the point in time that the momentum of the ball and the momentum of the fan while attempting to catch the ball ceases. A baseball, which is dislodged by incidental contact with an inanimate object or another person, before momentum has ceased, is not possessed. Incidental contact with another person is contact that is not intended by the other person. The first person to pick up a loose ball and secure it becomes its possessor."

Mr. Popov argues that this definition requires that a person seeking to establish possession must show unequivocal dominion and control, a standard rejected by several leading cases. Instead, he offers the perspectives of Professor Bernhardt and Professor Paul Finkelman who suggest that possession occurs when an individual intends to take control of a ball and manifests that intent by stopping the forward momentum of the ball whether or not complete control is achieved. Professors Finkelman and Bernhardt have correctly pointed out that some cases recognize possession even before absolute dominion and control is achieved. Those cases require the actor to be actively and ably engaged in efforts to establish complete control. Moreover, such efforts must be significant and they must be reasonably calculated to result in unequivocal dominion and control at some point in the near future.

This rule is applied in cases involving the hunting or fishing of wild animals or the salvage of sunken vessels. The hunting and fishing cases recognize that a mortally wounded animal may run for a distance before falling. The hunter acquires possession upon the act of wounding the animal not the eventual capture. Similarly, whalers acquire possession by landing a harpoon, not by subduing the animal. In the salvage cases, an individual may take possession of a wreck by exerting as much control "as its nature and situation permit." Inadequate efforts, however, will not support a claim of possession.

These rules are contextual in nature. They are crafted in response to the unique nature of the conduct they seek to regulate. Moreover, they are influenced by the custom and practice of each industry. The reason that absolute dominion and control is not required to establish possession in the cases cited by Mr. Popov is that such a rule would be unworkable and unreasonable. The "nature and situation" of the property at issue does not immediately lend itself to unequivocal dominion and control. It is impossible to wrap ones arms around a whale, a fleeing fox or a sunken ship.

The opposite is true of a baseball hit into the stands of a stadium. Not only is it physically possible for a person to acquire unequivocal dominion and control of an abandoned baseball, but fans generally expect a claimant to have accomplished as much. The custom and practice of the stands creates a reasonable expectation that a person will achieve full control of a ball before claiming possession. There is no reason for the legal rule to be inconsistent with that expectation. Therefore Gray's Rule is adopted as the definition of possession in this case.

The central tenant of Gray's Rule is that the actor must retain control of the ball after incidental contact with people and things. Mr. Popov has not established by a preponderance of the evidence that he would have retained control of the ball after all momentum ceased and after any incidental contact with people or objects. Consequently, he did not achieve full possession.

That finding, however, does not resolve the case. The reason we do not know whether Mr. Popov would have retained control of the ball is not because of incidental contact. It is because he was attacked. His efforts to establish possession were interrupted by the collective assault of a band of wrongdoers. A decision which ignored that fact would endorse the actions of the crowd by not repudiating them. Judicial rulings, particularly in cases that receive media attention, affect the way people conduct themselves. This case demands vindication of an important principle. We are a nation governed by law, not by brute force.

The legal question presented at this point is whether an action for conversion can proceed where the plaintiff has failed to establish possession or title. It can. An action for conversion may be brought where the plaintiff has title, possession or the right to possession. Here Mr. Popov seeks, in effect, a declaratory judgment that he has either possession or the right to possession. In addition he seeks the remedies of injunctive relief and a constructive trust. These are all actions in equity. A court sitting in equity has the authority to fashion rules and remedies designed to achieve fundamental fairness.

Consistent with this principle, the court adopts the following rule. Where an actor undertakes significant but incomplete steps to achieve possession of a piece of abandoned personal property and the effort is interrupted by the unlawful acts of others, the actor has a legally cognizable pre-possessory interest in the property. That pre-possessory interest constitutes a qualified right to possession which can support a cause of action for conversion.

Possession can be likened to a journey down a path. Mr. Popov began his journey unimpeded. He was fast approaching a fork in the road. A turn in one direction would lead to possession of the ball—he would complete the catch. A turn in the other direction would result in a failure to achieve possession—he would drop the ball. Our problem is that before Mr. Popov got to the point where the road forked, he was set upon by a gang of bandits, who dislodged the ball from his grasp.

Recognition of a legally protected pre-possessory interest, vests Mr. Popov with a qualified right to possession and enables him to advance a legitimate claim to the baseball based on a conversion theory. Moreover it addresses the harm done by the unlawful actions of the crowd. It does not, however, address the interests of Mr. Hayashi. The court is required to balance the interests of all parties. Mr. Hayashi was not a wrongdoer. He was a victim of the same bandits that attacked Mr. Popov. The difference is that he was able to extract himself from their assault and move to the side of the road. It was there that he discovered the loose ball. When he picked up and put it in his pocket he attained unequivocal dominion and control.

If Mr. Popov had achieved complete possession before Mr. Hayashi got the ball, those actions would not have divested Mr. Popov of any rights, nor would they have created any rights to which Mr. Hayashi could lay claim. Mr. Popov, however, was able to establish only a qualified pre-possessory interest in the ball. That interest does not establish a full right to possession that is protected from a subsequent legitimate claim. On the other hand, while Mr. Hayashi appears on the surface to have done everything necessary to claim full possession of the ball, the ball itself is encumbered by the qualified pre-possessory interest of Mr. Popov. At the time Mr. Hayashi came into possession of the ball, it had, in effect, a cloud on its title.

An award of the ball to Mr. Popov would be unfair to Mr. Hayashi. It would be premised on the assumption that Mr. Popov would have caught the ball. That assumption is not supported by the facts. An award of the ball to Mr. Hayashi would unfairly penalize Mr. Popov. It would be based on the assumption that Mr. Popov would have dropped the ball. That conclusion is also unsupported by the facts.

Both men have a superior claim to the ball as against all the world. Each man has a claim of equal dignity as to the other. We are, therefore, left with something of a dilemma.

Thankfully, there is a middle ground. The concept of equitable division has its roots in ancient Roman law. It is useful in that it "provides an equitable way to resolve competing claims which are equally strong." Moreover, "[i]t comports with what one instinctively feels to be fair." The principle at work here is that where more than one party has a valid claim to a single piece of property, the court will recognize an undivided interest in the property in proportion to the strength of the claim.

Exercise 2-9. *Popov v. Hayashi* Revisited

1. The disputed baseball was sold at an auction televised by ESPN in 2003 for $450,000. This amount was less than one-third the estimated $1.5 million that the parties had alleged at trial. Do you think the publicity affected the price? Hayashi reportedly promised his lawyers a contingency fee from a part of the proceeds.
2. The judge stressed that there was no wrongdoing on the part of either party to the lawsuit. What would have been the result if a member of the mob had grabbed the ball from Popov?
3. Compare Gray's Rule with the rules adopted by both Judge Tompkins and Judge Livingston.
4. The result in this case is very different from the all-or-nothing approach taken in *Pierson v. Post* or with the rule of first appropriation applied to natural resources. Equitable division represents a middle ground. Do you think it was a fair result?
5. Popov sued Hayashi for conversion, but he could not prevail on the claim unless he first proved that he owned the baseball. This should remind you of the claims of the Cayuga Nation for trespass and back rent. The court dismissed those claims because the Cayuga Nation could not establish possessory rights.

Equitable Remedies: Constructive Trusts and Equitable Division

The court in *Popov v. Hayashi* rejected the all-or-nothing approach to ownership reflected in *Pierson v. Post.* Instead of confirming ownership in Popov or Hayashi, the court ordered that they should share the property under the doctrine of equitable division. It is common in property cases for judges to consider equitable remedies. You have already studied the equitable defense of laches in connection with *Cayuga Indian Nation v. Pataki.* Throughout this course you will read cases where judges will invoke equitable principles and parties will request equitable remedies or assert equitable defenses. It is important to understand when to appeal to equity and how to use equitable defenses, but first it is necessary to brush up on a little history.

The Reception of Common Law

Our precedent-based common law legal system is inherited from England. Following the American Revolution, the newly constituted states "received" the existing body of English common law to the extent that it was not contrary to domestic law through statute or provisions in their state constitutions. This is why the early American cases routinely cite English precedent. As new states joined the Union, they also received the common law, with the exception of Louisiana, whose legal system also includes French and Spanish influences. Over the years, law in the United States has become increasingly codified, leaving less room for judge-made common law.

The influence of the English common law tradition, however, remains very strong in the area of property law. Judge-made doctrines, such as nuisance, continue to inform land use patterns alongside complex statutory schemes. Different types of ownership interests are referred to as "estates" and date back to the days of feudalism. Many property concepts still carry names derived from archaic French terms introduced at the time of the Norman Conquest.

Equity

An important feature of the English common law tradition was the distinction between law and equity. Law was the province of the Royal Courts and was governed by a strict system of stare decisis. The House of Lords, which was considered the highest court in the land, did not have the power to overrule its own opinions until 1966. A rigid adherence to precedent and legal maxims often created unworkable rules that produced a hardship on the parties. Equity developed in part to provide relief from the harshness of the common law. In the 16th century, the Lord Chancellor began to hear petitions from aggrieved parties who were not able to find relief in the courts of law. This practice developed into the Courts of Chancery where parties appealed to the "conscience" of the court and asked for fairness. Equity offered a parallel system of legal redress when there was no available or adequate remedy at law. A major difference between the Courts of Chancery and the Royal Courts was the types of remedies imposed. The primary remedy available in the Royal Courts was monetary damages. The Courts of Chancery, on the other hand, issued injunctions that would compel a party to perform a certain act or stop a particular behavior. Especially in the area of property law, there are many instances where an aggrieved party may not be made whole by money damages and might prefer an injunction.

In England, the courts of law and equity merged in the late 19th century. Today, U.S. federal courts and the courts of most states have also merged law and equity, although some distinctions remain. Only three states have separate courts of law and equity: Delaware, Mississippi, and Tennessee.

Equitable Remedies and Defenses

Legal damages are owed to a plaintiff as a matter of right, whereas equitable damages lie within the discretion of the court. Two of the most common equitable remedies are injunctive relief and specific performance. In the area of property law, the remedy of a constructive trust will be used to prevent unjust enrichment. All of these remedies are used when there is no available or adequate remedy at law. They are also subject to equitable defenses, such as unclean hands. The doctrine of unclean hands holds that "those who seek equity must do equity," meaning that the plaintiff must not be in the wrong. Other equitable defenses include estoppel, hardship, and laches.

A constructive trust is of particular importance to property law. It is a flexible remedy that is designed to prevent unjust enrichment that occurs when an individual benefits from his or her own wrongdoing and there is no adequate remedy at law. A constructive trust is not an actual trust, which will be discussed in greater detail in Chapter 5 when we discuss Estates in Land. Instead, it uses the structure of a trust to ensure fairness. A trust is a device that splits title to property between a beneficial owner, known as the beneficiary, and the trustee, who is a fiduciary. The trust holds legal title whereas the beneficiary is said to hold beneficial title. It is the job of the trustee to manage the trust property for the benefit of the beneficiary. If the trustee breaches his or her fiduciary duty or absconds with the trust property, the trustee is required to make the beneficiary whole.

Justice Cardozo referred to a constructive trust as "the formula through which the conscience of equity finds expression." *Beatty v. Guggenheim Exploration Co.*, 225 N.Y. 380 (1919). Take for example a gruesome case of patricide. Assume that a son murders his father in order to accelerate his inheritance. The terms of the father's will are clear: "I give my estate to my son, if he survives me. If not, I give my estate to my brother's children who survive me in equal shares." The only contingency in the father's will is that the son must survive him. Accordingly, title to the father's property will legally pass to the son under the terms of the father's will and there is no available remedy at law. Obviously, it is not fair to allow the son to profit from his wrongdoing. To prevent unjust enrichment, a court can impose a constructive trust on the property. The son will be declared the trustee of the property and will be deemed to hold the property in trust for the benefit of the next of kin entitled to take under the father's will. As constructive trustee, the court will then order the son to distribute the property to the next of kin and pay back any amounts that he may have used in order to make the beneficiaries whole.

Today every state, with the exception of New Hampshire, has enacted what is called a Slayer's Statute that deals with this type of situation, so it is no longer necessary to use a constructive trust. The typical Slayer's Statute provides that an heir or beneficiary under a will who is found to have intentionally killed the benefactor is deemed to have predeceased. In our example, the Slayer's Statute would have triggered the contingency in the father's will that the son had to be living at the time of the father's death in order to take under the will.

In *Popov v. Hayashi*, the court did not impose a constructive trust because it affirmatively found no wrongdoing on the part of either Popov or Hayashi, and a constructive trust is used to prevent unjust enrichment. Instead, the court employed the concept of equitable distribution to divide the proceeds from the sale of the baseball between the parties. This principle is typically used in the context of spousal property divisions upon divorce. In those cases, the property is not necessarily divided equally, but rather in accordance with the equities of the situation as set forth in the governing statute.

Intellectual Property

Intellectual property refers to creations of the mind or intellect, especially as they exist in the marketplace. It includes inventions, manufactured goods, artistic works, and designs. The three major areas of intellectual property are patents, trademarks, and copyrights. Even though some examples of intellectual property may have a tangible or physical form, such as a book or a machine, intellectual property is classified as intangible personal property. There is also a big difference between owning a book and owning the rights to the material in the book. The same can be said of the distinction between owning a machine and owning the rights to manufacture and market the machine.

The United States has a regime of federal laws that protect the proprietary rights of the creator or inventor of intellectual property. The protections are designed to encourage innovation by ensuring an inventor, creator, or author that her work will not be misappropriated by others for profit or gain. Article I, Section 8, clause 8 of the U.S. Constitution authorizes Congress to grant authors and inventors exclusive rights to their creations. Known as the Patent and Copyright Clause, it provides:

> The Congress shall have power ... To promote the progress of science and useful arts, by securing for limited times to authors and inventors the exclusive right to their respective writings and discoveries.

The major laws governing intellectual property are the U.S. Patent Act, 35 U.S.C. §§1 et seq, the U.S. Copyright Act, 17 U.S.C. §§101–810, and the Lanham (Trademark) Act, 15 U.S.C. §1051 et seq. Two different government agencies, the U.S. Patent and Trademark Office and the U.S. Copyright Office, administer the intellectual property laws.

A patent protects the inventor of "new and useful" inventions and discoveries, such as machines, manufactured goods, a particular process, or chemical combinations. 35 U.S.C. §101. Abstract ideas, laws of nature, and naturally occurring substances are not eligible for patent protection. A patent grants the inventor the exclusive right to profit from the patented product for a period as long as twenty years, depending on the type of patent. An inventor must apply for a patent with the U.S. Patent and Trademark Office. Once granted, a patent can be sold and transferred.

The law of copyright protects the creator of "original works of authorship." 17 U.S.C. §102. It covers artistic and intellectual works, sound recording, and architectural works. Copyright protection grants the creator of the work the right to sell, reproduce, perform and display the work. The protection generally lasts for 70 years after the creator's death. Unlike a patent, a copyright attaches automatically to "original works of authorship." Creators can register with the U.S. Copyright Office in order to take advantage of enhanced statutory protections. A copyright may be assigned or licensed.

A trademark is a symbol, design, logo, word, or phrase that identifies a particular company or brand of goods or services. Trademarks are the way that organizations express their commercial identity and make themselves easily recognizable to consumers. Trademark law protects the goodwill of a company by making sure that competitors can not adopt trademarks that are "confusingly similar." Once acquired, a trademark can be registered with the U.S. Patent and Trademark Office. As with copyright protection, registration is not required. However, registered trademarks receive greatly enhanced protections.

Because intellectual property is highly regulated by a complex statutory and regulatory scheme, it is not possible to describe the laws governing intellectual property in any detail in an introductory Property course. However, you may want to consider why the government provides special protection for the creators of intellectual property. What types of behavior are the laws designed to encourage? Are the laws the most efficient use of resources? What makes intellectual property different from natural resources, such as oil, or a fox or even a baseball?

Abandoned, Lost, and Mislaid Property

The prior section addressed the importance of capture, discovery, and labor in determining ownership. The cases involved things or resources that were unowned in a state of nature or created through an individual's labor. This section continues our discussion of personal property, as opposed to real property, but it involves items that were once owned. Here, the question presented is when an individual can become the owner of property that was once owned by another. The obvious answer is that an individual can receive property from another through purchase or gift. A transaction is a purchase when consideration is paid for the item. In the absence of consideration, the transaction is a gratuitous transfer or gift. A gift can occur during lifetime, which is referred to as an inter vivos gift, or at death through inheritance or by will.

Apart from purchase or gift, this section asks whether the old adage "finders keepers" has any precedent in property law. Property law in this area traditionally distinguishes among different types of found property; classifying property as abandoned, lost, mislaid, or treasure trove. Abandoned property is like the baseball in *Popov v. Hayashi*. It was once owned, but the true owner has evinced an intent to abandon the property and allow the next person to claim the property as his own. Lost property is simply what the name says—property that the true owner has lost. Mislaid property, however, is property that the true owner intentional placed somewhere, but can no longer find. The term treasure trove brings to mind a buried treasure chest filled with gold coins. It is almost always a form of currency that was concealed by the owner long ago. See if you can categorize the three items described below as either abandoned, lost, or mislaid.

1. You are walking down the hallway on your way to Property class and you spy a $20 bill on the floor. You look around and see no one else in the hallway. After placing your foot over the $20 bill, you reach down and place it in your pocket.

2. You are driving through a residential area and spy a lovely futon sitting out on the curb by the end of a driveway.

3. You are studying in the library and you spy a set of car keys and a half finished latte.

4. While digging in your parents' garden, you find a small box filled with foreign coins.

This section also addresses a central tenet of property law, namely that a thief never has good title—well, almost never. There is a limited exception where a true owner entrusts property to a merchant who deals with the same type of goods. Why would there be any exception to this rule? Wouldn't a rule that passed good title to a thief encourage wrongdoing?

Exercise 2-10. *Benjamin v. Linder Aviation*—Are Finders Really Keepers?

This case summarizes the four different types of found property at common law: abandoned, lost, mislaid, and treasure trove. It also applies a modern statute that provides for a "finder's fee" in certain circumstances. When reading the case, consider the rights of the various parties who assert a claim to the found property. Who do you think should have the superior claim?

Benjamin v. Lindner Aviation, Inc.

534 N.W.2d 400 (1995)

Ternus, J. Appellant, Heath Benjamin, found over $18,000 in currency inside the wing of an airplane. At the time of this discovery, appellee, State Central Bank, owned the plane and it was being serviced by appellee, Lindner Aviation, Inc. All three parties claimed the money as against the true owner. After a bench trial, the district court held that the currency was mislaid property and belonged to the owner of the plane. The court awarded a finder's fee to Benjamin. Benjamin appealed and Lindner Aviation and State Central Bank cross-appealed. We reverse on the bank's cross-appeal and otherwise affirm the judgment of the district court.

In April of 1992, State Central Bank became the owner of an airplane when the bank repossessed it from its prior owner who had defaulted on a loan. In August of that year, the bank took the plane to Lindner Aviation for a routine annual inspection. Benjamin worked for Lindner Aviation and did the inspection. As part of the inspection, Benjamin removed panels from the underside of the wings. Although these panels were to be removed annually as part of the routine inspection, a couple of the screws holding the panel on the left wing were so rusty that Benjamin had to use a drill to remove it. Benjamin testified that the panel probably had not been removed for several years.

Inside the left wing Benjamin discovered two packets approximately four inches high and wrapped in aluminum foil. He removed the packets from the wing and took off the foil wrapping. Inside the foil was paper currency, tied in string and wrapped in handkerchiefs. The currency was predominately twenty-dollar bills with mint dates before the 1960s, primarily in the 1950s. The money smelled musty.

Benjamin took one packet to his jeep and then reported what he had found to his supervisor, offering to divide the money with him. However, the supervisor reported the discovery to the owner of Lindner Aviation, William Engle. Engle insisted that they contact the authorities and he called the Department of Criminal Investigation. The money was eventually turned over to the Keokuk police department.

Two days later, Benjamin filed an affidavit with the county auditor claiming that he was the finder of the currency under the provisions of Iowa Code chapter 644 (1991). Lindner Aviation and the bank also filed claims to the money. The notices required by chapter 644 were published and posted. *See* Iowa Code §644.8 (1991). No one came forward within twelve months claiming to be the true owner of the money. §644.11 (if true owner does not claim property within twelve months, the right to the property vests in the finder).

Benjamin filed this declaratory judgment action against Lindner Aviation and the bank to establish his right to the property. The district court held that chapter 644 applies only to "lost" property and the money here was mislaid property. The court awarded the money to the bank, holding that it was entitled to possession of the money to the exclusion of all but the true owner. The court also held that Benjamin was a "finder" within the meaning of chapter 644 and awarded him a ten-percent finder's fee.

Benjamin appealed. He claims that the trial court should have found that the property was treasure trove or was lost or abandoned rather than mislaid, thereby entitling the finder to the property.

The bank and Lindner Aviation cross-appealed. Lindner Aviation claims that if the money is mislaid property, it is entitled to the money as the owner of the premises on which the money was found, the hangar where the plane was parked. It argues in the alternative that it is the finder, not Benjamin, because Benjamin discovered the money during his work for Lindner Aviation. The bank asserts in its cross-appeal that it owns the premises where the money was found—the airplane—and that no one is entitled to a finder's fee because chapter 644 does not apply to mislaid property.

Under the common law, there are four categories of found property: (1) abandoned property, (2) lost property, (3) mislaid property, and (4) treasure trove. The rights of a finder of property depend on how the found property is classified.

A. *Abandoned property.* Property is abandoned when the owner no longer wants to possess it. Abandonment is shown by proof that the owner intends to abandon the property and has voluntarily relinquished all right, title and interest in the property. Abandoned property belongs to the finder of the property against all others, including the former owner.

B. *Lost property.* "Property is lost when the owner unintentionally and involuntarily parts with its possession and does not know where it is." Stolen property found by someone who did not participate in the theft is lost property. Under chapter 644, lost property becomes the property of the finder once the statutory procedures are followed and the owner makes no claim within twelve months.

C. *Mislaid property.* Mislaid property is voluntarily put in a certain place by the owner who then overlooks or forgets where the property is. It differs from lost property in that the owner voluntarily and intentionally places mislaid property in the location where it is eventually found by another. In contrast, property is not considered lost unless the owner parts with it involuntarily. *see Hill v. Schrunk,* 207 Ore. 71 (Or. 1956) (carefully concealed currency was mislaid property, not lost property). The finder of mislaid property acquires no rights to the property. The right of possession of mislaid property belongs to the owner of the premises upon which the property is found, as against all persons other than the true owner.

D. *Treasure trove.* Treasure trove consists of coins or currency concealed by the owner. It includes an element of antiquity. To be classified as treasure trove, the property must have been hidden or concealed for such a length of time that the owner is probably dead or undiscoverable. Treasure trove belongs to the finder as against all but the true owner.

We think there was substantial evidence to find that the currency discovered by Benjamin was mislaid property. In [other] cases, we examined the location where the money was found as a factor in determining whether the money was lost property. Similarly, we [have] considered the manner in which the money had been secreted in deciding that it had not been abandoned. The place where Benjamin found the money and the manner in which it was hidden are also important here. The bills were carefully tied and wrapped and then concealed in a location that was accessible only by removing screws and a panel. These circumstances support an inference that the money was placed there intentionally. This inference supports the conclusion that the money was mislaid. *Jackson v. Steinberg,* 186 Ore. 129 (Or. 1948) (fact that $800 in currency was found concealed beneath the paper lining of a dresser indicates that money was intentionally concealed with intention of reclaiming it; therefore, property was mislaid, not lost); *Schley v. Couch,* 155 Tex. 195 (Tex. 1955) (holding that money found buried under garage floor was mislaid property as a matter of law because circumstances showed that money was placed there deliberately and court presumed that owner had either forgotten where he hid the money or had died before retrieving it).

The same facts that support the trial court's conclusion that the money was mislaid prevent us from ruling as a matter of law that the property was lost. Property is not considered lost unless considering the place where and the conditions under which the property is found, there is an inference that the property was left there unintentionally. Contrary to Benjamin's position, the circumstances here do not support a conclusion that the money was placed in the wing of the airplane unintentionally.

We also reject Benjamin's assertion that as a matter of law this money was abandoned property. Both logic and common sense suggest that it is unlikely someone would voluntarily part with over $18,000 with the intention of terminating his ownership. The location where this money was found is much more consistent with the conclusion that the owner of the property was placing the money there for safekeeping. We will not presume that an owner has abandoned his property when his conduct is consistent with a continued claim to the property. Therefore, we cannot rule that the district court erred in failing to find that the currency discovered by Benjamin was abandoned property.

Finally, we also conclude that the trial court was not obligated to decide that this money was treasure trove. Based on the dates of the currency, the money was no older than thirty-five years. The mint dates, the musty odor and the rusty condition of a few of the panel screws indicate that the money may have been hidden for some time. However, there was no evidence of the age of the airplane or the date of its last inspection. These facts may have shown that the money was concealed for a much shorter period of time.

Because the money discovered by Benjamin was properly found to be mislaid property, it belongs to the owner of the premises where it was found. Mislaid property is entrusted to the owner of the premises where it is found rather than the finder of the property because it is assumed that the true owner may eventually recall where he has placed his property and return there to reclaim it.

We think that the premises where the money was found is the airplane, not Lindner Aviation's hangar where the airplane happened to be parked when the money was discovered. The policy behind giving ownership of mislaid property to the owner of the premises where the property was mislaid supports this conclusion. If the true owner of the money attempts to locate it, he would initially look for the plane; it is unlikely he would begin his search by contacting businesses where the airplane might have been inspected. Therefore, we affirm the trial court's judgment that the bank, as the owner of the plane, has the right to possession of the property as against all but the true owner.

Benjamin claims that if he is not entitled to the money, he should be paid a ten percent finder's fee under section 644.13. The problem with this claim is that only the finder of "*lost* goods, money, bank notes, and other things" is rewarded with a finder's fee under chapter 644. Because the property found by Benjamin was mislaid property, not lost property, section 644.13 does not apply here. The trial court erred in awarding Benjamin a finder's fee.

AFFIRMED IN PART; REVERSED IN PART

Exercise 2-11. *Benjamin v. Linder Aviation* Revisited

1. As a matter of policy, why does the owner of the plane have a superior interest to the owner of the hanger where the plane was being repaired?
2. Would it make any difference if a thief had hidden the money in the plane? Would that change the chain of title?

3. Is it fair that Benjamin gets nothing when he did the right thing? Why did you think the Iowa state legislature chose not to include a finder's fee for mislaid property?
4. Why is this situation not a candidate for a constructive trust?

A Thief (Almost) Never Has Good Title

Given that you can't sell what you don't own, it makes sense that a thief cannot transfer good title to stolen property to a third party, even if that third party is unaware that the property is stolen and pays valuable consideration. The true owner is entitled to recover stolen property from a bona fide purchaser. The bona fide purchaser then has a claim for damages against the thief. The true owner gets the property back and the bona fide purchaser is entitled to damages.

The Uniform Commercial Code provides one important exception to this general rule. U.C.C. §2-403(2) provides that a bona fide purchaser can receive good title when the true owner entrusted the property to a merchant who generally deals with similar property. For example, a car owner drops his car off at the car dealer for an oil change, but the dealer sells the car to someone else. In that case, the true owner cannot recover the property. The bona fide purchaser gets to keep the property and the true owner has a case against the merchant/thief.

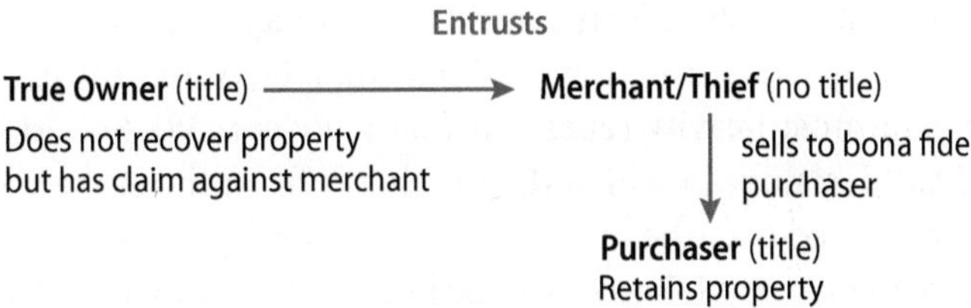

Exercise 2-12. *Alamo Rent-a-Car, Inc. v. Williamson*

This case applies the Florida version of U.C.C. "entruster" rule. U.C.C. §2-403(2). Can you think of other examples where the exception might apply? Does the exception enhance or diminish consumer confidence?

Alamo Rent-A-Car, Inc. v. Williamson Cadillac Company

613 So. 2d 517 Florida Court of Appeals (1993)

SCHWARTZ, Chief Judge. Alamo Rent-a-Car appeals from a summary judgment that Williamson Cadillac, which purchased an automobile from an individual who had leased the car from Alamo and sold it on the basis of a fraudulently obtained duplicate title, had superior rights to the car. We reverse with directions that judgment be entered for Alamo instead.

It is undisputed that, in a supremely run-of-the-mill transaction, Alamo rented a Cadillac for a week to a person named Frank Verdi for his individual use. It is undisputed also that, two days later, Verdi incorporated Verdi Fleet Systems, Inc., listing himself as sole director and registered agent. Verdi then forged an application for and received a duplicate title to the car and, three days after that (and two days after he was to have returned the car to Alamo) had his corporation sell it to Williamson, along with two other Cadillacs which had apparently been similarly obtained and titled. On these facts, Williamson cannot succeed.

It is of course the general rule that a thief such as Verdi cannot pass good title. Williamson's invocation of the exception to that rule contained in §672.403(2) is to no avail. That provision states:

> (2) Any entrusting of possession of goods to a merchant who deals in goods of that kind gives him power to transfer all rights of the entruster to a buyer in ordinary course of business.

This section does not apply because Alamo did not "entrust" the Cadillac to "a merchant who deals in goods of that kind." At the time he leased the car, Verdi was plainly not such a person; he, or rather his corporation, only became one two days later. Moreover, on an *a fortiori* basis, the vehicle could not have been "entrusted"— a term which itself connotes knowledge and volition—in the admitted absence of any indication that Alamo was aware of Verdi's unlawful business or intent. The very basis of §672.403(2) is to place on the owner the burden of losing his property if he knowingly takes the chance of delivering it to a person in the business of dealing with goods of that kind. This principle cannot apply to the present situation. The point is made by the distinction between these facts and those in the case on which Williamson most heavily relies, *Carlsen v. Rivera*, 382 So. 2d 825 (Fla. 4th DCA 1980). That decision, in which the purchaser from the embezzler of a leased vehicle indeed prevailed over the owner, rested entirely upon the fact that the lessor rented the car to one James McEnroe who he knew to be the owner of an automobile dealership. The principles applicable when this is *not* the case are well stated in *Touch of Class Leasing v. Mercedes-Benz of Canada, Inc.*, 248 N.J. Super. 426 (App. Div. 1991), cert. denied, 126 N.J. 390 (1991), which we are content to follow and adopt. The basis of our decision makes it unnecessary to treat Alamo's additional contentions that, given the circumstances of Williamson's acquisition of the car, it was not "a buyer in ordinary course of business" under §672.403(2), and that it could not secure title through the fraudulent duplicate title certificate under §? 319.29(1).

Reversed and remanded with directions.

Exercise 2-13. *Alamo Rent-a-Car, Inc. v. Williamson* Revisited

Why was Williamson not successful in its attempted application of the "entruster" rule? Was the car not entrusted? Was Verdi not a merchant? What if Verdi had incorporated Verdi Fleet Systems before he rented the car?

Adverse Possession and Related Concepts

In this section, we are going to shift our interest back to ownership rights in land. Although a thief never has good title, there are several instances where a trespasser may be granted ownership rights over the objections of the true owner. These instances are governed by the doctrines of adverse possession, prescriptive easement, and the improving trespasser. Initially, you may find it difficult to explain why these "land pirates" are treated so favorably, but the legal doctrines involved reflect the longstanding policy that the "best use of land is the use of land"—a policy that guided the settlement of the United States and its western expansion. As you read the cases, consider the continued utility of that policy. Is it appropriate for the 21st century?

Adverse Possession

As explained in Chapter 3, the hallmark of private property is the right to exclude non-owners. Landowners can enforce this right against trespassers under both tort law and criminal law. Adverse possession complicates our understanding of the relationship between owners and trespassers because, under certain circumstances, a trespasser who continuously uses property can become the owner of the property. Adverse possession rewards the productive use of property and penalizes the inattentive owner. It redistributes land to individuals who are using the property and, therefore, presumably value it more than the original owner who does not care enough about the property to enforce its boundaries.

Generally, a non-owner who enters the land of another without permission is a trespasser. The tort of trespass entitles a landowner to both compensatory and nominal damages. A trespasser who refuses to leave may also be guilty of a criminal offense, and the landowner can call the police to remove the trespasser. A non-owner who enters the land of another with the permission of the owner is a licensee, but if the permission is revoked, the licensee will become a trespasser and the same rules apply.

Under adverse possession, something altogether different occurs when a trespasser remains on the property for an extended period of time and uses it in a certain way. Instead of just compounding the offense and being branded an unrepentant wrongdoer, the longtime trespasser may become the owner of the property. The transformation to owner occurs by operation of law over the objection of the original titleholder and without any requirement to pay compensation. From the perspective of the original owner, adverse possession imposes a requirement that an owner must exercise due diligence and affirmatively enforce his right to exclude trespassers. As illustrated below, an owner has a number of options when confronted with a trespasser. If an owner sleeps on his rights and fails to enforce his boundaries, he may lose the property by adverse possession.

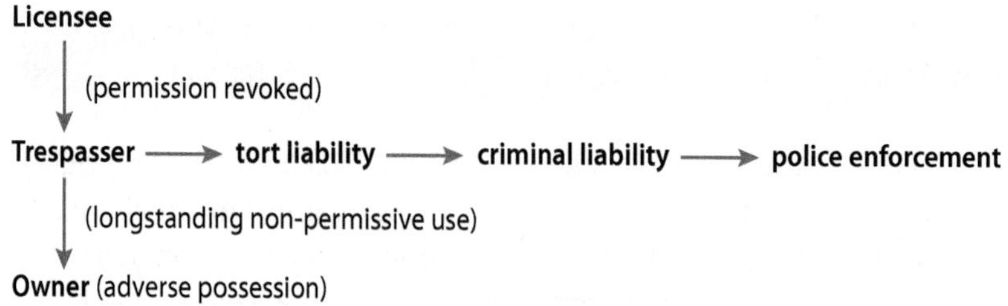

The requirements for adverse possession can be confusing, and the cases are very fact specific. There is also considerable variation among the states. Because of the importance of the interests at stake, most states require the trespasser to prove adverse possession by clear and convincing evidence, which is higher than the standard of a preponderance of the evidence that is typically used in civil cases. Adverse possession can be brought by the adverse possessor in order to have the court confirm title. Note that the court does not technically transfer title, since the act of possession transforms the trespasser into the owner. When the adverse possessor brings the case, it is said to be an action to "quiet title." A claim of adverse possession may also be raised as a defense to an action for trespass. This occurs when the original owner discovers the adverse possessor and attempts to have him removed as a trespasser. The adverse possessor can then raise the doctrine as a defense, claiming that he is actually the owner.

Here is an overview of the most common elements of adverse possession. You should also be sure to check local law whenever dealing with state-specific property concepts.

1. Possession. A key element is that of actual possession. The adverse possessor must occupy the property in a manner that is consistent with fee simple ownership. A fee simple absolute is the name of the highest form of property ownership. An individual who owns a fee simple absolute possesses all the sticks in the metaphorical bundle that is property. It makes sense that in order to dispossess the original owner, the adverse possessor must use the property in the same way as an owner in fee simple would use the property. In Chapter 5, you will learn more about the different types of estates in land that designate different degrees of ownership.

The adverse possessor must show that he used the property as the average owner would use the property. This includes engaging in significant activities to signal possessions: clearing the property, farming, building structures. One generally accepted way to show that the adverse possessor has occupied the land is by building a fence that encloses the property. The fence will also help determine the boundaries of the claim. Slightly different rules may apply if the adverse possessor holds property under a defective deed. In that case, the adverse possessor will have "color of title" and can claim the entire property subject to the deed.

2. Open and notorious. It is only fair to put the original owner on notice that a trespasser may be acquiring rights to the property. The requirement that the possession must be "open and notorious" is designed to provide such notice. There is no requirement that the original owner has actual notice. It is sufficient that the actions of the adverse possessor would alert a diligent owner. This requirement is related to the requirement of possession, since many of the activities that signal possession are also open and notorious: building, farming, enclosures. Activities that may not be sufficiently open and notorious would include occasional picnicking, hiking, selective planting or clearing of timber, or clearing refuse.

3. Exclusive. The adverse possessor must show that his use was exclusive, meaning that it was not shared with the original owner. This requirement is consistent with making sure that the adverse possessor is acting in a way that is consistent with fee simple ownership. The adverse possessor is not required to bar the original owner from the property and may occasionally allow others to use the property as would a typical owner. It is also possible for adverse possessors who occupy the land jointly to become co-owners. You will learn about the various forms of co-ownership in Chapter 4.

4. Continuous. The continuous requirement is also designed to make sure that the adverse possessor is acting like an average owner of the type of property in question. The requirement does not tie the adverse possessor to the land, but an extended absence may defeat a claim of adverse possession depending on the typical use of the property. For example, a vacation property may only be suitable for seasonal use. An adverse possessor of seasonal property would only have to use the property in season.

The doctrine of Tacking allows one adverse possessor to "tack" his claim to a prior adverse possessor if they are considered to be in privity. This occurs when one adverse possessor purports to transfer title (either by purchase or gift) to another.

5. Adverse or hostile. The adverse possessor must show that his use is non-permissive. The use of another's property is presumptively non-permissive. If the original owner granted the adverse possessor permission to be on the property, the claim will not prevail. If an adverse possessor was initially a licensee, then the adverse possessor must show express revocation of the grant of permission. Beyond the basic requirement of non-permissive use, the states impose different rules regarding how to determine when the use is adverse or hostile.

In order to prove adverse or hostile use, the majority of states simply require the absence of permission. Some states require that an adverse possessor must hold the property under a "claim of right," which means that the adverse possessor intended to take ownership of the property. Some states impose a good faith requirement, which seems to be the opposite of hostile. In these states only "innocent" adverse possessors who did not know that they were dispossessing the original owner are rewarded with ownership. Other states do not require good faith of all adverse possessors, but impose a shorter statutory period for adverse possessors acting in good faith. To further complicate matters, some states take the term hostile seriously. In Michigan, South Carolina, and Texas, an adverse possessor must prove that he knowingly intended to dispossess the original owner. The law in these states has been criticized for encouraging bad behavior.

6. Statutory period. The required period varies greatly among the states. The shortest period is five years, and the longest period is forty years. As noted above, some states impose different statutory periods depending on the circumstances. Just as the doctrine of Tacking can be used to assist an adverse possessor, many states will toll the statutory period if the original owner is under some form of disability, such as being underage or incapacitated.

A major exception to adverse possession is that government property is traditionally immune from claims of adverse possession. Some states have limited the scope of government immunity to instances where the property is being used for government functions. A federal statute allows claims for adverse possession against federally owned public lands where the property has been held in good faith and under color of title for at least twenty years. 43 U.S.C. § 1068.

How do you reconcile adverse possession with the rule that a thief never has good title?

Exercise 2-14. *Van Valkenburgh v. Lutz*

Van Valkenburgh v. Lutz is a classic case of adverse possession. It involves a dispute between two neighbors over boundaries. When trying to get to the bottom of a claim of adverse possession, it is always important to be able to visualize the property in question. Accordingly, as you read the initial statement of facts in the present case, map out the property. Start by drawing the triangular shape of the parcel. Fill in the parcel to show the different lots and the disputed encroachments. Then, because adverse possession is time sensitive, be sure to develop a time line that tracks the important events.

Van Valkenburgh v. Lutz

304 N.Y. 95 (1952)

DYE, J. These consolidated actions were brought to compel the removal of certain encroachments upon plaintiffs' lands, for delivery of possession and incidental relief. The subject property consists of four unimproved building lots designated as 19, 20, 21 and 22 in block 54 on the official tax map of the city of Yonkers, N.Y. These lots together form a parcel somewhat triangular in shape with dimensions of approximately 150 by 126 by 170 feet fronting on Gibson Place, a street to be laid out within the subdivision running in a northeasterly direction from Leroy Avenue and now surfaced for automobile travel as far as lots 26, 27 and 28. The subject premises were purchased by the plaintiffs from the city of Yonkers by deed dated April 14, 1947. At that time the defendants were, and had been since 1912, owners of premises designated as lots 14 and 15 in block 54, as shown on the same map. The defendants' lots front on Leroy Avenue and adjoin lot 19 owned by the plaintiffs at the rear boundary line. All of these lots, though differently numbered, appear on a map of the subdivision of the Murray Estate opened prior to 1912 and numbering 479 lots. At that time that part of the Murray subdivision was covered with a natural wild growth of brush and small trees.

The defendants interposed an answer denying generally the allegations of the complaint and alleging as an affirmative defense, and as a counterclaim, that William Lutz had acquired title to the subject premises by virtue of having held and possessed the same adversely to plaintiffs and predecessors for upwards of thirty years.

The issue thus joined was tried before Hon. FREDERICK P. CLOSE, Official Referee, who found that title to said lots "was perfected in William Lutz by virtue of adverse possession by the year 1935" and not thereafter disseized. The judgment entered thereon in favor of the defendants was affirmed in the Appellate Division, Second Department, without opinion, one Justice dissenting on the ground that the evidence was insufficient to establish title by adverse possession.

To acquire title to real property by adverse possession not founded upon a written instrument, it must be shown by clear and convincing proof that for at least fifteen years (formerly twenty years) there was an "actual" occupation under a claim of title, for it is only the premises so actually occupied "and no others" that are deemed to have been held adversely (Civ. Prac. Act, §§34, 38, 39). The essential elements of proof being either that the premises (1) are protected by a substantial inclosure, or are (2) usually cultivated or improved (Civ. Prac. Act, §40).

Concededly, there is no proof here that the subject premises were "protected by a substantial inclosure" which leaves for consideration only whether there is evidence showing that the premises were cultivated or improved sufficiently to satisfy the statute.

We think not. The proof concededly fails to show that the cultivation incident to the garden utilized the whole of the premises claimed. Such lack may not be supplied by inference on the showing that the cultivation of a smaller area, whose boundaries are neither defined nor its location fixed with certainty, "must have been * * * substantial" as several neighbors were "supplied * * * with vegetables". This introduces an element of speculation and surmise which may not be considered since the statute clearly limits the premises adversely held to those "actually" occupied "and no others" (Civ. Prac. Act, § 39) which we have recently interpreted as requiring definition by clear and positive proof.

Furthermore, on this record, the proof fails to show that the premises were improved (Civ. Prac. Act, § 40). According to the proof the small shed or shack (about 5 by 10 1/2 feet) which, as shown by survey map, was located on the subject premises about 14 feet from the Lutz boundary line. This was built in about the year 1923 and, as Lutz himself testified, he knew at the time it was not on his land and, his wife, a defendant here, also testified to the same effect.

The statute requires as an essential element of proof, recognized as fundamental on the concept of adversity since ancient times, that the occupation of premises be "under a claim of title" (Civ. Prac. Act, § 39), in other words, hostile, and when lacking will not operate to bar the legal title, no matter how long the occupation may have continued.

Similarly, the garage encroachment, extending a few inches over the boundary line, fails to supply proof of occupation by improvement. Lutz himself testified that when he built the garage he had no survey and thought he was getting it on his own property, which certainly falls short of establishing that he did it under a claim of title hostile to the true owner. The other acts committed by Lutz over the years, such as placing a portable chicken coop on the premises which he moved about, the cutting of brush and some of the trees, and the littering of the property with odds and ends of salvaged building materials, cast-off items of house furnishings and parts of automobiles which the defendants and their witnesses described as "personal belongings", "junk", "rubbish" and "debris", were acts which under no stretch of the imagination could be deemed an occupation by improvement within the meaning of the statute, and which, of course, are of no avail in establishing adverse possession.

[T]he proof fails to establish actual occupation for such a time or in such a manner as to establish title by adverse possession. The judgments should be reversed, the counterclaim dismissed and judgment directed to be entered in favor of plaintiff Joseph D. Van Valkenburgh for the relief prayed for in the complaint subject to the existing easement, with costs in all courts.

FULD, J. (dissenting). In my judgment, the weight of evidence lies with the determination made by the court at Special Term and affirmed by the Appellate Division.

Wild and overgrown when the Lutzes first moved into the neighborhood, the property was cleared by defendant's husband and had been, by 1916, the referee found, developed into a truck farm "of substantial size." Lutz, together with his children, worked the farm continuously until his death in 1948; indeed, after 1928, he had no other employment. Each year, a new crop was planted and the harvest of vegetables was sold to neighbors. Lutz also raised chickens on the premises, and constructed coops or sheds for them. Fruit trees were planted, and timber was cut from that portion of the property not used for the farm. On one of the lots, Lutz in 1920 built a one-room dwelling, in which his brother Charles has lived ever since.

Although disputing the referee's finding that the dimensions of Lutz's farm were substantial, the court's opinion fails to remark the plentiful evidence in support thereof. For instance, there is credible testimony in the record that "nearly all" of the property comprised by the four lots was cultivated during the period to which the referee's finding relates. A survey introduced in evidence indicates the very considerable extent to which the property was cultivated in 1950, and many witnesses testified that the farm was no larger at that time than it had ever been. There is evidence, moreover, that the cultivated area extended from the "traveled way" on *one side* of the property to a row of logs and brush—placed by Lutz for the express purpose of marking the farm's boundary—at the *opposite end* of the premises.

According to defendant's testimony, she and her husband, knowing that they did not have record title to the premises, intended from the first nevertheless to occupy the property as their own. Bearing this out is the fact that Lutz put down the row of logs and brush, which was over 100 feet in length, to mark the southwestern boundary of his farm; this marker, only roughly approximating the lot lines, extended beyond them into the bed of Gibson Place. The property was, moreover, known in the neighborhood as "Mr. Lutz's gardens", and the one-room dwelling on it as "Charlie's house"; the evidence clearly indicates that people living in the vicinity believed the property to be owned by Lutz. And it is undisputed that for upwards of thirty-five years—until 1947, when plaintiffs became the record owners—no other person ever asserted title to the parcel.

With evidence such as that in the record, I am at a loss to understand how this court can say that support is lacking for the finding that the premises had been occupied by Lutz under a claim of title. The referee was fully justified in concluding that the character of Lutz's possession was akin to that of a true owner and indicated, more dramatically and effectively than could words, an intent to claim the property as his own. Recognizing that "A claim of title may be made by acts alone, quite as effectively as by the most emphatic assertions", we have often sustained findings based on evidence of actual occupation and improvement of the property in the manner that "owners are accustomed to possess and improve their estates.

In short, there is ample evidence to sustain the finding that William Lutz actually occupied the property in suit for over fifteen years under a claim of title. Since, then, title vested in Lutz by 1935, the judgment must be affirmed.

I would affirm the judgment reached by both of the courts below.

Exercise 2-15. *Van Valkenburgh v. Lutz* Revisited

1. Revisit the key elements of adverse possession and ask how both the majority and the dissent applied these requirements. Do you agree with the majority or the dissent?

2. What else could Mr. and Mrs. Lutz have done to gain title by adverse possession?

Prescriptive Easements

In order to dispossess the original owner, an adverse possessor must act toward the property as would a typical owner in fee simple. Short of that, a prescriptive easement can arise when there is longstanding non-permissive *use*, but the conduct is not enough to qualify as possession (as would be expected of an owner). Instead of transforming a trespasser into an owner, a prescriptive easement grants a trespasser the right to use the property of another in the same way it had been used before without interference. A successful claimant owns an easement, but not fee ownership.

Chapter 10 will explore the rules governing easements in greater detail. Some key concepts are overviewed here. An easement is an interest in real property. Easements are generally affirmative in nature in that they authorize the use of someone else's property. A classic example would be a right of way across a neighbor's property. In such a case, the person who owns property subject to the easement (the servient estate holder) cannot exclude the easement owner from accessing their land as a passageway. There are two basic different kinds of easements: the benefit of an easement can attach to neighboring land, in which case they are called appurtenant; or they can be owned by an individual or an entity, in which case they are called in gross. Appurtenant easements run with the land and will benefit all future owners of the parcel to which it is attached. As an interest in real property, easements are covered by the Statute of Frauds and must be in writing to be enforceable. Prescriptive easements represent an important exception to this rule. Other exceptions to the writing requirement include easements by estoppel, easements implied by prior use and easements by necessity. All of these concepts are covered in Chapter 10 on Servitudes.

Additionally, just as easements can be created by satisfying the elements of prescription you are about to study, they can be terminated by these same principles as well. If a property owner interferes with the rights of an easement holder, they may be considered a trespasser on the easement. Because easements are interests in real property, they are subject to adverse possession or abandonment. Accordingly, an easement holder who does not stop a continuing trespass may lose her easement through adverse possession.

The elements that are necessary to prove acquisition of an easement by prescription are parallel to adverse possession except that two elements are different. First, the requirement of "possession" is changed to the requirement of "use." Second, the requirement for exclusive possession is modified or eliminated to account for the fact that an easement claimant might use the property of another at the same time the titled owner continues to use and enjoy their own property. That is the nature of easements—an easement owned has a limited property interest to engage in a particular activity and the servient estate owner retains the remaining interests. The next case highlights the distinction between a claim for adverse possession and a claim for a prescriptive easement.

Exercise 2-16. *Zuni Tribe v. Platt*

In *Zuni Tribe v. Platt*, the Zuni Tribe asserted a right to conduct a pilgrimage across private land to a sacred site. The Zuni Tribe had been conducting the pilgrimage every four years for hundreds of years. The court considers the rules governing both adverse possession and prescriptive easements.

United States on Behalf of the Zuni Tribe of New Mexico v. Platt

730 F. Supp. 318 (D.C. Ariz. 1990)

CARROLL, J. The Zuni Indians, as a part of their religion, make a regular periodic pilgrimage at the time of the summer solstice, on foot or horseback, from their reservation in northwest New Mexico to the mountain area the tribe calls Kohlu/wala:wa which is located in northeast Arizona. It is believed by the Zuni Indians that Kohlu/wala:wa is their place of origin, the basis for their religious life, and the home of their dead. These lands were lost to the Zuni Tribe as a result of an executive order in 1877, however, 1984 legislation, Public Law 98-408 § 4 (98 Stat. 1533), allowed the Tribe to acquire lands in Arizona for religious purposes. The legislation also allowed the Zuni Indians to acquire a permanent right of ingress and egress to Kohlu/wala:wa for traditional religious pilgrimages and ceremonies. As a part of the purchase of Kohlu/wala:wa, from Seven Springs Ranch Inc. the Zuni Tribe was granted a right of ingress and egress to the mountain connecting with an existing roadway from Hunt, Arizona. This point of access is on the west side of the mountain and would not enable the pilgrimage to have access to the area in the traditional manner.

There is historical evidence that the Zuni pilgrimage was occurring as early as 1540 A.D. The pilgrimage has been largely uncontested until recent times.

In 1985 defendant, Earl Platt, declared his intention of preventing the Zuni Indians from crossing his land on their pilgrimage. Earl Platt and the estate of Buena Platt (defendant), own or lease from the United States or the state of Arizona land in Apache County over which the Zuni Indians cross on their pilgrimage to Kohlu/wala:wa. On June 12, 1985 the United States on behalf of the Zuni Tribe instituted this action claiming a prescriptive easement by adverse possession across the Platt land.

The United States also sought a temporary restraining order, which was granted by Judge Copple on June 12, 1985, restraining the defendant from interfering with the Zuni pilgrimage. Another Temporary Restraining Order was entered on June 12, 1989 to restrain the defendant from interfering with the pilgrimage which was to take place on June 21–24, 1989.

The evidence presented at trial shows that the Zuni Indians have gone on their quadrennial pilgrimage, approximately every four years since, at least, the early twentieth century. There was direct evidence presented at trial, in the form of motion picture documentation, of the pilgrimage occurring in 1924. Furthermore, John Niiha, the Zuni Dance priest, testified that he has been on 11 pilgrimages since his first in approximately 1949. Another Zuni religious leader, Mecalite Wytsallaci, the Zuni Rain Priest of the North for the last 39 years, who is ninety-nine years old, testified that he went on a pilgrimage when he was a young man but has not participated in the pilgrimage since he has been the Rain Priest. Wytsallaci's testimony, indicates that he participated in a pilgrimage sometime prior to 1940. Since 1976 the Apache County Sheriff's office has set up a road block, north of St. Johns, on Highway 666, at the request of the Zuni Tribe, so as ensure the safety and privacy of the pilgrims as they cross the highway going to and coming from Kohlu/wala:wa on their pilgrimage. In 1985 the pilgrimage was conducted in the fifth year instead of the fourth, 1984, because, as the testimony indicates, the Zuni's did not want to jeopardize legislation pending in Congress whereby the Zuni Tribe could purchase Kohlu/wala:wa to be held in trust by the United States for the tribe.

Eighty Tribe members are selected to participate in the pilgrimage. However, due to age, health and other considerations not all actually go along. The pilgrimage party generally consists of forty to sixty Zuni Indians and twenty to forty horses. The pilgrims walk or ride horses, vehicles are not allowed in the pilgrimage procession. The Zuni pilgrimage begins at the Zuni Reservation, in Northwestern New Mexico, and follows a fairly direct path to Kohlu/wala:wa in Apache County, Arizona. The pilgrimage generally crosses the defendant's land[.] The total trek is 110 miles in length. It takes four days for the pilgrims to travel to Kohlu/wala:wa and return back to the reservation. The pilgrimage crosses approximately 18–20 miles of land owned or leased by the defendant Earl Platt.

The path or route used by the Zuni Indians, on their religious pilgrimage has been consistent and relatively unchanged. The plaintiffs concede that topographical changes may necessarily alter the route. However, man made obstacles will not cause the Zuni pilgrims to deviate from their customary path. This is evidenced by the fact the pilgrims cut or take down fences in their way.

The pathway used by the pilgrims is approximately fifty feet wide. The Zuni Indians use of the route in question is limited to a path or a place crossed enroot to Kohlu/wala:wa. Other than the path itself there are no points or landmarks of religious significance to the Zuni Indians on the defendant's land and the pilgrims do not camp on the defendant's land but they do stop for lunch on Platt land. There are a number of sites with religious significance to the Zuni Indians along the pilgrimage route east of the defendant's land.

The use of the property, by the Zuni Indians, along the pilgrimage route has been open visible and known to the community. Several witnesses who have been long time residents of the St. Johns area, which is in close proximity to the land in question, testified that they knew of the Zuni pilgrimage and that it was generally known throughout the community.

The Zuni Tribe, and the people going on the pilgrimage, believed that they had a right to cross the lands traversed by their established route. There has been no showing that they sought to cross lands under permission or by authority of other persons.

The Arizona statute defining adverse possession provides:

> "Adverse possession" means an actual and visible appropriation of the land, commenced and continued under a claim of right inconsistent with and hostile to the claim of another. A.R.S. § 12-521.

The Arizona statutes further provide that:

> A. A person who has a cause of action for recovery of any lands, tenements or hereditaments from a person having peaceable and adverse possession thereof, cultivating, using and enjoying such property, shall commence an action therefor within ten years after the cause of action accrues, and not afterward. A.R.S. § 12-526.

The Arizona statutes follow the generally held rule that in order for one to acquire right to property purely by adverse possession, such possession must be actual, open and notorious, hostile, under a claim of right, continuous for the statutory period of 10 years, and exclusive.

The Arizona Courts place the burden of proof on the party claiming the right to use another's land. Once the prima facie elements of prescription are met, the law presumes the use to be under a claim of right and not permissive. The burden of proving permissive use then falls upon the landowner.

The proof necessary to establish a prescriptive easement to use land is not the same as that to establish a claim of title by adverse possession. "It is only the use to which the premises are put which must be shown to be adverse, open and notorious. To the extent that the use is established, it, of course, is hostile to the title of the servient estate." Therefore, although the plaintiffs in this case must prove all the elements essential to title by prescription, their burden of proof must be measured in terms of the right to the use they claim, i.e. a very limited periodic use.

As stated above the plaintiffs must have proven, at trial, every element essential to adverse possession to establish a prescriptive easement over the pilgrimage route in question. Arizona case law does not provide a clear delineation as to the requirements of each element of adverse possession and often two or more requirements are analyzed in conjunction with each other.

The requirements of establishing actual possession and continuous possession are similar and inseparable and therefore they shall be considered together. Neither actual occupancy nor cultivation nor residence is necessary to constitute actual possession, and what acts may or may not constitute possession are necessarily varied and depend on the circumstances surrounding the case. In *Kay v. Biggs*, 13 Ariz. App. 172 (1970), the Arizona court of appeals held that two to three weeks of continuous possession during the summer every year coupled with other facts was sufficient to establish continuous possession and the adverse claim element required by statute. It should be noted in *Kay* the plaintiff sought and received title to the disputed parcel of land by adverse possession, not merely an easement.

The Zuni tribe has had actual possession of the route used for the religious pilgrimage for a short period of time every four years. They have had actual possession of the land in the sense that they have not recognized any other claim to the land at the time of the pilgrimage, as evidenced by their lack of deviation from the established route and disregard for fences or any other man made obstacle that blocks their course of travel. This Court also finds that the Zuni Tribe continually used a portion of the defendant's land for a short period of time every four years at least since 1924 and very probably for a period of time spanning many hundreds of years prior to that year.

Therefore, the plaintiffs have established the "actual" and "continuous" possession elements of their claim for adverse possession. Furthermore this "actual" possession has been continuous for over ten years which is required for a claim of a prescriptive right.

The open and notorious element of adverse possession requires that the acts of ownership must be of the character so as to indicate to the community in which the land is situated that it is in the exclusive possession and enjoyment of the claimant. There must be physical facts which openly evince and give notice of an intent to hold the land in hostile dominion and indicate to a prudent owner that an adverse claim is being asserted. However, an owner's actual knowledge of the adverse possession is equivalent to, and disposes with the necessity of open and notorious possession. Furthermore, presumption of notice or fact of notice upon the part of the title owner would arise to bar his right. Presumption of notice may arise when there is shown, under all facts and circumstances, a concurrence of the elements of adverse possession and the facts of use, possession and enjoyment indicating on the part of the claimant an intent to repudiate title and interest of the land owner.

The Zuni Tribe has not attempted to hide their pilgrimage or the route they were taking, although they do regard it as a personal and private activity. It was known generally throughout the community that the Zuni Indians took a pilgrimage every few years. It was also common knowledge in the community, generally, what route or over which lands the pilgrimage took place. Mrs. Hinkson, a resident of the St. John's area since 1938 and an owner of a ranch which the Zuni Indians cross on their pilgrimage, testified it was generally understood that the Zuni Tribe had set a precedent of crossing the land of ranchers that could not be changed even if owners of the land objected to such crossings or use of their property. The Zuni tribe also cut, tore down or placed gates in, fences on the property owned or leased by defendant and others.

This Court draws the reasonable inference, from all the facts and circumstances, that Earl Platt, the defendant in this case, was aware that a pilgrimage occurred, that it occurred approximately every four years and that the pilgrimage went across his property. The record shows that Earl Platt has owned or leased the property in question since the early 1940's.

Consequently, the Zuni Tribe's open and notorious use of Platt land and the inference that Earl Platt knew of such use satisfies and/or obviates the "open and notorious" element of an adverse possession.

It is contended by the plaintiffs that the Zuni's use of the Platt lands also fulfills the requirement of the "hostile" and "claim of right" elements of adverse possession. "Hostile" as applied to possession of realty does not connote ill will or evil intent, but merely a showing that the one in possession of the land claims exclusive rights thereto and denies by word or act the owner's title. Similarly a "claim of right" is:

> Nothing more than the intention of the party in possession to appropriate and use the land as his own to the exclusion of others irrespective of any semblance or shadow of actual title or right.

The record reflects, as discussed earlier, the Zuni pilgrims, at the time of their pilgrimage, claim exclusive right to the path they cross to Kohlu/wala:wa. The claim of right to temporary and periodic use of the defendant's land is evidenced by the cutting or pulling down of fences and the lack of deviation from the route. In recent years the Zuni Indians, with the aid of the Bureau of Land Management, placed gates in fences which impeded the pilgrimage route of the Zuni Indians. The use, by the pilgrims, of the defendant's land is "hostile" to Earl Platt's title. Also there was no evidence presented at trial which would indicate that the Zuni tribe sought permission to cross the land of Earl Platt. The evidence clearly illustrated that the Zuni Indians never sought permission to cross lands on their pilgrimage but rather it was believed said crossing was a matter of right.

The record leaves no doubt that the "hostile" and "claim of right" elements of adverse possession has been satisfied by the plaintiffs.

Insofar as the exclusivity of possession is required, in the context of the claim asserted here, it is reasonable to conclude that if people are occupying a tract of land at a particular time, another person or other people, cannot simultaneously occupy the same space. Therefore, the Zuni's participating in the quadrennial pilgrimage have exclusive possession of the land upon which they cross en route to Kohlu/wala:wa when they are crossing that land.

The Zuni Indian's use and possession of the Platt land has been actual, open and notorious, continuous and uninterrupted for at least 65 years and under a claim of right. Such use was known by the surrounding community.

It is clear from the record that the plaintiffs have established that the Zuni Indians meet the standards of adverse possession, set forth in A.R.S. § 12-521 and the applicable case law for purposes of the limited use sought. The Zuni Tribe is entitled to a prescriptive easement over the land of the defendant for the purposes of their quadrennial pilgrimage. The defendant presented no evidence and has not otherwise proven that the Zuni Indians' use of the land in question was permissive or otherwise.

Since the plaintiffs have established the Zuni Indians' right to a prescriptive easement this Court must determine the scope of that easement. The scope of a prescriptive easement is determined by the use through which it is acquired. Those using the land of another for the prescriptive period may acquire the right to continue such use, but do not acquire the right to make other uses of it.

Applying the above stated law this Court can only grant an easement for the use of defendant's land to the extent the use claimed has been proven or established at trial. Accordingly, IT IS ORDERED that the Zuni Tribe is granted an easement over the land owned by Earl Platt and the estate of Buena Platt, for 25 feet in either direction, of the route established by the October 27, 1987 Bureau of Land Management Survey, Exhibit 307.3, for the purposes of ingress to and egress from Kohlu/wala:wa by no more than 60 persons on foot or horseback.

IT IS FURTHER ORDERED the easement granted by this Court is limited to a 2 day period (one day each direction), during the summer solstice, once every four years to commence in 1993 and to continue on at 4 year intervals.

IT IS FURTHER ORDERED that the rights granted by this easement do not include the right to use defendant's water sources, nor does it include the right to light fires on the lands of the defendant.

IT IS FURTHER ORDERED that the Zuni Indian Tribe will be liable for any damage that occurs on defendant's property that is a result of the pilgrimage.

IT IS FURTHER ORDERED that the Zuni Tribe notify the defendant when the pilgrimage is going to occur at least 14 days prior to its commencement.

Exercise 2-17. *Zuni Tribe v. Platt* Revisited

The court granted an easement to the Zuni Tribe, but it also imposed certain restrictions to protect the interests of the private landowner. Do you think the court did a good job of balancing the competing interests?

The Improving Trespasser—*De minimis non curat lex*

The improving trespasser is a concept that is related to adverse possession, but it does not require longstanding use. It reflects the Latin maxim *de minimis non curat lex*, which means that the law will not concern itself with trifles.

The term improving trespasser conjures up images of a trespasser who decides to garden and clean up trash, but that interpretation is too literal. An improving trespasser refers to a non-owner who builds or constructs an improvement on the land of another without permission. When a building or other object encroaches on property, it is a continuing trespass, and the traditional remedy granted the owner of the property the absolute right to demand the removal of the encroachment. The modern approach is to apply a relative hardship doctrine where the court will balance the interests of the parties.

Take for example a neighbor who mistakenly builds a garage that encroaches on the adjoining property by two inches. Under the traditional rule, the neighboring landowner could compel the neighbor to remove the garage and cure the encroachment regardless of the cost. Under the doctrine of relative hardship, the court would refuse to grant an injunction compelling removal if the harm to the neighboring landowner is slight and the cost of removal is great. Instead, the court will order the improving trespasser to compensate the neighboring landowner by paying damages or compelling a sale of the land on which the encroachment sits. One major exception is that courts have not applied the relative hardship doctrine where the improving trespasser knowingly encroached on his neighbor's property. Before you read the next case, compare and contrast the doctrine of the improving trespasser with adverse possession so you are clear on the differences.

Exercise 2-18. *Yeakel v. Driscoll*

In *Yeakel v. Driscoll*, a newly built fire wall encroached on a neighbor's property by two inches for twelve feet. Do you consider this encroachment de minimus? How should we determine what qualifies as de minimus? Is it the quantum of the encroachment or of the resulting harm? How should we measure the severity of the harm?

Yeakel v. Driscoll

321 Pa. Super. 23 (1983)

Watkins, J. Plaintiff and defendants were owners of adjoining parcels of real estate in the City of Allentown. Each party owned one-half of a double home located adjacent to one another. The double home was constructed during the 1930's and contains a party wall separating the two homes together with rear porches which were separated by a cinder block wall. Having made plans to enclose their rear porch for energy conservation purposes, the defendants obtained the requisite building permit from the City of Allentown. The building permit required defendants to use a fire wall for that portion of the enclosure separating their property from that of the plaintiff. Two courses of decayed cinder block in the cinder block wall also had to be replaced. The fire wall between the properties was constructed by erecting it upon the cinder block wall which had previously existed between the rear porches. The work had commenced on August 30, 1979.

On September 6, 1979 plaintiff wrote a letter to a local newspaper complaining about the appearance of defendants' work. On September 25, 1979 plaintiff's attorney wrote to defendant complaining of their actions. By this time, work on the wall had been completed. On October 30, 1979, the plaintiff filed her Complaint in Equity against the defendants alleging that the new fire wall encroached several inches onto her property and requesting the court to order the defendants to refrain from entering onto her property, to remove the wall, and, to enjoin defendants from interfering in any way with the plaintiffs' use and occupancy of her property. The matter was heard by the court below on April 23, 1980. The hearing included a visit to the premises of the parties' by the Chancellor. Both parties agreed to the visit.

The Chancellor found that the defendant, John Driscoll, had discussed his plans with plaintiff's son prior to commencing the work. Plaintiff's son had owned plaintiff's property from 1972 until 1976 when he conveyed it to plaintiff. Defendants did not know that he was not the present owner. The plaintiff's son resided in plaintiff's home with her. The Chancellor also found that although defendants did remove a wooden frame or lip attached to the old cinder block wall which had provided support for a door of plaintiff's covering the steps at the rear exterior entrance to her basement, that defendant John Driscoll had obtained the approval of plaintiff's son to do so. He also found that plaintiff's son then extended plaintiff's rear porch and constructed a cover and locking door at the rear exterior entrance to her basement and same were secured by attaching them to defendants' concrete block wall. The Chancellor also held that the outer edge of defendants' new fire wall extended onto plaintiff's property for a distance of two inches on a skew approximately twelve (12) feet long from a point at the rear wall of plaintiff's dwelling to another point on the property line. The construction was in conformity with all City Codes. The Chancellor then went on to find that defendants' encroachment of a width of two (2) inches for twelve (12) feet constituted a "de minimus" or trivial one, applied the principal of "De minimus non curat Lex" to the case, and dismissed the plaintiff's complaint. Plaintiff appealed.

Plaintiff contends that she suffered real damages as a result of defendants' encroachment. She argues that she had never received water in her basement prior to defendants' work but that now, after a heavy rainfall, her basement becomes saturated with water. She attributes this condition to the defendants' work. She also claims that she is less secure in her home now because her new rear cellar door is not as good as the old one.

The heart of the instant action concerns the application of the doctrine of "de minimus" to this case. The doctrine is set forth in the maxim, "de minimus non curat lex" which means that the law will not concern itself with trifles. More specifically it means that a court will not grant equitable relief to a plaintiff who seeks a decree which will do him no good but which will work a hardship on another. [T]he court [below] found no nexus between the plaintiff's water problems and the defendant's fire wall. Thus, the removal of the fire wall from the two inches of plaintiff's property will not correct her water problem. Nor will the removal of the wall improve her security as the plaintiff's son has constructed a new cellar door in place of the old one. Thus, the only benefit to be gained by the plaintiff is to preserve her exclusivity to her two inches of property by forcing defendant to remove the fire wall from its present location. The City Codes of Allentown require the construction of a fire wall in such circumstances to protect property owners on both sides of the wall from a potential fire on the other side. Thus, we find that the court below did not commit reversible error when it weighed the equities involved in the case and decided that the removal or relocation of the wall (if that was possible) would do plaintiff no good and would work a hardship on another. The new wall replaced an old wall that had always been there. The new wall protects plaintiff, as well as, defendants. Such a wall was required by the City. Under these circumstances we find that the Chancellor did not err when he ruled that a two inch encroachment for a distance of twelve feet was subject to the "de minimus" maxim.

Order affirmed.

Brosky, Judge. I respectfully dissent. The majority opinion would make the equitable principle of *de minimis* applicable to cases in trespass *quare clausum fregit.* This is, in my view, contrary to the established law in Pennsylvania. Further, it violates several critical policy considerations. I would reverse the order of the court below and order the wall removed from appellant's land within a specified period of time.

The law in Pennsylvania on this subject dates back to the last century. In *Pile v. Pedrick,* 167 Pa. 296 (1895), the Supreme Court of this Commonwealth had before it a case legally identical to the one before us. There a wall was erected which encroached 1 3/8 inches onto the property of the adjoining landowner. In relevant part the opinion of the court states:

> For one inch and three eighths the ends of the stones in the wall are said to project beyond the division line. The defendants have no right at law or in equity to occupy land that does not belong to them and we do not see how the court below could have done otherwise than recognize and act upon this principle. They must remove their wall so that it shall be upon their land.

In *Pile* there is no suggestion of any doubt as to the result. Nor should there have been. This was in the face of an argument made by appellant that the wall should have been left as it was—for its removal would work a greater injury than damages at law.

While I believe that *Pile* governs the case before us, thus removing from this court's appraisal of its wisdom—I will briefly explore some of the other authority for this result and its underlying rationale.

Dean Prosser, perhaps the foremost authority on torts in twentieth century America, quoted in his hornbook the following statement. "... the common law, in considering liability for intrusions upon realty could not undertake to discriminate between the much and the little." Prosser, Law of Torts, 4th ed., (1971).

As in *Pile,* this has been found to be the rule even where little or no damage was suffered. The paucity of damage was held to be an insufficient reason to deny a mandatory injunction. This rule was also not voided by the fact that the expense to defendant in removing the trespassing object would be disproportionate to the damage to the plaintiff. In another case directly on point, the Supreme Court of our sister state, Arkansas, has held that the *de minimis* principle has no application to an encroachment caused by a brick wall leaning over a property line.

I dissent.

Exercise 2-19. *Yeakel v. Driscoll* Revisited

1. The majority notes that the plaintiff is requesting equitable relief in the form of an injunction. It then reasons that the court should not grant the relief when it "will do him no good, but work hardship on another." Do you agree?
2. The dissenting judge mentions a state supreme court case that is curiously absent from the majority opinion, *Pile v. Pedrick.* He also mentions that the absolute rule enunciated in *Pile* furthers important policy considerations. What policy interests are furthered by the absolute rule? What policy interests are furthered by the relative hardship rule?

Adverse Possession of Personal Property

Adverse possession most frequently arises in connection with disputes over real property, although it can also apply to personal property. Adverse possession is generally ill-suited to resolve disputes over personal property, because it is difficult to apply the open and notorious requirements. Unlike real property, personal property can be concealed. Adverse possession of real property is contingent on placing the original owner on sufficient notice. If the original owner fails to inspect his property and discover the trespasser, then the original owner may lose ownership. In the case of personal property, a thief could conceal the property for the statutory period and then claim ownership through adverse possession. What level of diligence does the original owner have to exercise in order to not lose ownership? When is an owner of personal property on notice that someone else is claiming ownership?

The courts have developed different approaches to address the question of notice. Some states have adopted a discovery rule that provides that the statutory period runs from the time the original owners discovers or should have discovered the location of the property. Other courts have adopted the demand rule that provides that the statutory period runs from the time when the original owner first makes a demand for the return of the property. The case below illustrates the difference between the two rules and the competing policy considerations.

Exercise 2-20. *Guggenheim Foundation v. Lubell*

A number of cases involving stolen artwork have grappled with the imperfect application of adverse possession to personal property claims. In these cases, it is typically a bona fide purchaser who asserts title to the artwork rather than the original thief. We know from earlier in the course that a thief never has good title, which means that he cannot pass good title to a bona fide purchaser. The true owner can recover the artwork from the bona fide purchaser, who then only has a claim for damages against the thief. Adverse possession provides a time limit where the true owner has a limited period to recover the artwork from either the thief or the bona fide purchaser. If the true owner fails to act within that period, the claim is barred. The question raised in Guggenheim *Found. v. Lubell* is when does that time limit begin to run.

Recall, also, that there is one limited exception where a thief can pass good title—where the true owner entrusts the property to a merchant who regularly deals in such property and the merchant turns out to be a thief. Adverse possession would not apply in a merchant case because the bona fide purchaser would have superior title. In the context of the art world, this situation could occur where an art collector lends a painting to a gallery owner who then turns out to be a thief and sells the painting to another collector. The true owner would have no claim against the bona fide purchaser, but could seek to recover damages from the gallery owner.

Guggenheim Foundation v. Lubell

77 N.Y.2d 311 (1991)

Wachtler, Chief Judge. The backdrop for this replevin action is the New York City art market, where masterpieces command extraordinary prices at auction and illicit dealing in stolen merchandise is an industry all its own. The Solomon R. Guggenheim Foundation, which operates the Guggenheim Museum in New York City, is seeking to recover a Chagall gouache worth an estimated $200,000. The Guggenheim believes that the gouache was stolen from its premises by a mailroom employee sometime in the late 1960s. The appellant Rachel Lubell and her husband, now deceased, bought the painting from a well-known Madison Avenue gallery in 1967 and have displayed it in their home for more than 20 years. Mrs. Lubell claims that before the Guggenheim's demand for its return in 1986, she had no reason to believe that the painting had been stolen.

On this appeal, we must decide if the museum's failure to take certain steps to locate the gouache is relevant to the appellant's Statute of Limitations defense. In effect, the appellant argues that the museum had a duty to use reasonable diligence to recover the gouache, that it did not do so, and that its cause of action in replevin is consequently barred by the Statute of Limitations. The Appellate Division rejected the appellant's argument. We agree with the Appellate Division that the timing of the museum's demand for the gouache and the appellant's refusal to return it are the only relevant factors in assessing the merits of the Statute of Limitations defense. We see no justification for undermining the clarity and predictability of this rule by carving out an exception where the chattel to be returned is a valuable piece of art.

The gouache, known alternately as *Menageries* or *Le Marchand de Bestiaux (The Cattle Dealer)*, was painted by Marc Chagall in 1912, in preparation for an oil painting also entitled *Le Marchand de Bestiaux*. It was donated to the museum in 1937 by Solomon R. Guggenheim.

The museum keeps track of its collection through the use of "accession cards," which indicate when individual pieces leave the museum on loan, when they are returned and when they are transferred between the museum and storage. The museum lent the painting to a number of other art museums over the years. The last such loan occurred in 1961–1962. The accession card for the painting indicates that it was seen in the museum on April 2, 1965. The next notation on the accession card is undated and indicates that the painting could not be located.

Precisely when the museum first learned that the gouache had been stolen is a matter of some dispute. The museum acknowledges that it discovered that the painting was not where it should be sometime in the late 1960s, but claims that it did not know that the painting had in fact been stolen until it undertook a complete inventory of the museum collection beginning in 1969 and ending in 1970. According to the museum, such an inventory was typically taken about once every 10 years. The appellant, on the other hand, argues that the museum knew as early as 1965 that the painting had been stolen. It is undisputed, however, that the Guggenheim did not inform other museums, galleries or artistic organizations of the theft, and additionally, did not notify the New York City Police, the FBI, Interpol or any other law enforcement authorities. The museum asserts that this was a tactical decision based upon its belief that to publicize the theft would succeed only in driving the gouache further underground and greatly diminishing the possibility that it would ever be recovered. In 1974, having concluded that all efforts to recover the gouache had been exhausted, the museum's Board of Trustees voted to "deaccession" the gouache, thereby removing it from the museum's records.

Mr. and Mrs. Lubell had purchased the painting from the Robert Elkon Gallery for $17,000 in May of 1967. The invoice and receipt indicated that the gouache had been in the collection of a named individual, who later turned out to be the museum mailroom employee suspected of the theft. They exhibited the painting twice, in 1967 and in 1981, both times at the Elkon Gallery. In 1985, a private art dealer brought a transparency of the painting to Sotheby's for an auction estimate. The person to whom the dealer showed the transparency had previously worked at the Guggenheim and recognized the gouache as a piece that was missing from the museum. She notified the museum, which traced the painting back to the defendant. On January 9, 1986, Thomas Messer, the museum's director, wrote a letter to the defendant demanding the return of the gouache. Mrs. Lubell refused to return the painting and the instant action for recovery of the painting, or, in the alternative, $200,000, was commenced on September 28, 1987.

In her answer, the appellant raised as affirmative defenses the Statute of Limitations, her status as a good-faith purchaser for value, adverse possession, laches, and the museum's culpable conduct. [T]he appellant argued that the replevin action to compel the return of the painting was barred by the three-year Statute of Limitations because the museum had done nothing to locate its property in the 20-year interval between the theft and the museum's fortuitous discovery that the painting was in Mrs. Lubell's possession. The trial court granted the appellant's cross motion for summary judgment, relying on *DeWeerth v. Baldinger*, 836 F.2d 103 (2d Cir. 1987), an opinion from the United States Court of Appeals for the Second Circuit. The trial court cited New York cases holding that a cause of action in replevin accrues when demand is made upon the possessor and the possessor refuses to return the chattel. The court reasoned, however, that in order to avoid prejudice to a good-faith purchaser, demand cannot be unreasonably delayed and that a property owner has an obligation to use reasonable efforts to locate its missing property to ensure that demand is not so delayed. Because the museum in this case had done nothing for 20 years but search its own premises, the court found that its conduct was unreasonable as a matter of law. Consequently, the court granted Mrs. Lubell's cross motion for summary judgment on the grounds that the museum's cause of action was time barred.

New York case law has long protected the right of the owner whose property has been stolen to recover that property, even if it is in the possession of a good-faith purchaser for value. There is a three-year Statute of Limitations for recovery of a chattel. The rule in this State is that a cause of action for replevin against the good-faith purchaser of a stolen chattel accrues when the true owner makes demand for return of the chattel and the person in possession of the chattel refuses to return it. Until demand is made and refused, possession of the stolen property by the good-faith purchaser for value is not considered wrongful. Although seemingly anomalous, a different rule applies when the stolen object is in the possession of the thief. In that situation, the Statute of Limitations runs from the time of the theft, even if the property owner was unaware of the theft at the time that it occurred.

In *DeWeerth v Baldinger*, which the trial court in this case relied upon in granting Mrs. Lubell's summary judgment motion, the Second Circuit took note of the fact that New York case law treats thieves and good-faith purchasers differently and looked to that difference as a basis for imposing a reasonable diligence requirement on the owners of stolen art. Although the court acknowledged that the question posed by the case was an open one, it declined to certify it to this Court, stating that it did not think that it "[would] recur with sufficient frequency to warrant use of the certification procedure." Actually, the issue has recurred several times in the three years since *DeWeerth* was decided, including the case now before us. We have reexamined the relevant New York case law and we conclude that the Second Circuit should not have imposed a duty of reasonable diligence on the owners of stolen artwork for purposes of the Statute of Limitations.

While the demand and refusal rule is not the only possible method of measuring the accrual of replevin claims, it does appear to be the rule that affords the most protection to the true owners of stolen property. Less protective measures would include running the three-year statutory period from the time of the theft even where a good-faith purchaser is in possession of the stolen chattel, or, alternatively, calculating the statutory period from the time that the good-faith purchaser obtains possession of the chattel. Other States that have considered this issue have applied a discovery rule to these cases, with the Statute of Limitations running from the time that the owner discovered or reasonably should have discovered the whereabouts of the work of art that had been stolen.

New York has already considered—and rejected—adoption of a discovery rule. In 1986, both houses of the New York State Legislature passed Assembly Bill 11462-A (Senate Bill 3274-B), which would have modified the demand and refusal rule and instituted a discovery rule in actions for recovery of art objects brought against certain not-for-profit institutions. This bill provided that the three-year Statute of Limitations would run from the time these institutions gave notice, in a manner specified by the statute, that they were in possession of a particular object. Governor Cuomo vetoed the measure, however, on advice of the United States Department of State, the United States Department of Justice and the United States Information Agency. In his veto message, the Governor expressed his concern that the statute "[did] not provide a reasonable opportunity for individuals or foreign governments to receive notice of a museum's acquisition and take action to recover it before their rights are extinguished." The Governor also stated that he had been advised by the State Department that the bill, if it went into effect, would have caused New York to become "a haven for cultural property stolen abroad since such objects [would] be immune from recovery under the limited time periods established by the bill."

The history of this bill and the concerns expressed by the Governor in vetoing it, when considered together with the abundant case law spelling out the demand and refusal rule, convince us that that rule remains the law in New York and that there is no reason to obscure its straightforward protection of true owners by creating a duty of reasonable diligence. Our case law already recognizes that the true owner, having discovered the location of its lost property, cannot unreasonably delay making demand upon the person in possession of that property. Here, however, where the demand and refusal is a substantive and not a procedural element of the cause of action, it would not be prudent to extend that case law and impose the additional duty of diligence before the true owner has reason to know where its missing chattel is to be found.

Further, the facts of this case reveal how difficult it would be to specify the type of conduct that would be required for a showing of reasonable diligence. Here, the parties hotly contest whether publicizing the theft would have turned up the gouache. According to the museum, some members of the art community believe that publicizing a theft exposes gaps in security and can lead to more thefts; the museum also argues that publicity often pushes a missing painting further underground. In light of the fact that members of the art community have apparently not reached a consensus on the best way to retrieve stolen art (*see*, Burnham, Art Theft: Its Scope, Its Impact and Its Control), it would be particularly inappropriate for this Court to spell out arbitrary rules of conduct that all true owners of stolen art work would have to follow to the letter if they wanted to preserve their right to pursue a cause of action in replevin. All owners of stolen property should not be expected to behave in the same way and should not be held to a common standard. The value of the property stolen, the manner in which it was stolen, and the type of institution from which it was stolen will all necessarily affect the manner in which a true owner will search for missing property. We conclude that it would be difficult, if not impossible, to craft a reasonable diligence requirement that could take into account all of these variables and that would not unduly burden the true owner.

Further, our decision today is in part influenced by our recognition that New York enjoys a worldwide reputation as a preeminent cultural center. To place the burden of locating stolen artwork on the true owner and to foreclose the rights of that owner to recover its property if the burden is not met would, we believe, encourage illicit trafficking in stolen art. Three years after the theft, any purchaser, good faith or not, would be able to hold onto stolen art work unless the true owner was able to establish that it had undertaken a reasonable search for the missing art. This shifting of the burden onto the wronged owner is inappropriate. In our opinion, the better rule gives the owner relatively greater protection and places the burden of investigating the provenance of a work of art on the potential purchaser.

Exercise 2-21. *Guggenheim Foundation v. Lubell* Revisited

1. The case mentions that three different federal agencies lobbied the Governor to veto legislation that would have imposed a discovery rule in New York State. Why was the federal government opposed to a discovery rule?
2. Assume you represent an art collector. What advice would you give your client before she purchases a work of art?
3. As we discussed in connection with the section on reparations and restitution, the Nazis confiscated vast amounts of personal property. Their systemic looting of artworks, especially from Jewish owners, has led to decades of claims from owners and descendants. The 2015 movie, *The Woman in Gold*, starring Helen Mirren, detailed the struggle of the descendant of the owner of a famous Klimt painting to regain ownership.

Chapter 3

Trespass—The Right to Exclude and the Right to Access

Introduction

The right to exclude non-owners is central to a system of private property. As we discussed in the prior Chapter, ownership is often conceptualized as a "bundle of sticks." Although the right to exclude is considered to be an essential "stick" in this bundle, it is far from absolute. We will see that this is also the case with the other "sticks" in the bundle. With respect to the right to exclude, there are a number of instances where non-owners may have a right to access the property of another. These instances include when there is some sort of necessity or where the law otherwise mandates access, such as in the case of public beach access or anti-discrimination commands. Accordingly, an owner's right to exclude is often balanced by a non-owner's right to access.

Owners ——→ Right to Exclude
v. v.
Non-Owners ——→ Right to Access

Chapter Problem: Exercise 3-1

Assume that you represent, Laura Henderson, who owns and operates a local convenience store, The Midtown Kwik-E-Mart. Laura has asked you to meet her at the store to discuss a few ideas she had about how to improve her customers' experience. You have represented her for a number of years, and she is accustomed to asking your advice on any fundamental changes to her business, but you have never visited the store. The store is located on a busy street with good foot traffic. You have to climb four steps to get to the front door where you notice two separate handwritten signs. The first signs reads: "No More Than Two (2) Students at ANY Time." The second sign reads, "Do NOT Give $$$$ to Panhandlers." As you are reading the signs, an older woman who appears to be homeless tries to hand you a five-dollar bill and says, "please buy me food. The store won't let me in."

When you see Laura, she thanks you for coming and then announces that she wants to install a buzzer on the front door "like they have in jewelry stores." Laura explains that she wants to be able to see her customers before she lets them in. She is often the only person working at the store, and she has recently begun to fear for her safety. Laura explains that "the neighborhood is changing—and not in a good way."

Keep this interaction in mind as you work through this Chapter. By the end of the Chapter, you should be able to advise Laura regarding her proposal to install a buzzer.

Overview of Chapter 3

In this Chapter, you will learn how courts balance the right of an owner to exclude with the right of a non-owner to access. You will also learn that these competing rights can be based on different sources of authority. For example, federal, state, and local non-discrimination statutes have significantly limited the common right to exclude for businesses that qualify as a "public accommodation." As you read the cases in this Chapter, it is important to keep track of both the rights asserted by the parties and the source of those rights. In other words, is the plaintiff asserting a common law right or one that has been created by statute? Also, it is always important to try to identify the policy objectives served by the law and be able to explain to your client why the law directs a particular answer.

The Chapter is divided into six subunits:

1. The Traditional Law of Trespass
2. Public Policy Limitations on the Right to Exclude Non-Owners
3. Property Open to the General Public
4. Non-Discrimination Laws
5. Beach Access and the Public Trust
6. Homelessness

The Traditional Law of Trespass

The owner of property has the right to exclude non-owners and deny them access to her property. This right is enforced through the tort of trespass. Trespass is defined as the intentional and unprivileged entry onto the land of another. An entry must be *intentional*, which means that an individual who is forcibly thrown onto the land of another or negligently enters the land of another will not be liable for trespass. In addition, the entry must also be *unprivileged*.

An entry is considered privileged when the individual has permission to enter or the law otherwise authorizes the entry. For example, an individual will generally not be liable for trespass if she enters the land of another to stop a crime or save a life. In the famous case of *Ploof v. Putnam*, 83 Vt. 494 (1910), the captain of a sloop was sailing with his wife and two minor children on Lake Champlain when a violent storm arose, and he tied the boat to a privately owned dock. The court held that the doctrine of necessity justified using the dock of another in order to seek shelter from the approaching storm. An individual may also be privileged to enter the land of another to recover personal property, which is sometimes referred to as chattel, provided that the property is not there as a result of that individual's actions or negligence.

When an owner of property grants an individual permission to enter her property, the grant of permission is called a *license*. The individual who is granted permission is referred to as the *licensee*. A license is considered a property interest, but it is relatively fragile, because the grantor of the license can revoke it for any reason, which is why a license is said to be revocable *at will*. A limited exception to this rule, called an easement by estoppel, is covered in Chapter 10. When you invite friends to a party at your apartment, you have granted them a license. The fact that the license is revocable at will means that you can decide when the party is over. A ticket to a sporting event or entertainment event is also considered a license. As soon as a license is revoked, the entry is no longer privileged. and the former licensee either must leave or become a trespasser.

In order to hold a non-owner liable for trespass in tort, an owner must file a lawsuit. If the lawsuit is successful, the owner will be entitled to damages. There are generally three different types of damages: nominal, compensatory, and punitive. Nominal damages are awarded when the plaintiff has not suffered any compensable harm, but has prevailed in her claim. Compensatory damages are designed to make the plaintiff whole for the harm suffered. Punitive damages are awarded over and above compensatory damages to punish the defendant for her conduct and deter future wrongdoers. In a trespass claim, the plaintiff is not required to show harm. The wrongful interference with the owner's right to exclude is sufficient to support a claim of trespass and will result in the award of nominal damages. The first case you will read, *Jacque v. Steenberg Homes*, presents a straightforward case of trespass and asks whether punitive damages are appropriate in a trespass case where the owners did not suffer any harm beyond the fact of the trespass.

Trespass is also a criminal offense. This gives an owner a powerful enforcement mechanism, because she can call the police to have a criminal trespasser removed forcibly. In some states, a non-owner must first be asked to leave and then refuse before being charged with criminal trespass. Trespass is typically a summary offense or a misdemeanor, although some states have enhanced penalties when the trespass involves specifics venues, such as schools or research facilities.

Here is a simple graph to illustrate what happens when a non-owner enters the property of another.

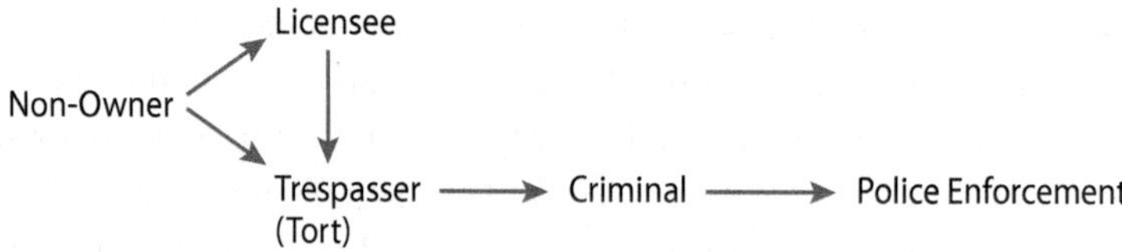

Ignoring for the moment issues of necessity and related privilege, a non-owner will either enter the property with permission as a licensee or without permission as a trespasser. Even if the non-owner enters as a licensee, he can become a trespasser, if the license is revoked. Once the non-owner is a trespasser in tort, he may be committing a criminal trespass. The owner then has the ability to call the police and have the non-owner forcibly removed. In this way, the owner of private property can use the power of the state to remove trespassers and enforce property boundaries.

Exercise 3-2. *Jacque v. Steenberg Homes*

Jacque v. Steenberg Homes presents a clear case of intentional trespass that involves both tort and criminal liability. The defendant concedes that it intentionally entered the plaintiff's land without permission.

1. Describe the property at issue.
2. What property right did the Jacques assert and on what authority?
3. Why did the Jacques refuse to grant permission to Steenberg Homes to cross their land? Does this seem like neighborly behavior?
4. Identify the general Wisconsin rule regarding the award of punitive damages in tort cases and explain the rationale for the rule.
5. Why do the Jacques claim that the rule should not apply in the case of intentional trespass?

Jacque v. Steenberg Homes, Inc.

563 N.W.2d 154 (Wis. 1997)

Bablitch, J. Steenberg Homes had a mobile home to deliver. Unfortunately for Harvey and Lois Jacque (the Jacques), the easiest route of delivery was across their land. Despite adamant protests by the Jacques, Steenberg plowed a path through the Jacques' snow-covered field and via that path, delivered the mobile home. Consequently, the Jacques sued Steenberg Homes for intentional trespass. At trial, Steenberg Homes conceded the intentional trespass, but argued that no compensatory damages had been proved, and that punitive damages could not be awarded without compensatory damages. Although the jury awarded the Jacques $1 in nominal damages and $100,000 in punitive damages, the circuit court set aside the jury's award of $100,000. The court of appeals affirmed, reluctantly concluding that it could not reinstate the punitive damages because it was bound by precedent establishing that an award of nominal damages will not sustain a punitive damage award. We conclude that when nominal damages are awarded for an intentional trespass to land, punitive damages may, in the discretion of the jury, be awarded. We further conclude that the $100,000 awarded by the jury is not excessive. Accordingly, we reverse and remand for reinstatement of the punitive damage award.

Plaintiffs, Lois and Harvey Jacques, are an elderly couple, now retired from farming, who own roughly 170 acres near Wilke's Lake in the town of Schleswig. The defendant, Steenberg Homes, Inc. (Steenberg), is in the business of selling mobile homes. In the fall of 1993, a neighbor of the Jacques purchased a mobile home from Steenberg. Delivery of the mobile home was included in the sales price.

Steenberg determined that the easiest route to deliver the mobile home was across the Jacques' land. Steenberg preferred transporting the home across the Jacques' land because the only alternative was a private road which was covered in up to seven feet of snow and contained a sharp curve which would require sets of "rollers" to be used when maneuvering the home around the curve. Steenberg asked the Jacques on several separate occasions whether it could move the home across the Jacques' farm field. The Jacques refused. The Jacques were sensitive about allowing others on their land because they had lost property valued at over $10,000 to other neighbors in an adverse possession action in the mid-1980's. Despite repeated refusals from the Jacques, Steenberg decided to sell the mobile home, which was to be used as a summer cottage, and delivered it on February 15, 1994.

On the morning of delivery, Mr. Jacque observed the mobile home parked on the corner of the town road adjacent to his property. He decided to find out where the movers planned to take the home. The movers, who were Steenberg employees, showed Mr. Jacque the path they planned to take with the mobile home to reach the neighbor's lot. The path cut across the Jacques' land. Mr. Jacque informed the movers that it was the Jacques' land they were planning to cross and that Steenberg did not have permission to cross their land. He told them that Steenberg had been refused permission to cross the Jacques' land.

At that point, the assistant manager asked Mr. Jacque how much money it would take to get permission. Mr. Jacque responded that it was not a question of money; the Jacques just did not want Steenberg to cross their land. Mr. Jacque testified that he told Steenberg to "Follow the road, that is what the road is for." Steenberg employees left the meeting without permission to cross the land.

At trial, one of Steenberg's employees testified that, upon coming out of the Jacques' home, the assistant manager stated: "I don't give a [expletive] what [Mr. Jacque] said, just get the home in there any way you can." The employees used a "bobcat" to cut a path through the Jacques' snow-covered field and hauled the home across the Jacques' land to the neighbor's lot.

When a neighbor informed the Jacques that Steenberg had, in fact, moved the mobile home across the Jacques' land, Mr. Jacque called the Manitowoc County Sheriff's Department. After interviewing the parties and observing the scene, an officer from the sheriff's department issued a $30 citation [for criminal trespass] to Steenberg's assistant manager.

The general rule was stated in *Barnard v. Cohen,* 165 Wis. 417, 162 N.W. 480 (1917), where the question presented was: "In an action for libel, can there be a recovery of punitory damages if only nominal compensatory damages are found?" [T]he *Barnard* court said no. *Barnard* continues to state the general rule of punitive damages in Wisconsin. The rationale for the compensatory damage requirement is that if the individual cannot show actual harm, he or she has but a nominal interest, hence, society has little interest in having the unlawful, but otherwise harmless, conduct deterred, therefore, punitive damages are inappropriate.

Steenberg contends that the rule established in *Barnard* prohibits a punitive damage award, as a matter of law, unless the plaintiff also receives compensatory damages. Because the Jacques did not receive a compensatory damage award, Steenberg contends that the punitive damage award must be set aside. The Jacques argue that the rationale for not allowing nominal damages to support a punitive damage award is inapposite when the wrongful act involved is an intentional trespass to land. The Jacques argue that both the individual and society have significant interests in deterring intentional trespass to land, regardless of the lack of measurable harm that results. We agree with the Jacques. An examination of the individual interests invaded by an intentional trespass to land, and society's interests in preventing intentional trespass to land, leads us to the conclusion that the *Barnard* rule should not apply when the tort supporting the award is intentional trespass to land.

The United States Supreme Court has recognized that the private landowner's right to exclude others from his or her land is "one of the most essential sticks in the bundle of rights that are commonly characterized as property." *Dolan v. City of Tigard,* 512 U.S. 374 (1994); (quoting *Kaiser Aetna v. United States,* 444 U.S. 164, 176, (1979)). This court has long recognized "every person['s] constitutional right to the exclusive enjoyment of his own property for any purpose which does not invade the rights of another person." Thus, both this court and the Supreme Court recognize the individual's legal right to exclude others from private property.

Yet a right is hollow if the legal system provides insufficient means to protect it. Harvey and Lois Jacque have the right to tell Steenberg Homes and any other trespasser, "No, you cannot cross our land." But that right has no practical meaning unless protected by the State. The law infers some damage from every direct entry upon the land of another. The law recognizes actual harm in every trespass to land whether or not compensatory damages are awarded. Thus, in the case of intentional trespass to land, the nominal damage award represents the recognition that, although immeasurable in mere dollars, actual harm has occurred.

Society has an interest in punishing and deterring intentional trespassers beyond that of protecting the interests of the individual landowner. Society has an interest in preserving the integrity of the legal system. Private landowners should feel confident that wrongdoers who trespass upon their land will be appropriately punished. When landowners have confidence in the legal system, they are less likely to resort to "self-help" remedies.

People expect wrongdoers to be appropriately punished. Punitive damages have the effect of bringing to punishment types of conduct that, though oppressive and hurtful to the individual, almost invariably go unpunished by the public prosecutor. The $30 forfeiture was certainly not an appropriate punishment for Steenberg's egregious trespass in the eyes of the Jacques. If punitive damages are not allowed in a situation like this, what punishment will prohibit the intentional trespass to land? Moreover, what is to stop Steenberg Homes from concluding, in the future, that delivering its mobile homes via an intentional trespass and paying the resulting Class B forfeiture, is not more profitable than obeying the law? Steenberg Homes plowed a path across the Jacques' land and dragged the mobile home across that path, in the face of the Jacques' adamant refusal. A $30 forfeiture and a $1 nominal damage award are unlikely to restrain Steenberg Homes from similar conduct in the future. An appropriate punitive damage award probably will.

In sum, as the court of appeals noted, the *Barnard* rule sends the wrong message to Steenberg Homes and any others who contemplate trespassing on the land of another. It implicitly tells them that they are free to go where they please, regardless of the landowner's wishes. As long as they cause no compensable harm, the only deterrent intentional trespassers face is the nominal damage award of $1 and the possibility of a Class B forfeiture. We conclude that both the private landowner and society have much more than a nominal interest in excluding others from private land. Intentional trespass to land causes actual harm to the individual, regardless of whether that harm can be measured in mere dollars. Consequently, the *Barnard* rationale will not support a refusal to allow punitive damages when the tort involved is an intentional trespass to land. Accordingly, assuming that the other requirements for punitive damages have been met, we hold that nominal damages may support a punitive damage award in an action for intentional trespass to land.

Our holding is supported by respected legal commentary. The Restatement (Second) of Torts supports the proposition that an award of nominal damages will support an award of punitive damages in a trespass to land action:

> The fact that the actor knows that his entry is without the consent of the possessor and without any other privilege to do so, while not necessary to make him liable, may affect the amount of damages recoverable against him, by showing such a complete disregard of the possessor's legally protected interest in the exclusive possession of his land as to justify the imposition of punitive in addition to nominal damages for even a harmless trespass, or in addition to compensatory damages for one which is harmful. *Restatement (Second) of Torts* § 163 cmt. e (1979).

The Restatement reiterates this position under the punitive damages section: nominal damages support an award of punitive damages "when a tort, such as trespass to land, is committed for an outrageous purpose, but no significant harm has resulted."

Without punitive damages, Steenberg has a financial incentive to trespass again. Our concern for deterrence is guided by our recognition of the nature of Steenberg's business. Steenberg sells and delivers mobile homes. It is, therefore, likely that they will again be faced with what was, apparently for them, a dilemma. Should they trespass and pay the forfeiture, which in this case was $30? Or, should they take the more costly course and obey the law? Today we alleviate the uncertainty for Steenberg Homes. We feel certain that the $100,000 will serve to encourage the latter course by removing the profit from the intentional trespass.

Reversed and remanded with direction.

Exercise 3-3. *Jacque v. Steenberg Homes* Revisited

1. The Wisconsin Supreme Court cites both the U.S. Supreme Court and the Second Restatement of Torts. Why are these sources of authority relevant to the case? What weight should courts give to the Restatement?
2. Why were criminal sanctions insufficient to deter future wrongdoing on the part of Steenberg Homes?
3. The court mentions that adequate punishment and deterrence for wrongdoing is necessary to maintain confidence in the legal system and discourage "self-help," which occurs when property owners take matters into their own hands. Why is it important to discourage self-help?
4. The court says that "both the private landowner and society have much more than a nominal interest in excluding others from private land." Do you agree?
5. In the United States, the use of the land of another is presumptively non-permissive. Why is this the default rule? Some countries have "right to roam" laws that mandate reasonable ingress to and egress from privately owned land. Why should the Jacques be able to increase significantly the cost of delivery when no actual harm would occur to their property? Is that fair?

Public Policy Limitations on the Right to Exclude Non-Owners

The right to exclude is by no means absolute. There are numerous instances where public policy concerns impose limitations on the right of a private property owner to exclude non-owners. As the New Jersey Supreme Court explains in the following case, *State v. Shack*, "[p]roperty interests serve human values." The cases in this section illustrate some of the countervailing pubic policy interests that argue in favor of restricting the right to exclude and recognizing a right of access for non-owners. The limitations on the right to exclude have sometimes been imposed by court decisions, which makes them common law or court-made limitations. These common law limitations include those articulated in both *State v. Shack* and *Food Lion v. ABC* (below after *State v. Shack*). They also include the well-established doctrine of necessity, where an intentional trespass is considered privileged when a non-owner enters the land of another to stop a crime or prevent bodily harm. Under this court-made doctrine, the societal interests in preventing crime or harm outweigh the societal interests in respecting property boundaries. Limitations on the right to exclude have also been imposed by federal, state, and local statutes, such as public accommodation laws that bar discrimination. As you read through these cases, consider the source of authority for each limitation. Is it a common law rule or a statutory exception? Does it amount to a right of access or merely restrict the right to exclude? Do you believe that these limitations are eroding private property rights or are they necessary to serve other human values?

Law students often find questions of public policy to be confusing, especially when they are struggling to identify the relevant facts and the holding. But it is just as important to be able to identify the public policy interests at stake in a case as it is to be able to identify the holding. Public policy is what provides the "why" behind the law—it is the reason or rationale for any given rule. When you represent a client, he will often want to know why the law prescribes a certain result, and it will be up to you to be able to explain it to him in plain English. Moreover, it is important to understand the public policy behind a rule in order to argue for its application or argue for an exception.

Take for example the prior case of *Jacque v. Steenberg*. The Jacques had to understand why the Wisconsin courts had adopted the *Barnard* rule in order to argue that it should not apply to intentional trespass. Instead of simply applying the *Barnard* rule regarding punitive damages in tort claims, the court first examined the rationale for the rule. It then determined that the rationale was not applicable to the case of intentional trespass, which raised different interests and concerns than other torts. The court chose not to follow the *Barnard* rule, but instead created an exception to the general rule that better addressed the public policy interests at stake in the case of intentional trespass. By examining the rationale—the why behind the rule—the court made certain that its decision reflected the strong public policy interest of respect for private property.

A court will often consider the consequences of a particular ruling before issuing a decision. This is the point when public policy concerns most clearly come into play. To return to *Jacque*, the court reasoned that if it followed the *Barnard* rule, it would not deter Steenberg from engaging in similar behavior in the future. In fact, Steenberg would have a "financial incentive" to trespass, because it would be less expensive for Steenberg to pay a small criminal fine and nominal damages whenever the shortest distance to a homesite was over the land of another. As a matter of public policy, the court found that such a result would be untenable. In the cases that follow, the courts apply the same sort of reasoning to the question of when to enforce the right to exclude non-owners.

Exercise 3-4. *State v. Shack*

The case of *State v. Shack* is a criminal case rather than a tort claim. The defendants, Shack and Tejeras, appealed their convictions for criminal trespass and raised several affirmative defenses that they claimed excused or justified the trespass. The following excerpt only addresses the state law claim that the right to exclude should be limited in this circumstance. The defendants also raised a defense under the U.S. Constitution on First Amendment grounds, as well as the Supremacy Clause. The New Jersey Supreme Court based its decision on state law and declined to reach the constitutional arguments. This is consistent with the general practice of constitutional avoidance, where courts avoid deciding constitutional issues if there is an alternative and more narrow ground to do so.

As you read the case, consider the following discussion points and questions.

1. Identify the competing property interests.
2. The defendant Shack was a lawyer. Why did he go to Tedesco's farm? Tedesco does not immediately order the defendants to leave, but instead imposes limitations on their visit. Why would a lawyer find the conditions that Tedesco imposed unacceptable?
3. Where does the court find evidence of public policy considerations that favor the defendants? Try to list all of the sources that the court draws on to reach its conclusion that the workers are a "highly disadvantaged segment of society."
4. What is the relationship between Tedesco and the seasonal workers? What property rights do the workers have? What property rights do the defendants have?
5. In *Jacque*, the court considered the criminal sanctions insufficient to deter future behavior. In *Shack*, the criminal fine is $50. Why would Shack and Tejeras appeal such a small fine?
6. What legal support does the court cite for its decision?

State of New Jersey v. Shack and Tejeras

277 A.2d 369 (N.J. 1971)

WEINTRAUB, J. Defendants entered upon private property to aid migrant farmworkers employed and housed there. Having refused to depart upon the demand of the owner, defendants were charged with violating N.J.S.A. § 2A:170-31 which provides that "[a]ny person who trespasses on any lands ... after being forbidden so to trespass by the owner ... is a disorderly person and shall be punished by a fine of not more than $50." Defendants were convicted in the Municipal Court of Deerfield Township and again on appeal in the County Court of Cumberland County on a trial *de novo.* We certified their further appeal before argument in the Appellate Division.

Complainant, Tedesco, a farmer, employs migrant workers for his seasonal needs. As part of their compensation, these workers are housed at a camp on his property.

Defendant Tejeras is a field worker for the Farm Workers Division of the Southwest Citizens Organization for Poverty Elimination, known by the acronym SCOPE, a nonprofit corporation funded by the Office of Economic Opportunity pursuant to an act of Congress. The role of SCOPE includes providing for the "health services of the migrant farm worker."

Defendant Shack is a staff attorney with the Farm Workers Division of Camden Regional Legal Services, Inc., known as "CRLS," also a nonprofit corporation funded by the Office of Economic Opportunity pursuant to an act of Congress. The mission of CRLS includes legal advice and representation for these workers.

Differences had developed between Tedesco and these defendants prior to the events which led to the trespass charges now before us. Hence when defendant Tejeras wanted to go upon Tedesco's farm to find a migrant worker who needed medical aid for the removal of 28 sutures, he called upon defendant Shack for his help with respect to the legalities involved. Shack, too, had a mission to perform on Tedesco's farm; he wanted to discuss a legal problem with another migrant worker there employed and housed. Defendants arranged to go to the farm together. Shack carried literature to inform the migrant farmworkers of the assistance available to them under federal statutes, but no mention seems to have been made of that literature when Shack was later confronted by Tedesco.

Defendants entered upon Tedesco's property and as they neared the camp site where the farmworkers were housed, they were confronted by Tedesco who inquired of their purpose. Tejeras and Shack stated their missions. In response, Tedesco offered to find the injured worker, and as to the worker who needed legal advice, Tedesco also offered to locate the man but insisted that the consultation would have to take place in Tedesco's office and in his presence. Defendants declined, saying they had the right to see the men in the privacy of their living quarters and without Tedesco's supervision. Tedesco thereupon summoned a State Trooper who, however, refused to remove defendants except upon Tedesco's written complaint. Tedesco then executed the formal complaints charging violations of the trespass statute.

Property rights serve human values. They are recognized to that end, and are limited by it. Title to real property cannot include dominion over the destiny of persons the owner permits to come upon the premises. Their well-being must remain the paramount concern of a system of law. Indeed the needs of the occupants may be so imperative and their strength so weak, that the law will deny the occupants the power to contract away what is deemed essential to their health, welfare, or dignity.

Here we are concerned with a highly disadvantaged segment of our society. We are told that every year farmworkers and their families numbering more than one million leave their home areas to fill the seasonal demand for farm labor in the United States. *The Migratory Farm Labor Problem in the United States* (1969 Report of Subcommittee on Migratory Labor of the United States Senate Committee on Labor and Public Welfare). The migrant farmworkers come to New Jersey in substantial numbers. The report just cited places at 55,700 the number of man-months of such employment in our State in 1968. The numbers of workers so employed here in that year are estimated at 1,300 in April; 6,500 in May; 9,800 in June; 10,600 in July; 12,100 in August; 9,600 in September; and 5,500 in October.

The migrant farmworkers are a community within but apart from the local scene. They are rootless and isolated. Although the need for their labors is evident, they are unorganized and without economic or political power. It is their plight alone that summoned government to their aid. In response, Congress provided under Title III-B of the Economic Opportunity Act of 1964 for "assistance for migrant and other seasonally employed farmworkers and their families." Section 2862 states "the purpose of this part is to assist migrant and seasonal farmworkers and their families to improve their living conditions and develop skills necessary for a productive and self-sufficient life in an increasingly complex and technological society." Section 2862(b)(1) provides for funding of programs "to meet the immediate needs of migrant and seasonal farmworkers and their families, such as day care for children, education, health services, improved housing and sanitation (including the provision and maintenance of emergency and temporary housing and sanitation facilities), legal advice and representation, and consumer training and counseling." As we have said, SCOPE is engaged in a program funded under this section, and CRLS also pursues the objectives of this section although, we gather, it is funded under § 2809(a)(3), which is not limited in its concern to the migrant and other seasonally employed farmworkers and seeks "to further the cause of justice among persons living in poverty by mobilizing the assistance of lawyers and legal institutions and by providing legal advice, legal representation, counseling, education, and other appropriate services."

These ends would not be gained if the intended beneficiaries could be insulated from efforts to reach them. It is in this framework that we must decide whether the camp operator's rights in his lands may stand between the migrant workers and those who would aid them. The key to that aid is communication. Since the migrant workers are outside the mainstream of the communities in which they are housed and are unaware of their rights and opportunities and of the services available to them, they can be reached only by positive efforts tailored to that end. *The Report of the Governor's Task Force on Migrant Farm Labor* (1968) noted that "One of the major problems related to seasonal farm labor is the lack of adequate direct information with regard to the availability of public services," and that "there is a dire need to provide the workers with basic educational and informational material in a language and style that can be readily understood by the migrant." The report stressed the problem of access and deplored the notion that property rights may stand as a barrier, saying

"In our judgment, 'no trespass' signs represent the last dying remnants of paternalistic behavior."

A man's right in his real property of course is not absolute. It was a maxim of the common law that one should so use his property as not to injure the rights of others—*Sic Utere Tuo ut Alienum Non Laedas.* Although hardly a precise solvent of actual controversies, the maxim does express the inevitable proposition that rights are relative and there must be an accommodation when they meet. Hence it has long been true that necessity, private or public, may justify entry upon the lands of another.

The subject is not static. As pointed out in 5 Powell, *Real Property* (Rohan 1970), while society will protect the owner in his permissible interests in land, yet

> [S]uch an owner must expect to find the absoluteness of his property rights curtailed by the organs of society, for the promotion of the best interests of others for whom these organs also operate as protective agencies. The necessity for such curtailments is greater in a modern industrialized and urbanized society than it was in the relatively simple American society of fifty, 100, or 200 years ago. The current balance between individualism and dominance of the social interest depends not only upon political and social ideologies, but also upon the physical and social facts of the time and place under discussion.

Professor Powell added in §746:

> As one looks back along the historic road traversed by the law of land in England and in America, one sees a change from the viewpoint that he who owns may do as he pleases with what he owns, to a position which hesitatingly embodies an ingredient of stewardship; which grudgingly, but steadily, broadens the recognized scope of social interests in the utilization of things.
>
> To one seeing history through the glasses of religion, these changes may seem to evidence increasing embodiments of the golden rule. To one thinking in terms of political and economic ideologies, they are likely to be labeled evidences of 'social enlightenment,' or of 'creeping socialism' or even of 'communistic infiltration,' according to the individual's assumed definitions and retained or acquired prejudices. With slight attention to words or labels, time marches on toward new adjustments between individualism and the social interests.

This process involves not only the accommodation between the right of the owner and the interests of the general public in his use of his property, but involves also an accommodation between the right of the owner and the right of individuals who are parties with him in consensual transactions relating to the use of the property. Accordingly substantial alterations have been made as between a landlord and his tenant. The argument in this case understandably included the question whether the migrant worker should be deemed to be a tenant and thus entitled to the tenant's right to receive visitors or whether his residence on the employer's property should be deemed to be merely incidental and in aid of his employment, and hence to involve no possessory interest in the realty. These cases did not reach employment situations at all comparable with the one before us. Nor did they involve the question whether an employee who is not a tenant may have visitors notwithstanding the employer's prohibition. Rather they were concerned with whether notice must be given to end the employee's right to remain upon the premises, with whether the employer may remove the discharged employee without court order, and with the availability of a particular judicial remedy to achieve his removal by process. We of course are not concerned here with the right of a migrant worker to remain on the employer's property after the employment is ended.

We see no profit in trying to decide upon a conventional category and then forcing the present subject into it. That approach would be artificial and distorting. The quest is for a fair adjustment of the competing needs of the parties, in the light of the realities of the relationship between the migrant worker and the operator of the housing facility.

Thus approaching the case, we find it unthinkable that the farmer-employer can assert a right to isolate the migrant worker in any respect significant for the worker's well-being. The farmer, of course, is entitled to pursue his farming activities without interference, and this defendants readily concede. But we see no legitimate need for a right in the farmer to deny the worker the opportunity for aid available from federal, State, or local services, or from recognized charitable groups seeking to assist him. Hence representatives of these agencies and organizations may enter upon the premises to seek out the worker at his living quarters. So, too, the migrant worker must be allowed to receive visitors there of his own choice, so long as there is no behavior hurtful to others, and members of the press may not be denied reasonable access to workers who do not object to seeing them.

It is not our purpose to open the employer's premises to the general public if in fact the employer himself has not done so. We do not say, for example, that solicitors or peddlers of all kinds may enter on their own; we may assume for the present that the employer may regulate their entry or bar them, at least if the employer's purpose is not to gain a commercial advantage for himself or if the regulation does not deprive the migrant worker of practical access to things he needs.

And we are mindful of the employer's interest in his own and in his employees' security. Hence he may reasonably require a visitor to identify himself, and also to state his general purpose if the migrant worker has not already informed him that the visitor is expected. But the employer may not deny the worker his privacy or interfere with his opportunity to live with dignity and to enjoy associations customary among our citizens. These rights are too fundamental to be denied on the basis of an interest in real property and too fragile to be left to the unequal bargaining strength of the parties. It follows that defendants here invaded no possessory right of the farmer-employer. Their conduct was therefore beyond the reach of the trespass statute. The judgments are accordingly reversed and the matters remanded to the County Court with directions to enter judgments of acquittal.

Exercise 3-5. *State v. Shack* Revisited

1. Did Tedesco lose his right to exclude all non-owners? Imagine you are counseling Tedesco on the importance of the court's opinion. Explain its parameters.
2. What does the court mean when it says that the defendants have "invaded no possessory right of the farmer-employer"?
3. Why do you think the court declined to reach the question of whether the workers should be considered "tenants"?
4. What does the court mean when it refers to "unequal bargaining power"? How does unequal bargaining power affect the ability to assert property rights?
5. Can you think of other occupations where housing is included as part of the salary or compensation package? What does this ruling mean for those occupations?
6. The court does not cite any New Jersey case law to support its decision. Instead, it cites a Latin maxim—*Sic Utere Tuo ut Alienum Non Laedas*—and a legal treatise. What persuasive value do these sources have?
7. Professor Powell makes the case that property law must change with the times to balance "adjustments between individualism and the social interests." Do you believe that the court struck the correct balance?

Investigative Journalism and the Law of Trespass

Exercise 3-6. *Food Lion, Inc. v. Capital Cities/ABC, Inc.*

In *Food Lion, Inc. v. Capital Cities/ABC, Inc.*, ABC reporters for the news magazine show *Primetime Live* went undercover at the supermarket chain Food Lion to investigate disturbing allegations about unsanitary handling of meat products. Food Lion later sued ABC and the reporters, claiming, among other things, that the reporters were liable for trespass when they secured jobs at Food Lion in the meat department and secretly video recorded food handling practices.

Investigative journalism has a long and storied history in the United States, dating back to the Progressive Era when reform-minded "muckrakers" exposed political and corporate corruption and shed light on various social ills. For example, Ida Tarbell's 1904 exposé on John D. Rockefeller, Sr. led to the 1911 Supreme Court case that broke up the Standard Oil, Co. monopoly. In the 1970s, a team of investigative journalists, Carl Bernstein and Bob Woodward of the *Washington Post*, brought down the Presidency of Richard M. Nixon in the aftermath of the Watergate scandal.

Like the reporters for *Primetime Live*, investigative journalists often go "undercover" in order to gather facts for their stories and exposés. In the 1880s, Nellie Bly had herself committed to an insane asylum in order to experience first hand the deplorable conditions and write about them for the *New York World*. A grand jury investigation led to stronger procedural safeguards and increased funding. Upton Sinclair worked undercover in Chicago meatpacking plants while writing his famous novel, *The Jungle*. The public uproar caused by the book led to federal regulation, including the Pure Food and Drug Act of 1906 and the eventual creation of the Federal Drug Administration (FDA). Although deception may be a longstanding tool of investigative reporting, there may also be legal consequences for those who knowingly deceive property owners, employers, and service providers.

The *Food Lion* case is a little different from the prior cases, because it is a decision by a federal court rather than a state court. The Fourth Circuit had diversity subject-matter jurisdiction because the litigants were citizens of different states and the amount in controversy exceeded $75,000. When a federal court sits in a diversity case, it is required to apply state law. In *Food Lion*, the Fourth Circuit grapples with the trespass law of the state of North Carolina. Be sure to look up any civil procedure terms with which you are not familiar, such as "remittitur."

1. The public typically applauds the efforts of the intrepid journalists who go undercover to expose wrongdoing, but what should the consequences be when their actions amount to trespass?
2. If the allegation of unsanitary food handling practices were true, they could pose a significant threat to public health and safety. Does the gravity of the potential harm justify the actions by the journalists? What if the allegations prove false?
3. In the days of online media and Twitter accounts, just about anyone can claim to be a journalist. What implications do online media and the ever-expanding Blogosphere have for the ruling in *Food Lion*? In addition to online media mavens, recent years have seen an increase in solicitude towards "whistleblowers," who seek to expose wrongdoing by leaking sensitive or confidential information to the press. Should whistleblowers also be afforded special treatment or given special consideration?
4. In the United States, the First Amendment to the U.S. Constitution guarantees Freedom of the Press, but that generally means that media should be free of government censorship or other restraints on their content. It does not grant members of the press special rights or privileges.

Food Lion, Inc. v. Capital Cities/ABC, Inc.

194 F.3d 505 (4th Cir. 1999)

Michael, J. Two ABC television reporters, after using false resumes to get jobs at Food Lion, Inc. supermarkets, secretly videotaped what appeared to be unwholesome food handling practices. Some of the video footage was used by ABC in a PrimeTime Live broadcast that was sharply critical of Food Lion. The grocery chain sued Capital Cities/ABC, Inc., American Broadcasting Companies, Inc., Richard Kaplan and Ira Rosen, producers of PrimeTime Live, and Lynne Dale and Susan Barnett, two reporters for the program (collectively, "ABC" or the "ABC defendants"). Food Lion did not sue for defamation, but focused on how ABC gathered its information through claims for fraud, breach of duty of loyalty, trespass, and unfair trade practices. Food Lion won at trial, and judgment for compensatory damages of $1,402 was entered on the various claims. Following a substantial (over $5 million) remittitur, the judgment provided for $315,000 in punitive damages. The ABC defendants appeal the district court's denial of their motion for judgment as a matter of law. Having considered the case, we affirm the judgment that Dale and Barnett committed a trespass.

In early 1992 producers of ABC's PrimeTime Live program received a report alleging that Food Lion stores were engaging in unsanitary meat-handling practices. The allegations were that Food Lion employees ground out-of-date beef together with new beef, bleached rank meat to remove its odor, and re-dated (and offered for sale) products not sold before their printed expiration date. The producers recognized that these allegations presented the potential for a powerful news story, and they decided to conduct an undercover investigation of Food Lion. ABC reporters Lynne Dale and Susan Barnett concluded that they would have a better chance of investigating the allegations if they could become Food Lion employees. With the approval of their superiors, they proceeded to apply for jobs with the grocery chain, submitting applications with false identities and references and fictitious local addresses. Notably, the applications fail to mention the reporters' concurrent employment with ABC and otherwise misrepresented their educational and employment experiences. Based on these applications, a South Carolina Food Lion store hired Barnett as a deli clerk in April 1992, and a North Carolina Food Lion store hired Dale as a meat wrapper trainee in May 1992.

Barnett worked for Food Lion for two weeks, and Dale for only one week. As they went about their assigned tasks for Food Lion, Dale and Barnett used tiny cameras and microphones concealed on their bodies to secretly record Food Lion employees treating, wrapping and labeling meat, cleaning machinery, and discussing the practices of the meat department. They gathered footage from the meat cutting room, the deli counter, the employee break room, and a manager's office. All told, in their three collective weeks as Food Lion employees, Dale and Barnett recorded approximately 45 hours of concealed camera footage.

Some of the videotape was eventually used in a November 5, 1992, broadcast of PrimeTime Live. ABC contends the footage confirmed many of the allegations initially leveled against Food Lion. The broadcast included, for example, videotape that appeared to show Food Lion employees repackaging and redating fish that had passed the expiration date, grinding expired beef with fresh beef, and applying barbecue sauce to chicken past its expiration date in order to mask the smell and sell it as fresh in the gourmet food section. The program included statements by former Food Lion employees alleging even more serious mishandling of meat at Food Lion stores across several states. The truth of the PrimeTime Live broadcast was not an issue in the litigation we now describe.

Food Lion sued ABC and the PrimeTime Live producers and reporters. Food Lion's suit focused not on the broadcast, as a defamation suit would, but on the methods ABC used to obtain the video footage. The grocery chain asserted claims of fraud, breach of the duty of loyalty, trespass, and unfair trade practices, seeking millions in compensatory damages.

We must first consider whether the ABC defendants can be held liable for trespass as a matter of North Carolina and South Carolina law and whether the North Carolina UTPA applies. As a federal court sitting in diversity, we are obliged to interpret and apply the substantive law of each state. *See Erie R.R. Co. v. Tompkins*, 304 U.S. 64 (1938). This process is more complicated here because neither state's highest court has applied its law to circumstances exactly like those presented in this case. Thus, we must offer our best judgment about what we believe those courts would do if faced with Food Lion's claims today.

ABC argues that it was error to allow the jury to hold Dale and Barnett liable for trespass on either of the independent grounds (1) that Food Lion's consent to their presence as employees was void because it was based on misrepresentations or (2) that Food Lion's consent was vitiated when Dale and Barnett breached the duty of loyalty. The jury found Dale and Barnett liable on both of these grounds and awarded Food Lion $1.00 in nominal damages, which is all that was sought in the circumstances.

In North and South Carolina, as elsewhere, it is a trespass to enter upon another's land without consent. Even consent gained by misrepresentation is sometimes sufficient. The consent to enter is canceled out, however, "if a wrongful act is done in excess of and in abuse of authorized entry."

We turn first to whether Dale and Barnett's consent to be in nonpublic areas of Food Lion property was void from the outset because of the resume misrepresentations. "Consent to an entry is often given legal effect" even though it was obtained by misrepresentation or concealed intentions. Without this result, a restaurant critic could not conceal his identity when he ordered a meal, or a browser pretend to be interested in merchandise that he could not afford to buy. Dinner guests would be trespassers if they were false friends who never would have been invited had the host known their true character, and a consumer who in an effort to bargain down an automobile dealer falsely claimed to be able to buy the same car elsewhere at a lower price would be a trespasser in a dealer's showroom.

Of course, many cases on the spectrum become much harder than these examples, and the courts of North and South Carolina have not considered the validity of a consent to enter land obtained by misrepresentation. Further, the various jurisdictions and authorities in this country are not of one mind in dealing with the issue.

[The court then considered another 4th Circuit case involving undercover activities on behalf of ABC, *Desnick v. ABC*, 44 F.3d 1345 (7th Cir. 1995).] We like *Desnick*'s thoughtful analysis about when a consent to enter that is based on misrepresentation may be given effect. In *Desnick* ABC sent persons posing as patients needing eye care to the plaintiffs' eye clinics, and the test patients secretly recorded their examinations. Some of the recordings were used in a PrimeTime Live segment that alleged intentional misdiagnosis and unnecessary cataract surgery. *Desnick* held that although the test patients misrepresented their purpose, their consent to enter was still valid because they did not invade "any of the specific interests [relating to peaceable possession of land] the tort of trespass seeks to protect:" the test patients entered offices "open to anyone expressing a desire for ophthalmic services" and videotaped doctors engaged in professional discussions with strangers, the testers; the testers did not disrupt the offices or invade anyone's private space; and the testers did not reveal the "intimate details of anybody's life." *Desnick* supported its conclusion with the following comparison:

> Testers are not trespassers even if they are private persons not acting under color of law. The situation of [ABC's] "testers" is analogous. Like testers seeking evidence of violation of anti-discrimination laws, [ABC's] test patients gained entry into the plaintiffs' premises by misrepresenting their purposes (more precisely by a misleading omission to disclose those purposes). But the entry was not invasive in the sense of infringing the kind of interest of the plaintiffs that the law of trespass protects; it was not an interference with the ownership or possession of land.

We return to the jury's first trespass finding in this case, which rested on a narrow ground. The jury found that Dale and Barnett were trespassers because they entered Food Lion's premises as employees with consent given because of the misrepresentations in their job applications. Although the consent cases as a class are inconsistent, we have not found any case suggesting that consent based on a resume misrepresentation turns a successful job applicant into a trespasser the moment she enters the employer's premises to begin work. The jury's finding of trespass therefore cannot be sustained on the grounds of resume misrepresentation.

There is a problem, however, with what Dale and Barnett did after they entered Food Lion's property. The jury also found that the reporters committed trespass by breaching their duty of loyalty to Food Lion "as a result of pursuing [their] investigation for ABC." We affirm the finding of trespass on this ground because the breach of duty of loyalty—triggered by the filming in non-public areas, which was adverse to Food Lion—was a wrongful act in excess of Dale and Barnett's authority to enter Food Lion's premises as employees.

[T]he North and South Carolina courts make clear that the law of trespass protects the peaceable enjoyment of property. It is consistent with the principle to hold that consent to enter is vitiated by a wrongful act that exceeds and abuses the privilege of entry. Here, both Dale and Barnett became employees of Food Lion with the certain consequence that they would breach their implied promises to serve Food Lion faithfully. They went into areas of the stores that were not open to the public and secretly videotaped, an act that was directly adverse to the interests of their second employer, Food Lion. Thus, they breached the duty of loyalty, thereby committing a wrongful act in abuse of their authority to be on Food Lion's property.

Exercise 3-7. *Food Lion, Inc. v. Capital Cities/ABC, Inc.* Revisited

1. Why did Food Lion not sue for defamation?
2. The court rules that the reporters were able to secure entry through misrepresentation. Where does the court draw the line and when did the actions of the reporters cross that line?
3. If you worked for a large media outlet and a reporter wanted to go undercover to pursue a story, what would you tell her?

The Power of Investigative Journalism—Animal Rights Activism

In recent years, animal rights activists have used undercover methods to bring attention to certain farming practices and the treatment of farm animals. In response to these exposés, some states have enacted laws that expressly forbid undercover activities in agriculture that are known as "ag-gag" laws. Idaho has a particularly aggressive ag-gag law that criminalizes taking photos or video at a farm or slaughterhouse without the owner's permission. The law was enacted after the NBC news program *Nightline* aired secretly shot footage of alleged abuses on an Idaho dairy farm. The Idaho law was challenged in federal court. *Animal Legal Def. Fund v. Otter*, 118 F. Supp. 3d 1195 (2015).

Property Open to the General Public

The traditional rule at common law was that innkeepers and common carriers were required to serve any customer who was able to pay for their services. William Blackstone wrote in his famous *Commentaries* that when:

> An innkeeper, or other victualer, hangs out a sign and opens his house to travelers, it is an implied engagement to entertain all persons who travel that way; and upon the universal *assumpsit* an action on the case will lie against him for damages, if he for good reason refuses to admit a traveler.

3 William Blackstone, *Commentaries on the Law of England* 164 (Univ. of Chicago 1979 reprint ed.) (1768). The act of hanging out a sign and advertising that one served the public seems to have severely limited the owner's right to exclude non-owners from his premises. The rationale for the common law rule was that innkeepers and common carriers often had a monopoly in any given locale and the refusal of service would place travelers at a grave risk. The rule furthered the policy that travelers should be able to venture from home overnight without concern that they would be arbitrarily refused service and left with no place to sleep. In this way, it is possible to see the right of reasonable access to inns and common carriers as a variation of the necessity doctrine discussed earlier in this Chapter. Without the rule, prospective customers would be at risk of harm and exposure.

Thinking this through in terms of property rights, a potential customer who enters a business held open to the general public does so as a licensee, because he is there by the implicit permission of the owner. The traditional common rule of reasonable access held that the license granted to a customer of an innkeeper or a common carrier was not revocable at will. The owner could only revoke the license for good cause, such as would be the case if the customer posed a danger to the owner or his other customers. This limitation on the owner's right to exclude was justified because of the potential risk to the customer if service were denied. A patron who was denied service was entitled to sue for damages.

English common law was followed in the Thirteen Colonies and was later "received" by the individual states when they obtained independence. As a result, pre-independence English common law continued to serve as the basis of the law in the United States to the extent that it was not expressly rejected by court case, statute, or constitutional provision. Accordingly, it is appropriate to begin the analysis of a business owner's right to exclude with Blackstone's *Commentaries*. However, quite a bit has happened since 1768, and the question remains whether, and under what circumstances, this traditional rule continues to govern property held open to the public.

There is some evidence that courts in a number of states extended the rule of reasonable access to other types of business establishments open to the general public. After the Civil War, however, state courts, especially in the South, began to apply a general rule of arbitrary exclusion that allowed business owners to exclude patrons for any reason or for no reason at all. Commentators suggest that the rule of arbitrary exclusion arose to negate the post-Civil War laws that required equal access to public accommodations for African Americans. In other words, the charge is that when states were required to grant African Americans the same access as was afforded white customers, state courts began to recognize an arbitrary right of exclusion. If businesses could arbitrarily exclude white customers, then they could also arbitrarily exclude African American customers as well.

Today the majority of states apply a right of arbitrary exclusion, although we will read a case from the New Jersey Supreme Court, *Uston v. Resorts*, that applies a right of reasonable access to establishments open to the general public. The rule of arbitrary exclusion allowed business owners to refuse access for any reason, including reasons motivated by prejudices and stereotypes. As we will see in the next section, the federal government, states, and local municipalities have passed statutes that prohibit discrimination based on certain protected characteristics in order to ensure equal access to public accommodations.

Exercise 3-8. *Uston v. Resorts International Hotel, Inc.*

The plaintiff in this case is Ken Uston, who was a famous blackjack player and card counter. Uston wrote numerous books on gambling and is credited with perfecting a method of team player card counting that was designed to tilt the odds in favor of the players, as opposed to the casino. As Uston's reputation grew, casinos banned him, as well as other individuals identified as card counters, from their premises. Uston sued casinos in both Nevada and New Jersey, claiming a right of reasonable access. Although the Nevada courts affirmed the casino's arbitrary right to exclude, the New Jersey Supreme Court recognized a reasonable right to access where an establishment is held open to the general public.

Uston's choice of venues may seem odd, but it reflected the spread of legalized gambling in the United States. Until the late 1970s, Nevada was the only state where gambling was legal. New Jersey permitted legalized gambling in Atlantic City in 1977 and the two destinations enjoyed a brief monopoly on casino gambling. Beginning in the late 1970s, Native American reservations asserted their sovereignty and authorized gambling, leading to the opening of reservation-based casinos. By the 1990s, states such as Illinois, Louisiana, and Indiana had legalized riverboat gambling. The case immediately following *Uston* involves riverboat gambling in Indiana.

As you read the *Uston* case, consider the following:

1. The full name of the defendant is Resorts International *Hotel*, Inc. Why doesn't Uston argue that Resorts should be subject to the innkeeper exception?
2. Consider the rationale behind the longstanding exception for innkeepers and common carriers. Can you think of ways to expand the rationale to include places of amusement or perhaps all establishments open to the general public?
3. How does the court characterize existing precedent regarding the right to exclude arbitrarily? What had changed in the 70 years since the court had last ruled on this question?

Uston v. Resorts International Hotel, Inc.

89 N.J. 163 (1982)

PASHMAN, J. Since January 30, 1979, appellant Resorts International Hotel, Inc. (Resorts) has excluded respondent, Kenneth Uston, from the blackjack tables in its casino because Uston's strategy increases his chances of winning money. Uston concedes that his strategy of card counting can tilt the odds in his favor. However, Uston contends that Resorts has no common law or statutory right to exclude him because of his strategy for playing blackjack.

Kenneth Uston is a renowned teacher and practitioner of a complex strategy for playing blackjack known as card counting. Card counters keep track of the playing cards as they are dealt and adjust their betting patterns when the odds are in their favor. When used over a period of time, this method allegedly ensures a profitable encounter with the casino.

[W]e feel constrained to refute any implication [that] the owners of places open to the public enjoy an absolute right to exclude patrons without good cause. We hold that the common law right to exclude is substantially limited by a competing common law right of reasonable access to public places.

Resorts claimed that it could exclude Uston because it had a common law right to exclude anyone at all for any reason. The right of an amusement place owner to exclude unwanted patrons and the patron's competing right of reasonable access both have deep roots in the common law. In this century, however, courts have disregarded the right of reasonable access in the common law of some jurisdictions at the time the Civil War Amendments and Civil Rights Act of 1866 were passed. As Justice Goldberg noted in his concurrence in *Bell v. Maryland*, 378 U.S. 226 (1964) "Underlying the congressional discussions and at the heart of the Fourteenth Amendment's guarantee of equal protection, was the assumption that the State by statute or by 'the good old common law' was obligated to guarantee all citizens access to places of public accommodation." *Id.*

The current majority American rule has for many years disregarded the right of reasonable access,[4] granting to proprietors of amusement places an absolute right arbitrarily to eject or exclude any person consistent with state and federal civil rights laws.

At one time, an absolute right of exclusion prevailed in this state, though more for reasons of deference to the noted English precedent of *Wood v. Leadbitter*, 13 M&W 838, 153 Eng.Rep. 351, (Ex.1845), than for reasons of policy. In *Shubert v. Nixon Amusement*, 83 N.J.L. 101 (Sup.Ct.1912), the former Supreme Court dismissed

4. The denial of freedom of reasonable access in some States following passage of the Fourteenth Amendment, and the creation of a common law freedom to arbitrarily exclude following invalidation of segregation statutes, suggest that the current majority rule may have had less than dignified origins.

a suit for damages resulting from plaintiff's ejection from defendants' theater. It hardly bears mention that our common law has evolved in the intervening 70 years. [T]he decisions of this Court have recognized that "the more private property is devoted to public use, the more it must accommodate the rights which inhere in individual members of the general public who use that property." *State v. Schmid*, 84 N.J. 535, 562 (1980).

In *State v. Shack*, 58 N.J. 297 (1971), the Court held that although an employer of migrant farm workers "may reasonably require" those visiting his employees to identify themselves, "the employer may not deny the worker his privacy or interfere with his opportunity to live with dignity and to enjoy associations customary among our citizens." The Court reversed the trespass convictions of an attorney and a social services worker who had entered the property to assist farmworkers there.

Schmid recognizes implicitly that when property owners open their premises to the general public in the pursuit of their own property interests, they have no right to exclude people unreasonably. On the contrary, they have a duty not to act in an arbitrary or discriminatory manner toward persons who come on their premises. That duty applies not only to common carriers, innkeepers, owners of gasoline service stations, or to private hospitals, but to all property owners who open their premises to the public. Property owners have no legitimate interest in unreasonably excluding particular members of the public when they open their premises for public use.

No party in this appeal questions the right of property owners to exclude from their premises those whose actions "disrupt the regular and essential operations of the [premises]," or threaten the security of the premises and its occupants. In some circumstances, proprietors have a duty to remove disorderly or otherwise dangerous persons from the premises. These common law principles enable the casino to bar from its entire facility, for instance, the disorderly, the intoxicated, and the repetitive petty offender.

Whether a decision to exclude is reasonable must be determined from the facts of each case. Respondent Uston does not threaten the security of any casino occupant. Nor has he disrupted the functioning of any casino operations. Absent a valid contrary rule by the Commission, Uston possesses the usual right of reasonable access to Resorts International's blackjack tables.

Exercise 3-9. *Uston v. Resorts International Hotel, Inc.* Revisited

In response to the decision in *Uston*, Atlantic City casinos altered the way Blackjack was played by adding additional decks of cards and taking other steps to minimize the potential for gain through card counting.

1. Under what circumstances could Resorts exclude Uston?

2. Why should Resorts be forced to serve a customer who is bad for business and clearly not in Resorts' economic interest? Would a restaurant with an "all you can eat buffet" have to admit a busload of competitive eaters?
3. The New Jersey Supreme Court ruled that "All property owners who open their premises to the public have no legitimate interest in unreasonably excluding particular members of the public when they open their premises for public use." Do you agree with the court? Is losing the right to exclude arbitrarily simply part of the cost of doing business in New Jersey?

Exercise 3-10. *Donovan v. Grand Victoria Casino & Resort*

The Indiana Supreme Court was faced with a similar case in 2010 involving an alleged card counter named Thomas Donovan and a riverboat casino.

1. You will see that the decision quotes Blackstone's *Commentaries*, but not the part about reasonable access quoted above.
2. The Indiana Supreme Court does not delve into the origin of the right to exclude arbitrarily. Instead, it applies what it refers to as a "long-standing principle of property law."
2. The court approvingly cites to an amicus curiae brief. Who do you think would have be interested enough in this litigation to file an amicus curiae brief on behalf of Grand Victoria Casino & Resort?

Donovan v. Grand Victoria Casino & Resort

934 N.E.2d 1111 (Ind. 2010)

Sullivan, J. An owner of an Indiana business has long had the absolute right to exclude a visitor or customer, subject only to applicable civil rights laws. This long-standing common law right of private property owners extends to the operator of a riverboat casino that wishes to exclude a patron for employing strategies designed to give the patron a statistical advantage over the casino.

Grand Victoria Casino & Resort, L.P. ("Grand Victoria"), owns and operates a riverboat casino located in Rising Sun, Indiana. One of the games offered by Grand Victoria is blackjack. Thomas P. Donovan supplements his income by playing blackjack in casinos. Donovan is a self-described "advantage player" who taught himself a strategy known as "card counting" that he employs when playing blackjack. Card counters keep track of the playing cards as they are dealt and adjust their betting patterns when the odds are in their favor. When used over a period of time, this method presumably ensures a more profitable encounter with the casino.

For a time, Grand Victoria allowed Donovan to play blackjack and card count if he wagered no more than $25 per hand. However, on August 4, 2006, Grand Victoria's director of table games advised Donovan that Grand Victoria had decided to ban Donovan from playing blackjack, though Donovan would still be allowed to play other casino games. After Donovan indicated that he would not comply with Grand Victoria's request, he was evicted and placed on Grand Victoria's list of excluded patrons.

Donovan filed suit against Grand Victoria, seeking a declaratory judgment that Grand Victoria could not exclude him from playing the game of blackjack for counting cards. The trial court granted summary judgment in favor of the casino. The Court of Appeals held that Grand Victoria had no right to exclude Donovan from blackjack for counting cards. Grand Victoria maintains that its exclusion of Donovan from the game of blackjack was proper because at common law the arbitrary exclusion of a patron from places of privately owned amusements was not actionable absent a statute prohibiting such exclusion. We agree. Grand Victoria enjoyed the common law right to exclude Donovan.

One of the time-honored principles of property law is the absolute and unconditional right of private property owners to exclude from their domain those entering without permission. See 2 William Blackstone, *Commentaries on the Laws of England* 2 (1766) (defining private property as "that sole and despotic dominion which one man claims and exercises over the external things of the world, in total exclusion of the right of any other individual in the universe"). In *Bailey v. Washington Theatre Co.*, this common law right was explicitly extended to proprietors of privately owned amusements. 218 Ind. 513 (1941). The patron in *Bailey* had sought an order compelling access to a privately owned theatre. In denying the patron relief, this Court held that "[t]he proprietor of a theater, unlike a carrier of passengers, is engaged in a strictly private business. He is under no implied obligation to serve the public and ... is under no duty to admit everyone who may apply and be willing to pay for a ticket." This long-standing principle of property law has been frequently reaffirmed, subject only to statutorily imposed prohibitions on exclusions for characteristics such as race and religion.

Donovan urges Indiana to adopt the New Jersey Supreme Court's decision of *Uston v. Resorts Int'l Hotel, Inc.*, 89 N.J. 163 (N.J. 1982). Uston had been excluded from a New Jersey casino for card counting. The *Uston* court held that any common law right the casino may have had to exclude Uston for these reasons was outweighed by Uston's right of access.

Indiana courts have never recognized a public right of access to private property. See *Wilhoite v. Melvin Simon & Assocs., Inc.*, 640 N.E.2d 382, 385 (Ind. Ct. App. 1994) ("There is no law, rule, or understanding stemming from Indiana law, federal law or other source creating a right to be admitted to private property.") In fact, *Wilhoite* rebuffed the view "that because [a proprietor] opens itself to the public, it loses its character as private property." *Id.* at 387 ("Nor does property lose its private character merely because the public is generally invited to use it for designated purposes.")).

Donovan argues that Grand Victoria opened its premises to the general public for tourism purposes and the arbitrary exclusion of patrons neither promotes tourism nor economic development. We are not persuaded. It seems to us just as likely—if not more so—that discouraging card counting enhances a casino's financial success and directly furthers the Legislature's express objective of promoting tourism and assisting economic development.

Other considerations counsel against adopting the position Donovan advances. In *Brooks v. Chicago Downs Association*, the Seventh Circuit recognized that although it is "arguably unfair" to allow a place of amusement arbitrarily to exclude patrons, there are sound public policy reasons in support of the common law rule of exclusion:

> [P]roprietors of amusement facilities, whose very survival depends on bringing the public into their place of amusement, are reasonable people who usually do not exclude their customers unless they have a reason to do so. What the proprietor of a race track does not want to have to do is prove or explain that his reason for exclusion is a just reason.

791 F.2d 512, 517 (1986). In the words of the Arizona Court of Appeals,

> We are not persuaded that the common law rule of exclusion should be changed. The policy upon which it is based is still convincing. The [casino] proprietor must be able to control admission to its facilities without risk of a lawsuit and the necessity of proving that every person excluded would actually engage in some unlawful activity.

Nation v. Apache Greyhound Park, 579 P.2d 580, 582 (1978); see also *Brief of Amicus Curiae* at 8 ("Such decisions are, and should be, matters of business judgment to be evaluated and remedied by competitive market forces, not courts.").

We affirm the judgment of the trial court.

Exercise 3-11. *Donovan v. Grand Victoria Casino & Resort* Revisited

1. The *Bailey* case cited in the opinion seems to recognize a right of reasonable access in the case of common carriers, but the court does not mention this exception. Why not?
2. The *Donovan* court ultimately trusts that market forces will constrain business owners from arbitrarily excluding patrons. Do you agree that decisions to exclude a customer "are, and should be, matters of business judgment to be evaluated and remedied by competitive market forces, not courts"?
3. *Uston* and *Donovan* represent the minority and majority rules, respectively. Property law often varies significantly from jurisdiction to jurisdiction. As a result, the answer to the question of whether a business owner has the right to exclude arbitrarily is going to be "it depends." Which approach do you prefer and why?

Non-Discrimination Laws

Although non-discrimination laws are most commonly associated with the employment context, there are numerous non-discrimination laws that apply to the property context. This section discusses non-discrimination laws and public accommodations. There are also non-discrimination laws that apply to housing and lending that are discussed later in the book. The public accommodation laws recognize that discrimination in the United States has long had a spatial component. During the period of Jim Crow, Southern states enacted laws mandating a separation of the races throughout public life: restrooms, parks, restaurants, buses, stores, and, of course, schools. In other states where segregation was not required by law, private business owners were free to discriminate on the basis of race.

Laws prohibiting discrimination in public accommodations have been enacted on the federal state and local level. They reach private conduct on privately owned property. In order to be subject to the law, a business must qualify as a public accommodation or an otherwise covered entity. A covered establishment may not discriminate against individuals who belong to a designated protected class. There are generally four parts of a public accommodation claim: 1) is the business covered by the law, 2) did the business "discriminate," 3) is the plaintiff a member of a protected class, and 4) do any exceptions apply.

Many state and local public accommodation laws are more expansive than the federal law in terms of the establishments covered by the law, the classes of individuals protected by the law, and the types of conduct that can qualify as discrimination. In other words, the federal public accommodation laws provide the minimum amount of protection that a business must provide. State and local laws are free to provide greater protection, meaning that the level of protection may vary from jurisdiction to jurisdiction. The Americans with Disabilities Act (ADA) also imposes affirmative duties on business owners to make their establishments physically accessible to individuals with disabilities. The ADA is discussed in greater detail in a following section.

The Four Parts of Public Accomodation Claims

1. Is the business covered by the law?
2. Did the business "discriminate"?
3. Is the plaintiff a member of a protected class?
4. Do any exceptions apply?

These non-discrimination laws have an impact on the property rights of business owners. The public accommodation laws have limited the common law right of business owners to exclude arbitrarily. In jurisdictions such as Indiana, where property owners can arbitrarily exclude customers, public accommodation laws impose an important limitation on the right to exclude. The owner of a covered establishment may exclude a customer for any reason or no reason, provided that the customer is not a member of a protected class. The ADA goes further and requires business owners to shoulder the costs of making their premises accessible to individuals with disabilities. In both instances, the law has chosen to strike the balance in favor of equal access.

The public accommodation laws reflect our strong commitment to equality that is embodied in the Equal Protection Clause of the Fourteenth Amendment to the U.S. Constitution. Broadly stated, the Fourteenth Amendment guarantees equal protection of the law and prohibits states from treating individuals differently absent a sufficient reason. The federal government is also prohibited from such behavior by the equal protection guarantees inherent in the Due Process Clause of the Fifth Amendment. The Constitution protects people from government action, but generally not from private action. Accordingly, Congress enacted the Civil Rights Act of 1964 to reach private discriminatory actions in the context of employment and public accommodations. Four years later, it enacted the Fair Housing Act to reach private discriminatory conduct in the housing market. Some states and municipalities had adopted non-discrimination laws prior to the Civil Rights Act of 1964.

The Civil Rights Act of 1964 was a major accomplishment of the Civil Rights movement and was motivated by widespread racial segregation and discriminatory practices. As you will learn in your Constitutional Law course, the Civil Rights Act of 1964 was not the first time that Congress had attempted to address the problem of private racially discriminatory conduct. During the period known as Reconstruction after the end of the Civil War, Congress tried to address private conduct. The Civil Rights Act of 1866 mandated equal treatment of all citizens with respect to the right to contract and to buy and sell real property. The Civil Rights Act of 1875 expanded this protection to include public accommodations and public transportation. Reconstruction ended in 1877 when the remaining federal troops where removed from Southern states in the aftermath of a hotly contested Presidential election. In 1883, in an eight-to-one opinion, the U.S. Supreme Court found the Civil Rights Act of 1875 to be unconstitutional in the *Civil Rights Cases*, 109 U.S. 3 (1883). The Court held that Congress did not have the enforcement power under the Fourteenth Amendment to regulate private actors. In *Plessey v. Ferguson*, 163 U.S. 537 (1896), the Court held in a seven-to-one opinion that state laws mandating racial segregation did not violate the Fourteenth Amendment, leading to the spread of Jim Crow laws and the systematic disenfranchisement of African Americans. Although *Brown v. Board of Education*, 347 U.S. 483 (1954), rejected *Plessey*'s doctrine of "separate but equal," the command of *Brown* was not sufficient to dismantle longstanding discriminatory practices.

When Congress enacted the Civil Rights Act of 1964, it based its authority on the Commerce Clause and not the enforcement provisions of the Fourteenth Amendment.

Given the history of the public accommodation laws, it may seem like they should be largely of historical interest. However, racial discriminatory behavior and profiling persists. The largest settlement of a public accommodations case occurred in the 1990s and not the 1960s. The restaurant chain Denny's paid $54 million to settle a claim of racial discrimination against customers. Ten years later, the restaurant chain Waffle House faced over 20 different lawsuits alleging violations of the federal public accommodations laws. These more recent cases typically involve behavior that is short of full exclusion, but instead may center on different terms of service, such as requiring certain customers to wait longer or to pay for their food before it is delivered to a table.

Federal Public Accommodation Protections

Exercise 3-12. Interpreting the Statute

The federal public accommodations laws are in Title II of the Civil Rights Act of 1964, which also contains the more famous Title VII prohibiting discrimination in employment. The relevant sections of the law are reproduced below. Read the excerpt carefully, and answer the following four questions:

1. Which businesses qualify as a "place of public accommodation"? What about the Kwik-E-Mart described in the Problem at the beginning of the Chapter?
2. What constitutes discrimination? Think of examples that you would use to describe the concept to a client.
3. Which classes of customers are protected by the statute?
4. What types of establishments are excluded from coverage and why?

42 U.S. Code § 2000a—Prohibition against discrimination or segregation in places of public accommodation

42 U.S.C. § 2000a Equal access

(a) All persons shall be entitled to the full and equal enjoyment of the goods, services, facilities, privileges, advantages, and accommodations of any place of public accommodation, as defined in this section, without discrimination on the ground of race, color, religion, or national origin.

42 U.S.C. § 2000a(b) Establishments affecting interstate commerce or supported in their activities by State action as places of public accommodation; lodgings; facilities principally engaged in selling food for consumption on the premises; gasoline stations; places of exhibition or entertainment; other covered establishments.

(b) Each of the following establishments is a place of public accommodation within this title if its operations affect commerce, or if discrimination or segregation by it is supported by State action:

(1) any inn, hotel, motel, or other establishment which provides lodging to transient guests, other than an establishment located within a building which contains not more than five rooms for rent or hire and which is actually occupied by the proprietor of such establishment as his residence.

(2) any restaurant, cafeteria, lunchroom, lunch counter, soda fountain, or other facility principally engaged in selling food for consumption on the premises, including, but not limited to, any such facility located on the premises of any retail establishment, or any gasoline station;

(3) any motion picture house, theater, concert hall, sports arena, stadium or other place of exhibition or entertainment; and

(4) any establishment (A)(i) which is physically located within the premises of any establishment otherwise covered by this subsection, or (ii) within the premises of which is physically located any such covered establishment and (B) which holds itself out as serving patrons of any such covered establishment.

42 U.S.C. § 2000a(e) Private establishments

The provisions of this title shall not apply to a private club or other establishment not in fact open to the public, except to the extent that the facilities of such establishment are made available to the customers or patrons of an establishment within the scope of subsection (b).

Exercise 3-13. *Denny v. Elizabeth Arden Salons, Inc.*—A "place of public accommodation"?

When a plaintiff brings a claim of discrimination under Title II of the Civil Rights Act of 1964, an initial question that must be answered is whether the establishment where the discriminatory treatment allegedly occurred qualifies as a "place of public accommodation." If the establishment clearly falls into one of the listed categories, such as a restaurant, hotel or movie theater, then the threshold question is easy to answer. However, when the statutory language is silent or ambiguous, then the court must determine whether the type of establishment in question is covered by the terms of the statute. This determination requires the court to engage in statutory interpretation.

Of course, when a court interprets a statute, it is not free to substitute its judgment for what it thinks the law should be. Rather, it must give effect to expressed congressional intent. In the words of the majority in *Denny v. Elizabeth Arden Salons, Inc.*, a court must "respect what Congress has said, not to put words in its mouth."

To determine the meaning of a statute, a court must start with the text. Applying the plain meaning rule, a court must generally give effect to the plain meaning of the statutory term unless it qualifies as a term of art. If the meaning is ambiguous, there are then a number of canons of statutory construction that courts can use to aid their interpretation. In certain instances, a court may also consider legislative history. The canons are designed to make sure that courts respect the distinct institutional roles of courts and legislatures. Whereas legislatures make the laws, courts interpret the laws.

The use of canons of construction dates back to the 16th century with Lord Coke's famous opinion in *Heydon's Case*. *Heydon's Case*, Y.B. 26 Eliz., fol. 7a, Pasch, (1584) 76 Eng. Rep. 637 (L.R. Exch.), and Blackstone commented favorably on the use of canons. Although canons were traditionally considered customary guidance rather than part of the common law, both individual states and the United States have codified many of the canons, giving them the force of law. Scholars suggest that the reliance on canons in U.S. Supreme Court cases have increased in recent years. James J. Brudney & Corey Ditslear, *Canons of Construction and the Elusive Quest for Neutral Reasoning*, 58 Vand. L. Rev. 1 (2005).

The following case presents an opportunity to gain familiarity with some of the canons of construction. The question presented is whether an Elizabeth Arden Salon qualifies as a "place of public accommodation" for purposes of the federal public accommodation law. Before reading the case, go back and look at the text of the statute set forth in the prior section. The statute itself is silent as to whether beauty salons or spas are covered. As you read the case, remember that the question is not whether the Elizabeth Arden Salon *should* be covered by the law's mandate of non-discrimination, but rather whether it *is* covered. Both the majority and the dissent are included to illustrate how what seems to be a simple question can be interpreted very differently.

Here is a list of some canons of construction that you might wish to consider as you read the case. The list is by no means exhaustive. You will see that some of the canons seem to contradict each other. Pay attention to how the opinions in the following case use or reject the canons listed below. How many can you identify?

Plain Meaning Rule—The starting point is almost always the "plain meaning" of the statute. Of course, the plain meaning of the statute is often open to debate. In order to determine plain meaning, judges will look to evidence of ordinary usage and will consult dictionaries.

Avoid an Absurd Result—This rule provides that a court should not follow the plain meaning if it would produce an absurd result that clearly was not contemplated by the legislature.

Terms of Art—Sometimes legislatures use words as terms of art with special definitions that might vary considerably from plain meaning or ordinary usage. Courts should not follow plan meaning where the legislature has provided a technical definition.

Statutory Purpose—Similar to the absurd result rule, this canon provides that when a statute is ambiguous, it should be interpreted in the way that is most consistent with the purpose of the statute. In other words, courts should not interpret words or phrases in isolation.

Expressio Unius—This phrase means that the "expression of one thing suggests the exclusion of others." It is useful when the legislature provides a list of examples or illustrations.

Noscitur a Sociis—This phrase means that courts should interpret a general term to be similar to more specific terms in a series of examples or illustrations.

Ejusdem Generis—This phrase means that courts should interpret a general term to reflect the overall nature of the class of objects described in more specific terms accompanying the general term.

Punctuation and Grammar—Legislatures are presumed to follow accepted rules of grammar and punctuation. Punctuation is considered intentional and will be given effect except in the case of a grammatical error. Such errors will not invalidate a statute.

Section Headings—Section headings within a statute may be considered in the construction of a statute, but they are not controlling.

Derogation of Common Law—Statutes in derogation of the common law should be strictly construed.

Remedial Laws—Statutes that are designed to remedy a wrong and are remedial in nature should be liberally construed.

Legislative History—Courts may consider legislative history under certain circumstance.

Denny v. Elizabeth Arden Salons, Inc.

456 F.3d 427 (4th Cir. 2006)

Wilkinson, J. In this case an African American woman bought her mother a gift package from a beauty salon and day spa. Upon visiting the salon to check on her mother and to add a hair coloring to the package, a receptionist told her that there was "a problem" because the salon did not "do black people's hair." The mother and daughter brought this suit against the salon under Title II of the Civil Rights Act of 1964, 42 U.S.C. § 2000a et seq. (2000) which prohibits racial discrimination in a "place of public accommodation." The district court granted summary judgment to the salon.

We hold that the district court properly dismissed plaintiffs' Title II claim, because the salon is not a "place of public accommodation," as that term is defined in the statute. Congress has clearly delineated those entities that fall within Title II's ambit, and we are not at liberty to go beyond what it has plainly enacted.

Plaintiffs are Seandria Denny and her mother, Jean Denny. They are African American. Defendant is Elizabeth Arden Salons, Inc., which operates Red Door Salon and Spa, an upscale beauty salon and day spa with locations in Virginia and several other states. The salon offers its customers a variety of different beauty services, including hair, skin, and nail care, makeup artistry, and massages, facials, and other body treatments.

The dispute in this case arose from incidents at a Red Door salon in the Tysons Corner Shopping Center in Northern Virginia. On May 26, 2002, Seandria Denny visited the salon to purchase a gift for her mother. She decided to buy Elizabeth Arden's $295 "Miracle Morning" package, which included a massage, facial, manicure, hair style, and lunch. Four days later, Jean Denny went to the salon to redeem her gift package. She received a facial and massage, and the salon then provided her with a salad for lunch. She obtained these services without incident, and planned to have her hair styled after lunch. When Seandria Denny [went to the salon] to see how her mother was doing the receptionist told her "[w]ell, Ms. Denny, I think we have a problem." The salon, she explained, did not "do black people's hair."

Title II entitles individuals "to the full and equal enjoyment of the goods, services, facilities, privileges, advantages, and accommodations of any place of public accommodation ... without discrimination or segregation on the ground of race, color, religion, or national origin." 42 U.S.C. § 2000a(a). It sets forth a comprehensive list of establishments that qualify as a "place of public accommodation," and in so doing excludes from its coverage those categories of establishments not listed. Places of public accommodation include: (1) hotels and other businesses providing "lodging to transient guests," (2) restaurants and other facilities "principally engaged in selling food for consumption on the premises," (3) "place[s] of exhibition or entertainment," and (4) establishments that are, *inter alia*, within a covered establishment. Whether an entity qualifies as a "place of public accommodation" can be a fact-intensive inquiry, because establishments differ markedly in their operations.

Plaintiffs rely on only one subsection of Title II's definition provision, contending that the salon is a "place of entertainment" under § 2000a(b)(3). Section 2000a(b)(3) defines "place of public accommodation" to include "any motion picture house, theater, concert hall, sports arena, stadium or other place of exhibition or entertainment."

We cannot agree with plaintiffs' argument. The plain text of the statute demonstrates that beauty salons are not covered by Title II. They are not mentioned in any of the numerous definitions of "place of public accommodation." They also bear little relation to those places of entertainment that are specifically listed, which strongly suggests that a salon would not fall within the catchall language "other place of exhibition or entertainment." 42 U.S.C. § 2000a(b)(3) As the Supreme Court has indicated, "the statutory language 'place of entertainment' should be given full effect according to its *generally accepted* meaning." A "place of entertainment" is one whose particular purpose is to entertain. *See The Random House Dictionary of the English Language* 1478 (2d ed. 1987) (defining "place" as, *inter alia*, "a space, area, or spot, *set apart or used for a particular purpose*: a place of worship; a place of entertainment") (emphasis added). Unlike a theater, concert hall, or sports arena—the purpose of the salon in this case is to offer its customers hair, skin, and body care. Visiting a salon does not fairly approximate the experience of attending a movie, symphony, or sporting match. Rather, the salon is more similar to businesses that offer tangible services, not entertainment.

Our friend in dissent would have us believe that Elizabeth Arden was doing anything other than styling hair and providing other beauty services, but such treatments were of course central to its business. Indeed, the styling of Jean Denny's hair is what this entire dispute is all about. This is not enough to transform a beauty salon into a "place of entertainment" remotely akin to the movies, concerts, and sports facilities Congress listed in the statute. Unfortunately, the dissent takes such an expansive view of the term "place of entertainment" that an automobile repair shop is apparently the only thing that does not fit within it.

The other subsections setting forth Title II's definition of "place of public accommodation" reinforce the ordinary textual reading that "place of entertainment" refers to those establishments designed to entertain. See 42 U.S.C. § 2000a(b). For Congress specifically included within Title II other service establishments, such as hotels and restaurants, and it chose not to cover with particularity facilities that sell salon services. If, however, Congress had intended for "place of entertainment" to encompass any service establishment with tangential entertainment value, there would have been no reason for Congress to include separate subsections for hotels, restaurants, and similar establishments in the statute. Thus to include in the statute all places where patrons might go in some part for relaxation, as the dissent would have it, renders unnecessary the entire exercise in statutory draftsmanship that Congress undertook in 42 U.S.C. § 2000a(b).

The case law delimiting the breadth of § 2000a(b)(3) also supports the plain and ordinary meaning of "place of entertainment." In *Daniel v. Paul*, 395 U.S. 298 (1969), the Supreme Court held that "a 232-acre amusement area with swimming, boating, sun bathing, picnicking, miniature golf, dancing facilities, and a snack bar" was a place of entertainment. The Court explained that the phrase should be interpreted in accord with its ordinary meaning to include both those "establishments where patrons are entertained as spectators or listeners" and "those where entertainment takes the form of direct participation in some sport or activity."The salon in this case—primarily offering body maintenance services with tangential entertainment value—does not readily compare to the "amusement business" in *Paul*, whose raison d'etre was to sell entertainment to its customers. Nor are the salon's services analogous to the great bulk of establishments that lower courts have held to be places of entertainment: most have had amusement and recreational elements front and center. [The court then lists cases dealing with: public parks, a community swimming facility, a roller skating rink, an amusement park, bowling alleys, golf courses and tennis courts.]

As the foregoing discussion of statutory text and case law makes clear, Title II approached the question of what is an establishment not through a generic definition, but through a series of extended lists. Indeed, § 2000a(b) lists no fewer than fourteen examples of establishments, and subsection (b)(3) lists no fewer than five different places of entertainment. Barber shops and beauty salons are sufficiently common and pervasive that we cannot casually attribute their omission to mere oversight. Indeed, it would have been easy enough for Congress to have included them.

We note, however, that we have interpreted the statute as it does read, not perhaps as it should read. One can think of good reasons why Title II should include both beauty salons and barber shops, even those catering to specific clienteles. That, however, is a matter for legislative debate. It remains our job to respect what Congress has said, not to put words in its mouth.

King, Circuit Judge, dissenting in part: In my view, the majority has erred in determining that the Elizabeth Arden Red Door Salon and Spa (the "Red Door Spa," or the "Spa") falls outside the ambit of the Civil Rights Act of 1964. As I see it, the majority's analysis suffers from two fatal errors. First, it fails to adhere to controlling precedent and accord proper effect to the broad statutory language of Title II Second, its reasoning relies on a crucial factual misapprehension—that the Red Door Spa is merely a hair salon when, in fact, it is much, much more.

The Red Door Spa, located directly across from the Tyson's Corner Shopping Center in Vienna, Virginia. According to its website, the Spa offers "a *complete* menu of salon and spa services," including "signature skincare, massage and body treatments, nail services, hair design, makeup artistry, and *much, much more*." These services include the "elemental balancing massage," which, the website declares, "has been called an 'out of body experience' by many of our guests." Moreover, one of the Spa's advertising brochures lists the various packages it offers—with names such as the "Red Door Rescue," the "Miracle Morning," and the "Executive Escape"—that include such services as "Purifying Scented Body Wrap[s]," "Desert Stone Massage[s]," and "Swedish Massage[s]."

The Public Accommodations Statute guarantees that, in this country, "[a]ll persons shall be entitled to the full and equal enjoyment of the goods, services, facilities, privileges, advantages, and accommodations of any place of public accommodation, as defined [herein]," irrespective of their race or color. 42 U.S.C. § 2000a(a). The Supreme Court has recognized that the Statute's "overriding purpose" is "to remove the daily affront and humiliation involved in discriminatory denials of access to facilities ostensibly open to the general public." *Daniel v. Paul*, 395 U.S. 298 (1969). Accordingly, the Court has mandated that we read the Statute carefully, in a manner consistent with its broad purpose and language.

Section 2000a(b) includes, as a place of public accommodation, "any motion picture house, theater, concert hall, sports arena, stadium *or other place of exhibition or entertainment*." And the Supreme Court, in addressing the Statute's breadth, has determined that "the statutory language 'place of entertainment' should be given full effect according to its generally accepted meaning." *Daniel*, 395 U.S. at 308. According to the Court, even though "most of the discussion in Congress regarding the coverage of [the Public Accommodations Statute] focused on places of spectator entertainment[,] ... a natural reading of its language would call for broader coverage." *Daniel*, 395 U.S. at 307-08. To illustrate, Justice Brennan quoted from *Webster's Third New International Dictionary*, defining "entertainment" as "the act of diverting, amusing, or causing someone's time to pass agreeably."

Pursuant to the settled principles of *Daniel*, the facilities enumerated as "place[s] of exhibition or entertainment" in § 2000a(b)(3) are unified by their common purpose of providing relaxation, amusement, recreation, and the like. And whether a particular business establishment constitutes such a "place of entertainment" is determined by a fact-bound inquiry into the facility's purposes. For example, few persons visit auto mechanics to be amused or diverted, and an auto mechanic's shop thus would not likely constitute a "place of entertainment" under the Public Accommodations Statute, even though it might provide its waiting customers with a television for casual viewing. By contrast, an amusement park—featuring roller coasters—derives its business from those who seek the thrills associated with speed and heights, and is thus "a place of entertainment" within the Statute, notwithstanding that its primary method of entertainment differs from that offered by motion picture houses, theaters, concert halls, or sports arenas.

My good friends in the majority erroneously conclude that the Red Door Spa is not a place of public accommodation, reasoning that "the plain text of the [S]tatute demonstrates that beauty salons are not covered by [it]," because "[t]hey are not mentioned in any of the numerous definitions of 'place of public accommodation,'" and "[t]hey also bear little relation to those places of entertainment that are specifically listed." The Court in *Daniel*, however, specifically rejected the ejusdem generis conclusion that places of entertainment "should be restricted to the primary objects of Congress' concern"—that is, motion picture houses, theaters, concert halls, sports arenas, and stadiums, as expressly enumerated in § 2000a(b)(3)—because "a natural reading" discloses the Statute's "broader coverage." Indeed, any business entity that has the specific purpose of providing "entertainment," as that term is generally understood, is covered by the Statute's broad reach.

The name "Elizabeth Arden Red Door Salon and Spa" implies a place where patrons come to relax and divert from their everyday lives. Through the years, the word "spa" has taken on many meanings, from the name of a Belgian town known for the curative properties of its mineral springs; to health baths containing hot, aerated water; to resorts that offer health and beauty treatments; to the modern "day spas" that provide patrons a temporary escape from daily life through massages, mud baths, steam treatments, and the like. It is entirely reasonable to conclude that Elizabeth Arden, in naming the Red Door Spa, used the term "spa" in its normal sense, and that a particular purpose of the Spa is providing services that relax, amuse, and divert its patrons.

Exercise 3-14. *Denny v. Elizabeth Arden Salons, Inc.* Revisited

Do you think that Elizabeth Arden Spa is a "place of entertainment" within the meaning of the federal public accommodations law? Do you agree with the majority that the Elizabeth Arden Spa is an establishment "primarily offering body maintenance services with tangential entertainment value" or do you agree with the dissent that the Red Door Spa is "in fact ... much, much more"? How did you arrive at your conclusion?

The plaintiffs also brought a claim under section 1981, the successor to the Civil Rights Act of 1866. A majority of the court affirmed their right to sue under section 1981. The majority explained that the disparate rulings reflected the distinction between section 1981 and Title II:

> While Title II clearly excludes this salon from coverage, section 1981 just as clearly governs racial animus in the making and enforcement of contracts. Our distinguished colleague in dissent simply overlooks the fact that the Reconstruction Congress and the 1964 Congress went about their work in different ways. The Reconstruction Congress wrote broadly, and we have given effect to that breadth as expressed in section 1981. The 1964 Congress also wrote broadly, but made clear through a series of specific references that Title II's reach, while ample, was not wholly without limit.

State and Local Public Accommodation Laws

As noted above, many state and local laws provide greater protection than the federal law. Since the federal law was enacted in 1964, many states and municipalities have amended their laws to include additional protected classes, including gender, marital status, sexual orientation, gender identity, military service, and source of income. They have also expanded the reach of their laws to cover many types of establishments that are not covered by the federal statute. Newer laws have rejected a literal notion of "place" to move beyond the requirement that a covered establishment must have an actual fixed "bricks and mortar" location. This type of expansion has obvious applications with the increase in e-commerce and the importance of the Internet, but it has also been used to reach non-profit organizations.

States and municipalities have chosen to provide greater protection than the federal government in all four of the core areas of inquiry: 1) the definition of place of public accommodation, 2) the scope and number of protected classes, 3) what actions constitute discrimination, and 4) the extent of exemptions for private and/or religious organizations. In the case of the last category, whether the state or municipality is providing greater protection may be a question of perspective. A more expansive set of exemptions may provide greater protection for private property rights, but arguably less protection for the right of equal public access. In certain circumstances, state and local public accommodation laws may impermissibly infringe on constitutionally protected rights, including the right to free association and expression guaranteed by the First Amendment.

Take, for example, the Minnesota public accommodation law. It includes "sex" as a protected category, unlike the federal law. The law also provides a more expansive definition of a "place of public accommodation," which is defined as "a business, accommodation, refreshment, entertainment, recreation, or transportation facility of any kind, whether licensed or not, whose goods, services, facilities, privileges, advantages or accommodations are extended, offered, sold, or otherwise made available to the public." Minn. Stat. 363.01, subd. 18; 363.03, subd. 3. Applying this expansive definition, the Minnesota Supreme Court ruled in 1981 that the Junior Chambers of Commerce, commonly known as the Jaycees, qualified as a *place* of public accommodation even though it was a non-profit membership organization. As a place a public accommodation, the court ruled that the Jaycees were required to admit women on the same terms as men. *U.S. Jaycees v. McClure*, 305 N.W.2d 764 (Minn. 1981). The Jaycees appealed the decision in federal court on constitutional grounds, alleging that the application of the Minnesota public accommodations law to the Jaycees violated their First Amendment right to freedom of association. The U.S. Supreme Court rejected this claim in *Roberts v. Jaycees*, 468 U.S. 609 (1984).

New Jersey also has a very expansive public accommodation law. In 1974, the New Jersey courts ruled that Little League constituted a place of public accommodation for purposes of its statute and was required to allow girls to play. *National Organization for Women, Essex Cnty. Chapter v. Little League Baseball, Inc.*, 318 A.2d 33, 35 (N.J. Super. Ct. App. Div. 1974). The historic case is excerpted in the following section. In 1999, the New Jersey Supreme Court held that the Boy Scouts organization qualified as a public accommodation and, therefore, could be required to refrain from discriminating on the basis of sexual orientation, which is a protected class under the New Jersey law. *Dale v. Boy Scouts of America*, 160 N.J. 562 (1999). The Boy Scouts appealed to the U.S. Supreme Court, arguing that the application of the New Jersey law impermissibly infringed on the organization's First Amendment right to free expression. *Dale v. Boy Scouts*, 530 U.S. 640 (2000). Unlike in *Roberts v. Jaycees*, the Court agreed with the Boy Scouts and held that the application of the New Jersey public accommodations law violated the organization's First Amendment right to free expression. Both cases illustrate a difficult balance between equality norms and constitutional guarantees.

Exercise 3-15. *National Organization for Women, Essex Cnty. Chapter v. Little League Baseball, Inc.*—The New Jersey Law Against Discrimination

As mentioned above, *NOW v. Little League* was a groundbreaking case that allowed girls to play Little League baseball, which had been restricted on the basis of sex. The case applied the public accommodation provisions of the New Jersey Law Against Discrimination (LAD) to Little League and held that the exclusion of girls constituted unlawful discrimination. Little League had argued that sex segregation was warranted for safety reasons because girls aged 8 to 12 were "physiologically inferior to boys" and would not be able to compete with boys safely or successfully. Expert witnesses successfully disputed that assertion. On the issue of physical ability, the court refused to "find as a fact that girls of ages 8–12 are not as a class subject to a materially greater hazard of injury while playing baseball than boys of that age group."

The broader statutory question presented was whether Little League qualified as a "place of public accommodation" under the LAD. Unlike the types of establishments enumerated in the federal public accommodations law, Little League did not have a fixed location nor was there a clearly defined physical space to which girls were being denied entry. The court's decision was possible because the LAD is drafted very differently from the federal law.

Before you read the excerpt from the case, review carefully the following sections of the New Jersey LAD. As you read the sections of the statute, think about how it differs from the federal public accommodations law. Which one do you think is better tailored to address the issue of unequal access to public accommodations? Consider how the LAD addresses the four core areas of a public accommodation law: 1) the definition of a place of public accommodation, 2) the scope and number of protected classes, 3) what actions constitute discrimination, and 4) the extent of exemptions for private and/or religious organizations. Do you agree with the New Jersey legislature's finding that "such discrimination threatens not only the rights and proper privileges of the inhabitants of the State but menaces the institutions and foundation of a free democratic State"?

New Jersey Law Against Discrimination

§ 10:5-3. Findings, declarations

The Legislature finds and declares that practices of discrimination against any of its inhabitants, because of race, creed, color, national origin, ancestry, age, sex, gender identity or expression, affectional or sexual orientation, marital status, familial status, liability for service in the Armed Forces of the United States, disability or nationality, are matters of concern to the government of the State, and that such discrimination threatens not only the rights and proper privileges of the inhabitants of the State but menaces the institutions and foundation of a free democratic State.

§ 10:5-4. Obtaining employment, accommodations and privileges without discrimination; civil right

All persons shall have the opportunity to obtain employment, and to obtain all the accommodations, advantages, facilities, and privileges of any place of public accommodation, publicly assisted housing accommodation, and other real property without discrimination because of race, creed, color, national origin, ancestry, age, marital status, affectional or sexual orientation, familial status, disability, nationality, sex, gender identity or expression or source of lawful income used for rental or mortgage payments, subject only to conditions and limitations applicable alike to all persons. This opportunity is recognized as and declared to be a civil right.

§ 10:5-5. Definitions relative to discrimination

l. "A place of public accommodation" shall include, but not be limited to: any tavern, roadhouse, hotel, motel, trailer camp, summer camp, day camp, or resort camp, whether for entertainment of transient guests or accommodation of those seeking health, recreation or rest; any producer, manufacturer, wholesaler, distributor, retail shop, store, establishment, or concession dealing with goods or services of any kind; any restaurant, eating house, or place where food is sold for consumption on the premises; any place maintained for the sale of ice cream, ice and fruit preparations or their derivatives, soda water or confections, or where any beverages of any kind are retailed for consumption on the premises; any garage, any public conveyance operated on land or water, or in the air, any stations and terminals thereof; any bathhouse, boardwalk, or seashore accommodation; any auditorium, meeting place, or hall; any theatre, motion-picture house, music hall, roof garden, skating rink, swimming pool, amusement and recreation park, fair, bowling alley, gymnasium, shooting gallery, billiard and pool parlor, or other place of amusement; any comfort station; any dispensary, clinic or hospital; any public library; any kindergarten, primary and secondary school, trade or business school, high school, academy, college and university, or any educational institution under the supervision of the State Board of Education, or the Commissioner of Education of the State of New Jersey. Nothing herein contained shall be construed to include or to apply to any institution, bona fide club, or place of accommodation, which is in its nature distinctly private; nor shall anything herein contained apply to any educational facility operated or maintained by a bona fide religious or sectarian institution[.]

National Organization for Women, Essex Cnty. Chapter v. Little League Baseball, Inc.

318 A.2d 33 (N.J. Super. Ct. App. Div. 1974)

Crawford, J. This is an appeal from an order and an amended order of the Division on Civil Rights, entered on a report, findings and recommendations by Sylvia B. Pressler, hearing officer, adopted by the Director of the Division, ordering Little League Baseball, Inc. ("Little League") and all local baseball leagues chartered by it in this State to admit girls aged 8 to 12 to participation in their baseball programs conducted in this State. These programs have heretofore been maintained solely for boys. The Division acted on a complaint of violation of the Law Against Discrimination, N.J.S.A. 10:5-1 et seq., and particularly section 10:5-12(f). That provision prohibits the denial by the operator of any "place of public accommodation" of any of its "accommodations, advantages, facilities or privileges" on account of "race, creed, color, national origin, ancestry, marital status or sex" except, in the case of sex, where the place of public accommodation "is in its nature reasonably restricted exclusively to individuals of one sex" (with a specification of a number of nonexclusive examples, discussed later in this opinion). Little League had not borne its burden of establishing that girls of 8 to 12 are so physiologically inferior to boys of the same age group as to preclude them as a class from competing as safely and successfully as boys in the game.Little League asserts it is not a "place of public accommodation" within the meaning of the statute, primarily because it is a membership organization which does not operate from any fixed parcel of real estate in New Jersey of which it had exclusive possession by ownership or lease. The hearing officer, in arriving at a contrary conclusion, held that the hallmark of a place of public accommodation was that "the public at large is invited," and she found that Little League issued an invitation to all boys in communities having local leagues. She found, further, that membership organizations, although not having a "specific pinpointable geographic area," are nevertheless places of public accommodation if, as Little League does, they offer advantages and facilities on the basis of a general, public invitation to join.We are satisfied that the determination of the Division on this issue is correct. The law is remedial and should be read with an approach sympathetic to its objectives. If this organization were not deemed a place of public accommodation it would be free to discriminate on the basis of race or religion as well as sex.The statutory noun "place" (of public accommodation) is a term of convenience, not of limitation. It is employed to reflect the fact that public accommodations are commonly provided at fixed "places," e.g., hotels, restaurants, swimming pools, etc. But a public conveyance, like a train, is a "place" of public accommodation although it has a moving situs. The "place" of public accommodation in the case of Little League is obviously the ball field at which tryouts are arranged, instructions given, practices held and games played. The statutory "accommodations, advantages, facilities and privileges" at the place of public accommodation, N.J.S.A. 10:5-12(f), is the entire agglomeration of the arrangements which Little League and its local chartered leagues make and the facilities they provide for the playing of baseball by the children. In *Fraser v. Robin Dee Day Camp*, 44 N.J.

480 (1965), the court held that day camps were places of public accommodation even before the statute listed them as such. The court noted that many of the specifically listed types of public accommodation were "educational or recreational" in nature, as were day camps. The same, of course, is true of Little League baseball. As to the educational nature of competitive athletics, see *Brenden v. Independent School District*, 477 F.2d 1292 (8th Cir. 1973).

Little League is a public accommodation because the invitation is open to children in the community at large, with no restriction (other than sex) whatever. It is public in the added sense that local governmental bodies characteristically make the playing areas available to the local leagues, ordinarily without charge.

In sum, we find no basis in anything argued by Little League to support a determination that, consistent with the underlying purpose of the statutory prohibition against denial of the facilities of places of public accommodation on account of sex, Little League by virtue of its nature may reasonably be permitted to be restricted to boys in the age category under consideration.

In so holding we note the justified characterization by the hearing officer of Little League as a "piece of public Americana." It has become synonymous with children's baseball—a sport which the Little League handbook proudly proclaims as America's national game. The record evidences the fact that substantial numbers of young girls want to partake in it and are qualified to do so competitively with boys of the same age. The logic of the statutory support for their aspirations is compelling.

Exercise 3-16. *National Organization for Women, Essex Cnty. Chapter v. Little League Baseball, Inc.* Revisited

1. Why wasn't the case against Little League brought under the federal public accommodations law?
2. Which canons of construction did the court employ? Could you argue for a different result?
3. In *Uston*, the New Jersey Supreme Court quoted approvingly from an earlier case that said: "the more private property is devoted to public use, the more it must accommodate the rights which inhere in individual members of the general public who use that property." Do you think this adequately explains the rationale for public accommodations laws? Are non-discrimination laws merely the cost of doing business?

The Americans with Disabilities Act

In 1990, Congress enacted broad legislation designed to address discrimination against persons with disabilities, the Americans with Disabilities Act (ADA). The

ADA prohibits discrimination in employment and public accommodations based on disability, but also imposes affirmative responsibilities on both employers and places of public accommodation to make reasonable accommodations and comply with certain accessibility requirements. Public accommodations are required to take affirmative steps to ensure that persons with disabilities are able to participate fully in public life. These affirmative responsibilities recognize that discrimination based on disability is often structural. Without addressing these structural barriers, any right of equal access would be illusory. Under the ADA, the privately owned places of public accommodation had to bear the costs associated with compliance.

With respect to any new construction commenced after the date of enactment of the ADA, covered facilities must comply with mandated accessibility guidelines. Existing structures were also required to remove certain "architectural barriers" provided such removal was "readily achievable," which is defined as " ... easily accomplished without much difficulty or expense." Where removal of the barriers is not "easily accomplished without much difficulty or expense," a covered establishment is still required "to make such goods, services, facilities, privileges, advantages, or accommodations available through alternative methods."

The following is an excerpt from the ADA. Compare the way the ADA defines "public accommodation" with the definition used in Title II of the Civil Rights Act of 1964.

42 U.S. Code § 12182—Prohibition of discrimination by public accommodations

(a) General rule

No individual shall be discriminated against on the basis of disability in the full and equal enjoyment of the goods, services, facilities, privileges, advantages, or accommodations of any place of public accommodation by any person who owns, leases (or leases to), or operates a place of public accommodation.

42 U.S. Code § 12181—Definitions

As used in this subchapter:

(7) Public accommodation

The following private entities are considered public accommodations for purposes of this subchapter, if the operations of such entities affect commerce—

(A) an inn, hotel, motel, or other place of lodging, except for an establishment located within a building that contains not more than five rooms for rent or hire and that is actually occupied by the proprietor of such establishment as the residence of such proprietor;

(B) a restaurant, bar, or other establishment serving food or drink;

(C) a motion picture house, theater, concert hall, stadium, or other place of exhibition or entertainment;

(D) an auditorium, convention center, lecture hall, or other place of public gathering;

(E) a bakery, grocery store, clothing store, hardware store, shopping center, or other sales or rental establishment;

(F) a laundromat, dry-cleaner, bank, barber shop, beauty shop, travel service, shoe repair service, funeral parlor, gas station, office of an accountant or lawyer, pharmacy, insurance office, professional office of a health care provider, hospital, or other service establishment;

(G) a terminal, depot, or other station used for specified public transportation;

(H) a museum, library, gallery, or other place of public display or collection;

(I) a park, zoo, amusement park, or other place of recreation;

(J) a nursery, elementary, secondary, undergraduate, or postgraduate private school, or other place of education;

(K) a day care center, senior citizen center, homeless shelter, food bank, adoption agency, or other social service center establishment; and

(L) a gymnasium, health spa, bowling alley, golf course, or other place of exercise or recreation.

42 U.S. Code § 12187—Exemptions for private clubs and religious organizations

The provisions of this subchapter shall not apply to private clubs or establishments exempted from coverage under title II of the Civil Rights Act of 1964 (42 U.S.C. 2000–a(e)) [42 U.S.C. 2000a et seq.] or to religious organizations or entities controlled by religious organizations, including places of worship.

Exercise 3-17. *National Federation of the Blind v. Target*—The Americans with Disabilities Act (ADA)

The ADA was enacted before the current explosion in e-commerce. Today, the online sale of goods and services is a significant portion of the economy. Some businesses, such as Amazon.com, sell exclusively online, whereas other businesses may have so-called "brick and mortar" stores, but also maintain an online presence for scheduling, sales, and information. If the ADA was designed to ensure full participation in public life by persons with disabilities, should the right of equal access extend to virtual or cyber places of public accommodation when so much of life's activities now take place online? For individuals who are blind or have certain learning disabilities, online content is inaccessible. The following case raises the issue of inaccessibility with respect to the website owned and operated by the retailer Target. Under the ADA, it is clear that each of the approximately 1,400 "brick and mortar" Target retail stores qualifies as a "public accommodation." The case asks whether Target's website is also a public accommodation.

National Federation of the Blind v. Target

452 F. Supp. 2d 946 (N.D. Cal. 2006)

PATEL, J. Plaintiffs National Federation of the Blind, National Federation of the Blind of California, Bruce Sexton, and all those similarly situated, filed this action against Target Corporation ("Target"), seeking declaratory, injunctive, and monetary relief. Plaintiffs claim that Target.com is inaccessible to the blind, and thereby violates federal law[] prohibiting discrimination against the disabled. Now before the court is defendant's motion to dismiss for failure to state a claim. Having considered the parties' arguments and submissions, and for the reasons set forth below, the court enters the following memorandum and order.

Target operates approximately 1,400 retail stores nationwide, including 205 stores in California. Target.com is a website owned and operated by Target. By visiting Target.com, customers can purchase many of the items available in Target stores. Target.com also allows a customer to perform functions related to Target stores. For example, through Target.com, a customer can access information on store locations and hours, refill a prescription or order photo prints for pick-up at a store, and print coupons to redeem at a store.

Plaintiffs allege that Target.com is not accessible to blind individuals. According to plaintiffs, designing a website to be accessible to the blind is technologically simple and not economically prohibitive. Protocols for designing an accessible internet site rely heavily on "alternative text": invisible code embedded beneath graphics. A blind individual can use screen reader software, which vocalizes the alternative text and describes the content of the webpage. Similarly, if the screen reader can read the navigation links, then a blind individual can navigate the site with a keyboard instead of a mouse. Plaintiffs allege that Target.com lacks these features that would enable the blind to use Target.com. Since the blind cannot use Target.com, they are denied full and equal access to Target stores, according to plaintiffs.

Defendant now moves to dismiss the complaint for failure to state a claim. Defendant claims that the Americans with Disabilities Act, 42 U.S.C. section 12182, ("ADA") covers access to only physical spaces. Since Target.com is not a physical space, defendant asserts that the complaint does not state a claim [under the ADA]. Title III of the ADA prevents discrimination against the disabled in places of public accommodation: "No individual shall be discriminated against on the basis of disability in the full and equal enjoyment of the goods, services, facilities, privileges, advantages, or accommodations of any place of public accommodation by any person who owns, leases (or leases to) or operates a place of public accommodation." 42 U.S.C. § 12182(a).

"Discrimination" under the ADA encompasses the denial of the opportunity, by the disabled, to participate in programs or services, and providing the disabled with separate, but unequal, goods or services. To ensure that the disabled have full and equal enjoyment of the goods and services of places of public accommodation, the ADA requires "reasonable modification" of "policies, practices, and procedures," the provision of auxiliary aids to ensure effective communication with the disabled, and the removal of architectural and communications barriers. The ADA thus departs from certain anti-discrimination statutes in requiring that places of public accommodation take affirmative steps to accommodate the disabled. H.R. Rep. No. 101-485, pt.2, at 104 (1990); 42 U.S.C. § 12182(b)(2)(A)(ii-iv).

Defendant contends that Target.com is not a place of public accommodation within the meaning of the ADA, and therefore plaintiffs cannot state a claim under the ADA. Specifically, defendant claims that the complaint is deficient because it does not allege that "individuals with vision impairments are denied access to one of Target's brick and mortar stores or the goods they contain." However, the complaint states that "due to Target's failure and refusal to remove access barriers to Target.com, blind individuals have been and are being denied equal access to Target stores, as well as to the numerous goods, services and benefits offered to the public through Target.com." Plaintiffs' legal theory is that unequal access to Target.com denies the blind the full enjoyment of the goods and services offered at Target stores, which are places of public accommodation.Defendant contends that even if Target.com is the alleged service of Target stores, plaintiffs still do not state a claim because they fail to assert that they are denied physical access to Target stores. Although a plaintiff may allege an ADA violation based on unequal access to a "service" of a place of public accommodation, courts have held that a plaintiff must allege that there is a "nexus" between the challenged service and the place of public accommodation. Under Ninth Circuit law, a "place of public accommodation," within the meaning of Title III, is a physical place.The Eleventh Circuit in *Rendon v. Valleycrest Prod., Ltd.* held that the telephone process for selecting contestants for "Who Wants to be a Millionaire" discriminated against people with hearing and other physical disabilities. 294 F.3d 1279, 1280-81 (11th Cir. 2002). The court found that the studio where the show was filmed was a place of public accommodation and that competing on the show was a privilege provided by the place of public accommodation. Thus, the court held that by using a discriminatory process for screening potential contestants, defendant was denying disabled persons equal enjoyment of a privilege (competing on the show) of a place of public accommodation (the studio).Defendant argues that the ADA prohibits only discrimination occurring on the premises of a place of public accommodation, and that "discrimination" is limited to the denial of physical entry to, or use of, a space. The ADA prohibits discrimination on the basis of disability "in the full and equal enjoyment of the goods, services, facilities, privileges, advantages or accommodations of any place of public accommodation." 42 U.S.C. § 12182(a) (emphasis added). The statute applies to the services of a place of public accommodation, not services in a place of public accommodation. To limit the ADA to discrimination in the provision of services occurring on the premises of a public accommodation would contradict the plain language of the statute. To the extent defendant argues that plaintiffs' claims are not cognizable because they occur away from a "place" of public accommodation, defendant's argument must fail.

In sum, the court finds that to the extent that plaintiffs allege that the inaccessibility of Target.com impedes the full and equal enjoyment of goods and services offered in Target stores, the plaintiffs state a claim, and the motion to dismiss is denied. To the extent that Target.com offers information and services unconnected to Target stores, which do not affect the enjoyment of goods and services offered in Target stores, the plaintiffs fail to state a claim under Title III of the ADA. Defendant's motion to dismiss this portion of plaintiffs' ADA claim is granted.

Exercise 3-18. *National Federation of the Blind v. Target* Revisited

Judge Patel applied a nexus test, holding that the plaintiffs had stated a cause of action to the extent that the inaccessibility of Target.com denied them full and equal access to the goods and services available in the brick and mortar Target retails stores. The court declined to find that Target.com was an independent public accommodation on the grounds that the ADA requires a physical place. This reading of the statute leaves online retailers currently beyond the scope of the ADA. Do you agree that the ADA requires a physical place?

Two years after the ruling, the National Federation for the Blind and Target reached a settlement. Target agreed to make certain changes to its website, established a $6,000,000 settlement fund, and agreed to pay attorney's fees and court costs which themselves exceeded $3,000,000. The lawsuit prompted many online retailers and service providers to make their websites more accessible, including Amazon.com and iTunes. Why would these providers take these steps when the ruling did not reach their activities?

In another interesting case from California, the Ninth Circuit ruled that a video game was not a public accommodation for purposes of the ADA. In *Stern v. Sony*, 459 Fed. Appx. 609 (9th Cir. 2011), the plaintiff alleged that "his visual impairments and the inaccessibility of Sony's video games prevent him from fully and equally enjoying the games." He argued that Sony should provide gamers that have visual disabilities with auxiliary visual and auditory cues through a free software patch. The company's failure to act, Stern alleged, violated the ADA. The court held that any connection between the video games and a physical place, such as Sony marketing events, was too tenuous to support a cause of action under the ADA.

Beach Access and the Public Trust Doctrine

Under the public trust doctrine, lands covered by tidal waters are deemed to be held in trust by the sovereign (i.e., the government) for the benefit of the general public. The doctrine has ancient roots, dating back to the time of Emperor Justinian. It was part of the English common law that then formed the basis of U.S. state law upon independence. The doctrine employs the legal fiction of a trust to describe the relationship of the parties. In the United States, the individual states are deemed to hold the tidal lands in trust for the benefit of the general public. As a deemed trustee, the government owes a fiduciary duty to the public to maintain and protect the trust property or resource. Although legal title to the tidal lands is vested in the state, the members of the general public are considered the beneficial owners of the property. This split of legal and beneficial (also known as equitable) title is characteristic of actual trust relationships, which are discussed in greater detail in Chapter 5.

The rationale for the Public Trust Doctrine is that the resource of the tidal lands was too valuable to permit private or even state ownership. Traditionally, the tidal lands were valuable resources for navigation, commerce, and fishing. More recently, land over which tidal waters ebb and flow have become important for their recreational value. Beaches and access to water provide the backbone of the tourism industry in a number of states. To reflect these changing values, states have gradually expanded their public trust doctrine to protect the recreational use of tidal lands. However, in some states, public access points to the beach are few and far between, making it difficult for the public to gain access to the public trust property. The demand for beach access has led to disputes in some states between the owners of private beachfront property and the beach-loving public. Some states have gone as far as to mandate public beach access over privately owned property.

As with many property issues, state law differs widely on the question of beach access, and the answer will depend on the state where the beach is located. Although states draw the line in different places, they all begin with a concept known as the mean high tide line. In most states, all land below the mean high tide line is held in trust for the public. Courts sometimes talk about this "line" interchangeably with the "line" between the dry and the wet sand, representing how high the tide had come in the night before. The mean high tide line is actually much more complicated and not immediately apparent to the naked eye. It is the arithmetic average of high-water heights observed by the National Oceanic and Atmospheric Administration (NOAA) over an 18.6-year Metonic cycle. It is the line that is formed by the intersection of the tidal plane of the mean high tide with the shore.

A few states use the mean low tide line to determine the public trust property. In these states, the public has a right to the tidal lands below the low tide mark, leaving only land that is covered by water. As a result, private property owners can own the beach to the mean low tide line. This is the rule followed by Maine, Massachusetts, and Virginia. These states also restrict the public use to the traditional pursuits of hunting, fishing, and navigation.

The states that follow the mean high tide line have different rules regarding whether members of the public enjoying the public trust property have a right to use the land above the mean high tide line, which is typically described as the dry sand beach. The majority of states do not grant any rights over the dry sand beach. Some states allow access across the privately owned dry sand beach, and others allow the public to use the dry sand beach as incidental to their enjoyment of the public trust property. The states that allow access through the use of privately owned dry sand beach have based their decisions on different laws. Courts in Hawaii, Oregon, and Texas have applied a doctrine known as customary use based on ancient, peaceful, uninterrupted and reasonable use of the beach. New Jersey courts have reasoned that in order for the public trust doctrine to be meaningful, the beach goers must have access to the dry sand for recreation purposes, and they must have access to the beach even if it is over privately owned property.

Exercise 3-19. *Raleigh Avenue Beach Association v. Atlantic Beach Club, Inc.*

New Jersey beaches have been a popular tourist destination since before the Civil War. Known for its 130 miles of sandy beach coastline, tourism is the third largest industry in the state. *Raleigh Avenue Beach Association v. Atlantic Beach Club, Inc.* represents a clash between private property interests and the beach-loving public.

1. The facts of the case are very technical and may be hard to follow if you are not familiar with the terminology. For this reason, it is a good idea to try to draw a map of the area in dispute based on the description provided by the court. You can then check your rendering against Google maps, but try to draw your own map first. It is good experience to try to translate the property terms into recognizable images.
2. Identify the key New Jersey cases that the court cited in the case and chart the evolution of the public trust doctrine in the state. Identify why each case is significant.
3. The ADA imposes affirmative duties on private property owners to make public accommodations accessible to persons with disabilities to ensure a meaningful right of access. In the following case, the court reasons that "reasonable access to the sea is integral to the public trust doctrine" and that without such access "the doctrine has no meaning." Do you agree?

Raleigh Avenue Beach Association v. Atlantis Beach Club, Inc.

185 N.J. 40, 879 A.2d 112 (2005)

Poritz, C.J. This case raises a question about the right of the public to use a 480-foot wide stretch of upland sand beach in Lower Township, Cape May County, owned by respondent Atlantis Beach Club, Inc., and operated as a private club. We hold today that, in the circumstances presented here, and on application of the factors set forth in *Matthews v. Bay Head Improvement Ass'n*, 95 N.J. 306, 326, cert. denied, *Bay Head Improvement Ass'n v. Matthews*, 469 U.S. 821 (1984), the public trust doctrine requires the Atlantis property to be open to the general public at a reasonable fee for services provided by the owner and approved by the Department of Environmental Protection.

Atlantis Beach Club, Inc. (Atlantis or Beach Club) is the successor in title to a Riparian Grant, dated January 17, 1907, from the State of New Jersey to the Cape May Real Estate Company. The grant encompassed a large area not relevant to this litigation except for certain submerged land that, in 1907, was located within the bed of Turtle Gut Inlet, a body of water that connected to the Atlantic Ocean. Today, the land is described on the Lower Township Municipal Tax Map as Block 730.02, Lot 1.02. No longer submerged, the lot extends to the mean high water line from a bulkhead running north/south along the western boundary of the property. That western boundary lies to the east of an unpaved section of Raleigh Avenue (which runs east/west), whereas the mean high water line serves as the boundary for Lot 1.03, which is entirely submerged beneath the ocean at high tide; Lot 1.02, however, consists of dry sand beach and protected dunes. The distance from the bulkhead (the western boundary of Lot 1.02) to the mean high water line is about 342 feet. Persons using the beach for recreational purposes cross over the bulkhead by walking on a boardwalk pathway that traverses the dunes and curves southward to the beach. The dry sand beach area lies beyond the dunes and extends to the mean high water line.

A pathway runs east/west along the unpaved section of Raleigh Avenue to the approximate midpoint of the bulkhead and then, as described, across the bulkhead and through the dunes. The La Vida del Mar Condominiums (La Vida), a four-story, twenty-four-unit condominium structure along Raleigh Avenue, stands immediately to the west of the bulkhead along the western boundary of the Atlantis property. Another four-story multiple unit condominium complex called the La Quinta del Mar sits to the south of La Vida and the path that runs from the end of the pavement on Raleigh Avenue and over the bulkhead. To the west of La Quinta del Mar are the Villa House and La Quinta Towers, both of which contain residential units. Seapointe Village (Seapointe) is located to the north of La Vida and consists of several structures, including a six-story, one-hundred-room hotel, and more than five hundred residential units. Seapointe occupies 63.4 acres, including the beach property to the north of the Atlantis beach.

The United States Coast Guard owns the property to the south of the Atlantis beach. That property is closed to the public from April 1 through August 15 to protect the piping plover, an endangered species, during breeding season. Although the Coast Guard beach is unavailable for most of the summer season, the property is open to the public the rest of the year.

Atlantis is located in the Diamond Beach neighborhood, a residential area of approximately three blocks by nine blocks that contains the only beach in Lower

Township facing the Atlantic Ocean. In addition to the beach access point on the Atlantis property at the end of Raleigh Avenue, there are two other access points in Diamond Beach north of Atlantis: one at the eastern end of Dune Drive and the other at the eastern end of Memphis Avenue. Access is blocked by condominium buildings located at the terminus of the other streets in the area. According to certifications filed by residents of La Quinta Towers in support of plaintiff Raleigh Avenue Beach Association (Association), the closest free entry to the beach is Dune Drive, a nine-block walk from Raleigh Avenue and a distance of approximately one-half mile. The beach access problem in Lower Township is further compounded by the limited number of parking spaces available in the Diamond Beach neighborhood.

Until 1996, the beach on the Atlantis property was open to the public free-of-charge. In the summer of 1996, however, Atlantis established a private beach club known at the time as Club Atlantis Enterprises. The club limited public access to its beach by charging a fee of $300 for six seasonal beach tags. As of July 2003, a sign posted on the gate at the entrance to the Atlantis beach read: "FREE PUBLIC ACCESS ENDS HERE/MEMBERSHIP AVAILABLE AT GATE." Atlantis's 2003 Rules and Regulations, also posted, provided the following warning:

> ANYONE ATTEMPTING TO USE, ENTER UPON OR CROSS OVER CLUB PROPERTY FOR ANY REASON WITHOUT CLUB PERMISSION OR WHO IS NOT IN POSSESSION OF A VALID TAG AND AUTHORIZED TO USE SUCH TAG WILL BE SUBJECT TO PROSECUTION, CIVIL AND OR CRIMINAL, TO THE FULLEST EXTENT PERMITTED BY LAW, INCLUDING ALL COSTS AND LEGAL FEES INCURRED BY THE CLUB.

Prior to the commencement of this litigation, the membership fee for new members and members who had joined the beach club in 2002 was set at $700 for the 2003 summer season. Members were entitled to eight beach tags per household. Atlantis also sold "Access Easements" at $10,000 each, paid in cash. Easement holders were required to pay an annual membership fee determined by dividing the actual costs associated with operating the beach club by the total number of members (both easement holders and yearly members) to arrive at the holder's proportionate share. According to a March 14, 2003 letter to members, the payment of membership fees or the purchase of an easement entitled them "to use and enjoy the [club] facilities," which included uniformed private security personnel on club grounds, as well as lifeguards on duty from June 21 through September 1, 2003, seven days a week, between the hours of 10:00 a.m. and 5:00 p.m.

On June 22, 2002, Tony Labrosciano was issued a summons for trespassing when he attempted to leave the wet sand area and walk across the Atlantis property to the eastern terminus of Raleigh Avenue in order to take the most direct route back to his home. On July 26, 2002, Atlantis filed an Order to Show Cause and Verified Complaint against Labrosciano, other unnamed persons, Lower Township, and the State of New Jersey, seeking, among other things, to enjoin Labrosciano and members of his class from "trespassing, entering onto and accessing" the Atlantis property, and declaring that Atlantis is not required to provide the public with access to or use of any portion of its property or the adjacent ocean.

The law we are asked to interpret in this case—the public trust doctrine—derives from the English common law principle that all of the land covered by tidal waters belongs to the sovereign held in trust for the people to use. *Borough of Neptune City v. Borough of Avon-by-the-Sea,* 61 N.J. 296 (1972). That common law principle, in turn, has roots

> in Roman jurisprudence, which held that "[b]y the law of nature[,] ... the air, running water, the sea, and consequently the shores of the sea," were "common to mankind." ... No one was forbidden access to the sea, and everyone could use the seashore "to dry his nets there, and haul them from the sea...." The seashore was not private property, but "subject to the same law as the sea itself, and the sand or ground beneath it." *Matthews, supra.*

In *Arnold v. Mundy,* 6 N.J.L. 1, 53 (E. & A.1821), the first case to affirm and reformulate the public trust doctrine in New Jersey, the Court explained that upon the Colonies' victory in the Revolutionary War, the English sovereign's rights to the tidal waters "became vested in the people of New Jersey as the sovereign of the country, and are now in their hands." *Arnold* addressed the plaintiff's claim to an oyster bed in the Raritan River adjacent to his farm in Perth Amboy. Chief Justice Kirkpatrick found that the land on which water ebbs and flows, including the land between the high and low water, belongs not to the owners of the lands adjacent to the water, but to the State, "to be held, protected, and regulated for the common use and benefit."

Early understanding of the scope of the public trust doctrine focused on the preservation of the "natural water resources" of New Jersey "for navigation and commerce ... and fishing, an important source of food." In *Neptune City,* the Court extended public rights in tidal lands "to recreational uses, including bathing, swimming and other shore activities." We invalidated a municipal ordinance that required non-residents of Avon-by-the-Sea to pay a higher fee than the residents of Avon were required to pay to access and use the town's beaches. The Court held:

> [A]t least where the upland sand area is owned by a municipality ... and dedicated to public beach purposes, a modern court must take the view that the public trust doctrine dictates that the beach and the ocean waters must be open to all on equal terms and without preference and that any contrary state or municipal action is impermissible.

Later, in *Matthews, supra* we considered "the extent of the public's interest in privately-owned dry sand beaches," which, we noted, "may [include both] a right to cross [such] privately owned ... beaches in order to gain access to the foreshore ... [and a] right to sunbathe and generally enjoy recreational activities" on the dry sands. We observed that New Jersey's beaches constitute a "unique" and "irreplaceable" resource, subject to increased pressure from population growth throughout the region and improved transportation to the shore. Concerned about the great demand and the limited number of beaches open to the public, we repeated:

> Exercise of the public's right to swim and bathe below the mean high water mark may depend upon a right to pass across the upland beach. Without some means of access the public right to use the foreshore would be meaningless. To say that the public trust doctrine entitles the public to swim in the ocean and to use the foreshore in connection therewith without assuring the public of a feasible access route would seriously impinge on, if not effectively eliminate, the rights of the public trust doctrine.

Matthews clearly articulates the concept already implicit in our case law that reasonable access to the sea is integral to the public trust doctrine. Indeed, as *Matthews* points out, without access the doctrine has no meaning.

That leaves the question raised in this case: whether use of the dry sand ancillary to use of the ocean for recreation purposes is also implicit in the rights that belong to the public under the doctrine. *Matthews* states unequivocally that a "bather's right in the upland sands is not limited to passage ... [and that] [r]easonable enjoyment of the foreshore and the sea cannot be realized unless some enjoyment of the dry sand area is also allowed." Because the activity of swimming "must be accompanied by intermittent periods of rest and relaxation beyond the water's edge," the lack of an area available to the public for that purpose "would seriously curtail and in many situations eliminate the right to the recreational use of the ocean." Although the *Matthews* Court did not compare that use of the dry sand to use associated with ancient fishing rights, it did point out that under Roman law, "everyone could use the seashore 'to dry his nets there, and haul them from the sea.... "' (quoting Justinian *Institutes* 2.1.1) (T. Sandars trans. 1st Am. ed. 1876). It follows, then, that use of the dry sand has long been a correlate to use of the ocean and is a component part of the rights associated with the public trust doctrine.

The factual context in which *Matthews* was decided was critical to the Court's holding. *Neptune City, supra* had held that the general public must be allowed to use a municipally-owned dry sand beach on equal terms with residents of the municipality. *Matthews* involved a private non-profit entity, the Bay Head Improvement Association (Improvement Association), that owned/leased and operated certain upland sand areas in the Borough of Bay Head for the recreational use of Bay Head residents only. The Improvement Association was closely connected with the municipality, which provided at various points in time, office space, liability insurance, and funding, among other things. That symbiotic relationship, as well as the public nature of the activities conducted by the Improvement Association, led the Court to conclude that the Improvement Association was in reality a "quasi-public body" bound by the *Neptune City* holding.

Although decided on narrow grounds, *Matthews* established the framework for application of the public trust doctrine to privately-owned upland sand beaches. The *Matthews* approach begins with the general principle that public use of the upland sands is "subject to an accommodation of the interests of the owner," and proceeds by setting forth criteria for a case-by-case consideration in respect of the appropriate level of accommodation. The Court's formulation bears repeating here:

> Archaic judicial responses are not an answer to a modern social problem. Rather, we perceive the public trust doctrine not to be "fixed or static," but one to "be molded and extended to meet changing conditions and needs of the public it was created to benefit." ...
>
> Precisely what privately-owned upland sand area will be available and required to satisfy the public's rights under the public trust doctrine will depend on the circumstances. Location of the dry sand area in relation to the foreshore, extent and availability of publicly-owned upland sand area, nature and extent of the public demand, and usage of the upland sand land by the owner are all factors to be weighed and considered in fixing the contours of the usage of the upper sand.
>
> Today, recognizing the increasing demand for our State's beaches and the dynamic nature of the public trust doctrine, we find that the public must be given both access to and use of privately-owned dry sand areas as reasonably necessary. While the public's rights in private beaches are not coextensive with the rights enjoyed in municipal beaches, private landowners may not in all instances prevent the public from exercising its rights under the public trust doctrine. The public must be afforded reasonable access to the foreshore as well as a suitable area for recreation on the dry sand.

We turn now to an application of the *Matthews* factors to the circumstances of this case in order to determine "what privately-owned upland sand area will be available and required to satisfy the public's rights under the public trust doctrine."

"Location of the dry sand area in relation to the foreshore":

The dry sand beach at the center of this controversy extends horizontally 480 feet from the Coast Guard property south of Atlantis to the Seapointe property north of Atlantis, and vertically, from three feet landward of the mean high water line about 339 feet to the dunes adjacent to the bulkhead and the Raleigh Avenue extension. It is easily reached by pedestrians using the path bisecting the Raleigh Avenue extension from the end of the paved roadway to the bulkhead.

"[E]xtent and availability of publicly-owned upland sand area":

There is no publicly-owned beach area in Lower Township, although it was represented to us at oral argument that there are public beaches in the "Wildwoods" north of Lower Township. The Borough of Wildwood Crest, immediately north of Lower Township, owns dry sand beach that is used by the public.

"[N]ature and extent of the public demand":

The Diamond Beach section of Lower Township is not large (three blocks by nine blocks), and parking is limited but available along the area streets. Local residents whose homes are within easy walking distance of Atlantis are members of the plaintiff Association, through which they have expressed their individual concerns about access and use. That there is enormous public interest in the New Jersey shore is well-known; tourism associated with New Jersey's beaches is a $16 billion annual industry.

"[U]sage of the upland sand land by the owner":

The more or less rectangular area of dry sand that constitutes the Atlantis beach has been closed to non-members of Atlantis from the summer of 1996 to May 4, 2004. As for the period prior to 1996, the general public used the beach without limitation or fee during the ten years between 1986 and 1996 and, it appears, enjoyed the same open access and use prior to 1986 (although the record is sparse on the issue of prior use). The La Vida condominiums, situated directly to the west of Atlantis, were constructed in 1986. Suffice it to say that the Atlantis beach was used by the public for many years.

In sum, based on the circumstances in this case and on application of the *Matthews* factors, we hold that the Atlantis upland sands must be available for use by the general public under the public trust doctrine. In so holding we highlight the longstanding public access to and use of the beach, the documented public demand, the lack of publicly-owned beaches in Lower Township, and the type of use by the current owner as a business enterprise.

Exercise 3-20. *Raleigh Avenue Beach Association v. Atlantic Beach Club, Inc.* Revisited

1. There is no doubt that this case expands the reach of the public trust doctrine in New Jersey. However, the application of the doctrine will always depend on the particular facts and circumstances. How well do you think the court did applying the law to the facts of the case?
2. Did the Atlantic Beach Club lose one of the sticks in its bundle of rights?
3. According to the court, on what terms can the public use the dry sand?
4. Recall that the Atlantic Beach Club was selling interests that they called "easements." How do you think the people who paid $10,000 for the "easements" reacted to the decision?
5. Is a beach a public accommodation under the Civil Rights Act of 1964? What about the New Jersey LAD? The ADA?

Homelessness

Homelessness is a major social problem in the United States. Although there are many reasons for homelessness, policy makers generally identify the lack of affordable housing as the main reason people experience homelessness, followed by poverty and unemployment. The U.S. Department of Housing and Urban Development (HUD) requires communities to conduct counts of homeless individuals on a single night in January. Known as a point-in-time count, this measure provides a snapshot of homelessness in the United States. For example, the 2014 point-in-time count revealed that there were 578,424 people experiencing homelessness. This translates to approximately 18 out of every 10,000 individuals living in the United States. Twenty-three percent of the homeless individuals were children under the age of 18. Nine percent of the homeless individuals were veterans. The majority of the homeless individuals were living in shelters, but 31 percent were living unsheltered in places not meant for human habitation such as an abandoned building or on the street.

By definition, homeless individuals do not have housing of their own. At night, those who are considered "sheltered" will either be sleeping at the homes of relatives or friends or at a facility run by the government or a non-profit organization. Those who are not "sheltered" may be squatting in the property of another or sleeping in public spaces, such as parks or highway underpasses. During the day, many of the homeless shelters require the residents to leave, leaving homeless individuals to wander in and out of public and private property.

The law of trespass and the right to exclude has obvious application to such living arrangements. The use of private property is presumptively non-permissive. Homeless individuals staying with relatives or friends only have a mere license that is revocable at will. Homeless individuals who are squatting or living in abandoned buildings are trespassing and are subject to arrest or removal. In most states, private business owners enjoy the arbitrary right to exclude, provided it does not violate any non-discrimination protections. Accordingly, a privately owned shopping mall would be able to exclude homeless individuals.

As members of the public, homeless individuals can access public spaces, such as parks, transportation hubs, and sidewalks. However, they are often denied access to these spaces by application of criminal laws designed to combat "vagrancy" or "loitering." When this occurs, homeless individuals have no place where they are entitled to rest because they are excluded from private property and driven from public spaces. They also have no place where they can conduct the essential elements of daily life: dressing, washing, toileting, and sleeping. To make matters worse, many jurisdictions criminalize these activities when they are conducted in public.

Exercise 3-21. *Pottinger v. City of Miami*

The following case is a class action filed on behalf of homeless people living in the City of Miami. The plaintiffs allege that the treatment of homeless individuals by the police violate the U.S. Constitution. Although the nuances of the constitutional claims presented are beyond the scope of this course, the case provides an illuminating discussion of the causes of homelessness and the government's responses to individuals who are homeless.

1. The court notes that "the majority of homeless individuals literally have no place to go." Think about all the things that you can do in your apartment that would be illegal if you did them in public.
2. Miami claims that it has a compelling interest "in keeping its parks and streets free of litter, vandalism and general deterioration; in preventing crime and ensuring safety in public parks; and in promoting tourism, business and the development of the downtown area." It further claims that all of these interests are "negatively affected by the presence of the homeless." How would you articulate the competing interests of the plaintiffs? How would you balance these interests?

Pottinger v. City of Miami

810 F. Supp. 1551 (S.D. Fla. 1992)

Atkins, Judge. Plaintiffs filed this action in December of 1988 on behalf of themselves and approximately 6,000 other homeless people living in the City of Miami. Plaintiffs' complaint alleges that the City of Miami ("defendant" or "City") has a custom, practice and policy of arresting, harassing and otherwise interfering with homeless people for engaging in basic activities of daily life—including sleeping and eating—in the public places where they are forced to live. Plaintiffs further claim that the City has arrested thousands of homeless people for such life-sustaining conduct under various City of Miami ordinances and Florida Statutes. In addition, plaintiffs assert that the city routinely seizes and destroys their property and has failed to follow its own inventory procedures regarding the seized personal property of homeless arrestees and homeless persons in general.

Plaintiffs allege that the property destruction and arrests, which often result in no criminal charges, prosecutions or convictions, violate their rights under the United States and Florida Constitutions. Because the arrested plaintiffs are released without further official process, the argument continues, plaintiffs never have the opportunity to raise such valid defenses as necessity or duress. As discussed below, plaintiffs contend that the city applies the ordinances or statutes under which they are arrested to homeless individuals as part of a custom and practice of driving the homeless from public places. Accordingly, plaintiffs do not argue that any of the ordinances should be stricken; instead, they ask that the City be enjoined from arresting homeless individuals for inoffensive conduct, such as sleeping or bathing, that they are forced to perform in public.

Upon careful review the evidence presented at trial and at prior proceedings and after weighing the various arguments presented throughout this litigation, the court finds that injunctive relief is warranted in this case for the following reasons, which are discussed more fully below. First, plaintiffs have shown that the City has a pattern and practice of arresting homeless people for the purpose of driving them from public areas. Second, the City's practice of arresting homeless individuals for harmless, involuntary conduct which they must perform in public is cruel and unusual in violation of the Eighth Amendment to the United States Constitution. Third, such arrests violate plaintiffs' due process rights because they reach innocent and inoffensive conduct. Fourth, the City's failure to follow its own written procedure for handling personal property when seizing or destroying the property of homeless individuals violates plaintiffs' fourth amendment rights. Fifth, the City's practice of arresting homeless individuals for performing essential, life-sustaining acts in public when they have absolutely no place to go effectively infringes on their fundamental right to travel in violation of the equal protection clause.

In essence, this litigation results from an inevitable conflict between the need of homeless individuals to perform essential, life-sustaining acts in public and the responsibility of the government to maintain orderly, aesthetically pleasing public parks and streets. The issues raised in this case reveal various aspects of this conflict which, unfortunately, has become intensified by the overwhelming increase in the number of homeless people in recent years and a corresponding decrease in federal aid to cities.

The plaintiffs are homeless men, women and children who live in the streets, parks and other public areas in the area of the City of Miami bordered on the North by Interstate 395, on the South by Flagler Street, on the East by Biscayne Bay, and on the West by Interstate 95. Professor James Wright, an expert in the sociology of the homeless, testified that most homeless individuals are profoundly poor, have high levels of mental or physical disability, and live in social isolation. He further testified that homeless individuals rarely, if ever, choose to be homeless. Generally, people become homeless as the result of a financial crisis or because of a mental or physical illness.

While a mental or physical illness may cause some people to become homeless, health problems are also aggravated by homelessness. Dr. Pedro J. Greer, Jr., Medical Director of the Camillus Health Concern and an expert in medical treatment of homeless individuals, testified that a higher incidence of all diseases exists among the homeless. For example, hypertension, gastro-intestinal disorders, tuberculosis and peripheral vascular disease occur at a much higher rate in homeless people. This is due to a variety of factors such as exposure to the elements, constant walking, sleeping and eating in unsanitary conditions, lack of sleep and poor nutrition. In addition, people without a home generally have no place to store medication, no clock to determine when to take a pill, and no water with which to take it. Medical treatment of the homeless is hampered by the lack of beds and other facilities in the areas where the homeless reside. Lack of transportation further enhances the difficulty of the homeless in obtaining follow-up medical care. Improper diet and the stress of living outside can also aggravate mental illnesses.

Substance abuse, a component of both physical and mental illness, is also a factor contributing to homelessness. Dr. Greer testified that studies have shown that people are genetically predisposed to alcoholism, but that no such genetic link has been established with regard to drug addictions. Substance abuse also may be a consequence of being homeless. Professor Wright testified that many homeless people do not begin drinking until they become homeless; they use alcohol as a self-medication to numb both psychological and physical pain.

Chronic unemployment is another problem that many homeless face. Joblessness among homeless individuals is exacerbated by certain barriers that impede them from searching for work, such as health problems, the fact that they have no place to bathe, no legal address, no transportation and no telephone.

Professor Wright also testified that the typical day in the life of a homeless individual is predominated by a quest to obtain food and shelter. Because the lines at feeding programs are often long, some homeless individuals skip meals because they will miss obtaining a space in a shelter if they wait for food. Dr. David F. Fike, a professor of social work and an expert on homelessness in Dade County, Florida, testified that the longer a person has been on the streets, the more likely it is that he or she will remain homeless.

The City has made laudable attempts, particularly in recent years, to assist the homeless. For example, the City resolved to participate, in conjunction with Dade County, the State of Florida and all agencies providing services to the homeless, in the development of an interim plan to provide resources to the homeless. In addition, the City stopped enforcing its ordinance against sleeping in public after an Eleventh Circuit ruling called into question the validity of a similar ordinance. However, many factors have frustrated the City's efforts to alleviate the problem of homelessness. Perhaps the most significant factor is the escalating number of homeless people.

The number of homeless individuals in Miami has grown at an alarming rate. According to Dr. Greer, the number of homeless treated medically at the Camillus Health Concern increased dramatically from 1984 to 1991. A disturbing aspect of the rise in homelessness is the increase in the number of families without shelter. One of the more poignant photographs in evidence shows two small children living beneath the I-395 overpass with their pregnant mother. As Dr. Greer commented, a second generation of homeless persons is being born right under our bridges.

The lack of low-income housing or shelter space cannot be underestimated as a factor contributing to homelessness. At the time of trial, Miami had fewer than 700 beds available in shelters for the homeless. Except for a fortunate few, most homeless individuals have no alternative to living in public areas.

The evidence presented at trial regarding the magnitude of the homelessness problem was overwhelming in itself. Then, shortly after the trial, one of the worst possible scenarios for homelessness occurred when Hurricane Andrew struck South Florida. Overnight, approximately 200,000 people were left without homes. In sum, this court has no difficulty in finding that the majority of homeless individuals literally have no place to go.

The City, as evidenced by the records presented at trial, has arrested thousands of homeless individuals from 1987 to 1990 for misdemeanors such as obstructing the sidewalk, loitering, and being in the park after hours. The records show that the City arrested homeless individuals for standing, sleeping or sitting on sidewalks in violation of City of Miami Code § 37-53.1 (prohibiting obstruction of sidewalks); for sleeping on benches, sidewalks or in parks in violation of Miami Code § 37-63 (prohibiting sleeping in public); for sleeping in the park in violation of Miami Code § 38-3 (prohibiting being in the park after hours); for loitering and prowling in violation of Florida Statutes § 856.032 and Miami Code §§ 37-34 and 35; and for sleeping, sitting or standing in public buildings in violation of Florida Statutes § 810.08, .09 (prohibiting trespassing).

The arrest records also show that many of the arrests for being in the park after hours were made less than an hour before the park was to reopen. In addition, the narrative sections of a majority of the arrest reports indicate that the individual arrestee was not disorderly, was not involved in any drug activity, and did not pose any apparent harm to anyone. Many of the records indicate that the arrestee was doing nothing more than sleeping. The testimony and the documentary evidence regarding the arrests of the homeless—in addition to the sheer volume of homeless people in the City of Miami and the dearth of shelter space—support plaintiffs' claim that there is no public place where they can perform basic, essential acts such as sleeping without the possibility of being arrested.

The interests advanced by the City to justify the arrests of homeless individuals for conduct such as congregating under bridges, lying down on public sidewalks or being in the park after hours may be summarized as follows. The City contends that it has a compelling interest in keeping its parks and streets free of litter, vandalism and general deterioration; in preventing crime and ensuring safety in public parks; and in promoting tourism, business and the development of the downtown area, which are negatively affected by the presence of the homeless. We must weigh these interests to determine whether or not they are compelling and, if so, whether they are accomplished through the least intrusive means.

Even assuming these asserted interests could be considered compelling, the City could certainly accomplish them through some manner that is less intrusive than arresting homeless individuals. Provision of alternative shelter and services would be the ideal means of accomplishing the same goals. However, in the absence of available shelter space or funds for services, the parks and streets could be cleaned and maintained without arresting the homeless. Similarly, promotion of tourism and business and the development of the downtown area could be accomplished without arresting the homeless for inoffensive conduct. Because the City's interests in maintaining public areas and in promoting tourism and business can be achieved without arresting homeless individuals, these interests cannot justify the burden that the arrests place on the right to travel.

The City further contends that it has a compelling interest in ensuring that its parks are free of crime. The court recognizes the tremendous responsibility that the

City has and agrees that the City's interest in this regard is a compelling one. However, the City has not shown that arresting the homeless for being in the park after hours when they have no place else to go is the least intrusive means of addressing the interest in crime prevention.

One court considered whether arresting homeless individuals for begging was a sufficiently narrow means of serving the government's interest in preserving public order and preventing crime. In *Loper v. New York City Police Dept.*, 802 F. Supp. 1029, the court stated as follows:

> A peaceful beggar poses no threat to society. The beggar has arguably only committed the offense of being needy. The message one or one hundred beggars sends society can be disturbing. If some portion of society is offended, the answer is not in criminalizing those people, debtor's prisons being long gone, but addressing the root cause of their existence. The root cause is not served by removing them from sight, however; society is then just able to pretend that they do not exist a little longer.

Similarly, although the idea of homeless people sleeping in public parks may disturb or offend some portion of society, the answer is not in arresting individuals who have arguably only committed the offense of being without shelter. There exist other means of preventing crime that are less drastic than arresting the homeless for harmless conduct that poses no threat to society.

The court finds that plaintiffs have established that the City has a policy and practice of arresting homeless individuals for the purpose of driving them from public areas. The court concludes that the City's practice of arresting homeless individuals for performing inoffensive conduct in public when they have no place to go is cruel and unusual in violation of the eighth amendment, is overbroad to the extent that it reaches innocent acts in violation of the due process clause of the fourteenth amendment and infringes on the fundamental right to travel in violation of the equal protection clause of the fourteenth amendment. For these reasons, the court finds that plaintiffs' claim for injunctive relief is warranted.

Obviously, the ideal solution would be to provide housing and services to the homeless. However, assembling and allocating such resources is a matter for the government—at all levels—to address, not for the court to decide. Rather, our immediate task is to fashion relief that accommodates the two predominant interests in this litigation. First, such relief must protect the homeless from one approach that clearly is not the answer to homelessness, that is, arresting homeless people for innocent, involuntary acts. Second, any relief granted must not unduly hamper the City's ability to preserve public order. For these reasons and for the reasons set forth above in the findings of fact and conclusions of law, it is

ORDERED AND ADJUDGED that

(1) The City's practice of arresting homeless individuals for the involuntary, harmless acts they are forced to perform in public is unconstitutional because such arrests are cruel and unusual in violation of the eighth amendment, reach innocent

and inoffensive conduct in violation of the due process clause of the fourteenth amendment and burden the fundamental right to travel in violation of the equal protection clause; and

(2) The City's practice of seizing and destroying the property of homeless individuals without following its own written procedure for handling found or seized personal property violates plaintiffs' rights under the fourth amendment.

Exercise 3-22. *Pottinger v. City of Miami* Revisited

The court granted the plaintiffs' request for injunctive relief and enjoined the police department "from arresting homeless individuals who are forced to live in public for performing innocent, harmless, inoffensive acts such as sleeping, eating, lying down or sitting" in at least two designated "safe zones" or "arrest-free" zones.

1. What did the court mean when it said that the "ideal solution" was a matter for the government and not the court to decide?
2. How well do you believe the court balanced the interests of the plaintiffs with the interests of the city?
3. During the Great Recession, the number of empty or abandoned properties in the United States increased dramatically. Homelessness also increased during this period. Why doesn't the government reallocate abandoned houses to homeless individuals? It would seem to be an easy solution to a major social problem.

PART THREE
Ownership Structures — Estates in Land

Chapter 4

Shared Property: Gifts, Concurrent Ownership and Family Property

Introduction

This chapter focuses on sharing property, where law, money and loving relationships frequently come together. People often choose to share property with someone they care about, including spouses, domestic partners, parents and children, siblings and friends. Property relationships recurrently flow from personal relationships. They can also shape the relationships and the individuals involved—both economically and socially. As you will see in this chapter, Property rules can be used as a tool for bringing people together and for taking care of loved ones. Conversely, the rules can also be used for separating out and advancing an individual's interests and desires, opening the door to conflict, struggles for power, and sometimes making the other owner(s) vulnerable to harm. This is everyday law that impacts a lot of people. As you learn the fundamentals of this body of law, consider how the rules impact individuals, inter-personal relationships and society. Are the rules beneficial and fair?

Overview of Chapter 4

This Chapter is divided into three subunits, each of which has its own Chapter Problem.

1. Gifts
2. Concurrent Ownership
3. Family Property Law

We begin with the law of gifts, where sharing takes its most altruistic form through a voluntary transfer that is not in exchange for something else. Next, you will learn about concurrent ownership where two or more people share rights to the same asset at the same time, such as a bank account or a home. This topic includes three standard forms of co-ownership: a tenancy in common; a joint tenancy with the right of survivorship, and—for married couples only—a tenancy by the entireties. Last, you will study Property laws that apply to married couples as well as to other intimate partner and family-type relationships.

Beyond the rules discussed here, notice that there are additional shared ownership structures developed elsewhere in this text (that sometimes overlap). For example, in the law of Estates in Land (Chapter 5), ownership is divided over time among several people who have distinct rights and obligations to the same property. Landlord-Tenant law (Chapter 6) is another example, where rights and responsibilities to the leased property are allocated between the parties so that a tenant has one set, while the landlord has another, distinct set. Also, in your study of Servitudes (Chapter 10) that helps govern neighbor relationships, you will find that non-owners sometimes have rights of access to or limited control over the use of another person's property. Finally, as you may study in other courses, many other resources are co-owned and managed as well, including businesses, non-profits, or the government (think beaches and national parks). A common conception of property is that it is owned and controlled individually. Yet, as you will see throughout this chapter, property ownership is very often shared.

Gifts

Chapter Problem: Exercise 4-1

Wendy Baker has come to your law office seeking your counsel. During your interview of her, you learn the following facts.

An elderly women named Neela has been close friends with the Baker family for twenty years. As she aged, her mind stayed sharp, but she became unable to care for herself physically. In Year One, Wendy Baker, who owns her home in her sole name, invited Neela to move in with her and her three children. Wendy invited Neela so she could assist Neela with her care needs, such as cooking and cleaning and driving her to medical appointments and elsewhere. Wendy was happy to help Neela and to have the pleasure of her company.

During the first few months Neela lived there, she was so grateful to the Baker family for their care and friendship that she paid the full cost of $30,000 for installing a swimming pool in the Baker's back yard. Although Neela knew she would never be able to use the pool herself, she was delighted because the Baker family children enjoyed the pool and used it often. The children called Neela their aunt, and Neela came to think of the Baker's home as her home too.

Everyone expected Neela to stay in the home for many years to come, until her death. It soon became clear that there was not enough space for everyone in the home, so in Year Two, Neela paid in full for an addition to be built onto the Baker's home that included a bedroom and bathroom for Neela, as well as a small living room. The addition was decorated according to Neela's design preferences. The new space was used primarily by Neela, but was also used occasionally by the rest of the family. The $60,000 cost of construction of the addition increased the value of the home by the same amount.

Wendy has come to you because she wants to write a will soon, leaving everything to her children. She wants to understand what her legal rights over the property are so she can decide how to proceed. As you learn the materials that follow, you will become prepared to evaluate the issues raised from this situation and advise Wendy. Be sure to identify and consider any relevant counter-arguments and possible alternative outcomes.

Another issue for you to grapple with is this: Wendy is considering bringing Neela to see you as a client so you can to help Neela with her estate planning as well. Think about whether you could represent them both. Do you see a potential conflict of interest? If so, might you be able to resolve it? (You will need to look up Model Rule of Professional Conduct 1.7.)

Lifetime Gifts

Gift giving is an everyday human experience that occurs in every culture in the world. Gifts are not only a source of economic value, but they can bring emotional satisfaction and connection as well, for both the giver and receiver. People often give away property with financial or sentimental value as a way of showing love and providing support. Indeed, much wealth is transferred by gift, often between family members. This section focuses on the law of gifts made during the lifetime of the owner (called *inter vivos* gifts).

Gifts that are given upon the death of the owner and gifts that are made by way of a trust are addressed only to a limited extent here and are governed by a distinct body of law that is typically studied in detail in a course such as Wills and Trusts. Gifts that are made at death by a will are called *testamentary* gifts. If a person dies without a will ("intestate"), then state statutes determine who will inherit property, with spouses, children and then other family members (typically related by blood) at the top of the list.

A gift is a voluntary and immediate transfer of something valuable from the gift giver (the donor) to the gift recipient (the donee) that is not in exchange for something else. Because it is a one way transfer and not a mutual exchange, a gift is distinguishable from a contract. Without an exchange (or "consideration" in contract law terms), a promise to make a gift in the future is simply not enforceable.

Gift	Contract
From me → to you	Exchange between me ⇄ and you

Inter vivos gifts must also be distinguished from gifts given at death. Testamentary gifts are completed only if they meet the basic requirements for a will: 1) a signed writing 2) with witnesses. In contrast, the legal requirements for making a lifetime gift are far more flexible. Except for real estate transactions (addressed elsewhere in this text), a writing is *not* required (although a writing surely can be helpful evidence), and a gift can even be inferred from the conduct of the parties involved.[1]

Picture this: it is the morning of your birthday, you walk out to your driveway and sitting there is a shiny new and expensive car, your favorite kind. It has a big red bow on it with a note that says "Happy Birthday [to you], love Mom" and includes the car keys. What a great surprise! But wait a minute: is the car now yours to keep? Can Mom change her mind and successfully take the car back?

The answer depends on whether each of the three elements for a completed gift are satisfied, as follows:

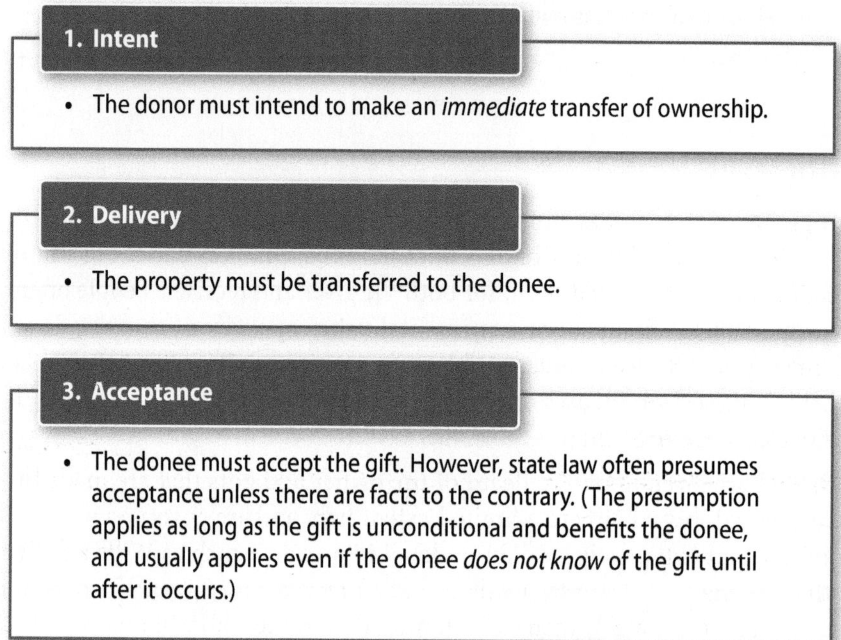

In the birthday car example, each element is satisfied. The gift recipient is now the owner of the car and Mom has transferred away the asset. Mom cannot change her mind because her gift once made is irrevocable.

What specific facts here support the donor's intent to give? (Remember that intent can be evidenced orally, in writing, or can be inferred.) What is the basis for finding the donee's acceptance? What about the delivery element? Any of the three different types of behaviors described below qualify as delivery. Which kind is present here?

---

1. In the chapter on real estate transactions, you will learn that real property transfers generally require a writing to be enforceable. There are also a number of exceptions to this.

a. Actual Delivery

- A physical transfer of the gift, such as handing over a hundred-dollar bill, a tie, or flowers.

b. Constructive Delivery

- The donee is given access to the gift, such as being provided the only key to open a locked box with the gift inside.

c. Symbolic Delivery

- Transfer of an item that represents or symbolizes the gift, such as a deed, a letter or a photo. For example, a handwritten note saying, "My dear son, because I am so proud of your recent graduation from college, I hereby give you the new car I bought at the dealer today," is likely to be effective delivery under modern law.

Now that you have begun to apply the rules, consider this question—what purpose does the delivery requirement probably serve?

Although three elements are required for a legally recognized gift, the donor's intent to transfer is most important. The delivery element should be understood with that in mind, because delivery is helpful evidence of intent to transfer, while lack of delivery calls intent into question. Some policymakers have even suggested elimination of the delivery requirement if the donor's intent to make a gift is established by clear and convincing evidence. *See* Restatement (Third) of Property: Wills and Other Donative Transfers § 6.2 (com. yy) (2003). However, most courts do not follow this approach—some form of delivery is still required.

Exercise 4-2. Identifying Completed Lifetime Gifts

Analyze the problems below to determine if there is a completed lifetime gift.

1. To celebrate a birthday, Grandfather hands his 25-year-old granddaughter an airplane ticket to Paris with her name on it. Elated, she takes the card and ticket, gives him a big hug and exclaims "Thank you so much Grandpa, this is my dream trip!"
2. Grandfather hands his 15-year-old granddaughter a card on her birthday. The signed card says, "I love you, Happy Birthday! My gift to you is a promise:

one day when you are older, I will buy you a ticket to Paris. I know that is the trip of your dreams."

3. A friend says to a friend, "I know you have long admired this necklace I am wearing. I am planning on giving it to you when I die."
4. A mother shows her diamond wedding ring to her son. She explains, "I will hold onto this ring while I am alive, but it is all yours when I die." (This one is controversial. Possibly yes: the son has been given a remainder interest, while the mother retains a life estate, see the *Gruen* case below.)

Exercise 4-3. *Gruen v. Gruen* — Distinguishing Gifts Made During Life or at Death

The *Gruen* case that follows is a real world example of how the basic rules apply. It also adds new layers to your ability to analyze whether the donor intends to make an immediate transfer of ownership (while he is alive, rather than only at death) and whether only a partial transfer is intended.

1. How should you analyze the intent element when the donor retains some rights to the item allegedly given away? As you will see in *Gruen* (and learn more about in Chapter 5, Estates in Land), it is possible for the donor to intend to immediately transfer some ownership rights to an item, even while the donor retains other rights, including the right of possession. An owner can disaggregate a larger set of property interests into component parts, and each part then is a separately identifiable interest in property. Whether a gift has been given depends on what the donor was thinking, and in this context, that can be hard to ascertain. Frequently, the issue comes up after the (alleged) donor has died, and one person claims to own the property through a completed lifetime gift (so that the donor no longer owns the property and is unable to give it away at death), and another person claims she is the rightful owner because of the donor's will.
2. As you read the case, for each element, identify the facts that support a finding of a completed gift, and compare those to the contrary facts. How is the controversy resolved?

Gruen v. Gruen

496 N.E.2d 869 (N.Y. 1986)

Simons, J. Plaintiff commenced this action seeking a declaration that he is the rightful owner of a painting which he alleges his father, now deceased, gave to him. He concedes that he has never had possession of the painting but asserts that his father made a valid gift of the title [giving the son a remainder interest] in 1963 reserving a life estate for himself [meaning the father has the right to possess the property until his death, at which time the son takes over the right of possession and owns all rights to the property]. His father retained possession of the painting until he died in 1980. Defendant, plaintiff's stepmother, has the painting now and has refused plaintiff's requests that she turn it over to him. She contends that the purported gift was testamentary in nature and invalid insofar as the formalities of a will were not met.... Following a seven-day nonjury trial, Special Term found that plaintiff had failed to establish any of the elements of an inter vivos gift ... [Conversely] [t]he Appellate Division held that a valid gift may be made reserving a life estate and, finding the elements of a gift established in this case.... [D]efendant appeals directly to this court ... from the subsequent final judgment entered in Supreme Court awarding plaintiff $2,500,000 in damages representing the value of the painting, plus interest. We now affirm.

The subject of the dispute is a work entitled "Schloss Kammer am Attersee II" painted by a noted Austrian modernist, Gustav Klimt. It was purchased by plaintiff's father, Victor Gruen, in 1959 for $8,000. On April 1, 1963 the elder Gruen, a successful architect with offices and residences in both New York City and Los Angeles during most of the time involved in this action, wrote a letter to plaintiff, then an undergraduate student at Harvard, stating that he was giving him the Klimt painting for his birthday but that he wished to retain the possession of it for his lifetime. This letter is not in evidence, apparently because plaintiff destroyed it on instructions from his father. Two other letters were received, however, one dated May 22, 1963 and the other April 1, 1963. Both had been dictated by Victor Gruen and sent together to plaintiff on or about May 22, 1963. The letter dated May 22, 1963 reads as follows:

> Dear Michael:
>
> I wrote you at the time of your birthday about the gift of the painting by Klimt. Now my lawyer tells me that because of the existing tax laws, it was wrong to mention in that letter that I want to use the painting as long as I live. Though I still want to use it, this should not appear in the letter. I am enclosing, therefore, a new letter and I ask you to send the old one back to me so that it can be destroyed.
>
> I know this is all very silly, but the lawyer and our accountant insist that they must have in their possession copies of a letter which will serve the purpose of making it possible for you, once I die, to get this picture without having to pay inheritance taxes on it.[2]
>
> Love,
>
> s/Victor.

2. The court notes later in the opinion that this tax advice was apparently mistaken.—Eds.

Gustav Klimt, *Schloss Kammer am Attersee II*

Enclosed with this letter was a substitute gift letter, dated April 1, 1963, which stated:

> Dear Michael:
>
> The 21st birthday, being an important event in life, should be celebrated accordingly. I therefore wish to give you as a present the oil painting by Gustav Klimt of Schloss Kammer which now hangs in the New York living room. You know that Lazette and I bought it some 5 or 6 years ago, and you always told us how much you liked it.
>
> Happy birthday again.
>
> Love,
>
> s/Victor.

Plaintiff never took possession of the painting nor did he seek to do so. Except for a brief period between 1964 and 1965 when it was on loan to art exhibits and when restoration work was performed on it, the painting remained in his father's possession, moving with him from New York City to Beverly Hills and finally to Vienna, Austria, where Victor Gruen died on February 14, 1980. Following Victor's death plaintiff requested possession of the Klimt painting and when defendant refused, he commenced this action.

[T]o make a valid inter vivos gift there must exist the intent on the part of the donor to make a present transfer; delivery of the gift, either actual or constructive to the donee; and acceptance by the donee. Second, the proponent of a gift has the burden of proving each of these elements by clear and convincing evidence.

Donative Intent

There is an important distinction between the intent with which an inter vivos gift is made and the intent to make a gift by will. An inter vivos gift requires that the donor intend to make an irrevocable present transfer of ownership; if the intention is to make a testamentary disposition effective only after death, the gift is invalid unless made by will. Defendant contends that the trial court was correct in finding that Victor did not intend to transfer any present interest in the painting to plaintiff in 1963 but only expressed an intention that plaintiff was to get the painting upon his death. The evidence is all but conclusive, however, that Victor intended to transfer ownership of the painting to plaintiff in 1963 but to retain a life estate in it and that he did, therefore, effectively transfer a remainder interest in the painting to plaintiff at that time. Although the original letter was not in evidence, testimony of its contents was received along with the substitute gift letter and its covering letter dated May 22, 1963. The three letters should be considered together as a single instrument and when they are they unambiguously establish that Victor Gruen intended to make a present gift of title to the painting at that time. But there was other evidence for after 1963 Victor made several statements orally and in writing indicating that he had previously given plaintiff the painting and that plaintiff owned it. Victor Gruen retained possession of the property, insured it, allowed others to exhibit it and made necessary repairs to it but those acts are not inconsistent with his retention of a life estate. Furthermore, whatever probative value could be attached to his statement that he had bequeathed the painting to his heirs, made 16 years later when he prepared an export license application so that he could take the painting out of Austria, is negated by the overwhelming evidence that he intended a present transfer of title in 1963. Victor's failure to file a gift tax return on the transaction was partially explained by allegedly erroneous legal advice he received, and while that omission sometimes may indicate that the donor had no intention of making a present gift, it does not necessarily do so and it is not dispositive in this case.

The correct test is "whether the maker intended the [gift] to have *no effect* until after the maker's death, or whether he intended it to transfer. As long as the evidence establishes an intent to make a present and irrevocable transfer of title or the right of ownership, there is a present transfer of some interest and the gift is effective immediately."

Delivery

In order to have a valid inter vivos gift, there must be a delivery of the gift, either by a physical delivery of the subject of the gift or a constructive or symbolic delivery such as by an instrument of gift, sufficient to divest the donor of dominion and control over the property. As the statement of the rule suggests, the requirement of delivery is not rigid or inflexible, but is to be applied in light of its purpose to avoid mistakes by donors and fraudulent claims by donees. Accordingly, what is sufficient to constitute delivery "must be tailored to suit the circumstances of the case." Defendant contends that when a tangible piece of personal property such as a painting is the subject of a gift, physical delivery of the painting itself is the best form of delivery and should be required. Here, of course, we have only delivery of Victor Gruen's letters which serve as instruments of gift. Defendant's statement of the rule as applied may be generally true, but it ignores the fact that what Victor Gruen gave plaintiff was not all rights to the Klimt painting, but only title to it with no right of possession until his death. Under these circumstances, it would be illogical for the law to require the donor to part with possession of the painting when that is exactly what he intends to retain.

Acceptance

Acceptance by the donee is essential to the validity of an inter vivos gift, but when a gift is of value to the donee, as it is here, the law will presume an acceptance on his part. Plaintiff did not rely on this presumption alone but also presented clear and convincing proof of his acceptance of a remainder interest in the Klimt painting by evidence that he had made several contemporaneous statements acknowledging the gift to his friends and associates, even showing some of them his father's gift letter, and that he had retained both letters for over 17 years to verify the gift after his father died. Defendant relied exclusively on affidavits filed by plaintiff in a matrimonial action with his former wife, in which plaintiff failed to list his interest in the painting as an asset. These affidavits were made over 10 years after acceptance was complete and they do not even approach the evidence in *Matter of Kelly* [285 N.Y. 139 (1941)] where the donee, immediately upon delivery of a diamond ring, rejected it as "too flashy." We agree with the Appellate Division that interpretation of the affidavit was too speculative to support a finding of rejection and overcome the substantial showing of acceptance by plaintiff.

Accordingly, the judgment appealed from and the order of the Appellate Division brought up for review should be affirmed, with costs.

Exercise 4-4. *Gruen* Revisited

1. What exactly is the holding of the case? How would your analysis of the case change if Victor had *said* this to Michael, "I wish to give you the Klimt painting upon my death"? Notice again that Victor was found to have gifted Michael part of his interest in the painting long before he died (Michael became the owner of the remainder interest in 1963, with possession postponed until Victor's death). You must carefully distinguish between a lifetime gift that is effective immediately, and one that takes effect only upon death.

2. Assume you represent Victor's wife (Michael's stepmother), what arguments would you make that there is no valid gift under these facts? What arguments should Michael's attorney make? Specifically, how would you address the fact that Victor kept the painting in his possession until his death?
3. Assuming a valid lifetime gift was made, could Victor have changed his mind and given the painting away in a will to someone else?
4. Brad and Pat were intimate partners, and Brad wanted to take their relationship to the next level. In a written and signed deed, Brad transferred title to his home from his name to Pat's name. They both traveled a lot for their jobs, and Pat was out of the country when Brad signed the deed. Brad was about to leave on a trip as well, and so put the deed in Pat's mailbox. The next day, Brad changed his mind. Analyze this fact situation and predict the outcome.

Conditional Gifts

You have just been exploring whether a gift is complete because there is intent to immediately transfer an ownership interest, delivery and acceptance. If so, the gift giver has relinquished his rights and typically cannot later take back the gift. However, there are some exceptions. It is possible to set up a conditional gift—so that if a condition is not met, the donee is not ultimately the owner and has to give back the gift. The discussion below addresses two recurring examples of conditional gifts—engagement rings and gifts *causa mortis* (gifts made with "death in view"). In Chapter 5 of this text, you will learn about other property structures that also allow donors to attach conditions to gifts.

Most states treat engagement rings as conditional gifts. Here is one scenario. A fortune cookie mysteriously arrives at the table. The woman at the table cracks open the cookie, and inside is a gorgeous and expensive diamond ring. The man at the table takes the ring, gets down on one knee, hands her the ring and asks the woman, "Will you marry me?" She exclaims "Yes I will!" and slips the ring on her finger. How lovely! Now consider what happens if the couple breaks up before they marry—who owns the ring?

The answer in most states is that the gift giver (the man) can rightfully claim ownership, and it doesn't matter who called off the engagement, or why. *See, e.g.*, *Lindh v. Surman*, 742 A.2d 643 (Pa. 1999). That is true even though when you apply the rules to the facts, it seems that the elements of a completed gift are satisfied. (Can you see why?) Most courts view engagement rings as implying a condition—it is as if the man said "I give you this ring now, but your ownership is based on the condition that we get married, and if we don't get married, then I own the ring."

Reflect for a moment on these rules. Do they reflect the likely expectations of modern couples? In other words, is the condition accurately implied? Also, does this rule raise any concerns about gender bias? *See Albinger v. Harris*, 48 P.3d 711 (2002) (finding it does, because typically men benefit from the rule, whereas women are harmed). Is this approach a good fit for same sex couples?

Another widely recognized conditional gift is a gift *causa mortis*—a gift that is based on an assumption that the donor will die soon. There are four elements needed: 1) donative intent; 2) delivery; 3) acceptance and 4) the donor's expectation of imminent death. If these criteria are met, then the donor can revoke the gift at *any* time until death. Also, if the donor has a miraculous recovery, in most states, the gift is presumptively revoked, and the donor may even have to redeliver the gift to ensure that the donee can keep it. Courts tend to be skeptical of these gifts—transfers shortly before death can trigger concerns about fraud.

Exercise 4-5. Evaluating Gifts *Causa Mortis*

Suppose an uncle realized he was having a serious heart attack. When his nephew met him at the hospital emergency room (and no other family members had yet arrived), he handed his nephew a valuable watch, saying it was his to keep. If the uncle recovers, who owns the watch? What if the uncle dies, can the nephew keep it?

Concurrent Ownership

Chapter Problem: Exercise 4-6

In January, Year 1, life-long friends Louise and Maria purchased property called "Mountain-Acre" as tenants in common. They moved into the residence together and shared the entire space even though Maria had contributed only 25% of the purchase price. There was no mortgage on the property.

Unfortunately, within a just a few weeks of moving into Mountainacre, Maria and Louise consistently had many angry verbal disagreements ranging across topics such as how to decorate their home to politics. Their friendship began to erode. Both women were frequently upset about this dynamic, but reacted in different ways. Taking advantage of Maria's unconfrontational nature, Louise would insult Maria recurrently, and sometimes would do so in front of guests and neighbors. On several occasions, Maria fled from the home in tears based on Louise's contentious behavior. Ultimately, after only one year, their relationship deteriorated to the point that they were no longer speaking. In January, Year 2, Louise could not tolerate the situation any longer and moved out.

Maria then lived at Mountainacre alone until January, Year 3. At that point, without saying a word to Maria and hoping it would make her unhappy, Louise invited her 21-year-old son Tyson to move into the home. Louise and Tyson agreed that Tyson could stay for at least 6 months in exchange for paying a modest amount of rent and doing some occasional work on the property such as mowing the lawn, cleaning the home and re-painting the whole house room by room. Tyson's labor and rent would be helpful, but mother and son both recognized that it would not come close to covering the $4,000 monthly rental value of the home. Maria was furious about Tyson moving in, and she soon moved out, leaving Tyson living in the home alone.

A senior partner at the law firm where you are an associate has asked that you determine what laws apply, how and what the likely legal outcomes are. After you have studied the materials on co-ownership, you will be in a position to share your evaluation of this fact situation.

Types of Co-Ownership

Concurrent ownership means that two or more people own the same asset at the same time, with each owner having the simultaneous right to possess the entire property. There are three basic types of concurrent ownership: tenancy in common; joint tenancy with the right of survivorship and tenancy by the entirety. The main features of these estates are overviewed immediately below, and then are explored in more detail in the subtopics that follow. Beyond these ownership structures, in the latter part of this chapter, you will study family property law, where common ownership is also sometimes recognized.

Why do people choose to own property together? Sharing property can be useful and efficient as well as emotionally satisfying. For intimate partners, sharing property can be an important part of building a life together. For friends, pooling some resources can build inter-personal connections and at the same time be cost effective. Multi-generational families also frequently share property. For example, older family members might co-own a home with the middle or younger generation. This provides a place to spend time together at the same time it creates shared responsibility for ongoing costs and maintenance. Intergenerational sharing like this is on the rise. As people live longer and the aging population grows, modern families regularly turn to co-ownership as an important way of caring for one another, and as a tool to assist with management of property. So, if family members share a bank account, either co-owner can manage the account, and that can be very helpful if one person becomes unable to do so independently. In addition, some types of co-ownership structures are used as a will substitute—because they have a survivorship feature that passes the share of the co-owner who dies to the surviving co-owner. Cumulatively, the benefits of co-ownership can be quite valuable. However, sharing property can also lead to conflicts. Decisions made by one co-owner can greatly impact another co-owner. Yet surprisingly, the legal regime has few mechanisms for collective decision-making. As you read more about co-ownership forms, be sure to take into account what risks come along with the benefits.

Tenancy in Common

The following transactions create a tenancy in common:

1. O to A and B.
2. O to A and B as tenants in common.
3. O to A and B with A having a 25% undivided share and B having a 75% undivided share.
4. O to A, B, and C.
5. O leases to A and B (who become roommates).
6. O dies without a will, and the property transfers by operation of law to O's five children by intestate succession.

Notice that a tenancy in common is the default co-ownership structure. The estate can be created without specific language identifying it and can arise simply from the circumstance of property being owned by more than one person.

Each co-owner has the right to possess the whole property. For example, if A wants to be in the kitchen at the same time B wants to be in the kitchen, neither can exclude the other—both are legally entitled to be in that space. In the absence of an agreement to the contrary, a right of co-possession to the entire property is a basic feature.

In addition, a tenant in common owns a portion (or share) of the underlying property. The shares are usually calculated based on how much each person contributed to the acquisition of the asset. If Sally paid 10% of the purchase price of a home, then her share is 10%. Some states initially presume equal shares based on the number of owners (*e.g.*, if there are two owners, each has a half share), but this is rebuttable with evidence of how much each contributed to acquisition costs. If a tenancy in common is created by way of a gift, then the share of ownership is dependent on how much the donor intended to transfer.

A tenant in common has the power to transfer his or her share independently, and can do so without the consent or knowledge of the other owner(s). Shares are transferable by gift or sale during life and at death. The deceased owner's share descends by will or intestate succession, often to his or her family.

If co-owners wants to end the property relationship altogether and the parties cannot agree on terms, any owner can seek a judicial partition. In a partition, a court can either physically divide the property or order a sale of the property and divide the proceeds. This allocation is based on the underlying shares of ownership.

Joint Tenancy with the Right of Survivorship

Like tenants in common, owners of a joint tenancy have a right to possess the entire property. The key distinguishing feature of this estate is the right of survivorship. If a co-owner dies with this property structure in place, his or her share is extinguished at death, and that share is absorbed by the other owner(s). A will cannot override this feature, because by taking title in this form, the parties have already determined that the survivor(s) among them will take ownership of the share of a predeceasing co-owner. This is sometimes called a poor person's will. Can you see why?

How is this estate created? Suppose O transfers Happyacre to "A and B as joint tenants with the right of survivorship." Most jurisdictions today will interpret this estate just as it is written. What if A owned a 40% share and B owned a 60% share? A joint tenancy would still exist under the modern approach that allows for differing shares and calculates shares based on contribution (just like for tenancies in common). However, some states retain older traditional rules and will not recognize a joint tenancy if there are owners with unequal shares. In such states, a court would find that a tenancy in common exists, even when a joint tenancy is clearly intended. This is because traditional rules require four unities to exist—the unities of time; title; interest; and possession, as follows:

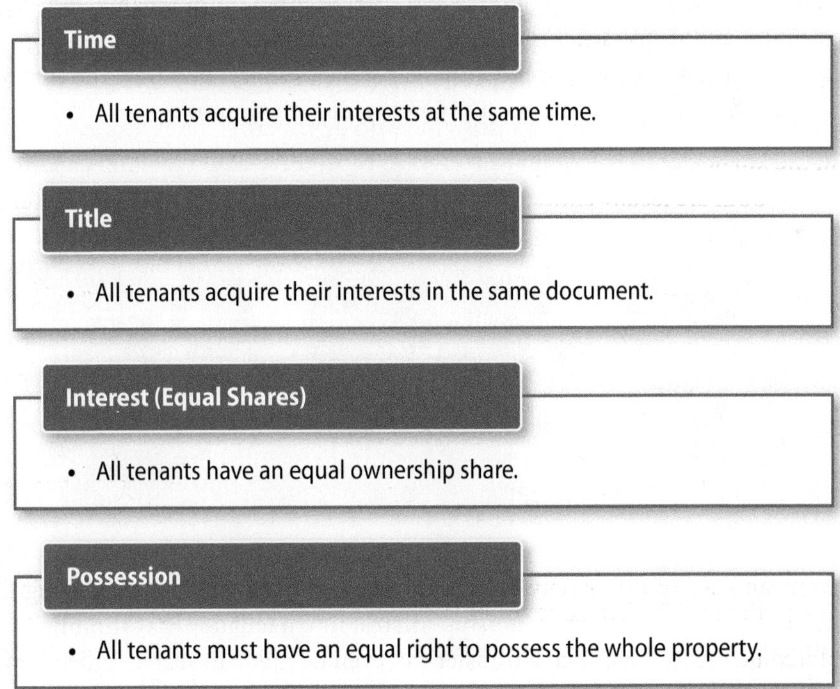

Time
• All tenants acquire their interests at the same time.
Title
• All tenants acquire their interests in the same document.
Interest (Equal Shares)
• All tenants have an equal ownership share.
Possession
• All tenants must have an equal right to possess the whole property.

Another common situation also causes unities problems. Assume a grandfather owns Black-Acre and wants to share ownership with his granddaughter. He signs a deed that provides "GF transfers Black-Acre to GF and GD as joint tenants with the right of survivorship, and not as tenants in common." Because the grandfather already owned Black-Acre before the transfer, he did not "acquire" his interest at the same time and in the same document as the granddaughter. This problem can be solved by use of a strawperson. The grandfather could transfer his interest to another person, and then that person could transfer the property to grandfather and granddaughter as joint tenants. In states that insist on the four unities, this cumbersome process is still necessary. The modern approach lets go of this. Many states now allow for self creation of a joint tenancy, so grandfather can just go ahead with his transaction as originally planned.

Another important characteristic of a joint tenancy is that the right of survivorship can easily be destroyed. Once a joint tenancy is in place, it can be changed—not by a will—but rather by the conduct of one of the owners during her lifetime. If a joint tenant transfers her share, then the ownership structure is *severed,* the right of survivorship is extinguished with regard to that share, and the grantee becomes a tenant in common with the other co-owners.

Assume a brother and two sisters co-own a home called Sibling-Acre in equal shares as joint tenants with the right of survivorship. Then the brother sells his interest to a friend. The friend owns now owns a ⅓ interest as a tenant in common with the sisters. If the friend dies, his interest will go to whoever inherits his property by will or intestate succession (not the sisters). In contrast, the sisters remain joint tenants with regard to each other, and if one sister dies, her interest evaporates and the surviving sister will then own a ⅔ share. The friend keeps his same ⅓ share, and now the surviving sister and the friend co-own the property as tenants in common.

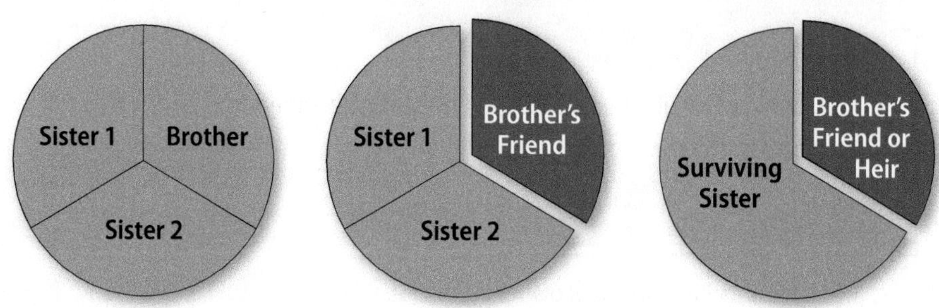

As you can see, joint tenants have the power to transfer their share during their lifetime, and can convert their ownership interest into a tenancy in common. As will be explored further below, such a transfer can even be made in secret. Indeed, many states allow self-declared transfers in a deed, so an owner can simply declare "I transfer from myself as joint tenant with a right of survivorship to myself as tenant in common." This makes the right of survivorship extinguishable during the lifetime of the co-owners. Owners can also end their property relationship by seeking a partition to divide the asset or its value.

Tenancy by the Entireties

Like the joint tenancy, a tenancy by the entireties includes a right of co-possession and a right of survivorship. The same unities have also typically been required. However, this estate has several unique features. First, only married couples can own property as tenants by the entireties. Participants must be in a legally recognized marriage under state law. Married same sex couples as well as opposite sex couples are eligible to own property this way. Second, a tenancy by the entireties and the right of survivorship *cannot* be disrupted (severed) by the choice of one spouse acting alone. Instead, a transfer of an interest in the property is valid only if both spouses agree. Only death, divorce or *mutual* consent will change the ownership form. Third, a judicial partition is unavailable unless it occurs through (or after) a divorce. Absent partition, a divorce automatically converts the estate into a tenancy in common. (This is because only married couples can own by the entireties, and a divorce dissolves the marriage). Fourth, this lock-in effect between spouses also provides some protection against creditors. In most states, the creditors of just one spouse cannot reach the property—it is immune from their claims. For example, if one spouse (the debtor spouse) borrows money from a bank and then defaults on the loan, the bank will *not* be able to seek collection for the loan against property held by the entireties.[3] You will study this feature in more detail later in this chapter. This estate is recognized in less than half the states today. Here is a summary overview.

The best practice for creating a tenancy by the entireties is, of course, to use explicit language. However, many states have a presumption that any transfer to a married couple will create this estate, even if the conveyance does not specifically say so. To overcome the presumption, there must be clear intent to create a different estate.

Resolving Ambiguities

Sometimes it is unclear what kind of co-ownership structure exists. How would you interpret a transfer that says "O to A and B as joint tenants in common" or "O to A and B jointly"? The grantor's intent generally determines which estate is created. That doesn't help much in these examples, however, because several differing interpretations are possible. Rules of interpretation can provide some assistance. A tenancy in common is the default type of ownership and will be presumed unless

3. One special creditor has been granted an exception to this rule. The government acting as a tax collector for one spouse's debt can reach tenancy by the entireties property. *See United States v. Craft*, 535 U.S. 274 (2002) (holding that a federal tax lien attached to the husband's interest in property owned in tenancy by the entireties even though the creditors of one spouse cannot reach the property under state law).

there is sufficient evidence that a different estate was intended. So assuming a tenancy in common exists is a good starting place for your analysis (but remember that can be overcome by contrary facts). Beyond this, there is a lot of variation about how to resolve ambiguities among the states. Some insist that explicit language must be used to create a joint tenancy, including a clear identification of the right of survivorship. The following language would be effective: "Otis hereby transfers Blackacre to Xavier and Yolanda as joint tenants in equal shares with the right of survivorship, and not as tenants in common." Other states are more flexible.

Another rule of interpretation to keep in mind (discussed earlier): in states that still require the four unities of time, title, interest and possession, and one of the unities, such as equal fractional shares is missing, a tenancy in common will be found even though a joint tenancy with a right of survivorship was clearly intended.

Exercise 4-7. Identifying Types of Co-Ownership

1. A father dies and leaves a valid will that says "I give Happy-Acre to my children A, B and C in equal shares." B then sells his interest to Z. Thereafter C dies leaving his property in a valid will to his favorite charity. Who owns what shares of Happy-Acre, and in what form?
2. A, B and C bought a residence called Serenity-Acre, contributing equal amounts to the purchase price. The deed to the house says "A, B & C as joint tenants with a right of survivorship, and not as tenants in common." B then sells his interest to Z. Thereafter C dies leaving his property in a valid will to his favorite charity. Who owns what shares of Serenity-Acre, and in what form? Would the result be different if there had been unequal shares of ownership at the time of purchase? (Hint: You need to apply the "four unities" to answer this.)
3. Husband and Wife bought a home together called Marriage-Acre and took title as tenants by the entireties. Without telling her husband, the wife wrote a deed to her secret boyfriend that said "I give my share of Marriage-Acre to Bob." Thereafter, the wife died. Who owns what shares of Marriage-Acre, and in what form? Would the result be different if Bob was a creditor attempting to collect a debt against Marriage-Acre?
4. Create a table or list with the core characteristics of each of the three types of co-ownership, including rules and language for creation, rights of possession, right to transfer during life and at death, and termination of the property relationship.
5. Be prepared to ask questions, give planning advice and draft language for a deed based on the following situation: Lou and Pat are an unmarried couple who have been together for four years. They are committed to staying together

indefinitely, and are in the process of buying a home they will share. Up until now, they have kept their finances separate, but expect that they will share finances to some extent once they move in together. They are considering whether to marry at some point, but are not sure they will do so. They both plan to contribute to the down payment. However, Pat has more income and more money for a downpayment than Lou. Still, they would like to own the house in equal shares. What advice do you have for how they should take title to the house? Draft options for specific language they should use in the deed.

Shared Bank Accounts

Many couples and family members share financial accounts through institutions including banks, and this practice is increasingly popular for multi-generational families. It can be a challenge to determine ownership and other rights to these accounts, and disputes frequently arise. Financial institutions usually offer their customers a limited set of choices for how to take title to the account, and sometimes those options are not a good fit for what the owner actually wants, or are simply misunderstood. There are a variety of different forms available, that go by a variety of names.

In particular, ascertaining the true ownership structure for a "joint bank account" or "joint bank account with right of survivorship" can be controversial and confusing. For example, consider the situation where a father creates a joint bank account by adding his daughter to an account he previously owned alone. What if the father contributed all the funds in the account? What if he was looking for his daughter's help managing the account? A shared bank account gives each person named on the account power to withdraw and manage the funds, so the daughter can indeed help her father. However, that doesn't resolve who owns the funds in the account. Management rights are distinct from ownership rights. So what does the daughter now own?

The ownership structure depends on what the father intended. There are a number of possibilities. First, it is possible the father intended a true joint tenancy with a right of survivorship account. That would mean that: a) he immediately gifted some of the funds to the daughter (perhaps half) and she can now consume her share as she wishes; and b) when one owner dies, the survivor owns the whole account. Another possibility is that the father wanted: a) help managing the asset; b) but to retain full ownership of the funds during his lifetime; and c) to have the balance of the account (if any) go to his daughter when he dies. If that is what the father intended, it is *not* a true joint tenancy with right of survivorship. (The daughter's present interest is missing.) The father was attempting to create a different package of rights and responsibilities—granting the daughter authority to act like a power of attorney or a trustee to manage the money for the father's benefit, and then a transfer only effective at death (which stands in for a will). Yet a bank may not offer or recognize this latter kind of account. Other options are that the father created a tenancy in common account (with its usual features), or an "agency account" that simply conferred management rights to the daughter but no ownership rights.

The property law system has to grapple with how to define ownership rights in circumstances like these. To repeat, the key inquiry is the intent of the parties. Of course, the formal language or category selected on the account is some evidence of intent. However, as you have learned, it not does not always reflect true intent—owners may greatly misunderstand how the accounts operate, and in any event title is not determinative. Many states follow two rules from the Uniform Probate Code that can help guide your analysis. First, an owner's share of a bank account is based on his or her contributions to the account, unless there is clear and convincing evidence of a gift, or of different intent. So a tenancy in common arrangement is presumed during the lifetime of the co-owners. *See* Uniform Probate Code §6-211 (2010). Second, the surviving joint tenant owns the balance in the account upon the death of the other owner, unless there is clear and convincing evidence to the contrary. *See* Uniform Probate Code §6-212 (2010).

Exercise 4-8. Evaluating Ownership of Shared Bank Accounts

1. To help crystalize your thinking in this complex area, which of the possibilities outlined for the father/daughter example above do the presumptions guide you to?
2. Now apply what you have learned to this practice problem:

   Diane has a close relationship with her mother Maud, who is now 85 years old and in good health. Contemplating her death and a possible period of incapacity in her future years, Maud asked Diane if she would help her manage her financial affairs. Diane happily agreed, and they went to Kelly Bank, Maud's financial institution, to open a joint account to replace the existing account solely in Maud's name. When they were at the bank, the bank teller presented them several choices for how to structure ownership of the account. Upon reflection, Maud chose a joint tenancy with right of survivorship account. She liked that option, because she understood from talking with the bank teller that with this kind of an account, Maud would retain ownership of the money in the account, but that it would transfer to Diane at her death. Maud alone funded the joint account with $100,000 transferred from the sole account now closed. Both Diane and Maud were signatories on the account, and thus, both were authorized to make withdrawals and manage the account. In the months following, when Maud asked her do so, Diane made several withdrawals from the account on Maud's behalf and for her benefit. Maud was very appreciative of the help.

About 6 months after opening bank account with her mother, Diane had an opportunity to realize her dream of opening her own coffee shop. She decided to go for it. However, Diane needed more money to start the business. Accordingly, Diane withdrew $10,000 from the Kelly Bank account. She did not ask, nor advise her mother of the withdrawal, because she was not sure her mother would agree it was a good idea. Diane figured this was a time when ignorance was bliss.

Assume Maud has come to you seeking your legal advice. Describe and evaluate for her the issues raised and your neutral analysis of these circumstances. In other words, be prepared to fully discuss all relevant and applicable law and facts regardless of who you predict will be successful. Be sure to raise any relevant counter-arguments and possible alternative outcomes.

Co-Tenant Rights and Obligations

This section addresses the rights and duties that apply to tenants in common and joint tenancies. The laws discussed here are the rules that apply by default. The parties can adjust or override these rules by contract. Tenants share both the costs and benefits of ownership. If there is a dispute, co-owners can seek a judicial accounting while ownership continues, or at its termination.

Sharing Costs, Benefits and Possession

Suppose two friends own equal shares of a vacation house in the mountains as tenants in common. What obligations do they have to pay for carrying costs such as a mortgage and annual real estate taxes? What about for necessary repairs or for an improvement such as adding on a new bathroom? What are the obligations if one owner uses the property all the time and the other never does? If the property is rented out to a third party, who is entitled to the income? Keep these questions in mind as you learn the rules and see them in action.

In addition to a share of the underlying value of the asset, each co-owner has the right to possess the entire property simultaneously with the other owners. Along with these benefits come obligations to pay a proportionate share of the operating costs of the property, including mortgage payments and taxes, as well as maintenance and necessary repairs. For example, with a $1,000 monthly mortgage on a property that is co-owned in half shares, each owner would be liable for $500 per month. Similarly, if the property had a leaky roof, both owners are responsible to pay the cost of repairing the roof, in the same proportion as the underlying ownership shares (so half shares if there are two owners, or one-third shares if there are three owners, etc.). Relatedly, co-owners have a duty not to commit "waste" by neglecting or destroying the property. You will learn about waste in Chapter 5, but note that it applies in a variety of contexts, including to co-owners.

What if one owner wanted to improve the property—such as adding a shed for storage? This would be considered an improvement. Unlike repairs and maintenance, co-owners are not required to share the costs of improvements. Instead, the added value from any improvements can be claimed later by the owner who made the investment.

Going back to the mountain vacation house example, what happens if one co-tenant chooses to possess the property, but the other chooses to stay away? This triggers another set of rules. First, in the majority of states, no rent is owed by the in-possession tenant to the out-of-possession tenant in such circumstances. This is because the non-possessing tenant has not been deprived of the right to possession—not using the property was voluntary. That said, the tenant who lives on the property does enjoy the added benefit of *sole* possession of the property, rather than shared possession. Given this, it seems unfair to require the non-possessing tenant to pay his full share of expenses. As a result, in many states, a credit against expenses is available to relieve the non-possessing tenant of some responsibility for payment. To summarize, the tenant who is not living in the mountain home would not be owed rent, but would have an expense credit. The rules change yet again if one owner "ousts" the other—by denying them access to the property. From that point on, rent is owed to the ousted tenant for that tenant's share of the rental value of the property. Ouster also starts the adverse possession clock running, and if the ouster goes on long enough without redress by the co-tenant whose rights have been violated, the ousting tenant becomes the sole owner.

Exercise 4-9. *Esteves* and *Olivas*

1. In the two cases and materials that follow, you will see many of these rules in action, and learn more about them. Make sure to identify and define each rule that is triggered.
2. In *Esteves*, pay special attention to the credit against expenses awarded to the son, Joao. How does the court justify the credit and how it is calculated?
3. In the *Olivas* case, how is ouster defined?
4. What effect does ouster have on the financial obligations between the owners?

Esteves v. Esteves

775 A.2d 163 (N.J. Super. 2001)

Lesemann, J. This appeal deals with the proper division of the proceeds from the sale of a one-family house held by a tenancy in common, with plaintiffs, the parents of defendant owning one-half of the house and defendant owning the other half.

The trial court held that plaintiffs, who had occupied the house by themselves for approximately eighteen years before it was sold, and had paid all of the expenses relating to the house during that period, were entitled to reimbursement from defendant for one-half of the sums they had paid, without any offset for the value of their occupancy. The net effect of that ruling amounted to a determination that plaintiffs were permitted to occupy the premises "rent free" for approximately eighteen years, while they paid one-half of the costs attributable to the house and defendant paid the other half. The trial court found that such a result was compelled by applicable law. We disagree, and conclude that when plaintiffs sought reimbursement from defendant for one-half of the costs of occupying and maintaining the premises, plaintiffs were required to allow defendant credit for the reasonable value of their occupancy of the house. Accordingly we reverse.

The case involves an unhappy family schism, but the facts, as found by the trial court and not disputed on appeal, are uncomplicated. In December 1980, plaintiffs Manuel and Flora Esteves, together with their son Joao Esteves, bought a house. They took title as tenants in common, with Manuel and Flora owning a one-half interest and Joao owning the other one-half. The purchase price was $34,500. Manuel and Flora paid $10,000 in cash as did Joao, and the parties took a mortgage loan for the remaining $14,500. They then moved into the house, and Joao undertook a considerable amount of work involving repairs and improvements while he lived there with his parents for somewhere between three months and eighteen months after closing. Joao then moved out and for approximately the next eighteen years, until the house was sold on February 26, 1998, Manuel and Flora lived there by themselves. At no time did they rent out any portion of the house.

Sale of the house produced net proceeds of $114,453.18. With the parties unable to agree on distribution of the proceeds, they agreed to each take $10,000 and deposit the remaining $94,453.18 in escrow. They then proceeded to trial, after which the trial court made the following findings and conclusions.

The court found that Manuel and Flora had paid out $17,336 in mortgage payments, including principal and interest; $14,353 for capital expenses; $21,599 for real estate taxes; $3,971 for sewer charges; and $4,633 for homeowners insurance. Those amounts totaled $61,892, and the court found that Joao was obligated to reimburse his parents for one-half that amount. However, the court also found that Joao had supplied labor with a value of $2,000 more than any labor expended by Manuel and Flora, and thus Joao was entitled to a credit for that amount. On the critical issue of credit for the value of plaintiffs' occupancy of the house, the court said this:

> I conclude there being no ouster of the defendant by the plaintiffs that there is no entitlement to the equivalent rent or rental value of the premises where the plaintiffs lived. The defendant could have continued to live there if he wanted to; he chose not to. And the law is clear that that being the case, he's not-there being no ouster, he's not entitled to anything for the rental value or what the rental could have been to the plaintiffs.

Over the years, there have been varying statements by our courts as to the rights and obligations of tenants in common respecting payment for maintenance of the parties' property and their rights and obligations respecting occupancy thereof. While those decisions may not always have been consistent, in *Baird v. Moore,* 50 N.J.Super. 156, 141 A.2d 324 (App. Div. 1958), this court, in a comprehensive, scholarly opinion by Judge Conford set out what we conceive to be the most appropriate, fair and practical rules to resolve such disputes. Those principles can be summarized as follows.

First, as a general proposition, on a sale of commonly owned property, an owner who has paid less than his pro-rata share of operating and maintenance expenses of the property, must account to co-owner who has contributed more than his pro-rata share, and that is true even if the former had been out of possession and the latter in possession of the property.

Second, the fact that one tenant in common occupies the property and the other does not, imposes no obligation on the former to make any contribution to the latter. All tenants in common have a right to occupy all of the property and if one chooses not to do so, that does not give him the right to impose an "occupancy" charge on the other.

Third, notwithstanding those general rules, when on a final accounting following sale, the tenant who had been in sole possession of the property demands contribution toward operating and maintenance expenses from his co-owner, fairness and equity dictate that the one seeking that contribution allow a corresponding credit for the value of his sole occupancy of the premises. To reject such a credit and nonetheless require a contribution to operating and maintenance expenses from someone who (like the defendant here) had enjoyed none of the benefits of occupancy would be patently unfair.

Finally, the party seeking the credit for the other's occupancy of the property has the burden of demonstrating the "actual rental value" of the property enjoyed by the occupying co-tenant.[2]

We believe the principles of *Baird* are sound and should be applied here. They support the trial court's conclusions as to defendant's obligation to contribute one-half of the $61,892 expended by his parents respecting the house they all owned. However, against that obligation, the court should offset a credit for the reasonable

2. The court in *Baird* also said that in any final accounting between the co-tenants, equitable considerations which would weigh against a simple mathematical balancing should be considered and could have an effect. Thus, *e.g.,* in *Baird,* where the co-tenants were brother and sister and the sister had expended extraordinary efforts to maintain the property for their mother and care for their mother in the property, those efforts were to be recognized in considering what if any occupancy credit should be imposed against the daughter. We see no such extraordinary equitable considerations here, but in the hearing which must follow the remand of this case, either party may submit evidence thereof for consideration by the trial court.

value of the occupancy enjoyed by the parents over the approximately eighteen years while they, and not their son, occupied the property. The obligation to present evidence of that value, which would normally be represented by rental value of the property, rests on the defendant. Although no such proof was presented at the prior trial, the uncertainty of the law in this area satisfies us that it would be unreasonable to deprive the defendant of the opportunity to do so now. Accordingly, the matter is reversed and remanded to the trial court for further proceedings at which the defendant shall have an opportunity to present evidence related to the value of the plaintiffs' sole occupancy of the property. We do not retain jurisdiction.

Olivas v. Olivas

780 P.2d 640 (N.M. Ct. App. 1989)

HARTZ, J. Respondent Sam Olivas (husband) appeals the property division in a divorce action. Petitioner Carolina Olivas (wife) and husband were divorced by a partial decree entered December 18, 1984. The district court did not enter its final order dividing property until August 31, 1987. The issues in this appeal arise, for the most part, as a consequence of the unusually lengthy delay between the divorce decree and the property division.

Husband appeals the rejection of his claims to compensation for his alleged constructive ouster from the community residence. We affirm.

Husband and wife separated in June 1983, about two months before wife filed her petition for dissolution of marriage. The district court found that husband "chose to move out of the family home, and he then maintained another home where he also had his office for his business." Husband contends that the district court erred in failing to find that he had been constructively ousted from the family home. He requested findings and conclusions that the constructive ouster by his wife entitled him to half of the reasonable rental value of the home from the time of the initial separation.

Husband and wife held the family home as community property during the marriage and as tenants in common after dissolution. Although wife was the exclusive occupant of the house after the separation, ordinarily a cotenant incurs no obligation to fellow cotenants by being the exclusive occupant of the premises.

> [I]t is a well-settled principle of the common law that the mere occupation by a tenant of the entire estate does not render him liable to his co-tenant for the use and occupation of any part of the common property. The reason is easily found. The right of each to occupy the premises is one of the incidents of a tenancy in common. Neither tenant can lawfully exclude the other. The occupation of one, so long as he does not exclude the other, is but the exercise of a legal right. If, for any reason, one does not choose to assert the right of common enjoyment, the other is not obliged to stay out; and if the sole occupation of one could render him liable therefor to the other, his legal right

> to the occupation would be dependent upon the caprice or indolence of his co-tenant, and this the law would not tolerate.

Williams v. Sinclair Refining Co., 39 N.M. 388, 392, 47 P.2d 910, 912 (1935) (quoting *Hamby v. Wall,* 48 Ark. 135, 137, 2 S.W. 705, 706 (1887)).

The result is otherwise, however, when the occupant has ousted the other cotenants. Although the term "ouster" suggests an affirmative physical act, even a reprehensible act, the obligation of the occupying cotenant to pay rent may arise in the absence of "actual" ouster when the realities of the situation, without there being any fault by either cotenant, prevent the cotenants from sharing occupancy. 4 G. Thompson, *Real Property* Section 1805, at 189 (J. Grimes Repl.1979) states:

> [B]efore a tenant in common can be liable to his cotenants for rent for the use and occupation of the common property, his occupancy must be such as amounts to a denial of the right of his cotenants to occupy the premises jointly with him, or the character of the property must be such as to make such joint occupancy impossible or impracticable.

Applying the notion of constructive ouster in the marital context is simply another way of saying that when the emotions of a divorce make it impossible for spouses to continue to share the marital residence pending a property division, the spouse who—often through mutual agreement—therefore departs the residence may be entitled to rent from the remaining spouse. Although one can say that the departing spouse has been constructively "ousted," the term should not suggest physical misconduct, or any fault whatsoever, on the part of the remaining spouse.

Common law precedents support the proposition that the remaining spouse should pay rent to the cotenant when both cannot be expected to live together on the property. For example, when it is impractical for all cotenants to occupy the premises jointly, it is unnecessary that those claiming rent from the cotenant in possession first demand the right to move in and occupy the premises. *See Oechsner v. Courcier,* 155 S.W.2d 963 (Tex.Civ.App.1941) (applying that principle when five heirs, with separate families totalling twenty-two members, were cotenants of a five-room cottage being occupied by one of the families). The impracticality of joint occupancy by the cotenants may result from the relations between the cotenants becoming "so strained and bitter that they could not continue to reside together in peace." [Citation omitted.] If, however, hostility flows only from the cotenant out of possession, ordinarily there would be no constructive ouster. In that circumstance the departing spouse has "abandoned" his or her interest in possession, rather than being excluded.

Husband had the burden of proving constructive ouster in this case. Therefore, we must sustain the district court's ruling against husband unless the evidence at trial was such as to *compel* the district court to find ouster. Although the evidence of hostility between the spouses may have sustained a finding by the district court of constructive ouster, there was substantial evidence to support the inference that husband's purpose in leaving the community residence was to live with a girlfriend and his departure was the reason wife filed for divorce; he was not pushed out but pulled. Also, the delay of several years before husband demanded any rent from wife supports an inference of abandonment of his interest in occupancy. In short, the evidence was conflicting and did not compel a finding of constructive ouster.

We recognize the ambiguity in the district court's finding that defendant "chose to move out." Such language could be consistent with husband's departure being the result of marital friction, in which case there generally would be constructive ouster. On the other hand, the language could also be construed as referring to husband's abandoning the home to live with another woman. We choose the second construction of the finding, because "[i]n the case of uncertain, doubtful or ambiguous findings, an appellate court is bound to indulge every presumption to sustain the judgment." [Citation omitted.] Moreover, it appeared from oral argument before this court that the issue of constructive ouster was framed in the district court in essentially the same manner as treated in this opinion. Therefore, we are comfortable in assuming that the district court applied the proper rule of law and in construing the district court's finding compatibly with its rejection of husband's proposed conclusion of law that there was a constructive ouster.

Exercise 4-10. *Esteves* and *Olivas* Revisited

1. Now you have resources to answer many of the questions raised earlier in this section.

   Suppose two people own equal shares of a house as tenants in common. Assume the carrying costs of property are $1,000 per month, and that if the property were rented out, the monthly rental value is $1,200.

   a. What obligations do the owners have to pay for carrying costs such as a mortgage and annual real estate taxes?

   b. What are the obligations if one owner uses the property all the time and the other never does? The rules vary depending on the context:

      (1) What rules are applied in *Esteves*, and what is the context that made those rules applicable? Specifically, when is a credit against expenses available, and how is it calculated? (In the above example, the maximum credit is $600—be sure you understand why.)

      (2) What rules are applied in *Olivas*, and what is the context that made those rules applicable?

      (3) Make a short outline of these rules.

2. An "actual" ouster occurs when there is an affirmative act of exclusion, such as changing the locks on the door and excluding a co-owner from the property. But *Olivas* demonstrates an alternative—a constructive ouster.

   a. How is constructive ouster defined?

b. Apply this rule to the facts from *Olivas*, generating arguments in favor of an ouster, and against.

c. Now consider, what if there had been no new romantic partner involved? How would that change your analysis?

d. The court in *Olivas* applied the doctrine of ouster to a married couple, but treated the spouses as if they were separate economic actors. Yet spouses typically share money extensively and allocate paid and unpaid labor as a team. Should the overall economic relationship between spouses be taken into account here?

3. What happens if an ouster goes on for the period of time required for adverse possession with the ousted tenant doing nothing to stop it in that period? (You need to apply the elements for adverse possession studied in Chapter 2.)

Transfers by One Co-Owner

As you learned earlier in this chapter, the extent of a co-owner's power to transfer her share depends on the kind of co-ownership structure that is in place. Recall that the main difference between tenants in common and joint tenants with the right of survivorship is the power to transfer at death. An owner of a tenancy in common has the power to transfer her share at their death. That is not the case with property owned as joint tenants. Instead, at the death of a co-tenant, the deceased person's interest will automatically pass to the surviving co-tenant(s). For example, if X and Y are joint tenants, and X dies, Y absorbs X's share and now owns the entire estate.

However, *both* tenants in common and joint tenants have the right to transfer their share freely during life, and can do so without the consent or even the knowledge of the other owner(s). This can occur by a transfer out of her entire interest by way of a gift or a sale. Another option for this group is to transfer out a lesser interest such as a lease, a mortgage or a life estate.

A lease by one co-tenant raises questions that are explored in Exercises 4-11 and 4-12 below, including the obligation to share rent.

Another issue that can arise if there is a transfer out by a joint tenant during his or her lifetime (before death) is whether the right of survivorship is destroyed. A lifetime transfer by a joint tenant can have a major impact, because not only is the share transferred to a new owner, but *if* there is a transfer out of *all* that the co-tenant owns, the structure of ownership is converted into a tenancy in common for the new owner and any remaining co-tenants. For example, if an owner has a one-third interest and transfers that interest to another, there is a severance, and it destroys the right of survivorship. The states disagree on whether a partial transfer out such as a mortgage or a lease will cause a severance—some finding it does, others finding it does not. You will learn more about severance in in Exercises 4-13 and 4-14 below.

Notice that the question of severance simply does not arise if there is a tenancy in common because there is no survivorship right to begin with. Nor can a severance occur in a tenancy by the entireties, because neither spouse can transfer an interest alone—mutual consent, the death of a spouse, or divorce is required to change the structure of ownership.

Leasing and Sharing Rent from Third Parties

Exercise 4-11. *Carr v. Deking*

Keep the following questions in mind as you read *Carr*.

1. What are the rights and obligations of the owners when one person wants to rent out the property and the other does not?
   a. Do both tenants have to agree to the rental to create a valid lease?
   b. What power does one tenant have to act alone?
   c. Does rent from a third party have to be shared? When?
2. Do the rules promote collaboration and cooperation or individual autonomy?

Carr v. Deking

765 P.2d 40 (1988 Wash. App.)

Green, J. The primary issue presented by this appeal is whether a tenant in common who refuses to join in a lease executed by the other tenant in common is entitled to eject the lessee.

Joel Carr and his father, George Carr, now deceased, owned a parcel of land in Lincoln County as tenants in common. From 1974 through 1986 the Carrs leased the land to Richard Deking pursuant to a year-to-year oral agreement receiving one-third of the annual crop as rent. The Carrs paid for one-third of the fertilizer. In 1986, Joel Carr informed Mr. Deking he wanted cash rent beginning with the 1987 crop year. Mr. Deking was not receptive to this proposal. In February 1987 Joel Carr wrote a letter to Mr. Deking to determine if he wanted to continue leasing the property. Mr. Deking did not respond. Instead he discussed the lease with George Carr. On February 18 Joel Carr went to his father's home and found Mr. Deking there discussing a possible 5-year lease. Joel Carr again indicated he wanted cash rent. Later that day, unbeknownst to Joel Carr, Mr. Deking and George Carr executed a written 10-year crop-share lease at the office of Mr. Deking's attorney. Under this lease, Mr. Deking agreed to pay all fertilizer costs. Joel Carr neither consented to nor ratified this lease and never authorized George Carr to act on his behalf.

In April Joel Carr gave notice to Mr. Deking that his tenancy would terminate at the end of the 1987 crop year. Mr. Deking responded that he would retain possession pursuant to the written lease with George Carr. In July Joel Carr commenced this action to declare that no valid lease existed, Mr. Deking had no right to farm the land and he should be required to vacate the land at the end of the 1987 crop year.

On August 21 Mr. Deking moved for summary judgment. He contended a lessee of one tenant in common cannot be ousted by the other tenant in common; and, therefore, Mr. Deking should be deemed a tenant in common with Joel Carr for the duration of the 10-year lease or until the premises are partitioned. Joel Carr also moved for summary judgment declaring the Deking-George Carr lease terminated. The court granted Mr. Deking's motion for summary judgment.

In reviewing a summary judgment, this court engages in the same inquiry as the trial court. Summary judgment can be granted only if the pleadings and depositions, together with affidavits, show there is no genuine issue as to any material fact and that the moving party is entitled to judgment as a matter of law. All facts submitted and all reasonable inferences must be considered in the light most favorable to the nonmoving party. Summary judgment should be granted only if, from all the evidence, reasonable persons could reach but one conclusion.

First, Joel Carr contends the court erred in refusing to eject Mr. Deking from the property on any of three bases: (1) He did not authorize or ratify the lease and, therefore, is not bound by it; (2) Mr. Deking is a stranger to the common title; and (3) the rights of Mr. Deking as lessee are subordinate to those of a nonjoining tenant in common. He argues public policy should prevent prospective lessees from going behind the back of one tenant in common to obtain a more favorable lease from the other.

On the other hand, it is Mr. Deking's position that George Carr could lawfully enter into a lease with respect to his own undivided one-half interest in the property, and Joel Carr was not entitled to bring an ejectment action to which George Carr did not agree. He asserts the proper remedy is partition, not ejectment. It is well settled that each tenant in common of real property may use, benefit and possess the entire property subject only to the equal rights of cotenants. Thus, a cotenant may lawfully lease his own interest in the common property to another without the consent of the other tenant and without his joining in the lease. The nonjoining cotenant is not bound by this lease of the common property to third persons. The lessee "steps into the shoes" of the leasing cotenant and becomes a tenant in common with the other owners for the duration of the lease. A nonjoining tenant may not demand exclusive possession as against the lessee, but may only demand to be let into co-possession.

Applying these principles, we find Joel Carr is not entitled to eject Mr. Deking from the property. The proper remedy is partition and until that occurs, Mr. Deking is entitled to farm the land under the lease. There is no indication that this property is not amenable to physical partition. Joel Carr clearly has the right to that remedy. Joel Carr cites no authority and none has been found which would render the lease ineffective as between the estate of George Carr and Mr. Deking.

In view of our holding that the trial court properly denied Joel Carr's effort to eject Mr. Deking, Joel Carr is entitled to the benefit of the Deking-George Carr lease, at his election, until a partition of the property occurs. However, Joel Carr cannot claim the benefits contained in the Deking-George Carr lease without also accepting the other terms of that lease. Consequently, we remand to the trial court to determine Joel Carr's election choice. If he elects to be governed until partition by the prior oral lease with Mr. Deking, then the trial court's ruling is affirmed. If Joel Carr elects to be governed until partition by the Deking-George Carr lease, then the judgment shall be so modified by the trial court.

Exercise 4-12. *Carr* Revisited

1. Be prepared to explain why George Carr was allowed to lease out the property without his son Joel's knowledge or consent, and over Joel's objection. What is the scope of the power of a co-tenant to lease?
2. Identify at least three rights that Joel Carr can still exercise even after his father leased out the property.
3. What obligations do co-owners have to share rent from a third party? Notice that a rent-sharing obligation arises only if the owners mutually agree to the lease and the renter obtains exclusive possession. Is rent shared if one owner participates in the lease and the other does not? The answer is no. Be sure you understand why.
4. Mother and Son co-own a vacation home at the beach. Son leases out the beach house for the months of June, July and August in Year 1 in exchange for $10,000 in rent. Son keeps the full rent for himself. The tenant believes she has the right to exclusive possession for the duration of the lease. If the Mother consents to the lease and makes a claim for rent against her son, will she prevail?
5. Why do the rules require so little cooperation or even disclosure of information given that the parties share the property?
6. What alternative rule(s) might be better?

Severance

Like a tenant in common, a joint tenant with a right of survivorship can freely transfer his share during the lifetime of the owner. (It is too late to attempt such a transfer at death.) This freedom includes the ability of one owner acting alone to sever a joint tenancy and extinguish the right of survivorship. A transfer out of a tenant's share to another person will accomplish this. At that point, the remaining co-tenant will own as a tenant in common with the new owner. Under the modern approach, a tenant can just transfer from herself as a joint tenant to herself as a tenant in common to produce the same result.

Note, however that the states are divided over whether a severance occurs or if instead a joint tenancy continues on intact, when a joint tenant transfers out less than their entire share (a fee simple) as with a mortgage or a lease. Some states conclude that a lease or a mortgage does affect a severance, and therefore, the owners become tenants in common. That means that the mortgage or the lease survives the death of the granting owner (just as it would for any tenancy in common). Other states reach the opposite conclusion. In such states, a lease or mortgage does *not* sever a joint tenancy. Accordingly, if the leasing or mortgaging owner dies first, then the lease or the mortgage disappears at death, and the surviving owner takes the property free of the lease or mortgage. So lenders and renters, beware!

Exercise 4-13. *Reicherter v. McCauley*

1. The next case shows how easy it can be to sever the right of survivorship by a declaration of one co-tenant to herself. Is it too easy?
2. Yet mortgages and leases in some states are not understood to cause a severance. Think about why that might be as you witness the clarity of intent Richard Reicherter expressed just before his death.
3. *Reicherter* also includes an example of a transfer by deed with effective delivery. This is typically required in a real estate transaction, as you will learn in Chapter 11. This is a fairly unusual example, because delivery is from the owner to himself, through his attorney. Refresh your recollection about the element of delivery for a completed gift that you studied in this chapter. Recall its purpose. It serves the same purpose here.

Reicherter v. McCauley

283 P.3d 219 (Kans. App. 2012)

Hill, J. In this appeal, we must decide if one joint tenant, 10 days before his death, can effectively destroy a joint tenancy interest in a tract of real estate and replace it with a tenancy in common by signing a quitclaim deed to himself and giving it to his lawyer for recording. Guided by the clearly manifested intent of the party making the conveyance here and because jointly owned property is freely transferable, we hold that the transfer of title was effective upon delivery of the deed to the grantor's lawyer for recording. We affirm the district court's ruling.

Richard F. Reicherter and his cousin, Douglas M. Reicherter, acquired an 80-acre farm in Marshall County in 1990, as joint tenants with rights of survivorship. Years later, when Richard was residing in a care facility, he signed a quitclaim deed on December 18, 2009, that conveyed his interest in the 80 acres to himself in an apparent attempt to sever the joint tenancy and create a tenancy in common. After signing,

Richard gave the deed to his attorney, Rodney Symmonds, for recording. On December 22, 2009, Symmonds mailed Richard's quitclaim deed along with a filing fee to the Marshall County Register of Deeds.

Then, Richard died on December 28, 2009. One day after his death, the Marshall County Register of Deeds recorded Richard's quitclaim deed. Douglas Reicherter was unaware that Richard had executed and filed a quitclaim deed until after Richard's death. There was no express agreement between Richard and Douglas preventing Richard from severing the joint tenancy.

Barbara J. McCauley was appointed executrix of Richard's estate. Naming McCauley as the defendant, Douglas and his wife filed a quiet title action in Marshall County seeking title to the entire 80-acre tract. McCauley counterclaimed claiming a half ownership interest and sought partition of the farm. Douglas opposed this action.

Both sides sought summary judgment. Ruling that Richard clearly intended to sever the joint tenancy and he could convey his interest to himself unimpeded and could thus create a tenancy in common, the district court granted Executrix McCauley's motion and denied Douglas' motion for summary judgment. The district court also held that the joint tenancy was severed when Richard, prior to his death, delivered the quitclaim deed to his attorney for filing.

Douglas Reicherter contends the unilateral attempt at self-conveyance by Richard was ineffective in destroying the joint tenancy ownership they had in the 80 acres. In Douglas' view, since the deed was not recorded until after Richard's death, it did not affect his surviving ownership of the entire tract as he had no prior notice of Richard's intent to sever the joint tenancy. He asks us to reverse the district court and order the court to quiet title to the 80 acres in his favor.

Executrix McCauley contends the joint tenancy to the tract was effectively severed and a tenancy in common was created when Richard signed the quitclaim deed to himself and then gave it to his lawyer for recording. In her view, Richard was not required to give notice to Douglas of his intent and recording the deed after Richard's death did not nullify Richard's intent of severing the joint tenancy. She asks us to affirm the district court.

Generally speaking, there are two ways to jointly own property in Kansas, either as tenants in common or as joint tenants with rights of survivorship. When considering the ownership of real estate, the law presumes a tenancy in common is created unless the deed or other conveyance creating the estate unequivocally conveys a joint tenancy to two or more persons or entities. There is no question here that before Richard's death, he and Douglas owned this 80-acre farm as joint tenants.

We have no doubt that Richard intended to sever the joint tenancy. At the summary judgment hearing, Douglas stipulated that the district court would not have to make a determination regarding Richard's intent because Richard demonstrated a clear intent to sever the joint tenancy by signing the quitclaim deed and giving it to his lawyer. Given that Richard's intent is not at issue, the remaining questions are whether self-conveyance is effective in Kansas and whether Richard's delivery of the quitclaim deed to his attorney effectively severed the joint tenancy or whether the failure to record the deed until after Richard's death thwarted Richard's intent.

No Kansas court has ruled on the issue of whether one joint tenant can unilaterally sever a joint tenancy by executing a quitclaim deed conveying his or her interest in the real estate to himself or herself as a tenant in common. For the three reasons given below, we hold that a joint tenant can self-convey and thus destroy a joint tenancy in this case where there are just two joint tenants.

First, under Kansas law, it is clear that any joint tenant may unilaterally sever his or her joint tenancy interest in real property and create a tenancy in common by conveying his or her interest to a third person. Had Richard conveyed his interests in this real estate to a third person the joint tenancy would have been changed to a tenancy in common with ownership of the tract held in common between that third party and Douglas upon delivery of the deed. We point this out to emphasize that whatever interest a joint owner has in real estate it is freely transferable, that is, it can be sold or given to someone else. There is no need for the party seeking transfer of ownership to first give notice to, or obtain the consent of, the remaining tenant to effectuate the conveyance.

Second, where the intent to create a joint tenancy is clearly manifested, a joint tenancy may be *created* by a transfer to persons as joint tenants from an owner or a joint owner *to himself or herself* and one or more persons as joint tenants. The Supreme Court ruled that a self-conveyance can create a joint tenancy. The all important factor is the clarity with which the grantor's intent is expressed at the time the transaction is initiated. Logically, we see no reason for a distinction between the method used to create or sever a joint tenancy. Just as a grantor can create a joint tenancy by unilaterally transferring ownership to himself or herself, so should a grantor be able to sever a joint tenancy through self-conveyance.

Third, other jurisdictions have found that unilateral self-conveyance severs a joint tenancy and have dispensed with the old requirements of deeding property to a straw man. We find their reasoning persuasive.

This reasoning leads us to rule in favor of Richard's estate. Upon effective delivery during the grantor's life, a quitclaim deed by a joint tenant to himself or herself as a tenant in common effectively severs the joint tenancy and creates a tenancy in common. Obviously, because of the facts of this case, we limit this ruling to a case where there are just two joint tenants.

Exercise 4-14. Revisiting *Reicherter* and More Complexities

1. Why is a joint tenancy sometimes called the ultimate gamble?
2. *Carr* and *Reicherter* both include secret transfers that most definitely impact the rights of the non-transferring owner. Both were affirmed by the court. Is that fair? Relatedly, do you have any ethical concerns for a lawyer who facilitates a secret severance? What if your client signed a deed purporting to

sever a joint tenancy and then asked you to hold onto the deed, and reveal its contents *only if* your client were to die before the other owner?

3. You represent Janet, who is in the process of buying a house with her sister Sue. Janet wants to own the property as joint tenants with the right of survivorship, but would like to foreclose the risk of severance. What ideas do you have for accomplishing this goal? Consider these possibilities: 1) a contract; or 2) a deed that says "Janet and Sue as concurrent life tenants, with the remainder interest to the survivor of them."

4. *Mortgages and Leases.* Let's return to a problem from earlier, with some new facts added. Mother and Son co-own a vacation home at the beach as joint tenants with the right of survivorship. Son leases out the beach house for the months of June, July and August in Year 1 in exchange for $10,000 in rent. Son keeps the full rent for himself. *New Facts*: Mother does not consent to the lease. In July, Year 1, Mother dies. Her will leaves all her property to her husband. You addressed the rent sharing question earlier. Focus now on the rules of severance and predict the alternative legal outcomes, depending on what state approach is applied. Now, change the facts again. What would happen if the son died first instead (on July 1)? In states where a lease does not cause a severance, the renters' rights to the lease would vanish. Can you see why?

Tenancies by the Entireties

A tenancy by the entireties operates quite differently in terms of the power to transfer. Some freedom to transfer is traded off for collective decision-making and security. As explained before, the estate cannot be severed by one spouse acting alone, and a partition is unavailable unless there is a divorce. Also, spouses who own as tenants by the entireties do not have the power to grant a third party any interest in the property without mutual consent. For example, a lease or mortgage granted by one spouse acting alone will not bind the property. One important consequence of this "lock in" feature is that a creditor cannot reach property held as tenants by the entireties when the debt is owed just by one spouse. The key point to understand for now is that if a creditor obtains a right to collect a debt against property (called a security interest or a lien), that right is a kind of property interest itself. Since one spouse alone cannot grant an interest in tenancy by the entireties property, no security interest will be recognized while the estate is intact. You will learn more about security interests including mortgages in Chapter 11.

Exercise 4-15. *Sawada v. Endo*

1. This next case vividly demonstrates the protection against creditors that typically accompanies a tenancy by the entireties. As you read, think about why such protection has been granted. What are the benefits of this? What are the costs?

2. *Sawada* also provides some insights into the history and evolution of the estate. A tenancy by the entireties originated in a system called coverture that viewed a husband and wife as one legal actor, and that actor was the husband. A woman's identity was subsumed at marriage, and the husband became the sole manager and owner of all property owned by either spouse. Many states abolished the entireties estate when coverture was abolished. Yet about half the states retained and modernized it. Does the modern version of the estate impact women differently (worse or better) than men today? Or has sex neutrality been achieved?

Sawada v. Endo

561 P.2d 1291 (Haw. 1977)

Menor, J. This is a civil action brought by the plaintiffs-appellants, Masako Sawada and Helen Sawada, in aid of execution of money judgments in their favor, seeking to set aside a conveyance of real property from judgment debtor Kokichi Endo to Samuel H. Endo and Toru Endo, defendants-appellees herein, on the ground that the conveyance as to the Sawadas was fraudulent.

On November 30, 1968, the Sawadas were injured when struck by a motor vehicle operated by Kokichi Endo. On June 17, 1969, Helen Sawada filed her complaint for damages against Kokichi Endo. Masako Sawada filed her suit against him on August 13, 1969. The complaint and summons in each case was served on Kokichi Endo on October 29, 1969.

On the date of the accident, Kokichi Endo was the owner, as a tenant by the entirety with his wife, Ume Endo, of a parcel of real property situate at Wahiawa, Oahu, Hawaii. By deed, dated July 26, 1969, Kokichi Endo and his wife conveyed the property to their sons, Samuel H. Endo and Toru Endo. This document was recorded in the Bureau of Conveyances on December 17, 1969. No consideration was paid by the grantees for the conveyance. Both were aware at the time of the conveyance that their father had been involved in an accident, and that he carried no liability insurance. Kokichi Endo and Ume Endo, while reserving no life interests therein, continued to reside on the premises.

On January 19, 1971 ... judgment was entered in favor of Helen Sawada and against Kokichi Endo in the sum of $8,846.46. At the same time, Masako Sawada was awarded judgment on her complaint in the amount of $16,199.28. Ume Endo, wife of Kokichi Endo, [died] on January 29, 1971. She was survived by her husband, Kokichi. Subsequently, after being frustrated in their attempts to obtain satisfaction of judgment from the personal property of Kokichi Endo, the Sawadas brought suit to set aside the conveyance which is the subject matter of this controversy. The trial court refused to set aside the conveyance, and the Sawadas appeal.

The determinative question in this case is, whether the interest of one spouse in real property, held in tenancy by the entireties, is subject to levy and execution by his or her individual creditors. This issue is one of first impression in this jurisdiction.

Hawaii has long recognized and continues to recognize the tenancy in common, the joint tenancy, and the tenancy by the entirety, as separate and distinct estates. The tenancy by the entirety is predicated upon the legal unity of husband and wife, and the estate is held by them in single ownership. They do not take by moieties, but both and each are seized of the whole estate.

A joint tenant has a specific, albeit undivided, interest in the property, and if he survives his cotenant he becomes the owner of a larger interest than he had prior to the death of the other joint tenant. But tenants by the entirety are each deemed to be seized of the entirety from the time of the creation of the estate. At common law, this taking of the "Whole estate" did not have the real significance that it does today, insofar as the rights of the wife in the property were concerned. For all practical purposes, the wife had no right during coverture to the use and enjoyment and exercise of ownership in the marital estate. All she possessed was her contingent right of survivorship.

The effect of the Married Women's Property Acts was to abrogate the husband's common law dominance over the marital estate and to place the wife on a level of equality with him as regards the exercise of ownership over the whole estate. The tenancy was and still is predicated upon the legal unity of husband and wife, but the Acts converted it into a unity of equals and not of unequals as at common law. No longer could the husband convey, lease, mortgage or otherwise encumber the property without her consent. The Acts confirmed her right to the use and enjoyment of the whole estate, and all the privileges that ownership of property confers, including the right to convey the property in its entirety, jointly with her husband, during the marriage relation. They also had the effect of insulating the wife's interest in the estate from the separate debts of her husband.

Neither husband nor wife has a separate divisible interest in the property held by the entirety that can be conveyed or reached by execution. A joint tenancy may be destroyed by voluntary alienation, or by levy and execution, or by compulsory partition, but a tenancy by the entirety may not. The indivisibility of the estate, except by joint action of the spouses, is an indispensable feature of the tenancy by the entirety.

We are not persuaded by the argument that it would be unfair to the creditors of either spouse to hold that the estate by the entirety may not, without the consent of both spouses, be levied upon for the separate debts of either spouse. No unfairness to the creditor in involved here.

Were we to view the matter strictly from the standpoint of public policy, we would still be constrained to hold as we have done here today. In *Fairclaw v. Forrest*, the court makes this observation:

> "The interest in family solidarity retains some influence upon the institution (of tenancy by the entirety). It is available only to husband and wife. It is a convenient mode of protecting a surviving spouse from inconvenient administration of the decedent's estate and from the other's improvident

> debts. It is in that protection the estate finds its peculiar and justifiable function." 130 F.2d at 833.

It is a matter of common knowledge that the demand for single-family residential lots has increased rapidly in recent years, and the magnitude of the problem is emphasized by the concentration of the bulk of fee simple land in the hands of a few. The shortage of single-family residential fee simple property is critical and government has seen fit to attempt to alleviate the problem through legislation. When a family can afford to own real property, it becomes their single most important asset. Encumbered as it usually is by a first mortgage, the fact remains that so long as it remains whole during the joint lives of the spouses, it is always available in its entirety for the benefit and use of the entire family. Loans for education and other emergency expenses, for example, may be obtained on the security of the marital estate. This would not be possible where a third party has become a tenant in common or a joint tenant with one of the spouses, or where the ownership of the contingent right of survivorship of one of the spouses in a third party has cast a cloud upon the title of the marital estate, making it virtually impossible to utilize the estate for these purposes.

If we were to select between a public policy favoring the creditors of one of the spouses and one favoring the interests of the family unit, we would not hesitate to choose the latter. But we need not make this choice for, as we pointed out earlier, by the very nature of the estate by the entirety as we view it, and as other courts of our sister jurisdictions have viewed it, "[a] unilaterally indestructible right of survivorship, an inability of one spouse to alienate his interest, and, importantly for this case, a broad immunity from claims of separate creditors remain among its vital incidents." [Citation omitted.]

Having determined that an estate by the entirety is not subject to the claims of the creditors of one of the spouses during their joint lives, we now hold that the conveyance of the marital property by Kokichi Endo and Ume Endo, husband and wife, to their sons, Samuel H. Endo and Toru Endo, was not in fraud of Kokichi Endo's judgment creditors.

KIDWELL, Justice, dissenting. The majority reaches its conclusion by holding that the effect of the Married Women's Act was to equalize the positions of the spouses by taking from the husband his common law right to transfer his interest, rather than by elevating the wife's right of alienation of her interest to place it on a position of equality with the husband's. I disagree. I believe that a better interpretation of the Married Women's Acts is that offered by the Supreme Court of New Jersey in *King v. Greene*, 30 N.J. 395, 412, 153 A.2d 49, 60 (1959):

> "It is clear that the Married Women's Act created an equality between the spouses in New Jersey, insofar as tenancies by the entirety are concerned. If, as we have previously concluded, the husband could alienate his right of survivorship at common law, the wife, by virtue of the act, can alienate her right of survivorship. And it follows, that if the wife takes equal rights with the husband in the estate, she must take equal disabilities. Such are the dictates

of common equality. Thus, the judgment creditors of either spouse may levy and execute upon their separate rights of survivorship."

One may speculate whether the courts which first chose the path to equality now followed by the majority might have felt an unexpressed aversion to entrusting a wife with as much control over her interest as had previously been granted to the husband with respect to his interest. Whatever may be the historical explanation for these decisions, I feel that the resultant restriction upon the freedom of the spouses to deal independently with their respective interests is both illogical and unnecessarily at odds with present policy trends. Accordingly, I would hold that the separate interest of the husband in entireties property, at least to the extent of his right of survivorship, is alienable by him and subject to attachment by his separate creditors, so that a voluntary conveyance of the husband's interest should be set aside where it is fraudulent as to such creditors, under applicable principles of the law of fraudulent conveyances.

Exercise 4-16. *Sawada* Revisited

1. Explain why the transfer by the Endos when they believed liability from the accident was looming was not a fraud on the tort victims as creditors?
2. *Policy Foundations.*
   a. What are the policy justifications that protect married couples who own as tenants by the entireties from legitimate creditors? Do you find them convincing?
   b. Should this form of ownership be more widely available? Should it also apply to other kinds of relationships, such as between parents and children? Or intimate partners who are not married?
3. *Sawada* reflects a typical approach. Without getting into the complexities, a small number of other states do allow a creditor to attach an interest to a limited extent, but that interest does not defeat the right to survivorship for the non-debtor spouse. *See, e.g., Capital Finance Co. Delaware Valley, Inc. v. Asterbadi*, 942 A.2d 21 (N.J. Super. 2008); *Covington v. Murray*, 416 S.W.2d 761 (Tenn. 1967).

Partition

People sometimes decide that it is best to terminate a co-ownership relationship. There are several options to achieve that. The property can be transferred to someone else, or the owners can agree to sell the property and divide the proceeds into shares. However, if the owners have conflicts that they cannot resolve, a judicial partition is available. If a partition claim is brought, a judge will either order the property physically divided into individually owned sub-parts (an "in-kind division") or order the property sold and allocate the proceeds.

An in-kind division is fairly easy if there is an undeveloped tract of land with all parts of equal value. So if X and Y owned a hundred acre parcel in equal shares either as tenants in common or as joint tenants, the court could simply divide ownership of 50 acres to X and the other 50 acres to Y. Of course, is quite difficult to physically divide a residence. Who gets the kitchen? Would it make any sense for the parties continue to live together? Probably not. On the other hand, as you will discover in the *Ark Land* case that follows, a forced sale has some potential downsides too.

Exercise 4-17. *Ark Land Co. v. Harper*

1. As you read *Ark Land*, be sure to extract the rules and policies that govern partition and identify the arguments each party makes or could make.
2. Also, consider several questions. Which method is preferred under the law? How hard is it to satisfy the requirements for a partition by sale?

Ark Land Co. v. Harper

599 S.E.2d 754 (W. Va. 2004)

Davis, J. This is an appeal by Rhonda Gail Harper, Edward Caudill, Rose M. Thompson, Edith D. Kitchen, Therman R. Caudill, John A. Caudill, Jr., Tammy Willis, and Lucille M. Miller (hereinafter collectively identified as the "Caudill heirs"), appellants/defendants below, from an order of the Circuit Court of Lincoln County. The circuit court's order authorized a partition and sale of real property jointly owned by the Caudill heirs and Ark Land Company (hereinafter referred to as "Ark Land"), appellee/plaintiff below. Here, the Caudill heirs contend that the legal precedents of this Court warrant partitioning the property in kind, not a sale. After a careful review of the briefs and record in this case, we agree with the Caudill heirs and reverse the circuit court.

This is a dispute involving approximately 75 acres of land situate in Lincoln County, West Virginia. The record indicates that "[t]he Caudill family has owned the land for nearly 100 years." The property "consists of a farmhouse, constructed around 1920, several small barns, and a garden[.]" Prior to 2001, the property was owned exclusively by the Caudill family. However, in 2001 Ark Land acquired a 67.5% undivided interest in the land by purchasing the property interests of several Caudill family members. Ark Land attempted to purchase the remaining property interests held by the Caudill heirs, but they refused to sell. Ark Land sought to purchase all of the property for the express purpose of extracting coal by surface mining. After the Caudill heirs refused to sell their interest in the land, Ark Land filed the complaint seeking to have the land partitioned and sold.

The dispositive issue is whether the evidence supported the circuit court's conclusion that the property could not be conveniently partitioned in kind, thus warranting a partition by sale. During the proceeding before the circuit court, the Caudill heirs presented expert testimony by Gary F. Acord, a mining engineer. Mr. Acord testified that the property could be partitioned in kind. Specifically, Mr. Acord testified that lands surrounding the family home did not have coal deposits and could therefore be partitioned from the remaining lands. On the other hand, Ark Land presented expert testimony which indicated that such a partition would entail several million dollars in additional costs in order to mine for coal.

We note at the outset that "[p]artition means the division of the land held in cotenancy into the cotenants' respective fractional shares. If the land cannot be fairly divided, then the entire estate may be sold and the proceeds appropriately divided." [Citation omitted.] Partition by sale, when it is not voluntary by all parties, can be a harsh result for the cotenant(s) who opposes the sale. This is because "'[a] particular piece of real estate cannot be replaced by any sum of money, however large; and one who wants a particular estate for a specific use, if deprived of his rights, cannot be said to receive an exact equivalent or complete indemnity by the payment of a sum of money.'" [Citations omitted.] Consequently, "[p]artition in kind ... is the preferred method of partition because it leaves cotenants holding the same estates as before and does not force a sale on unwilling cotenants." [Citation omitted.] The laws in all jurisdictions "appear to reflect this longstanding principle by providing a presumption of severance of common ownership in real property by partition in-kind[.]" [Citation omitted.]

This Court set out the following standard of proof that must be established to overcome the presumption of partition in kind:

> By virtue of W. Va.Code § 37-4-3, a party desiring to compel partition through sale is required to demonstrate [(1)] that the property cannot be conveniently partitioned in kind, [(2)] that the interests of one or more of the parties will be promoted by the sale, and [(3)] that the interests of the other parties will not be prejudiced by the sale. [Citation omitted.]

In its lengthy order requiring partition and sale, the circuit court addressed each of the three factors as follows:

> (14) That upon the Court's review and consideration of the entire record, even after the [Caudill heirs'] expert witness testified, the Court has determined that it is clearly evident that the subject property's nature, character, and amount are such that it cannot be conveniently, (that is "practically or justly") partitioned, or divided by allotment among its owners. Moreover, it is just and necessary to conclude that such a proposal as has been made by the [Caudill heirs], that of allotting the manor house and the surrounding "bottom land" unto the [Caudill heirs], cannot be affected

without undeniably prejudicing [Ark Land's] interests, in violation of the mandatory provisions of Code § 37-4-3; and,

(15) That while its uniform topography superficially suggests a division-in-kind, as proposed by Mr. Acord, the access road, the bottom lands and the relatively flat home site is, in fact, integral to establishing the fair market value of the subject property in its entirety, as its highest and best use as mining property, as shown by the uncontroverted testimony of [Ark Land's] experts Mr. Morgan and Mr. Terry; and,

(16) That from a review of the Commissioners' Report, it indicates that sale of the subject property will promote the interests of [Ark Land], "but may prejudice the best interest of the [Caudill heirs]." Obviously, from the legal principles and the reviewing standards set out above, the "best interests" of either party is not the standard upon which the Court must determine these issues. In that respect, it is undisputed that the remaining heirs, that are [the Caudill heirs] herein, do not wish to sell, or have the Court sell, their interests in the subject property, solely due to their sincere sentiment for it as the family's "home place". Other family members, however, did not feel the same way. Given the equally undisputed testimony of [Ark Land's] experts, it is just and reasonable for the Court to conclude that the interests of all the subject property's owners will not be financially prejudiced, but will be financially promoted, by sale of the subject property and distribution among them of the proceeds, according to their respective interests. The subject property's value as coal mining property, its uncontroverted highest and best use, would be substantially impaired by severing the family's "home place" and allotting it to them separately. Again, the evidence is not only a preponderance, but unrebutted, that Mr. Acord's proposal would greatly diminish the value of the subject property. Accordingly, the Court does hereby conclude as a matter of law that the subject property should be sold as a whole in its entirety, and that it cannot be partitioned in kind by allotment of part and a sale of the residue.

We are troubled by the circuit court's conclusion that partition by sale was necessary because the economic value of the property would be less if partitioned in kind. We have long held that the economic value of property *may* be a factor to consider in determining whether to partition in kind or to force a sale.

> Whether the aggregate value of the several parcels into which the whole premises must be divided will, when distributed among, and held in severalty by, the different parties, be materially less than the value of the same property if owned by one person, is a fair test by which to determine whether the interests of the parties will be promoted by a sale. [Citation omitted.]

However, our cases *do not* support the conclusion that economic value of property is the exclusive test for determining whether to partition in kind or to partition by sale. In view of the prior decisions of this Court, as well as the decisions from other jurisdictions, we now make clear and hold that, in a partition proceeding in which a party opposes the sale of property, the economic value of the property is not the exclusive test for deciding whether to partition in kind or by sale. Evidence of longstanding ownership, coupled with sentimental or emotional interests in the property, may also be considered in deciding whether the interests of the party opposing the sale will be prejudiced by the property's sale. This latter factor should ordinarily control when it is shown that the property can be partitioned in kind, though it may entail some economic inconvenience to the party seeking a sale.

In the instant case, the Caudill heirs were not concerned with the monetary value of the property. Their exclusive interest was grounded in the longstanding family ownership of the property and their emotional desire to keep their ancestral family home within the family. It is quite clear that this emotional interest would be prejudiced through a sale of the property.

The expert for the Caudill heirs testified that the ancestral family home could be partitioned from the property in such away as to not deprive Ark Land of any coal. The circuit court summarily and erroneously dismissed this uncontradicted fact because of the increased costs that Ark Land would incur as a result of a partition in kind. In view of our holding, the additional economic burden that would be imposed on Ark Land, as a result of partitioning in kind, is not determinative under the facts of this case.

The facts in this case reveal that, prior to 2001, Ark Land had no ownership interest in the property. Conversely, for nearly 100 years the Caudill heirs and their ancestors owned the property and used it for residential purposes. In 2001 Ark Land purchased ownership rights in the property from some Caudill family members. When the Caudill heirs refused to sell their ownership rights, Ark Land immediately sought to force a judicial sale of the property. In doing this, Ark Land established that its proposed use of the property, surface coal mining, gave greater value to the property. This showing is self-serving. In most instances, when a commercial entity purchases property because it believes it can make money from a specific use of the property, that property will increase in value based upon the expectations of the commercial entity. This self-created enhancement in the value of property cannot be the determinative factor in forcing a pre-existing co-owner to give up his/her rights in property. To have such a rule would permit commercial entities to always "evict" pre-existing co-owners, because a commercial entity's interest in property will invariably increase its value.

We are very sensitive to the fact that Ark Land will incur greater costs in conducting its business on the property as a result of partitioning in kind. However, Ark Land voluntarily took an economical gamble that it would be able to get all of the Caudill family members to sell their interests in the property. Ark Land's gamble failed. The Caudill heirs refused to sell their interests. The fact that Ark Land miscalculated on its ability to acquire outright all interests in the property cannot form the basis for depriving the Caudill heirs of their emotional interests in maintaining their ancestral family home. The additional cost to Ark Land that will result from a partitioning in kind simply does not impose the type of injurious inconvenience that would justify stripping the Caudill heirs of the emotional interest they have in preserving their ancestral family home.

In view of the foregoing, we find that the circuit court erred in determining that the property could not be partitioned in kind. We, therefore, reverse the circuit court's order requiring sale of the property. This case is remanded with directions to the circuit court to enter an order requiring the property to be partitioned in kind, consistent with the report and testimony of the Caudill heirs' mining engineer expert, Gary F. Acord.

MAYNARD, C.J., concurring, in part, and dissenting, in part. I concur with the new law created by the majority in this case. That is to say, I agree that evidence of longstanding ownership along with sentimental or emotional attachment to property are factors that should be considered and, in some instances, control the decision of whether to partition in kind or sale jointly-owned property which is the subject of a partition proceeding.

I dissent in this case, however, because I do not believe that evidence to support the application of those factors was presented here. In that regard, the record shows that none of the appellants have resided at the subject property for years. At most, the property has been used for weekend retreats. While this may have been the family "homeplace," a majority of the family has already sold their interests in the property to the appellee. Only a minority of the family members, the appellants, have refused to do so. I believe that the sporadic use of the property by the appellants in this case does not outweigh the economic inconvenience that the appellee will suffer as a result of this property being partitioned in kind.

I am also troubled by the majority's decision that this property should be partitioned in kind instead of being sold because I don't believe that such would have been the case were this property going to be put to some use other than coal mining. For instance, I think the majority's decision would have been different if this property was going to be used in the construction of a four-lane highway. Under those circumstances, I believe the majority would have concluded that such economic activity takes precedence over any long-term use or sentimental attachment to the property on the part of the appellants. In my opinion, coal mining is an equally important economic activity. This decision destroys the value of this land as coal mining property because the appellee would incur several million dollars in additional costs to continue its mining operations. As a result of the majority's decision in this case, many innocent coal miners will be out of work.

Exercise 4-18. *Ark Land* Revisited

1. If the court had ordered a partition by sale, can you guess who would have been an interested and economically powerful buyer at the auction? Would

the sale bring a fair price? Concerns about unequal economic power and a fair price arise because even though an auction is open to the public, the only bidders are very often interested parties and commercial actors.

2. What method of partition do you think a court is likely to choose if there are a good number of co-owners (such as 5 or 10 or 25) of a modest sized building or home? (Did you count how many Caudill heirs appealed?) Not surprisingly, even though the rules favor a partition in kind, partition by sale is more common.

Family Property Law

We now turn to our last major sub-topic of this chapter—sharing rules that govern property rights among family members. Our study includes fundamental legal principles that apply to 1) married couples and 2) to unmarried couples (sometimes called cohabitants) and other family or affinity relationships. As we will see, the laws governing these two groups are quite different.

Accordingly, be sure you understand when marriage laws are applicable versus the property laws for other family-type relationships. Marriage laws apply to spouses in a legally recognized marriage. In modern law, this includes both opposite and same sex couples. Marriages that comply with the formalities of a marriage license and solemnization (a ceremony conducted by a state-authorized officiant) will be recognized as valid. In a minority of states, it is also possible to enter into a valid marriage informally if the standards for a "common law marriage" are satisfied. Although there is some variation among the states, the usual requirements are a) intent to be a married couple and b) behavior like a married couple, including "holding out" to the public as spouses. For example, there is strong case for recognition of a common law marriage if a couple shares the same last name, are known as spouses at work or among family and friends, and they intertwine their lives financially and socially. Notice that intent can be implied from behavior. The possibility of a common law marriage can be raised even in the many states that have abolished it, because states will recognize a common law marriage that has been validly created in another state.

You are already familiar with many rules that families engage with from your study of gifts and concurrent ownership. You will continue to encounter those concepts in this section, but with new layers and rules added to the mix. The focus in this part is on situations where there is no co-ownership relationship established by title and no formal written contract between the parties. You will learn what the default rules provide (the laws that automatically apply, absent an exception), and what claims can be made. Note that these default rules may be overridden by a contract such as a prenuptial or cohabitation agreement. The standards for enforcement for such contracts vary and are not addressed here.

Chapter Problem: Exercise 4-19

1. Your supervising partner recently assigned you a new case, and you now represent Wendy Smith in her divorce action. Review the two documents that follow. After you study the materials in this sub-part, you will be prepared to evaluate and respond to the offer of settlement in the letter below, applying the law in place in the majority of states.
2. Assume next that the couple never married. How would that change your evaluation and response?
3. To strengthen your lawyering negotiation skills and strategies, it would be helpful to do some research on some fundamental negotiation principles, such as information gathering and attentive listening, developing a plan and selecting goals.

Kelly Rodriquez, Esquire
Family Law Practice Group, LLC,
57 Main Line Road
Landsburg, Maryland 87336
October 1, Year Ten

Ms. Wendy Smith

As you may know, I now represent your husband Harry Smith as his divorce attorney. We are hopeful that this will be an amicable process that will result in a mutually satisfactory agreement to settle the case. I understand that you and Harry have discussed grounds for divorce and both consent to a no-fault divorce. It is also terrific that you and he have reached consensus on custody matters and shared parenting time for your daughter Sonia (age 7) and son Jamie (age 5), with the children living with you about 65% of the time.

The next step is to address the economic issues in dissolving the marriage. If possible, we would like to resolve these issues outside of court, avoiding unnecessary costs, delays and the emotional escalation that can accompany litigation. That would likely make the process easier for the family and especially for your children.

A financial settlement should be pretty straightforward. As you have already agreed, Harry will pay $1,000 per month in child support, per the statewide child support guidelines. Each parent will pay a pro rata share of an after school child care program based on your respective incomes following the divorce. Beyond this, the family expenses have always been modest, and it is clear that both you and Harry are capable of self-support from employment. You both have college degrees and professional jobs, with Harry having recently graduated from law school and with you having worked throughout the marriage for Bank One and recently being promoted there as assistant manager. Accordingly, we believe no alimony is appropriate in this case.

In terms of property division, Harry is willing to split evenly the small amount of wealth that has accumulated during your 10 year marriage. As I understand it, you and Harry have the following property: (a) a home owned as tenants by the entireties, with equity of $70,000 after accounting for the mortgage; (b) your 401(k) retirement account worth $13,000; (c) $2,500 in a joint savings account; and d) two cars, one worth $4,000 and the other $6,000. There is also a $2,500 outstanding debt on the credit card in your sole name and, of course, Harry's law school loans. We propose Harry will be responsible to pay his education loans and the $2,500 credit card bill be assigned to you. For the house, we believe that Harry should be allocated $10,000 of the equity to reimburse him for the $10,000 down payment he contributed soon after marriage when you purchased your home, because that money originally came from an inheritance Harry received from his grandfather. The $60,000 remaining balance of the equity should be split, with each of you receiving $30,000. If you want to remain in the home, Harry is agreeable to that, but you will need to find a way to buy out Harry's interest in the home. For all other marital assets, we also propose an equal division. The only other asset left to discuss is your cabin in the mountains that you inherited five years ago that is now worth $75,000. Harry is willing to make no claim to that, except that he asks for reimbursement of $5,000 for the $10,000 that was paid from marital earnings for expenses of maintaining the cabin that you own in your sole name.

After you have had an opportunity to think this over, and perhaps to consult with an attorney of your own, should you wish to retain one, please let me know if this proposal is acceptable.

Sincerely,

Kelly Rodriquez

Kelly Rodriquez, Esquire

MEMO

From: Supervising Partner
To: The File
Re: Wendy Smith
Date: October 15, Year 10

Today I met with a new client, Wendy Smith, who is getting divorced. She recently received a settlement letter from the attorney who represents her husband Harry. My conversation with her yielded the information that follows.

At the time of the marriage, Wendy was 21 and had just graduated from a two-year community college. Harry was 23 and had just graduated from a university with a degree in political science. It was the first marriage for both parties. After the marriage, Wendy went to work as a bank teller at a salary of $25,000 a year and Harry worked as a sales representative for a phone company, earning $35,000 a year. Just after they married, the couple bought a modest home, using as a down payment a $10,000 gift from Harry's grandfather. According to Harry, the money was a gift to him by way of an advancement against an inheritance. According to Wendy, it was a gift to both of them; she remembers that the grandfather presented it to Harry at the couple's wedding reception and indicated that he wanted them to use it "to buy a house, have children, and continue the family name." Harry's grandfather has since died, and there is no other evidence on this question except for the fact that his grandfather's will made no provision for Harry.

Three years after the couple married, Wendy gave birth to a daughter, Sonia, now 7 years old. Two years after Sonia's birth, the couple had a son, Jamie, now 5 years old. Apart from three months of paid maternity leave after the birth of each child, Wendy continued to work at the bank. While the couple worked, Sonia and Jamie were initially in family day care and now attend a school-based after care program. Even with two incomes, Wendy and Harry found it difficult to make ends meet. Nonetheless, when Jamie was two years old, Harry decided he wanted to become a professional, because he was "sick and tired of getting no respect as a salesperson." Wendy concurred in the decision, largely because of the increased family income that she thought Harry's career switch would bring.

Accordingly, Harry enrolled as a full time student in law school. Wendy continued to work at the bank to support the family, and in addition to a scholarship Harry received that reduced his annual tuition, he obtained some educational loans to cover the balance of his tuition. Harry also worked part-time and during the summers. During Harry's three years in law school, the couple lived off of Wendy's salary and Harry's earnings from summer and part time jobs; Wendy's total gross earnings for those three years combined were $90,000 and Harry's total gross earnings for those three years combined were $20,000. To make ends meet, the family cut back significantly on their expenses, dipped into their modest savings and accepted some financial assistance from each spouse's parents.

Wendy's salary is $45,000 per year; Harry earns $75,000.

The property interests are as follows.

Matrimonial Home. Purchased for $100,000 soon after marriage. The current market value of the house is $140,000. The mortgage balance is $70,000; the mortgage payments are $800 per month; and taxes, repairs and maintenance cost approximately $2,400 per year.

Furnishings. These have a total worth of $10,000. All were purchased with the parties' salaries during the marriage. There are sufficient duplicates in the house to furnish an apartment minimally. The value of the duplicates is $2,000.

Retirement Accounts. Harry contributed $75 per month to a pension plan while working as a sales representative. His employer made no additional contribution. Harry's interest in the pension never vested; instead, when Harry left his sales job to attend law school, he received a lump sum payment of $5,800 (representing his pension contributions plus interest), which he used to pay part of his first year's law school tuition. Wendy has contributed to a 401k at the rate of $50 per month for the past eight years. Her employer has matched this with an additional $50 per month. Wendy's fully vested 401k is valued at approximately $13,000 (but it does fluctuate with the changing market)

Savings. The couple has a joint savings account of $2,500.

Cars. The couple owns two cars, both purchased during the marriage and both titled jointly. The two cars are: 1) a 6-year-old Subaru station wagon, valued at $4,000; and 2) a 4-year-old Honda sedan, valued at $6,000.

Liabilities. The parties are jointly liable on a credit card, with an outstanding balance of $2,500. Harry has student loans in his sole name. The obligation requires 60 monthly payments of $300. Since graduation, Harry has made eight monthly payments on his loan.

Married Couples

Immediately upon saying "I do" and entering into a legally valid marriage, a system of legal rules applies by default that greatly impacts the rights and responsibilities of spouses. This sub-part includes a brief discussion of laws and policies that are applicable during an intact marriage and at death, followed by a more detailed overview of divorce laws. An advanced and more in-depth study of these topics is the subject of other courses you might take such as Family Law and Wills and Trusts.

A bit of historical context may be helpful as you consider modern family law and policy. Marital property laws, along with views of gender roles, labor division in families and cultural norms around marriage, have undergone remarkable changes over time. Until the late nineteenth century, states maintained a system of "coverture" where men's dominance over women was a cornerstone of law and culture, and was seen as the natural order of things and as a core religious principle. Married women could not manage or own property or enter into contracts. Here is a description by jurist William Blackstone:

> By marriage, the husband and wife are one person in law: that is, the very being or legal existence of the woman is suspended during the marriage, or at least is incorporated and consolidated into that of the husband: under whose wing, protection, and cover, she performs everything; and is therefore called in our law-french a *feme-covert* ... under the protection and influence of her husband, her baron, or lord; and her condition during her marriage is called her coverture.... The husband is bound to provide his wife with necessaries by law, as much as himself; and, if she contracts debts for them, he is obliged to pay them; but for anything besides necessaries he is not chargeable.... The husband also by the old law, might give his wife moderate correction. For, as he is to answer for her misbehavior the law thought it reasonable to intrust him with this power of restraining her, by domestic chastisement, in the same moderation that a man is allowed to correct his apprentices or children....
>
> [E]ven the disabilities which the wife lies under are for the most part intended for her protection and benefit: so great a favourite is the female sex of the laws of England.

Commentaries on the Laws of England. Vol. 1, 442-445 (1765).

The Married Women's Property Acts, widely adopted by the start of the twentieth century, were an important step away from coverture. These laws allowed a married woman to own and manage property as if she were single, and gave control to women over their own earnings. However, practically speaking this was of limited help to many women of the time, who did not have earnings from employment and had no accumulated wealth of their own.

Women's legal and social status has greatly improved over time. In particular, large numbers of women have entered the workforce and contribute essential earnings to support their families. Still, even today, there are disparities in economic and social power between the sexes. For example, the gender gap in pay has hardly budged in a decade—women working full-time jobs earn about 80% of what men earn. This gap is even more pronounced for minority women. The gap also is larger when part-time workers and stay-at-home moms and caregivers for the elderly are taken into account. One (but certainly not the only) factor that explains the wage gap puzzle is how families allocate resources toward paid and unpaid work. Although the pattern is variable and shifting to some extent, women tend to do far more unpaid family care work, and men do more paid market work. This can translate into less economic power for women.

As you learn the fundamentals of property law in families, take some time to consider the extent to which contemporary law helps or hinders the economic security and social status of women and men, of children and others in need of family care. Consider too that traditional gender relationships ar not the only policy and cultural frontier in marriage law. The advent of same sex marriage that has now been recognized as a right with significant protections in the U.S. Constitution and the debate around the status of LGBTQ persons have raised significant questions about equality, dignity and the meanings and functions of civil marriage. Does marriage law serve its various constituents well and fairly? As you will see, important questions about the purpose and effects of property laws also arise in laws governing cohabitants and other family relationships.

Property Regimes During Marriage and at Death

In most states, very different property rules apply to married couples in different contexts: during an ongoing marriage; at death; and at divorce. Such states are called "separate property" or "title" states because the default rules *during marriage* and *at death* are that each spouse owns property separately and that the form of title to an asset determines ownership. So if one spouse alone is named on a bank account, or a car, or for real property or a retirement account, then that spouse is deemed the sole owner. Similarly, the earnings of a spouse are owned by the earner. The law assumes that spouses do *not* share property, unless they take title as co-owners. Of course, many spouses do own some assets jointly, in which case the rules of co-ownership studied earlier apply.

During an ongoing marriage, the separate property rules are supplemented by a reciprocal support obligation between spouses that is quite limited. Typically the obligation is to provide only items that are "necessary" in light of the resources of the family, and is only applicable if the spouse seeking support cannot pay the bill independently and the creditor (such as a hospital) seeks payment from the non-debtor spouse. Based on a theory of family privacy, the general rule is that the support obligation is not directly enforceable between the spouses while they remain married and living together. Pause here for a moment and consider the way many modern couples divide labor mentioned earlier. What effect might these rules have on a spouse with lower or no earnings?

If a married person dies, again, most states have a separate property system. That means the person who dies (called the decedent) is the sole owner of any property in his or her sole name or, if an asset is co-owned, then the particular rules of the co-ownership structure apply. Property owned at death passes according to a will or by a right of survivorship if one has been put in place. If not, intestate succession laws are triggered that typically give the decedent's estate in shares to spouses and lineal descendants (e.g., children, grandchildren) or, if none survive the decedent, then to other blood relatives. In summary, a spouse who dies can control the disposition of whatever property that spouse owns at death. However, if a spouse has a will and does not leave property to the surviving spouse, then the surviving spouse can elect against the will and take a share of the decedents estate. The "forced share," also known as an "elective share," varies by state, most typically it is one-third of the estate of the pre-deceasing spouse.

If a petition for divorce is filed, the separate property states convert to a "marital property" regime with "equitable distribution" of the estate that incorporates many core principles of community property, discussed next.

The nine community property states apply the same rules to married couples across all marital situations—during marriage, at death and at divorce. Community property law has a dual classification system that distinguishes shared property from separately owned property. In contrast to separate property states, title does not determine ownership, and all property that is acquired during marriage is presumed to be communal property. Exceptions to that norm must be proven and include property acquired before marriage and gifts or inheritances to one spouse, even during marriage. Separate property is owned individually by the spouse who has title to the asset. Each spouse co-owns community property from the date of acquisition and has the power to dispose of their 50% share (but not more) at all times, including at death. There is no elective share in community property states, because a spouse does not have the power to control the other spouse's half of the community property and so cannot attempt to disinherit the surviving spouse.

Let us step back and reflect on all this. Why does the legal system have rules that vary depending on the context of the marriage? Does it make sense to have different rules in place at death and during marriage versus at divorce?

Property Law at Divorce

At divorce, all states have adopted many basic principles of community property law. Specifically, at least some property is presumptively jointly owned and title does not control who owns property. Put another way, spouses often co-own some property even if title is in just one spouse's name. Most states have adopted a dual classification model that differentiates marital from separate property:

Marital Property

- All property acquired after the date of marriage until the end of the relationship (such as at separation or divorce, varies by state).

Separate Property

- Property acquired before marriage or after its dissolution, or by gift or inheritance to one spouse (or other exceptions, per statute).

A minority of states (fifteen) have a broader definition of community property and include all property whenever and however acquired as "in the pot" for distribution between spouses at divorce. In these so called "all property" or "hotchpot" states, even property that was owned by one spouse before marriage and kept in that spouse's name alone is subject to division. That said, legal decision-makers in hotchpot states may take into account when and how property was acquired when dividing property, and so the outcomes can be similar to those in marital or community property states.

There are three basic steps in a divorce that family lawyers frequently engage in to help their clients.

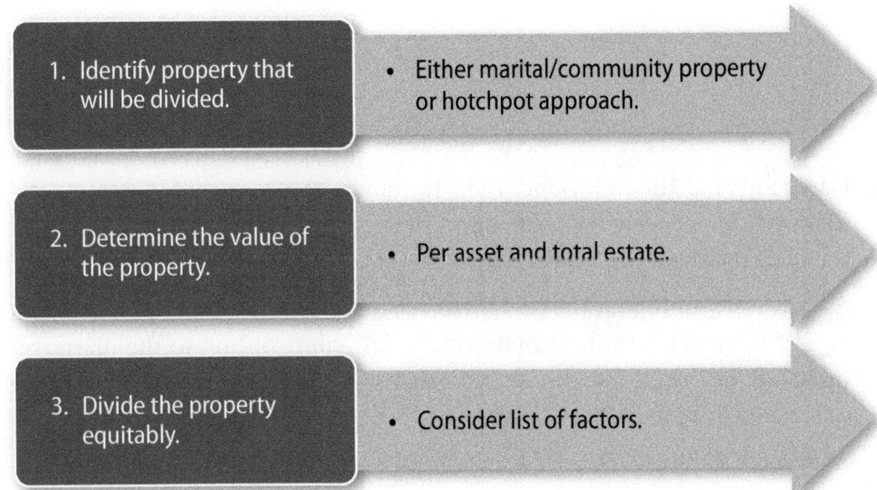

1. Identify property that will be divided.
Either marital/community property or hotchpot approach.
2. Determine the value of the property.
Per asset and total estate.
3. Divide the property equitably.
Consider list of factors.

You have already learned some basics for identifying divisible property and will learn more in the materials that follow. The valuation step is sometimes as easy as looking up how much money is in a bank account. It can also be complicated, such as valuing a small business, where an expert opinion might be appropriate and helpful. The last step is to allocate the property between the spouses. The vast majority of the states divide property based on what is "fair under the circumstances" based on a non-exhaustive list of factors to consider. That could mean an even or an uneven split depending on the facts. A few states mandate an equal division, and some states have a preference or presumption that equal is likely what is fair. What about debts? The same basic rules apply for characterizing liabilities—if the debt is acquired during marriage, there is a rebuttable presumption that it is a marital debt.

As you read the materials that follow, consider and look for answers to the following questions. What reasons might justify the legal assumption that married couples share ownership of property even when formal documents of title do not reflect that? How should property be allocated at divorce? What do you think should be considered or emphasized in legal decision-making?

Keep in mind that there is another piece of the economic puzzle for divorcing spouses—whether one spouse will have to pay the other alimony or, as it is frequently referred to today, "maintenance." This is a post-divorce obligation that can be awarded in addition to property division. Although the legal standards vary by state, typically alimony is payable if the claimant can demonstrate that he or she needs support to maintain the standard of living of the marriage, is unable to support herself or himself through reasonable employment and the other spouse has the ability to pay. In its contemporary applications, alimony awards, if granted at all, tend to be short in duration and modest in amount. Divorce lawyers and legal decision-makers view property division and alimony as a package, and might trade off some of one for the other as long as the cumulative result is appropriate. When calculating the value of the package, be aware that alimony is taxable to the recipient spouse, unlike property transfers.

Exercise 4-20. Understanding Equitable Distribution Statutes

1. Carefully read the Maryland and Montana statutes included below, and identify the property laws that apply at divorce, and which approach each state has for step one and three above.
2. As you read, note that the list of factors to determine what distribution is equitable breaks into three main categories: contribution to the marriage; financial resources or the lack of them; and, in some states, spousal misconduct or "fault."
3. Apply both statutes to the following fact situation and predict the legal outcomes. Maria was a successful lawyer for many years before she married Curtis. Just before the marriage, Maria owned a residence with no mortgage against it worth $300,000 and also had $200,000 saved in an account at First Bank in her sole name. During the marriage, the couple accumulated $250,000 of wealth from their earnings that is held in an account at Second Bank in Maria's sole name. Maria's residence also increased in value by $50,000 during the marriage.

Maryland Code, Family Law
[Marital property]

§ 8-201 Definitions

....

(e)(1) "Marital property" means the property, however titled, acquired by 1 or both parties during the marriage.

(2) "Marital property" includes any interest in real property held by the parties as tenants by the entirety unless the real property is excluded by valid agreement.

(3) Except as provided in paragraph (2) of this subsection, "marital property" does not include property:

(i) acquired before the marriage;

(ii) acquired by inheritance or gift from a third party;

(iii) excluded by valid agreement; or

(iv) directly traceable to any of these sources.

....

[Grant of award or transfer ownership of an interest in property]
§ 8-205. Marital property—Award

(a) Grant of award—

(1) Subject to the provisions of subsection (b) of this section, after the court determines which property is marital property, and the value of the marital property, the court may transfer ownership of an interest in property described in paragraph (2) of this subsection, grant a monetary award, or both, as an adjustment of the equities and rights of the parties concerning marital property, whether or not alimony is awarded.

[Required considerations]

(b) Factors in determining amount and method of payment or terms of transfer.—The court shall determine the amount and the method of payment of a monetary award, or the terms of the transfer of the interest in property described in subsection (a)(2) of this section, or both, after considering each of the following factors:

(1) the contributions, monetary and nonmonetary, of each party to the well-being of the family;

(2) the value of all property interests of each party;

(3) the economic circumstances of each party at the time the award is to be made;

(4) the circumstances that contributed to the estrangement of the parties;

(5) the duration of the marriage;

(6) the age of each party;

(7) the physical and mental condition of each party;

(8) how and when specific marital property or interest in property described in subsection (a)(2) of this section, was acquired, including the effort expended by each party in accumulating the marital property or the interest in property described in subsection (a)(2) of this section, or both;

(9) the contribution by either party of property described in § 8-201(e)(3) of this subtitle to the acquisition of real property held by the parties as tenants by the entirety;

(10) any award of alimony and any award or other provision that the court has made with respect to family use [of] personal property or the family home; and

(11) any other factor that the court considers necessary or appropriate to consider in order to arrive at a fair and equitable monetary award or transfer of an interest in property described in subsection (a)(2) of this section, or both.

....

Montana Code § 40-4-202

Division of property

(1) In a proceeding for dissolution of a marriage, legal separation, or division of property following a decree of dissolution of marriage or legal separation by a court

that lacked personal jurisdiction over the absent spouse or lacked jurisdiction to divide the property, the court, without regard to marital misconduct, shall, and in a proceeding for legal separation may, finally equitably apportion between the parties the property and assets belonging to either or both, however and whenever acquired and whether the title to the property and assets is in the name of the husband or wife or both.

....

Exercise 4-21. *Harper v. Harper*

The next case addresses the classification and division of property that is "hybrid" property, because the asset was acquired over a period of time, partly before marriage and partly during it. Be sure to work through the rules in this more complex situation. You will also discover some of the modern policy foundations for marital property law.

Harper v. Harper

448 A.2d 916 (Md. 1982)

DAVIDSON, J. This case presents two questions concerning the characterization and equitable distribution of certain property as marital property under Maryland Code §3–6A–01(e) of the Courts and Judicial Proceedings Article. More particularly, it initially presents the question whether real property, purchased under an installment contract and paid for in part before marriage and in part during marriage, is marital property. Additionally, it presents the question whether a marital residence constructed on that real property during marriage is marital property.

Section 3–6A–01(e) provides:

> "'Marital property' is *all property, however titled, acquired* by either or both spouses *during their marriage. It does not include property acquired prior to the marriage*, property acquired by inheritance or gift from a third party, or property excluded by valid agreement or *property directly traceable to any of these sources.*" (Emphasis added.)

In 1950 the petitioner, Sylvester E. Harper (husband), then unmarried, purchased an unimproved parcel of real property for a purchase price of approximately $355.00. The purchase was made under a land installment contract requiring a monthly payment of approximately $6.90. Before his marriage, the husband made all of the payments that came due.

On 3 November 1951, the husband married the respondent, Amaryllis M. Harper (wife). During the marriage, the husband continued to make all of the payments that came due until all of the requisite payments had been made.

In 1967 the husband personally built a house, costing approximately $21,600.00, upon the real property. That house was used by the parties as their marital residence. Although the wife's name appeared on the mortgage and she was legally obligated under it, the husband made all of the mortgage payments that came due on the marital residence. Additionally, the husband paid for all of the expenses associated with the upkeep and repair of the marital residence.

According to the wife, a substantial part of the payment on a previous house jointly owned by the parties was provided by her mother, and the proceeds of the sale of that house were used to finance the construction of the marital residence built in 1967. According to the husband's pleadings, he made all of the payments for the land, construction of the marital residence, and its upkeep. At all times, the property was titled solely in the husband's name.

At trial, there was evidence to show that there was an outstanding mortgage indebtedness of approximately $8,300.00 on the marital residence which was then appraised at a fair market value of approximately $65,500.00. There was no evidence to show the precise source and extent of the funds utilized during the marriage for payments for the land, construction of the marital residence, and its upkeep.

On 10 November 1980, a decree was entered granting the wife, among other things, an absolute divorce and a division of real property. More particularly, the trial court declared that the real property consisting of the lot with the marital residence upon it was marital property and ordered a sale in lieu of partition with each party receiving one-half of the proceeds of the sale. In reaching this result, the trial court said:

> In making a determination of ownership of real property under the applicable statutes upon granting a decree of divorce, the Court is guided by several factors including the contributions, both monetary and nonmonetary, made by each party to the well-being of the family; the value of the property interests of each spouse; the circumstances contributing to the estrangement of the parties; the duration of the marriage; the age and physical condition of the parties; and how and when the specific marital property was acquired. In this case, it is true that the Respondent provided the bulk of financial contributions toward acquiring the real property in question, however, the Complainant, as a wife and mother of some twenty-nine (29) years, made substantial nonmonetary contributions toward the marriage and the family during the time the said real property was acquired. Furthermore, this Court notes that the estrangement of the parties stemmed from the Respondent's cruel and abusive conduct toward the Complainant resulting in a divorce a mensa for constructive desertion. The length of the marriage in this case is considerable, spanning twenty-nine years of the parties' lives. The Court has also weighed the other factors mentioned above and concludes that the real property in question is marital property in which each spouse is entitled to a one-half share. For this reason the Court shall order a sale in lieu of partition of the said real property with an equitable distribution of the proceeds as prayed for by the Complainant.

The husband appealed to the Court of Special Appeals. In determining that the real property and marital residence were marital property, the Court of Special Appeals said:

> The thrust of appellant's argument on this issue is that since he acquired the lot, upon which the house was built, before the marriage, and since the house constituted a permanent improvement thereto, both the house and lot do not meet the statutory definition of marital property and thus the chancellor erred in concluding that this property was marital property. We disagree.
>
> With respect to the lot, while Mr. Harper had equitable title thereto prior to the marriage, ... it is clear that he acquired legal title after the marriage. It would appear, in fact, that since the marriage took place within a year of his execution of the land installment contract, the bulk of payment thereon took place after the marriage. In our view the lot was acquired during the marriage....
>
> With respect to the house built on the lot, after the parties had been married some sixteen years, it constituted a permanent improvement upon the lot; in fact, title in Mr. Harper's name was never changed although the parties talked about making that change. Having concluded the chancellor was correct in finding the lot to be marital property, it necessarily follows that the house erected thereon after the marriage of the parties would likewise, under the facts present here, be marital property. Indeed, not to conclude thusly would frustrate the very purpose of the marital property distribution act....

Harper, 431 A.2d at 764.

The husband filed a petition for a writ of certiorari that we granted. We shall reverse in part the judgment of the Court of Special Appeals.

Maryland's Property Disposition in Divorce and Annulment Act (Act) represents "a new legislative approach to the concept of marriage." [Citation omitted.] The Act was proposed by The Governor's Commission on Domestic Relations Laws which stated in its report to the Governor:

> *The Commission does not believe that the people of Maryland today hold the view that a spouse whose activities within the marriage do not include the production of income has 'never contributed anything toward the purchase of' property acquired by either or both spouses during the marriage.* Its members believe that non-monetary contributions within a marriage are real and should be recognized in the event that the marriage is dissolved or annulled. As homemaker and parent and housewife and handyman (of either sex), as a man and a woman having equal rights under the law united into one family unit, in which each owes a duty to contribute his or her best efforts to the marriage, the undertakings of each are for the benefit of the family unit. In most cases, each spouse makes a contribution entitled to recognition, even though the standards or methods of quantifying a spouse's non-monetary contribution are inexact.

Report of The Governor's Comm'n on Domestic Relations Laws, at 3 (1978) (emphasis added).

The Commission recognized that the marital residence is ordinarily the major asset of a marriage when it said:

> Experience shows that in the great majority of cases where property of any significance is involved, it consists of the family home, its contents, and one or more automobiles. It is an unusual case in which other investments of consequence are involved. A divorce law should be utilitarian—it should do the most good for the most people. Consequently, it is mainly the needs of the average person that must be addressed and satisfied.

Report of The Governor's Comm'n on Domestic Relations Laws, at 4 (1978).

Thus, the Commission expressly indicated that one of the remedial purposes of the proposed Act was to protect the interests of spouses who had made nonmonetary contributions to the marital residence. The proposed Act was designed to achieve this remedial purpose by "end[ing] the inequity inherent in Maryland's old 'title' system of dealing with the marital property of divorcing spouses." [Citation omitted.] The proposed Act established "the concept of 'marital property' as being all that property which was acquired by the parties during their marriage" and gave the court the power to "recognize non-monetary as well as monetary contributions of the parties to the marriage" in determining the value of and making an equitable distribution of the marital property.

[The court adopted the reasoning below from another jurisdiction.]

> The partnership theory, upon which the law of community property and this provision of the Uniform Marriage and Divorce Act is based, requires that the marital estate be entitled to a proportionate share in the value of property where its equity interest was partially acquired by marital funds. Where the marital estate chooses to invest its funds in certain property together with non-marital funds, the marital estate is entitled to a proportionate return on its investment.

(Citations omitted.)

We conclude that under the Maryland Act the appropriate analysis to be applied is the source of funds theory. Under that theory, when property is acquired by an expenditure of both nonmarital and marital property, the property is characterized as part nonmarital and part marital. Thus, a spouse contributing nonmarital property is entitled to an interest in the property in the ratio of the nonmarital investment to the total nonmarital and marital investment in the property. The remaining property is characterized as marital property and its value is subject to equitable distribution. Thus, the spouse who contributed nonmarital funds, and the marital unit that contributed marital funds each receive a proportionate and fair return on their investment.

We recognize that in order to apply the source of funds theory in Maryland, it is necessary to adopt ... an interpretation that defines the term "acquired," appearing in §3-6A-01(e), as the on-going process of making payment for property. Under this definition, characterization of property as nonmarital or marital depends upon the source of each contribution as payments are made, rather than the time at which legal or equitable title to or possession of the property is obtained.

Applying these principles to the instant case produces the following result. Ordinarily, under the three-step process provided by the Maryland Act, when real property is purchased and paid for in part before marriage and in part during marriage with nonmarital and marital funds, the property is nonmarital in part and marital in part. Additionally, ordinarily, when a marital residence is constructed upon that real property during marriage by the expenditure of nonmarital and marital property, the marital residence is nonmarital in part and marital in part. The property and the marital residence are nonmarital in the ratio that the nonmarital investment in the property and the residence bears to the total nonmarital and marital investment in the property and the residence. To the extent that the property and the residence are nonmarital, their value is not subject to equitable distribution. Similarly, the property and the marital residence are marital in the ratio that the marital investment in the property and the residence bears to the total nonmarital and marital investment in the property. To the extent that the property and the residence are marital, their value is subject to equitable distribution. When making an equitable distribution of the value of the marital property, the contributions, monetary and nonmonetary of each spouse, the value of thc property interests of each spouse, and the effort expended by each spouse in accumulating the marital property, among other things, shall be considered.

Exercise 4-22. *Harper* Revisited

1. Be sure you understand the main rule adopted by the court. Applying this, how would you characterize the equity in a house that was purchased before marriage, with the mortgage having been paid by the titled owner alone up to the date of marriage, and then paid during the marriage from a joint bank account into which both spouses funneled their earnings from employment?
2. How would you articulate to your client the rationale for why some property will be shared at divorce, and some property will be excluded?
3. If you represented Amaryllis and she was able to prove that she indeed contributed to the purchase of the marital residence with money that came from her mother, what argument would you make on her behalf in a dual classification state like Maryland?
4. In many divorces, at least one spouse is unrepresented. If you represent a client whose soon to be ex-spouse does not have an attorney and is not familiar with the laws of divorce, who offers to settle the case to his great disadvantage and contrary to the settled law in the area, what should or would you do?

More broadly, given that in many divorces one or both spouses are unrepresented ("*pro se*"), think about how the legal system might deal more effectively with the lack of information and legal expertise that lay people struggle with as they go through a difficult and often complicated process. What resources does your local or state court system have to address this phenomenon?

Exercise 4-23. *O'Brien v. O'Brien*

1. The next topic might be of particular interest to you. You will grapple with the following questions. Does a professional degree such as a law or medical degree earned during marriage qualify as property? If so, should it be considered, at least to some extent, a jointly acquired economic resource? If not, then should some other remedy be available for the spouse who did not earn the degree (the "supportive spouse")? What is fair? Do the rules and outcomes help or hurt the cause of equality between the sexes?
2. *O'Brien* reflects a minority view. Most states that have addressed the issue reach the opposite conclusions. A frequently cited case that describes the reasoning for this approach is *In re Marriage of Graham*, 574 P.2d 75 (Colo. 1978). As you read and evaluate the issues, develop a list of arguments for and against the view that enhanced earning power from a degree should be considered property that is sharable at divorce. Think about how you can incorporate the lessons of *Harper* into your analysis.

O'Brien v. O'Brien

489 N.E.2d 712 (N.Y. 1985)

Simons, J. In this divorce action, the parties' only asset of any consequence is the husband's newly acquired license to practice medicine. The principal issue presented is whether that license, acquired during their marriage, is marital property subject to equitable distribution under Domestic Relations Law § 236(B)(5). We now hold that plaintiff's medical license constitutes "marital property" within the meaning of Domestic Relations Law § 236(B)(1)(c) and that it is therefore subject to equitable distribution pursuant to subdivision 5 of that part.

Plaintiff and defendant married on April 3, 1971. At the time both were employed as teachers at the same private school. Defendant had a bachelor's degree and a temporary teaching certificate but required 18 months of postgraduate classes at an approximate cost of $3,000, excluding living expenses, to obtain permanent certification in New

York. She claimed, and the trial court found, that she had relinquished the opportunity to obtain permanent certification while plaintiff pursued his education. At the time of the marriage, plaintiff had completed only three and one-half years of college but shortly afterward he returned to school at night to earn his bachelor's degree and to complete sufficient premedical courses to enter medical school. In September 1973 the parties moved to Guadalajara, Mexico, where plaintiff became a full-time medical student. While he pursued his studies defendant held several teaching and tutorial positions and contributed her earnings to their joint expenses. The parties returned to New York in December 1976 so that plaintiff could complete the last two semesters of medical school and internship training here. After they returned, defendant resumed her former teaching position and she remained in it at the time this action was commenced. Plaintiff was licensed to practice medicine in October 1980. He commenced this action for divorce two months later. At the time of trial, he was a resident in general surgery.

During the marriage both parties contributed to paying the living and educational expenses and they received additional help from both of their families. They disagreed on the amounts of their respective contributions but it is undisputed that in addition to performing household work and managing the family finances defendant was gainfully employed throughout the marriage, that she contributed all of her earnings to their living and educational expenses and that her financial contributions exceeded those of plaintiff. The trial court found that she had contributed 76% of the parties' income exclusive of a $10,000 student loan obtained by defendant. Finding that plaintiff's medical degree and license are marital property, the court received evidence of its value and ordered a distributive award to defendant.

Defendant presented expert testimony that the present value of plaintiff's medical license was $472,000. Her expert testified that he arrived at this figure by comparing the average income of a college graduate and that of a general surgeon between 1985, when plaintiff's residency would end, and 2012, when he would reach age 65. After considering Federal income taxes, an inflation rate of 10% and a real interest rate of 3% he capitalized the difference in average earnings and reduced the amount to present value. He also gave his opinion that the present value of defendant's contribution to plaintiff's medical education was $103,390. Plaintiff offered no expert testimony on the subject.

The court, after considering the life-style that plaintiff would enjoy from the enhanced earning potential his medical license would bring and defendant's contributions and efforts toward attainment of it, made a distributive award to her of $188,800, representing 40% of the value of the license, and ordered it paid in 11 annual installments of various amounts beginning November 1, 1982 and ending November 1, 1992. The court also directed plaintiff to maintain a life insurance policy on his life for defendant's benefit for the unpaid balance of the award and it ordered plaintiff to pay defendant's counsel fees of $7,000 and her expert witness fee of $1,000. It did not award defendant maintenance.

A divided Appellate Division concluded that a professional license acquired during marriage is not marital property subject to distribution. It therefore modified the judgment by striking the trial court's determination that it is and by striking the provision ordering payment of the expert witness for evaluating the license and remitted the case for further proceedings. On these cross appeals, defendant seeks reinstatement of the judgment of the trial court.

The Equitable Distribution Law contemplates only two classes of property: marital property and separate property. The former, which is subject to equitable distribution, is defined broadly as "*all* property acquired by either or both spouses during the marriage and before the execution of a separation agreement or the commencement of a matrimonial action, *regardless of the form in which title is held*" (citation omitted). Plaintiff does not contend that his license is excluded from distribution because it is separate property; rather, he claims that it is not property at all but represents a personal attainment in acquiring knowledge. He rests his argument on decisions in similar cases from other jurisdictions and on his view that a license does not satisfy common-law concepts of property. Neither contention is controlling because decisions in other States rely principally on their own statutes, and the legislative history underlying them, and because the New York Legislature deliberately went beyond traditional property concepts when it formulated the Equitable Distribution Law Instead, our statute recognizes that spouses have an equitable claim to things of value arising out of the marital relationship and classifies them as subject to distribution by focusing on the marital status of the parties at the time of acquisition. Those things acquired during marriage and subject to distribution have been classified as "marital property" although, as one commentator has observed, they hardly fall within the traditional property concepts because there is no common-law property interest remotely resembling marital property. "It is a statutory creature, is of no meaning whatsoever during the normal course of a marriage and arises full-grown, like Athena, upon the signing of a separation agreement or the commencement of a matrimonial action. [Thus] [i]t is hardly surprising, and not at all relevant, that traditional common law property concepts do not fit in parsing the meaning of 'marital property'" [Citation omitted.] Having classified the "property" subject to distribution, the Legislature did not attempt to go further and define it but left it to the courts to determine.

Section 236 provides that in making an equitable distribution of marital property, "the court shall consider: (6) any equitable claim to, interest in, or direct or indirect contribution made to the acquisition of such marital property by the party not having title, including joint efforts or expenditures and contributions and services as a spouse, parent, wage earner and homemaker, and *to the career or career potential* of the other party." The words mean exactly what they say: that an interest in a profession or professional career potential is marital property which may be represented by direct or indirect contributions of the non-title-holding spouse, including financial contributions and nonfinancial contributions made by caring for the home and family.

Equitable distribution was based on the premise that a marriage is, among other things, an economic partnership to which both parties contribute as spouse, parent, wage earner or homemaker. Consistent with this purpose, and implicit in the statutory scheme as a whole, is the view that upon dissolution of the marriage there should be a winding up of the parties' economic affairs and a severance of their economic ties by an equitable distribution of the marital assets. Thus, the concept of alimony, which often served as a means of lifetime support and dependence for one spouse upon the other long after the marriage was over, was replaced with the concept of maintenance which seeks to allow "the recipient spouse an opportunity to achieve [economic] independence" (Assembly Memorandum, 1980 N.Y.Legis.Ann., at 130).

The determination that a professional license is marital property is also consistent with the conceptual base upon which the statute rests. As this case demonstrates, few undertakings during a marriage better qualify as the type of joint effort that the statute's economic partnership theory is intended to address than contributions toward one spouse's acquisition of a professional license. Working spouses are often required to contribute substantial income as wage earners, sacrifice their own educational or career goals and opportunities for child rearing, perform the bulk of household duties and responsibilities and forego the acquisition of marital assets that could have been accumulated if the professional spouse had been employed rather than occupied with the study and training necessary to acquire a professional license. In this case, nearly all of the parties' nine-year marriage was devoted to the acquisition of plaintiff's medical license and defendant played a major role in that project. She worked continuously during the marriage and contributed all of her earnings to their joint effort, she sacrificed her own educational and career opportunities, and she traveled with plaintiff to Mexico for three and one-half years while he attended medical school there. The Legislature has decided, by its explicit reference in the statute to the contributions of one spouse to the other's profession or career, that these contributions represent investments in the economic partnership of the marriage and that the product of the parties' joint efforts, the professional license, should be considered marital property.

Plaintiff's principal argument, adopted by the majority below, is that a professional license is not marital property because it does not fit within the traditional view of property as something which has an exchange value on the open market and is capable of sale, assignment or transfer. The position does not withstand analysis for at least two reasons. First, as we have observed, it ignores the fact that whether a professional license constitutes marital property is to be judged by the language of the statute which created this new species of property previously unknown at common law or under prior statutes. Thus, whether the license fits within traditional property concepts is of no consequence. Second, it is an overstatement to assert that a professional license could not be considered property even outside the context of section 236(B). A professional license is a valuable property right, reflected in the money, effort and lost opportunity for employment expended in its acquisition, and also in the enhanced earning capacity it affords its holder, which may not be revoked without due process of law. That a professional license has no market value is irrelevant. Obviously, a license may not be alienated as may other property and for that reason the working spouse's interest in it is limited. The Legislature has recognized that limitation, however, and has provided for an award in lieu of its actual distribution.

Plaintiff also contends that alternative remedies should be employed, such as an award of rehabilitative maintenance or reimbursement for direct financial contributions. The statute does not expressly authorize retrospective maintenance or rehabilitative awards and we have no occasion to decide in this case whether the authority to do so may ever be implied from its provisions. It is sufficient to observe that normally a working spouse should not be restricted to that relief because to do so frustrates the purposes underlying the Equitable Distribution Law. Limiting a working spouse to a maintenance award, either general or rehabilitative, not only is contrary to the economic partnership concept underlying the statute but also retains the uncertain and inequitable economic ties of dependence that the Legislature sought to extinguish by equitable distribution. Maintenance is subject to termination upon the recipient's remarriage and a working spouse may never receive adequate consideration for his or her contribution and may even be penalized for the decision to remarry if that is the only method of compensating the contribution. As one court said so well, "[t]he function of equitable distribution is to recognize that when a marriage ends, each of the spouses, based on the totality of the contributions made to it, has a stake in and right to a share of the marital assets accumulated while it endured, not because that share is needed, but because those assets represent the capital product of what was essentially a partnership entity" (citation omitted). The Legislature stated its intention to eliminate such inequities by providing that a supporting spouse's "direct or indirect contribution" be recognized, considered and rewarded.

Turning to the question of valuation, it has been suggested that even if a professional license is considered marital property, the working spouse is entitled only to reimbursement of his or her direct financial contributions. By parity of reasoning, a spouse's down payment on real estate or contribution to the purchase of securities would be limited to the money contributed, without any remuneration for any incremental value in the asset because of price appreciation. Such a result is completely at odds with the statute's requirement that the court give full consideration to both direct and indirect contributions. If the license is marital property, then the working spouse is entitled to an equitable portion of it, not a return of funds advanced. Its value is the enhanced earning capacity it affords the holder and although fixing the present value of that enhanced earning capacity may present problems, the problems are not insurmountable. Certainly they are no more difficult than computing tort damages for wrongful death or diminished earning capacity resulting from injury and they differ only in degree from the problems presented when valuing a professional practice for purposes of a distributive award, something the courts have not hesitated to do. The trial court retains the flexibility and discretion to structure the distributive award equitably.

Accordingly, in view of our holding that plaintiff's license to practice medicine is marital property, the order of the Appellate Division should be modified, with costs to defendant, by reinstating the judgment and the case remitted to the Appellate Division for determination of the facts, including the exercise of that court's discretion, and, as so modified, affirmed. Question certified answered in the negative.

MEYER, J., concurring. I concur in Judge Simons' opinion but write separately to point up for consideration by the Legislature the potential for unfairness involved in distributive awards based upon a license of a professional still in training.

[A property award] once made, is not subject to change. Yet a professional in training who is not finally committed to a career choice when the distributive award is made may be locked into a particular kind of practice simply because the monetary obligations imposed by the distributive award made on the basis of the trial judge's conclusion (prophecy may be a better word) as to what the career choice will be leaves him or her no alternative.

The present case points up the problem. A medical license is but a step toward the practice ultimately engaged in by its holder, which follows after internship, residency and, for particular specialties, board certification. Here it is undisputed that plaintiff was in a residency for general surgery at the time of the trial, but had the previous year done a residency in internal medicine. Defendant's expert based his opinion on the difference between the average income of a general surgeon and that of a college graduate of plaintiff's age and life expectancy, which the trial judge utilized, impliedly finding that plaintiff would engage in a surgical practice despite plaintiff's testimony that he was dissatisfied with the general surgery program he was in and was attempting to return to the internal medicine training he had been in the previous year. The trial judge had the right, of course, to discredit that testimony, but the point is that equitable distribution was not intended to permit a judge to make a career decision for a licensed spouse still in training. Yet the degree of speculation involved in the award made is emphasized by the testimony of the expert on which it was based. Asked whether his assumptions and calculations were in any way speculative, he replied: "Yes. They're speculative to the extent of, will Dr. O'Brien practice medicine? Will Dr. O'Brien earn more or less than the average surgeon earns? Will Dr. O'Brien live to age sixty-five? Will Dr. O'Brien have a heart attack or will he be injured in an automobile accident? Will he be disabled? I mean, there is a degree of speculation. That speculative aspect is no more to be taken into account, cannot be taken into account, and it's a question, again, Mr. Emanuelli, not for the expert but for the courts to decide. It's not my function nor could it be."

The equitable distribution provisions of the Domestic Relations Law were intended to provide flexibility so that equity could be done. But if the assumption as to career choice on which a distributive award payable over a number of years is based turns out not to be the fact (as, for example, should a general surgery trainee accidentally lose the use of his hand), it should be possible for the court to revise the distributive award to conform to the fact. And there will be no unfairness in so doing if either spouse can seek reconsideration, for the licensed spouse is more likely to seek reconsideration based on real, rather than imagined, cause if he or she knows that the nonlicensed spouse can seek not only reinstatement of the original award, but counsel fees in addition, should the purported circumstance on which a change is made turn out to have been feigned or to be illusory.

Exercise 4-24. *O'Brien* Revisited and Alternative Remedies

1. What did the court mean by saying marital property "arises full-grown, like Athena" once a divorce action has begun? It will help to recall from the discussion earlier that at divorce, separate property states convert to a marital property system.
2. Be prepared to argue for and against the reasoning in *O'Brien*. Why do you think a majority of states do not classify a degree as property?
3. Dr. O'Brien did not make the argument that the enhanced earnings from his degree are separate property. What arguments support a separate property claim to at least some of the earnings stream? Is going to professional school the main or only contribution to the value produced by having a degree? Did the lawyers make a mistake by neglecting this set of claims?
4. The concurring opinion critiques the assignment of a fixed value for the degree. A similar concern would arise if a law degree was treated as a marital asset and then the lawyer becomes a poet. As is true with many estimates of value, the assumptions underlying the estimate might not prove to be accurate. Part of the concern is that property division at divorce is a final judgment that is non-modifiable. In contrast, alimony is modifiable based on a change in circumstances. Can you think of a way to address the risk that the value assigned to the degree is too high, or too low?
5. *Alternative Approaches.* As explained, a majority of states disagree with *O'Brien* and reject the notion that a degree is a form of marital property. However, legal opinions in such states often do recognize that this result can be unfair, and suggest alternative remedies instead. The supporting spouse could claim a larger share of the marital property or ask for alimony. Yet these alternatives are often illusory. How much other property do you think a couple or family has after years of investing in education and training to earn a professional degree? Also, a supportive spouse may well be ineligible for maintenance (alimony). Recall that to be awarded alimony, the claimant must prove financial need, measured by the standard of living during the marriage (e.g., how much money does a typical law student have while in school?) and the inability to provide for herself through reasonable employment. Another factor is the other spouse's ability to pay. This is a difficult claim to make out, because in many cases of this type, the supportive spouse was the one who was employed and produced the earnings for the frugal lifestyle of the family. Also, as pointed out in *O'Brien*, alimony terminates if the recipient spouse remarries.

   To address these problems, some states have adopted a special form of relief such as "reimbursement alimony" that allows alimony to be paid (usually a fixed amount for a finite period of time) as a form of compensation for the contributions of the supportive spouse. Such a claim is frequently limited to reimbursement for direct financial contributions (such as tuition payments) only.

Analyze and predict the outcomes in *O'Brien* if the alternative approaches are applied.

Cohabitants and Other Family-Type Relationships

In the recent past, living with an unmarried partner was stigmatizing and, in many states, a crime. The practice of cohabitation and social acceptance of it have changed dramatically. Cohabitation is the new normal—for many as a testing ground and step toward marriage and for others as an alternative. Rates of cohabitation have grown exponentially, rising to about 7 million households in 2014, up from less than a million in the 1970s. There has also been a significant increase in non-marital childbearing, that often and increasingly occurs within unmarried couple unions.

There is a lot of variety among cohabitant groups and couples, including same sex and opposite sex couples. As one author of this text explains:

> Another aspect of this heterogeneity is that there are some sub-group differences associated with socio-economic class, race, and ethnicity. In particular, "[c]ohabitation remains more common among those with less education and for whom economic resources are more constrained." Cohabitation is significantly more common among African Americans and Hispanics than non-Hispanic Whites....
>
> [In terms of economic behavior,] there is a small subset of cohabitants who have a joint economy just as married couples overwhelmingly do, but there is also a large cohort who do not. As a group, unmarried partners are far more likely to keep their finances separate, to make economic decisions individually, and to calculate and account for expenses based on a fifty-fifty split. The exception is when unmarried couples live together raising their biological child(ren). In such relationships, a financial merger is evident just as it is with married couples. In terms of gendered labor specialization, it surely exists among cohabitants, but is less pronounced than among spouses.

Alicia Brokars Kelly, *Navigating Gender in Modern Intimate Partnership Law*, 14 J. L. & Fam. Stud. 1, 21, 25 (2012) (citations omitted).

The legal system remains in the process of debating and developing policy foundations and laws that appropriately regulate and respond to cohabitation. There are many open questions. Should unmarried couples be treated like married couples—or differently? Should there be uniform standards that can be applied to all unmarried couples? Or is a case by case analysis that is sensitive to factual variation best?

The materials in this section focus on two differing approaches in state laws when an unmarried couple breaks up. The majority of states merely recognize that cohabitants may make claims that are generally available to anyone in civil law. Specifically, claims for breach of contract (express and implied-in-fact), property claims such as partition for co-owners and a claim in equity for unjust enrichment are widely recognized. Beyond this, a small number of states recognize claims based on the nature of the relationship itself, and tend to treat unmarried couples like married couples. As long as the relationship is deemed sufficient, divorce-style property division may be ordered.

Another issue that has gotten less attention is how the law should regulate other family or family-type relationships. Such personal relationships can also include economic connections. Consider, for example, multi-generational relationships where caregiving, economic exchanges, sacrifices and gift giving all occur, and other non-sexual relationships such as between siblings and friends. As you read this section, think about whether contract law and equitable claims are a good fit for not only cohabitants, but for other family-type relationships, or whether there should be different or special rules for these various situations.

Exercise 4-25. *Watts v. Watts*

You will learn from this case the claims that are generally recognized between unmarried couples who live together, as well as some of the deliberations on policy issues. Look for at least four claims that a cohabitant might make.

Watts v. Watts

405 N.W.2d 303 (Wis. 1987)

Abrahamson, J. The case involves a dispute between Sue Ann Evans Watts, the plaintiff, and James Watts, the defendant, over their respective interests in property accumulated during their nonmarital cohabitation relationship which spanned 12 years and produced two children. The case presents an issue of first impression and comes to this court at the pleading stage of the case, before trial and before the facts have been determined.

The plaintiff commenced this action in 1982. The plaintiff's amended complaint alleges the following facts, which for purposes of this appeal must be accepted as true. The plaintiff and the defendant met in 1967, when she was 19 years old, was living with her parents and was working full time as a nurse's aide in preparation for a nursing career. Shortly after the parties met, the defendant persuaded the plaintiff to move into an apartment paid for by him and to quit her job. According to the amended complaint, the defendant "indicated" to the plaintiff that he would provide for her.

Early in 1969, the parties began living together in a "marriage-like" relationship, holding themselves out to the public as husband and wife. The plaintiff assumed the defendant's surname as her own. Subsequently, she gave birth to two children who were also given the defendant's surname. The parties filed joint income tax returns and maintained joint bank accounts asserting that they were husband and wife. The defendant insured the plaintiff as his wife on his medical insurance policy. He also took out a life insurance policy on her as his wife, naming himself as the beneficiary. The parties purchased real and personal property as husband and wife. The plaintiff executed documents and obligated herself on promissory notes to lending institutions as the defendant's wife.

During their relationship, the plaintiff contributed childcare and homemaking services, including cleaning, cooking, laundering, shopping, running errands, and maintaining the grounds surrounding the parties' home. Additionally, the plaintiff contributed personal property to the relationship which she owned at the beginning of the relationship or acquired through gifts or purchases during the relationship. She served as hostess for the defendant for social and business-related events. The amended complaint further asserts that periodically, between 1969 and 1975, the plaintiff cooked and cleaned for the defendant and his employees while his business, a landscaping service, was building and landscaping a golf course.

From 1973 to 1976, the plaintiff worked 20–25 hours per week at the defendant's office, performing duties as a receptionist, typist, and assistant bookkeeper. From 1976 to 1981, the plaintiff worked 40–60 hours per week at a business she started with the defendant's sister-in-law, then continued and managed the business herself after the dissolution of that partnership. The plaintiff further alleges that in 1981 the defendant made their relationship so intolerable that she was forced to move from their home and their relationship was irretrievably broken. Subsequently, the defendant barred the plaintiff from returning to her business.

The plaintiff alleges that during the parties' relationship, and because of her domestic and business contributions, the business and personal wealth of the couple increased. Furthermore, the plaintiff alleges that she never received any compensation for these contributions to the relationship and that the defendant indicated to the plaintiff both orally and through his conduct that he considered her to be his wife and that she would share equally in the increased wealth.

The plaintiff asserts that since the breakdown of the relationship the defendant has refused to share equally with her the wealth accumulated through their joint efforts or to compensate her in any way for her contributions to the relationship.

The plaintiff's first legal theory to support her claim against the property accumulated during the cohabitation is that the plaintiff, defendant, and their children constitute a "family," thus entitling the plaintiff to bring an action for property division [as if they were married].

On the basis of our analysis of sec. 767.255 and the Family Code which revealed no clear evidence that the legislature intended sec. 767.255 to apply to unmarried persons, we decline the invitation to extend the application of sec. 767.255 to unmarried cohabitants. We therefore hold that the plaintiff has not stated a claim for property division under sec. 767.255.

The plaintiff urges that the defendant, as a result of his own words and conduct, be estopped from asserting the lack of a legal marriage as a defense against the plaintiff's claim for property division under sec. 767.255. We do not think the parties' conduct should place them within the ambit of a statute which the legislature did not intend to govern them.

The plaintiff's third legal theory on which her claim rests is that she and the defendant had a contract to share equally the property accumulated during their relationship. The essence of the complaint is that the parties had a contract, either an express or implied in fact contract, which the defendant breached.

Wisconsin courts have long recognized the importance of freedom of contract and have endeavored to protect the right to contract. A contract will not be enforced, however, if it violates public policy. A declaration that the contract is against public policy should be made only after a careful balancing, in the light of all the circumstances, of the interest in enforcing a particular promise against the policy against enforcement.

The defendant appears to attack the plaintiff's contract theory on three grounds. First, the defendant apparently asserts that the court's recognition of plaintiff's contract claim for a share of the parties' property contravenes the Wisconsin Family Code. Second, the defendant asserts that the legislature, not the courts, should determine the property and contract rights of unmarried cohabiting parties. Third, the defendant intimates that the parties' relationship was immoral and illegal and that any recognition of a contract between the parties or plaintiff's claim for a share of the property accumulated during the cohabitation contravenes public policy.

The defendant rests his argument that judicial recognition of a contract between unmarried cohabitants for property division violates the Wisconsin Family Code on *Hewitt v. Hewitt,* 394 N.E.2d 1204 (1979). In *Hewitt* the Illinois Supreme Court concluded that judicial recognition of mutual property rights between unmarried cohabitants would violate the policy of the Illinois Marriage and Dissolution Act because enhancing the attractiveness of a private arrangement contravenes the Act's policy of strengthening and preserving the integrity of marriage. The Illinois court concluded that allowing such a contract claim would weaken the sanctity of marriage, put in doubt the rights of inheritance, and open the door to false pretenses of marriage.

[T]he *Hewitt* court made an unsupportable inferential leap when it found that cohabitation agreements run contrary to statutory policy and that the *Hewitt* court's approach is patently inconsistent with the principle that public policy limits are to be narrowly and exactly applied. We find no indication, however, that the Wisconsin legislature intended the Family Code to restrict in any way a court's resolution of property or contract disputes between unmarried cohabitants.

We turn to the defendant's third point, namely, that any contract between the parties regarding property division contravenes public policy because the contract is based on immoral or illegal sexual activity. Courts have generally refused to enforce contracts for which the sole consideration is sexual relations, sometimes referred to as "meretricious" relationships. While not condoning the illicit sexual relationship of the parties, many courts have recognized that the result of a court's refusal to enforce contract and property rights between unmarried cohabitants is that one party keeps all or most of the assets accumulated during the relationship, while the other party, no more or less "guilty," is deprived of property which he or she has helped to accumulate.

The plaintiff has alleged that she quit her job and abandoned her career training upon the defendant's promise to take care of her. A change in one party's circumstances in performance of the agreement may imply an agreement between the parties. In addition, the plaintiff alleges that she performed housekeeping, childbearing, childrearing, and other services related to the maintenance of the parties' home, in addition to various services for the defendant's business and her own business, for which she received no compensation. Courts have recognized that money, property, or services (including housekeeping or childrearing) may constitute adequate consideration independent of the parties' sexual relationship to support an agreement to share or transfer property.

According to the plaintiff's complaint, the parties cohabited for more than twelve years, held joint bank accounts, made joint purchases, filed joint income tax returns, and were listed as husband and wife on other legal documents. The joint ownership of property and the filing of joint income tax returns strongly implies that the parties intended their relationship to be in the nature of a joint enterprise, financially as well as personally.

Having reviewed the complaint and surveyed the law in this and other jurisdictions, we hold that the Family Code does not preclude an unmarried cohabitant from asserting contract and property claims against the other party to the cohabitation. We further conclude that public policy does not necessarily preclude an unmarried cohabitant from asserting a contract claim against the other party to the cohabitation so long as the claim exists independently of the sexual relationship and is supported by separate consideration. Accordingly, we conclude that the plaintiff in this case has pleaded the facts necessary to state a claim for damages resulting from the defendant's breach of an express or an implied in fact contract to share with the plaintiff the property accumulated through the efforts of both parties during their relationship. Once again, we do not judge the merits of the plaintiff's claim; we merely hold that she be given her day in court to prove her claim.

The plaintiff's fourth theory of recovery involves unjust enrichment. Essentially, she alleges that the defendant accepted and retained the benefit of services she provided knowing that she expected to share equally in the wealth accumulated during their relationship. She argues that it is unfair for the defendant to retain all the assets they accumulated under these circumstances and that a constructive trust should be imposed on the property as a result of the defendant's unjust enrichment.

Unlike claims for breach of an express or implied in fact contract, a claim of unjust enrichment does not arise out of an agreement entered into by the parties. Rather, an action for recovery based upon unjust enrichment is grounded on the moral principle that one who has received a benefit has a duty to make restitution where retaining such a benefit would be unjust. Because no express or implied in fact agreement exists between the parties, recovery based upon unjust enrichment is sometimes referred to as "quasi contract," or contract "implied in law" rather than "implied in fact."

In Wisconsin, an action for unjust enrichment, or quasi contract, is based upon proof of three elements: (1) a benefit conferred on the defendant by the plaintiff, (2) appreciation or knowledge by the defendant of the benefit, and (3) acceptance or retention of the benefit by the defendant under circumstances making it inequitable for the defendant to retain the benefit.

Many courts have held, and we now so hold, that unmarried cohabitants may raise claims based upon unjust enrichment following the termination of their relationships where one of the parties attempts to retain an unreasonable amount of the property acquired through the efforts of both.

In this case, the plaintiff alleges that she contributed both property and services to the parties' relationship. She claims that because of these contributions the parties' assets increased, but that she was never compensated for her contributions. She further alleges that the defendant, knowing that the plaintiff expected to share in the property accumulated, "accepted the services rendered to him by the plaintiff" and that it would be unfair under the circumstances to allow him to retain everything while she receives nothing. We conclude that the facts alleged are sufficient to state a claim for recovery based upon unjust enrichment.

As part of the plaintiff's unjust enrichment claim, she has asked that a constructive trust be imposed on the assets that the defendant acquired during their relationship. A constructive trust is an equitable device created by law to prevent unjust enrichment. [W]e hold that if the plaintiff can prove the elements of unjust enrichment to the satisfaction of the circuit court, she will be entitled to demonstrate further that a constructive trust should be imposed as a remedy.

The plaintiff's last alternative legal theory on which her claim rests is the doctrine of partition. The plaintiff has asserted in her complaint a claim for partition of "all real and personal property accumulated by the couple during their relationship according to the plaintiff's interest therein."

Chapter 820, Stats. 1985–86, provides for partition of personal property. Sec. 820.01 states in part: "When any of the owners of personal property in common shall desire to have a division and they are unable to agree upon the same an action may be commenced for that purpose." Sec. 820.01 thus states on its face that anyone owning property "in common" with someone else can maintain an action for partition of personal property held by the parties.

In this case, the plaintiff has alleged that she and the defendant were engaged in a joint venture or partnership, that they purchased real and personal property as husband

and wife, and that they intended to share all the property acquired during their relationship. In our opinion, these allegations, together with other facts alleged in the plaintiff's complaint (*e.g.*, the plaintiff's contributions to the acquisition of their property) and reasonable inferences therefrom, are sufficient under Wisconsin's liberal notice pleading rule to state a claim for an accounting of the property acquired during the parties' relationship and partition. We do not, of course, presume to judge the merits of the plaintiff's claim. Proof of her allegations must be made to the circuit court. We merely hold that the plaintiff has alleged sufficient facts in her complaint to state a claim for relief statutory or common law partition.

Exercise 4-26. *Watts* Revisited and Alternative Approaches

1. *Watts* represents the law of most states. Notice that marital property rules do not apply. There is no automatic legal relationship between the parties. Instead, the default rules for unmarried couples (and for other family-type relationships as well) assume separate finances—earnings are individually owned and title governs. However, a partner can attempt to prove otherwise by bringing forward a claim as recognized in *Watts*. Be prepared to fill out the chart below of the claims that cohabitants can make and be sure to include the required elements for each.

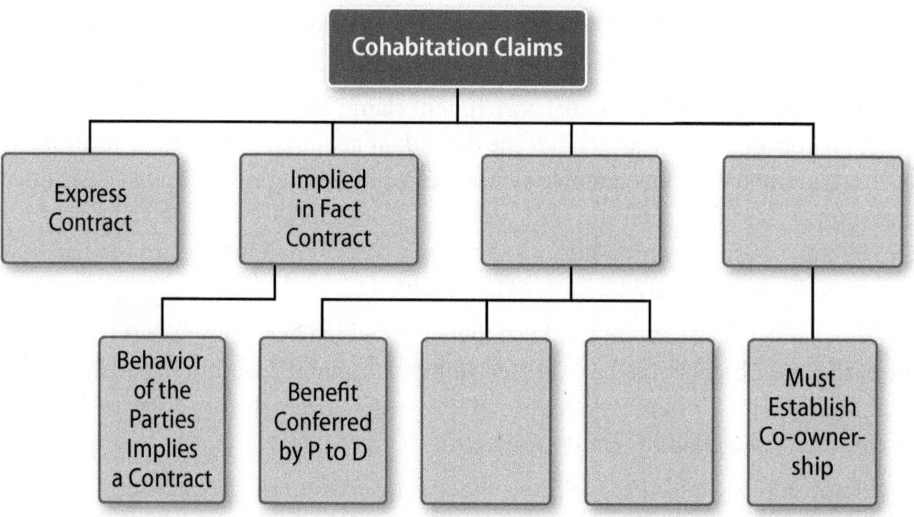

Remember too that in loving relationships, gifts often circulate. So you can add gifts to your list as well.

2. Recall the elements for a common law marriage. *Watts* would have made an excellent case for establishing an informally created marriage, but that was

not possible because Wisconsin does not recognize the doctrine. What would the outcome have been if the couple in *Watts* had been married? Compare that to the law and possible outcomes for unmarried couples in the majority of states.

3. Assuming Sue Ann wanted property rights to the wealth accumulated during the relationship, what legal advice would you have given her when she was contemplating moving in with James, and quitting her job? What advice would you have for James, assuming he wanted to keep his property separate from Sue Ann? It is possible to enter into a cohabitation agreement, which is likely to be enforceable under current law as long as it complies with contract law. It is unusual for couples to have such an agreement. Can you see why?

4. *Alternative Approaches.* A different approach has started to gain traction in a small number of other jurisdictions that treats unmarried couples similar to married couples. For example, the state of Washington allows for equitable distribution of property based on community property principles if a couple is in a "committed intimate partnership." This new legal status must be established by the applicant based on a list of factors that "include, but are not limited to: continuous cohabitation, duration of the relationship, purpose of the relationship, pooling of resources and services for joint projects, and the intent of the parties." *Connell v. Francisco*, 898 P.2d 831, 346 (1995) (citations omitted). However, alimony cannot be claimed based on this relationship status. In other countries such as Australia and the Netherlands, cohabitation also can trigger some marriage-like legal consequences. This approach is also being considered elsewhere, and a variation of it has been proposed by the American Law Institute. *See ALI Principles of the Law of Family Dissolution* §§6.01-6.06 (2002).

   Apply Washington's alternative regime to the facts of *Watts*. Which approach do you think is best and why?

5. *Palimony*. Another contrast to divorce law in the U.S. is that cohabitants cannot claim alimony unless there is a contract that promises support, also known as "palimony." Proving a contract then is key. States respond differently to such a claim. Some allow it, the same as any other contract claim. Other states, however, such as New Jersey, insist that a written contract be proved to make the claim viable, and will not recognize an implied promise for support.

Chapter 5

Estates in Land

Introduction

Estates in land are perhaps the most difficult part of the traditional law school Property course. An estate in land is a type of ownership interest in real property. The most common estate in land is a fee simple absolute, which represents the highest degree of ownership with the least amount of restrictions. The owner of a fee simple absolute holds all the sticks in the bundle for an indefinite period of time. Other types of estates in land are limited in duration, such as a life estate. Still other types of estates in land may vest or divest enjoyment of the real property upon the occurrence of an event.

Estates in land have deep historical roots dating back to the Norman Conquest in 1066. They have mystified law students and confounded attorneys for generations. Today, defeasible estates in land are used infrequently. As discussed in this Chapter, trusts offer greater flexibility and certainty of operation when a transferor wishes to condition the enjoyment of property on the occurrence of an event. It remains important to study and understand estates in land because they inform how our property law has developed and serve as the basis for various other legal relationships. Although you will likely never draft a legal estate in land other than a fee simple, you may encounter one drafted by an attorney from an earlier time. When you do, it will be important to recognize the estate and analyze it properly.

Chapter Problem: Exercise 5-1

You have an appointment with a new client, Mrs. Smith, who wants to talk about how she would like her property distributed when she dies. She is particularly interested in the disposition of a vacation home that has been in the family for several generations. Mrs. Smith is a widow. She has one son, Franklin, and two grandchildren. Although she would like to give the property to her son, he has had issues with gambling in the past and has declared bankruptcy. Franklin is divorced from his wife. Mrs. Smith explains that he is a good son and tries to be a good father to his young children aged 8 and 10. He is getting his life back together, and Mrs. Smith is optimistic that his latest business venture will take off and be successful.

As you read through this Chapter, consider what options you would present to Mrs. Smith regarding the disposition of her vacation property. Remember that you will want to disclose both the benefits and drawbacks of the various options.

Overview of Chapter 5

In this Chapter you will learn to identify the different estates in land. Estates in land are one area of property law where formalism still reigns. The estates system is an inflexible set of legal constructs that developed as a response to feudalism. The rules governing the creation of estates in land and the regulation of these estates are ill-suited to serve the contemporary needs of clients. As you read this Chapter, you will study instances where the law has evolved to better serve contemporary needs, including the public policy limitations placed on estates in land and various statutory reforms.

You will learn about these concepts in seven subunits:

1. Estates in Land
2. Trusts
3. The Rule Against Perpetuities
4. Other Regulatory Rules
5. Interpretation of Ambiguous Conveyances
6. Public Policy Limitations
7. Waste

Estates in Land

In earlier Chapters, we discussed the concept of fee simple ownership. In this Chapter, we will examine the other types of estates in land. Fee simple title represents the greatest ownership interest. In Chapter 2, we learned that you cannot sell or transfer more than you own, but you will see in this Chapter that you can transfer less than you own. You can retain an interest in the property for yourself or divide the property up among third parties over time. Just as property interests can be shared concurrently, they can also be shared over time. When this occurs, the property is said to have both present and future owners. This section provides the historical background for estates in land and introduces you to the major concepts. Although some of the concepts may seem impenetrable at first glance, much of the challenge in this area is simple vocabulary. Once you spend some time with the concepts and understand why they developed, it will be much easier to navigate among the different interests.

Historical Background

The estates system arose out of feudalism—a social structure where individuals were tied to the land and possession of the land was based on good behavior, rather than ownership. The system of feudalism centered on the exchange of land for military service or other feudal incidents. William the Conqueror, who was crowned William I after the Battle of Hastings in 1066, is often credited with introducing feudalism to England, although historians now say that feudalism predated the Norman Conquest. William I solidified feudalism as a means to control the country and divided the land up among the knights who had fought on his behalf. The various parcels of land were known as fiefdoms or fees.

The sovereign was the absolute owner of all the land, which he held pursuant to his allodial right. All others held property from the King. Land was the prime source of wealth and, therefore, how it was held and who controlled it was extremely important. Rights in the land were limited to a tenant's lifetime. There was no right allowing heirs to inherit, and land could not be sold. The limitation on the alienability of land led to a complex process known as subinfeudation that created a pyramidal structure of land tenure and social hierarchy where a tenant would take on subtenants who then would agree to assume some of the tenant's obligations. A subtenant could also take on subtenants who would, in turn, assume some of the first subtenant's feudal obligations.

In 1100, King Henry I established the inheritability of land upon the payment of a sum referred to as a "relief" that was often equal to one year's rent. Inheritance of land followed the rule of primogeniture where land passed to the oldest surviving son. Land would escheat to the lord upon the failure of issue or the commission of a felony. It would forfeit to the crown in the case of high treason. A New York case from 1852 described the process of subinfeudation as follows:

> At common law a feoffment in fee did not originally pass an estate in the sense in which the term is now understood. The purchaser took only a usufructary interest, without the power of alienation in prejudice of the lord. In default of heirs, the tenure became extinct and the land reverted to the lord. Under the system of English feudal tenures, all lands in the Kingdom, were supposed to be holden mediately or immediately of the King who was styled the "lord paramount", or above all. Such tenants as held under the King immediately, when they granted out portions of their lands to inferior persons, also became lords with respect to those inferior persons, since they were still tenants with respect to the King, and thus partaking of a middle nature were called "mense" or "middle lords". So, if the King granted a manor to A and A granted a portion of the land to B, now B was said to hold of A, and A of the King; or in other words, B held his lands immediately of A and mediately of the King. The King was therefore styled "Lord Paramount"; A was both tenant and lord, or a mesne lord, and B was called "tenant paravail", or the lowest tenant. Out of the feudal tenures or holdings sprung certain rights and incidents, among those which were fealty and escheat. Both these were

> incidents of socage tenure. Fealty is the obligation of fidelty which the tenant owed to the lord. Escheat was the reversion of the estate on a grant in fee simple upon a failure of the heirs of the owner. Fealty was annexed to and attendant on the reversion. They were inseparable. These incidents of feudal tenure belonged to the lord of whome the lands were immediately holden, that is to say, to him of whom the owner for the time being purchased. These grants were called subinfeudations.

De Peyster v. Michael, 6 N.Y. 457 (1852).

In 1290, the statute of *Quia Emptores* ended the practice of subinfeudation and required that the sale of land be absolute. It replaced the practice of subinfeudation with that of substitution where the grantor could not retain feudal rights over the land conveyed. The grantee assumed the obligations of the grantor to his lord, but did not assume any obligations to the grantor. In other words, the grantee stepped into the shoes of the grantor and assumed the grantor's obligations. Feudal obligations gradually lost their personal character, and feudal service was replaced with monetary feudal incidents. It was not until the 1540 Statute of Wills that real property could be devised by will. Until that time, the rules of inheritance were mandatory. If grantors wanted to avoid the rules of descent, they had to convey the property during their lifetimes.

One of the major forces in the development of the system of estates in land was the desire of landowners to avoid feudal incidents. Landowners would create future interests through a lifetime conveyance in an attempt to avoid the property passing by inheritance. If property passed by purchase rather than inheritance, it would not trigger the obligation to pay "just relief," which would be equivalent to our modern estate and inheritance taxes. Both the Rule in Shelley's Case and the Doctrine of Worthier Title, discussed later in this Chapter, represent legal responses to attempts by grantors to structure ownership in such a way to avoid feudal incidents.

The statute *Quia Emptores* promoted the free alienability of land, which is the keystone of common law property law. At the same time, it also empowered grantors to impose restrictions on future owners. This development created a tension between the interests of the present possessors and future generations that continues today. In 1285, the statute *De Donis Conditionalibus* created the fee tail that allowed land to descend through the lineal heirs of the grantee. If the line failed, the land would revert to the grantor's heirs. The recognition of fee tail responded to a grantor's desire to preserve property and keep it in the family. It also severely compromised the alienability of land and limited the enjoyment of the property for future generations.

In addition to fee tail, grantors were permitted to convey fee estates that would terminate on a future event and then revert back to the grantor or his heirs, such as a fee simple determinable and a fee simple subject to condition subsequent. Until 1536, however, it was not possible to shift the estate to a third party upon the occurrence (or non-occurrence) of an event. It could only go back to the grantor. A grantor could not create a contingent interest in a third party that would vest upon the termination of the current possessory estate. These types of interests in third parties are called executory interests. Grantors got around these limitations by employing a trust device known as a "use" that was enforceable in courts of equity. The 1536 Statute of Uses abolished this practice, but also authorized the creation of legal executory interests. Today such estates are referred to as a fee simple subject to an executory interest.

The rules governing estates in land were transplanted to U.S. law with the reception of common law, but there were some notable exceptions. For example, the practice of primogeniture was never widely accepted in the U.S. Despite the archaic nature of many of the rules, *stare decisis* assured that concepts were followed and served as the foundation of American property law. Courts dutifully applied such concepts as the Rule in Shelley's Case and the Doctrine of Worthier Title even though they were designed to stop the avoidance of long-discontinued feudal incidents and served no modern purpose.

In England, the Land Property Act of 1925 abolished legal estates in land with the exception of the fee simple absolute and the leasehold and required all future interests to be held in trust. Reform in the United States has been slower and more piecemeal, because it has proceeded on a state-by-state basis. Legal estates in land remain lawful in most jurisdictions, but the reform process has created wide regional variations among the different jurisdictions. Accordingly, when practicing in this area, it is always essential to consult local law.

Types of Estates in Land

Historically, estates in land were divided into two main categories: freehold estates that grant ownership and nonfreehold estates that grant possession or use for a limited duration. Nonfreehold estates are also called leaseholds. We will discuss leaseholds in detail in Chapter 6. Although leaseholds are considered to be a type of estate in land, they have increasingly been viewed by the courts and policymakers as contractual relationships as well. In Chapter 6, we will explore the laws applicable to leaseholds and the responsibilities and obligations of lessors and lessees, also known as landlords and tenants.

Within the category of freehold estates, some estates are limited by an individual's lifetime. These include life estates and fee tail. Other estates are called defeasible fees, because they terminate on the occurrence of an event at which point the property either reverts to the original grantor or shifts to a third party. There are three different types of defeasible fees: fee simple determinable, fee simple subject to a condition subsequent, and fee simple subject to an executory interest.

When a fee simple owner transfers her property, she can choose from among the different estates in land. As noted above, the transfer of property can either be *inter vivos* by deed or at death by will. The transferor is generally referred to as the grantor. For example, if a grantor wanted to transfer her property at death in fee simple to Thomas, her will would read: "I give Greenacre to Thomas in fee simple absolute." A transfer of real property by deed or will involves two parts: words of purchase and words of limitation. The words of purchase identify the grantee. The term purchase is a term of art and applies equally when the transfer is a gift. The words of limitation specify the quantum of the estate that is transferred.

I give Greenacre [to Thomas] [in fee simple absolute].

Words of purchase Words of limitation

If you were drafting a deed or a will, here is how you would express the different types of estates in land. In each case, the term "Greenacre" refers to the real property subject to the transfer. Thomas is the grantee, and Elliot is a third party. Can you identify the words of purchase and the words of limitation?

Fee Simple Absolute
Greenacre to Thomas in fee simple absolute.

Life Estate with a Remainder
Greenacre to Thomas for life, remainder to Elliot.

Fee Tail
Greenacre to Thomas and the heirs of his body.

Fee Simple Determinable
Greenacre to Thomas so long as not used for commercial purposes.

Fee Simple Subject to a Condition Subsequent
Greenacre to Thomas, provided it is not used for commercial purposes.

Fee Simple Subject to an Executory Limitation
Greenacre to Thomas, but if used for commercial purposes, then to Elliot.

Although a grantor is able to customize the transfer of real property by using one of the estates in land, she is not given unlimited flexibility. She must use a recognized fee and strictly adhere to the formalities for the creation of that fee. A grantor cannot mix and match estates. New estates will not be recognized. This is known as the Rule Against the Creation of New Estates. *Johnson v. Whiton*, 34 N.E. 542 (Mass. 1893).

Defeasible Fees Distinguished from Real Covenants and Easements

A defeasible fee is an estate that may terminate upon the occurrence or non-occurrence of an event. When the event that triggers defeasance occurs, the property then either goes back to the grantor or shifts to a third party.

It is important to distinguish estates in land from the real covenants and equitable servitudes covered in Chapter 10. Estates in land control the ownership of land, whereas real covenants control the use of land. It can often be confusing, because some of the triggering events used in common examples of defeasible estates "touch and concern" the land just as the restrictions imposed under real covenants.

For example, compare the following two provisions:

> *Greenacre to Thomas.* This property shall not be used for commercial purposes. This restriction shall run with the land and bind all future owners.
>
> *Greenacre to Thomas so long as Greenacre is not used for commercial purposes.*

The first provision is a grant of fee simple absolute followed by the creation a real covenant. The second provision creates a fee simple determinable. A key distinction between the two is what happens in each case if the trigger event occurs. In the case of the covenant, if Greenacre is used for commercial purposes, the grantor can sue for damages or injunctive relief. However, in the case of a fee simple determinable, the result is automatic reverter and immediate divestment.

The distinction in terms of remedy helps explain why legal estates in land are almost never seen in arm's length market transactions. The remedy of divestment is too harsh and final to be part of a bargained for exchange. For this reason, real covenants and equitable servitudes tend to arise in market transactions. Defeasible fees are more likely to be part of a gratuitous intra-family transfer.

The Recognized Estates in Land

This section explains the rules applicable to the recognized fees: fee simple absolute, life estates, fee tail, fee simple determinable, fee simple subject to a condition subsequent, and fee simple subject to an executory interest. A chart is provided at the end of this section that summarizes the various interests created under each of these estates in land.

Fee Simple Absolute

True to its name, fee simple absolute gives the owner the absolute power to sell or convey the property or devise the property under her will. It represents the largest and most comprehensive type of ownership. A fee simple absolute is considered to be of infinite duration, because it could last in perpetuity. At common law, the words of limitation that were required to create a fee simple absolute were "and his heirs." A grant of a fee simple absolute would read "Greenacre to A and his heirs." If the owner of Greenacre did not transfer the property, then at his death, the Greenacre would descend to his heirs through intestacy. The idea was that the estate could continue in perpetuity until one of the owners decided to transfer it.

Today it is no longer necessary to include the words "and his heirs" to create a fee simple absolute. A fee simple title will be presumed unless it is clear that the grantor had either retained an interest or created a future interest in a third party. The rule of construction that favors the larger interest is said to further the marketability of real property by disfavoring retained interests and future interests.

Here are examples of a fee simple absolute:

Greenacre to Thomas and his heirs.
Greenacre to Thomas in fee simple absolute.
Greenacre to Thomas in fee simple.
Greenacre to Thomas in fee.
Greenacre to Thomas.

Fee Tail

The estate of fee tail is used to maintain property within a single family line. It dates from 1285 and a statute known as *De Donis Conditionalibus.* Under fee tail, the property descends automatically to the oldest son. It could not be sold or transferred. If the family line failed and there were no descendants, the property would revert to the original grantor who had entailed the land. Since the original grantor would most likely be dead, the property would pass to collateral relatives, often distant cousins. If that makes you think of the popular British historical drama *Downton Abbey*, you are exactly right. Downton was entailed, but the Earl of Gratham only had three daughters: Mary, Edith, and Sybil. Because the Earl did not have any male heirs, Downton passed to a distant cousin, Mathew Crawley, who luckily married one of the Earl's daughters. Fee tail also figures in a number of classic novels, such as Jane Austen's *Pride and Prejudice* and George Elliot's *Middlemarch.*

In England, fee tail was abolished as a legal estate in land in 1925 by the Law of Property Act, along many of the archaic legal estates in land. Fee tail was never universally recognized in the United States. It has been abolished in all but four jurisdictions: Delaware, Maine, Massachusetts, and Rhode Island. In Delaware, Maine, and Massachusetts, entailed property can be sold or transferred, and the fee tail only applies in the event of intestacy. In Rhode Island, a fee tail is treated as a life estate with remainder in the life tenant's children. In all other states, an attempt to create a fee tail would most likely result in the creation of a fee simple absolute.

Here is an example of a fee tail:

Greenacre to Thomas and the heirs of his body.

Life Estates, Reversions, and Remainders

A life estate lasts for the duration of the life of the grantee. A life estate *pur autre vie* is measured by the life of a third party. The owner of a life estate is referred to as the "life tenant." Upon the expiration of a life estate, the property can revert back to the grantor or pass to a third party. If the property reverts back to the grantor, the grantor's interest is called a reversion. If the property passes to a third party, the interest is called a remainder, and the third party is referred to as the remainderman or remainderperson.

As explained above, most legal estates in land are no longer used today. Property typically conveys in fee simple. A legal life estate is an exception. It remains in use as a testamentary substitute, making it more likely that you might encounter one in your practice. However, most life estates today are conveyed in trust for estate planning purposes. For example, a spouse may leave her property in trust for the benefit of her surviving spouse, with remainder to her children. A transfer in trust can include all property, not just real property. Granting the surviving spouse a life estate will ensure that the surviving spouse has the benefit of the property for his or her lifetime, but is not permitted to alienate it or commit waste. If the surviving spouse remarries, the remainder is not subject to the new spouse's elective share and will not pass to the new spouse by intestacy. As a result, a transfer in trust can preserve and protect the property for the children of the deceased spouse. The section below on trusts outlines the benefits of using a trust and the negatives of using a legal life estate. This section discusses legal life estates that are created either by deed or by a testamentary devise.

A life tenant has the right to enjoy and possess the property during the term of the life estate. A life tenant can rent the property or transfer his life tenancy, but obviously cannot transfer more than he owns. If a life tenant transfers his life tenancy to a third party, the third party will take a life estate *pur autre vie*. Given the uncertainties attached to such an estate, these interests are not widely marketable.

Because the life tenant only holds a temporary right to enjoy and possess the property, he owes certain responsibilities to the future owners. Upon the expiration of a life estate, the future owner will take title in fee simple absolute unless the conveyance provides otherwise. The life tenant owes a duty to repair the property and may be held liable if he commits waste, which is discussed later in this Chapter. The life tenant is also responsible for taxes and other carrying charges of the property, but significant improvements or special assessments must be apportioned between the life tenant and the future owners.

Here are some examples of different types of life estates:

Greenacre to Thomas for life.

This is a life estate with a reversion in the grantor. It is not necessary for the grantor to specially retain a reversion. Anything that the grantor does not give away is deemed to be retained by the grantor. As a matter of drafting practice, it may be good advice to always spell out the grantor's intentions so there can be no ambiguity. In this case, the conveyance would read: *Greenacre to Thomas for life, reversion in the Grantor*. If the grantor is dead when the life tenant dies, the reversion will pass to the grantor's heirs. In the majority of jurisdictions, the grantor is able to transfer the reversion *inter vivos* or by will.

Greenacre to Thomas for Elliot's life.

This is a life estate *pur autre vie* with a reversion in the grantor. The life tenant's interest will terminate on the death of the measuring life, Elliot. A life estate *pur autre vie* can also be followed by a remainder. In which case, the conveyance would have to name the remainderman: *Greenacre to Thomas for Elliot's life, then to Emerson.*

> *Greenacre to Thomas for life, remainder to Elliot.*
>
> This is a life estate followed by a remainder, which is the most common formulation. In this case, the remainder is said to be "vested" because it will occur upon the termination of the preceding life estate and the identity of the remainderman is ascertained. If the remainderman does not survive the life tenant, the property will pass to the remainderman's heirs. The remainderman can also transfer his interest *inter vivos* or by will.

Remainders can either be vested, as in the case of Elliot's interest above, or they can be contingent. Complexities involving remainder interests frequently arise in the context of estate planning when a grantor wants to benefit a class of individuals, such as grandchildren. Transfers to a group of individuals, most often relatives of a particular degree, are referred to as class gifts.

Here is an example:

> *Greenacre to my daughter, Elliot, for life and then to my grandchildren in equal shares.*
>
> The remainder interest is considered to be contingent, because the takers are uncertain when the gift is made and the interest is created. The date when an interest is created depends on whether the gift is *inter vivos* or testamentary. An *inter vivos* gift is effective on the date of the transfer, whereas a testamentary gift under a will takes effect on the date of testator's death. In this case, the identity of the takers of the remainder interest will be clear only upon the death of the life tenant.

A contingent remainder also exists where the enjoyment of the remainder is subject to a condition precedent. Remainder interests pass by intestacy and are able to be transferred or devised regardless of whether they are vested or contingent, with the exception of where the identity of the remainderperson is unascertained. At common law, remainders were not transferrable *inter vivos*.

Here is an example:

> *Greenacre to my daughter, Elliot, for life and then to my granddaughter Emerson when she reaches 21 years of age.*
>
> In this case, the remainder is subject to a condition subsequent. Emerson must reach age 21. If Elliot dies and Emerson has not yet turned 21, the grantor retains a reversion until Emerson turns 21.

Contingent remainders are subject to additional rules that are discussed later in this Chapter, principally the Rule Against Perpetuities and the Doctrine of the Destructibility of Contingent Remainders. Contingent remainders are generally disfavored, because they impede the marketability of real property by clouding the title and introducing uncertainty as to future ownership. We will revisit the above example later in this Chapter and examine why it satisfies the Rule Against Perpetuities, provided Emerson was alive when the interest was created, but the gift to Emerson nonetheless fails under the Doctrine of the Destructibility of Contingent Remainders.

Vested remainders are also subject to additional classifications. In addition to vested remainders, there are also vested remainders subject to open and vested remainders subject to divestment. Unlike contingent remainders, vested remainders are not subject to the Rule Against Perpetuities, with the exception of vested remainders subject to open. Vested remainders are generally favored over contingent remainders. They are thought to add more certainty to the market because the identity of the future owner is known.

Here are some examples:

Greenacre to Thomas for life, then to Elliot.

This is a vested remainder. Elliot is ascertained, and her enjoyment is not subject to a condition precedent. Elliot will take possession upon the natural termination of the preceding life estate. The vested remainder is not subject to the Rule Against Perpetuities. Elliot can transfer her interest *inter vivos* or by will. If Elliot dies before Thomas and has not written a will, the interest will descend to her heirs by intestacy.

Greenacre to Thomas for life, then to Thomas' children.

If at the time the interest is created, Thomas has at least one child living, the remainder is vested. However, it is possible that Thomas may have other children. Accordingly, the remainder is said to be "vested subject to open," meaning that more people can join the class of future owners. A remainder that is vested subject to open is subject to the Rule Against Perpetuities.

Greenacre to Thomas for life, then to Elliot so long as the property is not used for commercial purposes.

This is a vested remainder subject to divestment because the remainder will be defeated if the property is used for commercial purposes. The grantor has retained a reversion by implication. A vested remainder subject to divestment is not subject to the Rule Against Perpetuities.

Fee Simple Determinable and Possibility of Reverter

A fee simple determinable terminates automatically upon the occurrence (or nonoccurrence) of a specific event. The property reverts back to the grantor or the grantor's heirs when the triggering event takes place. At common law, the possibility of reverter would descend through intestacy, but was not transferrable. The modern rule is that the possibility of reverter may also be transferred *inter vivos* or devised by will. If the possibility of reverter is transferred to a third party, it still retains its character as a reverter. A possibility of reverter is not subject to the common law Rule Against Perpetuities. Some jurisdictions have abolished the fee simple determinable, and any attempt to create such an estate in those jurisdictions will produce a fee simple absolute.

The downside of the automatic reverter is that the statute of limitations for adverse possession begins to run when the trigger event takes place. As explained in the following section on Trusts, a legal estate in land does not involve an impartial fiduciary who is charged with protecting the interests of both the present and future owners. In the case of a fee simple determinable, it is possible that the owner of the future interest may not discover that the triggering event occurred for some time after the event takes place. If the owner of the future interest fails to assert her interest in a timely manner, she runs the risk of losing it by adverse possession. Accordingly, owners of future interests must be vigilant and monitor the estates.

A fee simple determinable is about duration. In order to create a fee simple determinable, the grantor must use recognized words of limitation. The prescribed set of words and phrases that are sufficient to create a fee simple determinable are temporal in nature. They include: "so long as", "during", "while", and "until". The words or phrases are used within the granting clause. This differs from the construction of the fee simple subject to a condition subsequent discussed below, where the limitation is expressed in a separate clause separated by a comma. Although it may seem strange to place so much emphasis on a comma, it is important to remember that estates in land is an area of law where formalism still rules the day.

Here are some examples. Assume Thomas is in law school when the interest is created.

Greenacre to Thomas so long as he is enrolled in law school.
Greenace to Thomas during the time when he is in law school.
Greenacre to Thomas while he is in law school
Greenace to Thomas until he graduates from law school.

Fee Simple Subject to a Condition Subsequent and Right of Re-Entry

A fee simple subject to a condition subsequent does not terminate automatically upon the occurrence (or nonoccurrence) of a specific event. Instead, the grantor retains a right of re-entry. The triggering event gives the grantor the right to claim the estate in fee simple absolute. At common law, a right to re-entry would descend through intestacy, but was not transferrable. Today, the jurisdictions are split with regard to when a right to re-entry is transferrable. A majority of jurisdictions allow a right of re-entry to be devised by will. However, a majority of jurisdictions also prohibit the *inter vivos* transfer of a right to re-entry. A right of re-entry is not subject to the common law Rule Against Perpetuities.

The right of re-entry does not take effect immediately, which means that the statute of limitations for adverse possession does not begin to run when the trigger event takes place, as it does with a possibility of reverter. Instead, the owner of the right of re-entry must affirmatively assert his interest. It is not clear whether this difference translates to a definite advantage, because the owner of a right to re-entry who sleeps on her rights would be subject to an equitable defense of laches.

A fee simple subject to a condition subsequent requires the express creation of a condition that will terminate the estate. In order to create a fee simple subject to a condition subsequent, the grantor must use recognized words of limitation. The following set of phrases are sufficient to create a fee simple subject to a condition subsequent: "provided", "however", "if", "but if", "on condition that", and "in the event that". Unlike a fee simple determinable, the phrases are not used within the granting clause. They are used in the second clause separated by a comma. Again, these minor drafting points may seem insignificant, but this is an area ruled by formalism.

Here are some examples. Assume that Thomas is in law school at the time the interest is created.

Greenacre to Thomas, provided that he does not drop out of law school.
Greenacre to Thomas, but only if he does not drop out of law school.
Greenacre to Thomas, on condition that he does not drop out of law school.
Greenacre to Thomas, in the event that he stays in law school until he graduates.

Fee Simple Subject to an Executory Interest

A fee simple subject to an executory interest is an estate that terminates automatically upon the occurrence (or nonoccurrence) of a specific event and then shifts to a third party. The triggering event transfers fee simple ownership to the designated third party or his heirs. An executory interest descends through intestacy and is also transferrable *inter vivos* or by will. An executory interest is subject to the Rule Against Perpetuities.

There are two types of executory interests: shifting interests and springing interests. A shifting executory interest takes effect as soon as the triggering event occurs and the interest shifts to the third party. A springing executory interest does not vest immediately. Instead, there is a gap of time between the triggering event that terminates the estate and when the executory interest takes effect. In the case of a springing executory interest, the grantor retains a reversionary interest.

A fee simple subject to an executory interest is defined by the fact that a named third party has a future interest in the property. As noted above, the grantor may also have a retained interest in the property in the case of a springing executory interest. The words of limitation used to create a fee simple subject to an exectutory interest can be the phrases associated with either a fee simple determinable or a fee simple subject to a condition subsequent. The key component is the gift over to the third party upon the occurrence or nonoccurrence of an event.

Here are some examples of a shifting executory interest. Assume that Thomas is in law school at the time the interest is created.

Greenacre to Thomas, so long as he does not drop out of law school, then to Elliot.
Greenacre to Thomas, but if he does not graduate from law school, then to Elliot.

Here is an example of springing executory interest. Assume that Thomas is in law school at the time the interest is created and Elliot is 15 years of age.

Greenacre to Thomas, unless he drops out of law school, then to Elliot when she reaches the age of 21.

Exercise 5-2. Review Flow Chart of Estates in Land — Future Interests

Review the chart below. It will help guide you as you apply the laws and classify the estates.

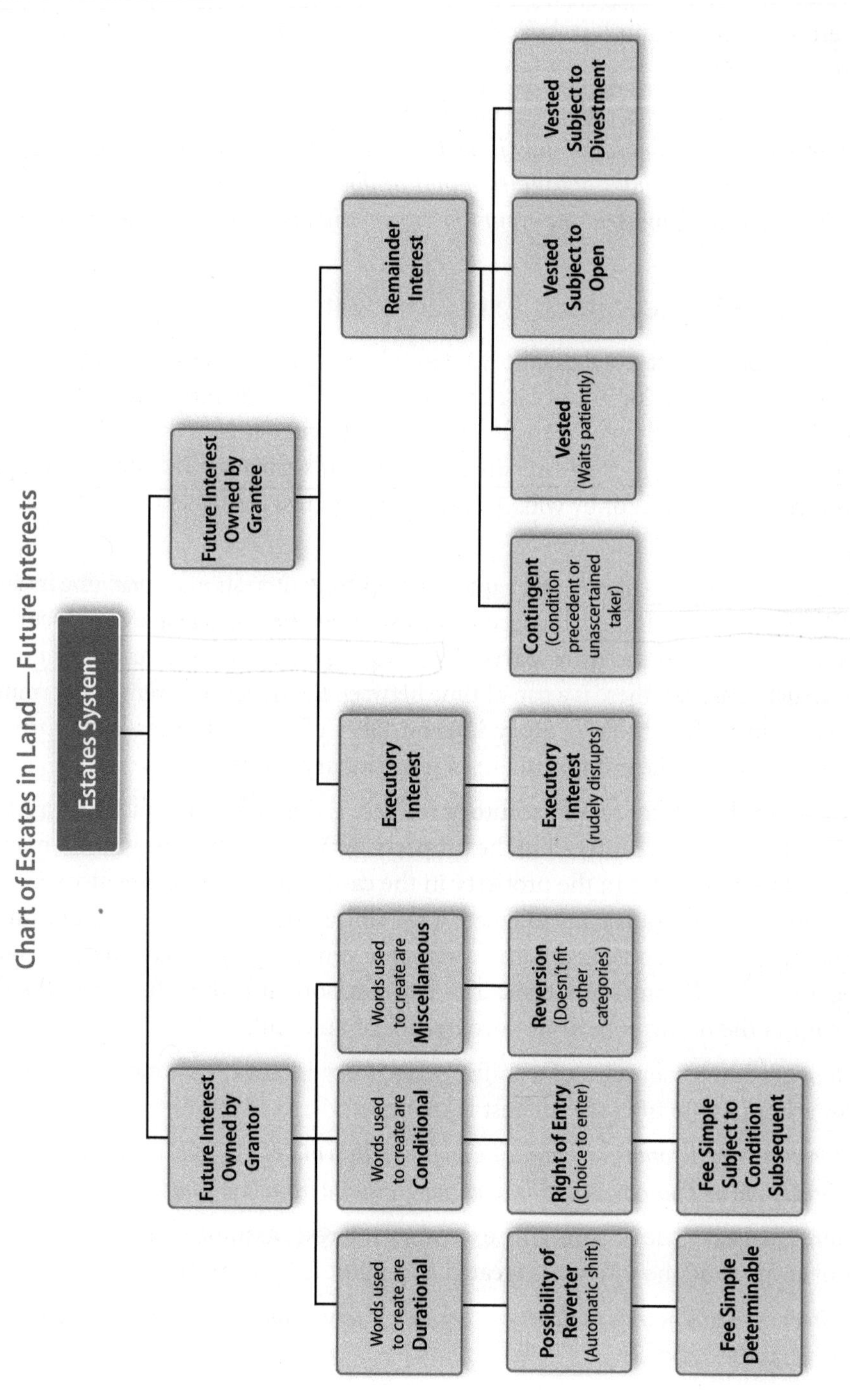

Exercise 5-3. Applying the Law of Estates

Apply the rules you have been learning to the following practice problems. Classify the estates (predict the outcome) created in the transfer of property as to all ownership interests that exist. You will need to be able to explain how you reach your conclusions, by applying the rules to the facts. The problems that follow are transfers of real property, known as Greenacre, by its owner, O.

1. "to A for life, then to B forever."
2. "to A and her heirs."
   a) If A's only child, B, runs up huge gambling debts, can B's creditors reach Blackacre?
   b) If A wishes to sell Greenacre and use the proceeds to take a trip around the world, can B stop her?
3. O devised Greenacre "to my wife, Wanda, for life, remainder to my daughter Deborah and her heirs." After O's death, Deborah died, leaving her mother, Wanda, as her sole heir. Deborah's will devised "all property I own at death" to a charity. Last year, Wanda died. Her executors (those she named in her will to carry out her testamentary intent) claim she owned Greenacre. The charity also claims ownership. Who wins?
4. "to A for life, then to B for life, then to C for life."
5. "to the United Church so long as the land is used for church purposes."
6. "to the United Church, on condition that the land is used for church purposes."
7. "to the United Church, provided that the land is used for church purposes, and if it is not so used, to Delvania Food Bank."
8. "to City, provided that the land is used for park purposes; otherwise to revert to the grantor."
9. "to City for the purpose of creating a public park."
10. "to City, and the City covenants and agrees that the land will be used solely for park purposes."
11. "to A for life, then to B and her heirs if B lives to attain the age of 25 years." B is 15 years old at the time of the conveyance.
12. "to A and his heirs, but if B marries then to B and her heirs."
13. " to A for life, remainder to B and her heirs."
14. "to A for life, remainder to B if she graduates college."
15. "to A for life, remainder to A's children and their heirs."
    a) assume A has no children at the time of conveyance.

b) assume A has one child at the time of conveyance.

16. "to A for life, then to B if he quits smoking, otherwise to C."

17. "to A for life, then to B, but if B starts smoking, to C."

Trusts

The estates discussed above are referred to as legal estates in land. The interests represented in the legal estates in land can also be created as equitable interests in trust. For example, it is possible to create a legal life estate either by deed or by will. It is also possible to create an equitable life estate in a trust. The trust can be created during the grantor's lifetime or under the grantor's will. England abolished legal estates in land in 1925, with the exception of the fee simple and leasehold. The English Law of Property Act of 1925 mandated that all life estates and future interests must be equitable interests held in trust. The holder of the possessory interest is deemed to hold the property in trust for the future owner. As a result, today there are only two types of legal estates in land recognized in England: a fee simple absolute and a leasehold.

Jurisdictions in the United States continue to recognize legal estates in land, although there has been some reform, such as the widespread abolishment of fee tail. However, the legal estates in land have many limitations and shortcomings that make them unattractive options for planning purposes. Trusts offer greater certainty of operation and protections for the parties. They will almost always be preferred to a creation of a legal estate in land with split present and future interests.

A trust represents a split of legal and equitable title. In order to create a trust, there must be a grantor, a trustee, a beneficiary, and a trust res or property. In certain situations, the grantor, trustee, and beneficiary can all be the same person. The trustee is a fiduciary who owes a duty to the beneficiaries to manage the property for their behalf.

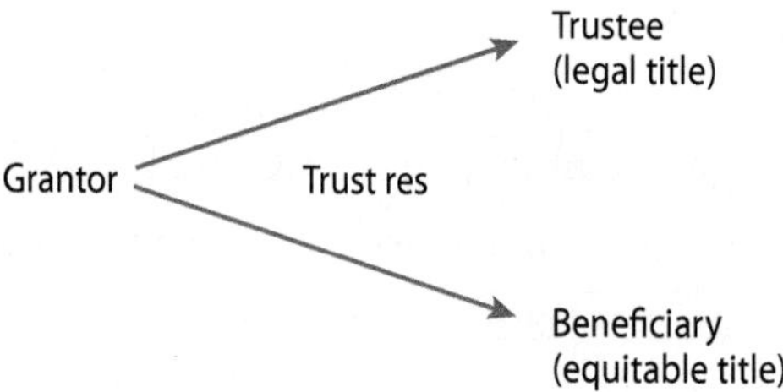

Where the beneficiaries include both present possessory interests and future interests, the trustee owes the beneficiaries a duty of impartiality. The trustee cannot favor one beneficiary or one class of beneficiaries over another. A trustee is liable for any loss that results from a breach of duty or failure to follow a prudent investment strategy.

It is a common estate planning tool to leave property, mostly likely investments, in trust for a surviving spouse and children. In this way, a trust provides much greater flexibility than an estate in land that is only available for real property. For example, a trust could provide a life estate for a surviving spouse followed by a life estate in children with remainder to grandchildren. As the life tenant, the surviving spouse would be entitled to income from the trust. The grantor could also give the surviving spouse or the trustee the power to invade principal on behalf of the surviving spouse. It is possible to grant the surviving spouse a power of appointment that authorizes her to designate who takes the remainder.

Trusts offer many advantages over legal estates in land. They provide certainty of operation, and the trustee has clearly defined duties. The trustee provides impartial management of the trust property, and there are clear statutory remedies for any breach of fiduciary duty. Trusts can be structured to be beyond the reach of creditors, unlike legal estates in land. Trusts are also not without drawbacks. A trust is a separate legal entity and also a separate taxable entity. There are expenses incurred in connection with a trust, including management fees and trustee commissions.

The Rule Against Perpetuities

The Rule Against Perpetuities limits the amount of time certain future interests can extend without vesting. It is designed to limit the reach of "dead hand control," which refers to the ability of grantors who are long dead to control the disposition of property. The Rule is designed to promote the free alienability of property. It prohibits grantors from burdening property with speculative and remote future interests in perpetuity. Accordingly, the Rule attempts to mediate important questions of inter-generational equity. It determines how long the present generation can deny future generations the ability to pass clear title to property.

The Rule dates from a 1682 case known as the *Duke of Norfolk's Case*. The decision enunciated a bright line rule that limited the length of time that certain future interests could take to vest. The Rule traditionally applies to contingent remainders, vested remainders subject to open, and executory interests. At common law, the Rule did not apply to grantor retained interests. All interests that could possibly fail to vest within the prescribed time frame are considered void *ab initio* and struck. The Rule applies to both legal estates in land that are created by deed or under a will and equitable interests that are held in trust. The Rule has also been applied to certain arm's length business transactions, such as rights of first refusal and options to purchase.

The Rule may be a bright line rule, but it is notoriously difficult to apply. Famously, a California court held in 1961 that it was not legal malpractice for an attorney to draft a will that violates the Rule Against Perpetuities. *Lucas v. Hamm*, 56 Cal. 2d 583 (Cal. App. 1961). This section explains the Rule and its various applications. It also outlines the statutory reforms that have either repealed or modified the Rule Against Perpetuities. Today, the Rule is of limited applicability, but it remains a favorite topic of bar examiners.

As of 2016, the majority of jurisdictions in the United States have abolished or radically reformed the Rule. Some jurisdictions have adopted a "wait and see" approach where an interest that violates the Rule will not be considered void *ab initio*, but will be struck if it in fact does violate the Rule in real time. Other jurisdictions have adopted the Uniform Statutory Rule Against Perpetuities that provides a flat time period of 90 years in which interests must vest. The latest trend among the states is to repeal the Rule in order to attract trust deposits to the state. When the first states relaxed the Rule in order to attract investment, it ignited a "race to the bottom" where states competed to enact laws that encouraged the exact type of "dead hand control" that the Rule was designed to limit.

The Classic Statement of the Rule

The classic statement of the Rule Against Perpetuities reads as follows:

> No interest is good unless it must vest, if at all, no later than 21 years after the death of some life-in-being at the creation of the interest.

Although the Rule aims to limit the ability of a grantor to control the disposition of property, it actually provides a grantor considerable leeway. Basically, a grantor can suspend the disposition of property for a lifetime plus 21 years. The addition of 21 years was necessary to allow a child to attain their majority, which at common law was 21 years of age. Today the age of majority is 18.

Here is an example:

> *Greenacre to my son for life, then to his children who reach 21 years of age.*

This example represents a fairly common estate planning device where the grantor desires to preserve property for his grandchildren by providing his children with a life estate. This scheme ensures that the child cannot alienate or encumber the property during his lifetime. The remainder to the grandchildren is then postponed until the grandchildren reach majority. This step avoids the necessity of appointing a guardian to manage the property for a minor remainderperson.

Three Steps to Applying the Rule

The application of the Rule Against Perpetuities takes three simple steps: 1) identify whether the future interest is subject to the Rule, 2) test the future interest, and 3) strike any offending provisions. You will find that if you break down the application of the Rule in this way, it is not as difficult as it seems.

- **Identify whether the interest is subject to the Rule.** At common law, grantor retained interests and vested remainders were exempt, although a few states have extended the scope of the Rule to include grantor retained interests. Accordingly, the first step in the application of the Rule is to eliminate those interests that are not subject to the Rule. Traditionally, those interests are reversions, rights of re-entry, possibilities of reverter, and most vested remainders. These interests would remain exempt even if they were transferred to a third party, because they retain their initial character. By process of elimination, it means that executory interests and contingent remainders are subject to the Rule. Vested remainders subject to open are also subject to the Rule. The Rule has also been applied to certain market-based real estate transactions, including rights of first refusal and options to purchase. The first case in this section, *Texaco Refining & Marketing, Inc. v. Samowitz*, 213 Conn. 676(1990), illustrates why the application of the Rule to market transactions is not appropriate and has been abolished in most jurisdictions.

The Rule does not apply when both the present possessory interest and the future interest are held by a charity. This exception favors transfers to charity and represents an incentive for grantors to transfer property to charities in perpetuity.

Here is an example:

Greenacre to Charity A, but if used for commercial purposes, then to Charity B.

- **Test the future interest.** If a future interest is subject to the Rule, you then have to test the interest to see if there is any possibility that the interest will not vest within the perpetuities period, which is a life-in-being plus 21 years. In order to apply this step, you have to identify the "measuring life" that will determine what constitutes a "life-in-being"; you also have to identify the trigger event that will cause the interest to vest.
- **Measuring life.** The measuring life must be a person who was in existence at the creation of the interest. In the case of an *inter vivos* transfer, the interest is created on the date the deed is effective. In the case of an interest created under a will, the interest is created when the will speaks, which is on the date of the testator's death. An interest created under an *inter vivos* trust is created on the date of the trust.

  The measuring life includes a period of gestation. In other words, if the life tenant is a child who is serving as the measuring life, it includes a child who is conceived, but not yet born. This is referred to as a child *en ventre sa mere*. There is also a second period of gestation added to the 21 years at the end of the perpetuities period. Accordingly, the perpetuities period can be expressed as:

  Period of gestation + life-in-being + 21 years + period of gestation

  The measuring life is generally an individual named in the transfer or a class (i.e., children) identified in the document, provided the class is closed. Technically, the measuring life could be any person alive (or in gestation) at the time of the creation of the interest. During the late 19th century, it became popular in England to use a Royal Lives Clause in trust documents. The Royal Lives Clause provided that the interest would vest or the trust would terminate on the death of the last surviving descendant of Queen Victoria who was alive (or in gestation) when the trust was created. Note that a testamentary trust is not created until the date of the testator's death.

- **Trigger event.** Once you have identified the measuring life, the next step is to identify the trigger event—the event that will cause the interest to vest (or not). The question is whether there is *any* possibility that this trigger event will not occur within a life-in-being plus 21 years. In this step, courts at common law have traditionally entertained some wild scenarios that were not at all probable and in many cases strained all credibility. These instances are covered separately below in the subsection titled "The Absurdities Created at Common Law."

  One way to approach this step of the analysis is to ask whether the trigger event is a life event, such as marriage or graduating from law school, or a restriction on the use of the property. When the trigger event is a restriction on the use of the property, it is likely that the future interest will violate the Rule Against Perpetuities, unless it is a grantor retained interest or a vested remainder that is not subject to open.

  Here is an example:

  Greenacre to Thomas so long as not used for commercial purposes, but if it is so used, then to Elliot.

  Remember that the interests held by both Thomas and Elliot will pass to their heirs through intestacy or are subject to transfer either *inter vivos* or by will. Neither interest terminates on the death of the named recipient. Either Thomas or Elliot could be the measuring life. The trigger event is that the property is used for commercial purposes. We don't know whether the property will ever be used for commercial purposes, and that uncertainty means that Elliot's interest may vest many years after both Thomas and Elliot are deceased and 21 years have passed.

  When the trigger event is instead a life event that can only occur during the lifetime of the measuring life, then you know that the future interest is good.

  Here are some examples:

  Greenacre to Thomas so long as he does not quit law school, but if he does quit law school, then to Elliot.

  In this case, we will know whether or not Elliot's interest vests within Thomas' lifetime. Elliot's interest may never vest if Thomas stays in law school and graduates, but the fact that the interest may never vest does not violate the Rule. The question is whether the uncertainty over vesting will be resolved within the perpetuities period. Thomas will either quit law school or stay in law school and graduate during his lifetime. If Thomas dies while still in law school, he has arguably satisfied the terms of the conveyance, and Greenacre should pass to his heirs in fee simple.

  Greenacre to Thomas, then to the first child of Elliot who graduates from law school.

  In this case, the answer depends on whether Elliot is alive at the creation of the interest. If Elliot is alive when the interest is created, then the future interest is void because Elliot will be presumed to be capable of having children regardless of her age. (This presumption at common law is embodied in the Fertile Octogenarian Rule, which is discussed below.) Graduating from law school must occur with the lifetime of Elliot's children, but if all possible children are not lives-in-being at the creation of the interest, it will fail to vest, if at all, within the perpetuities period. If Elliot is deceased when the interest is created, then the interest satisfies the Rule, because all of her children will be considered lives-in-being at the creation of the interest. The interest will then necessarily vest, if at all, within their lifetimes.

Greenacre to Thomas for life, then to the children of Elliot who reach age 21.

If Elliot is alive, but has no children, the interest is a contingent remainder. Elliot must have a child within his lifetime or nine months after his death. Accordingly, the interest does not violate the Rule. It will vest, if at all, within a life-in-being and 21 years.

Successive life estates should always raise a red flag and prompt careful analysis. A complicating factor is that individuals are presumed able to have children regardless of age, as discussed below.

- **Strike what violates the rule.** When you determine that an interest violates the Rule, the interest is void *ab initio* and has no effect. In order to determine what interest remains, it is necessary to examine the exact wording of the transfer. You then strike out the offending interest until there is a recognizable fee. As you will see below, this is one instance where seemingly minor drafting choices can make a important difference

Here are some examples:

Greenacre to Thomas so long as not used for commercial purposes[.]~~, but if it is so used, then to Elliot~~.

Thomas has a fee simple subject to an executory interest. Elliot's future interest violates the Rule Against Perpetuities, because there is no guarantee that the interest will vest with a life-in-being and 21 years. When you strike the offending interest, Thomas receives a fee simple determinable. The grantor retains a reversionary interest.

Greenacre to Thomas[.]~~, but if it is used for commercial purposes, then to Elliot.~~

In this case, Thomas and Elliot both have the same interests described in the example immediately above. However, there is a very different result when Elliot's interest is stricken. It is not sufficient to strike "then to Elliot" because what remains is not a recognizable estate.

Greenacre to Thomas, but if it is used for commercial purposes[.]~~, then to Elliot.~~

After striking "then to Elliot," what remains is not a recognizable estate in land. It is necessary to strike the entire condition in order to create a recognizable fee.

Greenacre to Thomas[.]~~, but if it is used for commercial purposes, then to Elliot.~~

Savings Clause

Given how complicated the Rule can be to apply, practitioners have developed savings clauses that are routinely inserted in trust documents to make sure that the trust does not inadvertently violate the Rule Against Perpetuities. The savings clause automatically terminates the trust at the expiration of the perpetuities period. The Royal Lives Clause discussed above is an example of a savings clause.

Here is an example:

> Notwithstanding anything contained to the contrary in this last will and testament, each trust created under this will (except such trusts as have heretofore vested in compliance with such rule or law) shall end, unless sooner terminated under other provisions of this will, twenty-one (21) years after the death of the last survivor of such of the beneficiaries hereunder as are living at the time of my death; and thereupon that the property held in trust shall be distributed free of all trust to the persons then entitled to receive the income and/or principal therefrom, in the proportion in which they are then entitled to receive such income.

The Will of Elvis Presley available at https://www.ibiblio.org/elvis/elvwill.html.

The Absurdities Created at Common Law

At common law, when courts applied the Rule Against Perpetuities, they would entertain any possibility—no matter how remote—that the interest would fail to vest within the perpetuities period. In a number of instances, courts entered the realm of the fanciful and constructed elaborate legal fictions that defied common sense and in some cases reality. These absurdities increased the criticism of the Rule that fueled much of the reform outlined in the following subsection.

- **Fertile octogenarian.** For purposes of the Rule Against Perpetuities, individuals are conclusively presumed to be cable of having children regardless of their age. *Jee v. Audley*, 1 Cox 324, 29 Eng. Rep. 1186 (Ch. 1787). On one hand, this functions as a bright line rule and means that courts do not have to make individual determinations of fertility. In the other hand, the presumption clearly defies reality.

  Here is an example:

  Greenacre to Elliot for life, and then to the first of Elliot's children to reach 25 years of age.

  Even if Elliot is 85 at the time the interest is created, she would be presumed capable of bearing a child the following year at age 86. Assume she dies the next year. Under these facts, the child, who was not a life in being at the creation of the interest, would reach 25 years of age beyond the perpetuities period. Accordingly, the interest would be void because it could conceivably not vest within the mandated perpetuities period of a life in being plus twenty-one years.

- **The unborn widow.** This rule follows the same sort of optimism that undergirds the fertile octogenarian.

  Here is an example:

  Greenacre to Thomas for life, then to Thomas' widow for life, then to Thomas' surviving children.

  Even if Thomas is 70 at the time of the conveyance and happily married, the future interest in his children is void because the Rule entertains any possibility—no matter how remote—that the interest will fail to vest within the perpetuities period. Under the unborn widow doctrine, it is considered possible that Thomas could divorce or be widowed and then marry someone who is not yet a life-in-being at the creation of the interest. Assuming Thomas remarries and then dies, a young widow could then continue to live for more than 21 years.

- **Slothful Executor.** This rule takes a somewhat dimmer view of human nature or at least human industry. It voids any gift that is directed to be made upon the distribution of an estate because it is possible that the administration of an estate may not occur within a life in being and 21 years. *In re Estate of Campbell*, 28 Cal. App. 2d 102 (Cal. App. 1938).

  Here is an example:

  Greenacre to Thomas upon the final distribution of my estate.

  The assumption is that the administration of the Testator's estate could drag on and on. Courts have held that there is no guarantee that the administration would be completed within the perpetuities period. Accordingly, the entire gift is void.

Perpetuities Reform

The absurd interpretations of the Rule, such as the fertile octogenarian and the unborn widow, led to extensive reform of the Rule Against Perpetuities. Today, only a handful of states retain the Rule in its common law form.

Perpetuities reform began in the middle of the 20th century with the adoption of the "wait-and-see approach." Under this approach, interests that could violate the Rule would not be declared void at the creation of the interest. Instead, they were preserved until the expiration of the perpetuities period. If they did not vest by the end of period, they would be declared void. However, if they did vest (or fail) prior to the expiration of the period, then they were considered valid. This modification ameliorated some of the harshest applications of the Rule Against Perpetuities. Pennsylvania was the first state to adopt the "wait-and-see" approach by statute in 1947. A number of states quickly followed. In 1979 the *Restatement (Second) of Property* endorsed the wait-and-see approach. The wait-and-see approach had the benefit of not voiding interests because of remote and improbable possibilities, such as the slothful executor. However, it continued to be difficult to determine the applicable perpetuities and then apply the Rule. As a result, the Rule remained a source of frustration for the practicing bar and clients.

The next major reform was the Uniform Statutory Rule Against Perpetuities that was finalized in 1986. The Uniform Rule provides a bright line rule that interests must vest within 90 years. It also provides an exemption for all commercial interests, such as options, as well as the traditional charitable exemption. The Uniform Rule has the advantage of eliminating the measuring life analysis in favor of a bright line rule, but it still provides an upper most limit on the duration of non-vested future interests. As of 2015, twenty-eight states and the District of Columbia had adopted the Uniform Statutory Rule Against Perpetuities.

By the end of the 1990s, the goal of perpetuities reform had changed. Instead of trying to make the Rule easier to apply, states began to repeal or significantly modify the Rule to encourage long-term trusts that are sometimes referred to as "Dynasty Trusts." The demand for these trusts is driven largely by federal transfer tax savings. Because a trust is governed by the law of the jurisdiction where the trustee is located, a grantor can choose which state law applies by hiring a corporate trustee with offices in the desired jurisdiction. The repeal of the Rule Against Perpetuities led to a "race to the bottom" as states competed to attract large trust deposits. As of 2015, eight states had repealed the Rulc. Another nine states have adopted longer perpetuities periods, sometimes only for property in trust. These extended periods range from 150 years in Washington State to 1,000 years in Colorado and Utah. Seventeen states retain the Rule, but have exempted certain trusts from its application. With the movement to repeal the Rule Against Perpetuities, public policy regarding future interests has come full circle.

Exercise 5-4. *Texaco Refining & Marketing, Inc. v. Samowitz*—Options to Purchase

Defeasible estates almost always arise in a donative context, meaning they are not generally the result of a market transactions and arms' length bargaining. The reason for this is that the stakes are too high. When a trigger event occurs in a defeasible fee, the result is forfeiture—termination of the possessory interests. The risk of forfeiture makes a defeasible estate not a sound investment. This differs from real covenants that are often found in non-donative marketplace transactions. Real covenants give rise to damages or injunctive relief, but not forfeiture.

The Rule Against Perpetuities is a check on the power of present possessors to exert dead hand control over future generations. Like defeasible fees, in general, the Rule Against Perpetuities is most applicable to donative intra-family transfers. However, there are some commercial or market-based interests that would seem to fall within the definition of interests subject to the Rule Against Perpetuities, such as rights of first refusal and options to purchase.

Courts have struggled with whether to exempt such interests from the application of the Rule on policy grounds. The Uniform Statutory Rule Against Perpetuities exempts most future interests created in non-donative transfers. The following case provides insight as to the reasoning employed by the courts when asked to void an option to purchase in a long-term commercial lease.

Texaco Refining & Marketing, Inc. v. Samowitz

213 Conn. 676 (1990)

Peters, C.J. This appeal concerns the validity, under General Statutes § 47-33a and the common law rule against perpetuities, of an option to purchase real property contained in a long-term commercial lease. The named plaintiff, Texaco Refining and Marketing, Inc., brought an action for specific performance of an option contract against the defendants, Jack Samowitz, Alex Klein, Sheila Klein, Gloria Walkoff and Marilyn Moss, as successors in interest to the lessor of a lease executed and recorded in 1964. The trial court rendered judgment for the plaintiff, and the defendants have appealed. We find no reversible error.

The trial court relied on a stipulation between the parties for its finding of facts. On June 3, 1964, the named plaintiff and Kay Realty Corporation, the predecessor in interest of the defendants, executed a lease for property in Southington. The term of the leasehold was fifteen years, subject to renewal by the lessee, the plaintiff, for three additional five year periods. The plaintiff exercised two of these options for renewal.

The provision of the lease at issue in this appeal granted the plaintiff "the exclusive right, at lessee's option, to purchase the demised premises ... at any time during the term of this lease or an extension or renewal thereof, from and after the 14th year of the initial term for the sum of $125,000." On August 14, 1987, during the second renewal period under the lease, the plaintiff gave notification, by certified mail, of its exercise of its option to purchase. When the defendants refused to transfer the property, the plaintiff brought this action, on December 30, 1987, for a judicial order of specific performance.

The trial court found that the plaintiff had demonstrated that it was ready, willing and able to perform its obligations under the contract, and that the option contained in its lease was supported by consideration. Noting that the terms of the lease had originally been negotiated by two corporations bargaining at arm's length, the court concluded that the option was enforceable. The court expressly considered and rejected both the statutory and the common law defenses that the defendants reassert in this appeal. Although we do not necessarily subscribe to the trial court's reasoning, we concur in its judgment on alternate grounds.

II

The defendants rely on the common law rule against perpetuities as their second argument for the unenforceability of the plaintiff's option to purchase their property. The rule against perpetuities states that "[n]o interest is good unless it must vest, if at all, not later than twenty-one years after some life in being at the creation of the interest." J. Gray, The Rule Against Perpetuities (4th Ed. 1942). The defendants maintain that the option in this case did not vest within the time span mandated by the rule. We disagree.

The trial court determined that the option in the lease agreement did not violate the rule against perpetuities by construing the lease agreement as a series of discrete undertakings, first for an initial fourteen year term, and thereafter for each renewal term. Because the option could be exercised only within one of these discrete terms, none of which exceeded twenty-one years in length, the court held that the interest in the option would necessarily vest within the time period specified by the rule against perpetuities.

Whatever might be the merits of the trial court's construction of the lease agreement, we prefer to consider a more basic question: do options in long-term leases fall within the jurisdiction of the rule against perpetuities? Our precedents indicate that the rule applies to an unrestricted option to purchase real property; but not to an option to renew the term of a real property lease. We have not, however, previously considered the relationship between the rule against perpetuities and an option to purchase contained in a long-term commercial lease of real property.

The defendants have offered no reason of policy why we should extend the ambit of the rule against perpetuities to cover an option to purchase contained in a commercial lease. "The underlying and fundamental purpose of the rule is founded on the public policy in favor of free alienability of property and against restricting its marketability over long periods of time by restraints on its alienation." 4 Restatement, Property (1944). An option coupled with a longterm commercial lease is consistent with these policy objectives because it stimulates improvement of the property and thus renders it more rather than less marketable.

We therefore conclude that an option to purchase contained in a commercial lease, at least if the option must be exercised within the leasehold term, is valid without regard to the rule against perpetuities. This position is consistent with the weight of authority in the United States. The commentators have, for a long time, unanimously supported what has become the majority view. The plaintiff's option in this case was, therefore, enforceable.

There is no error.

Exercise 5-5. *Texaco Refining* Revisited

The court ultimately determined that an option to purchase in a long-term commercial lease was consistent with the public policy supporting the Rule Against Perpetuities, namely free marketability of property. Rather than operating as a drag on title, the court found that the option coupled with a long-term commercial lease "stimulates improvement of the property and thus renders it more rather than less marketable." Do you agree with this analysis?

Other Regulatory Rules

In addition to the Rule Against Perpetuities, there are a number of other rules that limit the creation of estates in land and future interests. This section outlines the major rules that still have relevancy today: the Destructibility of Contingent Remainders, the Doctrine of Worthier Title, and the Rule in Shelley's Case.

Destructibility of Contingent Remainders

At common law, contingent remainders in real property were strongly disfavored because of the uncertainty they created. They would be deemed "destroyed" in three instances:

- Failure to vest. The contingent remainder failed to vest at the natural termination of the prior estate.

  Here is an example:

  Greenacre to Thomas for life, remainder to Elliot if Elliot reaches age 21 years.

  Thomas has a life estate and Elliot has a contingent remainder because its enjoyment is subject to a condition subsequent. The Grantor retains a reversion. If Thomas dies before Elliot turns 21, her interest will not immediately follow the life estate. Under this rule, her contingent remainder would be destroyed, and the Grantor's reversion would become possessory.

- Doctrine of Merger. Merger occurs when a party to a conveyance obtains all outstanding present and vested interests in a property. In such case, the individual takes the property in fee simple absolute. These situations arise when interests are transferred after the initial conveyance. Merger destroys contingent remainders, because it occurs when the same person holds all present interests and vested interests. Contingent interests are not taken into account.

  Here is an example:

  Greenacre to Thomas for life, remainder to Elliot if Elliot becomes a judge.

Thomas has a life estate and Elliot once again has a contingent remainder because enjoyment is subject to a condition subsequent. The Grantor retains a reversion. If the Grantor coveys his reversion to Thomas, and Elliot has not yet become a judge, the Doctrine of Merger awards Thomas a fee simple absolute, because Thomas holds the present interest (i.e., the life estate) and the vested interest (the reversion). Elliot's contingent remainder is destroyed.

- **Surrender of present interest.** The owner of the present possessory interest surrenders the interest before the contingent remainder vests.

  Here is an example:

  Greenacre to Thomas for life, remainder to Elliot when she marries.

  Thomas has a life estate which is a present possessory interest. Elliot has a contingent remainder, and the Grantor retains a reversion. If Thomas transfers his interest to the Grantor before Elliot marries, Elliot's contingent remainder is destroyed.

Today, many jurisdictions have abolished the Rule of the Destructibility of Contingent Remainders. In those jurisdictions, if a contingent remainder does not vest upon the termination of the prior estates, it becomes an executory interest. When applying the rule, it is important to be able to distinguish between contingent remainders and executory interests. A contingent remainder follows an estate that will terminate naturally upon the death of the present possessor—a life estate. It can also follow an estate of years.

Doctrine of Worthier Title

The Doctrine of Worthier Title prohibits the creation of a remainder in the grantor's heirs. The Doctrine applies in the case of a life estate or a term of years when the interests are created under the same instrument. The Doctrine creates a presumption that the grantor intended to retain a reversion, which can be rebutted by clear evidence. Today, the Doctrine only applies to *inter vivos* transfers.

Here is an example:

Greenacre to Thomas, remainder to the heirs of the Grantor.

Rule in *Shelley's Case*

The Rule in Shelley's Case takes its name from an English case from 1581 known, not surprisingly, as *Shelley's Case.* It prohibits the conveyance of a life estate followed by a remainder in the life tenant's heirs. It also applies to a transfer of a fee tail followed by a remainder in the heirs. The result under the Rule is that the life tenant takes a fee simple.

Here is an example:

Greenacre to Thomas for life and then to Thomas' heirs.

The Rule in Shelley's Case provides that Thomas takes both the life estate and the remainder. The Doctrine of Merger then holds that Thomas takes a fee simple. The creation of a remainder in Thomas' heirs is different from a remainder in Thomas' children. A living person does not have heirs. Accordingly, Thomas' heirs can only be determined when he dies. In contrast, a conveyance of a remainder to Thomas' children would be a vested remainder subject to open, assuming that Thomas has a child living at the creation of the interest.

Interpretation of Ambiguous Conveyances

The rules regulating estates in land and limiting the creation of future interests are designed to discourage concentration of wealth and the type of social hierarchy that characterized feudalism. In order to further these goals, courts adopted the Rule Against the Creation of New Estates. It channels grantors into one of the recognized fees. The channeling enhances certainty in the marketplace, because grantors are required to use easily recognizable fees that will be respected by the courts. When faced with a hybrid fee in 1893, Justice Holmes explained the Rule Against the Creation of New Estates. He wrote: "It would be most unfortunate and unexpected if it should be discovered at this late day that it was possible to impose such a qualification upon a fee[.]" *Johnson v. Whiton,* 34 N.E. 542 (Mass. 1893).

Even though grantors are required to use a recognized fee, there will be instances where the language used to create a fee is ambiguous. In such case, the courts will examine the language to determine which recognized fee the conveyance most closely approximates. Courts use rules of construction to assist them in this inquiry. The rules of construction reflect the strong policy in favor of free alienability of land. Where possible, courts will affirm the greater interest and avoid forfeiture. For example, if it were unclear whether the grantor intended a fee simple or a fee simple determinable, courts would rule in favor of the fee simple.

Another example of an area where ambiguity may arise is distinguishing between a defeasible fee and a real covenant. As we have discussed, a defeasible fee differs significantly from a real covenant in terms of remedy even though they may both focus on issues of land use. When the trigger event occurs in a defeasible fee, the result is forfeiture of the estate. In contrast, when the trigger event occurs in a real covenant, the remedy is going to be damages or possibly injunctive relief. There is no divestment. To the extent possible, courts will affirm a real covenant in order to avoid a forfeiture.

Exercise 5-6. *Hagaman v. Board of Education*

In the following case, the court was asked to construe a conveyance that is almost fifty years old. We can assume that the original grantors are no longer living. Their heir claimed that the conveyance created a defeasible fee and he possessed a reverter or a right of re-entry. The plaintiff asked the court to construe the conveyance as defeasible, but he seemed indifferent as to whether it was a fee simple determinable or a fee simple subject to a condition subsequent. Do you see a recognized estate in land?

Hagaman v. The Board of Education of the Township of Woodbridge

117 N.J. Super. 446 (1971)

LANE, JUDGE. The complaint seeks possession of real property conveyed by plaintiff's parents to defendant on October 20, 1925. Both parties moved for summary judgment. The trial court granted defendant's motion. The judgment that was entered "ORDERED that Summary Judgment be and is hereby granted to the defendant, Board of Education of the Township of Woodbridge dismissing plaintiff's complaint." Plaintiff appeals.

The deed to defendant contained a provision:

> It is the understanding of the parties to this conveyance that the hereinabove described land is conveyed solely for the purpose of being used for the erection and maintenance of a public school or schools and that the Board of Education of Woodbridge Township, N.J., will erect a school thereon on or before the school year of 1926 and use such building for school purposes.

From the affidavits and admissions in the pleadings it was uncontroverted that defendant erected a school building on the property and used the property for school purposes until approximately 1968. In that year the school building was closed. The students who formerly would have attended the school began to attend two new schools within the area. At the time of the trial the property in question was used as a recreational park or playground. It was equipped with swings, a sliding board, monkey bars and basketball courts. During the summer it was supervised by a full-time playground supervisor. Organized and supervised play activities were carried on. On March 2, 1971 after the judgment was rendered the school building was destroyed by fire.

Plaintiff argues that the deed expresses a clear and unequivocal intention to convey a fee simple determinable or a fee simple subject to a condition subsequent and that he is entitled to possession because the property is no longer being used for the maintenance of a public school.

In determining the meaning of a deed, prime consideration is the intent of the parties. An estate in fee simple determinable is an estate in fee simple which automatically determines upon the occurrence of a given event. The grantor retains a possibility of reverter upon the occurrence of the stated event. Generally, the intent to create such an estate is indicated by the use of words denoting duration of time such as "while," "during," "so long as." "The absence of some one of these phraseologies makes it likely that a court will find a covenant, a trust, or some other type of interest less drastic in its sanctions." 2 *Powell, Real Property.* [P]articular forms of expression standing alone and without resort to the purpose of the instrument in question are not determinative. Words of limitation merely stating the purpose for which the land is conveyed usually do not indicate an intent to create an estate in fee simple determinable although other language in the instrument, the amount of the consideration and the circumstances surrounding the conveyance may indicate such an intent. *Restatement, Property*, § 44, comment m. When a conveyance contains only a clause of condition or of covenant, such clause does not usually indicate an intent to create a fee simple determinable. *Restatement, Property* § 44, comment n.

An estate in fee simple subject to a condition subsequent is an estate in fee simple which upon the occurrence of a given event gives to the grantor or his successor in interest the right to reenter and terminate the estate. Upon the occurrence of the given event, the forfeiture of the estate is not automatic. The intent to create such an estate may be indicated by the use of such words as "on condition that," "provided that." Generally, an intent to create a fee simple subject to a condition subsequent is established when the conveyance contains one of the above phrases and a provision that if the given event occurs the grantor may enter and terminate or has a right to re-enter. "Conditions subsequent must be so created as to leave no doubt regarding the grantor's intention." 4 *Thompson, Real Property.* A mere statement of the use to which the conveyed land is to be devoted is not sufficient to create an estate in fee simple subject to a condition subsequent. Absent clear intention to create a fee simple subject to a condition subsequent, a conveyance with words of condition may be found to create a covenant, a trust, or a mere precatory expression.

Language in an instrument which is alleged to create a fee simple determinable or a fee simple subject to a condition subsequent is strictly construed. "A recognized rule of construction indicates that an instrument, when a choice exists, is to be construed against rather than in favor of a forfeiture."

If a choice is between an estate in fee simple determinable and an estate on condition subsequent, the latter is preferred. Where it is doubtful whether a clause in a deed is a covenant or a condition, the former is preferred. When a condition in a deed is relied upon to defeat an estate, it should be strictly construed and its violation must be clearly established. In the present case there are no words indicating an intent to create a fee simple determinable or a fee simple subject to a condition subsequent. There are no words creating either a right of re-entry or a possibility of a reversion.

Plaintiff does not have a right to possession to the property under the deed. This holding by the trial court was correct.

The judgment is affirmed.

Exercise 5-7. *Hagaman* Revisited

1. Assume you represented plaintiff's parents in the original transaction. How would you have drafted the deed to ensure that the grantors retained a right of reverter?
2. The court held that the deed provision quoted in the case did not constitute words of limitation sufficient to create a defeasible fee. If that were the case, what was the purpose and effect of the provision? Why did the grantors include it in the deed if it was not binding?
3. Precatory language expresses the wish, desire, or hope of a grantor. It does not represent a binding obligation or a limitation on the fee. Assume you represent the Board of Education. What weight do you advise your client that it needs to give to the precatory language contained in the deed?
4. What do you believe the grantors intended when they conveyed the property to the Board of Education?

Public Policy Limitations

The rules that we have discussed up until now all impose limits on the way that grantors can exercise "dead hand control." They restrict grantors to an inflexible set of recognized fees. They also limit the duration of certain future interests. They even tip the scales in favor of free alienability of land when courts are faced with ambiguous language. This section discusses a different type of limitations that can be imposed on estates in land. These limitations restrict what a grantor can do with his land as the present possessor in fee because of important public policy considerations. In other words, the limitations discussed in this section relate to why the grantor chose a particular restriction, not how the grantor expressed the restriction in the conveyance. They are concerned with the motivation for a particular restriction, not the technical language used to create the estate.

In this section, we will discuss three different instances where courts will void a restriction because it violates public policy: restraints on alienation; restraint on first marriage; and unreasonable restraints that interfere with family harmony. The present possessor in fee simple absolute has the power to customize a transfer and divide up the ownership of his property over time, provided he complies with the formal requirements discussed in the prior section. We saw how the Rule Against Perpetuities and other restrictions attempt to balance this power with the interests of future generations and the need to make property marketable by ensuring clear title. The rules in this section set forth another set of limitations on a grantor's power to control the disposition of his property beyond the grave. They are designed to blunt what has been referred to as the "cold and numbing influence of the dead hand." Sir Arthur Hobhouse, *The Dead Hand* (1880).

At the outset, it is important to understand why, and under what circumstances, a grantor would want to impose limitations on the future use of his property. Part of the motivation may be the belief that if you control the property, you also control the person. If grantors believe that they know best about what life choices their heirs should make, they may condition inheritance on certain behaviors or accomplishments. Their hope would be that their descendants would comply with the terms rather than forfeit the estates. Today it is relatively rare for a grantor to use a legal estate to incentivize heirs to behave in a certain way. For the reasons we discussed in the section on Trusts, legal estates in land are ill-suited to this purpose. However, incentive trusts remain a popular estate planning option. In a typical incentive trust, the grantor would condition a beneficiary's interest on certain behaviors, such as entering the family business or earning a law degree. Incentive trusts can also require that the beneficiary refrain from certain harmful behavior, such as substance abuse or gambling.

As you read through the cases, consider what public policy interests justify limiting the power of a present possessor in fee simple to utilize a recognized estate. Where do you strike the balance between the interests of present possessors and future owners?

Exercise 5-8. *Hankins v. Mathews* — Restraints on Alienation

Restraints on alienation fly in the face of the estates system, namely to promote the free marketability of land. A restraint on alienation is considered to be incompatible with a fee simple absolute. Such a restraint is considered "repugnant to the fee" and is void. Courts will sometimes approve a partial restraint on alienation when it is considered "reasonable."

As you read the case, consider whether the Rule Against Restraints on Alienation is really a public policy limitation. Is it perhaps more closely related to the limitation on the creation of new estates? Or is it an example of ambiguous language, because a deed cannot convey a fee simple and impose a restraint on alienation?

Hankins v. Mathews

221 Tenn. 190 (1968)

BURNETT, CHIEF JUSTICE. The parties will hereinafter be referred to as they appeared in the trial court; that is, James A. Hankins, et al., complainants, and Virgil Mathews, et al, defendants.

We are asked on this appeal to ascertain the legal consequences of certain provisions contained in the will of one A.A. Hankins. Mr. Hankins died testate on January 31, 1952, leaving a will, the pertinent provisions of which read as follows:

> Second. In the event my wife, Sarah Elizabeth should survive me I give, devise and bequeath to her all of my personal property of every nature, description and wherever located and all of my real estate, particularly such real estate as is described in said deeds recorded in Deed Book 528, Page 275 and Deed Book 236, Page 339 and Deed Book 273, Page 440 to have and to hold during her natural life and at her death to go to the persons hereinafter described.
>
> Fourth. I give and bequeath to my nephew, Jim Grubb, at the death of my wife, Sarah Elizabeth Hankins all of my personal property that the said Elizabeth Hankins has not used during her life "if she survives me" of every nature, description and whereever located. I further give and bequeath to my nephew the following real estate: One tract of land containing twenty five (25) acres more or less described in certain deed of P.H. Stanford and wife, Sally Stanford being deed dated March 18, 1914, recorded in Deed Book 273, Page 440 and a certain tract of land containing thirty (30) acres more or less described in a certain deed dated June 17, 1914 from D.M. Roberts and wife, Mary S. Roberts, recorded in Deed Book 236, Page 339. The said Jim Grubb is to keep this property in his possession ten years before he is able to sell, mortgage or in any other manner incumber [sic] and dispose of the same, and if he should attempt to do so, then in this event the said tracts of land shall revert to the heirs at law of A.A. Hankins.

After the death of Sarah Elizabeth Hankins, and within the ten year period thereafter, Jim Grubb executed certain deeds and leases in which he transferred the property in question to the defendants. The complainants then filed their original bill in the Chancery Court of Knox County, alleging that they are the sole heirs of A.A. Hankins and that by virtue of the attempted transfers from Jim Grubb to the defendants, the property, in accordance with the will of A.A. Hankins, had reverted to them. The complainants prayed that they be declared to be the lawful owners in fee simple of the entire thirty acre tract and of a one-half undivided interest in the twenty-five acre tract; that the twenty-five acre tract be partitioned or sold and the proceeds divided accordingly; that they be awarded certain rents and profits; that all the deeds to the defendants be declared void and removed as a cloud from the complainants' title and that the defendants be perpetually enjoined from setting up any claims with respect to the property.

The defendants demurred to the original bill on the ground that the restrictions placed by the testator on Jim Grubb's right to sell or otherwise encumber this real estate were "absolutely void as an illegal and unlawful attempt to restrain the alienation of said property."

The defendants insist that the testator, having given Jim Grubb a fee simple absolute estate in the property in one portion of his will, cannot subsequently divest said Grubb of important incidents of ownership such as the right to sell, mortgage or otherwise encumber the property. It is argued that these rights are inherent in a fee simple absolute estate in property and an attempt to take them away, even for a limited period, is an attempt to create an estate not recognized by the law.

The complainants insist, however, that the testator was only placing a reasonable restriction on the right of alienation, and that such reasonable restraints are in full accordance with the established law in this State.

After a thorough consideration of the problem we find ourselves inclined to agree with the propositions put forth by the defendants.

It should be emphasized before proceeding further that we are herein dealing with a total restriction upon the right of alienation, even though such restriction is only to last for ten years. We are not confronted with a situation similar to that presented in the case of *Overton v. Lea*, 108 Tenn. 505 (1902). In that case it was provided in the testator's will that property left to the beneficiary was never to come into the possession of the testator's sister or the sister's husband or anyone bearing the name of Kelly. The Supreme Court allowed the provision to stand on the ground that it was not inconsistent with the reasonable enjoyment of the fee. It was emphasized that the result would have been different had the restriction been a total one.

In *Andrews v. Hall*, 156 Neb. 817 (1953), the Supreme Court of Nebraska discusses estates subject to conditions in language which we consider adequate. It is there stated:

> We do not say that a testator may not create a vested fee simple estate subject to a condition subsequent, or a determinable or defeasible fee. What we do say is that a restriction against alienation of a vested fee simple estate is not any one of these, nor, since it is void, can it be used as the sole basis for the creation of any of these estates.

In our research we have found that the courts of practically all jurisdictions are in accord with the opinions expressed herein.

For the reasons discussed herein, we hold that the demurrer should be sustained and the case DISMISSED.

Exercise 5-9. *Hankins* Revisited

1. Courts will often approve a partial restraint on alienation. However, a total restraint on alienation for ten years is not considered a partial restraint. What would be an example of an acceptable partial restraint on alienation?
2. Can you think of any good reasons from a policy perspective that a grantor may want to restrict alienation for a period of years?

Exercise 5-10. *Casey v. Casey*—Unreasonable Restraints and Family Harmony

The following case involves what the court refers to as a "slight" restraint on alienation. It prohibits the sale or lease of the property to a single individual. The court is faced with the prospect of determining whether the restraint is reasonable. In order to do so, the court must determine why the restraint was imposed in the first place. Do you think it is appropriate for a court to inquire as to the motivation of the grantor/testator who is not available to testify on his own behalf? What considerations justify overriding an individual's right to testamentary freedom?

Casey v. Casey

287 Ark. 395 (1985)

Holt, Chief Justice. This case involves the interpretation of a restriction placed on a devise to appellee which, if violated, would shift the interest in the inheritance to appellants. The trial court held the restriction was invalid as an unreasonable restraint on alienation and too vague to be enforced and that appellee thus held the property in fee simple absolute.

Donald Casey, appellee, is the son of the testator, Fred Casey. The testator left $50.00 to each of six of his seven children and left the rest of his estate to appellee. In 1974, shortly before he died, the testator added a codicil which placed a restriction on appellee's inheritance. The appellee filed a petition to remove the cloud from the title in the Pope County Chancery Court on October 2, 1981 in which he sought to have the restriction declared void. The petition was challenged by appellants, who would take the property upon a violation of the restriction.

The testator's codicil stated in pertinent part:

> FIRST: ... Karen Kim Casey is the daughter of Donald J. Casey. It is my will that Karen Kim Casey shall never own or possess as a tenant, nor be on as a guest for more than one week per each calendar year any of the real estate which I have devised to my son, Donald J. Casey.
>
> SECOND: It is my intent to create a defeasible estate in Donald J. Casey in the nature of, and conditional limitation over, or executory devise, with the fact of termination depending upon the ownership or possession of Karen Kim Casey as set out above. It is my will that in the event Karen Kim Casey should ever own any part of the land which I heretofore bequeathed to Donald J. Casey or in the event she should ever possess said land as a tenant, or in the event she should ever be a guest on said land or any of it for more than one week of each calendar year, that the estate of Donald J. Casey immediately terminate as to that part of my real estate which I have devised and bequeathed to him and that said real estate shall immediately

become the property of Sam Casey in fee simple absolute and to his heirs and assigns forever. It is further my will to create a vested estate in Sam Casey and his heirs in fee simple absolute in the nature of the interest created by a springing or shifting use.

We agree with the trial court that the restriction is invalid. The trial court based its ruling in part on a finding that the phrase "never own or possess as a tenant" was vague, in that it could be read two ways, depending on whether a comma is inserted after "own." We see no vagueness or ambiguity, particularly when reading the will as a whole, but we do agree with the chancellor and find that the restriction is an unreasonable restraint on alienation.

A direct restraint is "a provision which, by its terms, prohibits or penalizes the exercise of the power of alienation." There are three types of direct restraints: disabling restraints, forfeiture restraints and promissory restraints. This case involves a forfeiture restraint, which exists when, by the terms of an instrument of transfer, the estate will be subject to forfeiture on alienation or will be terminated. In general, the courts adhere to the rule that all forfeiture restraints on the alienation of a legal fee simple interest in land are void. This rule operates to give full effect to the conveyance or devise except that the condition or limitation with respect to alienation is eliminated.

Restraints on alienation may be upheld if they are a reasonable means of accomplishing a legal and useful purpose. The Restatement of Property § 406 provides:

> The restraint on the alienation of a legal possessory estate in fee simple which is, or but for the restraint would be, indefeasible is valid if, and only if,
>
> (a) the restraint is a promissory restraint or a forfeiture restraint, and
>
> (b) the restraint is qualified so as to permit alienation to some though not all possible alienees, and
>
> (c) the restraint is reasonable under the circumstances, and
>
> (d) if the restraint is a forfeiture restraint, the requirements of the rule against perpetuities are satisfied.

4 Restatement of Property § 406 (1944).

Comment a to § 406 further states:

> To uphold restraints on the alienation of such estates it must appear that the objective sought to be accomplished by the imposition of the restraint is of sufficient social importance to outweigh the evils which flow from interfering with the power of alienation or that the curtailment of the power of alienation is so slight that no social danger is involved.

This rule applies even when the restraint on alienation is slight.

> All the circumstances of the conveyance should be considered in determining the reasonableness of the restraint. When present, the following factors support the conclusion that a restraint is unreasonable:
>
> 1. the restraint is capricious;

2. the restraint is imposed for spite or malice;

3. the one imposing the restraint has no interest in land that is benefited by the enforcement of the restraint;

4. the restraint is unlimited in duration;

5. the number of persons to whom alienation is prohibited is large.

Restatement § 406 comment i.

Applying these and other factors, we conclude that this restraint is unreasonable. The restraint did not protect any interest the testator had in the land while he was living, and only worked to keep his granddaughter off the land after his death. The duration of the restraint is limited to the lifetime of his granddaughter, who is 28, so it will likely remain for the entire period that appellee holds the land.

This is a case of first impression in Arkansas. In *Fleming v. Blount*, 202 Ark. 507 (1941), a forfeiture restraint was also at issue, but in that case we found the restraint was of short duration and served a worthwhile purpose. Further, the court held there that the testator's beneficiaries did not acquire fee simple title in the land. Therefore, that restraint was not contrary to any public policy and was valid. That case in no way suggests that a restraint such as the one before us now would be reasonable and does not offer precedent or guidelines for the situation now confronting us.

Here, there is no worthwhile purpose evident in this restraint; it appears to be capricious, and imposed for spite or malice. At trial, no one could explain why the testator harbored such animosity toward his granddaughter. Though the restraint is limited directly to only one person, the appellee's daughter would be a natural heir of appellee, which makes the restraint more significant. Further, to find that a restraint is reasonable on this factor alone would lead to difficult and arbitrary line-drawing in determining when a limited number of restricted transferees is too many.

For public policy reasons, some cases have held that provisions by which the acquisition or retention of property interests was made to depend on the separation of parent and minor child were illegal conditions. "A broader objection has appeared on occasion against any provision which tends to disrupt or interfere with family relations." *American Law of Property*, Vol. VI, § 27.19 (1974). Though this restraint does not require total separation of father and daughter, its obvious effect, if not purpose, is to interfere with family relations.

For these reasons, the restriction is invalid.

Affirmed.

Exercise 5-11. *Casey* Revisited

1. In *Hankins v. Mathews*, the plaintiffs objected to the sale of the property by the original devisee to the defendants. The plaintiffs claimed that the sale was

void because it violated the restrictions in the will. The procedural posture of *Casey* is different. Here, the original devisee is requesting the court to declare the restraint void and remove the cloud from his title. *Hankins* should be a reminder about how important it is to make sure that a purchaser can grant good title before completing the transaction.

2. How did the court determine that the restraint was "capricious and imposed for spite or malice"?
3. The court employs a slippery slope argument when it explains that, if it found the restraint reasonable because it was limited to one person, it "would lead to difficult and arbitrary line-drawing in determining when a limited number of restricted transferees is too many." Do you agree?

Exercise 5-12. *Shapira v. Union National Bank* — Rule Against Unreasonable Restraints on Marriage

A restraint on first marriage is generally void. The importance of promoting marriage is considered comparable to the importance of promoting the free alienability of property. Courts have held that some restraints on first marriage are reasonable. For example, if the transfer is designed to provide support until marriage, then it may be considered reasonable. The key is whether the purpose of the restraint is intended as a caprice or a penalty. If so, then the restraint is most likely void.

Parents or older relatives who have definite opinions regarding a descendant's choice of a spouse may find the ability to do so from beyond the grave too attractive to pass up. As a general matter, the law respects testamentary freedom. In *Shapira v. Union National Bank*, the court grapples with when restraints on marriage are reasonable. Again, it is a question of balancing the rights of present possessors with future generations. As you read the case, consider how you would feel if your parent conditioned your inheritance in a similar manner.

1. The first question is to ask from a legal standpoint is why the Rule Against Unreasonable Restraints on Marriage only applies to first marriages? It is common to provide a life estate for a surviving spouse that may be conditioned on re-marriage. Why is that sort of restraint on marriage permissible?
2. From a family perspective, you might also want to ask what sort of dynamics led to this result. Do you think Dan was surprised by the restriction in his father's will? If Dan's father had talked to him about this during his lifetime, what do you think Dan would have said?

3. Pay particular attention to the structure of Dr. Shapira's will. You should prepare an annotated family tree. Who are the other beneficiaries? Are they married? Where do they live?
4. When do you think a religious restriction on marriage should be considered reasonable? Remember that law serves human values.

Shapira v. Union National Bank

39 Ohio Misc. 28 (1974)

Henderson, Judge. This is an action for a declaratory judgment and the construction of the will of David Shapira, M.D., who died April 13, 1973, a resident of this county. By agreement of the parties, the case has been submitted upon the pleadings and the exhibit.

The portions of the will in controversy are as follows:

> *Item VIII.* All the rest, residue and remainder of my estate, real and personal, of every kind and description and wheresoever situated, which I may own or have the right to dispose of at the time of my decease, I give, devise and bequeath to my three (3) beloved children, to wit: Ruth Shapira Aharoni, of Tel Aviv, Israel, or wherever she may reside at the time of my death; to my son Daniel Jacob Shapira, and to my son Mark Benjamin Simon Shapira in equal shares, with the following qualifications:
>
> (b) My son Daniel Jacob Shapira should receive his share of the bequest only, if he is married at the time of my death to a Jewish girl whose both parents were Jewish. In the event that at the time of my death he is not married to a Jewish girl whose both parents were Jewish, then his share of this bequest should be kept by my executor for a period of not longer than seven (7) years and if my said son Daniel Jacob gets married within the seven year period to a Jewish girl whose both parents were Jewish, my executor is hereby instructed to turn over his share of my bequest to him. In the event, however, that my said son Daniel Jacob is unmarried within the seven (7) years after my death to a Jewish girl whose both parents were Jewish, or if he is married to a non Jewish girl, then his share of my estate, as provided in item 8 above should go to The State of Israel, absolutely.

The provision for the testator's other son Mark, is conditioned substantially similarly. Daniel Jacob Shapira, the plaintiff, alleges that the condition upon his inheritance is unconstitutional, contrary to public policy and unenforceable because of its unreasonableness, and that he should be given his bequest free of the restriction. Daniel is 21 years of age, unmarried and a student at Youngstown State University.

The provision in controversy is an executory devise or legacy, under which vesting of the estate of Daniel Jacob Shapira or the State of Israel is not intended to take place necessarily at the death of the testator, but rather conditionally, at a time not later than seven years after the testator's death. The executory aspect of the provision, though rather unusual, does not render it invalid.

PUBLIC POLICY

The condition that Daniel's share should be "turned over to him if he should marry a Jewish girl whose both parents were Jewish" constitutes a partial restraint upon marriage. If the condition were that the beneficiary not marry anyone, the restraint would be general or total, and, at least in the case of a first marriage, would be held to be contrary to public policy and void. A partial restraint of marriage which imposes only reasonable restrictions is valid, and not contrary to public policy. The great weight of authority in the United States is that gifts conditioned upon the beneficiary's marrying within a particular religious class or faith are reasonable.

Plaintiff contends, however, that in Ohio a condition such as the one in this case is void as against the public policy of this state. In Ohio, as elsewhere, a testator may not attach a condition to a gift which is in violation of public policy. There can be no question about the soundness of plaintiff's position that the public policy of Ohio favors freedom of religion and that it is guaranteed by Section 7, Article I of the Ohio Constitution, providing that "all men have a natural and indefeasible right to worship Almighty God according to the dictates of their own conscience." Plaintiff's position that the free choice of religious practice cannot be circumscribed or controlled by contract is substantiated by *Hackett v. Hackett*, 150 N.E.2d 431 (Ohio Ct. App. 1958). This case held that a covenant in a separation agreement, incorporated in a divorce decree, that the mother would rear a daughter in the Roman Catholic faith was unenforceable. However, the controversial condition in the case at bar is a partial restraint upon marriage and not a covenant to restrain the freedom of religious practice; and, of course, this court is not being asked to hold the plaintiff in contempt for failing to marry a Jewish girl of Jewish parentage.

Counsel contends that if "Dr. David Shapira, during his life, had tried to impose upon his son those restrictions set out in his Will he would have violated the public policy of Ohio as shown in *Hackett v. Hackett.* The public policy is equally violated by the restrictions Dr. Shapira has placed on his son by his Will." This would be true, by analogy, if Dr. Shapira, in his lifetime, had tried to force his son to marry a Jewish girl as the condition of a completed gift. But it is not true that if Dr. Shapira had agreed to make his son an inter-vivos gift if he married a Jewish girl within seven years, that his son could have forced him to make the gift free of the condition.

It is noted, furthermore, in this connection, that the courts of Pennsylvania distinguish between testamentary gifts conditioned upon the religious faith of the beneficiary and those conditioned upon marriage to persons of a particular religious faith. In *In re Clayton's Estate, supra* (13 D. & C. 413 [Phila. Co. Pa. 1930]), the court upheld a gift of a life estate conditioned upon the beneficiary's not marrying a woman of the Catholic faith. In its opinion the court distinguishes the earlier case of *Drace v. Klinedinst*, 275 Pa. 266 (1922), in which a life estate willed to grandchildren, provided they remained faithful to a particular religion, was held to violate the public policy of Pennsylvania. In *Clayton's Estate*, the court said that the condition concerning marriage did not affect the faith of the beneficiary, and that the condition, operating only on the choice of a wife, was too remote to be regarded as coercive of religious faith.

[Plaintiff cites the] case of *Maddox v. Maddox* [52 Va. (11 Grattan's) 804] (Va. 1854). The testator in this case willed a remainder to his niece if she remain a member of the Society of Friends. When the niece arrived at a marriageable age there were but five or six unmarried men of the society in the neighborhood in which she lived. She married a non-member and thus lost her own membership. The court held the condition to be an unreasonable restraint upon marriage and void, and that there being no gift over upon breach of the condition, the condition was in terrorem, and did not avoid the bequest. It can be seen that while the court considered the testamentary condition to be a restraint upon marriage, it was primarily one in restraint of religious faith. The court said that with the small number of eligible bachelors in the area the condition would have operated as a virtual prohibition of the niece's marrying, and that she could not be expected to "go abroad" in search of a helpmate or to be subjected to the chance of being sought after by a stranger. The court distinguished the facts of its case from those in England upholding conditions upon marriage by observing that England was "already overstocked with inhabitants" while this country had "an unbounded extent of territory, a large portion of which is yet unsettled, and in which increase of population is one of the main elements of national prosperity." The other ground upon which the Virginia court rested its decision, that the condition was in terrorem because of the absence of a gift over, is clearly not applicable to the case at bar, even if it were in accord with Ohio law, because of the gift over to the State of Israel contained in the Shapira will.

In arguing for the applicability of the *Maddox v. Maddox* test of reasonableness to the case at bar, counsel for the plaintiff asserts that the number of eligible Jewish females in this county would be an extremely small minority of the total population especially as compared with the comparatively much greater number in New York, whence have come many of the cases comprising the weight of authority upholding the validity of such clauses. There are no census figures in evidence. While this court could probably take judicial notice of the fact that the Jewish community is a minor, though important segment of our total local population, nevertheless the court is by no means justified in judicial knowledge that there is an insufficient number of eligible young ladies of Jewish parentage in this area from which Daniel would have a reasonable latitude of choice. And of course, Daniel is not at all confined in his choice to residents of this county, which is a very different circumstance in this day of travel by plane and freeway and communication by telephone, from the horse and buggy days of the 1854 *Maddox v. Maddox* decision. Consequently, the decision does not appear to be an appropriate yardstick of reasonableness under modern living conditions.

Plaintiff's counsel contends that the Shapira will falls within the principle of *Fineman v. Central National Bank* (1961) [175 N.E.2d 837], holding that the public policy of

Ohio does not countenance a bequest or devise conditioned on the beneficiary's obtaining a separation or divorce from his wife. Counsel argues that the Shapira condition would encourage the beneficiary to marry a qualified girl just to receive the bequest, and then to divorce her afterward. This possibility seems too remote to be a pertinent application of the policy against bequests conditioned upon divorce. Most other authorities agree with *Fineman v. Bank* that as a general proposition, a testamentary gift effective only on condition that the recipient divorce or separate from his or her spouse is against public policy and invalid. But no authorities have been found extending the principle to support plaintiff's position. Indeed, in measuring the reasonableness of the condition in question, both the father and the court should be able to assume that the son's motive would be proper. And surely the son should not gain the advantage of the avoidance of the condition by the possibility of his own impropriety.

Finally, counsel urges that the Shapira condition tends to pressure Daniel, by the reward of money, to marry within seven years without opportunity for mature reflection, and jeopardizes his college education. It seems to the court, on the contrary, that the seven year time limit would be a most reasonable grace period, and one which would give the son ample opportunity for exhaustive reflection and fulfillment of the condition without constraint or oppression. Daniel is no more being "blackmailed into a marriage by immediate financial gain," as suggested by counsel, than would be the beneficiary of a living gift or conveyance upon consideration of a future marriage—an arrangement which has long been sanctioned by the courts of this state.

In the opinion of this court, the provision made by the testator for the benefit of the State of Israel upon breach or failure of the condition is most significant for two reasons. First, it distinguishes this case from the bare forfeitures (including the technical in terrorem objection), and, in a way, from the vagueness and indefiniteness doctrine of some of the English cases. Second, and of greater importance, it demonstrates the depth of the testator's conviction. His purpose was not merely a negative one designed to punish his son for not carrying out his wishes. His unmistakable testamentary plan was that his possessions be used to encourage the preservation of the Jewish faith and blood, hopefully through his sons, but, if not, then through the State of Israel. Whether this judgment was wise is not for this court to determine. But it is the duty of this court to honor the testator's intention within the limitations of law and of public policy. The prerogative granted to a testator by the laws of this state to dispose of his estate according to his conscience is entitled to as much judicial protection and enforcement as the prerogative of a beneficiary to receive an inheritance.

It is the conclusion of this court that public policy should not, and does not preclude the fulfillment of Dr. Shapira's purpose, and that in accordance with the weight of authority in this country, the conditions contained in his will are reasonable restrictions upon marriage, and valid.

Exercise 5-13. *Shapira* Revisited

1. What estate did Dr. Shapira leave Dan? Is this a recognizable fee? Does it violate the Rule Against Perpetuities?
2. What do you think about what Dr. Shapira did with respect to Dan's inheritance? What if he had restricted Dan's choice of spouse to women or to members of the same race?
3. What does the court mean when it says that it takes judicial notice? The court mentions that times had changed "from the horse and buggy days" to "the day of travel by plane and freeway and communication by telephone." What advice do you think the judge would have given Dan today in the age of social media and the internet?
4. What is the significance of the gift over to the State of Israel?
5. Incentive trusts are very popular with wealthy families. What would you advise clients who wanted to set up an incentive trust that restricted their child's inheritance based on whether he pursued a certain major in college and then whether he went into the family business? With regard to Dr. Shapira's will, the court states "whether his judgment is wise is not for this court to determine." Is your role as a lawyer different?

Waste

Estates in land divide the ownership of property over time. Nowhere is that more clear than in the case of a life estate. A life tenant has the right to possess, use, and enjoy the property during her lifetime. However, a life tenant also owes a duty to the future owners of the property not to harm the property during her tenure. If a life tenant adversely affects the property, it is referred to as waste. Waste can be voluntary or permissive. Voluntary waste involves the commission of an act on the part of the life tenant. Permissive waste occurs when the life tenant allows the property to fall into a state of disrepair. An owner of a reversion or a vested remainder has standing to sue to for damages for past waste and to prevent future waste. A contingent remainderman has standing to sue to prevent future waste. Waste is an especially difficult problem to police in legal life estates.

Ameliorative waste occurs when the left tenant increases the value of the property by adding a permanent improvement. At common law, ameliorative waste was prohibited, but modern courts allow it where it does not impair the value of the remainder and either the remainderperson approved or the change was necessary due to a substantial and permanent change in the surrounding neighborhood.

Exercise 5-14. *Keesecker v. Bird*—Waste

Keesecker v. Bird demonstrates that waste in a legal life estate can be very difficult to regulate. In the absence of an impartial fiduciary, it is incumbent on the remainderman to take steps to safeguard his future interest. In some ways, this requirement is no different from the obligation we place on fee owners to inspect their property for trespassers or risk losing their property to adverse possession. As we have seen in earlier Chapters, if a property owner sleeps on her rights, she might just lose them.

1. When reading the case, it will be helpful to draw a family tree and prepare a time line. How was the remainderman related to the life tenant? Do you think that complicated the situation?
2. One of the defendants argues that the plaintiff's claims are barred by the statute of limitations. Could the other defendant have argued laches?
3. The case uses language that is specific to West Virginia when discussing the legal affairs of Emily Keesecker. Mrs. Keesecker was seriously injured in a car accident and, as a result, was not able to handle her own affairs. When an individual lacks capacity to make financial decision, the court will appoint a fiduciary, most often called a Guardian of the Estate, to act on the individual's behalf. When an individual lacks capacity to make personal decisions, including health care decisions, the court will also appoint a fiduciary, most often called a Guardian of the Person. The Guardian of the Estate may be the same person as the Guardian of the Person. Different jurisdictions refer to these fiduciaries by different names. The following case uses the term "Committee of the Estate" to refer to Mrs. Keesecker's Guardians.

Keesecker v. Bird

200 W. Va. 667 (1997)

Starcher, Justice. This case involves the application of summary judgment to claims of waste to a remainderman's interest in real and personal property. The plaintiff-appellant, Ward Keesecker, II, is the owner of a remainder interest in property bequeathed by will to Emily Keesecker for her life. The defendant-appellees, Walter M. Bird and Arch Steiner, were appointed by the circuit court of Arlington County, Virginia as the personal representatives over Emily Keesecker's affairs between 1981 and her death in 1993. The appellant alleges that the appellees, while overseeing Emily Keesecker's affairs, negligently allowed the property in the life estate to deteriorate, and subsequently permitted the property to be mostly destroyed.

I.
Facts and Background

In late 1974, Ward W. Keesecker, Sr., (Dr. Keesecker) and his second wife, Emily M. Keesecker, who were both residents of Morgan County, West Virginia, were involved in an automobile accident. Dr. Keesecker died from his injuries on January 24, 1975. Emily Keesecker was hospitalized and later moved to a nursing home where she remained until her death on May 15, 1993. Testimony by the parties indicates that she was comatose for the last nine years of her life.

In his will, Dr. Keesecker gave certain real and personal property to Emily Keesecker for her life, and upon her death the remainder was to go to his son (by his first marriage), appellant Ward W. Keesecker, II. The real property, Highwood House, was a large home located in Berkeley Springs, West Virginia with more than 20 rooms and four floors. One insurance agent inspected the home in 1984 and found it had a replacement cost of $361,878.00, while another agent estimated the replacement value at $207,981.00. The personal property in the life estate consisted of the contents of Highwood House. The appellant alleges that the home was filled with antiques.

At some point prior to 1981, Emily Keesecker was moved to a nursing home in Arlington County, Virginia. On May 1, 1981, the Circuit Court of Arlington County, Virginia, appointed appellee Arch Steiner as "Committee of the estate of Emily M. Keesecker." Mr. Steiner moved to Tennessee in 1986, and on June 26, 1986 the Circuit Court of Arlington County, Virginia entered an order relieving Mr. Steiner of his duties and appointing appellee Walter Bird as committee for Emily Keesecker. Mr. Steiner prepared a seven-page, single-spaced inventory listing the contents of each room of Highwood House and stated that these items were transferred to Mr. Bird. In his deposition, Mr. Bird acknowledged he inspected the house and signed the inventory list accepting the property.

Over the years of Mr. Bird's tenure as committee for the estate of Emily Keesecker, Highwood House was burglarized numerous times. Mr. Bird testified that he recalled reporting to the police more than a dozen thefts of personal property from Highwood House. No one was ever arrested for these burglaries. Mr. Bird also gave somewhat contradictory testimony about whether he sought indemnity for these losses from the homeowner's insurance company. He testified that he never made any claims for losses or damages to the insurance company for any of these breaking and enterings, but he later said he had simply called his insurance agent to report these crimes. Mr. Bird testified the insurance agent said he would get back to him, but he "never heard anything back."

Accounting statements filed by Mr. Bird reflect income from the rental of Highwood House between June 1986 and June 1990, in addition to Emily Keesecker's pension and social security checks. By 1990, it appears that Mr. Bird became unable to rent the Highwood property. He boarded up the windows and padlocked the doors. Because the property was unoccupied, the homeowner's insurance company canceled all insurance policies on Highwood House effective January 26, 1990.

On November 30, 1990, the Virginia Commissioner of Accounts wrote to Mr. Bird stating that the Commissioner would no longer approve disbursements from Mrs. Keesecker's estate account to pay for utilities, maintenance, or repairs to the house. The letter advised Mr. Bird to consider selling the house or abandoning it if it was of no value. It appears that Mr. Bird then listed the house with a local real estate company and indicated the selling price was $78,000.

On December 11, 1991, Mr. Bird wrote to appellant Ward Keesecker, II, saying that he had located a buyer willing to pay $78,000 for Highwood House and that he needed Mr. Keesecker to sign a contract approving the sale. Mr. Keesecker testified in his deposition that he received the letter but did not respond because he was not interested in selling his interest in the house. Two weeks after this letter was sent, on December 26, 1991, Highwood House was severely damaged in a fire of suspicious origin.

On April 17, 1992, Mr. Bird initiated a lawsuit against Mr. Keesecker to force the sale of the house. The complaint alleges that Mr. Bird had located a buyer for Highwood House, and because of the expense of upkeep for the house, it was in the best interest of Mrs. Keesecker (the life tenant) that the fee simple interest in the property be sold. Accordingly, appellee Bird asked that the trial court compel the sale of Highwood House, and use the interest and income from the sale proceeds for the support of Mrs. Keesecker. Appellant Keesecker answered the complaint and filed a counterclaim against appellee Bird and a third-party complaint against appellee Steiner alleging they committed waste to the property by failing to preserve Highwood House and its contents.

Subsequently, a second fire occurred at Highwood House on January 27, 1993, and while the extent of damage is not stated in the record, the testimony of the parties suggests that the house was virtually destroyed. Mrs. Keesecker died on May 15, 1993.

Both Mr. Bird and Mr. Steiner filed motions for summary judgment alleging that they were not proper parties to this action because they acted as fiduciaries and could not be held personally responsible for the debts of Emily Keesecker's estate. Accordingly, they insisted that the sole party defendant should be the estate of Mrs. Keesecker. Both appellees further argued that they did not commit waste, and could not be held responsible for waste even if it did occur. Lastly, Mr. Steiner alone argued that all claims against him were barred by the statute of limitation.

On August 18, 1995, the circuit court issued two brief orders granting Mr. Bird's and Mr. Steiner's motions for summary judgment. The circuit court dismissed the actions against Mr. Bird because he was "not a proper party to the instant litigation." The actions against Mr. Steiner were dismissed as barred by the statute of limitation. It is from these two orders that Mr. Keesecker now appeals

B.

The Circuit Court's Summary Judgment as to Appellee Steiner

Appellant Keesecker testified in his deposition that he was aware that his father's will had created a life estate of Highwood House for Emily Keesecker, "and upon her passing it would be mine and all the contents." During the period appellee Steiner managed Emily Keesecker's affairs, the appellant testified he would visit the Highwood property at least once a year. The appellant knew that Mr. Steiner was acting as his step mother's committee, and testified that Mr. Steiner had tried to buy his interest in the estate. During Mr. Steiner's tenure as committee, the appellant noted that the real property was falling into a state of disrepair, and that the personal property also was not being cared for. The appellant held the opinion that the "serious dilapidation of the house" commenced the day his father died in 1975.

The appellant was not immediately aware of the change of committee over his stepmother's estate in 1986. However, he testified in his deposition that he

> ... just had hearsay, people had said ... [and] I believed from what I had heard that Mr. Bird was managing the estate, which I guess I would assume was committee because Mr. Steiner had moved to Tennessee and left Mr. Bird in charge. That was my understanding.

Although the record is unclear on the exact date, it appears that during Mr. Bird's tenure as committee the appellant visited Highwood House. The appellant again found significant deterioration, finding bricks had fallen off a chimney and cut holes in the metal roof. He testified he repaired the holes to minimize damage to the house that would "obviously further deteriorate the house."

The appellant alleges that appellee Steiner's failure to make basic repairs to Highwood House and its contents between 1981 and 1986 constitutes waste under West Virginia law. The appellee argues that the appellant's claims, if any, are barred by the statute of limitation because the appellant waited nearly six years to initiate this action for waste. We agree with the appellee.

There are four steps to determining if a claim is barred by a statute of limitation. The first step in analyzing any statute of limitation question is to determine the applicable statute. Waste is a property damage tort consisting of an injury to the freehold by one rightfully in possession of land. Conversely, trespassing is an injury to the freehold by a stranger to the land. "This marks the distinction between waste and trespass." *Cecil v. Clark*, 49 W. Va. 459, 470 (1901). A plaintiff need not be in possession of the land to initiate action. The action is "not one to recover damages for injury to the possession of the land ... [but for] permanent injury done to the freehold...." *Crowder v. Fordyce Lumber Co.*, 93 Ark. 392, 394 (1910).

A life tenant owes a duty to a remainderman not to commit either voluntary or permissive waste. Waste is "any permanent or lasting injury done or permitted to be done by the holder of the particular estate to lands, houses, or other corporeal hereditaments, to the prejudice of the heir or of him in remainder or reversion." *Gwinn v. Rogers*, 92 W. Va. 533 (1922). "Waste, injury to the freehold by a tenant for life or years, is actionable at common law, whether it result from affirmative wrongful acts or mere omission to perform duty." *Talbott v. Southern Oil Co.*, 60 W. Va. 423 (1906). The term "waste" implies neglect or misconduct resulting in material damage to or loss of property, but does not include ordinary depreciation of property due to age and normal use over a comparatively short period of time. *Moore v. Phillips*, 6 Kan. App. 2d 94 (1981).

Injunctive relief is also available to restrain waste that is causing irremediable injury, an injury destructive to either the substance of the inheritance or that which gives it its chief value. We acknowledged the difficulty in defining irreparable injury in *Bettman v. Harness*, 42 W. Va. 433 (1896), when we stated:

> What is irreparable injury? It is impossible to define it inflexibly. Rights of property and its uses change so; so many new rights of property with new uses arise as time goes on.... The word "irreparable" means that which cannot be repaired, restored, or adequately compensated for in money, or where the compensation cannot be safely measured.

"Voluntary" or "commissive" waste involves the commission of the deliberate, willful or voluntary destruction or carrying away of something attached to the freehold. "Permissive waste" is the failure of the tenant, under the circumstances, to exercise the ordinary care of a prudent man for the preservation and protection of the estate. It appears that the appellant is alleging the appellees allowed permissive waste, an injury to property, to occur to Highwood House. Accordingly, the applicable statute of limitation in this case is found in W. Va. Code, 55-2-12(a) which requires that an action for damage to property be brought within two years of the date the action accrued.

The second step in evaluating a statute of limitation question is to establish when the requisite elements of the alleged tort occurred, such that the cause of action "accrued." In this case, assuming *arguendo* that appellee Steiner owed Emily Keesecker a duty to faithfully manage her life estate property in West Virginia, and a duty to not commit waste to the appellant's remainder interest in the property, the latest possible breach of that duty would have occurred in 1986 when he relinquished his committeeship to appellee Bird. Accordingly, any cause of action against appellee Steiner accrued in 1986, and any lawsuit for property damage would have had to have been filed by 1988.

The next step is to determine whether the plaintiff is entitled to the benefit of the ameliorative effects of the discovery rule. Under the "discovery rule," the statute of limitations is tolled until a claimant knows or by the exercise of reasonable diligence should know of his claim. It is clear that the appellant cannot benefit from the discovery rule. The appellant testified that he knew as far back as 1975 that the property was deteriorating, and that permanent damage was occurring to his remainder interest in the property throughout appellee Steiner's tenure as committee. Second, the appellant knew that Mr. Steiner was acting as his step-mother's committee, and knew that he may have been failing to properly care for Emily Keesecker's life estate property. Lastly, the appellant knew by 1986 that any breach of duty by the appellee was causing the alleged damage to the appellant's property interest. Hence, in 1986 or shortly thereafter, the appellant knew all of the elements of a possible cause of action—but failed to take any action. Therefore, the appellant is not entitled to the protection of the discovery rule.

Accordingly, we hold that the circuit court correctly ruled that any causes of action which the appellant may have had against appellee Steiner were barred by the statute of limitation.

IV

Conclusion

The circuit court's August 18, 1995 order as to appellee Steiner is affirmed. The circuit court's August 18, 1995 order as to appellee Bird is reversed, and the case is remanded for proceedings consistent with this opinion.

Affirmed in part, reversed in part, and remanded.

Exercise 5-15. *Keesecker* Revisited

1. Dr. Keesecker chose to use a legal life estate to provide for his wife. If you had represented him, what advice would you have given him regarding the disposition of his estate? What problem could have been avoided by the use of a trust?
2. If you had represented Ward Keesecker, Jr., what advice would you have given him when he first learned that he held a remainder interest? Be specific. How could that advice have prevented the unfortunate course of events that unfolded in *Keesecker*?

Chapter 6

Leasing Real Property

Introduction

Landlord-tenant law has changed radically in the last fifty years, moving from a regime that focused on landlord's rights to one that now has far reaching protections for residential tenants. Historically, a lease was viewed primarily as a property interest, an estate like those you studied in previous chapters. Property attributes still exist today—a tenant owns a current right to possess the property called a leasehold, and the landlord owns a future right to possess called a reversion, in addition to continued ownership of the underlying asset. However, as you will learn in this chapter, modern landlord-tenant relationships are regulated by a fairly complex hybrid of property law and contract law and, more recently, by consumer protection laws as well.

These changes mostly benefit domestic tenants and are designed to recognize the important human interests at stake concerning homes where individuals and families live. The law is also concerned with the lack of legal information and negotiation power a renter of housing might have. Although many of the same laws apply to commercial tenancies, not all do. Some protections such as the implied warranty of habitability are reserved for residential tenants only. This is because commercial tenants are thought to be more sophisticated consumers who are in a better position to protect their interests. Be sure to note any major legal differences between residential and commercial leases which are highlighted in this chapter.

Chapter Problem: Exercise 6-1

By the time you finish your study of this chapter, you will be prepared for the lawyering tasks assigned in this problem. For now, carefully review the complaint below and the summary of the supervising attorney's interview with the client. Keep this client situation in mind as you progress through the chapter and circle back to it at the end.

Your firm has been retained to represent Stefan Wakowski, a tenant who was recently served with the complaint in the file attached here. Your supervising attorney has asked you to evaluate the case to determine if the landlord's claims are likely to be successful and if there are any defenses or counter-claims the tenant could successfully bring. Be prepared to draft an answer to the complaint and to write a memorandum with your evaluation of the case for the senior attorney. Assume the parties' lease is consistent with the model lease in Exercise 6-5 below—and that the lease includes a term that attorney's fees for breach of the lease will be paid by the prevailing party.

Bernadette Kelly
Kelly & Associates LLC
123 Hill Road
Treetown, Delvania 95123

Attorney for the Plaintiff
ID NO. 987654

COMPLAINT

RECOVERY OF PROPERTY AND NON-PAYMENT OF RENT

JAMES PATEL	:	**IN THE COURT OF COMMON PLEAS**
Plaintiff/Landlord	:	
	:	**VALLEY COUNTY, DELVANIA**
vs.	:	
STEFAN WAKOWSKI	:	**CIVIL ACTION**
Defendant/Tenant	:	**NO. 123456**
	:	

Plaintiff alleges the following:

1. Plaintiff JAMES PATEL ("Landlord") is the owner of record of the rental property located at 345 Merry Lane, Oaks, Delvania 95133, in Valley County, Delvania.

2. The Defendant STEFAN WAKOWSKI is a tenant ("Tenant") and now resides in and has been in possession of these premises since April 1, Year One.

3. Landlord and Tenant entered into a written lease agreement ("Lease") on March 1, Year One agreeing to a one year fixed term of possession commencing on April 1, Year One and ending March 31, Year Two.

4. The landlord has registered the leasehold and notified tenant as required by D.S.A. 46:8.

5. Pursuant to the lease, the amount that must be paid by the tenant for these premises is $1,000, payable on the first day of each month in advance.

6. There is due, unpaid and owing from Tenant to Landlord rent as follows: $2,000 base rent for the months of May and June, Year One, and $250 in late charges for the months of May and June, Year One.

7. There is due, unpaid and owing from Tenant to Landlord $1,500 in attorney's fees and $250 filing costs.

8. The late charges, attorney's fees and other charges are permitted to be charged as rent for purposes of this action by federal, state and local law and by the lease.

9. The date that the next rent is due is July 1, Year One. If this case is scheduled for trial before that date, the total amount you must pay to have this complaint dismissed is $4,000. If this case is scheduled for trial on or after that date, the total amount you must pay to have this complaint dismissed is $5,000. Payment may be made to the landlord or the clerk of the court at any time before the trial date, but on the trial date payment must be made by 4:30 p.m. to get the case dismissed.

10. Landlord seeks a judgment for possession for non-payment of rent and forfeiture of the leasehold.

11. Tenant has not surrendered possession of the premises and Tenant holds over and continues in possession without the consent of Landlord.

12. A Notice to Quit/Demand For Possession has been personally served on TENANT on June 8, Year One.

WHEREFORE, Landlord demands judgment for

1. Immediate possession of the property against Tenant;

2. Past due rent of $2,000 plus $250 late fees;

3. Any rent owed and late fees owed but not paid between now and the trial, at the rate of $1,000 per month base rent and $125 per month late fees;

4. Filing costs of $250 and attorney's fees incurred to date of $1,500;

5. Reasonable attorney's fees incurred and owed but not paid between now and the trial,

6. For such other relief that the court shall deem proper.

Dated: June 10, Year One

Bernadette Kelly
Bernadette Kelly
Attorney for James Patel

MEMORANDUM

From: Senior Attorney
To: File
Date: June 10, Year One
Re: Stefan Wakowski

This is a summary of my interview with our client Stefan Wakowski. Mr. Wakowski has a number of problems with the rental property he is leasing.

The townhome he is renting is part of a large complex owned by his landlord James Patel. It has a small porch and the steps leading up to the porch and porch itself are eroding and starting to creak and move when walked on. One of the wooden planks on the top step is cracked so much that there is two-foot wide hole in it. Stefan and his guests have to be careful not to step there because a person could fall through. Also, the railing on the porch is missing on one side, making it possible to fall off the porch and drop down four feet to the ground below. The porch and steps are in this condition because of exposure to weather and not being maintained properly. The porch is also the only outdoor space for the property—and Stefan can't comfortably use it.

Also, somehow, bugs are getting inside the apartment. For a whole month earlier this spring, there were many ladybugs flying around. Most people find ladybug's harmless and kind of cute, but Stefan finds them creepy. Now the ladybugs are gone and there are bees getting inside. Stefan has been stung twice already. He is developing an allergy to bees where the site of the bee-sting swells up a lot. If his allergies were to worsen, this could become dangerous for him.

Last, Stefan is facing a situation I have not seen before with tenants. Another tenant named Gus lives right next door to Stefan. Gus rents his townhome from Mr. Patel as well. Gus's rental has a small back yard. Gus owns two dogs who he considers to be family members. Gus also has a "doggie day care" business that he runs out of his townhome. His job taking care of other people's dogs makes Gus enough money to support himself. On a typical weekday, during doggie day care hours, Gus cares for up to 6 visiting dogs who play inside his home or outside in the yard. When together as a group, the dogs bark very frequently and loudly. This goes on for several minutes at a time—when one dog starts barking the others follow and some howl. Since the townhomes have a shared wall between them, Stefan can hear the barking whether the dogs are inside or outside. The visiting dogs are there only weekdays and only from 9 a.m. to 5 p.m. It is pretty quiet in the evenings and on the weekends when Gus has only his two dogs there—they hardly ever bark when the other dogs are gone.

The noise of the dogs really bothers Stefan. He feels harassed by it. Stefan also works from home a lot and sometimes is unable to complete work phone calls because the dogs are so loud he cannot hear the person speaking to him.

Stefan has complained about all this to the landlord repeatedly. Mr. Patel says that he will not address or fix any of the issues and that Stefan needs to be more flexible. He said that dogs bark and that is a fact of life. All of this is the cause of Stefan's refusal to pay rent until the problems are resolved.

Overview of Chapter 6

This Chapter progresses from the commencement of a lease through its termination. It is divided into four (4) subunits.

1. Creating a Leasehold
2. Possession and Enjoyment of a Leasehold
3. Transferring a Leasehold
4. Ending a Tenancy

You will be introduced to fundamental legal principles and review sample documents that lay persons and lawyers frequently come across when renting housing. We begin with entering into a lease, including the types of leases, distinguishing leases from other categories of property, negotiation of terms and a brief introduction to anti-discrimination law in the Federal Fair Housing Act concerning selection and treatment of tenants. Next, for both landlords and tenants, you will learn about rights and duties surrounding possession, use, enjoyment and the physical condition of the leasehold. Here especially you will encounter the revolution in this area of law. You will also learn about the power to transfer a leasehold and the system that governs termination of the property relationship.

As is the practice throughout this book, your study focuses on the default rules that apply in the absence of an agreement. Many of the default rules concerning leases can be changed by contract. As we will see, however, there are some non-disclaimable protections for tenants that cannot be altered in a lease because to do so would violate public policy.

Creating a Leasehold

Types of Leaseholds

There are four types of leasehold estates: a term of years, a periodic tenancy, a tenancy at will, and a tenancy at sufferance.

Term of Years. This kind of lease lasts for a fixed period of time, with a definitive beginning and end date, such as one year or 6 months or 99 years. As you can see from the examples, the time period for a term of years lease need not be in years, it just needs to be specifically defined. A week-long vacation rental is another good illustration. The lease automatically terminates on the end date, unless the parties explicitly agree to extend the lease. This next rule might be surprising—a lease survives the death of either the landlord or the tenant. The right to possession for the term that the landlord has transferred out to the tenant and also the tenant's contractual obligation to pay rent will flow through at death to the estate of the deceased person. So if the landlord dies, the estate of the landlord (an entity that holds property interests that must be administered and distributed to heirs or devisees upon death) steps into the very same legal position as the landlord. The estate has the right to collect rent, and the tenant continues to have a right to possess the property until the end of the term. Similarly, if the tenant is the one who dies, then the obligation to pay rent and the right of possession flow to the tenant's estate.

Periodic Tenancy. This type of lease automatically renews unless one of the parties expressly terminates the lease. It has no definitive end date. Advance notice is required to end the lease. A common form of a periodic tenancy is a month to month lease. At the end of the month, if neither party gave notice to terminate, the lease renews for another month. This pattern continues on until and unless notice is given and the tenant vacates the premises. This lease type is implied if no fixed term and end point is identified. Oral leases or leases that simply provide for rent payable on the first of the month will be classified as month to month periodic tenancies, unless there is good evidence to the contrary. Another important and recurring example is when a term of years lease ends, but yet the tenant remains and pays rent monthly. At that point, the lease converts into a periodic tenancy.

How much notice must be given for an effective termination? Leases frequently provide for advance notice of 30, 60 or 90 days. If the lease does not specify the time frame, then the notice period will depend on the duration of the lease. For example, a month's notice is required to terminate a month to month lease. If a lease is year to year, 6 months advance notice of termination is typically required to avoid automatic renewal for another year. If notice is given too late, then the lease renews for the next period and then can be terminated. For example, assume 30 days advance notice is required, but the tenant gives notice only 15 days ahead. The lease will renew for another month and then end. The tenant will at that point be responsible to pay the remaining 6 weeks of rent. It is wise to give advance notice again to clarify the desire to end the lease. What property rights exist if the landlord or tenant dies while the lease is ongoing? As with a term of years lease, in most states, a periodic tenancy does not terminate at death. Instead, the same property relationship flows through to the estate of the decedent (the person who died). Again, the safest course is for the estate administrator to give proper notice if lease termination is desired.

At Will Tenancy. This is a tenancy that allows either party to terminate at any time—the lease continues only as long as either party desires. Advance notice is not required. That said, states typically have process protections for evicting tenants, and landlords are required to give at least some advance notice, such as 30 days, before a tenant must vacate the premises. In terms of notice, this makes an at will tenancy the functional equivalent of a periodic tenancy. An important difference that remains is that unlike the other kinds of leases, the death of one of the parties terminates the lease.

Tenancy at Sufferance. This category, also known as a holdover tenancy, refers to a tenant who was previously entitled to possession but wrongfully stayed beyond the termination of the leasehold. This means the tenant is entitled to the procedural safeguards of eviction and is in a different category than a trespasser who can be ejected from the premises by an owner using self-help or simply calling the police. Another issue that can come up is if the landlord accepts a check for rent during the holdover period. It is possible the lease will be deemed renewed. What advice would you give the landlord if she wants to collect rent for the holdover period but evict the tenant as soon as possible? (Think about what you might write on the back of a check.)

Exercise 6-2. Identifying Leaseholds

Analyze the problems below to determine what type of lease has been created and predict the legal outcomes.

1. Landlord and tenant agree to a lease with rent payable on the first of the month.
2. Landlord and tenant agree to a lease that starts on January 1, Year One and ends on June 1, Year Two, with rent payable on the first of the month.
3. Assume the same facts as in problem 2, except that the tenant remains in the apartment after June 1, Year Two and continues to pay rent on the first of the month for the next two months and the landlord accepts the rent. At that point the tenant would like to move out.

Distinguished from Other Interests

Legal categories in property law tend to be consequential because a set of rules and policies are triggered in some contexts but are quite different in others. Distinguishing property interests is a core task for law students learning the field and for practicing lawyers. A recurring and important question that we explore next is whether a lease or a license is created by a set of facts. An interest that is classified as a lease is governed by the body of law in this chapter, including substantive and process protections for tenants. You encounter licenses alongside other issues in several chapters in this text and they are addressed in more detail in Chapter 10 (Servitudes). A license is a grant of permission to enter property by an owner to a non-owner. The owner controls the grantee's access and can revoke permission. The non-owner has a very limited interest and can usually be excluded from the property at the will of the owner. For instance, if you invite someone over to your house for dinner, you have granted a license—and you can change your mind and announce that it is time for your guest to leave. Tickets to the movies, sporting events and skiing are also licenses. By contrast, a lease includes the "right to possess" property and is a larger, more significant property interest.

Exercise 6-3. *Vasquez v. Glassboro*

1. As you have been discovering elsewhere in this text, it can be difficult to precisely identify what constitutes possession. That is an important question in the next case. Before you start reading, identify some attributes you see as necessary or that exemplify "possession" in a typical rental situation. Then consider some situations that you think likely do not qualify as possession. An overnight guest perhaps? Other?
2. Carefully read the statute at issue in the case and work to interpret its meaning.
3. *Vasquez* vividly demonstrates how public policy can shape rules. You will see that the court has firmly in mind the profound impacts the law can have on migrant farmworkers. The case also introduces you to the serious concern of unequal bargaining in contract law more generally, and in landlord tenant law in particular. As you read this case and make your way through the entire chapter, be sure to evaluate the foundations that undergird the law and determine whether you find them convincing. Even if you agree, work to generate counter-arguments and policies. Your evaluation is more rigorous and sound if you examine various possibilities as part of your decision-making process.

Vasquez v. Glassboro Service Ass'n Inc.

415 A.2d 1156 (N.J. 1980)

Pollock, J. The primary issue is whether a farm labor service that employs migrant farmworkers from Puerto Rico and provides them with living quarters must dispossess a worker, not by self-help, but in a judicial proceeding after terminating his employment.

Natividad Vasquez, a Puerto Rican farmworker, instituted this action after he was dispossessed without notice following the termination of his employment by Glassboro Service Association, a farm labor service organization. Glassboro had employed Vasquez pursuant to a contract negotiated with the Puerto Rican Department of Labor. The Chancery Division ruled that Glassboro should not have dispossessed Vasquez by self-help, but in a summary dispossess proceeding.

We hold that a farm labor service may not use self-help, but must proceed in a judicial action to dispossess a farmworker who remains in possession of his living quarters after termination of his employment. We reach that conclusion although we hold that a migrant farmworker is not a tenant or otherwise included within N.J.S.A. 2A:18-61.1(m) pertaining to the dispossession of certain residential tenants. We hold further that the failure of the Glassboro contract to provide a migrant farmworker with a reasonable opportunity to find shelter before dispossession is against the public policy of the State, and we imply into the contract a provision for a reasonable time to find alternative housing. In resolving a dispute between a farmworker and a labor service, a court may grant time to the worker to find housing, direct the labor service to assist him in obtaining housing or provide him with return passage to Puerto Rico, or order other appropriate relief.

I.

Glassboro is a non-profit corporation comprised of farmers who contracted with Glassboro for migrant farm labor. The farmers called Glassboro as they needed workers to pick crops, and Glassboro transported workers from its labor camp to the farms. The length of time that a worker stayed at a farm varied, depending primarily on the time needed to pick a crop. Glassboro paid the worker his wages, and the farmer paid Glassboro for those wages plus a commission for Glassboro's services. Only men were hired; the workers' families remained in Puerto Rico. Glassboro paid a farmworker $2.40 per hour and charged him $23 per week for meals. The worker agreed to work eight hours a day for six days a week, plus overtime as mutually agreed.

The 1976 contract stated that a worker was to pay for his transportation from Puerto Rico. If he completed his contract, he would be reimbursed for the cost of transportation from and provided return transportation to Puerto Rico. If the worker did not fulfill his contract, Glassboro was not obliged to reimburse him for the cost of transportation. Although the contract provided that Glassboro would furnish a non-negotiable airplane ticket to Puerto Rico for a worker who became physically unfit, there was no comparable provision for a worker who was fired. The contract period was for 28 weeks, or until December 1, whichever came first.

The contract provided that, if an employee was to be discharged, a hearing was to occur no later than five days after the employee was given notice of termination. The contract did not require a minimum amount of time to elapse between notice and termination of employment.

The contract provided further for administrative review within the Puerto Rican Department of Labor whenever a worker had a complaint "regarding the breach, application, interpretation or compliance" with the contract. If the Secretary of Labor determined that Glassboro had "not adequately remedied the complaint," the Secretary could represent the worker and sue Glassboro.

Pursuant to the contract, Glassboro supplied living quarters for workers at its labor camp in New Jersey. Those quarters consisted of barracks housing up to 30 men. Each worker received a mattress, bedding, and a locker. The barracks were equipped with common toilets, showers, and lavatories. Although some farmers charged the workers for housing while the workers were at the farms, Glassboro did not impose any extra charge for housing at its labor camp. The contract did not require a migrant farmworker to live at Glassboro's labor camp. Nonetheless, the parties contemplated that the farmworker would reside at the labor camp.

In 1976, Vasquez was recruited in Puerto Rico and came to New Jersey to work for Glassboro. According to Glassboro's foreman, Vasquez's work was not satisfactory. On July 19, 1976, the foreman told Vasquez that he was to be discharged. A few hours later Vasquez had his "hearing" with the foreman and a field representative of the Puerto Rican Department of Labor. Thereafter the foreman decided to complete the discharge, a decision Vasquez does not challenge in this action. Although there were vacant spaces at the Glassboro barracks, Vasquez was not permitted to remain overnight. The foreman told him to gather his belongings and leave.

Unable to speak English and without funds to return to Puerto Rico, Vasquez sought the assistance of the Farmworkers Corporation, a federally funded non-profit corporation dedicated to the needs of farmworkers. He also consulted with the Farmworkers Rights Project of the Civil Liberties Education and Action Fund of the American Civil Liberties Union of New Jersey. A Rutgers law student returned with Vasquez to the camp and requested that Vasquez be allowed to remain overnight. The request was refused. Vasquez stayed with a friend who was participating in a job training program conducted by the Farmworkers Corporation.

The Farmworkers Rights Project filed a complaint on July 22, 1976, seeking an order permitting Vasquez to reenter his living quarters and enjoining defendants from depriving him of the use of the quarters except through judicial process. The complaint also sought damages, but Vasquez has abandoned that demand.

The trial court interpreted a provision of N.J.S.A. 2A:18-61.1 to apply to Vasquez. N.J.S.A. 2A:18-61.1 provides that a landlord may not remove a tenant except by establishing one of enumerated grounds as good cause. N.J.S.A. 2A:18-61.1(m) states good cause exists if "[T]he landlord or owner conditioned the tenancy upon and in consideration for the tenant's employment by the landlord or owner as superintendent, janitor or in some other capacity and such employment is being terminated." The court found Vasquez to be included within the phrase "in some other capacity" and ruled that Glassboro reinstate Vasquez to his living quarters.

Although Vasquez has since found housing, other workers have been evicted, one at 3:00 a.m. Shelter for dispossessed migrant farmworkers remains scarce. The Farmworkers Corporation estimates it provides emergency housing for approximately 500 workers each season.

Under the contract, once a worker's employment was ended, he had no right to stay at the camp. Glassboro had no obligation to arrange for alternative shelter. As with Vasquez, within the same day, Glassboro could notify a worker of the termination of his employment, meet with a representative of the Puerto Rican Department of Labor, complete the termination of the employment, and dispossess the employee.

The parties have urged that the dispossession of migrant farmworkers is likely to recur and have requested that we not treat the case as moot. We agree that the public interest requires that we resolve whether a migrant farmworker should be dispossessed from his living quarters through a judicial proceeding.

II.

At common law, one who occupied premises as an employee of the owner and received the use of the premises as part compensation for his services or under a contract of employment was not considered a tenant. The statute that the trial court found to be dispositive, N.J.S.A. 2A:18-61.1(m), modifies the common law rule by declaring an employee whose housing is conditioned upon employment to be a tenant. Consequently, an employee covered by the statute is entitled to three days' notice prior to institution of an eviction action. N.J.S.A. 2A:18-61.2(a). If N.J.S.A. 2A:18-61. 1(m) applied to Vasquez, he would have been entitled to three days' notice after termination of his employment and before commencement of an eviction action.

The initial question is whether the Legislature intended to include migrant farmworkers in the phrase "in some other capacity" in N.J.S.A. 2A:18-61.1(m). Neither the words of the statute nor the legislative history indicates that the Legislature contemplated including farmworkers within that phrase. Consequently, the meaning of the phrase may be gleaned by applying principles of statutory construction. Where general words follow a specific enumeration, the principle of ejusdem generis requires that the general words are applicable only to the same class of things already mentioned. In N.J.S.A. 2A:18-61.1(m), the general words "in some other capacity" follow the specific enumeration of "superintendent" and "janitor." We determine that, within the meaning of the statute, a farmworker does not belong to the same class of employees as a janitor or superintendent. A farmworker who possesses a mattress and locker in an unpartitioned barracks while waiting to be sent to work on a farm is different from a superintendent or janitor residing with his or her family in an apartment house. The farmworkers are all men who come from Puerto Rico without their families. They live in large barracks with no privacy, sleeping in bunks in an unpartitioned room and sharing toilets and showers. Their occupancy of the barracks is intermittent, since it is a base camp for use while they are awaiting assignment to farms.

[C]ases from other jurisdictions holding farmworkers to be tenants are distinguishable. They have described farmworkers as tenants in reaching the conclusion that the farmworkers have a right to information and services from third parties. This Court has already ruled, without characterizing migrant farmworkers as tenants, that they are entitled to receive visitors, members of the press, and persons providing charitable and governmental services. *State v. Shack*, 277 A.2d 369, 374 (N.J. 1971).

Our analysis of the words of the statute, the absence of any illuminating legislative history, and the application of principles of statutory construction lead to the conclusion that a migrant farmworker is not a tenant within the meaning of N.J.S.A. 2A:18-61.1(m). The special characteristics of migrant workers' housing, the absence of a contractual provision for the payment of rent, the lack of privacy, the intermittent occupancy, and the interdependence of employment and housing support this conclusion. Accordingly, we modify the judgment of the Appellate Division insofar as it holds that a migrant farmworker is a tenant within the meaning of the summary dispossess statute. However, our conclusion that Vasquez was not a tenant does not end our inquiry or preclude a finding that a farm labor service may dispossess a migrant farmworker only by judicial process.

III.

In ascertaining whether a farmworker is entitled to notice before dispossession, we turn next to the Glassboro contract. As stated above, the contract resulted from negotiations between the Puerto Rican Department of Labor and Glassboro. No migrant farmworker participated directly or through a labor union in the negotiations. The record does not demonstrate whether or not the Puerto Rican Department of Labor has the same interests as the migrant farmworkers. The Puerto Rican Department of Labor may have been concerned also about reducing unemployment in Puerto Rico by finding jobs for its residents on farms in New Jersey. Whatever the interests of the parties to the negotiations, a migrant farmworker was required to accept the contract as presented by Glassboro.

The contract in evidence is written in English. Although Vasquez spoke Spanish only, the record does not show that he received a Spanish translation of the contract. Nonetheless, he signed a copy of the contract.

Once a migrant farmworker came to Glassboro's labor camp in New Jersey, he depended on Glassboro for employment, transportation, food, and housing. He was separated by over 1300 miles from his home and family. Although an American citizen, he was isolated from most citizens in New Jersey by his inability to speak English. An invisible barrier separated a migrant farmworker from the rest of the State as he was shuttled from the labor camp to the farms. The lack of alternative housing emphasized the inequality between Glassboro and the migrant farmworkers. Once his employment ended, a farmworker lost not only his job but his shelter. The fear of discharge, and with it the loss of income, housing, and return passage to Puerto Rico permeated the contractual relationship. This is the setting in which we measure the contract against the public policy of the State.

Public policy eludes precise definition and may have diverse meanings in different contexts. The sources of public policy include federal and state legislation and judicial decisions. In the past, courts in New Jersey have refused to enforce contracts that violate the public policy of the State. No contract can be sustained if it is inconsistent with the public interest or detrimental to the common good. Contracts have been declared invalid because they violate statutes, promote crime, interfere with the administration of justice, encourage divorce, violate public morality, or restrain trade.

The courts and Legislature of New Jersey have demonstrated a progressive attitude in providing legal protection for migrant farmworkers. [There is legislation requiring water and toilets for workers and providing for safe and sanitary housing consitions] In 1979, the federal government, pursuant to OSHA [Occupational Safety and Health Act of 1970], assumed responsibility for inspection of many migrant labor camps. However, certain labor camps are still being inspected by New Jersey's Office of Agricultural Worker Compliance for the Federal Employment Service in order to comply with the federal requirement that housing be inspected prior to clearing any orders for interstate recruitment of migrant workers. The constant attention accorded by Congress and the State Legislature demonstrates a legislative concern for the well-being of migrant farmworkers.

In *Shack* this Court reversed convictions for trespass of a fieldworker and an attorney for organizations providing services for migrant farmworkers. Declining to characterize the migrant farmworker as either tenant or employee, Chief Justice Weintraub wrote:

> We see no profit in trying to decide upon a conventional category and then forcing the present subject into it. That approach would be artificial and distorting. The quest is for a fair adjustment of the competing needs of the parties, in the light of the realities of the relationship between the migrant worker and the operator of the housing facility. (*Shack*, *supra*, 277 A.2d at 374)

The Court weighed the property rights of the farmer against the rights of the farmworkers to information and services and found that the balance tipped in favor of the farmworker. Underlying that conclusion was recognition of the fundamental right of the farmworker to live with dignity. As in *Shack*, the appropriate result in this case arises from the status and the relationship of the parties.

The enlightened approach of the courts and the Legislature provides the context in which we assess the Glassboro contract and consider how a migrant farmworker should be dispossessed from his living quarters at a labor camp.

A basic tenet of the law of contracts is that courts should enforce contracts as made by the parties. However, application of that principle assumes that the parties are in positions of relative equality and that their consent is freely given. In recent years, courts have become increasingly sensitive to overreaching in contracts where there is an inequality in the status of the parties.

In a variety of situations, courts have revised contracts where there was an inequality in the bargaining power of the parties. The principle has been applied also to leases. In *Kuzmiak v. Brookchester*, 111 A.2d 425 (N.J. Super. Ct. App. Div.1955), the court invalidated a clause in an apartment lease exculpating a landlord from liability for negligence. More recently the inequality in bargaining power between landlord and tenant led this Court to comment that "lease agreements are frequently form contracts of adhesion. . . ." [Citation omitted.]

A migrant farmworker has even less bargaining power than a residential tenant. Although the contract did not require a migrant farmworker to live at the labor camp, the realities of his employment forced him to stay at the camp. Residence at the labor camp benefited not only the farmworker, but also Glassboro and its member farmers. It was more convenient for them if the workers resided at the camp: the pool of labor was at hand, and the workers could be transported conveniently to the farms. The contract assured Glassboro that there would be a labor source available on its property.

Under the contract, once a worker's employment was ended, he had no right to stay at the camp. Glassboro's possible need for the bed of a discharged farmworker, particularly during the growing season, is relevant, but not persuasive. In this case,

Glassboro had ample space for Vasquez, yet he was turned out of the barracks on the same day he was fired. The interest of neither the migrant farmworker nor the public is served by casting the worker adrift to fend for himself without reasonable time to find shelter.

The status of a worker seeking employment with Glassboro is analogous to that of a consumer who must accept a standardized form contract to purchase needed goods and services. Neither farmworkers nor consumers negotiate the terms of their contracts; both must accept the contracts as presented to them. In both instances, the contracts affect many people as well as the public interest.

A contract where one party, as here, must accept or reject the contract does not result from the consent of that party. It is a contract of adhesion:

> There being no private consent to support a contract of adhesion, its legitimacy rests entirely on its compliance with standards in the public interest. The individual who is subject to the obligations imposed by a standard form thus gains the assurance that the rules to which he is subject have received his consent either directly or through their conforming to higher public laws and standards made and enforced by the public institutions that legitimately govern him. (Slawson, *Standard Form Contracts and Democratic Control of Lawmaking Power*, 84 Harv. L. Rev. 529, 566 (1971))

The absence of a provision in the contract for reasonable time to find housing after termination of his employment bespeaks Glassboro's superior bargaining position. Further, by failing to provide for a reasonable time to find alternative housing, the contract is inconsistent with the enlightened attitude of the Legislature and the courts towards migrant farmworkers.

The crux of this case thus becomes the unconscionability of the contract as it is sought to be enforced against the migrant workers. The unconscionability of the contract inheres not only in its failure to provide a worker with a reasonable opportunity to find alternative housing, but in its disregard for his welfare after termination of his employment. The inherent inequity of the contract arouses a sense of injustice and invokes the equitable powers of the courts. In the absence of any concern demonstrated for the worker in the contract, public policy requires the implication of a provision for a reasonable time to find alternative housing.

IV.

At common law, on termination of employment, an employer could dispossess an employee who occupied premises incidental to his employment. To that extent, both an employer and landlord could use self-help to regain possession peaceably. The advantage to them was that they were assured of prompt restoration of the use of their property. However, an inherent vice in self-help is that it can lead to confrontations and breaches of the peace. In the absence of self-help, a landlord or employer at common law was remitted to an action in ejectment. The problem with ejectment is that it was slow and expensive.

With regard to real property occupied solely as a residence, the Legislature has resolved the dilemma by prohibiting entry without consent and by providing a summary dispossess proceeding. As explained above, migrant farmworkers are not tenants, and there is no comparable statute providing for their summary dispossession on termination of their employment. In fashioning a suitable remedy, we acknowledge that the realities of the relationship between the migrant worker and a farm labor service are unique and summon a judicial response unrestricted by conventional categories, such as employer-employee and landlord-tenant.

After oral argument, we requested the parties to submit supplemental briefs analyzing the applicability of the unlawful detainer statute to a farmworker who remains peaceably in possession of his living quarters following termination of his employment. One type of unlawful detainer statute, N.J.S.A., 2A:39-4, pertains to holdover tenants. Another unlawful detainer statute pertains to persons taking possession "without the consent of the owner or without color of title...." N.J.S.A. 2A:39-5. Although a migrant farmworker would qualify under the latter alternative as one who enters without color of title, the question remains whether he has "possession".

The meaning of "possession" varies with the context of its use. One writer suggests that "possession can only be usefully defined with reference to the purpose in hand; and that possession may have one meaning in one connection and another meaning in another." [Citation omitted.] Generally, a worker remains at Glassboro's camp only while waiting for assignment to a farm. Together with approximately 30 other men, he shared unpartitioned space in the barracks. We conclude that a migrant farmworker does not have possession of his living quarters within the meaning of N.J.S.A. 2A:39-5 and that the remedy of unlawful detainer is not available.

In the absence of a contractual provision or legislation addressing the plight of a migrant farmworker on termination of his employment, the courts, exercising equitable jurisdiction, should devise a remedy to fit the circumstances of each case. Depending on the circumstances, an equitable adjustment of the rights of the parties may vary from one case to another. An appropriate remedy might include time in addition to that implied in the contract, assistance in obtaining alternative housing, return passage to Puerto Rico, or some other form of relief. By abolishing self-help and requiring dispossession through a judicial proceeding, we provide a forum for an equitable resolution of a controversy between a farm labor service and a migrant farmworker on termination of the latter's employment.

We are mindful of the special considerations pertaining to migrant farmworkers and of the need for a prompt resolution of disputes between farmworkers and a farm labor service. In general, a summary action should be a more appropriate proceeding than a plenary action. In fact, the present case was instituted on complaint and order to show cause returnable three days later, at which time the court heard testimony, reserved decision, and rendered a written opinion seven days later. We conclude that a dispute concerning the dispossession of a migrant farmworker on termination of his employment, whether instituted by a farm labor service or, as here, by a farmworker, should proceed in a summary manner under R. 4:67.

Exercise 6-4. *Vasquez v. Glassboro* Revisited

1. Be prepared to explain why migrant workers do not qualify as tenants, based on lack of possession and the New Jersey statute. What arguments would you make as opposing counsel?
2. Exactly which public policies justify the court's imposition of new terms in the migrant worker's contract? How far does the court's reasoning extend to other contracts? For example, if you pay for an expensive hospital stay and have no bargaining power to determine the cost—might that be found an "unconscionable" adhesion contract that could be amended?
3. Do you think migrant workers are better off after the court's ruling? Could it be harmful?
4. Suppose a student Samara lives in dorm at a university. She is assigned her own room which has a private bathroom. Samara keeps a bed and desk and other personal effects in the room. She has a portable stove for cooking. She even obtained special permission for her cat to live with her when she is on campus. The university contract Samara signed provides that no student in a dorm has an entitlement to a particular room and that room assignments may change throughout the year. In addition, the university reserved the right to eject a student for any reason with 48 hours advance notice. Apply what you learned from *Vasquez* to this situation. This is a challenging undertaking. Be sure to consider alternative outcomes and focus on your reasoning.
5. Now draw on *Vasquez* to consider a different context. What policies are implicated for termination of a person's access to a continuing care retirement facility? The world is in the midst of what has been called a gray tsunami—a wave of population aging. Housing for elders is among many issues that are in need of careful attention in law and society. With increasing frequency, some older persons live in a community that combines residential living with health care, with options across a continuum from independent living, to assisted living, to more intensive nursing care. These situations may not fit neatly into existing property categories, such as a lease or a license.

   For example, in *Seabrook Village v. Murphy*, 853 A.2d 280 (N.J. Super. 2004), the Court held that a retirement community could not terminate a person's residency with just 60 days advance notice. The resident had paid $149,000 up front to live there along with monthly fees of over $1,000. There was a dispute about the fees, and the resident stopped paying the monthly fees until the controversy was resolved. The community sought to exclude the resident and even threatened to drop off the elderly resident at his son's home. The court held that the resident could only be involuntarily discharged after a hearing and proof of "just cause" (a difficult standard to meet set forth in legislation that specifically regulates such communities in New Jersey). *Seabrook* provided protections similar to those of tenants and perhaps more. Does this seem to strike the right balance between the interests of the residential health care facility and the residents?

Negotiating and Entering Into a Lease

This part highlights a range of issues that can arise in the process of entering into a lease.

Statute of Frauds. One basic consideration is whether a lease must be in writing. That depends on how long the lease term is. All states have a rule, called the Statute of Frauds, that requires real estate transactions to be in writing to be enforceable. Essential terms must be in the writing that is signed. Derived originally from English law, the idea is that a writing requirement will mitigate a possibly fraudulent claim against property because there will have to be written proof of an acquired interest. Another benefit is that this requirement promotes clarity about who owns what rights to property. The rule applies across many contexts and has evolved into a body of law, with exceptions. You will learn more about this in other chapters, particularly in Chapter 11—Real Estate Transactions. The modern Statute of Frauds for leases in most states is that a lease term of more than one year must be in writing to bind the parties. How does a month to month lease fit in? If a periodic tenancy ends up lasting for longer than one year because of renewals, the oral lease is valid as long as the original term is less than a year. So an unwritten monthly lease presents no problem. As lawyers know well, the best practice is to have a written lease in any event, so that the terms of the leasehold are clearly set out from the start.

Key Terms. Of course, the price of rent, the duration of the lease and the physical space are key issues in negotiating a lease. The amount of rent that can be charged is usually unregulated. However, a small number of municipalities (notably New York) have regulations that limit how much rent can be charged and increased. These laws are designed to balance the interests of landlords with access to housing for tenants. As to the physical space, we will see in the materials below that the law protects many aspects of a tenant's right to possession and enjoyment of a residential leasehold. This includes a landlord's duty to repair and an implied warranty of habitability that generally cannot be waived. As a result, there is very limited room for negotiation on such issues. This is an important counter-evolution to typical standard form leases that favor landlords. Usually, there is far more flexibility in commercial leases.

Security Deposits. The amount and management of security deposits are also regulated by legislation. Although the details vary, states often (1) limit a security deposit to no more than 2 months' rent; (2) require the landlord to place the money into an escrow account that earns interest; and (3) allow the landlord to use the deposit to pay for any damage to the property, with an accounting and refund of any balance due within a month after the lease ends.

Roommates Agreement? When there are two or more tenants who will share the lease, another issue to consider is whether the tenants should enter into a roommate agreement. A lease is designed to govern the relationship between landlords and tenants and not co-tenant relationships. A roommate agreement can assign responsibility for who pays what share of the rent, allocate the space, and assign duties such as cleaning and refraining from loud noises or other conduct that will disrupt quiet enjoyment of the living quarters. What is the property relationship between roommates in the absence of an agreement? Recall the default category for co-owned property you studied in Chapter 4—the roommates are tenants in common.

Exercise 6-5. Document Review—Model Lease

Below is a model standard form lease made available as part of a consumer guide from the Attorney General's office in Maine to help educate the public. The terms are more favorable to tenants than the typical form lease and drafted to be more easily understood by a non-lawyer. Review the lease carefully. Some of the terms will preview the materials studied next. By the end of the chapter, you should be able to evaluate and counsel a client about the meaning of the terms of the lease, the extent to which they depart from the default rules in landlord tenant law and make suggestions for terms that ought to be changed or negotiated further. To gain more experience, it would be helpful to find another lease (maybe your own) and compare it to this one.

Attorney General's Model Residential Lease
SAMPLE MAINE RESIDENTIAL LEASE

1. PARTIES TO THIS LEASE. The parties are: [names, addresses and phone numbers].

2. MANAGING AGENT. If the landlord employs an agent to manage this residence _______.

3. RESIDENCE LOCATION. This residence is a [house, apartment, mobile home] (check one). It is located at ______________________________.

4. LENGTH OF LEASE. The landlord will rent this residence to the tenant for ___________ months. This term shall begin on the _____ day of _________ 20_____, at noon and end on ______.

5. RENT PAYMENTS.

A. ***Rental Amount***. The rent for this residence is $ ____ a month. The tenant shall pay the rent for each month on the ____ day of that month.

B. ***Paying the Rent***. The rent should be paid to: ____ . The landlord may assess a penalty of __% (up to 4%) of the monthly rent once payment is 15 or more days late.

C. ***Additional Charges***. In addition to the monthly rent, the tenant also agrees to pay the landlord the following charges (describe the reason for the charge, the amount, and when it should be paid).

6. SECURITY DEPOSIT.

A. ***Amount of Security Deposit***. The tenant has agreed to pay the landlord $ ____ as a Security Deposit. (Enter amount not to exceed two months' rent.) The landlord will keep the Security Deposit separate from the landlord's own money.

B. ***Return of the Security Deposit***. The landlord will return the entire Security Deposit to the tenant at the end of the lease if the following conditions are met: (1) The apartment is in good condition except for (a) normal wear and tear or (b) damage not caused by the tenant, the tenant's family, invitees or guests; (2) The tenant does not owe any rent or utility charges which the tenant was required to pay directly to the landlord; and (3) The tenant has not caused the landlord expenses for storage and disposing of unclaimed property.

If the landlord deducts money from the tenant's Security Deposit, the landlord will provide the tenant a list of the items for which the tenant is being charged and return to the tenant the balance of the Security Deposit. The landlord will return the Security Deposit, or the remaining balance, to the tenant no more than thirty (30) days after the tenancy ends.

7. SERVICES PROVIDED BY THE LANDLORD. Utilities and services shall be paid by the parties as follows (examples listed).

8. FURNISHINGS PROVIDED BY THE LANDLORD. (These are examples not legal requirements.) Included are stove, refrigerator, drapes, smoke alarms, cable boxes, etc.

9. TENANT RESIDENTIAL RESPONSIBILITIES

A. ***Use Only as a Residence***. The tenant agrees that the residence will be used only as a residence, except for incidental use in trade or business (such as telephone solicitation of sales or arts and crafts created for profit). Such incidental uses will be allowed as long as they do not violate local zoning laws or affect the landlord's ability to obtain fire or liability insurance. The total number of persons residing in this residence cannot exceed ____.

B. ***Damage***. The tenant agrees not to damage the apartment, the building, the grounds or the common areas or to interfere with the rights of other tenants to live in their apartments in peace and quiet. Damage (other than normal wear and tear) caused by the tenant, the tenant's family, invitees, service animal or guests shall be repaired by the tenant at the tenant's expense. Upon the tenant's failure to make such repairs, the landlord, after reasonable written notice to the tenant, may make the repairs and the tenant shall be responsible to the landlord for their reasonable cost.

C. ***Alterations***. No alteration, addition or improvement to the residence shall be made by the tenant without the prior written consent by the landlord.

D. Tenant agrees to promptly notify the landlord if he knows, or suspects, an infestation of bedbugs in the unit and agrees to cooperate with the Landlord and any pest control agent to remediate.

10. LANDLORD RESIDENTIAL RESPONSIBILITIES

A. ***Legal Use of the Residence***. The landlord agrees not to interfere with the tenant's legal use of the residence.

B. ***Residence Must Be Fit to Live in.*** The landlord promises that the residence: (1) complies with applicable housing codes; (2) is fit to live in; and (3) is not dangerous to the life, health or safety of the occupants. The landlord agrees to: (insert list that parties agree to such as)

a. Maintain structural components, such as roofs, floors, and chimneys in reasonably good repair

b. Maintain dwelling in a reasonably weather tight condition

c. Provide adequate keys and locks

d. Keep common areas such as lobbies and stairwells clean and free of hazards

e. Keep electrical, plumbing and heating systems in good repair and maintain any appliances which are provided with the rental.

f. Test for radon

C. Landlord agrees to the following accommodations for tenant's disability (insert list).

11. LANDLORD ENTRY INTO THE RESIDENCE. Except for emergencies, the landlord may enter the apartment only during reasonable hours and after obtaining the tenant's consent at least 24 hours in advance. The tenant may not unreasonably withhold consent to the landlord to enter the residence.

12. BUILDING RULES. The tenant agrees to obey the following rules: (these are examples not legal requirements)

1. No smoking. 2. No pets (note service animals are not pets). 3. No parking, storage or accumulation of debris on the lawn/yard. 4. No candle burning. 5. Keep premises in a sanitary condition. 6. Maintain reasonable peace and quiet.

13. NOTIFYING THE LANDLORD OR TENANT. [Specify].

14. SUBLEASING. The tenant agrees not to sublease or assign this residence without the prior written consent of the landlord.

15. OCCUPANTS. The residents listed below shall be the sole occupants of the leased premises:

16. PETS. The tenant may___ may not___ (check one) maintain pets in the residence. If the tenant is allowed to have pets, only the following pets may live in the residence: [specify].

17. CONDITION OF RESIDENCE AT THE TIME LEASE IS SIGNED. Prior to signing this lease, the landlord and the tenant did___ did not___(check one) inspect together the residence. If they did inspect the residence, their findings were as follows: [describe].

18. WHEN THE LEASE ENDS. When the lease ends, the tenant agrees to return the residence in the same condition as it was at the start of the lease, except for normal wear and tear and except for those inspection items which were noted at the time this lease was signed and not repaired. The tenant will have to pay for damage to the residence only if the damage was caused by the tenant or the tenant's family, invitees, service animal or guests. The tenant shall remove all personal property and return the keys.

19. BREACH. Any violations of the provisions of this agreement by the Tenant will be deemed breach of the lease and the Landlord may pursue legal remedies including an action to evict the tenant. If the Landlord violates any provisions of this lease, the tenant may sue to enforce its terms. By signing this lease, the tenant does not waive any rights he has under the law.

http://www.maine.gov/ag/consumer/law_guide_article.shtml?id=27935.

Protection Against Discrimination

Suppose a landlord prefers blondes to brunettes, then a brunette applies for a rental, and the landlord refuses. How much legal power does a landlord have to select or refuse to lease to a tenant? Recall from the discussion of trespass in Chapter 3 that the right to exclude others is a core property right with strong legal protections. Even so, as you will continue to discover throughout this textbook, property rights such as the right to exclude do not give an owner absolute power. Rather, the law balances interests among property claimants in ways that vary, depending on the context. Because a landlord owns property, he or she has a default right to exclude. However, that power is limited and regulated in light of the importance of access to housing and to promote equality and discourage discrimination against groups of people who have historically suffered from exclusion.

This sub-part is a brief introduction to several fundamental legal principles and policies of the federal Fair Housing Act (FHA) concerning leasing. The FHA is a critically important statute that governs a landlord's right to exclude, including sales and rental of housing. It was adopted in 1968, soon after the death of Martin Luther King, as the last installment of civil rights statutes of that period. As Chapter 3 addresses, the Civil Rights Act of 1866[1] also provides protection against discrimination in real estate transactions as to race and national origin, and state and local laws may provide further safeguards beyond federal law. For example, some states prohibit discrimination based on sexual orientation, or based on marital status—categories that are missing from the FHA.

Exercise 6-6. Interpreting Statutes—The Federal Fair Housing Act

A key set of regulations regarding leasing from the federal Fair Housing Act are excerpted below. Note that there are some exceptions to the FHA—when discrimination is not actionable (not included in the excerpt). Two categories of property are generally exempt from the Act: (1) It does not apply to rooms or units in a dwelling that is owner-occupied and occupied by no more than four families living independently of each other, (2) nor to single family homes, as long as the owner has 3 or fewer such homes, does not use a real estate broker or salesperson and does not advertise in a way that violates the act.

Read the statute carefully and apply it to the following questions.

1. "All citizens of the United States shall have the same right, in every State and Territory, as is enjoyed by white citizens thereof to inherit, purchase, lease, sell, hold, and convey real and personal property." 42 U.S.C. § 1982.

1. Would there be a potentially meritorious cause of action if a landlord rented only to blondes?
2. What if a landlord refused to rent to a tenant and the tenant suspects it was because of race or religion or sex?
3. Is there a violation of the FHA if the landlord rents only to heterosexuals?
4. Is there a violation of the FHA if a landlord bans pets? What if having a pet assisted a tenant with a disability—such as a service or emotional support animal?
5. Could a landlord have a policy of renting to families with no more than two children?

42 U.S.C. § 3604

§ 3604. Discrimination in the sale or rental of housing and other prohibited practices

As made applicable by section 3603 of this title and except as exempted by sections 3603(b) and 3607 of this title, it shall be unlawful—

(a) To refuse to sell or rent after the making of a bona fide offer, or to refuse to negotiate for the sale or rental of, or otherwise make unavailable or deny, a dwelling to any person because of race, color, religion, sex, familial status [children living with parents or legal custodians and pregnant women], or national origin.

(b) To discriminate against any person in the terms, conditions, or privileges of sale or rental of a dwelling, or in the provision of services or facilities in connection therewith, because of race, color, religion, sex, familial status, or national origin.

(c) To make, print, or publish, or cause to be made, printed, or published any notice, statement, or advertisement, with respect to the sale or rental of a dwelling that indicates any preference, limitation, or discrimination based on race, color, religion, sex, handicap, familial status, or national origin, or an intention to make any such preference, limitation, or discrimination.

(d) To represent to any person because of race, color, religion, sex, handicap, familial status, or national origin that any dwelling is not available for inspection, sale, or rental when such dwelling is in fact so available.

(e) For profit, to induce or attempt to induce any person to sell or rent any dwelling by representations regarding the entry or prospective entry into the neighborhood of a person or persons of a particular race, color, religion, sex, handicap, familial status, or national origin.

(f)(1) To discriminate in the sale or rental, or to otherwise make unavailable or deny, a dwelling to any buyer or renter because of a handicap of—

(A) that buyer or renter [or person living with or associated with buyer or renter].

(2) To discriminate against any person in the terms, conditions, or privileges of sale or rental of a dwelling, or in the provision of services or facilities in connection with such dwelling, because of a handicap of that person [or same as above].

(3) For purposes of this subsection, discrimination includes—

(A) a refusal to permit, at the expense of the handicapped person, reasonable modifications of existing premises occupied or to be occupied by such person if such modifications may be necessary to afford such person full enjoyment of the premises except that, in the case of a rental, the landlord may where it is reasonable to do so condition permission for a modification on the renter agreeing to restore the interior of the premises to the condition that existed before the modification, reasonable wear and tear excepted.

(B) a refusal to make reasonable accommodations in rules, policies, practices, or services, when such accommodations may be necessary to afford such person equal opportunity to use and enjoy a dwelling....

Exercise 6-7. *Sullivan v. Hernandez*

Even in cases where discrimination is apparent, it can be difficult for a tenant to prove intentional discrimination. As we will see in the next case, courts have developed an approach that allows for claims under the FHA when direct evidence may not be available. As you read *Sullivan*, consider the following questions.

1. What is the three step approach to proving intentional discrimination under the FHA? Be sure to identify what the tenant must prove and when and how the burden of proof shifts from the tenant to the landlord and then shifts back.
2. What facts support a finding of discrimination here?

Sullivan v. Hernandez

215 F. Supp. 2d 635 (D. Md. 2002)

Motz, J. In this action Harold and Carla Sullivan allege that they were unlawfully discriminated against on the basis of race and disability in violation of the Fair Housing Act, 42 U.S.C. § 3601, *et seq.* ("FHA"), and the Civil Rights Act of 1866, 42 U.S.C. § 1981, *et seq.* (" section 1981") when their application for rental housing was rejected. They have brought suit against Jan Hernandez, Noah & Cummings Property Management, Inc. ("Noah & Cummings"), Susan Ronan, and Long and Foster Real Estate, Inc. ("Long and Foster"). Hernandez and Noah & Cummings joined Ronald and Maureen Carroll as third-party defendants. Discovery has been completed, and the defendants and the Carrolls have filed a joint motion for summary judgment. Plaintiffs have filed a cross-motion for summary judgment as to their claims for disability discrimination. For the reasons that follow, I will deny both motions.

On December 31, 1998, the Sullivans, who are both African-American, met with Hernandez, an agent for Noah & Cummings, in order to discuss rental properties. After the Sullivans and Hernandez spoke, Hernandez took the Sullivans to view several properties. One property viewed by the Sullivans was 503 Curry Ford Road, owned by the Carrolls. After viewing this property, the Sullivans completed a rental application for it on December 31, 1998. Subsequently, Hernandez delivered the application to Susan Ronan, an agent for Long and Foster who listed the Carrolls' property. Ronan asserts that she did not receive the Sullivans' application until January 4, 1999.

A few days before Ronan allegedly received the Sullivans' application, Ronan received a rental application for the Carrolls' property from Partha Bagchi. Long and Foster personnel then obtained background information on the Sullivans and Bagchi, including credit reports, information about the rental history of the applicants, and information about the applicants' employment. Specifically, the reports indicated that (1) Bagchi's salary was $90,000 compared to the Sullivans' collective salary of approximately $50,000, (2) the Sullivans' had a reserve in mutual funds and bank accounts totaling approximately $27,000, (3) there were two negative credit reports in Mrs. Sullivan's history, (4) Mrs. Sullivan had one prior bankruptcy, and (5) on one prior occasion Bagchi violated a rental lease by vacating a premises more than six months prior to the lease's expiration without landlord approval. On January 8, 2002, Ronan read the reports to Mr. Carroll. After listening to these reports, the Carrolls chose to rent the home to Bagchi.

Courts have adapted the *McDonnell-Douglas* framework to housing discrimination claims. Thus, in order to survive summary judgment, the Sullivans must allege sufficient facts to establish a prima facie case of housing discrimination. To establish a prima facie case of housing discrimination, the plaintiff must prove that: (1) he or she is a member of a statutorily protected class; (2) he or she applied for and was qualified to rent or purchase certain property or housing; (3) he or she was rejected; and (4) the housing or rental property remained available thereafter. The first three elements are undisputed. The Sullivans are African-American. Additionally, the Sullivans applied to rent the Carroll's property, were qualified to rent the property, and their application was rejected.

The defendants and third-party defendants (to whom, for ease of presentation, I will collectively refer as "defendants") dispute the final element of a prima facie case. They contend that the Sullivans cannot establish that the rental property remained available because another application was accepted immediately after their application was rejected. That argument fails because it would allow a discriminating party to avoid a discrimination suit simply by accepting another application. The final element of a prima facie case does not require a plaintiff to establish that the property remained available indefinitely or for a long period. It simply requires a plaintiff to show that the property remained available immediately after the application in question was received. Here, the property was available when the Sullivans' application was received by the Carrolls and their real estate agent, Ronan, even though Bagchi's application was subsequently accepted. Thus, the Sullivans have established a prima facie case of housing discrimination.

The burden shifts to the defendants to offer a legitimate, non-discriminatory explanation for selecting Bagchi's application. In an affidavit submitted in support of defendants' summary judgment motion, Mr. Carroll states that he selected Bagchi's application because he believed that: (1) Bagchi had a stronger credit history than the Sullivans; (2) Bagchi had a greater income than the Sullivans; (3) several creditors reported that Mrs. Sullivan had not paid her debts; and (4) Mrs. Sullivan had declared bankruptcy. Although the Sullivans debate the merits of which applicant was better qualified financially, on its face Carroll's explanation is both reasonable and non-discriminatory.

Thus, the burden shifts back to the Sullivans to establish that the Carrolls' explanation is pretextual. A plaintiff may establish pretext by demonstrating that "the employer's proffered explanation is unworthy of credence." [Citations omitted.] In this case, the Carrolls initially offered an explanation for selecting Bagchi's application over the Sullivans which is inconsistent with the more recent affidavit Mr. Carroll has submitted. In their answers to interrogatories, they cited three factors that led to their decision: Bagchi's financial and "fully qualified" status, the fact that Ronan recommended Bagchi's application, and the fact that Bagchi's application was received first. When confronted with potential disputes over two of these factors, the Carrolls retreated and dwindled their explanation down to one factor: Bagchi's financial status.

A reasonable jury could find that the shift in the Carrolls' position was not incidental and raises a question concerning defendants' motivation. First, there is an inconsistency regarding Ronan's role in the decision to choose Bagchi's application. In their interrogatory answers, the Carrolls stated that they chose to enter into a lease with Mr. Bagchi because "Mr. Bagchi's application was recommended to us by our trusted real estate agent, Ms. Ronan." (*See* Pl.Ex. 4 at 5.) In contrast, in his current explanation, Mr. Carroll downplays Ronan's role in the decision. In fact, Mr. Carroll's recent affidavit, makes no reference to advice from Ronan. (*See* Def.Ex. 5 ¶¶ 6–8.) The reason for this change may be that defendants now realize that Ronan, but not the Carrolls, had reviewed the rental application, which included copies of the Sullivans' drivers' licenses. By detaching Ronan from the decision to choose Bagchi, the defendants are able to argue (and, in fact, do argue) that the decision to choose Bagchi could not have been discriminatory because Mr. Carroll made the decision without knowledge of the Sullivans' race.

Second, there is an inconsistency regarding the timing of the applications. In their interrogatory answers, the Carrolls stated that they chose Bagchi's application because it "was the first that [they] received." (*See* Pl. Ex. 4 at 5.) Mr. Carroll's later affidavit, however, makes no reference to the order in which the applications were received. This is significant because the evidence is contradictory concerning when Ronan received the Sullivans' application. Ronan testified that she did not receive the application from Hernandez until January 4, 2002. (Ronan Dep. at 41–42, Pl. Ex. 10.) Hernandez, on the other hand, testified that she dropped the application off at

Ronan's office on December 31, 2001. (Hernandez Dep. at 29–34, Pl. Ex. 9.) Again, an inconsistency is presented that could lead a reasonable jury to infer that the legitimate, nondiscriminatory explanation offered by the defendants is pretextual. Accordingly, I will deny the defendants' motion for summary judgment.

I will now briefly address the Sullivans' contention that they should be granted a summary judgment claim for disability discrimination. The Carrolls rejected the Sullivans' application, in part, because of Carla Sullivan's credit history and prior bankruptcy. This negative credit history was allegedly due to Carla Sullivan's disability. The Sullivans argue that simply because Mr. Carroll knew that the Sullivans' income was from disability payments, the defendants must be held per se liable for housing discrimination. They cite no authority for this proposition, and I find it entirely unpersuasive.

Possession and Enjoyment of a Leasehold

In this part of the chapter, you will learn the body of law governing both landlord and tenant rights and duties concerning possession and enjoyment of a leasehold.

Delivering Possession

Imagine you have rented an apartment in a new town where you have a great new job that starts soon. Having driven a long distance in a rental truck with all your belongings, you arrive at your new place only to discover that a previous tenant is still living in the apartment. You cannot move in and have nowhere to go. Is the landlord accountable to solve this problem or are you? As you might expect, under the law of most states, the landlord is responsible to deliver *actual* possession of the leasehold and, if need be, evict the holdover tenant. Failure to do so is a breach of contract. In such a situation, the tenant may choose to terminate the lease and seek compensatory damages for any losses incurred. Alternatively, the tenant can affirm the lease and be compensated for any damages such as a higher cost for renting temporary housing. Sensibly, the tenant will not have to pay rent until the space is actually available. As always, however, you should be sure to research the law of the state where a controversy like this arises, because a minority of states take the opposite approach and view removal of the wayward tenant as the new tenant's problem, find no breach of contract and still require the tenant to pay rent.

The Implied Warranty of Habitability

By the 1970s, widespread adoption of an implied warranty of habitability ushered in a new era in residential landlord-tenant law concerning the quality and physical condition of leaseholds. In almost all states today, landlords are generally responsible to provide a minimum baseline of health, safety and functionality in rental properties where tenants and their families live. This obligation is implied and in most states cannot be waived. This complements local housing codes in place nationwide that also require safe and fit housing—but gives tenants a tool for direct enforcement against landlords. As we will see, tenants have a range of remedies available for breach of the warranty, including ending the lease or withholding rent. The longstanding doctrine of constructive eviction—that prohibits landlords from interfering with a tenant's right of possession and quiet enjoyment—provides another avenue of protection. Constructive eviction will be addressed in a sub-section that follows.

Under the previous regime, landlords had no duty to make rental housing fit for habitation, nor to maintain and repair the premises. *Caveat lessee* or "let the tenant beware" ruled the period. Residential rentals were treated like agricultural leases from the middle ages, where the bare right of possession of the land was the heart of the transfer and all that was required of the landlord. Finding it profitable to avoid repairs or shift them to tenants, many landlords refused to obligate themselves to make repairs in a lease. Tenants were rarely able to bargain for or enforce better terms. In addition, lease clauses were deemed independent of each other, so that if a landlord breached the contract, the tenant still had a duty to pay rent. Consider this infamous example from traditional property law: a rental home burns down so that the tenant and his family have nowhere to live. The result? Applying *caveat lessee*, rent is due to the landlord just the same as before. Can you see why?

This system frequently led to disastrous outcomes for tenants and for public health. Housing conditions, especially in urban areas, were deplorable. Tenants were often living in overcrowded spaces, without the basic necessities of life such as heat and running water and living with raw sewage, vermin and filth. Disease was rampant, including cholera, yellow fever, tuberculosis and polio. Some cities responded by adopting housing codes that mandated necessities such as water, heat, water-tight apartments, safe electrical wiring and operational plumbing. However, enforcement and penalties against landlords were typically weak and ineffective. Additionally, tenants were afraid to complain for fear of retribution—of losing their homes or suffering rent increases that they could not afford.

As you study the materials and cases here, you will learn the current legal scheme as well as the foundations for this reversal of course. You will also bear witness to some of the stories of tenants' struggles against the dangerous and often inhumane conditions that were prevalent and legally permissible before the reforms. As the name suggests, the implied warranty concerns habitability and it applies to residential leases.

Exercise 6-8. *Javins v. First National Realty Corp.* and *Hilder v. St. Peter*

1. *Javins* was a catalyst for transformation of landlords' duty to repair and tenants' rights and remedies. As you read the case, identify and evaluate the court's reasoning. More generally, consider too what roles are appropriate for judges.

Can and should judges be agents of dramatic legal change? If so, what principles justify that?

2. In *Hilder*, pay special attention to the description of Ella Hilder's experiences and those of her children. Notice that the *Javins* opinion did not include any details of the living conditions of the tenants. In contrast, *Hilder*'s depiction offers an opportunity for a deeper understanding and perhaps a more persuasive foundation for this legal movement. Do you find the personal storytelling here to be an effective lawyering strategy? What other value(s) might it have?
3. The appalling living conditions endured by tenants such as the Hilder family raises a critically important question that arises throughout this chapter—to what extent is modern law an effective tool for actually improving the lives of tenants in sub-standard rentals?
4. *Hilder* provides a helpful overview of the content and operation of the implied warranty of habitability. As you read, be sure to identify and apply the principles of law.

Javins v. First National Realty Corporation

428 F.2d 1071 (D.C. Cir. 1970)

J. Skelly Wright. These cases present the question whether housing code violations which arise during the term of a lease have any effect upon the tenant's obligation to pay rent. We hold that a warranty of habitability, measured by the standards set out in the Housing Regulations for the District of Columbia, is implied by operation of law into leases of urban dwelling units covered by those Regulations and that breach of this warranty gives rise to the usual remedies for breach of contract.

I

By separate written leases, each of the appellants rented an apartment in a three-building apartment complex in Northwest Washington known as Clifton Terrace. The landlord, First National Realty Corporation, filed separate actions seeking possession on the ground that each of the appellants had defaulted in the payment of rent due for the month of April. The tenants, appellants here, admitted that they had not paid the landlord any rent for April. However, they alleged numerous violations of the Housing Regulations as "an equitable defense or (a) claim by way of recoupment ..." They offered to prove [1500 violations of the Housing Regulations in the building].

II

Since, in traditional analysis, a lease was the conveyance of an interest in land, courts have usually utilized the special rules governing real property transactions to resolve controversies involving leases. However, as the Supreme Court has noted in another context, "the body of private property law ... more than almost any other branch of law, has been shaped by distinctions whose validity is largely historical." [Citations omitted.] Courts have a duty to reappraise old doctrines in the light of the facts and values of contemporary life—particularly old common law doctrines which the courts themselves created and developed. As we have said before, "The continued vitality of the common law ... depends upon its ability to reflect contemporary community values and ethics." [Citation omitted.]

The assumption of landlord-tenant law, derived from feudal property law, that a lease primarily conveyed to the tenant an interest in land may have been reasonable in a rural, agrarian society; it may continue to be reasonable in some leases involving farming or commercial land. In these cases, the value of the lease to the tenant is the land itself. But in the case of the modern apartment dweller, the value of the lease is that it gives him a place to live. The city dweller who seeks to lease an apartment on the third floor of a tenement has little interest in the land 30 or 40 feet below, or even in the bare right to possession within the four walls of his apartment. When American city dwellers, both rich and poor, seek "shelter" today, they seek a well known package of goods and services—a package which includes not merely walls and ceilings, but also adequate heat, light and ventilation, serviceable plumbing facilities, secure windows and doors, proper sanitation, and proper maintenance.

III

Modern contract law has recognized that the buyer of goods and services in an industrialized society must rely upon the skill and honesty of the supplier to assure that goods and services purchased are of adequate quality. In interpreting most contracts, courts have sought to protect the legitimate expectations of the buyer and have steadily widened the seller's responsibility for the quality of goods and services through implied warranties of fitness and merchantability.

The rigid doctrines of real property law have tended to inhibit the application of implied warranties to transactions involving real estate. Now, however, courts have begun to hold sellers and developers of real property responsible for the quality of their product. For example, builders of new homes have recently been held liable to purchasers for improper construction on the ground that the builders had breached an implied warranty of fitness. In other cases courts have held builders of new homes liable for breach of an implied warranty that all local building regulations had been complied with.

Despite this trend in the sale of real estate, many courts have been unwilling to imply warranties of quality, specifically a warranty of habitability, into leases of apartments. Recent decisions have offered no convincing explanation for their refusal; rather they have relied without discussion upon the old common law rule that the lessor is not obligated to repair unless he covenants to do so in the written lease contract. In our judgment, the old no-repair rule cannot coexist with the obligations imposed on the landlord by a typical modern housing code, and must be abandoned in favor of an implied warranty of habitability. In the District of Columbia, the standards of this warranty are set out in the Housing Regulations.

IV

A.

In our judgment the common law itself must recognize the landlord's obligation to keep his premises in a habitable condition. This conclusion is compelled by three separate considerations. First, we believe that the old rule was based on certain factual assumptions which are no longer true; on its own terms, it can no longer be justified. Second, we believe that the consumer protection cases discussed above require that the old rule be abandoned in order to bring residential landlord-tenant law into harmony with the principles on which those cases rest. Third, we think that the nature of today's urban housing market also dictates abandonment of the old rule.

The common law rule absolving the lessor of all obligation to repair originated in the early Middle Ages. Such a rule was perhaps well suited to an agrarian economy; the land was more important than whatever small living structure was included in the leasehold, and the tenant farmer was fully capable of making repairs himself. Court decisions in the late 1800's began to recognize that the factual assumptions of the common law were no longer accurate in some cases. For example, the common law, since it assumed that the land was the most important part of the leasehold, required a tenant to pay rent even if any building on the land was destroyed. Faced with such a rule and the ludicrous results it produced, in 1863 the New York Court of Appeals declined to hold that an upper story tenant was obliged to continue paying rent after his apartment building burned down. The court simply pointed out that the urban tenant had no interest in the land, only in the attached building. [S]ome courts began some time ago to question the common law's assumptions that the land was the most important feature of a leasehold and that the tenant could feasibly make any necessary repairs himself.

It is overdue for courts to admit that these assumptions are no longer true with regard to all urban housing. Today's urban tenants, the vast majority of whom live in multiple dwelling houses, are interested, not in the land, but solely in "a house suitable for occupation." Furthermore, today's city dweller usually has a single, specialized skill unrelated to maintenance work; he is unable to make repairs like the "jack-of-all-trades" farmer who was the common law's model of the lessee. Further, unlike his agrarian predecessor who often remained on one piece of land for his entire life, urban tenants today are more mobile than ever before. A tenant's tenure in a specific apartment will often not be sufficient to justify efforts at repairs. In addition, the increasing complexity of today's dwellings renders them much more difficult to repair than the structures of earlier times. In a multiple dwelling repair may require access to equipment and areas in the control of the landlord. Low and middle income tenants, even if they were interested in making repairs, would be unable to obtain any financing for major repairs since they have no long-term interest in the property.

Our approach to the common law of landlord and tenant ought to be aided by principles derived from the consumer protection cases referred to above. In a lease contract, a tenant seeks to purchase from his landlord shelter for a specified period of time. The landlord sells housing as a commercial businessman and has much greater opportunity, incentive and capacity to inspect and maintain the condition of his building. Moreover, the tenant must rely upon the skill and bona fides of his landlord at least as much as a car buyer must rely upon the car manufacturer. In dealing with major problems, such as heating, plumbing, electrical or structural defects, the tenant's position corresponds precisely with "the ordinary consumer who cannot be expected to have the knowledge or capacity or even the opportunity to make adequate inspection of mechanical instrumentalities, like automobiles, and to decide for himself whether they are reasonably fit for the designed purpose." [Citation omitted.]

Since a lease contract specifies a particular period of time during which the tenant has a right to use his apartment for shelter, he may legitimately expect that the apartment will be fit for habitation for the time period for which it is rented. We point out that in the present cases there is no allegation that appellants' apartments were in poor condition or in violation of the housing code at the commencement of the leases. Since the lessees continue to pay the same rent, they were entitled to expect that the landlord would continue to keep the premises in their beginning condition during the lease term. It is precisely such expectations that the law now recognizes as deserving of formal, legal protection.

Even beyond the rationale of traditional products liability law, the relationship of landlord and tenant suggests further compelling reasons for the law's protection of the tenants' legitimate expectations of quality. The inequality in bargaining power between landlord and tenant has been well documented. Tenants have very little leverage to enforce demands for better housing. Various impediments to competition in the rental housing market, such as racial and class discrimination and standardized form leases, mean that landlords place tenants in a take it or leave it situation. The increasingly severe shortage of adequate housing further increases the landlord's bargaining power and escalates the need for maintaining and improving the existing stock. Finally, the findings by various studies of the social impact of bad housing has led to the realization that poor housing is detrimental to the whole society, not merely to the unlucky ones who must suffer the daily indignity of living in a slum.

Thus we are led by our inspection of the relevant legal principles and precedents to the conclusion that the old common law rule imposing an obligation upon the lessee to repair during the lease term was really never intended to apply to residential urban leaseholds. Contract principles established in other areas of the law provide a more rational framework for the apportionment of landlord-tenant responsibilities; they strongly suggest that a warranty of habitability be implied into all contracts for urban dwellings.

B.

We believe, in any event, that the District's housing code requires that a warranty of habitability be implied in the leases of all housing that it covers. The housing code—formally designated the Housing Regulations of the District of Columbia—was established and authorized by the Commissioners of the District of Columbia on

August 11, 1955. Since that time, the code has been updated by numerous orders of the Commissioners. The 75 pages of the Regulations provide a comprehensive regulatory scheme setting forth in some detail: (a) the standards which housing in the District of Columbia must meet; (b) which party, the lessor or the lessee, must meet each standard; and (c) a system of inspections, notifications and criminal penalties. The Regulations themselves are silent on the question of private remedies.

Two previous decisions of this court, however, have held that the Housing Regulations create legal rights and duties enforceable in tort by private parties. In *Whetzel v. Jess Fisher Management Co.*, 108 U.S.App.D.C. 385, 282 F.2d 943 (1960), we followed the leading case of *Altz v. Leiberson*, 233 N.Y. 16, 134 N.E. 703 (1922), in holding (1) that the housing code altered the common law rule and imposed a duty to repair upon the landlord, and (2) that a right of action accrued to a tenant injured by the landlord's breach of this duty. As Judge Cardozo wrote in *Leiberson*:

> ... We may be sure that the framers of this statute, when regulating tenement life, had uppermost in thought the care of those who are unable to care for themselves. The Legislature must have known that unless repairs in the rooms of the poor were made by the landlord, they would not be made by any one....

[Citation omitted]

The District of Columbia Court of Appeals gave further effect to the Housing Regulations in *Brown v. Southall Realty Co.*, 237 A.2d 834 (1968). There the landlord knew at the time the lease was signed that housing code violations existed which rendered the apartment "unsafe and unsanitary." Viewing the lease as a contract, the District of Columbia Court of Appeals held that the premises were let in violation of Sections 2304 and 2501 of the Regulations and that the lease, therefore, was void as an illegal contract. In the light of *Brown*, it is clear not only that the housing code creates privately enforceable duties as held in *Whetzel*, but that the basic validity of every housing contract depends upon substantial compliance with the housing code at the beginning of the lease term. The *Brown* court relied particularly upon Section 2501 of the Regulations which provides:

> Every premises accommodating one or more habitations shall be maintained and kept in repair so as to provide decent living accommodations for the occupants. This part of this Code contemplates more than mere basic repairs and maintenance to keep out the elements; its purpose is to include repairs and maintenance designed to make a premises or neighborhood healthy and safe.

By its terms, this section applies to maintenance and repair during the lease term. Under the *Brown* holding, serious failure to comply with this section before the lease term begins renders the contract void. We think it untenable to find that this section has no effect on the contract after it has been signed. To the contrary, by signing the lease the landlord has undertaken a continuing obligation to the tenant to maintain the premises in accordance with all applicable law.

The duties imposed by the Housing Regulations may not be waived or shifted by agreement if the Regulations specifically place the duty upon the lessor. Criminal penalties are provided if these duties are ignored. This regulatory structure was established by the Commissioners because, in their judgment, the grave conditions in the housing market required serious action. Yet official enforcement of the housing code has been far from uniformly effective. Innumerable studies have documented the desperate condition of rental housing in the District of Columbia and in the nation.

We therefore hold that the Housing Regulations imply a warranty of habitability, measured by the standards which they set out, into leases of all housing that they cover.

V

In the present cases, the landlord sued for possession for nonpayment of rent. Under contract principles, however, the tenant's obligation to pay rent is dependent upon the landlord's performance of his obligations, including his warranty to maintain the premises in habitable condition. In order to determine whether any rent is owed to the landlord, the tenants must be given an opportunity to prove the housing code violations alleged as breach of the landlord's warranty.

At trial, the finder of fact must make two findings: (1) whether the alleged violations existed during the period for which past due rent is claimed, and (2) what portion, if any or all, of the tenant's obligation to pay rent was suspended by the landlord's breach. If no part of the tenant's rental obligation is found to have been suspended, then a judgment for possession may issue forthwith. On the other hand, if the jury determines that the entire rental obligation has been extinguished by the landlord's total breach, then the action for possession on the ground of nonpayment must fail.

The jury may find that part of the tenant's rental obligation has been suspended but that part of the unpaid back rent is indeed owed to the landlord. In these circumstances, no judgment for possession should issue if the tenant agrees to pay the partial rent found to be due. If the tenant refuses to pay the partial amount, a judgment for possession may then be entered.

Hilder v. St. Peter

478 A.2d 202 (Vt. 1984)

Billings, C.J. The facts are uncontested. In October, 1974, plaintiff began occupying an apartment at defendants' 10–12 Church Street apartment building in Rutland with her three children and new-born grandson. Plaintiff orally agreed to pay defendant Stuart St. Peter $140 a month and a damage deposit of $50; plaintiff paid defendant the first month's rent and the damage deposit prior to moving in. Plaintiff has paid all rent due under her tenancy. Because the previous tenants had left behind garbage and items of personal belongings, defendant offered to refund plaintiff's damage deposit if she would clean the apartment herself prior to taking possession. Plaintiff did clean the apartment, but never received her deposit back because the defendant denied ever receiving it. Upon moving into the apartment, plaintiff discovered a broken kitchen window. Defendant promised to repair it, but after waiting a week and fearing that her two year old child might cut herself on the shards of glass, plaintiff repaired the window at her own expense. Although defendant promised to provide a front door key, he never did. For a period of time, whenever plaintiff left the apartment, a member of her family would remain behind for security reasons. Eventually, plaintiff purchased and installed a padlock, again at her own expense. After moving in, plaintiff discovered that the bathroom toilet was clogged with paper and feces and would flush only by dumping pails of water into it. Although plaintiff repeatedly complained about the toilet, and defendant promised to have it repaired, the toilet remained clogged and mechanically inoperable throughout the period of plaintiff's tenancy. In addition, the bathroom light and wall outlet were inoperable. Again, the defendant agreed to repair the fixtures, but never did. In order to have light in the bathroom, plaintiff attached a fixture to the wall and connected it to an extension cord that was plugged into an adjoining room. Plaintiff also discovered that water leaked from the water pipes of the upstairs apartment down the ceilings and walls of both her kitchen and back bedroom. Again, defendant promised to fix the leakage, but never did. As a result of this leakage, a large section of plaster fell from the back bedroom ceiling onto her bed and her grandson's crib. Other sections of plaster remained dangling from the ceiling. This condition was brought to the attention of the defendant, but he never corrected it. Fearing that the remaining plaster might fall when the room was occupied, plaintiff moved her and her grandson's bedroom furniture into the living room and ceased using the back bedroom. During the summer months an odor of raw sewage permeated plaintiff's apartment. The odor was so strong that the plaintiff was ashamed to have company in her apartment. Responding to plaintiff's complaints, Rutland City workers unearthed a broken sewage pipe in the basement of defendants' building. Raw sewage littered the floor of the basement, but defendant failed to clean it up. Plaintiff also discovered that the electric service for her furnace was attached to her breaker box, although defendant had agreed, at the commencement of plaintiff's tenancy, to furnish heat.

... [I]t would be wrong for the law to continue to impose the doctrine of caveat lessee on residential leases.

> The modern view favors a new approach which recognizes that a lease is essentially a contract between the landlord and the tenant wherein the landlord promises to deliver and maintain the demised premises in habitable condition and the tenant promises to pay rent for such habitable premises. These promises constitute interdependent and mutual considerations. Thus, the tenant's obligation to pay rent is predicated on the landlord's obligation to deliver and maintain the premises in habitable condition.

Boston Housing Authority v. Hemingway, 363 Mass. 184, 198, 293 N.E.2d 831, 842 (1973).

Recognition of residential leases as contracts embodying the mutual covenants of habitability and payment of rent does not represent an abrupt change in Vermont law. Our case law has previously recognized that contract remedies are available for breaches of lease agreements. More significantly, our legislature, in establishing local housing authorities, 24 V.S.A. § 4003, has officially recognized the need for assuring the existence of adequate housing.

> [S]ubstandard and decadent areas exist in certain portions of the state of Vermont and ... there is not ... an adequate supply of decent, safe and sanitary housing for persons of low income and/or elderly persons of low income, available for rents which such persons can afford to pay ... this situation tends to cause an increase and spread of communicable and chronic disease ... [and] constitutes a menace to the health, safety, welfare and comfort of the inhabitants of the state and is detrimental to property values in the localities in which it exists....

24 V.S.A. § 4001(4).

Therefore, we now hold expressly that in the rental of any residential dwelling unit an implied warranty exists in the lease, whether oral or written, that the landlord will deliver over and maintain, throughout the period of the tenancy, premises that are safe, clean and fit for human habitation. This warranty of habitability is implied in tenancies for a specific period or at will. Additionally, the implied warranty of habitability covers all latent and patent defects in the essential facilities of the residential unit [including common spaces]. This means that a tenant who enters into a lease agreement with knowledge of any defect in the essential facilities cannot be said to have assumed the risk, thereby losing the protection of the warranty. Nor can this implied warranty of habitability be waived by any written provision in the lease or by oral agreement.

In determining whether there has been a breach of the implied warranty of habitability, the courts may first look to any relevant local or municipal housing code; they may also make reference to the minimum housing code standards enunciated in 24 V.S.A. § 5003(c)(1)–5003(c)(5). A substantial violation of an applicable housing code shall constitute prima facie evidence that there has been a breach of the warranty of habitability. "[O]ne or two minor violations standing alone which do not affect" the health or safety of the tenant, shall be considered de minimus and not a breach of the warranty. [Citations omitted.] In addition, the landlord will not be liable for defects caused by the tenant.

However, these codes and standards merely provide a starting point in determining whether there has been a breach. Not all towns and municipalities have housing codes; where there are codes, the particular problem complained of may not be addressed. In determining whether there has been a breach of the implied warranty of habitability, courts should inquire whether the claimed defect has an impact on the safety or health of the tenant.

In order to bring a cause of action for breach of the implied warranty of habitability, the tenant must first show that he or she notified the landlord "of the deficiency or defect not known to the landlord and [allowed] a reasonable time for its correction." [Citation omitted.]

Because we hold that the lease of a residential dwelling creates a contractual relationship between the landlord and tenant, the standard contract remedies of rescission, reformation and damages are available to the tenant when suing for breach of the implied warranty of habitability. The measure of damages shall be the difference between the value of the dwelling as warranted and the value of the dwelling as it exists in its defective condition. In determining the fair rental value of the dwelling as warranted, the court may look to the agreed upon rent as evidence on this issue. "[I]n residential lease disputes involving a breach of the implied warranty of habitability, public policy militates against requiring expert testimony" concerning the value of the defect. [Citation omitted.] The tenant will be liable only for "the reasonable rental value [if any] of the property in its imperfect condition during his period of occupancy." [Citation omitted.]

We also find persuasive the reasoning of some commentators that damages should be allowed for a tenant's discomfort and annoyance arising from the landlord's breach of the implied warranty of habitability. See Moskovitz, *The Implied Warranty of Habitability: A New Doctrine Raising New Issues,* 62 Calif. L. Rev. 1444, 1470–73 (1974) (hereinafter cited as *A New Doctrine*); *A Dream Deferred,* [48 UMKC L. Rev. 237, 238 (1980)] *supra,* at 250–51. Damages for annoyance and discomfort are reasonable in light of the fact that

> the residential tenant who has suffered a breach of the warranty ... cannot bathe as frequently as he would like or at all if there is inadequate hot water; he must worry about rodents harassing his children or spreading disease if the premises are infested; or he must avoid certain rooms or worry about catching a cold if there is inadequate weather protection or heat. Thus, discomfort and annoyance are the common injuries caused by each breach and hence the true nature of the general damages the tenant is claiming.

Moskovitz, *A New Doctrine, supra,* at 1470–71. Damages for discomfort and annoyance may be difficult to compute; however, "[t]he trier [of fact] is not to be deterred from this duty by the fact that the damages are not susceptible of reduction to an exact money standard." [Citation omitted.]

Another remedy available to the tenant when there has been a breach of the implied warranty of habitability is to withhold the payment of future rent. The burden and expense of bringing suit will then be on the landlord who can better afford to bring the action. In an action for ejectment for nonpayment of rent, 12 V.S.A. § 4773, "[t]he trier of fact, upon evaluating the seriousness of the breach and the ramification of the defect upon the health and safety of the tenant, will abate the rent at the landlord's expense in accordance with its findings." *A Dream Deferred, supra,* at 248. The tenant must show that: (1) the landlord had notice of the previously unknown defect and failed, within a reasonable time, to repair it; and (2) the defect, affecting habitability, existed during the time for which rent was withheld. Whether a portion, all or none of the rent will be awarded to the landlord will depend on the findings relative to the extent and duration of the breach. Of course, once the landlord corrects the defect, the tenant's obligation to pay rent becomes due again.

Additionally, we hold that when the landlord is notified of the defect but fails to repair it within a reasonable amount of time, and the tenant subsequently repairs the defect, the tenant may deduct the expense of the repair from future rent.

In addition to general damages, we hold that punitive damages may be available to a tenant in the appropriate case. Although punitive damages are generally not recoverable in actions for breach of contract, there are cases in which the breach is of such a willful and wanton or fraudulent nature as to make appropriate the award of exemplary damages. A willful and wanton or fraudulent breach may be shown "by conduct manifesting personal ill will, or carried out under circumstances of insult or oppression, or even by conduct manifesting ... a reckless or wanton disregard of [one's] rights...." [Citation omitted.] When a landlord, after receiving notice of a defect, fails to repair the facility that is essential to the health and safety of his or her tenant, an award of punitive damages is proper.

> The purpose of punitive damages ... is to punish conduct which is morally culpable.... Such an award serves to deter a wrongdoer ... from repetitions of the same or similar actions. And it tends to encourage prosecution of a claim by a victim who might not otherwise incur the expense or inconvenience of private action.... The public benefit and a display of ethical indignation are among the ends of the policy to grant punitive damages.

Davis v. Williams, 92 Misc.2d 1051, 402 N.Y.S.2d 92, 94 (N.Y.Civ.Ct.1977).

In the instant case, the trial court's award of damages, based in part on a breach of the implied warranty of habitability, was not a misapplication of the law relative to habitability. Because of our holding in this case, the doctrine of constructive eviction, wherein the tenant must abandon in order to escape liability for rent, is no longer viable. When, as in the instant case, the tenant seeks, not to escape rent liability, but to receive compensatory damages in the amount of rent already paid, abandonment is similarly unnecessary. Under our holding, when a landlord breaches the implied warranty of habitability, the tenant may withhold future rent, and may also seek damages in the amount of rent previously paid.

In its conclusions of law the trial court stated that the defendants' failure to make repairs was compensable by damages to the extent of reimbursement of all rent paid and additional compensatory damages. The court awarded plaintiff a total of $4,945.00; $3,445.00 represents the entire amount of rent plaintiff paid, plus the $50.00 deposit. This appears to leave $1500.00 as the "additional compensatory damages." However, although the court made findings which clearly demonstrate the appropriateness of an award of compensatory damages, there is no indication as to how the court reached a figure of $1500.00. It is "crucial that this Court and the parties be able to determine what was decided and how the decision was reached." [Citation omitted.]

Additionally, the court denied an award to plaintiff of punitive damages on the ground that the evidence failed to support a finding of willful and wanton or fraudulent conduct. The facts in this case, which defendants do not contest, evince a pattern of intentional conduct on the part of defendants for which the term "slumlord" surely was coined. Defendants' conduct was culpable and demeaning to plaintiff and clearly expressive of a wanton disregard of plaintiff's rights. The trial court found that defendants were aware of defects in the essential facilities of plaintiff's apartment, promised plaintiff that repairs would be made, but never fulfilled those promises. The court also found that plaintiff continued, throughout her tenancy, to pay her rent, often in the face of verbal threats made by defendant Stuart St. Peter. These findings point to the "bad spirit and wrong intention" of the defendants, [citation omitted] and would support a finding of willful and wanton or fraudulent conduct, contrary to the conclusions of law and judgment of the trial judge. However, the plaintiff did not appeal the court's denial of punitive damages, and issues not appealed and briefed are waived.

Affirmed in part; reversed in part and remanded for hearing on additional compensable damages, consistent with the views herein.

Exercise 6-9. Understanding the Warranty and Remedies for Breach

1. *Rationale for the Warranty.* Identify at least three justifications offered in *Javins* or *Hilder* for the shift to an implied warranty of habitability. Note further that a waiver of the warranty typically is unenforceable as a matter of public policy. Do you find the rationales persuasive? Does the mandatory warranty actually help tenants? Who ultimately bears the cost of doing repairs? Is it fair to impose these duties on landlords?
2. *Definition and Scope of the Warranty.* Take care to note that the warranty focuses on habitability and so governs residential properties. It does not generally apply to commercial rentals. What exactly does the warranty include? As *Javins* demonstrates, in some states, the warranty is co-extensive with building and housing codes—meaning a significant housing code violation constitutes a breach. In other states, the standard is broader, as we saw in *Hilder.* A housing code violation certainly can qualify as a breach. Beyond that, however, a defect that makes a rental unfit for residential use is a breach, whether there is a housing code violation or not. For another example of how to define the warranty, review clause 10 of the sample lease in Exercise 6-5 above. Now determine whether the following situations present actionable claims. A cockroach infestation? Bedbugs? Secondhand smoke recurrently flowing through the air vents between apartments? No or broken air conditioning? Worn and peeling paint?
3. *Mechanics and Remedies.* Ella Hilder repeatedly notified the landlord of the terrible conditions in her apartment. Typically, notice to the landlord is required to trigger the tenant's rights, and the landlord then has reasonable time to cure the defect. Be sure to research individual state laws, because there is some variation on exactly when a breach occurs.

   Once a breach occurs, tenants have a variety of remedies available. Consider the list below and fill in any gaps. Which options seem best for a client like Ella Hilder? Why?

Recission of the Contract

- The landlord's breach of the warranty entitles the tenant to end the lease and be relieved of the obligation to pay future rent. Therefore, one option is to move out and stop paying rent.

Repair & Deduct

- How would you explain this to a client?

Rent Withholding/Abatement

- The tenant is also entitled to stay and withold rent. Accordingly, what will the result be if the landlord brings an action for eviction for non--payment of rent? Tenants need to be aware that some statutes regulate rent witholding. It is wise to set aside the withheld rent in case a court determines that some rent is owed. In some states, such rent must be deposited into an escrow account.
- A court might find that rent should be reduced rather than eliminated entirely for the period of the breach. Methods for calculating rent abatement vary. One pragamatic approach that avoids the need for expert witnesses is to apply a precentage reduction of rent that approximates the reduction in usable space or value. As explained in *Hilder*, courts also may consider the fair market value of the leasehold in its defective condition compared to the rental value if the property were in compliance with the warranty.

Injunction or Specific Performance

- As equity requires, a court can order that the landlord make repairs or other specific acts be performed. (Courts have even ordered landlords to live in the space!)

Administrative Remedies

- A tenant may be able to call the local housing authority for an inspection. The government can then take action and require the landlord to make repairs.

Damages

- A tenant can seek compensatory damages. This includes reimbursement of lost rental value (that has been paid for), any losses to personal property such as furniture or technology, and excess costs of alternative housing.
- Might damages be paid to account for a tenant's discomfort and annoyance from breach? Yes, in some states (as Hilder explains).
- Might damages be paid to account for a tenant's discomfort and annoyance from breach? Yes, in some states (as Hilder explains).
- Punitive damages are also available if the landlord's breach was intentional or willful and wanton or fraudulent in disregard of human safety and welfare.

4. *A more general right to adequate housing?* The implied warranty of habitability applies to rental properties that tenants have secured. It does not include a more general right to *access* adequate housing. Indeed, no right to housing has been found in the U.S. Constitution. *See Lindsay v. Normet*, 405 U.S. 56 (1972). However, several international human rights instruments and some other nations do provide for a right to adequate housing. For example, chapter 2, section 26 of the South African Constitution declares that "everyone has the right to have access to adequate housing." Also, a right to an adequate standard of living for individual and family health and well-being that includes food, clothing and housing is recognized in the Universal Declaration of Human Rights (Article 25) and the International Covenant on Economic, Social and Cultural Rights (both adopted by the United Nations). Should protections for adequate housing be expanded in the U.S.?

The Covenant of Quiet Enjoyment and Constructive Eviction

Imagine you rent a basement office for your law practice where you also store client files and evidence. Your office building is old, and there are recurrent leaks that sometimes leave standing water in parts of your office space, making those parts unusable for periods of time. The exposure to water also produces mold. Some of your files and client evidence have gotten wet and been compromised. Some of your co-workers are allergic to mold and struggling with health issues as a result. You have repeatedly notified your landlord of the problems, and he has engaged in some modest efforts to fix the leaks and redress the mold. However, these attempts fail to resolve the defects. The landlord is not willing to incur the expenses of more major repairs. (This fact situation draws on *Village Commons, LLC v. Marion County Prosecutors Office*, 882 N.E.2d 210 (Ind. Ct. App. 2008.))

What can the tenant do? Put simply, tenants have a right to peace and quiet—and if the landlord fails to provide it, tenants can move out or sue. More specifically, *both* commercial and residential leases include an *implied covenant of quiet enjoyment.* (Note that this is unlike the implied warranty of habitability which applies to residential leases only.) If a landlord's actions or inaction cause substantial interference with use and enjoyment of the leasehold, then a tenant has been "constructively evicted." The idea is that a tenant's use and possession rights have been disrupted in a way that is the functional equivalent of an actual eviction. By failing to provide quiet enjoyment, it is as if the landlord is forcing the tenant to move out. As a result of the landlord's breach, the tenant may abandon the tenancy and be relieved of the obligation to pay rent. This reflects a change from the former regime that treated landlord and tenant duties as independent—now they are dependent. This means a breach by the landlord releases the tenant from the lease and from rent.

Traditional law required a tenant to abandon the premises to claim constructive eviction. However, under the modern approach, the tenant has another option besides leaving—the tenant can stay and sue for breach and seek damages such as lost rental value. However, tenants need to be careful about how they exercise this option and take action (sue) within a reasonable time. Otherwise, staying in the leasehold might be seen as evidence that the interference was not "substantial" enough to constitute constructive eviction or may be deemed a waiver of the claim.

Another issue that can come up is whether a landlord's actions qualify as an actual eviction. You will study eviction at the end of this chapter. Changing the locks on the door and excluding a tenant would be an eviction. This would be deemed wrongful in the usual case, because landlords cannot use self-help to evict and must instead use established legal processes and obtain a court order for eviction. Less extremely, suppose a landlord obstructed a tenant's access to part of the rental property? Say there was a rooftop garden in an apartment, but the landlord closed it down. Or, what if the landlord decided to use 10% of the square footage of a space rented to a tenant? When there is a *partial* actual eviction like in these examples, traditional law allows the tenant to stop paying rent entirely, even if the tenant stays. Perhaps not surprisingly, the modern rule is that the tenant will be awarded rent abatement (a reduction) instead. As we will see in the *Minjack* case studied next, it is possible to have a partial constructive eviction that may result in a partial rent obligation if the tenant stays.

Exercise 6-10. *Minjack v. Randolph*

As you read *Minjack,* engage the questions and activities that follow.

1. Identify each element of constructive eviction and apply the rules to the facts. Specifically, determine why the landlord is accountable. Notice as well how the court addresses and adjusts the abandonment element.
2. Identify the various ways constructive eviction can be raised either as the basis for a tenant's claim or as a defense. Also, identify the available remedies.

Minjack Co. v. Randolph

528 N.Y.S.2d 554 (N.Y. App. Div. 1988)

In July of 1983 petitioner-landlord commenced the within summary non-payment proceeding against respondents Randolph and Kikuchi, tenants of a loft space on the fourth floor of petitioner's building on West 20th Street in Manhattan, alleging non-payment of rent since July 1981. The tenants' answer set forth as affirmative defenses that because they were unable to use two-thirds of the loft space due to the landlord's renovations and other conditions, they were entitled to an abatement of two-thirds of the rent, and that as to the remaining one-third space, they were entitled to a further rent abatement due to the landlord's failure to supply essential services. The tenants also counterclaimed for breach of warranty of habitability, seeking both actual and punitive damages and attorney's fees.

A trial was held in Civil Court before Justice Saxe in November of 1983. It was stipulated that rent was due and owing from October 1981 through November 1983 in the amount of $12,787 ($200 due for October 1981, $450 due each month from November 1981 through December 1982, and $567 per month since January 1983).

Respondents commenced residency of the loft space in 1976 pursuant to a commercial lease. Petitioner offered a commercial lease even though at the time of the signing of the lease the building was used predominantly for residential purposes and the respondents had informed petitioner that they would use the loft as their residence. The loft space measures 1700 square feet, approximately two-thirds of which is used as a music studio for Mr. Kikuchi, where he composes, rehearses and stores his very expensive electronic equipment and musical instruments. The remainder of the space is used as the tenants' residence.

Late in 1977, the fifth floor tenant began to operate a health spa equipment business which included the display of fully working jacuzzis, bathtubs, and saunas. The jacuzzis and bathtubs were filled to capacity with water. From November 1977 through February 1982, respondents suffered at least 40 separate water leaks from the fifth floor. At times the water literally poured into the bedroom and bedroom closets of respondents' loft, ruining their clothes and other items. Water leaked as well into the kitchen, the bathroom and onto Mr. Kikuchi's grand piano and other musical instruments. Respondents' complaints to petitioner went unheeded.

In January of 1978 the fifth-floor tenant began to sandblast the walls, causing sand to seep through openings around pipes and cracks in the ceiling and into respondent's loft. The sand, which continued to fall into the loft even as the parties went to trial, got into respondent's clothes, bed, food and even their eyes.

In September of 1981 the landlord commenced construction work in the building to convert the building into a Class A multiple building. To convert the freight elevator into a passenger elevator, petitioner had the elevator shaft on respondent's side of the building removed. The workers threw debris down the elevator shaft, raising "huge clouds of dust" which came pouring into the loft and settled everywhere, on respondents' clothes, bed, food, toothbrushes and musical equipment. The musical equipment had to be covered at all times to protect it from the dust. Respondents began to suffer from eye and sinus problems, nausea, and soreness in their throats from the inhalation of the dust. Respondents attempted to shield themselves somewhat from the dust by putting up plastic sheets, only to have the workmen rip them down.

To demonstrate the hazardous nature of some of the construction work, respondents introduced evidence that as the landlord's workers were demolishing the stairs from the seventh floor down, no warning signs were posted, causing one visitor to come perilously close to falling through a hole in the stairs. The workers jackhammered a new entrance to the loft, permitting the debris to fall directly onto the floor of respondents' loft. The workmen would mix cement right on respondents' floor. A new entrance door to the loft was sloppily installed without a door sill, and loose bricks were left around the frame. A day later, brick fragments and concrete fell on tenant Randolph's head as she closed the door.

The record contains many more examples of dangerous construction and other conduct interfering with respondents' ability to use and enjoy possession of their loft. From 1981 until the time of trial, Kikuchi was completely unable to use the music studio portion of the loft. His musical instruments had been kept covered and protected against the sand and later the dust since 1978.

The jury rendered a verdict awarding respondents a rent abatement of 80% for July 1981 through November 1983, as compensatory damages on the theory of constructive eviction from the music studio portion of the loft; a 40% rent abatement for January 1981 through November 1983, on the remainder of the rent due for the residential portion of the premises, on a theory of breach of warranty of habitability; a 10% rent abatement on the rent attributable to the residential portion of the premises for all of 1979, on a breach of warranty of habitability theory; and punitive damages in the amount of $20,000. After trial the court granted respondents' motion made pursuant to Real Property Law Sec. 234 for reasonable attorney's fees, awarding respondents $5000. The court also granted petitioner's motion to set aside the verdict and for other relief, only to the extent of reducing the award for punitive damages to $5000. Final judgment was entered on March 23, 1984.

On appeal to the Appellate Term that court reversed the judgment. Holding that the doctrine of constructive eviction could not provide a defense to this non-payment proceeding, because tenants had not abandoned possession of the demised premises, the court reversed the jury's award as to the 80% rent abatement predicated on the constructive eviction theory. The court ordered a new trial on the counterclaim for breach of warranty of habitability, concluding it likely that the jury's consideration of the constructive eviction claim impacted on the breach of warranty of habitability claim. The court also struck down the award of punitive damages, concluding that, even if punitive damages could properly be awarded in habitability cases, the facts herein did not support a finding of "high moral culpability" or "criminal indifference to civil obligations," [citations omitted] so as to warrant punitive damages. [Citations omitted.] We reverse and hold that the tenants were entitled to avail themselves of the doctrine of constructive eviction based on their abandonment of a portion of the premises and that the award for punitive damages was permissible and warranted by these facts.

We agree with the holding and reasoning of *East Haven Associates v. Gurian*, 64 Misc.2d 276, 313 N.Y.S.2d 276, that a tenant may assert as a defense to the nonpayment of rent the doctrine of constructive eviction, even if he or she has abandoned only a portion of the demised premises due to the landlord's acts in making that portion of the premises unusable by the tenant. It is not contrary to ... any established precedent to hold that when the tenant is constructively evicted from a portion of the premises by the landlord's actions, he should not be obligated to pay the full amount of the rent. Indeed "compelling considerations of social policy and fairness" dictate such a result. [Citations omitted.]

As for petitioner's argument on appeal that the tenants never abandoned any portion of the premises and, in fact, continued to use the entire loft even up until the day of trial, we note that this assertion is unaccompanied by any citation to the record. This was no mere inadvertent error, for there is absolutely nothing in the record to support such a claim. The evidence at trial fully supported a finding that respondents were compelled to abandon the music studio portion of the loft due to "the landlord's wrongful acts [which] substantially and materially deprive[d] the tenant[s] of the beneficial use and enjoyment" of that portion of the loft. [Citations omitted.]

Petitioner does, however, correctly point out that as the constructive eviction claim was asserted as a defense to the nonpayment of rent and respondents did not request an abatement for any months other than those in which they did not pay rent, the jury's award of an 80% rent abatement as to the months July, August, September and half of October of 1981 must be stricken.

The award for punitive damages, as reduced by the Civil Court to $5000, should be reinstated as well. Although generally in breach of contract claims the damages to be awarded are compensatory, in certain instances punitive damages may be awarded when to do so would "deter morally culpable conduct." [Citations omitted.] Accordingly, the issue of punitive damages was properly submitted to the jury, and we are satisfied that this record supports the jury's finding of morally culpable conduct in light of the dangerous and offensive manner in which the landlord permitted the construction work to be performed, the landlord's indifference to the health and safety of others, and its disregard for the rights of others, so as to imply even a criminal indifference to civil obligations. One particularly egregious example of the landlord's wanton disregard for the safety of others was the way in which the stair demolition was performed: steps were removed and no warning sign even posted. The landlord's indifference and lack of response to the tenants' repeated complaints of dust, sand and water leak problems demonstrated a complete indifference to their health and safety and a lack of concern for the damage these conditions could cause to the tenants' valuable personal property. Such indifference must be viewed as rising to the level of high moral culpability. Accordingly, the award of punitive damages is sustained.

We likewise reject petitioner's argument that respondents cannot rely on their lease in order to recover attorney's fees pursuant to the provisions of Real Property Law Sec. 234. This is an action under the lease and this lease has not been voided. Furthermore, residential occupants of lofts are afforded the same protections available to other residential tenants under the Real Property Law (*see* Multiple Dwelling Law Sec. 286[11]). Thus, the award for attorney's fees was proper.

Except to eliminate any rent abatement for July through mid-October of 1981, the Civil Court judgment should be reinstated.

Exercise 6-11. *Minjack* Revisited and Landlord's Potential Liability for the Acts of Others

1. *Risk assessment.* Assume the tenants in *Minjack* seek your counsel after one year of these difficulties and, despite them, they want to stay in the property. What questions would you have for them? What risks would you advise them about if they do stay?
2. Make a list of the options and remedies a tenant has if they have a meritorious claim for constrictive eviction.
3. *Landlord's Liability for Another's Conduct.* The traditional rule is that landlords are not responsible for the acts of third parties. However, the trend in recent years is to find the landlord in breach if her conduct or the conduct of someone *attributable to* the landlord interferes with quiet enjoyment. This is the approach in the *Second Restatement of Property* that holds a landlord liable not only for their own conduct, but for the conduct of others on the landlord's property if the conduct "could be legally controlled" by the landlord. In the each of the fact situations below, consider whether and why a landlord might be held accountable when the disruption to quiet enjoyment of the property is caused in the first instance by someone other than the landlord.
   a) Construction workers hired by the landlord make noise and dust that make it exceedingly difficult to engage in basic living activities such as sleep and conversation and preparing food.
   b) One tenant of the landlord operates a bar and restaurant with live music on the bottom floor of an apartment building that causes noise and vibration for another tenant of the same landlord who lives above the bar. This makes make it exceedingly difficult for the upstairs tenant to engage in basic living activities such as sleep and conversation and preparing food. Each tenant signed a lease that includes a standard clause that says: "Tenant promises to conduct herself on the premises and to require other persons on the premises to conduct themselves in a manner that will not disturb the peaceful enjoyment of other tenants or neighbors." *See Blackett v. Olanoff*, 358 N.E.2d 817 (Mass. 1976) (finding landlord liable).
   c) A tenant who lives on a lower level of an apartment building smokes frequently and daily in the apartment. This causes secondhand smoke to travel into the apartment of the tenant upstairs who greatly dislikes the smell and is concerned about the health risk from exposure to the smoke. The upstairs tenant complains to the landlord, who does nothing.

d) A salon and spa business rented commercial space in a small shopping center in the suburbs. The distinguishing selling point for the business is that they provide a serene environment where customers can truly relax. Another business moves into the same shopping center. The business is a trampoline and recreation facility that caters to children and young adults with indoor and outdoor space. The business draws large numbers of children who make a lot of noise running around and laughing and sometimes screaming with joy and excitement. What difference would it make if the landlord who rented to the spa was *not* the same landlord who rented out space to the trampoline park? Rather than, or in addition to, suing the landlord for breach of contract, consider whether the salon might be able to successfully bring a nuisance claim against the trampoline park. (Nuisance law is addressed in Chapter 7.)

e) What if a tenant in an apartment complex recurrently stalks and sexually harasses another tenant in the common spaces of the complex (such as the hallways and parking lots)? If the tenant complains to the landlord and the landlord comes to seek your counsel—what advice would you give? In addition to the rules governing the leasehold, you will also want to consider a landlord's potential tort liability, discussed in the subsection below.

4. *Comparing the Covenant of Quiet Enjoyment to the Implied Warranty of Habitability.* Fill out the chart below to identify the differences and similarities between these two doctrines. Keep in mind that a tenant might have experiences that trigger viable claims under both.

Covenant of Quiet Enjoyment	**Implied Warranty of Habitability**
Promises:	Promises:
Applies to:	Applies to: residential leases only

Tort Liability for Personal Injury

Following the arc of the implied warranty of habitability, tort liability for landlords is another area of law that undergone significant change. Landlords were traditionally immune to liability for personal injury based on an agricultural model of leases that assumed the tenant was in control of and responsible for the condition of the rental premises. That model has been abandoned with the law's recognition of the implied warranty of habitability, the landlord's duty to repair and the expansion of the landlord's liability in constructive eviction cases—including for the conduct of others in some instances. Tort liability has similarly shifted.

As explained earlier, states allow for compensatory damages for breach of the warranty of habitability, and some states make pain and discomfort losses available as a part of that claim (as we saw in *Hilder*). More generally, many states now simply apply negligence principles to residential landlords. The landlord has a duty to use reasonable care, along with other duties such as the duty to repair and maintain habitability. So, for example, if a landlord fails to properly repair a leaky roof and the roof collapses and causes a personal injury such as broken arm or a concussion, the landlord can be held liable for negligence. In another example, a landlord was found liable for allowing toxic mold to cause personal injury to a tenant. *New Haverford Partnership v. Stroot*, 772 A.2d 792 (Del. 2001). Additionally, the awful problem of children being poisoned by lead paint has resulted in federal as well as state regulation. The Residential Lead-Based Paint Hazard Reduction Act requires owners of most buildings built before 1978 to disclose the presence of any known lead based paint and, in any event, to provide a pamphlet warning of the possibility. *See* 42 U.S.C. §§4851-4856.

Whether the landlord had the ability to control the premises is a central issue. (We saw that this question is important in constructive eviction claims as well.) How far liability extends in the case of criminal conduct by a third party that occurs on the leased property is controversial. What if there is a criminal attack by a stranger against a tenant in the dark hallway inside an apartment building? The answer under traditional law is that the landlord is not obligated to protect tenants from criminal behavior. However, the clear trend in modern law is to hold a landlord liable if the landlord failed to exercise reasonable care to prevent foreseeable attacks, particularly in common areas. The landlord's conduct will be evaluated and in order to comply with the law should include secure locks and doors, adequate lights in hallways and parking lots and other appropriate safeguards.

Beyond general negligence, landlords are also potentially liable for other torts. As long as the elements of the cause of action can be proved, a tenant can sue for intentional infliction of emotional distress or negligent infliction. This usually involves "extreme and outrageous" conduct such as a lack of heat or a severe pest infestation. What if an injury occurs but the landlord is not at fault for having been negligent? Landlords are not generally held strictly liable for personal injuries that occur on the leased property. There are occasional exceptions to this in state laws. However, Louisiana is the only state that currently imposes strict liability on landlords as a first principle.

Consumer Protection Laws

Modern landlord and tenant relationships are regulated not only by specific statutes and doctrines but increasingly by more general consumer protection laws as well. Depending on state law, tenants may be able to bring a claim as a consumer of housing against a landlord for unfair or deceptive trade practices.

Some examples of landlord activities that have been found to constitute unfair or deceptive trade practices are: inclusion of an unenforceable clause in a lease (such as a waiver of the implied warranty of habitability); failing to maintain a leasehold that is fit for habitation; collecting rent when property is uninhabitable; violating fair debt collection rules; making a false claim for damages against a security deposit; and an eviction or other adverse action against a tenant in retaliation for complaints about substandard housing conditions. (You will study retaliatory eviction at the end of this chapter.) A tenant might want to bring such a claim, perhaps in addition to others, because consumer protection laws may allow for higher awards such as treble damages, punitive damages and recovery of attorney's fees. As always, state specific research is needed if your client's situation presents these issues.

Tenant's Restrictions on Use

There are a number of laws that regulate the tenant's use and possession of a leasehold.

Illegal Uses. Leases include an implied covenant by the tenant not to use the property for illegal purposes, such as drug related criminal activity. If the landlord and tenant both know about and agree to the illegal use, then the lease is void. If the tenant alone is responsible for the illegal use, then the tenant is in breach of the contract and the landlord can seek an eviction or damages and other remedies.

The Duty Not to Commit Waste. Another obligation is the tenant's duty not to commit waste. Put simply, tenants have a duty not to harm the rental property. More specifically, tenants must leave the property intact—and exercise reasonable care to keep the property in substantially the same condition as it was when the leasehold began. There is an exception for "normal wear and tear," meaning tenants are not accountable for erosion of the property from ordinary use such as carpets or paint getting dirty (although lease terms may depart from this default rule). In contrast, a tenant who causes a sizable hole in a wall—even accidentally—has committed waste. The landlord can insist that the tenant repair the wall or pay for the expense of having someone else repair it. The duty not to commit waste preserves the landlord's right to enjoy possession and the value of the property in the future. Note however, that this duty is quite limited in the context of residential leases. It does not change the general rule that landlords, not tenants, are responsible overall for maintaining and repairing the leasehold.

The doctrine of waste applies to a number of other contexts as well. It governs relationships among current possessors of property and future possessors, when property ownership is divided over time. Waste is addressed in some detail in the study of estates in land in Chapter 5. For example, a life tenant (who has the current right to possess the property until their death) has a duty not to harm the property and indeed to proactively maintain the property, thus ensuring that possession of the property can be enjoyed in the future and its value is maintained for the remainderperson. Similarly, co-owners of property also have a duty not to commit waste (shared property is addressed in Chapter 4).

No Removal of Fixtures, Except Trade Fixtures. A fixture is an item of personal property that is permanently attached to a building or land (real property). Fixtures generally become a part of the underlying property to which they are affixed. Accordingly, fixtures for leased property become owned by the landowner. For example, if a tenant installs a built-in bookcase so that the structure of the bookcase and shelves is permanently attached to the wall, the bookcase is a fixture and ownership of it transfers to the landlord. A free standing bookcase that a tenant brings into a rental property is not a fixture and belongs to the tenant at the end of leasehold. Sometimes it is unclear whether an item is a fixture. If the property can be removed easily without damage to the land or building, it is not a fixture. Conversely, if removal is difficult, expensive and harms the property, it qualifies as a fixture. Once again, these are default rules that can be contracted around.

All of this governs ownership. If there is no agreement between the landlord and tenant about how to handle fixtures, consider the possibility that a tenant may have another way of recovering the value of a fixture. If a tenant invests money and labor by installing a fixture that becomes the landlord's property, a tenant may attempt to recover the value of the improvement by claiming unjust enrichment resulting in a constructive trust. Unjust enrichment claims can arise in a variety of contexts—if a benefit is conferred on a property owner by another person and if the claimant can demonstrate it is unfair to allow the owner to retain the (full) benefit. For example, as explained in Chapter 4 on Sharing Property, this is a claim a cohabitant may be able to make at termination of an intimate partner relationship (if the facts warrant it).

"Trade fixtures" are an exception to the general rules you just learned. Trade fixtures are used in a business that has rented commercial space, such as a restaurant owner that installs booths and tables and new kitchen appliances. Unless the parties agree otherwise, trade fixtures belong to the *renter* and are removable by the tenant.

Duty Not to Cause a Nuisance. As explained in Chapter 7, a person who owns or possesses property can be sued for nuisance if their activities on the property are found to cause "unreasonable harm." This is a tort claim that arises in the absence of a contract. Adding to this, many leases today include a specific promise by the tenant "not to disturb the quiet enjoyment of neighbors or other tenants, or to cause a nuisance." A clause like this makes a tenant who causes a nuisance potentially liable for breach of contract (as well as the tort of nuisance) and gives the landlord authority to enforce the contract by way of an injunction or damages or by seeking an eviction.

Covenants in the Lease. A tenant may agree to restrictions on use in a lease. Additionally, the property may be bound by "real covenants" that restrict certain uses by a tenant because of promises created earlier by a predecessor property owner that flow through to bind anyone who possesses the property. You will learn about real covenants in Chapter 10. Some examples of lease covenants are a restriction on a tenant to use the leasehold only for residential purposes—or even a rule that requires a tenant to use only "curtains with a white back facing out the window."

Transferring a Leasehold

Assume a landlord owns an apartment building with 20 apartments, or a small shopping center. What happens if a landlord desires to sell her property interest (her "reversion")? Now assume instead that tenant Tim just landed a wonderful new job 1,000 miles away from the apartment he rents now that has a fixed term. Can Tim transfer the leasehold to another tenant to replace him?

The general rule is that both the landlord's reversion and the tenant's leasehold are transferable. Alienability is a core policy in this area of law, much as we have seen across property law. Nevertheless, as you will discover in the materials that follow, the tenant's default right to alienability can be—and often is—modified by contract. Many leases today have a standard clause that limits a *tenant's right to transfer*—and authorizes a transfer only if the landlord consents. This balances a tenant's interest in alienability with the landlord's continuing and future interests in the property. The modern trend requires the landlord to have a commercially reasonable basis for refusing consent, unless the lease explicitly says otherwise.

A landlord's right to transfer is typically unrestrained. A landlord is empowered to give away or sell an apartment building or commercial space during life or to transfer her interest at death to another. The new owner has the same rights as the original landlord—including the right to collect rent and enforce the lease terms. The new landlord is bound to any pre-existing leases and cannot end the lease except in the usual course. For example, a tenant with 6 months remaining on a term of years lease is entitled to remain in the apartment until the end of the term. The transfer of ownership of the reversion does not change that. Similarly, for a month to month lease, the landlord would have to give 30 days' advance notice of termination or otherwise comply with the advance notice period specified in the lease.

What happens to a tenant's interest in a leasehold if there is a mortgage against the property and the landlord fails to pay? You will study mortgages in Chapter 11 on Real Estate Transactions. For now, you just need to understand some basic principles applicable to the context of landlord-tenant law. When a borrower of money secures a loan by granting a mortgage against property and then defaults, the lender (typically a bank) has the right to seek a foreclosure. This means the bank can force the sale of the property in order to collect the debt. Will a lease survive a foreclosure? That depends on whether the lease or the mortgage is first in time. If a fixed term lease was created before the granting of the mortgage, it will survive foreclosure. If the mortgage was granted before the lease, or, if a lease says the mortgage will have priority even for mortgages that are granted *after* the lease, then the lease can be terminated at foreclosure. Many tenants have had to face the possibility of losing their rental units due to the large increase in foreclosures in recent years that accompanied the downturn in the economy and the subprime mortgage crises. In some jurisdictions, new laws have been adopted to add protections to tenants in this situation. This area of law is in flux. Indeed, there was federal law with significant protections for tenants in place starting in 2009 that has since expired. See Protecting Tenants at Foreclosure Act (PTFA), 12 U.S.C. § 5220. As always, if you encounter these kinds of questions in your legal practice, be sure to do specific research and keep up with any changes in the law.

The next subsections focus on the body of law governing a tenant's transfer of a leasehold, including assignment and subletting and when a landlord is empowered to consent or refuse a tenant's proposed transfer.

Assignment or Subletting the Lease

As we continue to see, the right to transfer is a highly important attribute of property. Accordingly, a tenant has the power to transfer the leasehold unless this power is altered in the lease. There are two methods by which a tenant can transfer a leasehold interest to another tenant—by either assignment or sublet. An assignment occurs when the original tenant (identified here as T-1) transfers his entire interest in the leasehold to a subsequent tenant (who we will call T-2). In contrast, in a sublease, T-1 transfers only part of his leasehold interest to T-2, and T-1 retains some portion of the estate. These two methods can produce surprisingly different legal outcomes, so they must be distinguished and studied carefully. Be aware that there may be state law variations that depart from the majority rules discussed here.

Exercise 6-12. Distinguishing Between Assignments and Subleases

1. *Classifying the Transfer.* Here are some simple examples that focus on the duration of the right of possession of the leasehold.
   a. Assume a coffee shop owner (T-1) has a 12 month term of years lease. After enjoying the leasehold for the first 3 months of the lease, T-1 transfers his rights to the rental space to another tenant who will take over the coffee shop for the remainder of the term (the last 9 months). This transfer is an assignment.
   b. Now assume instead that T-1 transfers to T-2 the right to possess the leasehold for months 4 through 9 but retains his rights to possession for the last 3 months. This is a sublease. What if T-2 retained possession for the final two weeks?
   c. What if T-1 rented 10,000 square feet of space for two years and then transferred 5,000 square feet to T-2 for the remainder of the term—but T-1 retained the other 5,000 for himself? Most states would classify the transfer as an assignment—of part of the space.

Be sure you understand these examples and how they differ. It is generally the substance of the transfer rather than the label that determines which kind of transfer has occurred. Rather than or in addition to this objective test, some courts today will also consider the intent of the parties.

2. *Legal Outcomes.* You need to distinguish an assignment from a sublease, because the two types of transfer can produce different legal results. The key issue is who the landlord can sue directly for missed rent or other monetary damages. With a sublease, T-2 is not directly liable to the landlord for rent or other economic damages. In contrast, with an assignment, a landlord can directly sue T-2 for lost rent and other damages.

Note that regardless of the type of transfer, the landlord can sue T-2 to regain possession by way of an injunction for eviction. Also important, the landlord can always sue *T-1* for any unpaid rent during the period of the lease, because T-1 is contractually obligated to pay rent for the term, and an assignment or a sublease does not transfer that personal promise.

Again then, the essential difference in legal outcomes is that with an assignment, the landlord can directly sue *both* T-1 and T-2 for rent that was due and not paid. With a sublease, the landlord can only sue T-1 and not T-2. (Then T-1 could sue T-2 based on their contract.)

To understand this more deeply, we need to look at the relationships created by an assignment or a sublease.

a. Assignments: An assignment creates a triangular relationship among T-1, T-2 and the landlord, as explained here.

Assume L and T-1 enter into a 2 year fixed term lease with rent of $1,000 per month. Two distinct relationships were created in the original lease (often called the master lease). The parties have a direct contractual relationship because of the exchange of promises that were made—such as possession in exchange for rent. This relationship is called "privity of contract." The landlord and tenant also have a shared property relationship, because each owns a property interest in the rental space—the landlord having the reversion and the tenant having the leasehold estate. This relationship is called "privity of estate."

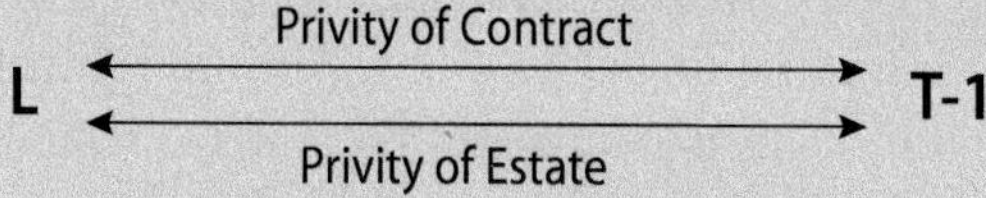

With one year remaining on the master lease, now assume T-1 transfers all his rights to the leasehold to T-2 in exchange for rent of $1,200 per month. This is an assignment. It is deemed to be a transfer of the entire property relationship T-1 had previously, meaning that that T-2 is now viewed as being in privity of estate with the landlord and T-1 is not. At the same time, T-1 and T-2 have created a contractual relationship between them. However, there is no direct contractual relationship between T-2 and L. Yet T-1 remains in a contractual relationship with L.

Here is an illustration of the relationships created by an assignment.

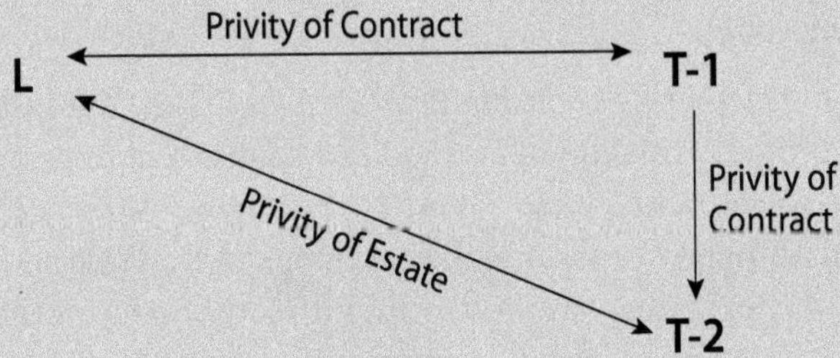

You should be ready now to answer these questions.

i) Who is the owner of the extra $200 per month in rent paid by T-2 to T-1? (Recall that T-1 owes $1,000 in rent to L but T-2 pays $1,200 in rent to T-1.)

ii) Now assume T-2 fails to the pay rent to T-1, and as a result, T-1 does not pay L. L can sue T-1, as well as T-2 to collect the unpaid rent (up to $1,000 per month maximum). Articulate the basis for the L's lawsuits against T-1 and against T-2.

b. Subleases. Subleases do not create a triangular relationship among the parties, but rather two separate relationships, because of lack of privity of estate.

Assume L and T-1 enter into a 2 year fixed term lease with rent of $1,000 per month. This creates both privity of estate and privity of contract between L and T-1, just the same as explained above for assignments. Now assume at the end of year one of the master lease that T-1 transfers to T-2 possession of the leasehold for 6 months and T-1 retains the right of possession for the last 6 months. This is a sublease. Because all of T-1's rights to the property are not transferred to T-2, the law concludes that L and T-1 remain in privity of estate and there is no privity of estate (or insufficient privity) between L and T-2. If T-2 fails to pay rent and so T-1 fails to pay rent, the result is that L can sue T-1 but *cannot* sue T-2 directly for money damages including unpaid rent.

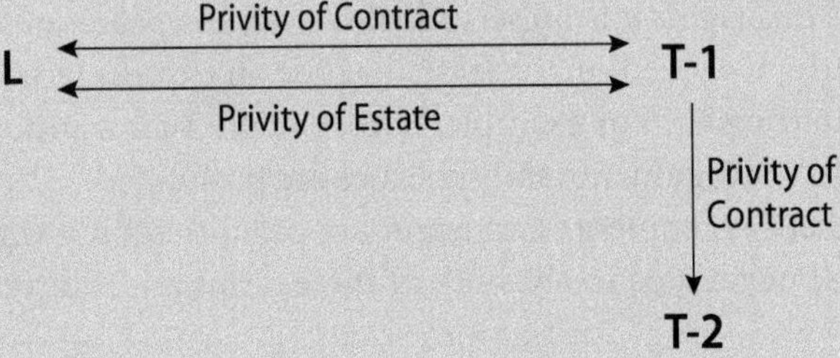

You might find this to be quite a technical distinction. It is. It remains in modern law based more on history than good reason. You will encounter privity of estate in other areas of property law as well—primarily in your study of real covenants and equitable servitudes (Chapter 10). The trend is to minimize or eliminate the impact of the concept, but it still has a lingering role in many states.

c. *Potential Contractual Relationship Between L and T-2.* You just learned that the default property rules do not recognize a contractual relationship between L and T-2. However, of course, L and T-2 can agree otherwise. For example if T-2 explicitly agrees to assume the covenants in the lease and the landlord agrees, then the parties have a contract directly between them. Another possibility is that a contract will be implied based on a third party beneficiary theory. If T-2 promises to pay rent directly to the landlord in the contract between T-1 and T-2, then the landlord is a beneficiary of the promises made between T-1 and T-2. As such, the landlord can sue to enforce the promise and can sue T-2 directly for unpaid rent.

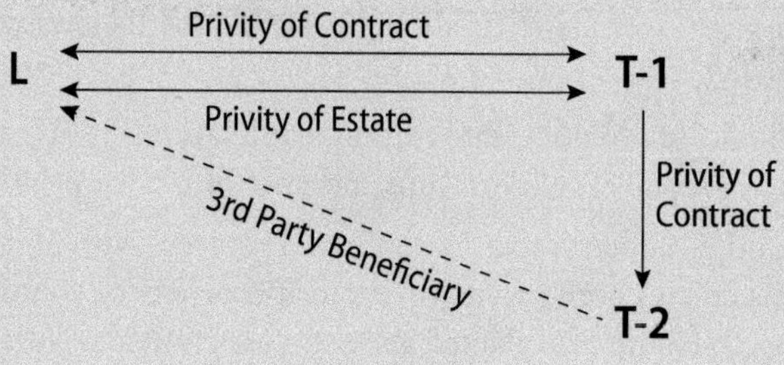

Limitations on Transfers—Landlord Consent

It is often the case that a commercial tenant desires to transfer a leasehold. What if the landlord objects? As you have just learned, the general rule is that a tenant has the power to freely transfer his interest through an assignment or sublease. If a lease does not address this right, it is preserved. However, the power of alienation can be modified by contract. Indeed, many leases include an express term that restricts the tenant's power to transfer. For example, a lease might ban transfers completely by saying "all transfers, assignments and subleases are prohibited." Alternatively, a lease might provide that "assignments and leases are permitted only with the landlord's prior approval." If negotiated freely, both of these terms are enforceable.

Exercise 6-13. *Kendall v. Ernest Pestana*

The enforceability and meaning of a "landlord consent clause" is the subject of the next case. The core question explored is whether a term in a lease that provides for transfers only with the landlord's consent means that the landlord can withhold consent only if it is reasonable to do so. As you read *Kendall,* be sure to identify the two alternative approaches to answering to this question. This is an evolving area of law and, as *Kendall* makes clear, states differ.

Kendall v. Ernest Pestana

709 P.2d 837 (Cal. 1985)

This case concerns the effect of a provision in a commercial lease that the lessee may not assign the lease or sublet the premises without the lessor's prior written consent. The question we address is whether, in the absence of a provision that such consent will not be unreasonably withheld, a lessor may unreasonably and arbitrarily withhold his or her consent to an assignment. This is a question of first impression in this court.

This case arises on appeal from an order sustaining a demurrer without leave to amend. We review the allegations of the complaint applying the established principle that a demurrer "admits the truth of all material factual allegations in the complaint...." [Citation omitted.]

The allegations of the complaint may be summarized as follows. The lease at issue is for 14,400 square feet of hangar space at the San Jose Municipal Airport. The City of San Jose, as owner of the property, leased it to Irving and Janice Perlitch, who in turn assigned their interest to respondent Ernest Pestana, Inc. Prior to assigning their interest to respondent, the Perlitches entered into a 25-year sublease with one Robert Bixler commencing on January 1, 1970. The sublease covered an original five-year term plus four 5-year options to renew. The rental rate was to be increased every 10 years in the same proportion as rents increased on the master lease from the City of San Jose. The premises were to be used by Bixler for the purpose of conducting an airplane maintenance business.

Bixler conducted such a business under the name "Flight Services" until, in 1981, he agreed to sell the business to appellants Jack Kendall, Grady O'Hara and Vicki O'Hara. The proposed sale included the business and the equipment, inventory and improvements on the property, together with the existing lease. The proposed assignees had a stronger financial statement and greater net worth than the current lessee, Bixler, and they were willing to be bound by the terms of the lease.

The lease provided that written consent of the lessor was required before the lessee could assign his interest, and that failure to obtain such consent rendered the lease voidable at the option of the lessor. Accordingly, Bixler requested consent from the Perlitches' successor-in-interest, respondent Ernest Pestana, Inc. Respondent refused to consent to the assignment and maintained that it had an absolute right arbitrarily to refuse any such request. The complaint recites that respondent demanded "increased rent and other more onerous terms" as a condition of consenting to Bixler's transfer of interest.

The proposed assignees brought suit for declaratory and injunctive relief and damages seeking, inter alia, a declaration "that the refusal of ERNEST PESTANA, INC. to consent to the assignment of the lease is unreasonable and is an unlawful restraint on the freedom of alienation...." The trial court sustained a demurrer to the complaint without leave to amend and this appeal followed.

II.

The law generally favors free alienability of property, and California follows the common law rule that a leasehold interest is freely alienable. Contractual restrictions on the alienability of leasehold interests are, however, permitted. "Such restrictions are justified as reasonable protection of the interests of the lessor as to who shall possess and manage property in which he has a reversionary interest and from which he is deriving income." [Citations omitted]

The common law's hostility toward restraints on alienation has caused such restraints on leasehold interests to be strictly construed against the lessor. This is particularly true where the restraint in question is a "forfeiture restraint," under which the lessor has the option to terminate the lease if an assignment is made without his or her consent. Nevertheless, a majority of jurisdictions have long adhered to the rule that where a lease contains an approval clause (a clause stating that the lease cannot be assigned without the prior consent of the lessor), the lessor may arbitrarily refuse to approve a proposed assignee no matter how suitable the assignee appears to be and no matter how unreasonable the lessor's objection. The harsh consequences of this rule have often been avoided through application of the doctrines of waiver and estoppel, under which the lessor may be found to have waived (or be estopped from asserting) the right to refuse consent to assignment.

The traditional majority rule has come under steady attack in recent years. A growing minority of jurisdictions now hold that where a lease provides for assignment only with the prior consent of the lessor, such consent may be withheld *only where the lessor has a commercially reasonable objection to the assignment*, even in the absence of a provision in the lease stating that consent to assignment will not be unreasonably withheld. For the reasons discussed below, we conclude that the minority rule is the preferable position.

III.

The impetus for change in the majority rule has come from two directions, reflecting the dual nature of a lease as a conveyance of a leasehold interest and a contract. The policy against restraints on alienation pertains to leases in their nature as *conveyances*. Numerous courts and commentators have recognized that "[i]n recent times the necessity of permitting reasonable alienation of commercial space has become paramount in our increasingly urban society." [Citation omitted.] Civil Code section 711 provides: "Conditions restraining alienation, when repugnant to the interest created, are void." It is well settled that this rule is not absolute in its application, but forbids only *unreasonable* restraints on alienation. [Citations omitted.] Reasonableness is determined by comparing the justification for a particular restraint on alienation with the quantum of restraint actually imposed by it.

The Restatement Second of Property adopts the minority rule on the validity of approval clauses in leases: "A restraint on alienation without the consent of the landlord of a tenant's interest in leased property is valid, *but the landlord's consent to an alienation by the tenant cannot be withheld unreasonably,* unless a freely negotiated provision in the lease gives the landlord an absolute right to withhold consent." (Rest.2d Property, § 15.2(2) (1977), italics added.) A comment to the section explains: "The landlord may have an understandable concern about certain personal qualities of a tenant, particularly his reputation for meeting his financial obligations. The preservation of the values that go into the personal selection of the tenant justifies upholding a provision in the lease that curtails the right of the tenant to put anyone else in his place by transferring his interest, but this justification does not go to the point of allowing the landlord arbitrarily and without reason to refuse to allow the tenant to transfer an interest in leased property." (*Id.*, com. a.) Under the Restatement rule, the lessor's interest in the character of his or her tenant is protected by the lessor's right to object to a proposed assignee on reasonable commercial grounds. The lessor's interests are also protected by the fact that the original lessee remains liable to the lessor as a surety even if the lessor consents to the assignment and the assignee expressly assumes the obligations of the lease.

The second impetus for change in the majority rule comes from the nature of a lease as a *contract.* "[T]here has been an increased recognition of and emphasis on the duty of good faith and fair dealing inherent in every contract." [Citation omitted.] Thus, "[i]n every contract there is an implied covenant that neither party shall do anything which will have the effect of destroying or injuring the right of the other party to receive the fruits of the contract...." [Citation omitted.] "[W]here a contract confers on one party a discretionary power affecting the rights of the other, a duty is imposed to exercise that discretion in good faith and in accordance with fair dealing." [Citation omitted.] Here the lessor retains the discretionary power to approve or disapprove an assignee proposed by the other party to the contract; this discretionary power should therefore be exercised in accordance with commercially reasonable standards. "Where a lessee is entitled to sublet under common law, but has agreed to limit that right by first acquiring the consent of the landlord, we believe the lessee has a right to expect that consent will not be unreasonably withheld." [Citation omitted.]

Under the minority rule, the determination whether a lessor's refusal to consent was reasonable is a question of fact. Some of the factors that the trier of fact may properly consider in applying the standards of good faith and commercial reasonableness are: financial responsibility of the proposed assignee; suitability of the use for the particular property; legality of the proposed use; need for alteration of the premises; and nature of the occupancy, i.e., office, factory, clinic, etc.

Denying consent solely on the basis of personal taste, convenience or sensibility is not commercially reasonable. Nor is it reasonable to deny consent "in order that the landlord may charge a higher rent than originally contracted for." [Citation omitted.] This is because the lessor's desire for a better bargain than contracted for has nothing to do with the permissible purposes of the restraint on alienation—to protect the lessor's interest in the preservation of the property and the performance of the lease covenants.

In contrast to the policy reasons advanced in favor of the minority rule, the majority rule has traditionally been justified on three grounds. Respondent raises a fourth argument in its favor as well. None of these do we find compelling.

First, it is said that a lease is a conveyance of an interest in real property, and that the lessor, having exercised a personal choice in the selection of a tenant and provided that no substitute shall be acceptable without prior consent, is under no obligation to look to anyone but the lessee for the rent. This argument is based on traditional rules of conveyancing and on concepts of freedom of ownership and control over one's property.

A lessor's freedom at common law to look to no one but the lessee for the rent has, however, been undermined by the adoption in California of a rule that lessors—like all other contracting parties—have a duty to mitigate damages upon the lessee's abandonment of the property by seeking a substitute lessee. Furthermore, the values that go into the personal selection of a lessee are preserved under the minority rule in the lessor's right to refuse consent to assignment on any commercially reasonable grounds. Such grounds include not only the obvious objections to an assignee's financial stability or proposed use of the premises, but a variety of other commercially reasonable objections as well. The lessor's interests are further protected by the fact that the original lessee remains a guarantor of the performance of the assignee.

The second justification advanced in support of the majority rule is that an approval clause is an unambiguous reservation of absolute discretion in the lessor over assignments of the lease. The lessee could have bargained for the addition of a reasonableness clause to the lease (i.e., "consent to assignment will not be unreasonably withheld"). The lessee having failed to do so, the law should not rewrite the parties' contract for them.

Numerous authorities have taken a different view of the meaning and effect of an approval clause in a lease, indicating that the clause is not "clear and unambiguous," as respondent suggests. "It would seem to be the better law that when a lease restricts a lessee's rights by requiring consent before these rights can be exercised, *it must have been in the contemplation of the parties that the lessor be required to give some reason for withholding consent.*" [Citation omitted.] In light of the interpretations given to approval clauses in the cases cited above, and in light of the increasing number of jurisdictions that have adopted the minority rule in the last 15 years, the assertion that an approval clause "clearly and unambiguously" grants the lessor absolute discretion over assignments is untenable. It is not a rewriting of a contract, as respondent suggests, to recognize the obligations imposed by the duty of good faith and fair dealing, which duty is implied by law in every contract.

The third justification advanced in support of the majority rule is essentially based on the doctrine of stare decisis. It is argued that the courts should not depart from the common law majority rule because "many leases now in effect covering a substantial amount of real property and creating valuable property rights were carefully prepared by competent counsel in reliance upon the majority viewpoint." [Citation omitted.] As pointed out above, however, the majority viewpoint has been far from universally held and has never been adopted by this court. Moreover, the trend in favor of the minority rule should come as no surprise to observers of the changing state of real property law in the 20th century. The minority rule is part of an increasing recognition of the contractual nature of leases and the implications in terms of contractual duties that flow therefrom. We would be remiss in our duty if we declined to question a view held by the majority of jurisdictions simply because it is held by a majority. [T]he "vitality [of the common law] can flourish only so long as the courts remain alert to their obligation and opportunity to change the common law when reason and equity demand it." [Citation omitted.]

A final argument in favor of the majority rule is advanced by respondent and stated as follows: "Both tradition and sound public policy dictate that the lessor has a right, under circumstances such as these, to realize the increased value of his property." Respondent essentially argues that any increase in the market value of real property during the term of a lease properly belongs to the lessor, not the lessee. We reject this assertion. One California commentator has written: "[W]hen the lessee executed the lease he acquired the contractual right for the exclusive use of the premises, and all of the benefits and detriment attendant to possession, for the term of the contract. He took the downside risk that he would be paying too much rent if there should be a depression in the rental market.... Why should he be deprived of the contractual benefits of the lease because of the fortuitous inflation in the marketplace[?] By reaping the benefits he does not deprive the landlord of anything to which the landlord was otherwise entitled. The landlord agreed to dispose of possession for the limited term and he could not reasonably anticipate any more than what was given to him by the terms of the lease. His reversionary estate will benefit from the increased value from the inflation in any event, at least upon the expiration of the lease." [Citation omitted.]

Respondent here is trying to get *more* than it bargained for in the lease. A lessor is free to build periodic rent increases into a lease, as the lessor did here. Any increased value of the property beyond this "belongs" to the lessor only in the sense, as explained above, that the lessor's reversionary estate will benefit from it upon the expiration of the lease. We must therefore reject respondent's argument in this regard.

IV.

In conclusion, both the policy against restraints on alienation and the implied contractual duty of good faith and fair dealing militate in favor of adoption of the rule that where a commercial lease provides for assignment only with the prior consent of the lessor, such consent may be withheld only where the lessor has a commercially reasonable objection to the assignee or the proposed use. Under this rule, appellants have stated a cause of action against respondent Ernest Pestana, Inc.

Exercise 6-14. Evaluating and Applying Limits on Transfers

1. Assume you represent a landlord who wishes to maintain maximum control over a tenant's transfer. What specific language would you recommend the landlord seek to include in a lease?
2. How will a court interpret the following clauses in a freely negotiated lease? Fill out the unanswered questions below and determine the reasoning for each.
   a) "Tenant may not transfer, assign or sublet the leasehold."

      Answer: This is enforceable even though it is clearly a restraint on alienation.

   b) "Tenant may not transfer, assign or sublet the leasehold without the landlord's prior consent. The landlord can withhold consent for any reason or for no reason whatsoever, even if doing so would be arbitrary and unreasonable."

      Answer:

   c) "Tenant may not transfer, assign or sublet the leasehold without the landlord's prior consent."

      Answer:

   i) Under the traditional approach, the landlord can withhold consent even if doing so is commercially unreasonable.

   ii) How will the language be interpreted under the minority/modern approach (adopted in *Kendall*)?

   d) What result if a lease does not address the tenant's power of alienation?
3. *When Is a Landlord Commercially Unreasonable*? Suppose a landlord rented space to a tenant for a shoe shop with a lease that includes a clause providing for transfers of the leasehold only with the landlord's consent. About half way through the fixed term, the tenant proposes an assignment of the lease to a new tenant with better financial resources than the original tenant. The new tenant plans on opening a meat and cheese store. The landlord refuses to consent for two reasons. First, the landlord is concerned that the store will not be successful because there are a number of other stores that sell the same products. Second, the landlord is a vegan who does not eat meat or cheese because she has a moral objection to using animals as food and she doesn't want her property used this way. Will the landlord's denial of consent be found to be commercially reasonable?

4. *Residential Leases.* Residential landlords have not generally been held to the same standard as commercial landlords. So a landlord who withholds consent to a proposed sublease or assignment need not have a "commercially reasonable" basis. Why might that be so? Can you think of an argument for why reasonableness should be required for residential landlords?

Ending a Tenancy

Many leases end without controversy. For example, a tenant in a term of years rental might simply vacate the property at the end of the lease. Or, a landlord might give appropriate notice to a month to month tenant who then timely departs. This last section of the chapter addresses several more controversial issues that can arise at the end of a tenancy. First, you will learn the rights and duties of the parties if a tenant abandons the premises before the end of the term and stops paying rent. Next, you will learn about the laws and policies of eviction, including the prohibition on retaliation against a tenant for asserting claims to a habitable premises. Last, you will study some common regulations concerning security deposits.

Tenant Abandonment and Landlord's Duty to Mitigate

Imagine if a tenant gets a great new job in another state or falls in love and wants to relocate to live with a romantic partner. What are the rights and duties of the landlord if the tenant wants to end the lease early? It is possible that the parties could come to an agreement around this and the landlord could accept "surrender" of the leasehold and excuse the tenant from future liability for rent and other damages. Of course, a landlord may not be inclined to do this. After all, the tenant did promise to pay rent for the period of the leasehold and now desires a change in the lease terms. Accordingly, if a tenant vacates the premises early and fails to pay rent, this "abandonment" is an actionable breach of contract. Even so, as the next case demonstrates, at the same time modern law provides some significant protections to landlords, it also affords protection to the breaching tenant and to the interests of society.

Exercise 6-15. *Sommer v. Kridel*

Sommer v. Kridell is another important case in landlord-tenant law that reflects major change. As you read, determine what the law was before and after the case and why the reforms were adopted. Additionally, identify and evaluate exactly what obligations a landlord has to mitigate the damages caused by a tenant's abandonment.

Sommer v. Kridell

378 A.2d 767 (N.J. 1977)

Pashman, J. We granted certification in these cases to consider whether a landlord seeking damages from a defaulting tenant is under a duty to mitigate damages by making reasonable efforts to re-let an apartment wrongfully vacated by the tenant. Separate parts of the Appellate Division held that, in accordance with their respective leases, the landlords in both cases could recover rents due under the leases regardless of whether they had attempted to re-let the vacated apartments. Although they were of different minds as to the fairness of this result, both parts agreed that it was dictated by *Joyce v. Bauman*, 113 N.J.L. 438, 174 A. 693 (E. & A. 1934), a decision by the former Court of Errors and Appeals. We now reverse and hold that a landlord does have an obligation to make a reasonable effort to mitigate damages in such a situation. We therefore overrule *Joyce v. Bauman* to the extent that it is inconsistent with our decision today.

I.

This case was tried on stipulated facts. On March 10, 1972 the defendant, James Kridel, entered into a lease with the plaintiff, Abraham Sommer, owner of the "Pierre Apartments" in Hackensack, to rent apartment 6-L in that building. The term of the lease was from May 1, 1972 until April 30, 1974, with a rent concession for the first six weeks, so that the first month's rent was not due until June 15, 1972. [Assignments and subleases were prohibited.]

One week after signing the agreement, Kridel paid Sommer $690. Half of that sum was used to satisfy the first month's rent. The remainder was paid under the lease provision requiring a security deposit of $345. Although defendant had expected to begin occupancy around May 1, his plans were changed. He wrote to Sommer on May 19, 1972, explaining

> I was to be married on June 3, 1972. Unhappily the engagement was broken and the wedding plans cancelled. Both parents were to assume responsibility for the rent after our marriage. I was discharged from the U.S. Army in October 1971 and am now a student. I have no funds of my own, and am supported by my stepfather.
>
> In view of the above, I cannot take possession of the apartment and am surrendering all rights to it. Never having received a key, I cannot return same to you.
>
> I beg your understanding and compassion in releasing me from the lease, and will of course, in consideration thereof, forfeit the 2 month's rent already paid.
>
> Please notify me at your earliest convenience.

Plaintiff did not answer the letter.

Subsequently, a third party went to the apartment house and inquired about renting apartment 6-L. Although the parties agreed that she was ready, willing and able to rent the apartment, the person in charge told her that the apartment was not being shown since it was already rented to Kridel. In fact, the landlord did not re-enter the apartment or exhibit it to anyone until August 1, 1973. At that time it was rented to a new tenant for a term beginning on September 1, 1973. The new rental was for $345 per month with a six week concession similar to that granted Kridel.

Prior to re-letting the new premises, plaintiff sued Kridel in August 1972, demanding $7,590, the total amount due for the full two-year term of the lease. Following a mistrial, plaintiff filed an amended complaint asking for $5,865, the amount due between May 1, 1972 and September 1, 1973. The amended complaint included no reduction in the claim to reflect the six week concession provided for in the lease or the $690 payment made to plaintiff after signing the agreement. Defendant filed an amended answer to the complaint, alleging that plaintiff breached the contract, failed to mitigate damages and accepted defendant's surrender of the premises. He also counterclaimed to demand repayment of the $345 paid as a security deposit.

The trial judge ruled in favor of defendant. Despite his conclusion that the lease had been drawn to reflect "the 'settled law' of this state," he found that "justice and fair dealing" imposed upon the landlord the duty to attempt to re-let the premises and thereby mitigate damages. He also held that plaintiff's failure to make any response to defendant's unequivocal offer of surrender was tantamount to an acceptance, thereby terminating the tenancy and any obligation to pay rent. As a result, he dismissed both the complaint and the counterclaim. The Appellate Division reversed in a per curiam opinion, and we granted certification.

[In another case] the Appellate Division affirmed the trial court, holding that it was bound by prior precedents. Nevertheless, it freely criticized the rule which it found itself obliged to follow:

> There appears to be no reason in equity or justice to perpetuate such an unrealistic and uneconomic rule of law which encourages an owner to let valuable rented space lie fallow because he is assured of full recovery from a defaulting tenant. Since courts in New Jersey and elsewhere have abandoned ancient real property concepts and applied ordinary contract principles in other conflicts between landlord and tenant there is no sound reason for a continuation of a special real property rule to the issue of mitigation. * * *

[138 N.J.Super. at 273-74, 350 A.2d at 519; citations omitted.]

II

As the lower courts in both appeals found, the weight of authority in this State supports the rule that a landlord is under no duty to mitigate damages caused by a defaulting tenant. This rule has been followed in a majority of states. Nevertheless, while there is still a split of authority over this question, the trend among recent cases appears to be in favor of a mitigation requirement.

The majority rule is based on principles of property law which equate a lease with a transfer of a property interest in the owner's estate. Under this rationale the lease conveys to a tenant an interest in the property which forecloses any control by the landlord; thus, it would be anomalous to require the landlord to concern himself with the tenant's abandonment of his own property.

Yet the distinction between a lease for ordinary residential purposes and an ordinary contract can no longer be considered viable. As Professor Powell observed, evolving "social factors have exerted increasing influence on the law of estates for years." 2 Powell on Real Property (1977 ed.), § 221(1) at 180-81. The result has been that

> [t]he complexities of city life, and the proliferated problems of modern society in general, have created new problems for lessors and lessees and these have been commonly handled by specific clauses in leases. This growth in the number and detail of specific lease covenants has reintroduced into the law of estates for years a predominantly contractual ingredient.

Id. at 181.

Application of the contract rule requiring mitigation of damages to a residential lease may be justified as a matter of basic fairness. Professor McCormick first commented upon the inequity under the majority rule when he predicted in 1925 that eventually

> the logic, inescapable according to the standards of a "jurisprudence of conceptions" which permits the landlord to stand idly by the vacant, abandoned premises and treat them as the property of the tenant and recover full rent, while yield to the more realistic notions of social advantage which in other fields of the law have forbidden a recovery for damages which the plaintiff by reasonable efforts could have avoided.

McCormick, "The Rights of the Landlord Upon Abandonment of the Premises by the Tenant," 23 Mich.L.Rev. 211, 221-22 (1925). Various courts have adopted this position.

The pre-existing rule cannot be predicated upon the possibility that a landlord may lose the opportunity to rent another empty apartment because he must first rent the apartment vacated by the defaulting tenant. Even where the breach occurs in a multi-dwelling building, each apartment may have unique qualities which make it attractive to certain individuals. Significantly, in *Sommer v. Kridel*, there was a specific request to rent the apartment vacated by the defendant; there is no reason to believe that absent this vacancy the landlord could have succeeded in renting a different apartment to this individual.

We therefore hold that antiquated real property concepts which served as the basis for the pre-existing rule, shall no longer be controlling where there is a claim for damages under a residential lease. Such claims must be governed by more modern notions of fairness and equity. A landlord has a duty to mitigate damages where he seeks to recover rents due from a defaulting tenant.

If the landlord has other vacant apartments besides the one which the tenant has abandoned, the landlord's duty to mitigate consists of making reasonable efforts to re-let the apartment. In such cases he must treat the apartment in question as if it was one of his vacant stock.

As part of his cause of action, the landlord shall be required to carry the burden of proving that he used reasonable diligence in attempting to re-let the premises. We note that there has been a divergence of opinion concerning the allocation of the burden of proof on this issue. While generally in contract actions the breaching party has the burden of proving that damages are capable of mitigation, here the landlord will be in a better position to demonstrate whether he exercised reasonable diligence in attempting to re-let the premises.

III

The *Sommer v. Kridel* case presents a classic example of the unfairness which occurs when a landlord has no responsibility to minimize damages. Sommer waited 15 months and allowed $4658.50 in damages to accrue before attempting to re-let the apartment. Despite the availability of a tenant who was ready, willing and able to rent the apartment, the landlord needlessly increased the damages by turning her away. While a tenant will not necessarily be excused from his obligations under a lease simply by finding another person who is willing to rent the vacated premises, here there has been no showing that the new tenant would not have been suitable. We therefore find that plaintiff could have avoided the damages which eventually accrued, and that the defendant was relieved of his duty to continue paying rent. Ordinarily we would require the tenant to bear the cost of any reasonable expenses incurred by a landlord in attempting to re-let the premises, but no such expenses were incurred in this case.

Eviction

Eviction is the legal process landlords use to recover possession of the leased property by requiring a tenant to vacate. Typically, an action for eviction stems from a tenant's failure to pay rent. An eviction might also be based on a tenant's violation of a lease covenant—like making excessive noise.

It used to be that a landlord could use self-help to evict a tenant—by calling the police and changing the locks on the door. Now the general rule is that tenants can be evicted only through a judicial process. To try and accommodate the landlord's interests while still providing judicial supervision, most states have statutes that provide for an expedited or "summary" process to make litigation faster and simpler. These statutes have a variety of names such as unlawful detainer, summary ejectment or forcible entry and detainer. It might take roughly 90 days for such a case to come to a conclusion. However, landlords do not generally have an obligation to renew a lease. A few states require a landlord to have "just cause" to end a tenancy whether by eviction or non-renewal. For an example of the process of eviction, review again the complaint in the Chapter Problem 6-1.

Prohibited Retaliation

Tenants have a defense against eviction if the landlord is seeking to dispossess the tenant in retaliation for asserting their rights to the implied warranty of habitability or complaining about the quality or condition of the property. What reasons might there be for this law?

Exercise 6-16. *Hillview Associates v. Bloomquist*

Carefully extract the statutory law from the next case to identify the elements that must be proved for a cause of action for retaliatory eviction and the application of the rules. As you read, work to articulate the policy foundations of the law and consider whether it effectively serves those goals.

Hillview Associates v. Bloomquist

440 N.W.2d 867 (Iowa 1989)

ANDREASEN, J. This appeal concerns the eviction of tenants from the Gracious Estates Mobile Home Park. The affirmative defense of retaliatory eviction and other defenses raised by the tenants were rejected by the district court. On appeal we reverse the district court as to six tenants and affirm the result of the district court order as to two other tenants.

The underlying action on this appeal is an equitable forcible entry and detainer action. Our review of this action is de novo. We review both the facts and the law and determine, based on the credible evidence, rights anew on those propositions properly presented. In equity cases, especially when considering the credibility of witnesses, we give weight to the trial court's findings of fact, but we are not bound by them. Where the defendant raises an affirmative defense, the defendant has the burden of proving that defense by a preponderance of the evidence. In determining if the burden of proof has been established, we consider all evidence, both in support and contrary to the proposition, and then weigh each to determine which is more convincing.

Gracious Estates Mobile Home Park (Gracious Estates) is located in Des Moines. It is owned by Hillview Associates (Hillview), a partnership based in California. The general partner of Hillview is William Cavanaugh, a resident of California. Management of Gracious Estates has been delegated to a company known as Tandem Management Services, Inc. (Tandem), also owned by Cavanaugh and the other general partners of Hillview. Tandem employed Kathy Nitz as a regional manager, Gennie Smith as park manager and Doug Cavanaugh as property manager at Gracious Estates.

In January 1987 tenants at Gracious Estates began to meet informally to discuss their concerns over the physical condition of the trailer court and recent increases in rent. On January 28, 1987, the first meeting of a tenant's association was held in the clubhouse of Gracious Estates, and approximately 125 tenants came to the meeting. This meeting resulted in an agenda of specific concerns for the health, safety and quality of living in Gracious Estates. A volunteer leadership committee was established for the association, now known as the Gracious Estates Tenant's Association. In the course of organizing and articulating complaints, tenants contacted the Iowa Attorney General's office and their state representative.

On February 9, 1987, a meeting was held between approximately five members of the association, Ms. Nitz and the park maintenance supervisor. The tenants lodged several complaints at this meeting. This meeting lasted approximately one hour and was relatively calm. The relationship between the tenant's association and the management of Gracious Estates began to erode. The tenants were frustrated with the lack of action taken by the management of Gracious Estates.

A meeting with Ms. Nitz was scheduled for April 15, 1987. A meeting did occur on April 15 between representatives of the tenants association and Ms. Nitz. This "meeting" was held in Nitz's private office and lasted approximately five to ten minutes. The discussion quickly disintegrated into a shouting match which climaxed in a physical altercation between Nitz and one of the tenants, Kimber Davenport.

After this meeting, the management of the trailer court served ultimatums on all tenants requiring them to sign the park rules or be evicted. Management also sought out tenants not in the tenant's association in an attempt to start a rival tenants' association favorable to management. On April 22, 1987, Hillview served a thirty-day notice of termination on the following tenants: Tom and Sandra Bloomquist; Kimber and Reva Davenport; Richard and Nellie Swartz; and Donald and Judith Ray. At least one member of each of these married couples was present at the April 15 meeting. A former secretary of Ms. Nitz testified that "they'd [management] get these now, and then the rest later. That way it wouldn't look like they were doing it because they were members of an association."

Hillview later discovered that the thirty-day notice did not provide specific grounds for termination as required by statute. On June 4, 1987, Hillview again served each of these tenants with a notice of termination which provided a sixty-day period for them to leave. At the end of the sixty-day period, the tenants remained in possession. Hillview then served three-day notices to quit. The tenants remained in the park and Hillview filed a forcible entry and detainer action.

In this summary action for forcible entry and detainer, the tenants raised the defenses of retaliatory eviction and waiver. The trial court rejected these defenses and entered an equitable decree ordering the tenants to remove their mobile homes from the park. The cases of all eight tenants were consolidated for trial and remain consolidated on appeal.

The Iowa Legislature adopted remedial legislation for mobile home tenants in the Mobile Home Parks Residential Landlord and Tenant Act. The purpose of this act is to "simplify, clarify and establish the law governing the rental of mobile home spaces and rights and obligations of landlord and tenant." [Citation omitted.] This law also acts to "encourage landlord and tenant to maintain and improve the quality of mobile home living." [Citation omitted.] This act is recognition that the mobile home tenant is bargaining for more than simply a portion of real estate, and therefore, this act provides certain considerations unique to a mobile home rental situation.

The Iowa Mobile Home Act prohibits retaliatory conduct by landlords:

> 1. Except as provided in this section, a landlord shall not retaliate by increasing rent or decreasing services or by bringing or threatening to bring an action for possession or by failing to renew a rental agreement after any of the following:
>
> (a) The tenant has complained to a governmental agency charged with responsibility for enforcement of a building or housing code of a violation applicable to the mobile home park materially affecting health and safety. For this subsection to apply, a complaint filed with a governmental body must be in good faith.
>
> (b) The tenant has complained to the landlord of a violation under section 562B.16.
>
> (c) The tenant has organized or become a member of a tenant's union or similar organization.
>
> (d) For exercising any of the rights and remedies pursuant to this chapter.
>
> 2. If the landlord acts in violation of subsection 1 of this section, the tenant is entitled to the remedies provided in section 562B.24 and has a defense in an action for possession. In an action by or against the tenant, evidence of a complaint within six months prior to the alleged act of retaliation creates a presumption that the landlord's conduct was in retaliation. The presumption does not arise if the tenant made the complaint after notice of termination of the rental agreement. For the purpose of this subsection, "presumption" means that the trier of fact must find the existence of the fact presumed unless and until evidence is introduced which would support a finding of its nonexistence.
>
> 3. Notwithstanding subsections 1 and 2 of this section, a landlord may bring an action for possession if either of the following occurs:
>
> (a) The violation of the applicable building or housing code was caused primarily by lack of reasonable care by the tenant or other person in the household or upon the premises with the tenant's consent.
>
> (b) The tenant is in default of rent three days after rent is due. The maintenance of the action does not release the landlord from liability under section 562B.22, subsection 2.

Iowa Code § 562B.32 (1987). This act also provides for termination by either party without cause, so long as a sixty-day notice is provided in writing.

In 1968 the United States Court of Appeals for the District of Columbia held that a landlord was not free to evict a tenant in retaliation for the tenant's report of housing code violations. As a matter of statutory construction and for reasons of public policy, such an eviction would not be permitted. However, a tenant who proves a retaliatory purpose is not entitled to remain in possession in perpetuity. If the illegal purpose is dissipated, the landlord can, in the absence of legislation or a binding contract, evict the tenant for legitimate reasons or even for no reason at all. The question of permissible or impermissible purpose is one of fact for the court or jury.

In 1979 the Iowa Legislature adopted the Uniform Residential Landlord and Tenant Act and the Mobile Home Parks Residential Landlord and Tenant Act. Both acts prohibit retaliatory conduct. In an action by or against the tenant, evidence of a complaint within six months prior to the alleged act of retaliation creates a presumption that the landlord's conduct was in retaliation. For the purpose of the statutory subsection "presumption" means the trier of fact must find the existence of the fact presumed unless and until evidence is introduced which could support a finding of its nonexistence.

As a matter of statutory construction, we hold this statutory presumption imposes a burden upon the landlord to produce evidence of legitimate nonretaliatory reasons to overcome the presumption. The tenant may then be afforded a full and fair opportunity to demonstrate pretext. The burden of proof of the affirmative defense of retaliatory termination of the lease remains upon the tenant. If the landlord does not meet the burden of producing evidence of a nonretaliatory reason for termination, the statutory presumption would compel a finding of retaliatory lease termination. If the landlord does produce evidence of a nonretaliatory purpose for terminating the lease, then the fact-finder must determine from all the evidence whether a retaliatory termination has been proven by a preponderance of the evidence. Although the burden of producing evidence shifts to the landlord once the tenant has offered evidence of a complaint within six months of the notice of termination, the burden of proof remains with the tenant to establish the affirmative defense.

In deciding whether a tenant has established a defense of retaliatory eviction, we consider the following factors, among others, tending to show the landlord's primary motivation was not retaliatory.

(a) The landlord's decision was a reasonable exercise of business judgment;

(b) The landlord in good faith desires to dispose of the entire leased property free of all tenants;

(c) The landlord in good faith desires to make a different use of the leased property;

(d) The landlord lacks the financial ability to repair the leased property and therefore, in good faith, wishes to have it free of any tenant;

(e) The landlord was unaware of the tenant's activities which were protected by statute;

(f) The landlord did not act at the first opportunity after he learned of the tenant's conduct;

(g) The landlord's act was not discriminatory.

Restatement (Second) of Property § 14.8 comment f (1977).

We find the tenants have offered substantial evidence of a retaliatory termination. They were active, vocal members of a newly-formed tenant's association. They made good faith complaints about the landlord's failure to maintain the mobile home park in a clean and safe condition. An employee of the landlord testified that certain leases were terminated because the tenants were active members of the tenants association. In response, the landlord has offered substantial evidence of a nonretaliatory reason for termination. The tenants who actively participated in the disturbance and physical abuse of Ms. Nitz during the April 15 meeting were notified of lease termination, other active members of the association were not.

According to Ms. Nitz, the tenants surrounded her desk on April 15 and implored her to call California. One of the tenants, Kimber Davenport, placed both hands in the middle of Nitz's desk, leaned over the desk, shouted that Nitz had a "truck-driver's mentality" and that she wasn't a lady. Nitz asked the tenants to leave and all but Mr. and Mrs. Rathburn refused. Ms. Nitz then left her office and, after a cooling-off period, returned and demanded that the other tenants leave the office. She again demanded that they leave and threatened to call the police if they did not. The tenants began to leave. Mr. Davenport was the last to leave, and as he left he continued the verbal abuse of Ms. Nitz and gestured to her with his finger close to her face. According to Ms. Nitz, she pushed his finger away and Davenport struck her in the face, knocking her into a doorjam. At that point, another tenant, Don Carlson, entered the room and physically removed Davenport.

Davenport's testimony concerning the April 15 meeting was very different from Ms. Nitz's testimony. Davenport testified at the forcible entry and detainer trial that he was polite and reasonable during this meeting. Further, he claimed that he did not place his hands on Nitz's desk, shout at her, or strike her. Rather, he testified that he pushed her away with an open hand. Davenport's testimony loses credibility when it is compared with his prior testimony in a criminal case concerning this incident. In his prior testimony, Davenport admitted that he placed his hands in the middle of Ms. Nitz's desk, shouted insults at her, and struck her.

Several conclusions can fairly be drawn from the evidence. First, the April 15 meeting was initiated by members of a tenant's association in an attempt to address grievances with the management of the trailer court. This meeting disintegrated into a shouting match. The tenants were told to leave three times and they left only after a threat to call the police. We, like the trial court, conclude that Davenport did strike Ms. Nitz in the face as he left the room. He was the principal agitator, quickly leaving the topic of improvements for the park and launching into a personal attack on Ms. Nitz.

Under Iowa law, tenants may organize and join a tenant's association free from fear of retaliation. The tenants may participate in activities designed to legitimately coerce a landlord into taking action to improve living conditions. The presumption of retaliatory eviction in Iowa Code section 562B.32 protects legitimate activities of tenant unions or similar organizations.

The resolution of landlord-tenant grievances will normally involve some conflicts and friction between the parties. Arguments, even heated arguments with raised voices, cannot fairly be described as being in violation of proper conduct. There is, however, a limit to the type of conduct that will be tolerated. Kimber Davenport crossed beyond the line of legitimate behavior. Davenport has failed to establish by a preponderance of the evidence that the termination of his lease was retaliatory. The termination of the Davenports' lease was legitimate and thus cannot be said to be retaliation arising from his complaints or union activities.

Although the statutory presumption of retaliation has been neutralized by the evidence produced by Hillview, we find the evidence of retaliatory eviction concerning tenants Bloomquist, Swartz, and Ray, to be more convincing. Although they were present at the April 15 meeting and did participate in the arguments, they did not encourage or participate in the assault of Ms. Nitz. The landlord's response by an attempted termination of their leases can reasonably be attributed to their active membership in the tenant's organization and in response to legitimate complaints they had made.

We reject Hillview's argument that there must be specific intent to retaliate on the part of Hillview's general partner before the tenants can prevail on a defense of retaliatory eviction. The evidence reveals that the local and regional managers of Gracious Estates made the decision to evict these tenants. The general partner ratified this decision without direct participation in the decision-making process.

The acts of an agent are attributable to the principal. In this situation, to require specific intent by the general partner of a multi-state real estate business would frustrate the intention of Iowa Code section 562B.32. Hillview's interpretation would allow mid-level managers to retaliate against tenant associations and seek refuge by keeping top-level directors uninformed of specific disputes with individual tenants. Tenants Bloomquist, Swartz, and Ray have established by a preponderance of the evidence their affirmative defense of retaliatory eviction. Tenants Davenport have not.

This is an appeal from the court's ruling and judgment in an equitable forcible entry and detainer action. We find the landlord is not entitled to an order of removal of tenants Bloomquist, Swartz and Ray because the tenants have established their affirmative defense of retaliatory termination.

We find tenant Davenport has not established the affirmative defenses of retaliatory termination or statutory waiver. The trial court ruling holding the plaintiffs were entitled to possession of Kimber and Reva Davenport's described premises is affirmed and an order for removal may issue.

We tax eighty percent of the costs of this appeal against Hillview Associates and twenty percent against Kimber and Reva Davenport.

Security Deposits

Exercise 6-17. Extracting Rules from Statutes

We discussed the basics of security deposits regulation earlier. Here is a statute from Delaware that addresses the issues in some detail. What are thc limits on how much a landlord can require for a security deposit for a residential lease?

25 Del. Code § 5514 Security deposit.

(a)(1) A landlord may require the payment of security deposit.

(2) No landlord may require a security deposit in excess of 1 month's rent where the rental agreement is for 1 year or more.

(3) No landlord may require a security deposit in excess of 1 month's rent (with the exception of federally-assisted housing regulations), for primary residential tenancies of undefined terms or month to month where the tenancy has lasted 1 year or more. After the expiration of 1 year, the landlord shall immediately return, as a credit to the tenant, any security deposit amount in excess of 1 month's rent, including such amount which when combined with the amount of any surety bond is in excess of 1 month's rent.

(4) The security deposit limits set forth above shall not apply to furnished rental units.

(b) Each security deposit shall be placed by the landlord in an escrow bank account in a federally-insured banking institution with an office that accepts deposits within the State. Such account shall be designated as a security deposits account and shall not be used in the operation of any business by the landlord. The landlord shall disclose to the tenant the location of the security deposit account. The security deposit principal shall be held and administered for the benefit of the tenant, and the tenant's claim to such money shall be prior to that of any creditor of the landlord, including, but not limited to, a trustee in bankruptcy, even if such money is commingled.

(c) The purpose of the security deposit shall be:

(1) To reimburse the landlord for actual damages caused to the premises by the tenant which exceed normal wear and tear, or which cannot be corrected by painting and ordinary cleaning; and/or

(2) To pay the landlord for all rental arrearage due under the rental agreement, including late charges and rental due for premature termination or abandonment of the rental agreement by the tenant; and/or

(3) To reimburse the landlord for all reasonable expenses incurred in renovating and rerenting the premises caused by the premature termination of the rental agreement by the tenants, which includes termination pursuant

to § 5314 of this title, providing that reimbursement caused by termination pursuant to § 5314 of this title shall not exceed 1 month's rent.

(d) Where a tenant is required to pay a fee to determine the tenant's credit worthiness, such fee is an application fee. A landlord may charge an application fee, not to exceed the greater of either 10 percent of the monthly rent for the rental unit or $50, to determine a tenant's credit worthiness. The landlord shall, upon receipt of any money paid as an application fee, furnish a receipt to the tenant for the full amount paid by the tenant, and shall maintain for a period of at least 2 years, complete records of all application fees charged and amounts received for each such fee. Where the landlord unlawfully demands more than the allowable application fee, the tenant shall be entitled to damages equal to double the amount charged as an application fee by the landlord.

(e) If the landlord is not entitled to all or any portion of the security deposit, the landlord shall remit the security deposit within 20 days of the expiration or termination of the rental agreement.

(f) Within 20 days after the termination or expiration of any rental agreement, the landlord shall provide the tenant with an itemized list of damages to the premises and the estimated costs of repair for each and shall tender payment for the difference between the security deposit and such costs of repair of damage to the premises. Failure to do so shall constitute an acknowledgment by the landlord that no payment for damages is due. Tenant's acceptance of a payment submitted with an itemized list of damages shall constitute agreement on the damages as specified by the landlord, unless the tenant, within 10 days of the tenant's receipt of such tender of payment, objects in writing to the amount withheld by the landlord.

(g) Penalties.—

(1) Failure to remit the security deposit or the difference between the security deposit and the amount set forth in the list of damages within 20 days from the expiration or termination of the rental agreement shall entitle the tenant to double the amount wrongfully withheld.

(2) Failure by a landlord to disclose the location of the security deposit account within 20 days of a written request by a tenant or failure by the landlord to deposit the security deposit in a federally-insured financial institution with an office that accepts deposits within the State, shall constitute forfeiture of the security deposit by the landlord to the tenant. Failure by the landlord to return the full security deposit to the tenant within 20 days from the effective date of forfeiture shall entitle the tenant to double the amount of the security deposit.

(h) All communications and notices, including the return of any security deposit under this section, shall be directed to the landlord at the address specified in the rental agreement and to the tenant at an address specified in the rental agreement or to a forwarding address, if provided in writing by the tenant at or prior to the termination of the rental agreement. Failure by the tenant to provide such address shall relieve the landlord of landlord's responsibility to give notice herein and landlord's liability for double the amount of the security deposit as provided herein, but the landlord shall continue to be liable to the tenant for any unused portion of the security deposit; provided, that the tenant shall make a claim in writing to the landlord within 1 year from the termination or expiration of the rental agreement.

PART FOUR
Public Land Use Law

Chapter 7

Nuisance

Introduction

The law of nuisance balances the right to use property with a corresponding right to quiet enjoyment. Although the right to use one's property is an essential property right, it is not absolute. The right to use your property is limited by your neighbor's right to quiet enjoyment and vice versa. In order to balance these rights, the law of nuisance considers the utility of the offending conduct and the gravity of complained harm. Today, many jurisdictions have enacted zoning ordinances that are designed to avoid nuisance before it happens by separating incompatible uses. Neighbors also routinely enter into private agreements regarding land use restrictions. In addition, properties in housing developments and condominium projects are often subject to reciprocal covenants that restrict land use. Despite these trends, nuisance remains an important doctrine because it regulates land use among neighbors in the absence of a private agreement or a relevant statutory provision.

Neighbor A ⟶ Right to Use

v. v.

Neighbor B ⟶ Right to Quiet Enjoyment

Chapter Problem: Exercise 7-1

Assume you represent Megan Taylor who owns a semi-detached house located at 118 E. Moreland Avenue. She lives in the house with her eight year old son. Megan's house shares a common wall with 120 E. Moreland Avenue, which is owned by Sheila Smith. At the back of each house there is a deck that extends to the backyard. Sheila has rented the house to three students at a local college. The lease states that the students are not permitted to smoke inside the house, but they may smoke on the back deck. They also play loud music and have frequent parties in the back yard. After a party, the back yard is littered with trash and red Solo cups. Megan reports that the students are very slow to clean up the mess.

Megan has complained to Sheila and to the tenants about the noise and the smoke. Megan says that the secondhand smoke aggravates her son's asthma. She no longer allows her son to play in their backyard, and she has to keep all of her windows closed to keep the smoke out of her house. Megan reports that the noise from the parties sometimes makes it impossible to sleep. She also objects to the profanities that the students use, which is another reason that she doesn't let her son play outside. Megan worries that the presence of a student rental right next door will decrease the fair market value of her property.

Megan has retained you to help her resolve her dispute with Sheila and the students. As always, the first step is to identify the property in question. You should then identify the competing rights asserted by the parties. As you read through this chapter, you will be able to evaluate what authority each side has to support their claims. By the end of this chapter, you should be in a position to determine whether Megan would be successful in a nuisance action.

Overview of Chapter 7

In this chapter, you will learn how courts balance the competing right of an owner to use his property with the right of a neighbor or other affected individuals to quiet enjoyment. Nuisance is among the oldest of the common law actions. One of the reasons it has retained is relevance through the centuries is that the doctrine is flexible. It asks questions regarding the utility of the conduct and the gravity of the harm that necessarily incorporate contemporary standards.

The Chapter is divided into three subunits:

1. The Law of Nuisance
2. Statutory Reforms: Right to Farm Laws and Public Nuisance
3. Utility and Harm in a Contemporary Context: Alternative Energy

The Law of Nuisance

The tort of nuisance is a common law concept. Based on the maxim that one cannot use his property to harm another—*sic utere tuo, ut alienum non laedas*—nuisance restricts unreasonable land use that causes harm to neighbors. Nuisance recognizes that our actions have consequences, and we are part of a community. As the poet John Donne famously wrote:

> No man is an island,
> Entire of itself,
> Every man is a piece of the continent,
> A part of the main.

Later in the chapter we will discuss statutory reforms to the nuisance doctrine, and later in the course, we will consider private agreements entered into regarding land use, referred to as covenants or easements, and zoning. Both statutes and private agreements may balance the interests differently by providing greater protection for the right to use or the right to quiet enjoyment.

Nuisance is a flexible common standard that regulates relations among neighbors in the absence of a controlling statute or private agreement. Nuisance empowers neighbors to restrict the ability of neighboring property owners to engage in otherwise lawful conduct on their own property. It does not simply give neighbors a veto power, but rather requires the court to balance the gravity of the alleged harm with the utility of the offending conduct. The ability of your neighbor to dictate what you could and could not do on your property would greatly reduce the value of private property and unreasonably interfere with your right to use your property. The challenge presented by nuisance is striking the right balance between the right to use and the right to quiet enjoyment.

The Restatement (Second) of Torts is clear that nuisance does not provide relief for every minor annoyance or complaint raised by your neighbor.

> Life in an organized society, and especially in populous communities, involves an unavoidable clash of individual interests. Practically all human activity, unless carried on in a wilderness, interferes to some extent with others.... It is an obvious truth that each individual in a community must put up with a certain amount of annoyance, inconvenience, and interference and must take a certain amount of risk in order that all may get on together.

Restatement (Second) of Torts § 822, comment g.

In order to understand nuisance, it is helpful to differentiate nuisance from the related torts of trespass and negligence. It is also important to understand how the courts evaluate the gravity of the alleged harm and the utility of the offending conduct. Depending upon the circumstances, courts may award damages, injunctive relief, or some combination of the two. This section provides an overview of the basic legal concepts involved in nuisance claims. Two later sections deal with statutory reforms and the challenges presented by technology.

Distinguished from Trespass

As you recall from Chapter 3, trespass is defined as the intentional and unprivileged entry onto the land of another. The key to trespass is the physical invasion of a possessory interest. Recall that nominal damages are allowed for trespass, and there is no requirement of substantial harm. Trespass protects the important right to exclude which is considered the hallmark of private property. Nuisance on the other hand does not require a physical invasion. To illustrate the difference, imagine two neighbors living side-by-side: Neighbor A and Neighbor B. Neighbor A insists on playing very loud music day and night. Neighbor B finds the racket highly disturbing. He can't sleep or work with all the commotion.

There is no physical invasion because Neighbor A never sets foot on Neighbor B's property, but the sound of the music does not stop at the property line. In fact, Neighbor B complains that the music is so loud that it is as if Neighbor A were inside Neighbor B's house. On the other hand, Neighbor A complains that his actions are perfectly legal. Even though Neighbor A has not set foot on Neighbor B's property, nuisance places limits on what Neighbor A can do on his own property. If Neighbor A's conduct unreasonably interferes with Neighbor B's right to quiet enjoyment, the law of nuisance may require Neighbor A to pay damages or support an injunction requiring him to stop his behavior.

The distinction between trespass and nuisance has been tested in cases involving environmental concerns, such as odors and pollution. Although these cases present no physical invasion in the traditional sense, scientific advancements have made it possible for plaintiffs to argue that offending odors and pollution are comprised of microscopic particles that cross property lines. The first case you will read includes an extended discussion of the difference between trespass and nuisance in the environmental context and how courts have responded to requests to extend trespass to include microscopic particles. The growing trend is to allow plaintiffs to proceed under both nuisance and trespass.

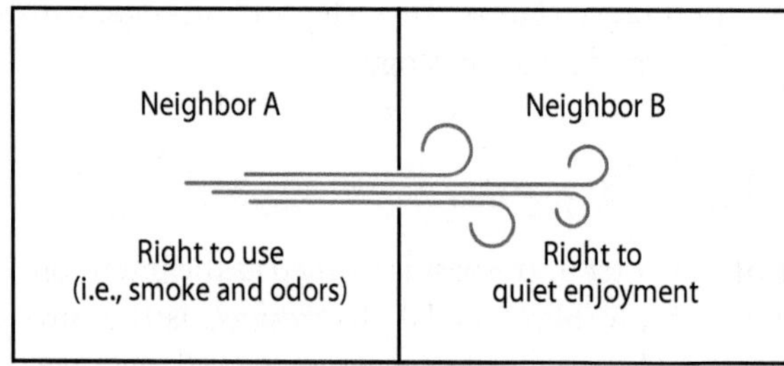

Distinguished from Negligence

Nuisance is also different from negligence. Negligence involves the failure to exercise the level of care that a reasonable or prudent person would exercise in the same circumstances. In the case of nuisance, there is no requirement that the offending neighbor breach a legal duty of conduct or that the resulting harm is foreseeable. Neighbor A's actions could be both lawful and not negligent, yet still constitute a nuisance if they cause an unreasonable interference with Neighbor B's right to quiet enjoyment. One way to think about this distinction is that the primary focus of a nuisance action is not the offending conduct, but the impact of the offending conduct on neighboring property owners.

Balancing Competing Interests

The Restatement (Second) of Torts provides that liability in nuisance arises from an "intentional and unreasonable" interference with "another's interest in the private use and enjoyment of land." § 822. There are exceptions for conduct that is ultra hazardous or otherwise negligent or reckless, in which case unintentional conduct can give rise to liability. Conduct is considered "unreasonable" when "the gravity of the harm outweighs the utility of the actor's conduct." There is an exception for ultra hazardous activity, such as blasting or storing toxic waste. In those cases, nuisance law imposes strict liability and will likely enjoin the conduct regardless of its potential utility.

Balancing the competing interests requires a very fact specific inquiry. The Restatement (Second) of Torts identifies five separate factors to be considered when evaluating the gravity of the harm:(a) the extent of the harm involved; (b) the character of the harm involved; (c) the social value that the law attaches to the type of use or enjoyment invaded; (d) the suitability of the particular use or enjoyment invaded to the character of the locality; and (e) the burden on the person harmed of avoiding the harm. *Restatement (Second) of Torts* § 827. It also identifies three factors to be considered when evaluating the utility of the conduct: (a) the social value that the law attaches to the primary purpose of the conduct; (b) the suitability of the conduct to the character of the locality; and (c) the impracticability of preventing or avoiding the invasion. *Restatement (Second) of Torts* § 828. As you read through the cases in this chapter, try to identify which factors the courts give the most weight. Often, the utility of the conduct is simply being able to exercise the right to use the property. Some conduct is considered to have no utility, such as the building of spite fences which serve no purpose other than to block a neighbor's view—on spite.

The Restatement (Second) of Torts also recognizes a private cause of action for public nuisance. A public nuisance is conduct that causes "an unreasonable interference with a right common to the general public." *Restatement (Second) of Torts* § 821B(1). Historically, government officials were responsible for abating public nuisances, many of which were later codified as minor criminal offenses. A private property owner would only be permitted to bring a cause of action for public nuisance if she suffered a particular harm. The Restatement (Second) of Torts reflects the trend of courts to allow private individuals to bring claims, and many states have enacted statutes specifically authorizing such lawsuits.

Remember that in a nuisance claim the offending conduct does not have to be unlawful or negligent. To some extent, nuisance law regulates conduct that is simply in the wrong place at the wrong time. In the 1926 landmark U.S. Supreme Court case *Euclid v. Ambler Realty*, 272 U.S. 365 (1926), Justice Sutherland gave us the colorful metaphor of a "pig in the parlor" when he explained "A nuisance may be merely a right thing in the wrong place—like a pig in the parlor instead of the barnyard." The balancing of the interests is designed to determine whether the pig is indeed in the parlor or the barnyard.

When evaluating the alleged harm, courts take into account the maxim we studied in connection with the doctrine of the Improving Trespasser in Chapter 2—the law will not concern itself with trifles or *de minimis non curat lex.* Courts will rarely provide relief for purely aesthetic harm or claims that a neighbor's conduct has reduced a property's fair market value. Accordingly, you might be out of luck if your neighbor decides to stop mowing his lawn or paints his house bright purple. Of course, the conduct causing the aesthetic harm or decline in fair market value could be prohibited by a statute or private agreement, even though they are most likely not actionable under common law nuisance. For example, many municipalities have zoning ordinances that prohibit allowing a lawn to go back to a state of nature and require periodic mowing. Some municipalities also have historic districts where only historically accurate paint colors are allowed. Homeowners' associations generally have rules that require homeowners to maintain their property within certain guidelines.

Nuisance law will also not provide relief where the complaining property owner is engaged in what is considered a "hypersensitive use." For example, a court has denied a nuisance claim brought by a neighboring property owner who had an extremely rare allergy to certain fumes emitted by railroad ties that were near his property. *Jenkins v. CSX Transportation, Inc.*, 906 S.W.2d 460 (Tenn. Ct. App. 1995). In a series of cases, courts have denied a claim of nuisance brought by owners of drive-in movie theaters alleging that outdoor lights from a neighboring property harmed the quality of the movie-going experience. *Belmar Drive-In Theatre Co. v. Illinois State Toll Highway Comm'n*, 34 Ill. 2d 544 (1966); *Lynn Open Air Theatre, Inc. v. Sea Crest Cadillac-Pontiac, Inc.*, 1 Mass. App. Ct. 186 (1973); *Amphitheaters, Inc. v. Portland Meadows*, 184 Or. 336 (1948); *Sheridan Drive-In Theatre, Inc. v. State*, 384 P.2d 597 (Wyo. 1963).

When a plaintiff moves next to the property and is aware of the offending conduct, the plaintiff is said to have "come to the nuisance." In cases where a plaintiff has "come to the nuisance," it is much harder to sustain a claim of nuisance against the property owner who was there first. The doctrine partly recognizes the concept of first in time, first in right that we saw in connection with the use of natural resources in Chapter 2. It also presumes that the complaining land owner had fair notice of the potential nuisance before she moved in.

If we change the facts slightly in our hypothetical about Neighbor A and Neighbor B and the loud music, it is easy to illustrate the concept of coming to the nuisance.

Assume that Neighbor A owns and operates a bar and restaurant named A's place that has live music several nights a week. A's place is a community institution and has been in business at that location for over thirty years. Neighbor B buys the property next door for a good price.

When he made the purchase, he was fully aware of A's Place and its reputation for hosting live (and loud) music several times a week. Neighbor B renovates the property and moves in. He then sues Neighbor A alleging that the music unreasonably interferes with his right to quiet enjoyment. Under these facts, Neighbor B's claim may be denied on the grounds that he came to the nuisance because Neighbor B knew what he was getting into when he bought the property.

Although courts are reluctant to allow a newcomer to veto a longstanding use in the community, plaintiffs can overcome the presumption against relief by showing that the nuisance is severe or the character of the community has changed. The expansion of the suburbs and exburbs into traditional rural areas has given rise to conflict between farmers and property owners and developers. To follow Justice Sutherland's metaphor, take the example of a pig farm. Pig farms are known to emit very strong odors. When located in a predominantly rural area where population density is low, the offending smells may not reach another property.

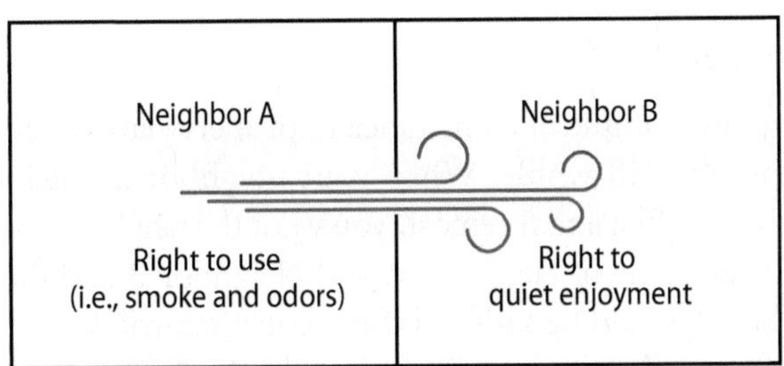

However, when housing developments begin to pop up in the immediate vicinity of the pig farmer, the farmer may find that he is no longer in a barnyard, but rather smack dab in the middle of someone's parlor.

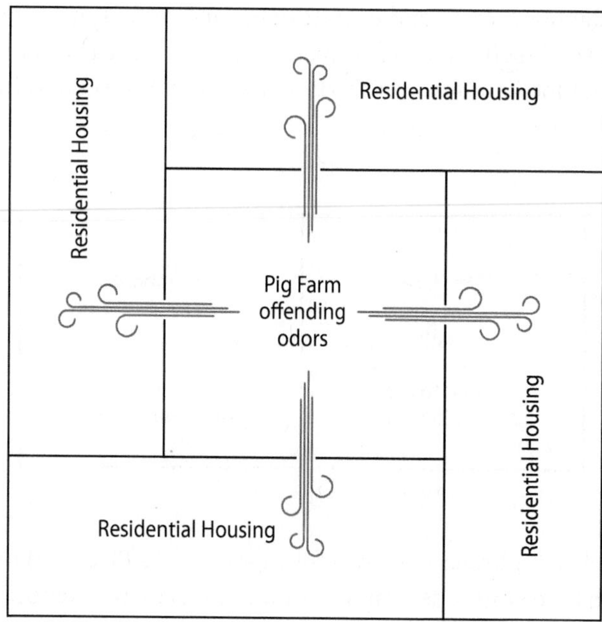

As state courts became increasingly willing to entertain nuisance suits from newcomers, a number of states passed "Right to Farm Laws" that make coming to the nuisance an absolute bar to a nuisance claim in the case of farming and related activities. This is discussed in greater detail later in this chapter.

Remedies

Once a court decides that the gravity of the harm outweighs the utility of the conduct, the court must determine the appropriate remedy. There are generally three types of relief that courts award in a nuisance action:

- Damages
- Injunction
- Purchased Injunction

Nuisance is a good example of an instance in property law where money damages may not make the plaintiff whole. When your neighbor is engaging in offending conduct, it is likely that, first and foremost, you want the neighbor to stop the conduct. Going back to our example of Neighbor A and Neighbor B and the loud music. Do you think Neighbor B would be satisfied if the court awarded damages, but allowed Neighbor A to continue the conduct? Traditionally, damages are restricted to the loss of property rights and do not extend to items that could be included in an award for negligence, such as emotional distress. In the case of residential property, a common measure of damages is lost rental value—the difference in the fair market rental value of the property with and without the nuisance. Commercial establishments can also make a case for lost profits.

Damages may provide sufficient relief when the offending conduct is in the past, but money damages may provide cold comfort for an aggrieved property owner when the conduct is ongoing. Courts will award damages and refuse to grant injunctive relief where the offending conduct is unreasonable, but also has high social utility. This was the case in *Boomer v. Atlantic Cement Co.*, where the highest court in the New York ruled that a cement factory was a nuisance, but refused to enjoin the conduct and instead awarded damages for the pollution it caused. *Boomer v. Atlantic Cement Co.*, 257 N.E.2d 870 (N.Y. 1970). The court reasoned that injunctive relief would have been a "drastic remedy" when it compared the extent of the permanent damage caused to the complaining property owners ($185,000) to the $45 million invested in the factory and the 350 jobs at stake. This decision is often pointed to as an example of the use of cost-benefit analysis in the context of property law.

Courts engage in a similar cost-benefit analysis when deciding whether to order a purchased injunction. A purchased injunction is considered the appropriate remedy when the conduct is unreasonable, but it would not be fair to impose the costs associated with stopping the conduct on the defendant, such as when the plaintiff came to the nuisance. The plaintiff is then given the option. He will be granted injunctive relief, provided he pays damages to the defendant. In this way, the plaintiff can be said to have "purchased" an injunction. As you read through the cases, be sure to pay special attention to the remedies requested and awarded.

Exercise 7-2. *Babb v. Lee County Landfill* — Trespass or Nuisance?

The following case provides an extended discussion of the distinction between nuisance and trespass. The decision from the South Carolina Supreme Court arose from a somewhat unusual procedural posture. The lawsuit between the plaintiffs and the offending landfill was filed in federal court, but involved underlying questions of state law. The federal District Court found that the South Carolina case law was not clear regarding the distinction between nuisance and trespass and certified questions of law to be resolved by the state court. Federal courts tasked with applying state law may certify questions of law to be resolved by the state court in the absence of clear precedent.

Babb, Elstrom, and Jackson v. Lee County Landfill

405 S.C. 129 (2013)

HEARN, JUSTICE. Brought in federal district court on claims arising from offensive odors migrating from a landfill onto the plaintiffs' properties, this case comes to this Court for the resolution of several issues of law. Specifically, we consider the measure of damages for trespass and nuisance claims [and] the requirement that a physical, tangible invasion occur for a trespass to arise.

FACTUAL/PROCEDURAL HISTORY

The plaintiffs, six individuals residing near a landfill operated by defendant Lee County Landfill SC, LLC (the Landfill) in Bishopville, South Carolina, initiated this action seeking to recover for substantial interference with the use and enjoyment of their property caused by odors emanating from the landfill. The plaintiffs asserted nuisance, trespass, and negligence claims based on the odors. Both before and during trial, the plaintiffs abandoned all claims for loss of use, diminution in property value, and personal injury, leaving only annoyance, discomfort, inconvenience, interference with enjoyment of their property, loss of enjoyment of life, and interference with mental tranquility as their damages claims.

Following a trial, the jury awarded the plaintiffs actual or compensatory damages totaling $532,500 on their negligence, trespass, and nuisance claims, with three plaintiffs receiving $77,500 and three receiving $100,000. The jury also awarded each plaintiff $300,000 in punitive damages. The Landfill filed motions for judgment as a matter of law or alternatively for a new trial. After determining that South Carolina precedent was not clear on state law issues raised in the post-trial motions, the District Court certified [two] questions to this Court.

LAW/ANALYSIS

I. TEMPORARY TRESPASS AND NUISANCE DAMAGES

The first question asks whether the lost rental value of property is the maximum amount of damages recoverable for a temporary trespass or nuisance. While the Landfill argues that the temporary trespass and nuisance damages are limited to the lost rental value of the property, the plaintiffs argue that in addition to this measure of damages, they can also recover separate damages for annoyance, discomfort, and inconvenience. Specifically, the plaintiffs argue they can recover for "damages to the person incurred through the loss of enjoyment of the property." We answer this question in the affirmative, holding the damages recoverable for a temporary trespass or nuisance are limited to lost rental value.

From their earliest inception through the present day, the actions of trespass and nuisance have been limited to one's interest in property, rather than providing any protection to one's person. Trespass, as that term is used here,[2] arose from the medieval assize of novel disseisin[3] which was created for the protection of a landowner's interest in the exclusive possession of land. Glanville, the great medieval legal scholar who was the first to comment upon the assize of novel disseisin, wrote that it existed to aid a person when another "unjustly and without a Judgment, has disseised another

2. While trespass may mean any "unlawful act committed against the person or property of another," and in that sense is the mother of all common law tort liability, we use it here in the form in which it is now generally used to mean an action to recover for an unlawful entry by another onto one's real property. *Black's Law Dictionary* 1541 (8th ed. 1999). With the development of tort law over the intervening centuries, those other forms of trespass have become their own distinct causes of action with their own names.

3. "Disseisin" is "[t]he act of wrongfully depriving someone of the freehold possession of property." *Black's Law Dictionary* 506 (8th ed. 1999).

of his Freehold." R. Glanville, *The Treatise on the Laws and Customs of the Realm of England*, bk. XIII, ch. XXXII (John Beames trans. 1900). Thus, Glanville recognized the assize as limited to protection of one's property interests.

Developing from the assize of novel disseisin came the assize of nuisance, modern nuisance's medieval ancestor. *See Restatement (Second) of Torts* § 821D (1979). The new writ also protected a landowner from interference with his rights in land and "closely resembled the modern cause of action for private nuisance, providing redress for interference with the use and enjoyment of plaintiff's land resulting from acts committed on the defendant's land." Jeff L. Lewin, *Boomer and the American Law of Nuisance*, 54 ALB. L. REV. 189, 193 (1990).

Blackstone, writing centuries later, described a trespass as a "species ... of real injuries, or wrongs that affect a man's lands, tenements, or hereditaments." 3 William Blackstone, *Commentaries* *209. He went on to describe a trespass as "an entry on another man's ground without a lawful authority, and doing some damage, however inconsiderable, to his real property," and explained that the trespass cause of action protects a property owner's right to exclusive possession of his land. Blackstone also wrote that a nuisance was a "real injur[y] to a man's lands and tenements," describing a private nuisance as "anything done to the hurt or annoyance of the lands, tenements, or hereditaments of another." Thus, Blackstone recognized trespass and nuisance as actions protecting and limited to one's property rights.

Arising from that common law heritage, under South Carolina law trespass and nuisance are limited to the protection of property interests. A trespass is any interference with "one's right to the exclusive, peaceable possession of his property." *Ravan v. Greenville Cnty.*, 315 S.C. 447, 463 (Ct. App. 1993). A nuisance, trespass's counterpart, provides a remedy for invasions of a property owner's right to the use and enjoyment of his property. *Clark v. Greenville Cnty.*, 313 S.C. 205, 209 (1993) ("Nuisance law is based on the premise that '[e]very citizen holds his property subject to the implied obligation that he will use it in such a way as not to prevent others from enjoying the use of their property.'").

Furthermore, the Restatement (Second) of Torts bolsters this conclusion by recognizing that those causes of action are limited to one's property rights, stating that "[a] trespass is an invasion of the interest in the exclusive possession of land, as by entry upon it. A nuisance is an interference with the interest in the private use and enjoyment of the land...." *Restatement (Second) of Torts* § 821D (1979). It goes on to provide:

> Interest in "use and enjoyment" also comprehends the pleasure, comfort and enjoyment that a person normally derives from the occupancy of land. Freedom from discomfort and annoyance while using lands is often as important to a person as freedom from physical interruption with his use or freedom from detrimental change in the physical condition of the land itself. This interest in freedom from annoyance and discomfort in the use of land is to be distinguished from the interest in freedom from emotional distress. The latter is purely an interest of personality and receives limited legal

protection, whereas the former is essentially an interest in the usability of land.... *Id.*

To the extent South Carolina's trespass and nuisance case law discusses annoyance, discomfort, interference with the enjoyment of property, loss of enjoyment of life, or interference with mental tranquility, those cases speak in terms of injury to one's property interest in the use and enjoyment of property. For example, in *Woods v. Rock Hill Fertilizer Co.*, 102 S.C. 442 (1915), the plaintiff brought a nuisance action against a fertilizer plant near her home based on odors, dust, and small particles emanating from the plant. The Court held that allegations the plaintiff's mother and sister lived with her and suffered annoyance and discomfort due to the plant were relevant only because they tended to show "the nature and extent of the plaintiff's damages, since she has the right to have them live with her and enjoy the comforts of her home." Thus, the Court found the annoyance and discomfort allegations were relevant because they went to the harm to the plaintiff's property interest in the use and enjoyment of her property.

In *Lever v. Wilder Mobile Homes, Inc.*, 283 S.C. 452 (Ct. App. 1984), the plaintiff brought a nuisance action alleging the defendant's sewage lagoon emitted offensive odors and leaked sewage into the plaintiff's fish pond, polluting the pond and killing his fish. The defendant appealed the denial of its motions for directed verdict and judgment notwithstanding the verdict. The court of appeals found evidence establishing a nuisance in the form of testimony that the plaintiff could no longer host family picnics or church groups on the property and could no longer garden there. That evidence was not considered because of the harm the plaintiff suffered personally, but because it represented a loss of use and enjoyment of the property, as shown by the court relating the alleged harm back to the ability to use and enjoy the property.

Thus, from their inception through to today, trespass and nuisance have been actions limited to the protection of one's property interests. They have never served to protect against harms to one's person.[4] To permit plaintiffs to recover for annoyance and discomfort to their person as a component of trespass or nuisance damages, as opposed to as related to their property interests, would be to unhinge trespass and nuisance from the traditional property locus and transform them into personal injury causes of action. Not only would it represent a drastic expansion of trespass and nuisance beyond the realm of property, it would also represent a fundamental change in our tort law jurisprudence which does not permit recovery for sheer annoyance and discomfort. In short, allowing recovery for personal annoyance and discomfort under the guise of trespass and nuisance would be the stealth recognition of an entirely new tort.

The damages recoverable for trespass and nuisance being strictly limited to damages to one's property interests, the only proper measure of them is the value of the property. A well-known principle of property law is that property consists of a bundle of rights.

4. Rather, over time the common law developed numerous causes of action—for example, battery and negligence—to permit a plaintiff to recover for harm to his person. Of course, a trespass or nuisance plaintiff also has those causes of action available to him to recover for harm to his person in addition to harm to his land.

The value of a piece of property is the value of all of the rights one obtains through ownership of the property. Thus, included in the value of property are the rights of exclusive possession and use and enjoyment protected by the trespass and nuisance causes of action respectively. To the extent those interests are harmed by a temporary trespass or nuisance, the harm would be reflected in the lost rental value of the property.

In other words, lost rental value includes the annoyance and discomfort experienced as the result of a temporary trespass or nuisance. The lost rental value of the property is the difference between the rental value absent the trespass or nuisance and the rental value with the trespass or nuisance. The rental value with the trespass or nuisance present would be less, in part, because a hypothetical renter would have to suffer the annoyance and discomfort of the nuisance or trespass. Thus, the lost rental value measures the monetary value of the harm to the property interest. Furthermore, because lost rental value includes damages caused by annoyance or discomfort, to permit a plaintiff to recover both the lost rental value plus an additional sum for annoyance and discomfort would be to permit a double recovery.

II. TRESPASS FROM INVISIBLE ODORS

The second certified question asks whether South Carolina law recognizes a cause of action for trespass solely from invisible odors, rather than from a physical invasion such as dust or water. The plaintiffs argue South Carolina has abandoned the traditional rule that a trespass requires an invasion of property by a physical, tangible thing, and thus, the Court should recognize odors as constituting a trespass. The Landfill argues for the traditional rule, asserting that odors, due to their intangibility, cannot constitute a trespass, but rather, only may give rise to a nuisance cause of action. We hold that South Carolina adheres to the traditional rule requiring an invasion by a physical, tangible thing for a trespass to exist, and accordingly, hold that odors cannot give rise to a trespass claim.

We first note the relevant distinctions between the trespass and nuisance causes of action which presumably give rise to the plaintiffs' arguments that intangible intrusions should be sufficient to constitute a trespass. First, recovery under a nuisance claim requires proof of actual and substantial injury, whereas trespass entitles a plaintiff to nominal damages even in the absence of any actual injury. Also, in order to rise to the level of an actionable nuisance, the interference or inconvenience must be unreasonable. The unreasonableness requirement reflects the unavoidable reality that persons must suffer some inconvenience and annoyance from their neighbors for modern life to carry on. For trespass, there is no requirement of unreasonableness. Rather, any trespass, however small and insignificant, gives rise to an actionable claim.

This Court has yet to consider the tangible versus intangible distinction for trespass actions. The traditional common law rule, the dimensional test, provides that a trespass only exists where the invasion of land occurs through a physical, tangible object. Under that rule, intangible matter or energy, such as smoke, noise, light, and vibration, are insufficient to constitute a trespass. More specifically, under that rule, courts have held that odors do not give rise to a trespass cause of action because they are intangible.

In reaction to modern science's understanding of microscopic and atomic particles, a divergent line of decisions have discarded the dimensional test and permitted recovery for trespass without regard to whether the intrusion was by a tangible object, but rather by considering the nature of the interest harmed. [In *Martin v. Reynolds Aluminum*, 221 Ore. 86, 342 P.2d 790 (Or. 1959), the Oregon Supreme Court considered] a trespass action against an aluminum smelter for fluoride gases and microscopic particulates they alleged the smelter emitted, which traveled through the air and settled on the plaintiffs' property. Dispensing with the dimensional test, the Oregon Supreme Court held the intrusion of fluoride was a trespass despite its intangible nature. The court reasoned that while the fluoride particles were individually minute and invisible, each particle that entered the plaintiffs' property was a physical intrusion, and but for their size, would undoubtedly give rise to a trespass action. The court also noted cases finding intrusions by very small objects constituted a trespass, citing cases in which shot from a gun, particles of molten lead, spray from a cooling tower, and soot were held to be a trespass. Additionally, the court cited cases in which vibrations of the soil and concussion of the air created a trespass. The court then concluded that drawing a line between tangible and intangible intrusions had become arbitrary in light of modern science, writing:

> It is quite possible that in an earlier day when science had not yet peered into the molecular and atomic world of small particles, the courts could not fit an invasion through unseen physical instrumentalities into the requirement that a trespass can result only from a *direct* invasion. But in this atomic age even the uneducated know the great and awful force contained in the atom and what it can do to a man's property if it is released. In fact, the now famous equation $E=mc^2$ has taught us that mass and energy are equivalents and that our concept of "things" must be reframed.

In light of those considerations, the court held the determination of whether an invasion of the right to exclusive possession occurred, and thus whether a trespass occurred, is best determined by consideration of the energy and force of the thing intruding upon a plaintiff's land.

The next seminal decision in the divergent line was *Borland v. Sanders Lead Co., Inc.*, 369 So. 2d 523 (Ala. 1979), where the plaintiffs sued a lead smelter for lead and sulfoxide emissions they alleged settled on and damaged their property. After a discussion of *Martin*, the court noted that in adopting the *Martin* holding it "might appear, at first blush, ... that every property owner in this State would have a cause of action against any neighboring industry which emitted particulate matter into the atmosphere, or even a passing motorist, whose exhaust emissions come to rest upon another's property." However, the court found that *Martin*'s substantiality requirement obviates that concern.

However, we find persuasive the Michigan Court of Appeals' rejection of this divergent line of decisions in *Adams v. Cleveland-Cliffs Iron Co.*, 602 N.W.2d 215 (Mich. App. 1999). There, the court adhered to the dimensional test, holding that intangible invasions are properly characterized as giving rise to nuisance or negligence actions and cannot give rise to a trespass action. The court first noted that courts rejecting the dimensional test have been troubled by the principle that nominal damages are available for trespass, and in order to avoid "subjecting manufacturing plants to potential liability to every landowner on whose parcel some incidental residue of industrial activity might come to rest, these courts have grafted onto the law of trespass a requirement of actual and substantial damages." But in adopting the substantiality requirement, those courts transmute the trespass cause of action into the nuisance cause of action. The court went on to explain that "[w]here the possessor of land is menaced by noise, vibrations, or ambient dust, smoke, soot, or fumes, the possessory interest implicated is that of use and enjoyment, not exclusion, and the vehicle through which a plaintiff normally should seek a remedy is the doctrine of nuisance." Finally, the court found that the substantiality requirement inherent in the divergent view endangers the sanctity of the right to exclusive possession, explaining: "The law should not require a property owner to justify exercising the right to exclude. To countenance the erosion of presumed damages in cases of trespass is to endanger the right of exclusion itself." Accordingly, the court concluded it would retain the dimensional test because it safeguards "genuine claims of trespass and keep[s] the line between the torts of trespass and nuisance from fading into a wavering and uncertain ambiguity."

We acknowledge that the dimensional test is an imperfect rule. It does not comport with modern science's understanding of matter and the relationship between matter and energy. However, we question whether any rule can perfectly distinguish between those things that intrude upon the right to exclusive possession of land and those that do not. The right to exclusive possession is an artificial construct incapable of precise definition or measurement and thus, defies the creation of a perfect rule to measure intrusions upon it.

Property is commonly conceptualized as a bundle of rights, and among the rights some are particularly fundamental and as such receive greater protection than others. For example, because human society cannot function without persons experiencing some reduction in the use and enjoyment of their property due to others' use of nearby property, nuisance law only protects landowners against substantial harm from others using their property unreasonably. However, the right of exclusive possession is fundamental. Without it, other rights in the bundle would be rendered nearly worthless. For example, one's ability to use and enjoy property would be severely curtailed by others being permitted to come onto the property freely and do as they please. Accordingly, the common law has traditionally accorded absolute protection to the right of exclusive possession through trespass's provision of liability and damages for any trespass, no matter how insignificant. We believe the distinction between trespass and nuisance is important due to the extra protection needed for the right of exclusive possession. The dimensional test, while not perfect, provides a workable rule that roughly tracks the line between those things that interfere with the right to exclusive possession, and thus, are a trespass, and those that merely interfere with the right to use and enjoyment, and thus, are a nuisance.

For these reasons, we answer this question in the negative. South Carolina does not recognize a trespass cause of action for invisible odors. Rather, South Carolina hews to the traditional dimensional test and only recognizes intrusions by physical, tangible things as capable of constituting a trespass.

CONCLUSION

For the reasons stated, we answer the certified questions as follows. As to question one, we hold the damages recoverable for a temporary trespass or nuisance claim are limited to the lost rental value of the property. As to question two, we hold a trespass exists only when an intrusion is made by a physical, tangible thing.

Exercise 7-3. *Babb* Revisited

1. Both trespass and nuisance are torts. Do you agree that damages should be limited to the loss of the use of property? Will loss of rental value make a property owner whole? How do you distinguish between "annoyance and discomfort in the use of land" and "emotional distress"? Can the two be interrelated?
2. The Restatement Second of Torts provides: "Freedom from discomfort and annoyance while using lands is often as important to a person as freedom from physical interruption with his use or freedom from detrimental change in the physical condition of the land itself." If this is true, then why does the court insist on maintaining the distinction between the two actions? Do you think the distinction is warranted given the scientific understanding of particles? Is it accurate to say that particles are not tangible?
3. The South Carolina Supreme Court is unwilling to dispense with the dimensional test for fear of imposing disabling liability on industry. Do you agree?
4. The growing trend among the states is to allow plaintiffs to proceed under both nuisance and trespass in cases involving microscopic particles.

Exercise 7-4. *Page County Appliance Ctr. v. Honeywell*— Hypersensitive Use

In negligence claims and criminal law, the "eggshell plaintiff" rule provides that you must take your victim as you find him. This is not the case in nuisance law, where a defendant can claim that his conduct is not unreasonable because the plaintiff is engaged in a hypersensitive use. *Page County Appliance Center, Inc. v. Honeywell, Inc.* involves an allegation of hypersensitive use, but it also illustrates how complicated a nuisance claim can be when multiple parties are involved.

In order to understand the following case, it is important to be aware of the state of technology in 1980. Computers were not commonplace, but they were very important for travel agents to be able to make and manage reservations, particularly with the airlines. Page County Appliance sold televisions, and you can assume that it had a huge wall of televisions on display like you would see today at a Best Buy or a comparable store. One major difference is that in 1980, very few places in the United States had cable television. Instead, television signals traveled through the air and were received with the assistance of antennae. There were also only three major networks and PBS. In order to sell the televisions, it was important to have good reception. After all, what customer would buy a television with a fuzzy picture?

1. For this case, you will want to build a diagram to illustrate the relationships between and among the parties.
2. The case does not give us sufficient information to draw a map of the properties, but it always helps to try to envision the property in question. Here, we can assume that Page County Appliance was in a strip of commercial retail properties, including Central Travel, where the nuisance originated. The nuisance started when Kay Crowell, the owner of Central Travel, acquired a new computer.

Page County Appliance Center, Inc. v. Honeywell, Inc.

347 N.W.2d 171 (Iowa 1984)

Reynoldson, J. Plaintiff Page County Appliance Center, Inc. (Appliance Center), sued Honeywell, Inc. (Honeywell), and ITT Electronic Travel Services, Inc. (ITT), for nuisance and tortious interference with business relations. Defendants appeal from judgment entered on jury verdicts awarding compensatory and punitive damages. Honeywell appeals from a judgment rendered against it on ITT's cross-claim for indemnification. We reverse and remand for new trial.

Appliance Center has owned and operated an appliance store in Shenandoah, Iowa, since 1953. In 1975 the store was acquired by John Pearson, who sold televisions, stereos, and a variety of appliances. Before 1980 Pearson had no reception trouble with his display televisions. In early January 1980, however, ITT placed one of its computers with Central Travel Service in Shenandoah as part of a nationwide plan to lease computers to retail travel agents. Central Travel was separated by only one other business from the Appliance Center. This ITT computer was manufactured, installed, and maintained by Honeywell.

Thereafter many of Pearson's customers told him his display television pictures were bad; on two of the three channels available in Shenandoah he had a difficult time "getting a picture that was fit to watch." After unsuccessfully attempting several remedial measures, in late January 1980, he finally traced the interference to the operations of Central Travel's computer. Both defendants concede Pearson's problems were caused by radiation leaking from the Honeywell computer.

Pearson discussed the problem with Kay Crowell, owner of Central Travel. She placed a call to ITT's president in New York. Although he was unavailable, ITT personnel apparently notified Honeywell. ITT's only contact with Pearson was through a telephone call some ten months later. At that time Pearson told ITT's sales representative that Honeywell was working on the problem; he made no effort to follow up on ITT's interest in the problem.

Honeywell indeed was working to correct the situation, and had been since February 1980. Honeywell technicians made repeated trips to make various unsuccessful adjustments to the computer. They found the computer was operating properly; the interference-causing radiation was a design and not a service problem. Pearson then telephoned Armando Benitez, the technicians' supervisor. Pearson testified Benitez told him Honeywell was "way over budget" on the Central Travel computer and that "if you don't like it, you can move."

Nonetheless, in early fall of 1980 Honeywell sent out Phil Brzozoski, one of its engineers from Boston. According to Pearson, when he asked Brzozoski why it had taken him so long to come, the latter replied he would not have been there at all had Pearson not instituted suit; that was the way big business worked. Kay Crowell, admittedly Pearson's friend, testified Brzozoski told her the delay was "good business." Pearson in fact did not bring suit until December 22, 1980, although his counsel sent demand letters to Honeywell and ITT in October 1980. At trial a top Honeywell employee testified it was not company policy to await lawsuits before taking remedial action.

The Honeywell engineers effected a 70 percent improvement in the television reception by certain modifications of the computer in the fall of 1980. Pearson, still dissatisfied, started this action in December. While the suit was pending, Honeywell further modified the computer, finally alleviating Pearson's problems in May 1982.

At trial a Honeywell senior staff engineer admitted the technology to manufacture a non-radiation-emitting computer was available long before it developed this computer, but opined it would have been neither cost nor consumer effective to utilize that technology. He testified Honeywell believed it had corrected Pearson's problems in the fall of 1980.

The Appliance Center's case against Honeywell and ITT finally was submitted to the jury on the theories of nuisance and tortious interference with prospective business relations. It asked for only injunctive relief against Kay Crowell, doing business as Central Travel Service. The latter's motion for summary judgment was sustained. The jury found for the Appliance Center against the remaining defendants on both theories, and further found the Appliance Center should recover \$71,000 in compensatory damages and \$150,000 in exemplary damages. Following jury trial, Kay Crowell's cross-claim against Honeywell and ITT's cross-claim against Honeywell were submitted to the court. Crowell's cross-claim was dismissed. She did not appeal and is not involved in this proceeding. Trial court awarded ITT full indemnity against Honeywell, in the amount of $221,000, together with attorney fees and costs. Both defendants appeal from the judgment in favor of Appliance Center; Honeywell additionally appeals from the judgment awarding ITT indemnity.

Defendants raise a number of claimed trial court errors, discussed in the divisions that follow.

I. Should Trial Court Have Granted Defendants' Motions for Directed Verdict and for Judgment Notwithstanding the Verdict on the Nuisance Count

A. ITT argues trial court should have granted its motions for directed verdict because the Appliance Center property was being used for a purpose peculiarly sensitive to computer emissions, and because plaintiff did not prove ITT substantially participated in the creation or maintenance of the alleged nuisance.

Certain general principles govern our review here. In considering the propriety of a motion for directed verdict the court views the evidence in the light most favorable to the party against whom the motion is made. We examine the evidence in the same light to determine whether there was a jury issue.

Our analysis of ITT's first contention must start with Iowa Code section 657.1, which in relevant part states:

> Whatever is ... an obstruction to the free use of property, so as essentially to interfere with the ... enjoyment of ... property, is a nuisance, and a civil action by ordinary proceedings may be brought to enjoin and abate the same and to recover damages sustained on account thereof.

Narrowing our focus, we note the Appliance Center is alleging a "private nuisance," that is, an actionable interference with a person's interest in the private use and enjoyment of his or her property. It also is apparent that if Central Travel's computer emissions constitute a nuisance it is a "nuisance per accidens, or in fact"—a lawful activity conducted in such a manner as to be a nuisance.

Principles governing our consideration of nuisance claims are well established. One's use of property should not unreasonably interfere with or disturb a neighbor's comfortable and reasonable use and enjoyment of his or her estate. A fair test of whether the operation of a lawful trade or industry constitutes a nuisance is the reasonableness of conducting it in the manner, at the place, and under the circumstances shown by the evidence. Each case turns on its own facts and ordinarily the ultimate issue is one of fact, not law. The existence of a nuisance is not affected by the intention of its creator not to injure anyone. *Patz*, 196 N.W.2d at 561. Priority of occupation and location—"who was there first"—is a circumstance of considerable weight.

When the alleged nuisance is claimed to be offensive to the person, courts apply the standard of "normal persons in a particular locality" to measure the existence of a nuisance. This normalcy standard also is applied where the use of property is claimed to be affected. "The plaintiff cannot, by devoting his own land to an unusually sensitive use, ... make a nuisance out of conduct of the adjoining defendant which would otherwise be harmless." W. Prosser, The Law of Torts § 87, at 579 (4th ed. 1971).

In the case before us, ITT asserts the Appliance Center's display televisions constituted a hypersensitive use of its premises as a matter of law, and equates this situation to cases involving light thrown on outdoor theater screens in which light-throwing defendants have carried the day. *See Belmar Drive-In Theatre Co. v. Illinois State Toll Highway Commission*, 34 Ill. 2d 544 (1966); *Lynn Open Air Theatre, Inc. v. Sea Crest Cadillac-Pontiac, Inc.*, 1 Mass. App. Ct. 186 (1973); *Amphitheaters, Inc. v. Portland Meadows*, 184 Or. 336 (1948); *Sheridan Drive-In Theatre, Inc. v. State*, 384 P.2d 597 (Wyo. 1963). Several of those cases are distinguishable both on facts and by the way the issue was raised.

We cannot equate the rare outdoor theater screen with the ubiquitous television that exists, in various numbers, in almost every home. Clearly, the presence of televisions on any premises is not such an abnormal condition that we can say, as a matter of law, that the owner has engaged in a peculiarly sensitive use of the property. This consideration, as well as related considerations of unreasonableness, gravity of harm, utility of conduct, and priority of occupation, are factual determinations that should have been submitted to the jury in this case. We find no trial court error in refusing to direct a verdict on this ground.

ITT's second contention asserts trial court should have directed a verdict in its favor because it did not participate in the creation or maintenance of the alleged nuisance. We have noted ITT was engaged in a multimillion dollar, national program to lease computers to travel agencies. It owned this computer and leased it to Central Travel. It was to ITT that the agency first turned when the effect of the computer radiation became apparent. ITT continued to collect its lease payments; the computer did not operate for the benefit of Crowell alone. The jury could have found ITT evidenced some measure of its responsibility, as owner of the computer, in contacting Honeywell and making belated inquiries regarding Appliance Center's problems both to Pearson and Crowell.

It is no ground for directed verdict that the computer was leased to Central Travel. "One is subject to liability for a nuisance caused by an activity, not only when he carries on the activity but also when he participates to a substantial extent in carrying it on." Restatement (Second) of Torts § 834 (1979). Even one who contracts out nuisance-causing work to independent contractors may have the duty, upon notice, "to take reasonably prompt and efficient means to suppress the nuisance." *Shannon v. Missouri Valley Limestone Co.*, 255 Iowa 528 (1963). A failure to act under circumstances in which one is under a duty to take positive action to prevent or abate the invasion of the private interest may make one liable, and this may include a lessor or licensor.

An action for damages for nuisance need not be predicated on negligence. Nuisance ordinarily is considered as a condition, and not as an act or failure to act on the part of the responsible party. A person responsible for a harmful condition found to be a nuisance may be liable even though that person has used the highest possible degree of care to prevent or minimize the effect.

Where there is reasonable doubt whether one of several persons is substantially participating in carrying on an activity, the question is for the trier of fact. We hold such reasonable doubt existed on the record made in this case, and trial court did not err in refusing to direct a verdict on this ground.

Our holding on the two issues discussed above disposes of ITT's contention trial court should have granted its motion for judgment notwithstanding the verdict, posited on the same grounds.

B. Honeywell asserts trial court should have granted its motion for directed verdict because, even though it manufactured the computer, Central Travel and ITT were in control of the instrument at all relevant times; thus Honeywell did not have the legal right to terminate its use. Honeywell devotes ten and one-half pages of its brief to this thesis without mentioning that it had an ongoing contract to service and maintain the computer.

Much of what we have written in subdivision I(A) applies here. Again, the issue is one of material participation. Honeywell's design permitted radiation to escape this computer, although technology was available to minimize this effect. Apparently factors of cost and ease of service access weighed more in the design decision. Honeywell was the only party with the technological know-how to control the radiation leakage. Its maintenance contract with ITT clearly absolved it of any liability if anyone else made any alterations or additions to the equipment, and reserved the right to terminate the agreement should that occur. As with ITT, we think Honeywell's material participation was an issue for the finder of fact.

Both Honeywell and ITT objected because the court did not submit to the jury the issue whether Appliance Center was devoting its premises to an unusually sensitive use. We hold defendants were entitled to have this question resolved by the jury.

We reverse and remand with instructions to set aside the judgment in favor of Appliance Center against Honeywell and ITT, and the judgment entered on ITT's cross-claim against Honeywell. Defendants shall be granted a new trial in conformance with this opinion.

REVERSED AND REMANDED WITH INSTRUCTIONS.

Exercise 7-5. *Page* Revisited

1. When Kay Crowell sat down at her keyboard, she had no idea that her computer terminal would leak radiation that would interfere with the reception of the televisions on display in Page County Appliance. Why did Page County only request injunctive relief against Kay?

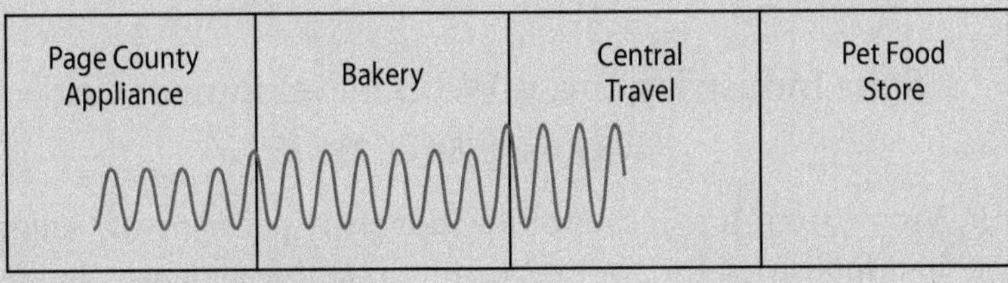

2. The court states that "We cannot equate the rare outdoor theater screen with the ubiquitous television that exists, in various numbers, in almost every home." Although this may be true, do you think home television use is the same as a display wall full of television sets? Note that the court holds that the question of whether the plaintiff is engaged in a hypersensitive use is a question of fact.
3. Both ITT and Honeywell appealed the failure of the lower court to declare a directed verdict in their favor. The court grants a new trial that will determine the questions regarding hypersensitive use and material participation. Assuming the television display is not a hypersensitive use, who do you think is ultimately responsible for the nuisance? Honeywell? ITT? Kay Cromwell?
4. Were you surprised that "a Honeywell senior staff engineer admitted the technology to manufacture a non-radiation-emitting computer was available long before it developed this computer, but opined it would have been neither cost nor consumer effective to utilize that technology"?

Exercise 7-6. *Spur Indus., Inc. v. Del E. Webb Dev. Co.* — Coming to the Nuisance

1. *Spur Industries* provides a classic example of a housing development that encroaches on a previously rural community. Rather than barring the nuisance claim outright, the court crafts an unusual remedy that is designed to balance the competing interest of the parties. Do you believe that plaintiffs who knowingly come to a nuisance should be barred from bringing a nuisance action?
2. *Spur Industries* also illustrates how fact specific nuisance claims can be. You should be sure to chart a timeline so you can keep track of the order in which the events unfolded. Remember that who was there first is important, but not always controlling.
3. Unlike *Page County Appliance*, this case provides a detailed description of the property in question and presents an excellent opportunity for you to practice visualizing the property. Try your hand at mapping out the area in interest. It will provide a helpful reference as you work through the facts.

Spur Industries, Inc. v. Webb Development Co.

108 Ariz. 178 (1972)

Cameron, Vice Chief Justice. From a judgment permanently enjoining the defendant, Spur Industries, Inc., from operating a cattle feedlot near the plaintiff Del

E. Webb Development Company's Sun City, Spur appeals. Webb cross-appeals. Although numerous issues are raised, we feel that it is necessary to answer only two questions. They are:

> 1. Where the operation of a business, such as a cattle feedlot is lawful in the first instance, but becomes a nuisance by reason of a nearby residential area, may the feedlot operation be enjoined in an action brought by the developer of the residential area?
>
> 2. Assuming that the nuisance may be enjoined, may the developer of a completely new town or urban area in a previously agricultural area be required to indemnify the operator of the feedlot who must move or cease operation because of the presence of the residential area created by the developer?

The facts necessary for a determination of this matter on appeal are as follows. The area in question is located in Maricopa County, Arizona, some 14 to 15 miles west of the urban area of Phoenix, on the Phoenix-Wickenburg Highway, also known as Grand Avenue. About two miles south of Grand Avenue is Olive Avenue which runs east and west. 111th Avenue runs north and south as does the Agua Fria River immediately to the west.

Farming started in this area about 1911. In 1929, with the completion of the Carl Pleasant Dam, gravity flow water became available to the property located to the west of the Agua Fria River, though land to the east remained dependent upon well water for irrigation. By 1950, the only urban areas in the vicinity were the agriculturally related communities of Peoria, E1 Mirage, and Surprise located along Grand Avenue. Along 111th Avenue, approximately one mile south of Grand Avenue and 1 1/2 miles north of Olive Avenue, the community of Youngtown was commenced in 1954. Youngtown is a retirement community appealing primarily to senior citizens.

In 1956, Spur's predecessors in interest, H. Marion Welborn and the Northside Hay Mill and Trading Company, developed feedlots, about 1/2 mile south of Olive Avenue, in an area between the confluence of the usually dry Agua Fria and New Rivers. The area is well suited for cattle feeding and in 1959, there were 25 cattle feeding pens or dairy operations within a 7 mile radius of the location developed by Spur's predecessors. In April and May of 1959, the Northside Hay Mill was feeding between 6,000 and 7,000 head of cattle and Welborn approximately 1,500 head on a combined area of 35 acres.

In May of 1959, Del Webb began to plan the development of an urban area to be known as Sun City. For this purpose, the Marinette and the Santa Fe Ranches, some 20,000 acres of farmland, were purchased for $15,000,000 or $750.00 per acre. This price was considerably less than the price of land located near the urban area of Phoenix, and along with the success of Youngtown was a factor influencing the decision to purchase the property in question.

By September 1959, Del Webb had started construction of a golf course south of Grand Avenue and Spur's predecessors had started to level ground for more feedlot area. In 1960, Spur purchased the property in question and began a rebuilding and expansion program extending both to the north and south of the original facilities. By 1962, Spur's expansion program was completed and had expanded from approximately 35 acres to 114 acres.

Accompanied by an extensive advertising campaign, homes were first offered by Del Webb in January 1960 and the first unit to be completed was south of Grand Avenue and approximately 2 ½ miles north of Spur. By 2 May 1960, there were 450 to 500 houses completed or under construction. At this time, Del Webb did not consider odors from the Spur feed pens a problem and Del Webb continued to develop in a southerly direction, until sales resistance became so great that the parcels were difficult if not impossible to sell. Thomas E. Breen, Vice President and General Manager of the housing division of Del Webb, testified at deposition as follows:

> Q Did you ever have any discussions with Tony Cole at or about the time the sales office was opened south of Peoria concerning the problem in sales as the development came closer towards the feed lots?
>
> A Not at the time that that facility was opened. That was subsequent to that.
>
> Q All right, what is it that you recall about conversations with Cole on that subject?
>
> A Well, when the feed lot problem became a bigger problem, which, really, to the best of my recollection, commenced to become a serious problem in 1963, and there was some talk about not developing that area because of sales resistance, and to my recollection we shifted—we had planned at that time to the eastern portion of the property, and it was a consideration.
>
> Q Was any specific suggestion made by Mr. Cole as to the line of demarcation that should be drawn or anything of that type exactly where the development should cease?
>
> A I don't recall anything specific as far as the definite line would be, other than, you know, that it would be advisable to stay out of the southwestern portion there because of sales resistance.
>
> Q And to the best of your recollection, this was in about 1963?
>
> A That would be my recollection, yes.
>
> Q As you recall it, what was the reason that the suggestion was not adopted to stop developing towards the southwest of the development?
>
> A Well, as far as I know, that decision was made subsequent to that time.
>
> Q Right. But I mean at that time?
>
> A Well, at that time what I am really referring to is more of a long-range planning than immediate planning, and I think it was the case of just trying to figure out how far you could go with it before you really ran into a lot of sales resistance and found a necessity to shift the direction.

Q So the plan was to go as far as you could until the resistance got to the point where you couldn't go any further?

A I would say that is reasonable, yes.

By December 1967, Del Webb's property had extended south to Olive Avenue and Spur was within 500 feet of Olive Avenue to the north. Del Webb filed its original complaint alleging that in excess of 1,300 lots in the southwest portion were unfit for development for sale as residential lots because of the operation of the Spur feedlot.

Del Webb's suit complained that the Spur feeding operation was a public nuisance because of the flies and the odor which were drifting or being blown by the prevailing south to north wind over the southern portion of Sun City. At the time of the suit, Spur was feeding between 20,000 and 30,000 head of cattle, and the facts amply support the finding of the trial court that the feed pens had become a nuisance to the people who resided in the southern part of Del Webb's development. The testimony indicated that cattle in a commercial feedlot will produce 35 to 40 pounds of wet manure per day, per head, or over a million pounds of wet manure per day for 30,000 head of cattle, and that despite the admittedly good feedlot management and good housekeeping practices by Spur, the resulting odor and flies produced an annoying if not unhealthy situation as far as the senior citizens of southern Sun City were concerned. There is no doubt that some of the citizens of Sun City were unable to enjoy the outdoor living which Del Webb had advertised and that Del Webb was faced with sales resistance from prospective purchasers as well as strong and persistent complaints from the people who had purchased homes in that area.

MAY SPUR BE ENJOINED?

The difference between a private nuisance and a public nuisance is generally one of degree. A private nuisance is one affecting a single individual or a definite small number of persons in the enjoyment of private rights not common to the public, while a public nuisance is one affecting the rights enjoyed by citizens as a part of the public. To constitute a public nuisance, the nuisance must affect a considerable number of people or an entire community or neighborhood.

Where the injury is slight, the remedy for minor inconveniences lies in an action for damages rather than in one for an injunction. Moreover, some courts have held, in the "balancing of conveniences" cases, that damages may be the sole remedy. We have no difficulty in agreeing with the conclusion of the trial court that Spur's operation was an enjoinable public nuisance as far as the people in the southern portion of Del Webb's Sun City were concerned.

§36-601, subsec. A reads as follows:

§36-601. Public nuisances dangerous to public health

A. The following conditions are specifically declared public nuisances dangerous to the public health:

1. Any condition or place in populous areas which constitutes a breeding place for flies, rodents, mosquitoes and other insects which are capable of

> carrying and transmitting disease-causing organisms to any person or persons.

By this statute, before an otherwise lawful (and necessary) business may be declared a public nuisance, there must be a "populous" area in which people are injured:

> [I]t hardly admits a doubt that, in determining the question as to whether a lawful occupation is so conducted as to constitute a nuisance as a matter of fact, the locality and surroundings are of the first importance. A business which is not per se a public nuisance may become such by being carried on at a place where the health, comfort, or convenience of a populous neighborhood is affected. * * * What might amount to a serious nuisance in one locality by reason of the density of the population, or character of the neighborhood affected, may in another place and under different surroundings be deemed proper and unobjectionable. *MacDonald v. Perry,* 32 Ariz. 39 (1927).

It is clear that as to the citizens of Sun City, the operation of Spur's feedlot was both a public and a private nuisance. They could have successfully maintained an action to abate the nuisance. Del Webb, having shown a special injury in the loss of sales, had a standing to bring suit to enjoin the nuisance. The judgment of the trial court permanently enjoining the operation of the feedlot is affirmed.

MUST DEL WEBB INDEMNIFY SPUR?

A suit to enjoin a nuisance sounds in equity and the courts have long recognized a special responsibility to the public when acting as a court of equity. In addition to protecting the public interest, however, courts of equity are concerned with protecting the operator of a lawfully, albeit noxious, business from the result of a knowing and willful encroachment by others near his business.

In the so-called "coming to the nuisance" cases, the courts have held that the residential landowner may not have relief if he knowingly came into a neighborhood reserved for industrial or agricultural endeavors and has been damaged thereby:

> Plaintiffs chose to live in an area uncontrolled by zoning laws or restrictive covenants and remote from urban development. In such an area plaintiffs cannot complain that legitimate agricultural pursuits are being carried on in the vicinity, nor can plaintiffs, having chosen to build in an agricultural area, complain that the agricultural pursuits carried on in the area depreciate the value of their homes. The area being *primarily agricultural*, any opinion reflecting the value of such property must take this factor into account. The standards affecting the value of residence property in an urban setting, subject to zoning controls and controlled planning techniques, cannot be the standards by which agricultural properties are judged.
>
> People employed in a city who build their homes in suburban areas of the county beyond the limits of a city and zoning regulations do so for a reason. Some do so to avoid the high taxation rate imposed by cities, or to avoid special assessments for street, sewer and water projects. They usually build on improved or hard surface highways, which have been built either at state

> or county expense and thereby avoid special assessments for these improvements. It may be that they desire to get away from the congestion of traffic, smoke, noise, foul air and the many other annoyances of city life. But with all these advantages in going beyond the area which is zoned and restricted to protect them in their homes, they must be prepared to take the disadvantages. *Dill v. Excel Packing Company,* 183 Kan. 513 (1958).

And:

> [A] party cannot justly call upon the law to make that place suitable for his residence which was not so when he selected it. *Gilbert v. Showerman,* 23 Mich. 448 (1871).

Were Webb the only party injured, we would feel justified in holding that the doctrine of "coming to the nuisance" would have been a bar to the relief asked by Webb, and, on the other hand, had Spur located the feedlot near the outskirts of a city and had the city grown toward the feedlot, Spur would have to suffer the cost of abating the nuisance as to those people locating within the growth pattern of the expanding city:

> The case affords, perhaps, an example where a business established at a place remote from population is gradually surrounded and becomes part of a populous center, so that a business which formerly was not an interference with the rights of others has become so by the encroachment of the population. *City of Ft. Smith v. Western Hide & Fur Co.,* 153 Ark. 99 (1922).

We agree, however, with the Massachusetts court that:

> The law of nuisance affords no rigid rule to be applied in all instances. It is elastic. It undertakes to require only that which is fair and reasonable under all the circumstances. In a commonwealth like this, which depends for its material prosperity so largely on the continued growth and enlargement of manufacturing of diverse varieties, 'extreme rights' cannot be enforced. *Stevens v. Rockport Granite Co.*, 216 Mass. 486 (1914).

There was no indication in the instant case at the time Spur and its predecessors located in western Maricopa County that a new city would spring up, full-blown, alongside the feeding operation and that the developer of that city would ask the court to order Spur to move because of the new city. Spur is required to move not because of any wrongdoing on the part of Spur, but because of a proper and legitimate regard of the courts for the rights and interests of the public.

Del Webb, on the other hand, is entitled to the relief prayed for (a permanent injunction), not because Webb is blameless, but because of the damage to the people who have been encouraged to purchase homes in Sun City. It does not equitably or legally follow, however, that Webb, being entitled to the injunction, is then free of any liability to Spur if Webb has in fact been the cause of the damage Spur has sustained. It does not seem harsh to require a developer, who has taken advantage of the lesser land values in a rural area as well as the availability of large tracts of land on which to build and develop a new town or city in the area, to indemnify those who are forced to leave as a result.

Having brought people to the nuisance to the foreseeable detriment of Spur, Webb must indemnify Spur for a reasonable amount of the cost of moving or shutting down. It should be noted that this relief to Spur is limited to a case wherein a developer has, with foreseeability, brought into a previously agricultural or industrial area the population which makes necessary the granting of an injunction against a lawful business and for which the business has no adequate relief.

It is therefore the decision of this court that the matter be remanded to the trial court for a hearing upon the damages sustained by the defendant Spur as a reasonable and direct result of the granting of the permanent injunction. Since the result of the appeal may appear novel and both sides have obtained a measure of relief, it is ordered that each side will bear its own costs.

Affirmed in part, reversed in part, and remanded for further proceedings consistent with this opinion.

Exercise 7-7. *Spur* Revisited

1. The opinion quotes testimony, statutory language, and persuasive authority from other states. Consider the weight that the court puts on the different sources.
2. An appellate court is not the finder of fact, which is why the supreme court of Arizona remands the case to the trial court to determine the damages that will be sustained by Spur Industries. Recall that the court in *Page County Appliance* also remanded the case to the trial court for factual findings.
3. The court in *Spur Industries* says that Webb is not "blameless," but nonetheless grants a permanent injunction. If Webb has unclean hands, why does the court grant injunctive relief? Can Webb refuse to pay the damages?

Statutory Reforms: Right to Farm Laws and Public Nuisance

Nuisance is one of the earliest common law causes of action, dating back to medieval times. The Restatement Second of Torts provides an overview of the judge-made case law in the area of nuisance. Many states have codified their common law of nuisance through statutes. In both *Page County Appliance* and *Spur Industries*, the court was dealing with a statutory definition of nuisance. In *Page County*, the relevant statutory provision was the definition of private nuisance, whereas *Spur Industries* involved an alleged public nuisance. This section discusses some of these statutory developments and notes instances where the statutory provisions have diverged from the traditional common law rules.

In *Page County*, the court quotes a statutory provision that sets forth a traditional definition of nuisance and makes it clear that both injunctive relief and damages are available. Other state statutes have codified the rule regarding coming to the nuisance. These provisions codify the common law presumption against a claim brought by a plaintiff who came to the nuisance. As we saw in *Spur Industries*, however, courts are sometimes willing to enjoin a longstanding use even when the plaintiff came to the nuisance with full knowledge of the offending conduct. A rash of cases similar to *Spur Industries*, where residential developments encroached on traditionally rural communities, caused state legislatures to take notice. Today, all fifty states have enacted some form of "Right to Farm" legislation designed to protect prior agricultural uses from nuisance claims.

For example, if Webb Development had filed its claim against Spur Industries today, it would have had to overcome the Right to Farm Law enacted by the Arizona legislature. Ariz. Rev. Stat. §§3-111 to 3-112. The law provides that prior agricultural uses are presumed reasonable for purposes of nuisance law. However, nuisance can provide relief if the activity has "substantial adverse effect on the public health and safety." Take a look at the language of the statute. Do you think that Webb Development would have prevailed if the Right to Farm Law had been in place at the time?

§3-111. Definitions. In this chapter, unless the context otherwise requires:

1. "Agricultural operations" means all activities by the owner, lessee, agent, independent contractor and supplier conducted on any facility for the production of crops, livestock, poultry, livestock products or poultry products.

2. "Farmland" means land devoted primarily to the production for commercial purposes of livestock or agricultural commodities.

§3-112. Agricultural operations; nuisance liability

A. Agricultural operations conducted on farmland that are consistent with good agricultural practices and established prior to surrounding nonagricultural uses are presumed to be reasonable and do not constitute a nuisance unless the agricultural operation has a substantial adverse effect on the public health and safety.

B. Agricultural operations undertaken in conformity with federal, state and local laws and regulations are presumed to be good agricultural practice and not adversely affecting the public health and safety.

The terms and scope of the Right to Farm Laws vary from state to state. The case in this section, *Shore v. Maple Lane Farms*, requires the court to interpret the scope the "farm operations" that are protected under the Tennessee Right to Farm law.

Another area where there has been significant statutory reform is in the area of public nuisance. As mentioned earlier, at common law, only government officials could seek to abate a public nuisance, and this remains largely true today. However, many of the traditional types of activities that were considered public nuisances are now prohibited by public health or safety codes and environmental regulations or are considered summary criminal offenses. For example, in Pennsylvania a public nuisance is a misdemeanor of the second degree. 18 Pa. Code § 6504. Although the statute fails to define what constitutes a "public nuisance," the courts have adopted the definition provided by the Restatement Second of Torts: "an unreasonable interference with a right common to the general public." Restatement (Second) Torts § 821B. It further provides that an activity unreasonably interferes with a public right if "the conduct involves a significant interference with the public health, the public safety, the public peace, the public comfort or the public convenience." *Restatement (Second) Torts* § 821B, comment (b).

Other states have enacted legislation that designates certain activities as a public nuisance per se. Iowa has a very detailed statute that defines a public nuisance to include: "The depositing or storing of flammable junk, such as old rags, rope, cordage, rubber, bones, and paper, by dealers in such articles within the fire limits of a city, unless in a building of fireproof construction[.]" Iowa Code § 657.2(9). In slightly more colorful language, the Iowa statute also includes: "[h]ouses of ill fame, kept for the purpose of prostitution and lewdness, gambling houses, places resorted to by persons participating in criminal gang activity ... or places resorted to by persons using controlled substances ... in violation of law, or houses where drunkenness, quarreling, fighting, or breaches of the peace are carried on or permitted to the disturbance of others." Iowa Code § 657.2(6).

The Restatement (Second) of Torts recognizes the right of private individuals to bring a public nuisance claim in certain circumstances. There are two different rules depending upon whether the relief requested is damages or an injunction.

> § 821C. Who Can Recover for Public Nuisance
>
> (1) In order to recover damages in an individual action for a public nuisance, one must have suffered harm of a kind different from that suffered by other members of the public exercising the right common to the general public that was the subject of interference.
>
> (2) In order to maintain a proceeding to enjoin to abate a public nuisance, one must
>
> (a) have the right to recover damages, as indicated in Subsection (1), or
>
> (b) have authority as a public official or public agency to represent the state or a political subdivision in the matter, or
>
> (c) have standing to sue as a representative of the general public, as a citizen in a citizen's action or as a member of a class in a class action.

Some states have enacted legislation authorizing private individuals to bring an action for abatement against a public nuisance. New York law provides that a private individual who either owns or leases property in the vicinity of "real property used or occupied in whole or in part as a bawdy-house, or house or place of assignation for lewd persons, or for purposes of prostitution, or for any illegal trade, business or manufacture" can sue individually to evict the tenants or occupants of the offending property. N.Y. R.P.A.P.L. 715. In *Kellner v. Cappellini*, a New York state court approved a summary procedure brought by neighbors to evict the residents of a notorious "crack den." *Kellner v. Cappellini*, 135 Misc. 2d 759 (N.Y. Misc. 1986). In *Kellner*, the pro se petitioners argued that the property was being used for drug sales and drug-related activity and the "illegal activities [had] attracted large numbers of drug buyers and users into their neighborhood and disrupted a once quiet block of brownstones and turned the area into a drug market." *Id.* at 760.

The public nuisance doctrine has empowered community members and public officials to bring actions to abate public nuisances where safety codes, environmental regulations, or the criminal law have proven ineffective. Because nuisance reaches lawful conduct, government officials have also used public nuisance claims as an innovative way to address larger social problems. State and local officials have brought public nuisance cases against the manufacturers of lead pigment for childhood lead poisoning and the manufacturers of firearms for gun violence. *See, e.g., State of Rhode Island v. Lead Industires Ass., Inc.*, 951 A.2d 428 (R.I. 2008); *City of Cincinnati v. Beretta U.S.A., Corp.*, 768 N.E.2d 1136, 1142 (Ohio 2002). California sued car manufacturers for contributing to global warming. *California People v. General Motors Corp.*, 2007 WL 2726871 (N.D. Cal. 2007). Most recently, cities hard hit by the Great Recession and the crash of the real estate market sued mortgage lenders to recoup the costs associated with the mass foreclosures. *City of Cleveland v. Deutsche Bank Trust Co.*, No. 2008 cv 00139 (N.D. Ohio Jan. 16, 2008).

Exercise 7-8. *Shore v. Maple Farms* — Right to Farm Laws

1. The following case calls for both a map and a timeline. As with the other nuisance cases we have seen, *Shore v. Maple Lane Farms, LLC* is very fact specific. Unlike the other cases, however, the viability of the plaintiff's case depends on the interpretation of a Right to Farm law.
2. As you read the case, pay attention to how the court interprets the statute. Do you recognize any of the statutory construction rules from Chapter 3?
3. The case involves the Tennessee Right to Farm Act that protects "farm operations" from nuisance suits by creating a rebuttable presumption that "farm operations" are not a nuisance. Applying the "plain meaning rule," what types of activities do you think of when you hear the term "farm operations"? Do you think the meaning of the term can change over time?

Shore v. Maple Lane Farms, LLC

411 S.W.3d 405 (Tenn. 2013)

William C. Koch, Jr., Judge. This appeal involves a dispute over the noise from amplified music concerts being conducted on farm land in rural Blount County. After the business owners who hosted the concerts defied the county zoning authority's order limiting the concerts to one per year, a neighboring property owner filed suit in the Chancery Court for Blount County seeking to abate the concerts as a common-law nuisance. The trial court granted the defendants' motion for an involuntary dismissal at the close of the plaintiff's proof, finding that the Tennessee Right to Farm Act, Tenn. Code Ann. §§ 43-26-101 to -104 (2007), precluded nuisance liability. The Court of Appeals affirmed. We granted the plaintiff homeowner permission to appeal. We hold that the trial court erred by granting the motion to dismiss because the plaintiff homeowner presented a prima facie case of common-law nuisance.

OPINION

I.

Beginning in the mid-1980s, Robert Schmidt and his family acquired approximately 225 acres of property on Maple Lane in the Greenback area of Blount County and began operating Maple Lane Farms. The farm raised cattle, corn, vegetables, strawberries, and pumpkins.

Over the years, however, Mr. Schmidt began to offer public attractions on the farm to increase revenue. Between 2006 and 2008, these attractions accounted for approximately 75% of the total revenue of Maple Lane Farms. Each spring, Maple Lane Farms hosted a Strawberry Jam Festival that offered activities, including strawberry picking, face painting, rock climbing, inflatables, and other games. Each fall, the farm presented a multi-week festival with attractions that included a corn maze, a pick-your-own pumpkin patch, hayrides, antique shows, and pageants. At some point, Mr. Schmidt began hosting amplified music concerts during the spring and fall festivals.

In May 2003, Velda J. Shore, a retiree from Middle Tennessee, moved to the Mountain Meadows subdivision adjacent to Maple Lane Farms. Ms. Shore, who was in her mid-seventies, believed that Nashville had become too crowded and wanted to find a home "with a little piece of land where I could work it and get out and grow something." Her one-half acre tract is on a bluff overlooking Maple Lane Farms, approximately 150 feet from the Maple Lane Farms boundary line. The back and side of her house are mostly windows that enable Ms. Shore to enjoy views of the mountains and the lake.

Before she purchased her property, Ms. Shore was informed that there was no commercial activity in the area. After she moved into her new home, Ms. Shore discovered that Maple Lane Farms operated a corn maze in the fall that was open to the public and that hayrides and a pick-your-own pumpkin patch were also available. She did not find these activities bothersome and, in fact, "enjoyed seeing the children and the tractor pulling the wagon around to get the pumpkins."

According to Ms. Shore, the spring and fall activities at Maple Lane Farms expanded significantly between 2006 and 2008. Mr. Schmidt began offering all-terrain vehicle demonstrations and helicopter rides that provided the passengers with an opportunity to see the corn maze from the air. The helicopters flew directly over Ms. Shore's house. In addition, Mr. Schmidt began presenting fireworks displays at night and hosting a number of open-air concerts featuring amplified music. These concerts occurred during the day and at night.

Ms. Shore became increasingly concerned about the noise from the concerts, as well as the congestion on the roads and the trash left by the persons who attended the events at Maple Lane Farms. She testified that she could hear the "boom, boom, boom, boom" of the music throughout her home. Ms. Shore also testified that she left her home during the daytime concerts to escape the noise. However, she could not escape the noise during the nighttime concerts because she could not drive at night. Ms. Shore testified that, because of the noise, she was forced to keep her windows and doors closed and remain inside during "the best time ... of the year to have your doors and windows open or to sit out on the deck or on the front porch."

On October 8, 2007, Ms. Shore sent a letter to the Blount County Commission regarding the activities at Maple Lane Farms. At the time, Mr. Schmidt's fall festival was in full swing. Ms. Shore compared her circumstances to "living close to another 'Dollywood,'" and described the loud music, the noise, and the helicopter flights. She wrote that she did not desire Maple Lane Farms to "close down their festivities." Rather, she asked for "reasonable accommodation, where each may enjoy the land where they have put their life savings."

II.

This appeal comes to us from the trial court's order granting Mr. Schmidt's motion for involuntary dismissal at the close of Ms. Shore's proof. The first issue is whether Ms. Shore presented a prima facie case of nuisance based on activities at Maple Lane Farms that are not otherwise exempted from nuisance claims by the Tennessee Right to Farm Act. Interpreting the scope of the Act involves an issue of law.

III.

We turn to Ms. Shore's common-law nuisance claim. Because of the procedural posture of this case, the resolution of this issue hinges more on the meaning and application of the Tennessee Right to Farm Act than on the strength of Ms. Shore's evidence.

A.

The right to the free use and enjoyment of property has long been recognized as an important facet of ownership. However, this right is not an unrestricted license to use property without regard for the impact of the use on others. The legal maxim—*sic utere tuo ut alienum non laeda*—directs landowners not to use their property in a way that injures the lawful rights of others. Thus, since the earliest days, Tennessee's courts have recognized that "[e]very individual, indeed, has a right to make the most profitable use of that which is his own, so that he does not injure others in the enjoyment of what is theirs." *Neal v. Henry*, 19 Tenn. (Meigs) 17 (1838). This longstanding principle is the cornerstone of a common-law nuisance claim.

A common-law nuisance is a tort characterized by interference with the use or enjoyment of the property of another. W. Page Keeton et al., *Prosser & Keeton on the Law of Torts* § 87, at 619 (5th ed. 1984). A nuisance is anything that annoys or disturbs the free use of one's property or that renders the property's ordinary use or physical occupation uncomfortable. It extends to everything that endangers life or health, gives offense to the senses, violates the laws of decency, or obstructs the reasonable and comfortable use of the property.

As long as an interference with the use or enjoyment of property is substantial and unreasonable enough to be offensive or inconvenient, virtually any disturbance of the use or enjoyment of the property may amount to a nuisance. However, an activity or use of property that constitutes a nuisance in one context may not constitute a nuisance in another context. Whether an activity or use of property amounts to an unreasonable invasion of another's legally protected interests depends on the circumstances of each case, such as the character of the surroundings, the nature, utility, and social value of the use, and the nature and extent of the harm involved.

Whether a particular activity or use of property is a nuisance is measured by its effect on a "normal person," not by its effect on the "hypersensitive." *Jenkins v. CSX Transp., Inc.*, 906 S.W.2d 460 (Tenn. Ct. App. 1995). Rather, the standard for determining whether a particular activity or use of property is a nuisance is "its effect upon persons of ordinary health and sensibilities, and ordinary modes of living, and not upon those who, on the one hand, are morbid or fastidious or peculiarly susceptible to the thing complained of, or, on the other hand, are unusually insensible thereto." *Id.* Thus, as Professors Prosser and Keeton have noted, "[i]f normal persons living in the area or community would regard the invasion in question as definitely offensive, seriously annoying, or intolerable, then the invasion is both significant and unreasonable."

With respect to noise in particular, no person is entitled to absolute quiet in the enjoyment of his or her property. Rather, a person may insist only upon the degree of quietness consistent with the locality in which he or she dwells or conducts business. Nevertheless, excessive noise may constitute a nuisance when it imposes discomfort beyond the reasonable limit dictated by surrounding conditions. While lawful and useful businesses should not be adversely affected based on "trifling and imaginary" annoyances that might "offend the taste or disturb the nerves of a fastidious or over refined person," the law does not countenance anyone being driven from their home or being compelled to live in discomfort.

Whether a particular level of noise constitutes a nuisance depends on a variety of circumstances. Among the relevant circumstances are the locality, the character of the neighborhood, the nature of the use causing the noise, the extent and frequency of the injury, the time of day when the noise occurs, and the effects on the enjoyment of life, health, and property of those affected by the noise.

The appropriate remedies for nuisance include damages and injunctive relief. Damages and injunctive relief are not mutually exclusive.

B.

Right-to-farm laws are a nationwide phenomenon. They took hold in the late 1970s in response to accelerating conversion of farmland to non-agricultural uses. These laws reflected that reversing the loss of productive farmland was high on the national policy agenda.

The concern over the loss of productive farmland triggered an array of different legislative solutions. One of these solutions was to encourage farmers to continue farming by offering them various forms of tax relief. At its core, the tax relief approach functions by assessing land used for farming at less than its fair market value. The Tennessee General Assembly provided this sort of tax relief to farmers when it enacted the Agricultural, Forest and Open Space Land Act of 1976.

Another solution addressed the perception that nuisance lawsuits were a contributing factor to the loss of farmland. The spread of non-agricultural uses of property, particularly residential developments, into formerly agricultural areas resulted in increased friction between farmers and their non-farmer neighbors. Nuisance complaints often followed, levied by individuals who built homes in rural areas and then objected to noises, odors, dust, chemical use, and slow-moving machinery associated with agricultural uses of the land. Right-to-farm laws became the most common legislative solution to this perceived problem.

In the beginning, these right-to-farm laws amounted to little more than a codification of the common-law concept of "coming to a nuisance." While they were not patterned after a uniform or model act, one of their central tenets was that "if an agricultural operation was not a nuisance prior to changed conditions (e.g., non-farm residential development) in the surrounding area, then it cannot become a public or private nuisance because of changing conditions." Thus, these laws reflected a legislative policy judgment that the traditional balancing of varying factors—the character of the surroundings, the nature, utility, and social value of the uses or activities, and the nature and extent of the harm involved—intrinsic to determining the existence of a nuisance should ordinarily be tipped toward agriculture in the case of conflicting uses of land.

C.

When it enacted the Agricultural, Forest and Open Space Land Act of 1976, the Tennessee General Assembly found that "[m]any prime agricultural and forest lands in Tennessee, valuable for producing food and fiber for a hungry world, are being permanently lost for any agricultural purposes and that these lands constitute important economic, physical, social, and esthetic assets to the surrounding lands and to the people of Tennessee." Tenn. Code Ann. § 67-5-1002(3). Six years later, based on this finding, the General Assembly enacted the Tennessee Right to Farm Act.

The Tennessee Right to Farm Act protects farms and farm operations from nuisance claims by creating a rebuttable presumption that they are not nuisances.

D.

A threshold question regarding Ms. Shore's nuisance claim—one seemingly overlooked by both the trial court and the Court of Appeals—is whether the Tennessee Right to Farm Act applies to the activity at issue in this case. The lower courts appear to have assumed that all the activities occurring at Maple Lane Farms would be covered by the Act as long as some threshold amount of agricultural activity was occurring somewhere on the farm. Working from this assumption, the lower courts turned their attention to deciding whether Ms. Shore had presented sufficient evidence—focused on generally accepted agricultural practices—to rebut the presumption in Tenn. Code Ann. § 43-26-103(a) that the amplified music concerts presented at Maple Lane Farms were not nuisances. The Tennessee Right to Farm Act does not bear out this approach.

The Tennessee Right to Farm Act does not extend nuisance protection to all activities occurring on a farm. Rather, the Act provides nuisance protection only to "the land, buildings, and machinery used in the commercial production of farm products and nursery stock" and to certain defined activities characterized as "farm operation[s]." Had the General Assembly intended to extend broader protection against nuisance suits to things other than the land, buildings, and machinery used in the commercial production of farm products or nursery stock or to activities other than "farm operations," it would have used broader language than what appears in Tenn. Code Ann. § 43-26-103(a). Although we have determined that the occurrence of some farming activity at Maple Lane Farms is not sufficient to shield all activities occurring at Maple Lane Farms from nuisance suits, our work is not complete. We must still determine whether the activity being complained of in this case—the amplified music concerts—qualifies as a "farm operation" for the purpose of the Tennessee Right to Farm Act.

Resolving this question requires us to interpret and apply the provisions of the Tennessee Right to Farm Act. Our role in construing a statute is to "ascertain and give effect to the legislative intent without unduly restricting or expanding a statute's coverage beyond its intended scope." To do so, we focus initially on the statute's words, giving these words their natural and ordinary meaning in light of their statutory context. We must avoid any "forced or subtle construction that would limit or extend the meaning of the language." Every word in a statute is presumed to have meaning and purpose, and the statute must be construed in its entirety.

If the statutory language is clear and unambiguous, we apply the statute's plain language in its normal and accepted use. However, when the statutory language is unclear, we may refer to a number of sources beyond the statutory text to aid our endeavor. We may consider, among other things, the broader statutory scheme, the history and purpose of the legislation, public policy, historical facts preceding or contemporaneous with the enactment of the statute, earlier versions of the statute, the caption of the act, and the legislative history of the statute.

E.

The Tennessee Right to Farm Act insulates farm operations from nuisance suits. As used in the Act, "farm operation" is a broad term intended to include all activities connected "with the commercial production of farm products or nursery stock." Tenn. Code Ann. § 43-26-102(2). The statutory definition includes specific examples of the sorts of activities covered by the Act, and among these activities is "noise." We need not resort to dictionaries to decide that "noise" emanates from the amplified music concerts presented at Maple Lane Farms. Accordingly, the Tennessee Right to Farm Act would apply to the noise generated by the concerts at Maple Lane Farms if these concerts are somehow connected "with the commercial production of farm products or nursery stock."

Both the trial court and the Court of Appeals, considering the essentially undisputed evidence in the record, characterized the concerts at Maple Lane Farms as "marketing." The trial court observed that the concerts were "a right clever marketing operation." The Court of Appeals viewed the concerts as "a marketing and promotion effort to further the income of the farming operation and to put the farm in the minds of the public." We agree with this characterization. Thus, the question becomes whether marketing activities are part of the "commercial production of farm products or nursery stock."

We find it significant that the General Assembly chose to use the word "production" alone in its definition of "farm operation." It did not include "marketing," as other states have done in similar contexts. Marketing activities are not mentioned elsewhere in the Tennessee Right to Farm Act, and we have found no reference to marketing in the legislative history of the Act or any of its amendments. Based on the text and the legislative history of the Tennessee Right to Farm Act, no conclusion can be reached other than that, when it enacted the Act, the General Assembly was focused on the activities related to the production of farm products—that is to say, growing or raising these products. The General Assembly was not focused on the marketing of farm products for sale.

Despite the absence of a specific mention of "marketing" in the Tennessee Right to Farm Act, marketing activities, such as the concerts at issue in this case, could be covered by the Act if they occur "in connection with" producing (growing or raising) the farm products produced at Maple Lane Farms, such as cattle, corn, vegetables, strawberries, and pumpkins. The language of the Act provides precious little guidance with regard to the type of "connection" the General Assembly envisioned.

Noise that at first blush may not appear to be connected with the production of farm products could turn out to be just that under careful analysis. For example, "a dog next door which makes night hideous with his howls" would ordinarily be considered to be a quintessential nuisance because it interferes with the right to the undisturbed enjoyment of the premises. However, the same howls by a dog guarding livestock might be protected from nuisance liability precisely because they are connected with raising the livestock. *See Hood River Cnty. v. Mazzara*, 193 Ore. App. 272 (Or. Ct. App. 2004) (finding the barking of a dog to be a legitimate farming practice rather than a nuisance because the dog was engaged in guarding livestock). Accordingly, we will resort to the legislative history of the Tennessee Right to Farm Act to ascertain whether the General Assembly envisioned that marketing activities were somehow "connected with" the production of farm products.

Three years before it enacted the Tennessee Right to Farm Act, the General Assembly enacted statutes intended to shield feedlots, dairy farms, and egg production houses from nuisance claims. Subject to certain requirements and conditions, these statutes provided feedlots, dairy farms, and egg production houses with an "absolute defense" against nuisance suits. *See* Tenn. Code Ann. §44-18-102(a).

As originally introduced, the Tennessee Right to Farm Act contained a similar provision providing an "absolute defense" to nuisance suits for farms and farm operations. Several members of the General Assembly balked at creating an absolute defense to nuisance suits for farms and farm operations. Members expressed concern about allowing farmers to assert this defense after they changed their farming activities, for example, from raising crops to raising swine. To address these concerns, the sponsors agreed to amend the bill to create a rebuttable presumption instead of an absolute defense. This amendment enabled the sponsors to garner enough votes to enact the Tennessee Right to Farm Act.

A limited discussion of nuisances caused by noise occurred in the Senate during the debate regarding the extent to which changes in farm operations should be permitted. Senator Tommy Burks, the bill's primary Senate sponsor, explained that one purpose of the legislation was to provide nuisance protection for a change in farming practice that generated noise that a neighbor might find disturbing. There was no discussion regarding noise generated by any activities other than farming.

As a general matter, we decline to broadly construe statutes that are in derogation of the common law. The common law may not be altered by statute any further than the statute declares or necessarily requires. Therefore, without some clear indication to the contrary, we will not presume that the General Assembly intended to change the common law by implication.

Despite our diligent search, we have found nothing that suggests the General Assembly considered noise from amplified music concerts held on a farm to necessarily have a connection with producing farm products. Nor have we found any basis to conclude that the General Assembly considered music concerts to be some sort of farm operation. The plain language of the Tennessee Right to Farm Act reflects a close connection between producing farm products and the conditions or activities shielded by the Act. Accordingly, we decline to give the same broad interpretation to the Tennessee Right to Farm Act that was given by the courts below.

The essentially unrebutted evidence of Ms. Shore's case-in-chief provides a factual basis for finding that the music concerts at issue bore no relation to the production of cattle, corn, vegetables, strawberries, or pumpkins at Maple Lane Farms. Frank Leuthold, a retired professor from the University of Tennessee College of Agriculture, testified that the concerts hosted by Maple Lane Farms had nothing to do with producing its farm products. The trial court made no specific findings in this regard. As such, we review the record to determine where the preponderance of the evidence lies. Simply put, Professor Leuthold's testimony is entirely consistent with our interpretation of the Tennessee Right to Farm Act, and we find no proof in the record that preponderates against his testimony. Accordingly, we conclude that the record reflects that the rebuttable presumption in Tenn. Code Ann. § 43-26-103(a) does not apply to the amplified music concerts held at Maple Lane Farms.

F.

Having determined that, based on the record in this case, the Tennessee Right to Farm Act does not apply to the music concerts held at Maple Lane Farms, we return to the question of whether Ms. Shore presented a prima facie case of nuisance sufficient to survive a motion for involuntary dismissal. We have determined that Ms. Shore's nuisance claim should not have been dismissed at the close of her proof.

Ms. Shore testified that concerts being held at Maple Lane Farms disrupted her use and enjoyment of her property. With regard to 2008, Ms. Shore identified two days in the spring associated with the Strawberry Jam Festival and three weekends in the fall. With regard to 2009, she identified three concerts, although she did state that the music was not as loud in 2009 as it had been in earlier years. With regard to 2010, Ms. Shore identified the concerts offered in conjunction with the Strawberry Jam Festival. She testified that the concerts had an adverse effect on her health, including a quickened pulse, headaches, and nausea. She also offered medical testimony from her primary care physician that the events at Maple Lane Farms significantly increased her stress level and anxiety, caused problems with her sleeping, and made life more difficult for her overall. In addition, Ms. Shore stated her belief that the activities had decreased the value of her property.

In addition to her own testimony, Ms. Shore presented the testimony of three other neighbors of Maple Lane Farms. Mr. Hartman testified that the concerts were so loud that he could not hear the television or have a telephone conversation, even when his home was completely shut. He also testified that he escaped the noise by leaving his home during the concerts. Like Mr. Hartman, Mr. Johnson stated that the concerts were so loud that he could not hear his television, even when in his basement, and that the noise prevented him from falling asleep. Also like Mr. Hartman, Mr. Johnson testified that he would often leave his home during the concerts. Finally, Ms. Hayden testified that the concerts bothered her and were so loud that she could feel vibrations in her chest. She also stated that the concerts interfered with her ability to read in her own home.

In the context of this case, nuisance liability attaches to conduct that is a legal cause of an invasion of another's interest in the use and enjoyment of land, where the invasion is substantial and unreasonable. In our view, Ms. Shore presented prima facie evidence of nuisance. Mr. Schmidt made a conscious decision to hold multiple concerts even after the Board's decision. The noise from these concerts invaded the interests of his neighbors, including Ms. Shore, in the use and enjoyment of their property. Ms. Shore was forced out of her home during daytime concerts, and she was a hostage to the noise at night. While Mr. Schmidt takes issue with Ms. Shore's failure to present testimony from others living in her particular subdivision, we do not believe such proof was required. Certainly Mr. Schmidt can put forward such proof if he believes it will be helpful to his case. Considering all the evidence currently in the record, we find that Ms. Shore presented a prima facie case of nuisance.

V.

We reverse the judgments of the trial court and the Court of Appeals involuntarily dismissing Ms. Shore's complaint and remand the case for further proceedings consistent with this opinion.

Exercise 7-9. *Shore v. Maple Farms* Revisited

1. The Tennessee Supreme Court holds that the existence of some farming operations will not shield all the activities on the property. In making that determination, the court considers: "the broader statutory scheme, the history and purpose of the legislation, public policy, historical facts preceding or contemporaneous with the enactment of the statute, earlier versions of the statute, the caption of the act, and the legislative history of the statute."
2. Why did the legislature decide not to provide an absolute defense as it did in the case of feedlots and other specific agricultural activities?
3. In March 2014, the Tennessee General Assembly amended the definition of agriculture in state law to include "entertainment activities conducted in conjunction with, but secondary to, commercial production of farm products and nursery stock, when such activities occur on land used for the commercial production of farm products and nursery stock."

Utility and Harm in a Contemporary Context: Alternative Energy

Many of the classic examples of nuisance involve industrial or agricultural uses that neighbors have considered noxious, such as copper smelting, animal rendering, oil refining, pig farming, and cement plants. Today, these activities are regulated by health and safety codes and environmental regulations, which means that aggrieved property owners can appeal to government officials for relief without resorting to potentially costly litigation. Common law nuisance remains available should the regulatory system fail to provide relief.

As new industries and commercial practices develop, however, regulation often lags behind. An individual whose quiet enjoyment is harmed by the lawful conduct of his neighbor may have no choice but to resort to a common claim of nuisance. Take for example, the popularity of drones. If your neighbor is a drone enthusiast who is constantly flying her drones through your back yard, do you have a claim for nuisance or trespass or both? What if your neighbor's drone does not cross your property line, but still makes an incessant noise and photographs you and your family without permission? In the absence of statutory or regulatory authority, the dispute will be resolved through a claim of common law nuisance.

Nuisance may be particularly well suited to resolve contemporary claims involving new industries and technologies because it takes into account the social utility of the conduct when balancing the competing interests. Indeed, its incorporation of contemporary values may be one of the reasons that common law nuisance has remained such an important part of Anglo-American property law through the centuries. The doctrine that once resolved encroachments on the royal domain has retained its vitality and today may be used to mediate disputes over your neighbor's pack of drones or that giant wind turbine in her front yard. Restatement (Second) of Torts provides that the "social value that the law attaches to the primary purpose of the conduct" is one of three factors to be considered when measuring the utility of the conduct. *Restatement (Second) of Torts* § 828(a). The other two factors are: the suitability of the conduct to the character of the locality, and the impracticability of preventing or avoiding the invasion. *Id.*

As you will see from the following cases, the flexibility of the nuisance doctrine is sometimes limited by is its common law character. Because nuisance is a common law tort, the law of nuisance has developed through case law and is subject to stare decisis. Controlling precedent adds a historical dimension to nuisance law that runs counter to its otherwise contemporary orientation. For example, how can a court adequately measure the gravity of harm caused by blocking solar panels when binding precedent provides that obstruction of light and air does not interfere with quiet enjoyment? The courts in the following cases are presented with novel situations and narrow precedent. As you read the cases in this section, consider how well the courts balance not only the competing interests of the parties, but also the competing institutional roles of the judiciary and the legislature.

Exercise 7-10. *Fountainbleau Hotel Corp. v. Forty-Five Twenty-Five, Inc.* — Rights to "Light and Air"

The next case takes us to Miami Beach at a time of great development and promise. It involves a dispute between two iconic hotels—The Fountainbleau and the Eden Roc. A map is essential to understanding the dispute and the interests at stake. It is also helpful to be aware of some historical context. In the 1950s, we did not understand the detrimental effects of prolonged exposure to the sun. People would lie out in the sun to get a tan while on vacation. Coming back from a Florida vacation with a tan was a status symbol, especially in the winter.

As you read the case, pay particular attention to the alleged harm to the Eden Roc. How would you quantify the alleged harm?

Fontainebleau Hotel Corp. v. Forty-Five Twenty-Five, Inc.

114 So. 2d 357 (Fla. App. 1959)

Per Curiam. This is an interlocutory appeal from an order temporarily enjoining the appellants from continuing with the construction of a fourteen-story addition to the Fontainebleau Hotel, owned and operated by the appellants. Appellee, plaintiff below, owns the Eden Roc Hotel, which was constructed in 1955, about a year after the Fontainebleau, and adjoins the Fontainebleau on the north. Both are luxury hotels, facing the Atlantic Ocean. The proposed addition to the Fontainebleau is being constructed twenty feet from its north property line, 130 feet from the mean high water mark of the Atlantic Ocean, and 76 feet 8 inches from the ocean bulkhead line. The 14-story tower will extend 160 feet above grade in height and is 416 feet long from east to west. During the winter months, from around two o'clock in the afternoon for the remainder of the day, the shadow of the addition will extend over the cabana, swimming pool, and sunbathing areas of the Eden Roc, which are located in the southern portion of its property.

In this action, plaintiff-appellee sought to enjoin the defendants-appellants from proceeding with the construction of the addition to the Fontainebleau (it appears to have been roughly eight stories high at the time suit was filed), alleging that the construction would interfere with the light and air on the beach in front of the Eden Roc and cast a shadow of such size as to render the beach wholly unfitted for the use and enjoyment of its guests, to the irreparable injury of the plaintiff; further, that the construction of such addition on the north side of defendants' property, rather than the south side, was actuated by malice and ill will on the part of the defendants' president toward the plaintiff's president; and that the construction was in violation of a building ordinance requiring a 100-foot setback from the ocean.

The chancellor heard considerable testimony on the issues made by the complaint and the answer and, as noted, entered a temporary injunction restraining the defendants from continuing with the construction of the addition. His reason for so doing was stated by him, in a memorandum opinion, as follows:

> In granting the temporary injunction in this case the Court wishes to make several things very clear. The ruling is not based on any alleged presumptive title nor prescriptive right of the plaintiff to light and air nor is it based on any deed restrictions nor recorded plats in the title of the plaintiff nor of the defendant nor of any plat of record. It is not based on any zoning ordinance nor on any provision of the building code of the City of Miami Beach nor on the decision of any court, nisi prius or appellate. It is based solely on the proposition that no one has a right to use his property to the injury of another. In this case it is clear from the evidence that the proposed use by the Fontainebleau will materially damage the Eden Roc. There is evidence indicating that the construction of the proposed annex by the Fontainebleau is malicious or deliberate for the purpose of injuring the

> Eden Roc, but it is scarcely sufficient, standing alone, to afford a basis for equitable relief.

This is indeed a novel application of the maxim *sic utere tuo ut alienum non laedas.* This maxim does not mean that one must never use his own property in such a way as to do any injury to his neighbor. It means only that one must use his property so as not to injure the lawful *rights* of another. In *Reaver v. Martin Theatres*, 52 So.2d 682 (Fla. 1951), under this maxim, it was stated that "it is well settled that a property owner may put his own property to any reasonable and lawful use, so long as he does not thereby deprive the adjoining landowner of any right of enjoyment of his property *which is recognized and protected by law, and so long as his use is not such a one as the law will pronounce a nuisance.*" [Emphasis supplied.]

No American decision has been cited, and independent research has revealed none, in which it has been held that—in the absence of some contractual or statutory obligation—a landowner has a legal right to the free flow of light and air across the adjoining land of his neighbor.

There being, then, no legal right to the free flow of light and air from the adjoining land, it is universally held that where a structure serves a useful and beneficial purpose, it does not give rise to a cause of action, either for damages or for an injunction under the maxim *sic utere tuo ut alienum non laedas,* even though it causes injury to another by cutting off the light and air and interfering with the view that would otherwise be available over adjoining land in its natural state, regardless of the fact that the structure may have been erected partly for spite.

We see no reason for departing from this universal rule. If, as contended on behalf of plaintiff, public policy demands that a landowner in the Miami Beach area refrain from constructing buildings on his premises that will cast a shadow on the adjoining premises, an amendment of its comprehensive planning and zoning ordinance, applicable to the public as a whole, is the means by which such purpose should be achieved. But to change the universal rule—and the custom followed in this state since its inception—that adjoining landowners have an equal right under the law to build to the line of their respective tracts and to such a height as is desired by them (in in absence, of course, of building restrictions or regulations) amounts, in our opinion, to judicial legislation. So use your own as not to injure another's property is, indeed, a sound and salutary principle for the promotion of justice, but it may not and should not be applied so as gratuitously to confer upon an adjacent property owner incorporeal rights incidental to his ownership of land which the law does not sanction.

Since it affirmatively appears that the plaintiff has not established a cause of action against the defendants by reason of the structure here in question, the order granting a temporary injunction should be and it is hereby reversed with directions to dismiss the complaint.

Reversed with directions.

Exercise 7-11. *Fountainbleau Hotel Corp.* Revisited

1. Nuisance actions require courts to balance the gravity of the harm with the utility of the conduct. Here, the court seemed to assign a trivial value to "light and air." Did it fail to take into account the specific context of the dispute? Who wants to go to a Miami Beach hotel that has a shady beach? The value of "light and air" to a Miami Beach hotel is very high. Rather than considering the contemporary value of "light and air" to the plaintiff, the court relied on past precedent and refused to diverge from the accepted rule for fear of engaging in "judicial legislation."
2. Did the court miss the competitive benefit enjoyed by Fountainbleu if the Eden Roc beach is rendered unusable? What is more valuable to the City of Miami: more hotel rooms or beaches without shade?
3. The court explains that structures erected partly for spite still have utility. Such mixed motive structures should be distinguished from "spite fences" that are generally held to have no utility because they were built solely for spite and no one has the right to use her property to harm another. Spite fences are structures that serve no useful purpose of the owner and are really designed simply to block a neighbor's view. Accordingly, spite fences will generally be enjoyed because they are considered to have zero utility.

Exercise 7-12. *Prah v. Maretti*—Solar Energy

1. In *Fountainbleu,* the court did not agree that access to "light and air" was part of the plaintiff's right to quiet enjoyment even though it was arguably an essential component of its commercial enterprise. In the next case, the plaintiff needs access to "light and air" for a different, but no less essential reason—solar power. As you read the case, consider how both the majority and the dissent characterize the gravity of the harm.
2. The majority and dissenting opinions express different views of the institutional role of the judiciary. It should remind you of the debate between Judge Thompkins and Judge Livingston in *Pierson v. Post.* One big difference is that here the judicial activist pens the majority opinion. Which judge most closely reflects your views regarding the role of the judiciary?

Prah v. Maretti

108 Wis. 2d 223 (1982)

Abrahamson, J. This appeal from a judgment of the circuit court for Waukesha county, Max Raskin, circuit judge, was certified to this court by the court of appeals, sec. (Rule) 809.61, Stats. 1979-80, as presenting an issue of first impression, namely, whether an owner of a solar-heated residence states a claim upon which relief can be granted when he asserts that his neighbor's proposed construction of a residence (which conforms to existing deed restrictions and local ordinances) interferes with his access to an unobstructed path for sunlight across the neighbor's property. This case thus involves a conflict between one landowner (Glenn Prah, the plaintiff) interested in unobstructed access to sun-light across adjoining property as a natural source of energy and an adjoining landowner (Richard D. Maretti, the defendant) interested in the development of his land.

The circuit court concluded that the plaintiff presented no claim upon which relief could be granted and granted summary judgment for the defendant. We reverse the judgment of the circuit court and remand the cause to the circuit court for further proceedings.

I.

According to the complaint, the plaintiff is the owner of a residence which was constructed during the years 1978-1979. The complaint alleges that the residence has a solar system which includes collectors on the roof to supply energy for heat and hot water and that after the plaintiff built his solar-heated house, the defendant purchased the lot adjacent to and immediately to the south of the plaintiff's lot and commenced planning construction of a home. The complaint further states that when the plaintiff learned of defendant's plans to build the house he advised the defendant that if the house were built at the proposed location, defendant's house would substantially and adversely affect the integrity of plaintiff's solar system and could cause plaintiff other damage. Nevertheless, the defendant began construction. The complaint further alleges that the plaintiff is entitled to "unrestricted use of the sun and its solar power" and demands judgment for injunctive relief and damages.

The record made on the motion reveals the following additional facts: Plaintiff's home

was the first residence built in the subdivision, and although plaintiff did not build his house in the center of the lot it was built in accordance with applicable restrictions. Plaintiff advised defendant that if the defendant's home were built at the proposed site it would cause a shadowing effect on the solar collectors which would reduce the efficiency of the system and possibly damage the system. To avoid these adverse effects, plaintiff requested defendant to locate his home an additional several feet away from the plaintiff's lot line, the exact number being disputed. Plaintiff and defendant failed to reach an agreement on the location of defendant's home before defendant started construction.

The circuit court denied plaintiff's motion for injunctive relief, declared it would entertain a motion for summary judgment and thereafter entered judgment in favor of the defendant.

III.

In testing the sufficiency of the complaint the facts pleaded by the plaintiff, and all reasonable inferences therefrom, are accepted as true. The pleadings are to be liberally construed with a view to substantial justice to the parties and the complaint should be dismissed as legally insufficient only if "it is quite clear that under no circumstances can the plaintiff recover."

As to the claim of private nuisance the circuit court concluded that the law of private nuisance requires the court to make "a comparative evaluation of the conflicting interests and to weigh the gravity of the harm to the plaintiff against the utility of the defendant's conduct." The circuit court concluded: "A comparative evaluation of the conflicting interests, keeping in mind the omissions and commissions of both Prah and Maretti, indicates that defendant's conduct does not cause the gravity of the harm which the plaintiff himself may well have avoided by proper planning." The circuit court also concluded that sec. 844.01 does not apply to a home constructed in accordance with deed and municipal ordinance requirements. Further, the circuit court rejected the prior appropriation doctrine as "an intrusion of judicial egoism over legislative passivity."

We consider first whether the complaint states a claim for relief based on common law private nuisance. This state has long recognized that an owner of land does not have an absolute or unlimited right to use the land in a way which injures the rights of others. The rights of neighboring landowners are relative; the uses by one must not unreasonably impair the uses or enjoyment of the other. When one landowner's use of his or her property unreasonably interferes with another's enjoyment of his or her property, that use is said to be a private nuisance.

The private nuisance doctrine has traditionally been employed in this state to balance the conflicting rights of landowners, and this court has recently adopted the analysis of private nuisance set forth in the Restatement (Second) of Torts. The Restatement defines private nuisance as "a nontrespassory invasion of another's interest in the private use and enjoyment of land." Restatement (Second) of Torts Sec. 821D (1977). The phrase "interest in the private use and enjoyment of land" as used in sec. 821D is broadly defined to include any disturbance of the enjoyment of property.

Although the defendant's obstruction of the plaintiff's access to sunlight appears to fall within the Restatement's broad concept of a private nuisance as a nontrespassory invasion of another's interest in the private use and enjoyment of land, the defendant asserts that he has a right to develop his property in compliance with statutes, ordinances and private covenants without regard to the effect of such development upon the plaintiff's access to sunlight. In essence, the defendant is asking this court to hold that the private nuisance doctrine is not applicable in the instant case and that his right to develop his land is a right which is per se superior to his neighbor's interest in access to sunlight. This position is expressed in the maxim "cujus est solum, ejus est usque ad coelum et ad infernos," that is, the owner of land owns up to the sky and down to the center of the earth. The rights of the surface owner are, however, not unlimited.

The defendant is not completely correct in asserting that the common law did not protect a landowner's access to sunlight across adjoining property. At English common law a landowner could acquire a right to receive sunlight across adjoining land by both express agreement and under the judge-made doctrine of "ancient lights." Under the doctrine of ancient lights if the landowner had received sunlight across adjoining property for a specified period of time, the landowner was entitled to continue to receive unobstructed access to sunlight across the adjoining property. Under the doctrine the landowner acquired a negative prescriptive easement and could prevent the adjoining landowner from obstructing access to light.

Although American courts have not been as receptive to protecting a landowner's access to sunlight as the English courts, American courts have afforded some protection to a landowner's interest in access to sunlight. American courts honor express easements to sunlight. American courts initially enforced the English common law doctrine of ancient lights, but later every state which considered the doctrine repudiated it as inconsistent with the needs of a developing country. Indeed, for just that reason this court concluded that an easement to light and air over adjacent property could not be created or acquired by prescription and has been unwilling to recognize such an easement by implication.

Many jurisdictions in this country have protected a landowner from malicious obstruction of access to light (the spite fence cases) under the common law private nuisance doctrine. If an activity is motivated by malice it lacks utility and the harm it causes others outweighs any social values. Thus a landowner's interest in sunlight has been protected in this country by common law private nuisance law at least in the narrow context of the modern American rule invalidating spite fences.

This court's reluctance in the nineteenth and early part of the twentieth century to provide broader protection for a landowner's access to sunlight was premised on three policy considerations. First, the right of landowners to use their property as they wished, as long as they did not cause physical damage to a neighbor, was jealously guarded.

Second, sunlight was valued only for aesthetic enjoyment or as illumination. Since artificial light could be used for illumination, loss of sunlight was at most a personal annoyance which was given little, if any, weight by society.

Third, society had a significant interest in not restricting or impeding land development. This court repeatedly emphasized that in the growth period of the nineteenth and early twentieth centuries change is to be expected and is essential to property and that recognition of a right to sunlight would hinder property development. The court expressed this concept as follows:

> As the city grows, large grounds appurtenant to residences must be cut up to supply more residences.... The cistern, the outhouse, the cesspool, and the private drain must disappear in deference to the public waterworks and sewer; the terrace and the garden, to the need for more complete occupancy....

> Strict limitation [on the recognition of easements of light and air over adjacent premises is] in accord with the popular conception upon which real estate has been and is daily being conveyed in Wisconsin and to be essential to easy and rapid development at least of our municipalities.

Considering these three policies, this court concluded that in the absence of an express agreement granting access to sunlight, a landowner's obstruction of another's access to sunlight was not actionable. These three policies are no longer fully accepted or applicable. They reflect factual circumstances and social priorities that are now obsolete.

First, society has increasingly regulated the use of land by the landowner for the general welfare. *Euclid v. Ambler Realty Co.*, 272 U.S. 365 (1926).

Second, access to sunlight has taken on a new significance in recent years. In this case the plaintiff seeks to protect access to sunlight, not for aesthetic reasons or as a source of illumination but as a source of energy. Access to sunlight as an energy source is of significance both to the landowner who invests in solar collectors and to a society which has an interest in developing alternative sources of energy. The federal government has also recognized the importance of solar energy and currently encourages its utilization by means of tax benefits, direct subsidies and government loans for solar projects.

Third, the policy of favoring unhindered private development in an expanding economy is no longer in harmony with the realities of our society. The need for easy and rapid development is not as great today as it once was, while our perception of the value of sunlight as a source of energy has increased significantly.

Courts should not implement obsolete policies that have lost their vigor over the course of the years. The law of private nuisance is better suited to resolve landowners' disputes about property development in the 1980's than is a rigid rule which does not recognize a landowner's interest in access to sunlight. As we said in *Ballstadt v. Pagel*, 202 Wis. 484 (1930), "What is regarded in law as constituting a nuisance in modern times would no doubt have been tolerated without question in former times."

In *Bielski v. Schulze*, 16 Wis. 2d 1 (1962), this court said: "Inherent in the common law is a dynamic principle which allows it to grow and to tailor itself to meet changing needs within the doctrine of stare decisis, which, if correctly understood, was not static and did not forever prevent the courts from reversing themselves or from applying principles of common law to new situations as the need arose. If this were not so, we must succumb to a rule that a judge should let others 'long dead and unaware of the problems of the age in which he lives, do his thinking for him.'"

"The genius of the common law is its ability to adapt itself to the changing needs of society." *Moran v. Quality Aluminum Casting Co.*, 34 Wis. 2d 542 (1967).

Yet the defendant would have us ignore the flexible private nuisance law as a means of resolving the dispute between the landowners in this case and would have us adopt an approach of favoring the unrestricted development of land and of applying a rigid and inflexible rule protecting his right to build on his land and disregarding any interest of the plaintiff in the use and enjoyment of his land. This we refuse to do.

We therefore hold that private nuisance law, that is, the reasonable use doctrine as set forth in the Restatement, is applicable to the instant case. Recognition of a nuisance claim for unreasonable obstruction of access to sunlight will not prevent land development or unduly hinder the use of adjoining land. It will promote the reasonable use and enjoyment of land in a manner suitable to the 1980's. That obstruction of access to light might be found to constitute a nuisance in certain circumstances does not mean that it will be or must be found to constitute a nuisance under all circumstances. The result in each case depends on whether the conduct complained of is unreasonable.

Accordingly we hold that the plaintiff in this case has stated a claim under which relief can be granted. Nonetheless we do not determine whether the plaintiff in this case is entitled to relief. In order to be entitled to relief the plain-tiff must prove the elements required to establish actionable nuisance, and the conduct of the defendant herein must be judged by the reasonable use doctrine.

Because the plaintiff has stated a claim of common law private nuisance upon which relief can be granted, the judgment of the circuit court must be reversed. We reverse the judgment of the circuit court dismissing the complaint and remand the matter to circuit court for further proceedings not inconsistent with this opinion.

CALLOW, J. DISSENTING. The majority has adopted the Restatement's reasonable use doctrine to grant an owner of a solar heated home a cause of action against his neighbor who, in acting entirely within the applicable ordinances and statutes, seeks to design and build his home in such a location that it may, at various times during the day, shade the plaintiff's solar collector, thereby impeding the efficiency of his heating system during several months of the year. Because I believe the facts of this case clearly reveal that a cause of action for private nuisance will not lie, I dissent.

The majority then concludes that this court's past reluctance to extend protection to a landowner's access to sunlight beyond the spite fence cases is based on obsolete policies which have lost their vigor over the course of the years. The three obsolete policies cited by the majority are: (1) Right of landowners to use their property as they desire as long as no physical damage is done to a neighbor; (2) In the past, sunlight was valued only for aesthetic value, not a source of energy; and (3) Society has a significant interest in not impeding land development. The majority has failed to convince me that these policies are obsolete.

It is a fundamental principle of law that a "landowner owns at least as much of the space above the ground as he can occupy or use in connection with the land." *United States v. Causby*, 328 U.S. 256 (1946). I firmly believe that a landowner's right to use his property within the limits of ordinances, statutes, and restrictions of record where such use is necessary to serve his legitimate needs is a fundamental precept of a free society which this court should strive to uphold.

The majority cites two zoning cases to support the conclusion that society has increasingly regulated private land use in the name of public welfare. The cases involving the use of police power and eminent domain are clearly distinguishable from the present situation as they relate to interference with a private right solely for the public health, safety, morals, or welfare. In the instant case, we are dealing with an action which seeks to restrict the defendant's private right to use his property, notwithstanding a complete lack of notice of restriction to the defendant and the defendant's compliance with applicable ordinances and statutes. The plaintiff who knew of the potential problem before the defendant acquired the land seeks to impose such use restriction to accommodate his personal, private benefit—a benefit which could have been accommodated by the plaintiff locating his home in a different place on his property or by acquiring the land in question when it was for sale prior to its acquisition by the defendant.

I know of no cases repudiating policies favoring the right of a landowner to use his property as he lawfully desires or which declare such policies are "no longer fully accepted or applicable" in this context. The right of a property owner to lawful enjoyment of his property should be vigorously protected, particularly in those cases where the adjacent property owner could have insulated himself from the alleged problem by acquiring the land as a defense to the potential problem or by provident use of his own property.

The majority concludes that sunlight has not heretofore been accorded the status of a source of energy, and consequently it has taken on a new significance in recent years. Solar energy for home heating is at this time sparingly used and of questionable economic value because solar collectors are not mass produced, and consequently, they are very costly. Their limited efficiency may explain the lack of production.

Regarding the third policy the majority apparently believes is obsolete (that society has a significant interest in not restricting land development), I concede the law may be tending to recognize the value of aesthetics over increased volume development and that an individual may not use his land in such a way as to harm the public. The instant case, however, deals with a private benefit. While the majority's policy arguments may be directed to a cause of action for public nuisance, we are presented with a private nuisance case which I believe is distinguishable in this regard.

I would submit that any policy decisions in this area are best left for the legislature. I would concur with these observations of the trial judge: "While temptation lingers for the court to declare by judicial fiat what is right and what should be done, under the facts in this case, such action under our form of constitutional government where the three branches each have their defined jurisdiction and power, would be an intrusion of judicial egoism over legislative passivity."

I conclude that plaintiff's solar heating system is an unusually sensitive use. In other words, the defendant's proposed construction of his home, under ordinary circumstances, would not interfere with the use and enjoyment of the usual person's property. "The plaintiff cannot, by devoting his own land to an unusually sensitive use, such as a drive-in motion picture theater easily affected by light, make a nuisance out of conduct of the adjoining defendant which would otherwise be harmless."

Because I do not believe that the facts of the present case give rise to a cause of action for private nuisance, I dissent.

Exercise 7-13. *Prah* Revisited

1. The plaintiff built the first house in the subdivision. The plaintiff told the defendant that where he chose to build his house could interfere with the plaintiff's access to sunlight. Nuisance traditionally measures the social utility of the offending conduct, but what about the social utility of the quiet enjoyment? Here, the plaintiff wants unobstructed access to light and air in order to power his solar energy system. How should the court take that into account? Do you think that it is significant that the defendant had notice that his conduct could harm his neighbor? If you had represented the plaintiff, where would you have advised him to situate his house on the lot given the state of the law when he built the house?
2. Why is the English common law doctrine of "ancient lights" inconsistent with the needs of a developing nation?
3. In the United States, neighbors can enter into an express agreement that preserves the right to a view. As you will see in Chapter 10, an easement for light and air is an exception to the rule that negative easements are not recognized. An easement for light and air is not available through prescription on the grounds that a landowner would not have notice that there were negative easements on the property because a negative easement involves the right to stop your neighbor from doing something. In other words, if your neighbor is not doing something, how can he be on notice that he is not permitted to do what he is not doing?
4. Do you agree that "Courts should not implement obsolete policies that have lost their vigor over the course of the years"? Or should change in the law of a certain magnitude be left to the legislature?
5. The dissent concludes that plaintiff's solar power system is an unusually sensitive use. Could the same have been said of Eden Roc's beach?
6. The majority identifies three reasons for refusing to follow the traditional rule that a landowner has no right to light and air. Identify each reason and evaluate how well the dissent rebuts the majority's rationale.

Exercise 7-14. *Sowers v. Forest Hills Subdivision* — Wind Turbines

1. *Prah v. Maretti* was decided in 1982. During the oil embargo and the gas crisis of the 1970s, it became clear that our dependence on foreign oil was a national security concern. Federal energy policy shifted to encourage the development of sustainable energy sources, such as solar power. Today, global warming and environmental concerns have renewed our interest in sustainable energy.

The next case involves another form of sustainable energy—wind power. When an individual homeowner installs a solar system, her house is outfitted with solar panels that are typically unobtrusive and mounted on a roof. Wind power, on the other hand, requires large wind turbines that the Nevada Supreme Court characterized as "gigantic."

2. The decision grapples with two basic principles of nuisance law: no relief for aesthetic harm and relief for diminution in property value. Consider how the court evaluates these concerns given the reality of a 75-foot-tall wind turbine.

Sowers v. Forest Hills Subdivision

294 P.3d 427 (Nev. 2013)

Hardesty, J. In this appeal, we address whether the district court properly concluded that, under the particular circumstances and surroundings of the case, a proposed residential wind turbine would constitute a nuisance warranting a permanent injunction against its construction. Below, respondents Forest Hills Subdivision, Ann Hall, and Karl Hall (collectively] the Halls) sought to permanently enjoin their neighbor, appellant Rick Sowers, from constructing a wind turbine on his residential property, asserting that the proposed turbine would constitute a nuisance. The district court agreed and granted the permanent injunction.

We conclude that, in this case, substantial evidence exists to support the district court's conclusion that the proposed wind turbine constitutes a nuisance. We also determine that the wind turbine at issue would create a nuisance in fact. In reaching our conclusion, we hold that the aesthetics of a wind turbine alone are not grounds for finding a nuisance. However, we conclude that a nuisance in fact may be found when the aesthetics are combined with other factors, such as noise, shadow flicker, and diminution in property value. In this case, the district court heard testimony about the aesthetics of the proposed wind turbine, the noise and shadow flicker it would create, and its potential to diminish surrounding property values. Based on this evidence, we conclude that substantial evidence supports the district court's finding that the proposed residential wind turbine would be a nuisance in fact. Thus, we affirm the order granting a permanent injunction prohibiting its construction.

FACTS AND PROCEDURAL HISTORY

Sowers informed residents of the Forest Hills Subdivision that he planned to construct a wind turbine on his residential property. After this announcement, Sowers' neighbors, the Halls, and the Forest Hills Subdivision filed a complaint in district court claiming that the proposed wind turbine posed a potential nuisance because it would generate constant noise and obstruct the views of neighboring properties. The Halls sought to permanently enjoin construction of the wind turbine and requested preliminary injunctive relief.

At the preliminary injunction hearing, the district court heard testimony that the subdivision was a very quiet area, and that the turbine would obstruct Mr. Hall's view and create noise and shadow flicker.[3] Another resident, who was also a licensed realtor, testified that the proposed wind turbine would diminish property values in the neighborhood. A renewable energy specialist testified that the proposed wind turbine would likely generate the same level of noise as "the hum of a highway," and a contractor hired to construct the turbine testified that there was no way to mitigate the shadow flicker caused by the wind turbine.

The district court then conducted a site visit to the location of a comparable wind turbine. At this site visit, Sowers brought a decibel-reading machine that indicated that the noise from the wind turbine did not exceed 5 decibels from 100 feet away. A neighbor to that wind turbine testified that it produced some noise and shadow flicker, but that the turbine did not bother him. The district court also visited Sowers' home in Forest Hills, the proposed site for his wind turbine, but noted there was no way for Sowers to test the possible decibel level at that location.

Following the preliminary injunction hearing, the district court granted the permanent injunction. The district court heavily considered its visit to the site of the comparable turbine and its observation that it "was astonished by the size of the structure and the 'overwhelming impression of gigantism.'" The district court also considered that the Forest Hills Subdivision had panoramic views and was a very quiet neighborhood, and that the proposed wind turbine would likely lower property values in the area. Based on these findings and the site visits, the district court held that the proposed wind turbine constituted a nuisance because the turbine would substantially interfere with the neighboring residents' enjoyment and use of their property. As such, the district court ordered a permanent injunction enjoining construction of the wind turbine. Sowers now appeals.

DISCUSSION

On appeal, Sowers argues that the district court improperly concluded that the proposed wind turbine constituted a nuisance and improperly granted the permanent injunction. We disagree.

A nuisance is "[a]nything which is injurious to health, or indecent and offensive to the senses, or an obstruction to the free use of property, so as to interfere with the comfortable enjoyment of life or property." NRS 40.140(1)(a). There are several kinds of nuisances, two of which are pertinent to this discussion. A nuisance at law, also called a nuisance per se, is "a nuisance at all times and under any circumstances, regardless of location or surroundings." *See* 66 C.J.S. Nuisances § 4 (2013). A nuisance in fact, also called a nuisance per accidens, is "one which becomes a nuisance by reasons of circumstances and surroundings." *Id.*

---

3. "Shadow flicker" refers to the alternating pattern of light and dark shadows occurring when the blades of a wind turbine rotate in the line of sight of the sun. These shadows often create a flickering or strobe effect.

We recognize that the Washoe County Development Code permits the construction of private wind turbines in residential areas if such turbines otherwise comply with the requirements of the Code. See generally Washoe County Code Ch. 326 (2010). We are also cognizant of this state's aggressive policy favoring renewable energy sources, such as wind turbines. See NRS 278.02077. We further acknowledge the testimony from the neighbor of the person owning the comparable wind turbine who said that the turbine did not bother him. Based on these considerations, we do not believe that wind turbines are severe interferences in all circumstances, and thus wind turbines are not nuisances at law.

However, even when a structure or act is not a nuisance per se, "[a] nuisance may arise from a lawful activity conducted in an unreasonable and improper manner." 66 C.J.S. Nuisances § 16 (2012) (footnote omitted). Thus, a wind turbine may "be or become a nuisance by reason of the improper or negligent manner in which it is conducted, or by reason of its locality, as where it is done or conducted in a place where it necessarily tends to the damage of another's property." *Id.* Accordingly, "a fair test as to whether a business or a particular use of a property in connection with the operation of the business constitutes a nuisance[] is the reasonableness or unreasonableness of the operation or use in relation to the particular locality and under all existing circumstances." *Burch v. Nedpower Mount Storm, LLC*, 220 W. Va. 443 (W. Va. 2007).

"When deciding whether one's use of his or her property is a nuisance to his neighbors, it is necessary to balance the competing interests of the landowners, using a commonsense approach." 66 C.J.S. Nuisances § 13 (2012). Although we recognize that preserving a residential neighborhood's character is an important and substantial interest for subdivision homeowners, we have consistently held that a landowner does not have a right to light, air, or view. Thus, in resolving this issue on appeal, we must determine whether the proposed wind turbine is "so unreasonable and substantial as to amount to a nuisance and warrant an injunction" by balancing "the gravity of the harm to the plaintiff against the utility of the defendant's conduct, both to himself and to the community." *Cook v. Sullivan*, 149 N.H. 774 (N.H. 2003).

Substantial evidence supports the district court's conclusion that the proposed wind turbine is a nuisance in fact. The determination of whether an activity constitutes a nuisance is generally a question of fact. This court will uphold the factual findings of the district court as long as these findings are not clearly erroneous and are supported by substantial evidence.

To sustain a claim for private nuisance, an interference with one's use and enjoyment of land must be both substantial and unreasonable. Interference is substantial "'[i]f normal persons living in the community would regard the [alleged nuisance] as definitively offensive, seriously annoying or intolerable.'" *Rattigan v. Wile*, 445 Mass. 850 (Mass. 2006) (quoting Restatement (Second) of Torts § 821F cmt. d (1979)). Interference is unreasonable when "the gravity of the harm outweighs the social value of the activity alleged to cause the harm." *Burch*, 647 S.E.2d at 887.

In the small body of national caselaw regarding wind turbines, noise and diminution of property values are the most universally considered factors in determining whether a private nuisance exists. Some states also consider the presence of shadow flicker in combination with noise and property value reduction. We have not previously addressed whether the aesthetics of a wind turbine is a proper consideration in determining the existence of a nuisance. We adopt the view of several jurisdictions that hold aesthetics alone cannot form the basis of a private nuisance claim. The reason for this general rule, with which we agree, is that aesthetic considerations are fraught with subjectivity. But we also adopt *Burch v. Nedpower*'s holding that aesthetics-based complaints can be one of several factors to consider, because we agree with the rationale of that court when it stated: "'Unsightly things are not to be banned solely on that account. Many of them are necessary in carrying on the proper activities of organized society. But such things should be properly placed, and not so located as to be unduly offensive to neighbors or to the public.'" 647 S.E.2d at 891. Thus, while Sowers is correct that the large proportions of the turbine alone cannot form the basis of a nuisance finding, the district may properly consider the enormity of the object as one factor in its decision.

Noise

In a case with similar facts from another jurisdiction, the Superior Court of New Jersey held that a residential wind turbine located in a quiet neighborhood constituted a nuisance solely on the basis of the constant loud noise that the turbine generated. *Rose v. Chaikin*, 187 N.J. Super. 210 (N.J. Super. Ct. Ch. Div. 1982). In *Rose*, the Superior Court found that the distinctive sound of the wind turbine produced a heightened level of intrusiveness because the neighborhood was quiet, separated from commercial and heavier residential noise, and the residents had specifically chosen to live in the area due to the peacefulness the community afforded. We conclude that the citizens who were protected in *Rose* are analogous to the Halls and other Forest Hills residents, as the district court heard testimony of several persons living in the Forest Hills Subdivision that the subdivision was very quiet, and they were concerned that the level of noise from the wind turbine would change the character of the neighborhood they had sought to live in. Since a renewable energy expert testified that the noise created by the turbine would be similar to that of the hum on a nearby highway, there is some evidence that the quiet would most likely be gone. Based on this evidence, the district court could have determined that the proposed wind turbine constitutes a nuisance as a source of excessive noise.

Diminution to property value

Burch also allows for the consideration of potentially diminished property values where it is shown that a landowner's use and enjoyment of his or her property may be infringed. Since the district court received testimony from subdivision residents that they feared an impact on the use and enjoyment of their property, it was fair for the district court to also take into account potential harm to property values. Thus, it was acceptable to include in its findings and conclusions the opinion of the real estate agent who testified that properties in proximity to wind turbines decreased in value.

Aesthetics and shadow flicker

A district court may consider the aesthetics of the wind turbine only if factors other than unsightliness or obstruction of views are claimed. In *Burch*, the West Virginia court noted that shadow flicker was a kind of aesthetic concern that could be considered in conjunction with other factors. It further anticipated how a commercial wind turbine facility abutting a neighborhood could constitute a private nuisance where constant shadow flicker was likely to ruin the enjoyment of residents. Here, Karl Hall testified that the wind turbine would create a shadow flicker on his property, and the contractor hired to construct the wind turbine testified that there is no way to mitigate shadow flicker. Thus, it was not clearly erroneous for the district court to consider shadow flicker.

Nor was it error for the district court to consider the size of the proposed wind turbine. Evidence was heard from a representative of the company who was supposed to construct the turbine indicating that the height of the proposed turbine exceeded 75 feet. The district court got to experience just how tall 75 feet is during its site visit to a comparable wind turbine. With this perspective, the site visit to Sowers' property revealed that his proposed turbine would be a significant imposition on the Halls' ability to use their property, as their land, which lays lower than Sowers' land, would now have a sizeable obstacle overshadowing it. Since evidence of other factors was presented, it was proper for the district court to add into its consideration the presence of shadow flicker and the size of the turbine and the impact on views.

As such, we conclude that this evidence concerning the noise, diminution in property value, shadow flicker, and aesthetics far outweighs any potential utility of the proposed wind turbine within the Forest Hills Subdivision. We recognize that the utility of the wind turbine is the fact that it is an alternative energy source, which Nevada's public policy favors. However, an NV Energy representative informed the court that only Sowers would benefit from this alternative energy source since any energy credit for the turbine's use would only be extended to Sowers' property, and not to the other subdivision residents. Thus, we conclude that the wind turbine's utility within the community is far outweighed by its potential harm to the Forest Hills Subdivision residents.

We conclude that the proposed wind turbine constitutes a nuisance in fact. Accordingly, we affirm the district court's order granting a permanent injunction.

Exercise 7-15. *Sowers* Revisited

A representative from Nevada Energy informed the court that "only Sowers would benefit from this alternative energy source since any energy credit for the turbine's use would only be extended to Sowers' property, and not to the other subdivision residents." Do you agree with this statement?

Chapter 8

Zoning

Introduction

Since the late 19th century, local governments in the United States have engaged in comprehensive zoning as a way to promote rational development and sound land use policies. Comprehensive zoning helped cities to manage their growing populations while also encouraging commercial and industrial activity. It shaped the suburbs and bedroom communities that sprung up after World War II. Despite its many benefits, it has also been criticized for operating as an exclusionary device that has fostered income inequality and segregation.

A central goal of zoning is to separate incompatible uses and thereby prevent nuisance before it happens. With its bright line rules and clearly drawn boundaries, zoning also offers an ease of administration and certainty that is not available in a private nuisance claim. As we saw in the prior chapter, nuisance claims are highly fact-specific and often result in lengthy and costly litigation. Even with the advent of zoning, nuisance claims remain an important way for property owners to enforce their right to quiet enjoyment. The principals of common law nuisance have also informed zoning rules and practice from the earliest court cases upholding the first comprehensive codes.

Chapter Problem: Exercise 8-1

Assume you represent Civitas, nonprofit organization that owns and operates community group homes for adults with developmental disabilities. Two Civitas group homes are located in Falls Township, and it has just purchased a third property that it plans to develop as a group home. Each group home houses four adults with developmental disabilities and two "house parents." The group homes are in large single-family dwellings. All three properties are located within a three-block radius. The close proximity makes it easier to plan coordinated events and share services.

State and federal policy strongly encourages community living for adults with developmental disabilities in a residential setting. The move toward community living represents an important shift in policy that began in the 1970s. Prior to that time, adults with developmental disabilities were housed in large state-run institutions. Social expectations regarding the optimal type of housing changed with the emergence of the disability rights movement and high profile scandals regarding the care provided at some of the institutions. This led to a push towards de-institutionalization and normalization that favored a "least restrictive" alternative approach to housing options. A wide range of state and federal laws and regulations encourage and regulate community living options.

Civitas has contacted you because Falls Township amended its zoning ordinance to require a mandatory dispersal of residential group homes. Under the ordinance, group homes must be separated by at least one-half mile. The two existing group homes do not satisfy this requirement. The third property is also located too close to the other two properties to qualify. The stated purpose of the ordinance is to prevent a clustering of group homes that could re-create an institutional environment. Your client reports that the neighbors have been hostile to the group homes and had lobbied the local council to prevent the opening of the third residential group home. By the end of this chapter, you should be able to advise Citivas with respect to how this new ordinance will impact its operations and whether the organization has any recourse.

Overview of Chapter 6

The power to zone derives from the states' inherent police power. This chapter explores the scope of that power. It explains the zoning process, including provisions that are designed to make allowances for hardship and prior nonconforming uses. It also examines some of the instances where the zoning process is used in an exclusionary manner to keep certain uses and individuals out of a particular community. As you read through the cases, it is important to remember that zoning is state action that triggers constitutional protections. Accordingly, every zoning action potentially raises both federal and state constitutional concerns.

The Chapter is divided into four subunits:

1. The Power to Zone
2. The Zoning Process
3. Exclusionary Zoning: Federal and State Law
4. NIMBY—Not In My Backyard

The Power to Zone

Zoning is an exercise of police power reserved to the states under the Tenth Amendment of the U.S. Constitution. The individual states are empowered to regulate issues related to health, safety, and general welfare within their borders. Zoning restricts the use of private property (i.e., use zoning) and prescribes rules regarding the size or height of structures, minimum lot size, and setback requirements (i.e., area zoning). The states have delegated the power to promulgate, implement and enforce zoning laws to the county or city level. Local control is thought to be desirable because it is more likely that the local governing body will be familiar with the needs of the particular city or county. The process of delegation is typically accomplished through a zoning enabling act. Some state constitutions specifically address land use issues. The zoning enabling act typically requires localities to adopt both a comprehensive plan and a zoning ordinance. The comprehensive plan is often prepared by the local planning board or commission, which then recommends the plan to the local governing body, such as a city council or county commissioners.

The term zoning refers to the different districts or zones within a municipality or county that are designated for a particular use, such as residential, commercial, industrial, and agricultural uses. Within these broad categories there are other distinctions. For example, a residential designation generally includes a zone where only single-family dwellings are permitted, often designated R-1. In addition, there may be a residential zone where two-family homes are allowed and a third zone where multi-family units are permitted. Often the uses will be structured as a pyramid with priority given to the most favored use, such that a single-family dwelling would be permitted in a zone designated as multi-family, but an apartment building would not be permitted in a zone designated single-family (R-1) or two-family (R-2). In addition to demarcating different areas for different uses, zoning codes generally provide detailed guidelines for structures that are permitted within each zone, including height and size.

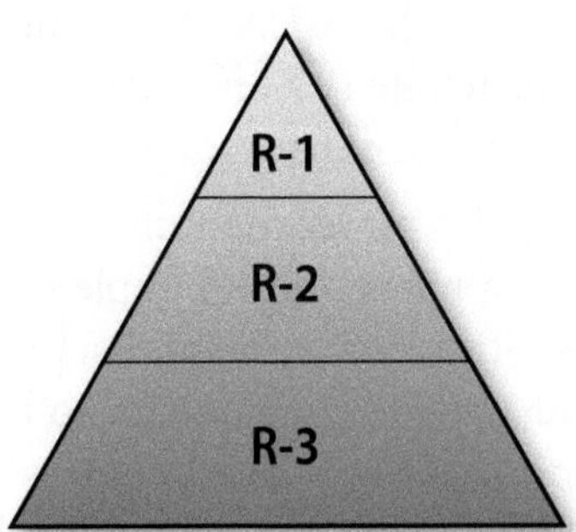

In order to get a sense of the different types of restrictions, you should Google the zoning map for your city or county. Here is a very stylized version of a zoning map using a standard pie chart. You can see the major use categories separated by clear boundaries. Zoning maps often use different colors to signify the different use districts.

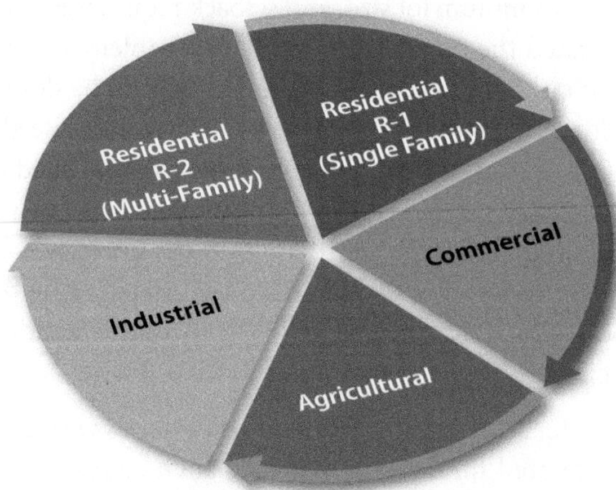

History

New York City enacted the first city-wide zoning ordinance in 1916. It was adopted in response to the pubic outcry over the construction of the 42-story Equitable Building at 120 Broadway in Manhattan. The building had no setbacks and towered over its neighbors, blocking views and access to light. New York City did not limit the height of future skyscrapers, but instead imposed setback rules that were designed to ensure access to light and air. The impact of these setback rules can be seen in the design of some of the tiered skyscrapers of the period that had a large base and then floors that decreased in size the higher they went.

The New York City zoning ordinance became a model that was adopted by other growing metropolitan areas. In 1922, the U.S. Department of Commerce issued the Standard State Zoning Enabling Act. By 1926, nineteen states had adopted substantially similar legislation. Today, all fifty states have zoning enabling acts.

A zoning enabling act delegates power to municipalities to prepare and adopt a comprehensive plan and zoning regulations to implement and enforce the plan. It also provides for the creation of a planning commission. The planning commission is authorized to consider and approve amendments to the zoning regulations. The members of the commission may be appointed or elected or some combination of the two, with particular officials serving ex officio. As explained later in this chapter, zoning regulations typically have provisions for individual property owners to petition for a variance or special use permit in case of hardship. Zoning regulations also provide exceptions for prior nonconforming uses.

Constitutionality

The growing popularity of comprehensive planning did not sit well with some property owners who believed that zoning diminished their property rights. In 1926, the U.S. Supreme Court resolved these objections in the landmark case of *Village of Euclid v. Ambler Realty Co.* A property owner had challenged a comprehensive zoning scheme on the grounds that it violated the Fourteenth Amendment to the U.S. Constitution because it represented a denial of property without due process and state interference with private rights. The Court upheld the comprehensive plan as a reasonable exercise of the Village of Euclid's police power. It noted that a zoning scheme would only be declared unconstitutional where the "provisions are clearly arbitrary and unreasonable, having no substantial relation to the public health, safety, morals, or general welfare."

The decision in *Village of Euclid v. Ambler Realty Co.* further accelerated the trend toward the adoption of comprehensive planning. The case resolved the fundamental question regarding the constitutionality of comprehensive zoning schemes, but specific aspects of certain zoning plans and provisions have continued to be subject to both state and federal constitutional challenges. Some of these challenges are discussed later in this chapter.

Limitations

The form of comprehensive zoning that was approved by the Court in *Village of Euclid v. Ambler Realty Co.* is referred to as "Euclidian zoning." Although it is by far the most common form of zoning in the United States, it is not without its detractors. Some commentators object to zoning as an infringement of private property rights. Houston is the largest U.S. city without a comprehensive zoning plan. In the absence of comprehensive zoning, land use can be regulated through private contractual agreements, such as the restrictive covenants and equitable servitudes covered in Chapter 10.

Environmentalists have blamed zoning for urban sprawl and suburbs that are car dependent and not pedestrian friendly. Social justice advocates have charged that zoning has regulated noxious uses to low-income areas and communities of color while systematically excluding low- and middle-income housing from desirable neighborhoods. Comprehensive zoning sometimes reflects a "not in my backyard" or "NIMBY" impulse where communities zone out important, but undesirable uses, such as halfway houses or group homes. A number of these themes are explored later in this chapter.

Exercise 8-2. *Village of Euclid v. Ambler Realty Co.*

The *Village of Euclid v. Ambler Reality Co.* was a landmark U.S. Supreme Court case that had a profound influence on land use policy across the United States. The unanimous decision upheld the constitutionality of comprehensive zoning. The case provides a detailed description of the zoning ordinance, which was a classic example of what is now referred to "Euclidian zoning." As you read the case, consider the level of detail included in the ordinance, both in terms of use restrictions and area restrictions.

The plaintiff challenged the comprehensive zoning plan adopted by the Village of Euclid on the grounds that it constituted a deprivation of property without due process and a denial of equal protection under the Fourteenth Amendment to the U.S. Constitution. The Court applied what we now refer to as a rational basis test—the lowest level of judicial scrutiny. It asked whether the ordinance was arbitrary and unreasonable and had no substantial relation to the public health, safety, morals, or general welfare.

Do you believe that a comprehensive zoning scheme diminishes the rights of private property owners?

Village of Euclid v. Ambler Reality Co.

272 U.S. 365 (1926)

Mr. Justice Sutherland delivered the opinion of the Court. The Village of Euclid is an Ohio municipal corporation. It adjoins and practically is a suburb of the City of Cleveland. Its estimated population is between 5,000 and 10,000, and its area from twelve to fourteen square miles, the greater part of which is farm lands or unimproved acreage. It lies, roughly, in the form of a parallelogram measuring approximately three and one-half miles each way. East and west it is traversed by three principal highways: Euclid Avenue, through the southerly border, St. Clair Avenue, through the central portion, and Lake Shore Boulevard, through the northerly border in close proximity to the shore of Lake Erie. The Nickel Plate railroad lies from 1,500 to 1,800 feet north of Euclid Avenue, and the Lake Shore railroad 1,600 feet farther to the north. The three highways and the two railroads are substantially parallel.

Appellee is the owner of a tract of land containing 68 acres, situated in the westerly end of the village, abutting on Euclid Avenue to the south and the Nickel Plate railroad to the north. Adjoining this tract, both on the east and on the west, there have been laid out restricted residential plats upon which residences have been erected.

On November 13, 1922, an ordinance was adopted by the Village Council, establishing a comprehensive zoning plan for regulating and restricting the location of trades, industries, apartment houses, two-family houses, single family houses, etc., the lot area to be built upon, the size and height of buildings, etc.

The entire area of the village is divided by the ordinance into six classes of use districts, denominated U-1 to U-6, inclusive; three classes of height districts, denominated H-1 to H-3, inclusive; and four classes of area districts, denominated A-1 to A-4, inclusive. The use districts are classified in respect of the buildings which may be erected within their respective limits, as follows: U-1 is restricted to single family dwellings, public parks, water towers and reservoirs, sub-urban and interurban electric railway passenger stations and rights of way, and farming, non-commercial greenhouse nurseries and truck gardening; U-2 is extended to include two-family dwellings; U-3 is further extended to include apartment houses, hotels, churches, schools, public libraries, museums, private clubs, community center buildings, hospitals, sanitariums, public playgrounds and recreation buildings, and a city hall and courthouse; U-4 is further extended to include banks, offices, studios, telephone exchanges, fire and police stations, restaurants, theatres and moving picture shows, retail stores and shops, sales offices, sample rooms, wholesale stores for hardware, drugs and groceries, stations for gasoline and oil (not exceeding 1,000 gallons storage) and for ice delivery, skating rinks and dance halls, electric substations, job and newspaper printing, public garages for motor vehicles, stables and wagon sheds (not exceeding five horses, wagons or motor trucks) and distributing stations for central store and commercial enterprises; U-5 is further extended to include billboards and advertising signs (if permitted), warehouses, ice and ice cream manufacturing and cold storage plants, bottling works, milk bottling and central distribution stations, laundries, carpet cleaning, dry cleaning and dyeing establishments, blacksmith, horseshoeing, wagon and motor vehicle repair shops, freight stations, street car barns, stables and wagon sheds (for more than five horses, wagons or motor trucks), and wholesale produce markets and salesrooms; U-6 is further extended to include plants for sewage disposal and for producing gas, garbage and refuse incineration, scrap iron, junk, scrap paper and rag storage, aviation fields, cemeteries, crematories, penal and correctional institutions, insane and feeble minded institutions, storage of oil and gasoline (not to exceed 25,000 gallons), and manufacturing and industrial operations of any kind other than, and any public utility not included in, a class U-1, U-2, U-3, U-4 or U-5 use. There is a seventh class of uses which is prohibited altogether.

Class U-1 is the only district in which buildings are restricted to those enumerated. In the other classes the uses are cumulative; that is to say, uses in class U-2 include those enumerated in the preceding class, U-1; class U-3 includes uses enumerated in the preceding classes, U-2 and U-1; and so on. In addition to the enumerated uses, the ordinance provides for accessory uses, that is, for uses customarily incident to the principal use, such as private garages. Many regulations are provided in respect of such accessory uses.

The classification of area districts is: In A-1 districts, dwellings or apartment houses to accommodate more than one family must have at least 5,000 square feet for interior lots and at least 4,000 square feet for corner lots; in A-2 districts, the area must be at least 2,500 square feet for interior lots, and 2,000 square feet for corner lots; in A-3 districts, the limits are 1,250 and 1,000 square feet, respectively; in A-4 districts, the limits are 900 and 700 square feet, respectively. The ordinance contains, in great variety and detail, provisions in respect of width of lots, front, side and rear yards, and other matters, including restrictions and regulations as to the use of bill boards, sign boards and advertising signs.

Appellee's tract of land comes under U-2, U-3 and U-6. The first strip of 620 feet immediately north of Euclid Avenue falls in class U-2, the next 130 feet to the north, in U-3, and the remainder in U-6. The uses of the first 620 feet, therefore, do not include apartment houses, hotels, churches, schools, or other public and semi-public buildings, or other uses enumerated in respect of U-3 to U-6, inclusive. The uses of the next 130 feet include all of these, but exclude industries, theatres, banks, shops, and the various other uses set forth in respect of U-4 to U-6, inclusive.

Annexed to the ordinance, and made a part of it, is a zone map, showing the location and limits of the various use, height and area districts, from which it appears that the three classes overlap one another; that is to say, for example, both U-5 and U-6 use districts are in A-4 area districts, but the former is in H-2 and the latter in H-3 height districts. The plan is a complicated one and can be better understood by an inspection of the map, though it does not seem necessary to reproduce it for present purposes.

The lands lying between the two railroads for the entire length of the village area and extending some distance on either side to the north and south, having an average width of about 1,600 feet, are left open, with slight exceptions, for industrial and all other uses. This includes the larger part of appellee's tract. Approximately one-sixth of the area of the entire village is included in U-5 and U-6 use districts. That part of the village lying south of Euclid Avenue is principally in U-1 districts. The lands lying north of Euclid Avenue and bordering on the long strip just described are included in U-1, U-2, U-3 and U-4 districts, principally in U-2.

The enforcement of the ordinance is entrusted to the inspector of buildings, under rules and regulations of the board of zoning appeals. Meetings of the board are public, and minutes of its proceedings are kept. It is authorized to adopt rules and regulations to carry into effect provisions of the ordinance. Decisions of the inspector of buildings may be appealed to the board by any person claiming to be adversely affected by any such decision. The board is given power in specific cases of practical difficulty or unnecessary hardship to interpret the ordinance in harmony with its general purpose and intent, so that the public health, safety and general welfare may be secure and substantial justice done. Penalties are prescribed for violations, and it is provided that the various provisions are to be regarded as independent and the holding of any provision to be unconstitutional, void or ineffective shall not affect any of the others.

The ordinance is assailed on the grounds that it is in derogation of § 1 of the Fourteenth Amendment to the Federal Constitution in that it deprives appellee of liberty and property without due process of law and denies it the equal protection of the law, and that it offends against certain provisions of the Constitution of the State of Ohio. The prayer of the bill is for an injunction restraining the enforcement of the ordinance and all attempts to impose or maintain as to appellee's property any of the restrictions, limitations or conditions. The court below held the ordinance to be unconstitutional and void, and enjoined its enforcement.

Building zone laws are of modern origin. They began in this country about twenty-five years ago. Until recent years, urban life was comparatively simple; but with the great increase and concentration of population, problems have developed, and constantly are developing, which require, and will continue to require, additional restrictions in respect of the use and occupation of private lands in urban communities. Regulations, the wisdom, necessity and validity of which, as applied to existing conditions, are so apparent that they are now uniformly sustained, a century ago, or even half a century ago, probably would have been rejected as arbitrary and oppressive. Such regulations are sustained, under the complex conditions of our day, for reasons analogous to those which justify traffic regulations, which, before the advent of automobiles and rapid transit street railways, would have been condemned as fatally arbitrary and unreasonable. And in this there is no inconsistency, for while the meaning of constitutional guaranties never varies, the scope of their application must expand or contract to meet the new and different conditions which are constantly coming within the field of their operation. In a changing world, it is impossible that it should be otherwise. But although a degree of elasticity is thus imparted, not to the meaning, but to the application of constitutional principles, statutes and ordinances, which, after giving due weight to the new conditions, are found clearly not to conform to the Constitution, of course, must fall.

The ordinance now under review, and all similar laws and regulations, must find their justification in some aspect of the police power, asserted for the public welfare. The line which in this field separates the legitimate from the illegitimate assumption of power is not capable of precise delimitation. It varies with circumstances and conditions. A regulatory zoning ordinance, which would be clearly valid as applied to the great cities, might be clearly invalid as applied to rural communities. In solving doubts, the maxim *sic utere tuo ut alienum non laedas*, which lies at the foundation of so much of the common law of nuisances, ordinarily will furnish a fairly helpful clew. And the law of nuisances, like-wise, may be consulted, not for the purpose of controlling, but for the helpful aid of its analogies in the process of ascertaining the scope of, the power. Thus the question whether the power exists to forbid the erection of a building of a particular kind or for a particular use, like the question whether a particular thing is a nuisance, is to be determined, not by an abstract consideration of the building or of the thing considered apart, but by considering it in connection with the circumstances and the locality. A nuisance may be merely a right thing in the wrong place,—like a pig in the parlor instead of the barnyard. If the validity of the legislative classification for zoning purposes be fairly debatable, the legislative judgment must be allowed to control.

There is no serious difference of opinion in respect of the validity of laws and regulations fixing the height of buildings within reasonable limits, the character of materials and methods of construction, and the adjoining area which must be left open, in order to minimize the danger of fire or collapse, the evils of over-crowding, and the like, and excluding from residential sections offensive trades, industries and structures likely to create nuisances.

Here, however, the exclusion is in general terms of all industrial establishments, and it may thereby happen that not only offensive or dangerous industries will be excluded, but those which are neither offensive nor dangerous will share the same fate. But this is no more than happens in respect of many practice-forbidding laws which this Court has up-held although drawn in general terms so as to include individual cases that may turn out to be innocuous in themselves. The inclusion of a reasonable margin to insure effective enforcement, will not put upon a law, otherwise valid, the stamp of invalidity. Such laws may also find their justification in the fact that, in some fields, the bad fades into the good by such insensible degrees that the two are not capable of being readily distinguished and separated in terms of legislation. In the light of these considerations, we are not prepared to say that the end in view was not sufficient to justify the general rule of the ordinance, although some industries of an innocent character might fall within the proscribed class. It can not be said that the ordinance in this respect "passes the bounds of reason and assumes the character of a merely arbitrary fiat." *Purity Extract Co. v. Lynch*, 226 U.S. 192, 204. Moreover, the restrictive provisions of the ordinance in this particular may be sustained upon the principles applicable to the broader exclusion from residential districts of all business and trade structures, presently to be discussed.

We find no difficulty in sustaining restrictions of the kind thus far reviewed. The serious question in the case arises over the provisions of the ordinance excluding from residential districts, apartment houses, business houses, retail stores and shops, and other like establishments. This question involves the validity of what is really the crux of the more recent zoning legislation, namely, the creation and maintenance of residential districts, from which business and trade of every sort, including hotels and apartment houses, are excluded. Upon that question, this Court has not thus far spoken. The decisions of the state courts are numerous and conflicting; but those which broadly sustain the power greatly outnumber those which deny altogether or narrowly limit it; and it is very apparent that there is a constantly increasing tendency in the direction of the broader view.

The matter of zoning has received much attention at the hands of commissions and experts, and the results of their investigations have been set forth in comprehensive reports. These reports, which bear every evidence of pains-taking consideration, concur in the view that the segregation of residential, business, and industrial buildings will make it easier to provide fire apparatus suitable for the character and intensity of the development in each section; that it will increase the safety and security of home life; greatly tend to prevent street accidents, especially to children, by reducing the traffic and resulting confusion in residential sections; decrease noise and other conditions which produce or intensify nervous disorders; preserve a more favorable environment in which to rear children, etc. With particular reference to apartment houses, it is pointed out that the development of detached house sections is greatly retarded by the coming of apartment houses, which has sometimes resulted in destroying the entire section for private house purposes; that in such sections very often the apartment house is a mere parasite, constructed in order to take advantage of the open spaces and attractive surroundings created by the residential character of the district. Moreover, the coming of one apartment house is followed by others, interfering by their height and bulk with the free circulation of air and monopolizing the rays of the sun which otherwise would fall upon the smaller homes, and bringing, as their necessary accompaniments, the disturbing noises incident to increased traffic and business, and the occupation, by means of moving and parked automobiles, of larger portions of the streets, thus detracting from their safety and depriving children of the tlineprivilege of quiet and open spaces for play, enjoyed by those in more favored localities,—until, finally, the residential character of the neighborhood and its desirability as a place of detached residences are utterly destroyed. Under these circumstances, apartment houses, which in a different environment would be not only entirely unobjectionable but highly desirable, come very near to being nuisances.

If these reasons, thus summarized, do not demonstrate the wisdom or sound policy in all respects of those restrictions which we have indicated as pertinent to the inquiry, at least, the reasons are sufficiently cogent to preclude us from saying, as it must be said before the ordinance can be declared unconstitutional, that such provisions are clearly arbitrary and unreasonable, having no substantial relation to the public health, safety, morals, or general welfare.

Decree reversed.

Exercise 8-3. *Village of Euclid v. Ambler Reality Co.* Revisited

1. The Village of Euclid designated use districts (U-1 to U-6), height districts (H-1 to H-3), and area districts (A-1 to A-4). The plaintiff primarily objected to the ordinance due to the use restrictions. One goal of comprehensive zoning is to minimize nuisance. Review the different uses that the ordinance has grouped together in the different use districts. How well do you think the plan furthers the goal of preventing nuisance before it happens? Do you see any potential friction? Also, many of the designated uses are specific to 1923. How well do you think the ordinance will be able to adapt to changing times?
2. The law of nuisance also provided justification for the exercise of police power to regulate land use and development. As Justice Sutherland explained in his opinion:

   > In solving doubts, the maxim *sic utere tuo ut alienum non laedes* [use your own property in such a manner as not to injure that of another], which lies at the foundation of so much of the common law of nuisances, ordinarily will furnish a fairly helpful clew [sic]. And the law of nuisances, likewise, may be consulted, not for the purpose of controlling, but for the helpful aid of its analogies in the process of ascertaining the scope of, the [police] power.

The Zoning Process

The central feature of any zoning scheme is the comprehensive plan. The comprehensive plan is developed by the planning commission and approved by the local legislative body. It divides the municipality into use districts and prescribes area restrictions and requirements. It also provides a description of the goals and plans for future development. The zoning ordinance is the local law that is designed to implement and enforce the comprehensive plan. Generally, amendments to the zoning ordinance must be consistent with the comprehensive plan.

In certain circumstances, property owners may petition the planning commission or the local elected governing body to rezone their property. These requests are evaluated with respect to whether they are consistent with the comprehensive plan. However, municipalities will sometimes negotiate with developers and exact concessions in exchange for a favorable change in zoning. This form of contract or conditional zoning is subject to challenge on the grounds that it constitutes illegal spot zoning. Spot zoning has been challenged on numerous grounds, including procedural and constitutional objections. It also undermines the comprehensive plan and smacks of preferential treatment. Some commentators contend that contract or conditional zoning provides certain benefits because Euclidian zoning is otherwise too inflexible.

The administrative body that administers the zoning code is generally called the zoning board or zoning board of adjustment. The members may be the same as the members of the planning commission. It hears requests from property owners for individual exceptions to the zoning law. If these requests are based on hardship, they are typically referred to as variances. In certain instances, a particular use may be authorized by the zoning board only if certain conditions are met. In such cases, a property owner would be requesting a special use permit. In addition, zoning laws generally carve out exceptions for prior nonconforming uses. Property owners are entitled to appeal decisions of the zoning board in court. Some jurisdictions have an administrative body that hears the appeals and serves as an intermediate step. If individualized relief is not forthcoming, a property owner can petition the planning commission or legislative body to rezone the property.

The cases in the next section deal with spot zoning, contract zoning, and variances. The zoning process often involves strong community involvement. Neighbors, community groups, and other stakeholders frequently attend meetings of local zoning authorities and monitor their decisions closely. They may lobby both the zoning authority and the local governing body regarding land use planning priorities and environmental concerns. The first case involves a case brought by a community organization challenging the approval of a rezoning request.

Exercise 8-4. *Save Our Rural Environment v. Snohomish County*— Spot Zoning

1. "Spot zoning results when a zoning ordinance creates a small island of property with restrictions on its use different from those imposed on the surrounding property." *Jaffe v. City of Davenport,* 179 N.W.2d 554, 556 (Iowa 1970). Spot zoning is not necessarily invalid. It will be upheld if there is reasonable basis

to treat the rezoned property differently from the surrounding property, and the restriction is consistent with the comprehensive plan and a valid exercise of the police power.

2. The following case involves a nonprofit organization, Save Our Rural Environment (SORE), that was formed to represent the interests of residents who objected to the rezoning. The presence of nonprofit community organizations is common in zoning matters. Planning commission hearings are open to the public. Nonprofit organizations and community groups will often organize to present a united front at the hearings and communicate their positions to the members of the commission. You will note that in this case, the planning commission recommended against the requested rezoning. As you read the case, consider what factors would cause the Snohomish County Council to reject the recommendation of the planning commission. How will the County benefit from the proposed development? How might it be harmed?

Save Our Rural Environment v. Snohomish County

662 P.2d 816 (Wash. 1983)

Dolliver, J. Plaintiff Save Our Rural Environment (SORE) is a Washington nonprofit corporation, organized to oppose the rezone of certain land in Snohomish County. Plaintiff appeals from a Snohomish County Superior Court decision denying its petition for review of the amendment by the Snohomish County Council of its comprehensive plan and subsequent rezone of a parcel of land near Lake Stevens known as the "Soper Hill Site." Plaintiff SORE originally filed its appeal in Division One of the Court of Appeals. This court granted defendants' motion to transfer and accelerate review. We affirm the decision of the Snohomish County Superior Court.

On July 23, 1979, Snohomish County adopted the Snohomish/Lake Stevens Area Comprehensive Plan, as authorized by RCW 36.70.340. The Soper Hill site is included in the comprehensive plan area and was designated suburban residential in the comprehensive plan.

In August 1979, a representative of Hewlett-Packard Company wrote the Snohomish County Board of Commissioners proposing development of an electronics manufacturing facility on the Soper Hill site. The Hewlett-Packard representative suggested amending the Snohomish/Lake Stevens Area Comprehensive Plan to provide for a business park zone so as to enable construction of the electronics manufacturing facility on the Soper Hill site.

In April 1980, the Snohomish County Planning Department issued draft environmental impact statements for the proposed comprehensive plan amendment and for Hewlett-Packard's business park proposal. The county planning commission conducted public hearings on the proposal. After the hearings, a majority of the planning commission recommended against amendment of the comprehensive plan.

The Snohomish County Council then held its own hearings and rejected the planning commission's recommendation. In late December 1980, the county council formally enacted the comprehensive plan amendment. The council required, however, that any business park rezone applicant satisfy three conditions related to controlling drainage, buffering of agricultural lands, and resolving expected road and traffic problems in the area.

Following enactment of the comprehensive plan amendment, Hewlett-Packard filed a preliminary development plan and rezone application as required by Snohomish County Code 18.55.040. A county hearing examiner held public hearings on the preliminary development plan and rezone application in February and March 1981. On April 3, 1981, the hearing examiner issued his final report and recommendation on the Soper Hill rezone request. The hearing examiner concluded the rezone satisfied all requirements of the County's business park zone, the County road ordinance, and the council's three criteria established in the comprehensive plan amendment. On May 14, 1981, the Snohomish County Council unanimously adopted the Soper Hill rezone.

SORE challenged the comprehensive plan amendment and Soper Hill rezone by filing in King County Superior Court a petition for review of the Snohomish County Council decisions. The King County Superior Court determined the ends of justice would be better served by transferring the case to Snohomish County Superior Court and granted defendants' motion for change of venue. The Snohomish County Superior Court ruled in favor of defendants on all issues presented. We affirm.

I

We first consider whether the Soper Hill rezone constitutes illegal spot zoning. Spot zoning has been consistently defined to be zoning action by which a smaller area is singled out of a larger area or district and specially zoned for a use classification totally different from and inconsistent with the classification of surrounding land, and not in accordance with the comprehensive plan. We first considered and condemned spot zoning in *State ex rel. Miller v. Cain*, 40 Wn.2d 216 (1952), although we warned in that case against laying down a hard and fast rule that all spot zoning is illegal. When faced with a challenge to a county's rezone action on the grounds the rezone constitutes an illegal spot zone, the main inquiry of the court is whether the zoning action bears a substantial relationship to the general welfare of the affected community. Only where the spot zone grants a discriminatory benefit to one or a group of owners to the detriment of their neighbors or the community at large without adequate public advantage or justification will the county's rezone be overturned.

We are convinced the Soper Hill rezone bears a substantial relationship to the general welfare of Snohomish County. The County's business park zoning classification provides a flexible means to broaden the industrial base of the region and to produce energy and travel time savings for employees. There is no question as to the careful and comprehensive nature of the deliberations in the enactment of the amendment to the comprehensive plan and the rezone. After examining the voluminous record in the present case, we conclude it demonstrates the Soper Hill rezone will operate to benefit the general welfare and that it is in conformance with the Snohomish/Lake Stevens Area Comprehensive Plan. Consequently, we reject plaintiff's contention the Soper Hill rezone constitutes an illegal spot zone.

We are aware of the growing disenchantment with traditional "Euclidean" zoning philosophy and practices under which a municipality is divided into different types of zoning districts, each of which is assigned particular uses. The purpose of traditional zoning is to protect the public health, safety, and welfare and to minimize conflicts between incompatible uses. Traditional zoning concepts, however, generally do not meet the community's present and future land use needs for water and sewage, roads and community services, and fail to protect the environment. Modern land use controls such as Snohomish County's business park zone ordinance are an attempt to anticipate changing patterns of land development and to overcome the inadequacies and inflexibility of orthodox zoning regulations.

IV

Finally, the record indicates Snohomish County fully complied with the requirements to consider the effects of its land use decisions on the entire affected community. All neighboring jurisdictions were consulted; all those which responded supported the proposal for a business park at the Soper Hill site. Furthermore, the Snohomish County Council properly considered and acted to mitigate the effects of its land use decisions on the entire affected area. The County took traffic counts, quantified and disclosed levels of traffic service, numbers of accidents, projected population increases, and effects on public services for the entire affected area. As a result of its determinations, the Snohomish County Council imposed conditions that the rezone applicant must satisfy, all directed to mitigate the projected environmental impacts on the affected area. The county also obtained commitments from the State of Washington for road improvements to state facilities in the area. Only after rezone conditions were met and the State commitment to improve highways in the area was secured did the County allow the project to proceed.

All procedures were carefully followed and all requirements have been met by Snohomish County. The rezone of the Soper Hill site is valid.

Affirmed.

Exercise 8-5. *Save Our Rural Environment* Revisited

1. Hewlett-Packard wanted to build an electronic manufacturing plant on property that was zoned as suburban residential. Rezoning is a more complicated process that requires the amendment of the zoning ordinance. Why did Hewlett-Packard request rezoning instead of a variance?

2. What weight did the court give to the fact that the planning commission had recommended against rezoning?
3. Does this decision represent a rejection of traditional Euclidian zoning?

Exercise 8-6. *Rando v. Town of North Attleboro* — Contract Zoning

Rando v. Town of North Attleboro also involves rezoning at the behest of a developer. In this case, the town of North Attleboro received a number of concessions from the developer who proposed to build a 260,000 acre shopping mall and multi-screen movie theater. Building such a large project can be a complicated undertaking. It is common for the developer and the local authorities to work together on issues related to infrastructure and the like. It also makes sense that the municipality would want to exercise some degree of control over the scope and nature of the project.

Contract zoning, where rezoning is exchanged for a quid pro quo, is generally invalid as either an illegal delegation of police powers or an attempt to influence the rezoning process itself. As you read the following case, consider whether the traditional restrictions on contract zoning adequately protect the interests of the residents. How would you define contract zoning to balance the interests of both developers and the residents?

Rando v. Town of North Attleboro

44 Mass. App. Ct. 603 (1998)

Perretta, J. Article 51 of the town meeting warrant, an amendment to the zoning by-law, was enacted by the defendant town of North Attleborough (town) after approval by the required two-thirds vote at the representative town meeting held October 23, 1993. The amendment changed approximately thirty-seven acres of land from a residential to a commercial zoning district. It was approved by the Attorney General, and notice of that approval was posted by the town clerk conformably with G.L. c. 40, § 32. See G.L. c. 40A, § 5. The plaintiffs then brought this action in the Land Court pursuant to G.L. c. 40A, § 4, and G.L. c. 231A, § 1. The trial judge found that the adoption of the amendment was a valid exercise of local zoning power and dismissed the plaintiffs' complaint. As below, the plaintiffs' principal arguments on appeal are that the amendment constitutes "contract" zoning in violation of the Massachusetts Constitution and G.L. c. 40A, and that the town failed to follow its own "master plan" established pursuant to G.L. c. 41, § 81D. We affirm the judgment.

1. *The facts.* We relate the facts as found by the trial judge. The plaintiffs reside at 31 Newport Avenue, Attleboro. Their property contains about eleven acres, all situated in Attleboro, and abuts the line dividing North Attleborough and Attleboro. Alfred Carpionato, the defendant-intervener, is a developer who owns approximately eighty-two contiguous acres of land in North Attleborough. This land abuts the Attleboro line as well as part of the plaintiffs' property.

On August 13, 1993, Carpionato, acting pursuant to G.L. c. 40A, § 5, filed a warrant article with the North Attleborough selectmen seeking to include on the October town meeting agenda a rezoning of approximately thirty-seven acres of land (locus) from an R-30 residential district to a C-60 commercial zoning district. The plaintiffs' property does not abut the locus but is adjacent to a parcel of fourteen and one-half acres owned by Carpionato that will remain in the R-30 district. The locus is situated on the easterly side of Route 1, contiguous to land zoned C-60. A small mall, known as "Fashion Crossing," is located directly north of the locus, and a Walmart store is directly to the south. Also, there is a Bradlees store directly across Route 1 from the locus, and the Emerald Square Mall is diagonally across Route 1 from the locus.

Carpionato plans to develop the locus into a 260,000 square foot shopping mall and multiscreen movie complex. Under the town's 1974 zoning regulations, a 600-foot wide commercial strip fronting both sides of Route 1 was established within the R-30 residential district. Consequently, as rezoned, the locus effectively increases the width of the existing commercial strip along Route 1.

Prior to the October town meeting, Carpionato voluntarily made various proposals to State and town authorities which, as alleged, were intended to mitigate the potential impact of his planned commercial development. Those proposals included the creation of a fourteen and one-half acre "no build" buffer zone in an area to remain zoned as R-30, thereby shielding neighbors to the east, including the plaintiffs, from the C-60 district; provision for traffic improvements; the establishment of a "mitigation fund" for the town in the amount of $ 260,000; the payment in mitigation of an amount between $ 400,000 and $ 450,000 to the Massachusetts Highway Department for roadway improvements; and an agreement not to seek a tax abatement on any of the rezoned land for a period of five years.

3. *Contract zoning.* " 'Illegal contract zoning is said to involve the process by which a local government enters into an agreement with a developer whereby the government extracts a performance or promise from the developer in exchange for its agreement to rezone the property' ... [and] ... 'is disapproved of largely on the basis of the principle that a municipality may not contract away its police power to regulate on behalf of the general welfare.' " Bobrowski, Massachusetts Land Use and Planning Law at § 3.4.4 (1993), quoting from 1A Rathkopf, Zoning and Planning §§ 29A-25 and 29A-27 (4th ed. 1982). The plaintiffs argue that the zoning amendment is invalid because the town illegally bargained away its police powers in exchange for Carpionato's various proposals, as memorialized in the "restrictive covenant," "deed restriction," and "mitigation covenant," all of which were subject to an escrow agreement until the amendment was approved, without change, by the town and the Attorney General.

A remarkably similar argument was presented in *Sylvania Elec. Prod. Inc. v. Newton*, 344 Mass. 428 (1962), where the prospective developer of a tract of land, Sylvania, sought a zoning amendment changing the classification of the land from residential to limited manufacturing. After discussions with zoning officials, Sylvania voluntarily agreed to impose on the tract various conditions and use restrictions in addition to those already made applicable under the zoning ordinance to land within a limited manufacturing district. Those additional conditions and restrictions were as follows. Sylvania, which held an option to purchase the tract in issue, agreed to cede three acres of the parcel to the Oak Hill Park Association. Those three acres were to be retained in the residential district for a period of thirty years. Sylvania's agreement was to be set out in a deed to be attached to a proposed option agreement by which Sylvania would give the city a thirty-year option to purchase, for $300, a thirty-acre strip of land which was adjacent to land belonging to the Metropolitan District Commission. Sylvania also proposed other restrictions, including creation of a "buffer zone" upon which no buildings could be erected, limitation of the floor area of the planned buildings, and establishment of a pattern of traffic in connection with the construction of the premises. After the board of alderman enacted the zoning amendment, Sylvania recorded the option agreement and attached deed form. The court [upheld] the validity of the zoning amendment.

The plaintiffs argue that there is an "extraneous consideration" in the present case which removes it from *Sylvania* and renders the town meeting vote an invalid exercise of zoning power, viz., Carpionato's agreement to pay $260,000 directly to the town without that money being specifically tied to any projected costs to the town as a result of the development. As noted in *Sylvania,* conditioning a zoning amendment upon a required payment into a municipality's general fund "could impeach the enacting vote" on the basis that it was not made "solely in respect of rezoning the locus."

We do not think a payment that is promised by the developer rather than required by the municipality and that is reasonably intended to meet public needs arising out of the proposed development can be viewed as an "extraneous influence" upon a zoning decision. Carpionato's "mitigation covenant" acknowledged that the zoning amendment, if enacted, would allow commercial development on the locus which, in turn, "will have substantial impact on the Town," and that "in order to mitigate the effect of such rezoning, and the resultant commercial development that will take place thereafter on the Town, [Carpionato] hereby covenants ... [to] make a gift to the Town" of $260,000, said amount calculated on the basis of $1 per square foot of retail space available in the building or buildings erected on the locus.

Although the plaintiffs rely heavily on the use of the word "gift" in the covenant, there was evidence to show that the money was intended to mitigate the impact of the development upon the town. In a letter sent to the town's planning board, Carpionato expressly stated that the money was being given to mitigate the impact of the development in the "surrounding neighborhoods and the entire North Attleborough community." While he advised the planning board that he had numerous suggestions as to how the money could be used, such as the repairing and repaving of Route 1, he also stated that "it would be inappropriate for us to tell the Town what it needs."

There was also the testimony of John Kokot, the executive vice president of Carpionato Properties, Inc., and Robert Daylor, a site planner as well as a registered professional engineer and a registered land surveyor. Kokot testified that, because there was no set formula or methodology by which to determine the amount of any mitigation offer, he arrived at the figure of $260,000 ($1 per square foot) on the basis of information about the proposed development itself, the mitigation offer made in the development of Emerald Square Mall, and opinions obtained from various people in North Attleborough. Daylor testified that mitigation money is frequently used "for trade-off of density in the commercial zone," such as sidewalks, bicycle trails, or just green space and open space.

Finally, the minutes of the town meeting discussion concerning passage of Article 51 do not support the claim of "extraneous influence." Those minutes show that Kokot spoke at the meeting and detailed not only what Carpionato was required by various State authorities to do in order to mitigate the impact of the development, especially in respect to a predictable traffic increase, but also what more he was volunteering to do. Consistent with the sentiment expressed in the earlier mentioned letter to the town's planning board, Kokot told the town meeting representatives, "I don't want to get involved in the personal solution, all I want to do is pay for it." The minutes indicate that one issue for debate by the town meeting representatives was the conflict between protecting the residential zone and increasing the tax base and employment opportunities. The details of that debate were not recorded and are, instead, reflected in the minutes as "much discussion."

Applying the analysis set out in *Sylvania*, to the evidence before us, we conclude that the trial judge was not in error in finding that two-thirds plus one of the town meeting members were not improperly influenced to act on behalf of the developer rather than in the best interests of the town.

Judgment affirmed.

Exercise 8-7. *Rando v. Town of North Attleboro* Revisited

1. Do the concessions agreed to in *Rando* remind you of the purchased injunctions that we discussed in Chapter 7? Recall that in *Spur Industries*, the plaintiffs were able to enjoin the offending use, but were required to pay damages to the defendant for the costs associated with suspending operations. Here, the developer is able to proceed with the project, but is required to mitigate the public costs associated with the project.

2. How can you tell the difference between the "mitigation fund" and a good old-fashioned bribe? Is that what the court was trying to get at with its discussion of "extraneous influence"?

Exercise 8-8. *Cochran v. Fairfax County of Board of Zoning Appeals* — Variances

The last two cases involved rezoning that requires an amendment to the zoning ordinance. *Cochran v. Fairfax County Board of Zoning Appeals* involves three consolidated appeals from a request for a variance. The administrative body charged with administering the zoning law is typically authorized to issue a variance to an individual property owner upon a showing of hardship. Interested parties, including neighbors, are entitled to appeal the decision.

The three fact patterns discussed in *Cochran* are illustrative of the types of instances where property owners will request a variance. In the first two cases, neighbors objected to the grant of a variance. In the third case, the Board of Zoning Appeals appealed a court decision that overturned its denial of a variance. As you read the cases, consider what you think should be required to establish the existence of "hardship."

Cochran v. Fairfax County of Board of Zoning Appeals

594 S.E.2d 571 (Va. 2004)

Russell, J. These three cases involve decisions by local boards of zoning appeals (collectively and individually, BZA) upon applications for variances from the local zoning ordinances. Although the facts and proceedings differ in each case, and will be discussed separately, the governing principles of law are the same. We therefore consider and decide the cases in a single opinion.

THE FAIRFAX CASE

Michael R. Bratti was the owner of a tract of land containing approximately 20,470 square feet, in the McLean area of Fairfax County. The property was zoned R-2, a residential classification permitting two dwelling units per acre, and was improved by a home in which Bratti had resided for eight years. The zoning ordinance required side yard setbacks of at least 15 feet from the property lines. Bratti's existing home fit well within the setbacks.

Bratti filed an application with the BZA for four variances. He proposed to demolish his existing home and erect a much larger house on the site. The proposed structure would come within 13 feet of the northerly property line, rather than the 15 feet required by the ordinance, and would be further extended into the setback area by three exterior chimneys which would extend beyond the northerly wall of the house. The proposed house would be 71 feet wide and 76 feet from front to back. The proposed encroachment into the side yard setback would extend the entire 76 foot depth of the house.

It was undisputed that Bratti's proposed house could be built upon the existing lot without any need for a variance by simply moving it two feet to the south, plus the additional distance required by the chimneys. Bratti explained to the Board, however, that he desired to have a "side-load" garage on the south side of his house and that a reduction of two feet of open space on the south side would make it inconvenient for vehicles to turn into the garage. The present house had a "front-load" garage which opened directly toward the street. When it was pointed out to Bratti that he could avoid this problem by reconfiguring his proposed house to contain a "front-load" garage, he responded that such a house would have less "curb appeal" than the design he proposed.

If the house were built in its proposed location, but reduced in size by two feet to comply with the zoning ordinance, there would be a resulting loss of 152 square feet of living space. There were two relatively level areas shown on the plans for the proposed dwelling, one in front of the house and one in the rear. It was conceded that an additional 152 square feet of living space could have been constructed in either of these areas, but Bratti explained that he wanted to use the level area in front of the house as a play area for children and for additional parking, and that he was unwilling to encroach upon the level area in the rear because he desired to use it as a large outdoor courtyard which he said was "the central idea in the house."

The proposed dwelling had two stories. A third story could have been added as a matter of right, without variances. Bratti conceded that this could easily be done and would more than accommodate the 152 square feet lost by compliance with the zoning ordinance, but that it would be aesthetically undesirable, causing the house to appear to be a "towering structure" as seen from the street.

Over the opposition of a number of neighbors, the BZA granted all four variances. The objecting neighbors petitioned the circuit court for certiorari. The Board of Supervisors of Fairfax County obtained leave of court to enter the case as an additional petitioner, opposing the variances. The court, after a hearing, affirmed the decision of the BZA and entered an order dismissing the petition for writ of certiorari. The objecting neighbors and the Board of Supervisors brought this appeal.

THE PULASKI CASE

Jack D. Nunley and Diana M. Nunley owned a corner lot in the Town of Pulaski that contained .6248 acre. The lot was bounded by public streets on three sides. A street 40 feet wide ran along the front of the property and the intersection of that street with a street approximately 30 feet wide formed the southeastern corner of the lot. The 30-foot street ran northward from the intersection, forming the eastern boundary of the lot, and then curved to the west to form the lot's northern boundary.

The curvature was gradual, having a radius of 34.53 feet. This curve formed the northeasterly corner of the lot.

The property was zoned R-1, a residential classification which contained a special provision relating to corner lots:

> The side yard on the side facing the side street shall be at least 15 feet from both main and accessory structures. Town of Pulaski, Va., Zoning Ordinance, art. IV § 2.6.2 (2002).

The Nunleys petitioned the BZA for a variance from the required 15-foot set back to zero feet, in order to construct a garage at the northeast corner of the lot, the northeast corner of which would be placed tangent to the curving property line. There was no existing garage on the property, and the Nunleys explained that placing a garage in this location would provide the easiest access to the street. The topography of the lot was difficult, the curve along the 30-foot street lying at a considerable elevation above the floor level of the existing house. The garage could be constructed closer to the house without the need for a variance, but this would require construction of a ramp that would add considerably to the expense of the project. Also, the Nunleys explained, there was a stone retaining wall, five feet in height, behind the house that would be weakened or destroyed if the garage were to be built closer to the house.

Neighbors objected, pointing out to the BZA that the construction of the garage so close to the corner would create a blind area that would be dangerous for traffic coming around the curve on the 30-foot street. They also complained that it would be an "eyesore" and would destroy existing vegetation.

The BZA eventually granted the Nunleys a modified variance, permitting an accessory structure no closer than five feet from the northern projected boundary and no closer than 15 feet from the eastern projected boundary of the property. The modified variance also provided that construction should not "alter or destroy the aesthetic looks of existing vegetation bordering the northern projected boundary" of the property.

Virginia C. MacNeal, a neighbor who had objected to the variance before the BZA, filed a petition for certiorari in the circuit court. The court, in a letter opinion, affirmed the decision of the BZA and denied the petition for certiorari. Virginia C. MacNeal brought this appeal.

THE VIRGINIA BEACH CASE

Jack and Rebecca Pennington owned a 1.25-acre parcel of land in a subdivision known as Avalon Terrace, in the City of Virginia Beach. The property was improved by their home, in which they had lived for many years, and a detached garage containing 528 square feet which they had built in 1972. The property was zoned R-10, a single-family residential classification permitting four dwelling units per acre. The ordinance contained a limitation on "accessory structures" by requiring that they "do not exceed five hundred (500) square feet of floor area or twenty (20) percent of the floor area of the principal structure, whichever is greater." The size of the Penningtons' home was such that the 500 square-foot limitation applied to their property.

The Penningtons applied to the BZA for a variance permitting accessory structures containing a total of 816 square feet, in lieu of the 500-square foot limitation. They explained that the purpose of the request was to permit the construction of a storage shed, 12 by 24 feet, adjacent to the garage, and also to bring into conformity the 28 square feet by which the existing garage exceeded the limitation imposed by the zoning ordinance.

The Penningtons could have built the storage shed as an appendage or as an addition to the existing house without the need for any variance, but their representative explained to the BZA that their lot was so large that the shed would be nearly invisible from the street and would have no impact upon neighboring properties. He contended that the obvious purpose of the size limitation on accessory structures, as contained in the ordinance, was to inhibit the erection of large, unsightly outbuildings on small lots. He pointed out that the Penningtons' lot was so large that four dwelling sites could be carved out of it, and that therefore the impact of a small additional outbuilding would be minimal and would not contravene the spirit of the zoning ordinance. He also pointed out that a number of the neighbors were related to the Penningtons and that no neighbors had any objection to their request.

The zoning administrator of the City of Virginia Beach opposed the request, pointing out that there was no need for a variance because the desired storage shed could be built as an appurtenance to the existing house. The zoning administrator had no objection to a variance to the extent of the 28 square feet needed to bring the existing garage into conformity with the zoning ordinance. The BZA granted the variance to bring the garage into conformity, but denied the remainder of the Penningtons' request on the ground that no "hardship" existed.

The Penningtons filed a petition for certiorari in the circuit court. The court ruled that a hardship existed, overruled the decision of the BZA and granted the Penningtons' requested variance. The BZA brought this appeal.

ANALYSIS

Zoning is a valid exercise of the police power of the Commonwealth. *West Brothers Brick Co. v. Alexandria*, 169 Va. 271 (1937). Zoning ordinances, of necessity, regulate land use uniformly within large districts. It is impracticable to tailor such ordinances to meet the condition of each individual parcel within the district. The size, shape, topography or other conditions affecting such a parcel may, if the zoning ordinance is applied to it as written, render it relatively useless. Thus, a zoning ordinance, valid on its face, might be unconstitutional as applied to an individual parcel, in violation of Article 1, § 11 of the Constitution of Virginia.

Because a facially valid zoning ordinance may prove unconstitutional in application to a particular landowner, some device is needed to protect landowners' rights without destroying the viability of zoning ordinances. The variance traditionally has been designed to serve this function. In this role, the variance aptly has been called an "escape hatch" or "escape valve." A statute may, of course, authorize variances in cases where an ordinance's application to particular property is not unconstitutional. However, the language used in Code § 15.1-495(b) to define "unnecessary hardship" clearly indicates that the General Assembly intended that variances be granted *only in cases where application of zoning restrictions would appear to be constitutionally impermissible.* Therefore, the BZA has authority to grant variances only to avoid an unconstitutional result. We said in *Commonwealth v. County Utilities*, 223 Va. 534 (1982):

> All citizens hold property subject to the proper exercise of police power for the common good. Even where such an exercise results in substantial diminution of property values, an owner has no right to compensation therefor. In *Penn Central Transportation Co. v. City of New York*, 438 U.S. 104 (1978), the Supreme Court held that no taking occurs in the circumstances unless the regulation interferes with *all reasonable beneficial uses of the property, taken as a whole. Id.* at 542, (emphasis added).

The BZA, when considering an application for a variance, acts only in an administrative capacity. Under fundamental constitutional principles, administrative officials and agencies are empowered to act only in accordance with standards prescribed by the legislative branch of government. To hold otherwise would be to substitute the will of individuals for the rule of law. The General Assembly has prescribed such standards regulating the authority of the BZA to grant variances by enacting Code § 15.2-2309(2) which provides, in pertinent part:

Boards of zoning appeals shall have the following powers and duties:

> ... (2) To authorize ... such variance as defined in § 15.2-2201 from the terms of the ordinance as will not be contrary to the public interest, when, owing to special conditions a literal enforcement of the provisions will result in unnecessary hardship; ... as follows:
>
> ... where by reason of exceptional topographic conditions or other extraordinary situation or condition of the piece of property ... the strict application of the terms of the ordinance would effectively prohibit or unreasonably restrict the utilization of the property or where the board is satisfied, upon the evidence heard by it, that the granting of the variance will alleviate a clearly demonstrable hardship approaching confiscation, as distinguished from a special privilege or convenience sought by the applicant....

No such variance shall be authorized by the board unless it finds: (a) That the strict application of the ordinance would produce undue hardship.... Adhering to the rule in *Packer*, we construe the statutory terms "effectively prohibit or unreasonably restrict the utilization of the property," "unnecessary hardship" and "undue hardship" in that light and hold that the BZA has no authority to grant a variance unless the effect of the zoning ordinance, as applied to the piece of property under consideration, would, in the absence of a variance, "interfere with all reasonable beneficial uses of the property, taken as a whole."

CONCLUSION

Notwithstanding the presumption of correctness to which the decision of the BZA is entitled, each of the present cases fails to meet the foregoing standard. The proposed house in Fairfax could have been reconfigured or moved two feet to the south, avoiding the need for a variance. Indeed, the project could simply have been abandoned and the existing use continued in effect. The proposed garage in Pulaski could have been moved to another location on the lot, or the project abandoned. The shed in Virginia Beach could have been built as an addition to the existing house, or the project abandoned. Without any variances, each of the properties retained substantial beneficial uses and substantial value. The effect of the respective zoning ordinances upon them in no sense "interfered with all reasonable beneficial uses of the property, taken as a whole."

Compelling reasons were presented in favor of each of the applications for variances: The desires of the owners, supported by careful planning to minimize harmful effects to neighboring properties; probable aesthetic improvements to the neighborhood as a whole, together with a probable increase in the local tax base; greatly increased expense to the owners if the plans were reconfigured to meet the requirements of the zoning ordinances; lack of opposition, or even support of the application by neighbors; and serious personal need, by the owners, for the proposed modification.

When the impact of the zoning ordinance is so severe as to meet the foregoing standard, the BZA becomes vested with wide discretion in tailoring a variance that will alleviate the "hardship" while remaining "in harmony with the intended spirit and purpose of the ordinance." Code § 15.2-2309(2). Factors such as those advanced in support of the variances in these cases are appropriate for consideration by the BZA in a case that falls within that discretionary power, but they are immaterial in a case in which the BZA has no authority to act. The threshold question for the BZA in considering an application for a variance as well as for a court reviewing its decision, is whether the effect of the zoning ordinance upon the property under consideration, as it stands, interferes with "all reasonable beneficial uses of the property, taken as a whole." If the answer is in the negative, the BZA has no authority to go further.

For these reasons, we will reverse the judgments of the circuit courts in each of the cases, vacate the resolutions of the Boards of Zoning Appeals of the County of Fairfax and the Town of Pulaski, respectively, reinstate the resolution of the Board of Zoning Appeals of the City of Virginia Beach, and enter final judgments here.

Exercise 8-9. *Cochran* Revisited

1. All three of the cases presented in *Cochran* involved what are referred to as "nonuse variances" as opposed to "use variances." A nonuse variance provides relief from set back rules, lot requirements, height restrictions, and the like, whereas a use variance would potentially allow "a pig in a parlor." Some jurisdictions do not permit use variances on the theory that they directly

undermine the comprehensive plan. *Matthew v. Smith*, 707 S.W.2d 411 (Mo. 1986).

2. Two of the cases involved objecting neighbors. The zoning ordinance and the appeals process provide a degree of certainty and ease of operation that is not present in a common law nuisance case. That said, assuming the variances had been upheld, would the neighbors have been able to bring a claim for common law nuisance?

Exclusionary Zoning: Federal and State Law

Zoning is by its very nature exclusionary. As Justice Douglas explained in *Village of Belle Terre v. Boraas*: "every line drawn by a legislature leaves some out that might well have been included." *Village of Belle Terre v. Boraas*, 416 U.S. 1 (1974). In the early 20th century, some American cities enacted racially restrictive zoning laws, including Atlanta, Chicago, and Richmond. These laws replicated on a macro scale the private racially restrictive covenants that were already in place in many neighborhoods. The U.S. Supreme Court invalidated racially restrictive zoning in 1917. *Buchanan v. Warley*, 245 U.S. 60 (1917). In *Buchanan v. Warley*, the Court unanimously held that a Louisville, Kentucky ordinance that prohibited the sale of real property in white majority neighborhoods to African Americans violated the Fourteenth Amendment. Property owners continued to encumber property with racially restrictive private covenants. The Court invalidated private racially restrictive covenants in 1948 in *Shelley v. Kraemer*, 334 U.S. 1 (1948).

Today, the term "exclusionary zoning" most often refers to zoning schemes that operate to prohibit low- and middle-income people from living in certain communities. The rapid suburbanization that occurred after World War II was largely framed by Euclidian zoning. Comprehensive planning controlled the development of the suburbs and bedroom communities that sprung up around urban centers. As middle class white residents of urban areas relocated to the suburbs, they left low-income minority residents in declining urban centers.

Comprehensive plans can make certain communities out of reach for low- and even middle-income residents through both use and area restrictions. For example, a comprehensive plan could fail to provide for multi-family housing or townhouses. Single-family dwellings are generally more expensive to either purchase or rent. In addition, area restrictions such as minimum lot size can increase the cost of housing, making it prohibitive for low- and middle-income individuals.

In the 1970s, community groups and other activists began to challenge these zoning schemes. In many instances, access to suburban communities also meant access to superior school districts and safer neighborhoods. Communities defended their comprehensive plans on fiscal grounds, noting a desire to maintain a strong tax base and preserve property values. You will see in the first case, *Village of Arlington*

Heights v. Metropolitan, that the U.S. Supreme Court has rejected constitutional challenges to exclusionary zoning schemes. However, some states have been more receptive to challenges brought under their state constitutions and have mandated inclusionary zoning for low- and middle-income residents. Although this represents a minority trend, some jurisdictions have enacted inclusionary zoning provisions that require a certain number or percentage of units within a given development to be reserved for low- or middle-income residents. As you read the cases in this section, consider how we should balance the importance of access to opportunity with the ability of a community to set the terms and the pace of its development.

Exercise 8-10. *Village of Arlington Heights v. Metropolitan* — Federal Law

Village of Euclid v. Ambler Realty, Co. established the constitutionality of comprehensive zoning. Although comprehensive zoning schemes represent a valid exercise of police power, we saw in the prior section that the application of these schemes to individual property owners may still be challenged. The challenges to zoning laws as they are applied can be based on procedural deficiencies or claims that the action is inconsistent with the comprehensive plan. Both of these claims can potentially raise constitutional issues. The cases in this section are addressing broader claims than the individual complaints adjudicated in the prior section. The exclusionary zoning challenges allege that an entire comprehensive plan is unconstitutional because of the effect the plan has on the composition of the community.

The following case involves the denial of a rezoning request. Plaintiffs alleged that the denial was racially discriminatory and violated the Fourteenth Amendment to the U.S. Constitution. As you read the case, pay particular attention to the standard of proof that the plaintiffs must meet and the difference between discriminatory effect and discriminatory purpose.

In Chapter 3, we discussed that, in some instances, non-owners have a right to access. Do you see any parallel policy considerations in the exclusionary zoning cases?

Village of Arlington Heights v. Metropolitan

429 U.S. 252 (1977)

Mr. Justice Powell delivered the opinion of the Court. In 1971 respondent Metropolitan Housing Development Corporation (MHDC) applied to petitioner, the Village of Arlington Heights, Ill., for the rezoning of a 15-acre parcel from single-family to multiple-family classification. Using federal financial assistance, MHDC planned to build 190 clustered townhouse units for low- and moderate-income tenants.

The Village denied the rezoning request. MHDC, joined by other plaintiffs who are also respondents here, brought suit in the United States District Court for the Northern District of Illinois. They alleged that the denial was racially discriminatory and that it violated, inter alia, the Fourteenth Amendment. Following a bench trial, the District Court entered judgment for the Village, and respondents appealed. The Court of Appeals for the Seventh Circuit reversed, finding that the "ultimate effect" of the denial was racially discriminatory, and that the refusal to rezone therefore violated the Fourteenth Amendment. We granted the Village's petition for certiorari and now reverse.

I

Arlington Heights is a suburb of Chicago, located about 26 miles northwest of the downtown Loop area. Most of the land in Arlington Heights is zoned for detached single-family homes, and this is in fact the prevailing land use. The Village experienced substantial growth during the 1960's, but, like other communities in northwest Cook County, its population of racial minority groups remained quite low. According to the 1970 census, only 27 of the Village's 64,000 residents were black.

The Clerics of St. Viator, a religious order (Order), own an 80-acre parcel just east of the center of Arlington Heights. Part of the site is occupied by the Viatorian high school, and part by the Order's three-story novitiate building, which houses dormitories and a Montessori school. Much of the site, however, remains vacant. Since 1959, when the Village first adopted a zoning ordinance, all the land surrounding the Viatorian property has been zoned R-3, a singlefamily specification with relatively small minimum lot-size requirements. On three sides of the Viatorian land there are single-family homes just across a street; to the east the Viatorian property directly adjoins the backyards of other single-family homes.

The Order decided in 1970 to devote some of its land to low- and moderate-income housing. Investigation revealed that the most expeditious way to build such housing was to work through a nonprofit developer experienced in the use of federal housing subsidies under § 236 of the National Housing Act, 48 Stat. 1246, as added and amended, 12 U.S.C. § 1715z-1.

New commitments under § 236 were suspended in 1973 by executive decision, and they have not been revived. Projects which formerly could claim § 236 assistance, however, will now generally be eligible for aid under § 8 of the United States Housing Act of 1937, as amended by § 201(a) of the Housing and Community Development Act of 1974, 42 U.S.C. § 1437f (1970 ed., Supp. V), and by the Housing Authorization Act of 1976, § 2, 90 Stat. 1068. Under the § 8 program, the Department of Housing and Urban Development contracts to pay the owner of the housing units a sum which will make up the difference between a fair market rent for the area and the amount contributed by the low-income tenant. The eligible tenant family pays between 15% and 25% of its gross income for rent. Respondents indicated at oral argument that, despite the demise of the § 236 program, construction of the MHDC project could proceed under § 8 if zoning clearance is now granted.

MHDC is such a developer. It was organized in 1968 by several prominent Chicago citizens for the purpose of building low- and moderate-income housing throughout the Chicago area. In 1970 MHDC was in the process of building one § 236 development near Arlington Heights and already had provided some federally assisted housing on a smaller scale in other parts of the Chicago area.

After some negotiation, MHDC and the Order entered into a 99-year lease and an accompanying agreement of sale covering a 15-acre site in the southeast corner of the Viatorian property. MHDC became the lessee immediately, but the sale agreement was contingent upon MHDC's securing zoning clearances from the Village and § 236 housing assistance from the Federal Government. If MHDC proved unsuccessful in securing either, both the lease and the contract of sale would lapse. The agreement established a bargain purchase price of $300,000, low enough to comply with federal limitations governing land-acquisition costs for § 236 housing. MHDC engaged an architect and proceeded with the project, to be known as Lincoln Green. The plans called for 20 two-story buildings with a total of 190 units, each unit having its own private entrance from the outside. One hundred of the units would have a single bedroom, thought likely to attract elderly citizens. The remainder would have two, three, or four bedrooms. A large portion of the site would remain open, with shrubs and trees to screen the homes abutting the property to the east.

The planned development did not conform to the Village's zoning ordinance and could not be built unless Arlington Heights rezoned the parcel to R-5, its multiple-family housing classification. Accordingly, MHDC filed with the Village Plan Commission a petition for rezoning, accompanied by supporting materials describing the development and specifying that it would be subsidized under § 236. The materials made clear that one requirement under § 236 is an affirmative marketing plan designed to assure that a subsidized development is racially integrated. MHDC also submitted studies demonstrating the need for housing of this type and analyzing the probable impact of the development. To prepare for the hearings before the Plan Commission and to assure compliance with the Village building code, fire regulations, and related requirements, MHDC consulted with the Village staff for preliminary review of the development. The parties have stipulated that every change recommended during such consultations was incorporated into the plans.

During the spring of 1971, the Plan Commission considered the proposal at a series of three public meetings, which drew large crowds. Although many of those attending were quite vocal and demonstrative in opposition to Lincoln Green, a number of individuals and representatives of community groups spoke in support of rezoning. Some of the comments, both from opponents and supporters, addressed what was referred to as the "social issue"—the desirability or undesirability of introducing at this location in Arlington Heights low- and moderate-income housing, housing that would probably be racially integrated.

Many of the opponents, however, focused on the zoning aspects of the petition, stressing two arguments. First, the area always had been zoned single-family, and the neighboring citizens had built or purchased there in reliance on that classification.

Rezoning threatened to cause a measurable drop in property value for neighboring sites. Second, the Village's apartment policy, adopted by the Village Board in 1962 and amended in 1970, called for R-5 zoning primarily to serve as a buffer between single-family development and land uses thought incompatible, such as commercial or manufacturing districts. Lincoln Green did not meet this requirement, as it adjoined no commercial or manufacturing district.

At the close of the third meeting, the Plan Commission adopted a motion to recommend to the Village's Board of Trustees that it deny the request. The motion stated: "While the need for low and moderate income housing may exist in Arlington Heights or its environs, the Plan Commission would be derelict in recommending it at the proposed location." Two members voted against the motion and submitted a minority report, stressing that in their view the change to accommodate Lincoln Green represented "good zoning." The Village Board met on September 28, 1971, to consider MHDC's request and the recommendation of the Plan Commission. After a public hearing, the Board denied the rezoning by a 6-1 vote.

The following June MHDC and three Negro individuals filed this lawsuit against the Village, seeking declaratory and injunctive relief. A second nonprofit corporation and an individual of Mexican-American descent intervened as plaintiffs. The trial resulted in a judgment for petitioners. Assuming that MHDC had standing to bring the suit, the District Court held that the petitioners were not motivated by racial discrimination or intent to discriminate against low income groups when they denied rezoning, but rather by a desire "to protect property values and the integrity of the Village's zoning plan." The District Court concluded also that the denial would not have a racially discriminatory effect.

A divided Court of Appeals reversed. It first approved the District Court's finding that the defendants were motivated by a concern for the integrity of the zoning plan, rather than by racial discrimination. Deciding whether their refusal to rezone would have discriminatory effects was more complex. The court observed that the refusal would have a disproportionate impact on blacks. Based upon family income, blacks constituted 40% of those Chicago area residents who were eligible to become tenants of Lincoln Green, although they composed a far lower percentage of total area population. The court reasoned, however, that under our decision in *James v. Valtierra*, 402 U.S. 137 (1971), such a disparity in racial impact alone does not call for strict scrutiny of a municipality's decision that prevents the construction of the low-cost housing.

There was another level to the court's analysis of allegedly discriminatory results. Invoking language from *Kennedy Park Homes Assn. v. City of Lackawanna*, 436 F.2d 108, 112 (Cir. 2d 1970), cert. denied, 401 U.S. 1010 (1971), the Court of Appeals ruled that the denial of rezoning must be examined in light of its "historical context and ultimate effect." Northwest Cook County was enjoying rapid growth in employment opportunities and population, but it continued to exhibit a high degree of residential segregation. The court held that Arlington Heights could not simply ignore this problem. Indeed, it found that the Village had been "exploiting" the situation by allowing itself to become a nearly all-white community. The Village had no other current plans for building low- and moderate-income housing, and no other R-5 parcels in the Village were available to MHDC at an economically feasible price.

III

Our decision last Term in *Washington v. Davis*, 426 U.S. 229 (1976), made it clear that official action will not be held unconstitutional solely because it results in a racially disproportionate impact. "Disproportionate impact is not irrelevant, but it is not the sole touchstone of an invidious racial discrimination." Proof of racially discriminatory intent or purpose is required to show a violation of the Equal Protection Clause. Although some contrary indications may be drawn from some of our cases, the holding in *Davis* reaffirmed a principle well established in a variety of contexts.

Davis does not require a plaintiff to prove that the challenged action rested solely on racially discriminatory purposes. Rarely can it be said that a legislature or administrative body operating under a broad mandate made a decision motivated solely by a single concern, or even that a particular purpose was the "dominant" or "primary" one. In fact, it is because legislators and administrators are properly concerned with balancing numerous competing considerations that courts refrain from reviewing the merits of their decisions, absent a showing of arbitrariness or irrationality. But racial discrimination is not just another competing consideration. When there is a proof that a discriminatory purpose has been a motivating factor in the decision, this judicial deference is no longer justified.

Determining whether invidious discriminatory purpose was a motivating factor demands a sensitive inquiry into such circumstantial and direct evidence of intent as may be available. The impact of the official action—whether it "bears more heavily on one race than another," *Washington v. Davis*—may provide an important starting point. Sometimes a clear pattern, unexplainable on grounds other than race, emerges from the effect of the state action even when the governing legislation appears neutral on its face. The evidentiary inquiry is then relatively easy. But such cases are rare. Absent a pattern as stark as that in *Gomillion* [*v. Lightfoot*, 364 U.S. 339 (1960),] or *Yick Wo* [*v. Hopkins*, 118 U.S. 356 (1886)], impact alone is not determinative, and the Court must look to other evidence.

The historical background of the decision is one evidentiary source, particularly if it reveals a series of official actions taken for invidious purposes. For example, if the property involved here always had been zoned R-5 but suddenly was changed to R-3 when the town learned of MHDC's plans to erect integrated housing, we would have a far different case. Departures from the normal procedural sequence also might afford evidence that improper purposes are playing a role. Substantive departures too may be relevant, particularly if the factors usually considered important by the decisionmaker strongly favor a decision contrary to the one reached.

The legislative or administrative history may be highly relevant, especially where there are contemporary statements by members of the decisionmaking body, minutes of its meetings, or reports. In some extraordinary instances the members might be called to the stand at trial to testify concerning the purpose of the official action, although even then such testimony frequently will be barred by privilege.

The foregoing summary identifies, without purporting to be exhaustive, subjects of proper inquiry in determining whether racially discriminatory intent existed. With these in mind, we now address the case before us.

IV

In making its findings on this issue, the District Court noted that some of the opponents of Lincoln Green who spoke at the various hearings might have been motivated by opposition to minority groups. The court held, however, that the evidence "does not warrant the conclusion that this motivated the defendants." On appeal the Court of Appeals focused primarily on respondents' claim that the Village's buffer policy had not been consistently applied and was being invoked with a strictness here that could only demonstrate some other underlying motive. The court concluded that the buffer policy, though not always applied with perfect consistency, had on several occasions formed the basis for the Board's decision to deny other rezoning proposals. "The evidence does not necessitate a finding that Arlington Heights administered this policy in a discriminatory manner." The Court of Appeals therefore approved the District Court's findings concerning the Village's purposes in denying rezoning to MHDC.

We also have reviewed the evidence. The impact of the Village's decision does arguably bear more heavily on racial minorities. Minorities constitute 18% of the Chicago area population, and 40% of the income groups said to be eligible for Lincoln Green. But there is little about the sequence of events leading up to the decision that would spark suspicion. The area around the Viatorian property has been zoned R-3 since 1959, the year when Arlington Heights first adopted a zoning map. Single-family homes surround the 80-acre site, and the Village is undeniably committed to single-family homes as its dominant residential land use. The rezoning request progressed according to the usual procedures. The Plan Commission even scheduled two additional hearings, at least in part to accommodate MHDC and permit it to supplement its presentation with answers to questions generated at the first hearing.

The statements by the Plan Commission and Village Board members, as reflected in the official minutes, focused almost exclusively on the zoning aspects of the MHDC petition, and the zoning factors on which they relied are not novel criteria in the Village's rezoning decisions. There is no reason to doubt that there has been reliance by some neighboring property owners on the maintenance of single-family zoning in the vicinity. The Village originally adopted its buffer policy long before MHDC entered the picture and has applied the policy too consistently for us to infer discriminatory purpose from its application in this case. Finally, MHDC called one member of the Village Board to the stand at trial. Nothing in her testimony supports an inference of invidious purpose.

In sum, the evidence does not warrant overturning the concurrent findings of both courts below. Respondents simply failed to carry their burden of proving that discriminatory purpose was a motivating factor in the Village's decision. This conclusion ends the constitutional inquiry. The Court of Appeals' further finding that the Village's decision carried a discriminatory "ultimate effect" is without independent constitutional significance.

Proof that the decision by the Village was motivated in part by a racially discriminatory purpose would not necessarily have required invalidation of the challenged decision. Such proof would, however, have shifted to the Village the burden of establishing that the same decision would have resulted even had the impermissible purpose not been considered. If this were established, the complaining party in a case of this kind no longer fairly could attribute the injury complained of to improper consideration of a discriminatory purpose. In such circumstances, there would be no justification for judicial interference with the challenged decision. But in this case respondents failed to make the required threshold showing.

Exercise 8-11. *Village of Arlington* Revisited

1. *Village of Arlington* clarifies that proof of racially discriminatory intent or purpose is required to prove a violation of the Equal Protection Clause. Consider what types of evidence would be sufficient to show a discriminatory intent or purpose.
2. The Court mentions that sometimes the result may be so stark that the pattern is inexplicable on any other grounds than racial discrimination, but notes that these cases are rare. As examples of these rare instances, the Court cites *Yick Wo v. Hopkins*, 118 U.S. 356 (1886), and *Gomillion v. Lightfoot*, 364 U.S. 339 (1960), where facially neutral laws were stuck down. *Gomillion* was a voting rights case involving a gerrymandered district designed to reduce the influence of African American voters. *Yick Wo* challenged a facially neutral San Francisco zoning ordinance. The ordinance prohibited the operation of a laundry business in a wooden building unless the owner applied for and received a permit. The law had a disproportionate impact on Chinese Americans. Nearly ninety-seven percent of the laundries in San Francisco at the time were in wooden buildings and seventy-five percent of the laundries were owned by Chinese Americans. Two hundred of the Chinese-owned laundries applied for a permit, and all of the requests were denied. In contrast, only one of the requests for a permit from a non-Chinese applicant was denied. The Court ruled that

   > Though the law itself be fair on its face and impartial in appearance, yet, if it is applied and administered by public authority with an evil eye and an unequal hand, so as practically to make unjust and illegal discriminations between persons in similar circumstances, material to

their rights, the denial of equal justice is still within the prohibition of the Constitution.

3. In *Yick Wo*, the Court took particular care to note the extent of the longstanding investment that the Chinese American owners had made in the laundries. Can you make a case that reasonable investment backed expectations also played a role in *Village of Arlington*?

Exercise 8-12. *Southern Burlington County NAACP v. Township of Mount Laurel*—State Law

Inclusionary zoning cases have had greater success at the state level. The following case from the New Jersey Supreme Court represents a minority view. As we have seen in other instances, state constitutions are free to provide greater protections than the federal Constitution. In *Southern Burlington County NAACP v. Township of Mount Laurel* (known as *Mount Laurel I*), the plaintiffs challenged the comprehensive zoning plan of the Township of Mount Laurel, New Jersey under the New Jersey Constitution.

In Chapter 3, we read several cases from the New Jersey Supreme Court dealing with issues related to a non-owner's right of access: *State v. Shack*, *Uston v. Resorts*, and *National Organization for Women, Essex Cnty. Chapter v. Little League Baseball, Inc.* In these cases, the New Jersey Supreme Court ruled in favor of access. As you read the following case, consider whether the policies favoring access should also apply to communities.

Southern Burlington County NAACP v. Township of Mount Laurel

67 N.J. 151 (1975)

HALL, J. This case attacks the system of land use regulation by defendant Township of Mount Laurel on the ground that low and moderate income families are thereby unlawfully excluded from the municipality. The trial court so found and declared the township zoning ordinance totally invalid. Its judgment went on, in line with the requests for affirmative relief, to order the municipality to make studies of the housing needs of low and moderate income persons presently or formerly residing in the community in substandard housing, as well as those in such income classifications presently employed in the township and living elsewhere or reasonably expected to be employed therein in the future, and to present a plan of affirmative public action designed "to enable and encourage the satisfaction of the indicated needs.: Jurisdiction was retained for judicial consideration and approval of such a plan and for the entry of a final order requiring its implementation.

The implications of the issue presented are indeed broad and far-reaching, extending much beyond these particular plaintiffs and the boundaries of this particular municipality.

There is not the slightest doubt that New Jersey has been, and continues to be, faced with a desperate need for housing, especially of decent living accommodations economically suitable for low and moderate income families. The situation was characterized as a "crisis" and fully explored and documented by Governor Cahill in two special messages to the Legislature—*A Blueprint for Housing in New Jersey* (1970) and *New Horizons in Housing* (1972).

Plaintiffs represent the minority group poor (black and Hispanic) seeking such quarters. But they are not the only category of persons barred from so many municipalities by reason of restrictive land use regulations. We have reference to young and elderly couples, single persons and large, growing families not in the poverty class, but who still cannot afford the only kinds of housing realistically permitted in most places—relatively high-priced, single-family detached dwellings on sizeable lots and, in some municipalities, expensive apartments. We will, therefore, consider the case from the wider viewpoint that the effect of Mount Laurel's land use regulation has been to prevent various categories of persons from living in the township because of the limited extent of their income and resources. In this connection, we accept the representation of the municipality's counsel at oral argument that the regulatory scheme was not adopted with any desire or intent to exclude prospective residents on the obviously illegal basis of race, origin or believed social incompatibility.

As already intimated, the issue here is not confined to Mount Laurel. The same question arises with respect to any number of other municipalities of sizeable land area outside the central cities and older built-up suburbs of our North and South Jersey metropolitan areas (and surrounding some of the smaller cities outside those areas as well) which, like Mount Laurel, have substantially shed rural characteristics and have undergone great population increase since World War II, or are now in the process of doing so, but still are not completely developed and remain in the path of inevitable future residential, commercial and industrial demand and growth. Most such municipalities, with but relatively insignificant variation in details, present generally comparable physical situations, courses of municipal policies, practices, enactments and results and human, governmental and legal problems arising therefrom. It is in the context of communities now of this type or which become so in the future, rather than with central cities or older built-up suburbs or areas still rural and likely to continue to be for some time yet, that we deal with the question raised.

[The township's] candid position is that, conceding its land use regulation was intended to result and has resulted in economic discrimination and exclusion of substantial segments of the area population, its policies and practices are in the best present and future fiscal interest of the municipality and its inhabitants and are legally permissible and justified. It further asserts that the trial court was without power to direct the affirmative relief it did.

I
The Facts

Mount Laurel is a flat, sprawling township, 22 square miles, or about 14,000 acres, in area, on the west central edge of Burlington County. It is roughly triangular in shape, with its base, approximately eight miles long, extending in a northeasterly-southwesterly direction roughly parallel with and a few miles east of the Delaware River. Part of its southerly side abuts Cherry Hill in Camden County. That section of the township is about seven miles from the boundary line of the city of Camden and not more than 10 miles from the Benjamin Franklin Bridge crossing the river to Philadelphia.

In 1950, the township had a population of 2817, only about 600 more people than it had in 1940. It was then, as it had been for decades, primarily a rural agricultural area with no sizeable settlements or commercial or industrial enterprises. The populace generally lived in individual houses scattered along country roads. There were several pockets of poverty, with deteriorating or dilapidated housing (apparently 300 or so units of which remain today in equally poor condition). After 1950, as in so many other municipalities similarly situated, residential development and some commerce and industry began to come in. By 1960 the population had almost doubled to 5249 and by 1970 had more than doubled again to 11,221. These new residents were, of course, "outsiders" from the nearby central cities and older suburbs or from more distant places drawn here by reason of employment in the region. The township is now definitely a part of the outer ring of the South Jersey metropolitan area, which area we define as those portions of Camden, Burlington and Gloucester Counties within a semicircle having a radius of 20 miles or so from the heart of Camden city. And 65% of the township is still vacant land or in agricultural use.

The growth of the township has been spurred by the construction or improvement of main highways through or near it. The New Jersey Turnpike, and now route I-295, a freeway paralleling the turnpike, traverse the municipality near its base, with the main Camden-Philadelphia turnpike interchange at the corner nearest Camden. State route 73 runs at right angles to the turnpike at the interchange and route 38 slices through the northeasterly section. Routes 70 and U.S. 130 are not far away. This highway network gives the township a most strategic location from the standpoint of transport of goods and people by truck and private car. There is no other means of transportation.

The location and nature of development has been, as usual, controlled by the local zoning enactments. The general ordinance presently in force, which was declared invalid by the trial court, was adopted in 1964. We understand that earlier enactments provided, however, basically the same scheme but were less restrictive as to residential development. The growth pattern dictated by the ordinance is typical.

Under the present ordinance, 29.2% of all the land in the township, or 4,121 acres, is zoned for industry. This amounts to 2,800 more acres than were so zoned by the 1954 ordinance. The industrial districts comprise most of the land on both sides of the turnpike and routes I-295, 73 and 38. Only industry meeting specified performance standards is permitted. The effect is to limit the use substantially to light manufacturing, research, distribution of goods, offices and the like. Some non-industrial uses, such as agriculture, farm dwellings, motels, a harness racetrack, and certain retail sales and service establishments, are permitted in this zone. The amount of land zoned for retail business use under the general ordinance is relatively small—169 acres, or 1.2% of the total. Some of it is near the turnpike interchange; most of the rest is allocated to a handful of neighborhood commercial districts. While the greater part of the land so zoned appears to be in use, there is no major shopping center or concentrated retail commercial area—"downtown"—in the township.

The balance of the land area, almost 10,000 acres, has been developed until recently in the conventional form of major subdivisions. The general ordinance provides for four residential zones, designated R-1, R-1D, R-2 and R-3. All permit only single-family, detached dwellings, one house per lot—the usual form of grid development. Attached townhouses, apartments (except on farms for agricultural workers) and mobile homes are not allowed anywhere in the township under the general ordinance. This dwelling development, resulting in the previously mentioned quadrupling of the population, has been largely confined to the R-1 and R-2 districts in two sections—the northeasterly and southwesterly corners adjacent to the turnpike and other major highways. The result has been quite intensive development of these sections, but at a low density. The dwellings are substantial; the average value in 1971 was $ 32,500 and is undoubtedly much higher today.

The general ordinance requirements, while not as restrictive as those in many similar municipalities, nonetheless realistically allow only homes within the financial reach of persons of at least middle income.

The record thoroughly substantiates the findings of the trial court that over the years Mount Laurel "has acted affirmatively to control development and to attract a selective type of growth" and that "through its zoning ordinances has exhibited economic discrimination in that the poor have been deprived of adequate housing and the opportunity to secure the construction of subsidized housing, and has used federal, state, county and local finances and resources solely for the betterment of middle and upper-income persons."

There cannot be the slightest doubt that the reason for this course of conduct has been to keep down local taxes on *property* (Mount Laurel is not a high tax municipality) and that the policy was carried out without regard for nonfiscal considerations with respect to *people*, either within or without its boundaries. This conclusion is demonstrated not only by what was done and what happened, as we have related, but also by innumerable direct statements of municipal officials at public meetings over the years which are found in the exhibits. The trial court referred to a number of them. No official testified to the contrary.

This policy of land use regulation for a fiscal end derives from New Jersey's tax structure, which has imposed on local real estate most of the cost of municipal and county government and of the primary and secondary education of the municipality's children. The latter expense is much the largest, so, basically, the fewer the school children, the lower the tax rate. Sizeable industrial and commercial ratables are eagerly sought and homes and the lots on which they are situate are required to be large enough, through minimum lot sizes and minimum floor areas, to have substantial value in order to produce greater tax revenues to meet school costs. Large families who cannot afford to buy large houses and must live in cheaper rental accommodations are definitely not wanted, so we find drastic bedroom restrictions for, or complete prohibition of, multi-family or other feasible housing for those of lesser income.

This pattern of land use regulation has been adopted for the same purpose in developing municipality after developing municipality. Almost every one acts solely in its own selfish and parochial interest and in effect builds a wall around itself to keep out those people or entities not adding favorably to the tax base, despite the location of the municipality or the demand for varied kinds of housing. There has been no effective intermunicipal or area planning or land use regulation. All of this is amply demonstrated by the evidence in this case as to Camden, Burlington and Gloucester counties. One incongruous result is the picture of developing municipalities rendering it impossible for lower paid employees of industries they have eagerly sought and welcomed with open arms (and, in Mount Laurel's case, even some of its own lower paid municipal employees) to live in the community where they work.

II
The Legal Issue

The legal question before us, as earlier indicated, is whether a developing municipality like Mount Laurel may validly, by a system of land use regulation, make it physically and economically impossible to provide low and moderate income housing in the municipality for the various categories of persons who need and want it and thereby, as Mount Laurel has, exclude such people from living within its confines because of the limited extent of their income and resources. Necessarily implicated are the broader questions of the right of such municipalities to limit the kinds of available housing and of any obligation to make possible a variety and choice of types of living accommodations.

We conclude that every such municipality must, by its land use regulations, presumptively make realistically possible an appropriate variety and choice of housing. More specifically, presumptively it cannot foreclose the opportunity of the classes of people mentioned for low and moderate income housing and in its regulations must affirmatively afford that opportunity, at least to the extent of the municipality's fair share of the present and prospective regional need therefor. These obligations must be met unless the particular municipality can sustain the heavy burden of demonstrating peculiar circumstances which dictate that it should not be required so to do.

We reach this conclusion under state law and so do not find it necessary to consider federal constitutional grounds urged by plaintiffs. We begin with some fundamental principles as applied to the scene before us.

Land use regulation is encompassed within the state's police power. Our constitutions have expressly so provided since an amendment in 1927. That amendment, now Art. IV, sec. VI, par. 2 of the 1947 Constitution, authorized legislative delegation of the power to municipalities (other than counties), but reserved the legislative right to repeal or alter the delegation (which we take it means repeal or alteration in whole or in part). The legislative delegation of the zoning power followed in 1928, by adoption of the standard zoning enabling act, now found, with subsequent amendments, in N.J.S.A. 40:55-30 to 51.

It is elementary theory that all police power enactments, no matter at what level of government, must conform to the basic state constitutional requirements of substantive due process and equal protection of the laws. These are inherent in Art. I, par. 1 of our Constitution, the requirements of which may be more demanding than those of the federal Constitution. It is required that, affirmatively, a zoning regulation, like any police power enactment, must promote public health, safety, morals or the general welfare. (The last term seems broad enough to encompass the others). Conversely, a zoning enactment which is contrary to the general welfare is invalid. Indeed these considerations are specifically set forth in the zoning enabling act as among the various purposes of zoning for which regulations must be designed. N.J.S.A. 40:55-32. Their inclusion therein really adds little; the same requirement would exist even if they were omitted. If a zoning regulation violates the enabling act in this respect, it is also theoretically invalid under the state constitution. We say "theoretically" because, as a matter of policy, we do not treat the validity of most land use ordinance provisions as involving matters of constitutional dimension; that classification is confined to major questions of fundamental import. We consider the basic importance of housing and local regulations restricting its availability to substantial segments of the population to fall within the latter category.

The demarcation between the valid and the invalid in the field of land use regulation is difficult to determine, not always clear and subject to change. It is fundamental and not to be forgotten that the zoning power is a police power of the state and the local authority is acting only as a delegate of that power and is restricted in the same manner as is the state. So, when regulation does have a substantial external impact, the welfare of the state's citizens beyond the borders of the particular municipality cannot be disregarded and must be recognized and served.

It is plain beyond dispute that proper provision for adequate housing of all categories of people is certainly an absolute essential in promotion of the general welfare required in all local land use regulation. Further the universal and constant need for such housing is so important and of such broad public interest that the general welfare which developing municipalities like Mount Laurel must consider extends beyond their boundaries and cannot be parochially confined to the claimed good of the particular municipality. It has to follow that, broadly speaking, the presumptive obligation arises for each such municipality affirmatively to plan and provide, by its land use regulations, the reasonable opportunity for an appropriate variety and choice of housing, including, of course, low and moderate cost housing, to meet the needs, desires and resources of all categories of people who may desire to live within its boundaries. Negatively, it may not adopt regulations or policies which thwart or preclude that opportunity.

It is also entirely clear, as we pointed out earlier, that most developing municipalities, including Mount Laurel, have not met their affirmative or negative obligations, primarily for local fiscal reasons. In sum, we are satisfied beyond any doubt that, by reason of the basic importance of appropriate housing and the longstanding pressing need for it, especially in the low and moderate cost category, and of the exclusionary zoning practices of so many municipalities, conditions have changed, and judicial attitudes must be altered from that espoused in [earlier cases] to require a broader view of the general welfare and the presumptive obligation on the part of developing municipalities at least to afford the opportunity by land use regulations for appropriate housing for all.

Mount Laurel's zoning ordinance is also so restrictive in its minimum lot area, lot frontage and building size requirements, earlier detailed, as to preclude single-family housing for even moderate income families. Again it is evident these requirements increase the size and so the cost of housing. The conclusion is irresistible that Mount Laurel permits only such middle and upper income housing as it believes will have sufficient taxable value to come close to paying its own governmental way.

Akin to large lot, single-family zoning restricting the population is the zoning of very large amounts of land for industrial and related uses. Mount Laurel has set aside almost 30% of its area, over 4,100 acres, for that purpose; the only residential use allowed is for farm dwellings. In almost a decade only about 100 acres have been developed industrially. Despite the township's strategic location for motor transportation purposes, as intimated earlier, it seems plain that the likelihood of anywhere near the whole of the zoned area being used for the intended purpose in the foreseeable future is remote indeed and that an unreasonable amount of land has thereby been removed from possible residential development, again seemingly for local fiscal reasons.

Without further elaboration at this point, our opinion is that Mount Laurel's zoning ordinance is presumptively contrary to the general welfare and outside the intended scope of the zoning power in the particulars mentioned. A facial showing of invalidity is thus established, shifting to the municipality the burden of establishing valid superseding reasons for its action and non-action. We now examine the reasons it advances.

The township's principal reason in support of its zoning plan and ordinance housing provisions, advanced especially strongly at oral argument, is the fiscal one previously adverted to, *i.e.*, that by reason of New Jersey's tax structure which substantially finances municipal governmental and educational costs from taxes on local real property, every municipality may, by the exercise of the zoning power, allow only such uses and to such extent as will be beneficial to the local tax rate. In other words, the position is that any municipality may zone extensively to seek and encourage the "good" tax ratables of industry and commerce, and limit the permissible types of housing to those having the fewest school children or to those providing sufficient value to attain or approach paying their own way taxwise.

We have no hesitancy in now saying, and do so emphatically, that, considering the basic importance of the opportunity for appropriate housing for all classes of our citizenry, no municipality may exclude or limit categories of housing for that reason or purpose. While we fully recognize the increasingly heavy burden of local taxes for municipal governmental and school costs on homeowners, relief from the consequences of this tax system will have to be furnished by other branches of government. It cannot legitimately be accomplished by restricting types of housing through the zoning process in developing municipalities.

The propriety of zoning ordinance limitations on housing for ecological or environmental reasons seems also to be suggested by Mount Laurel in support of the one-half acre minimum lot size in that very considerable portion of the township still available for residential development. It is said that the area is without sewer or water utilities and that the soil is such that this plot size is required for safe individual lot sewage disposal and water supply. The short answer is that, this being flat land and readily amenable to such utility installations, the township could require them as improvements by developers or install them under the special assessment or other appropriate statutory procedure. The present environmental situation of the area is, therefore, no sufficient excuse in itself for limiting housing therein to single-family dwellings on large lots. This is not to say that land use regulations should not take due account of ecological or environmental factors or problems. Quite the contrary. Their importance, at last being recognized, should always be considered. Generally only a relatively small portion of a developing municipality will be involved, for, to have a valid effect, the danger and impact must be substantial and very real (the construction of every building or the improvement of every plot has some environmental impact)—not simply a makeweight to support exclusionary housing measures or preclude growth—and the regulation adopted must be only that reasonably necessary for public protection of a vital interest. Otherwise difficult additional problems relating to a "taking" of a property owner's land may arise.

By way of summary, what we have said comes down to this. As a developing municipality, Mount Laurel must, by its land use regulations, make realistically possible the opportunity for an appropriate variety and choice of housing for all categories of people who may desire to live there, of course including those of low and moderate income. It must permit multi-family housing, without bedroom or similar restrictions, as well as small dwellings on very small lots, low cost housing of other types and, in general, high density zoning, without artificial and unjustifiable minimum requirements as to lot size, building size and the like, to meet the full panoply of these needs. Certainly when a municipality zones for industry and commerce for local tax benefit purposes, it without question must zone to permit adequate housing within the means of the employees involved in such uses. (If planned unit developments are authorized, one would assume that each must include a reasonable amount of low and moderate income housing in its residential "mix," unless opportunity for such housing has already been realistically provided for elsewhere in the municipality.) The amount of land removed from residential use by allocation to industrial and commercial purposes must be reasonably related to the present and future potential for such purposes. In other words, such municipalities must zone primarily for the living welfare of people and not for the benefit of the local tax rate.

There is no reason why developing municipalities like Mount Laurel, required by this opinion to afford the opportunity for all types of housing to meet the needs of various categories of people, may not become and remain attractive, viable communities providing good living and adequate services for all their residents in the kind of atmosphere which a democracy and free institutions demand. They can have industrial sections, commercial sections and sections for every kind of housing from low cost and multi-family to lots of more than an acre with very expensive homes. Proper planning and governmental cooperation can prevent over-intensive and too sudden development, insure against future suburban sprawl and slums and assure the preservation of open space and local beauty. We do not intend that developing municipalities shall be overwhelmed by voracious land speculators and developers if they use the powers which they have intelligently and in the broad public interest. Under our holdings today, they can be better communities for all than they previously have been.

Exercise 8-13. *Southern Burlington County NAACP* Revisited

1. Mount Laurel is a bedroom community outside of Philadelphia. It experienced tremendous growth in population in the twenty-five years prior to the court challenge. The growth was controlled and orchestrated by its comprehensive land use system. The individuals who bought homes and invested in the community arguably relied on this land use system and the vision of Mount Laurel expressed in its comprehensive plan. How should we weigh their investment-backed expectations?
2. The New Jersey Supreme Court imposed an affirmative obligation on New Jersey municipalities to "make realistically possible an appropriate variety and choice of housing." On what authority does the court base this ruling?
3. Not surprisingly, this case, known as *Mount Laurel I,* opened the door for similar lawsuits to be filed against other municipalities. The same plaintiffs later sued Mount Laurel for its alleged failure to implement the affirmative duty imposed on it by *Mount Laurel I.* That case reached the New Jersey Supreme Court in 1983 and is known as *Mount Laurel II.* In *Mount Laurel II,* the court outlined a number of potential remedies and established mechanisms to resolve claims, such as specialized courts. The New Jersey State legislature enacted the Fair Housing Act in 1985 that created the Council on Affordable Housing (COAH). The COAH assists municipalities comply with their obligations to provide affordable housing.

Exercise 8-14. *Britton v. Town of Chester*—The Remedy

Mount Laurel II authorized a "builder's remedy" whereby the court could allow a builder to continue with a higher density project than authorized by local zoning, provided a sufficient number of units were set aside for low- or moderate-income residents.

In *Britton v. Town of Chester*, the Town of Chester, New Hampshire, challenged a court ruling that permitted a builder to proceed with a multi-family housing project on a parcel of property not zoned for multi-family use. The town challenged the ruling on the grounds that it violated the separation of powers. In numerous cases, we have seen courts defer to the legislature out of respect for their judicial role. Here, the court is accused of going too far and usurping the authority of the legislature.

Britton v. Town of Chester

134 N.H. 434 (1991)

BATCHELDER, J. In this appeal, the defendant, the Town of Chester (the town), challenges a ruling by the Master (R. Peter Shapiro, Esq.), approved by the Superior Court (Gray, J.), that the Chester Zoning Ordinance is invalid and unconstitutional. In addition, the town argues that the relief granted to plaintiff Remillard, permitting him to construct multi-family housing on a parcel not currently zoned for such development, violates the separation of powers provision of the New Hampshire Constitution, N.H. Const. pt. I, art. 37, and creates an unreasonable use for this parcel. We modify the trial court's ruling that the ordinance as a whole is invalid, but we affirm the granting of specific relief to plaintiff Remillard as well as the court's ruling that the ordinance, on the facts of this case, is unlawful as applied.

The plaintiffs brought a petition in 1985, for declaratory and injunctive relief, challenging the validity of the multi-family housing provisions of the Chester Zoning Ordinance. The master's report, filed after a hearing, contains extensive factual findings which we summarize here. The town of Chester lies in the west-central portion of Rockingham County, thirteen miles east of the city of Manchester. Primary highway access is provided by New Hampshire Routes 102 and 121. The available housing stock is principally single-family homes. There is no municipal sewer or water service, and other municipal services remain modest. The town has not encouraged industrial or commercial development; it is a "bedroom community," with the majority of its labor force commuting to Manchester. Because of its close proximity to job centers and the ready availability of vacant land, the town is projected to have among the highest growth rates in New Hampshire over the next two decades.

The United States Department of Housing and Urban Development, having settled upon the median income for non-metropolitan Rockingham County as a yardstick, has determined that a low-income family in Chester is a household with annual earnings of $16,500 or less, and a moderate-income family has annual earnings of $16,501 to $25,680. Various federal and State government agencies have also determined that low- and moderate-income families should not pay in excess of 30% of their gross income for rent. Thus, a low-income family in Chester should pay less than $4,950 annually, and a moderate-income family in Chester should pay between $4,951 and $7,704 annually, for housing.

The plaintiffs in this case are a group of low- and moderate-income people who have been unsuccessful in finding affordable, adequate housing in the town, and a builder who, the master found, is committed to the construction of such housing. At trial, two plaintiffs testified as representative members of the group of low- and moderate-income people. Plaintiff George Edwards is a woodcutter who grew up in the town. He lives in Chester with his wife and three minor children in a one-bedroom, thirty-foot by eight-foot camper trailer with no running water. Their annual income is $14,040, which places them in the low-income category. Roger McFarland grew up and works in the town. He lives in Derry with his wife and three teenage children in a two-bedroom apartment which is too small to meet their needs. He and his wife both work, and their combined annual income is $24,000. Under the area standards, the McFarlands are a moderate-income family. Raymond Remillard is the plaintiff home builder. A long-time resident of the town, he owns an undeveloped twenty-three-acre parcel of land on Route 102 in the town's eastern section. Since 1979, he has attempted to obtain permission from the town to build a moderate-sized multi-family housing development on his land.

The zoning ordinance in effect at the beginning of this action in 1985 provided for a single-family home on a two-acre lot or a duplex on a three-acre lot, and it excluded multi-family housing from all five zoning districts in the town. In July 1986, the town amended its zoning ordinance to allow multi-family housing. Article six of the amended ordinance now permits multi-family housing as part of a "planned residential development" (PRD), a form of multi-family housing required to include a variety of housing types, such as single-family homes, duplexes, and multi-family structures.

After a hearing, the master recommended that judgment be ordered for the plaintiffs; that the town's land use ordinances, including the zoning ordinance, be ruled invalid; and that plaintiff Remillard be awarded a "builder's remedy." We will uphold the findings and rulings of a court-approved master's recommendation unless they are unsupported by the evidence or are erroneous as a matter of law. The test on appeal is not whether we would have found as the master did, but whether there was evidence on which he could reasonably base his finding.

We first turn to the ordinance itself, because it does, on its face, permit the type of development that the plaintiffs argue is being prohibited. The master found, however, that the ordinance placed an unreasonable barrier to the development of affordable housing for low- and moderate-income families. Under the ordinance, PRDs are allowed on tracts of not less than twenty acres in two designated "R-2" (medium-density residential) zoning districts. Due to existing home construction and environmental considerations, such as wet-lands and steep slopes, only slightly more than half of all the land in the two R-2 districts could reasonably be used for multi-family development. This constitutes only 1.73% of the land in the town. This fact standing alone does not, in the confines of this case, give rise to an entitlement to a legal remedy for those who seek to provide multi-family housing. However, it does serve to point out that the two R-2 districts are, in reality, less likely to be developed than would appear from a reading of the ordinance. A reviewing court must read the entire ordinance in the light of these facts.

In *Beck v. Town of Raymond*, 118 N.H. 793, 394 A.2d 847 (1978) this court sent a message to zoning bodies that "[t]owns may not refuse to confront the future by building a moat around themselves and pulling up the drawbridge." Id. The town of Chester appears willing to lower that bridge only for people who can afford a single-family home on a two-acre lot or a duplex on a three-acre lot. Others are realistically prohibited from crossing. Municipalities are not isolated enclaves, far removed from the concerns of the area in which they are situated. As subdivisions of the State, they do not exist solely to serve their own residents, and their regulations should promote the general welfare, both within and without their boundaries. Therefore, we interpret the general welfare provision of the zoning enabling statute, RSA 674:16, to include the welfare of the "community," as defined in this case, in which a municipality is located and of which it forms a part.

A municipality's power to zone property to promote the health, safety, and general welfare of the community is delegated to it by the State, and the municipality must, therefore, exercise this power in conformance with the enabling legislation. Because the Chester Zoning Ordinance does not provide for the lawful needs of the community, in that it flies in the face of the general welfare provision of RSA 674:16 and is, therefore, at odds with the statute upon which it is grounded, we hold that, as applied to the facts of this case, the ordinance is an invalid exercise of the power delegated to the town pursuant to RSA 674:16-30. We so hold because of the master's finding that "there are no substantial and compelling reasons that would warrant the Town of Chester, through its land use ordinances, from fulfilling its obligation to provide low[-] and moderate[-]income families within the community and a proportionate share of same within its region from a realistic opportunity to obtain affordable housing."

As to the specific relief granted to plaintiff Remillard, the town contends that the court's order effectively rezones the parcel in violation of the separation of powers provision found in part I, article 37 of the New Hampshire Constitution. It further asserts that, even if it were lawful for a court to rezone or grant specific relief, plaintiff Remillard's proposed development does not qualify for such a remedy.

The trial court has the power, subject to our review for abuse of discretion, to order definitive relief for plaintiff Remillard. In *Soares v. Town of Atkinson*, 129 N.H. 313, 529 A.2d 867 (1987), we upheld the master's finding that granting a "builder's remedy," *i.e.*, allowing the plaintiff builder to complete his project as proposed, is discretionary. In this appeal, the master found such relief to be appropriate, and the town has not carried its burden on appeal to persuade us to the contrary. A successful plaintiff is entitled to relief which rewards his or her efforts in testing the legality of the ordinance and prevents retributive action by the municipality, such as correcting the illegality but taking pains to leave the plaintiff unbenefitted.

The master relied on *Southern Burlington County N.A.A.C.P. v. Township of Mount Laurel*, 92 N.J. 158, 456 A.2d 390 (1983) (*Mt. Laurel II*), in determining that plaintiff Remillard was entitled to build his development as proposed. In *Mount Laurel I*, the New Jersey Supreme Court held that the municipality's zoning ordinance violated the general welfare provision of its State Constitution by not affording a realistic opportunity for the construction of its "fair share" of the present and prospective regional need for low- and moderate-income housing. *Mt. Laurel II* was a return to the New Jersey Supreme Court, eight years later, prompted by the realization that *Mt. Laurel I* had not resulted in realistic housing opportunities for low- and moderate-income people, but in "paper, process, witnesses, trials and appeals." The court noted that the "builder's remedy," which effectively grants a building permit to a plaintiff/developer, based on the development proposal, as long as other local regulations are followed, should be made more readily available to insure that low- and moderate-income housing is actually built.

Since 1979, plaintiff Remillard has attempted to obtain permission to build a moderate-sized multi-family housing development on his land in Chester. He is committed to setting aside a minimum of ten of the forty-eight units for low- and moderate-income tenants for twenty years. "Equity will not suffer a wrong without a remedy." 2 Pomeroy's Equity Jurisprudence § 423 (5th ed. 1941). Hence, we hold that the "builder's remedy" is appropriate in this case, both to compensate the developer who has invested substantial time and resources in pursuing this litigation, and as the most likely means of insuring that low- and moderate-income housing is actually built.

Although we determine that the "builder's remedy" is appropriate in this case, we do not adopt the *Mt. Laurel* analysis for determining whether such a remedy will be granted. Instead, we find the rule developed in *Sinclair Pipe Line Co. v. Richton Park*, 19 Ill. 2d 370, 167 N.E.2d 406 (1960), is the better rule as it eliminates the calculation of arbitrary mathematical quotas which *Mt. Laurel* requires. That rule is followed with some variation by the supreme courts of several other States and awards relief to the plaintiff builder if his development is found to be reasonable, *i.e.*, providing a realistic opportunity for the construction of low- and moderate-income housing and consistent with sound zoning concepts and environmental concerns. Once an existing zoning ordinance is found invalid in whole or in part, whether on constitutional grounds or, as here, on grounds of statutory construction and application, the court may provide relief in the form of a declaration that the plaintiff builder's proposed use is reasonable, and the municipality may not interfere with it. Plaintiff must bear the burden of proving reasonable use by a preponderance of the evidence. Once the plaintiff's burden has been met, he will be permitted to proceed with the proposed development, provided he complies with all other applicable regulations.

The town's argument that the specific relief granted to plaintiff Remillard violates the separation of powers provision found in part I, article 37 of the New Hampshire Constitution, to the extent that the trial court exercised legislative power specifically delegated to the local zoning authority, is without merit. The rule we adopt today does not produce this result. This rule will permit the municipality to continue to control its own development, so long as it does so for the general welfare of the community. It will also accommodate the construction of low- and moderate-income housing that had been unlawfully excluded.

The zoning ordinance evolved as an innovative means to counter the problems of uncontrolled growth. It was never conceived to be a device to facilitate the use of governmental power to prevent access to a municipality by "outsiders of any disadvantaged social or economic group." *Beck, supra.* The town of Chester has adopted a zoning ordinance which is blatantly exclusionary. This court will not condone the town's conduct.

Affirmed in part and reversed in part.

Exercise 8-15. *Britton* Revisited

1. The plaintiff-homebuilder had attempted to develop the property for multi-family use since 1979. The court specifically mentions that the remedy is appropriate, because the plaintiff-homebuilder "has invested substantial time and resources in pursuing this litigation." Do you think that is sufficient justification?
2. Although the New Hampshire Supreme Court cites *Mount Laurel II* approvingly, it adopts a different standard for determining when a builder's remedy is appropriate. It rejected the mathematical method set forth in *Mount Laurel II* for determining a community's fair share. Instead, the court adopted the "reasonable" approach enunciated by the Illinois Supreme Court. It seems that the New Hampshire Supreme Court chose to adopt a flexible standard over a bright-line rule. Do you see advantages to both approaches? Disadvantages?

NIMBY—Not In My Back Yard

In *Britton v. Chester*, the Supreme Court of New Hampshire quoted with approval a prior opinion that had warned "[t]owns may not refuse to confront the future by building a moat around themselves and pulling up the drawbridge." The acronym NIMBY has been applied to efforts by communities to keep out certain uses that the residents deem undesirable. In many instances, these targeted uses have high social utility. For example, communities have attempted to keep out domestic violence shelters, group homes, and halfway houses. Communities have also attempted to block industrial development that may have negative externalities, such landfills, quarries, incinerators, and toxic waste dumps. Prisons are another proposed use that can incite community outrage, as can adult entertainment establishments, even when their activities are protected by the First Amendment. In many of these cases, the offending use provides an important service and needs to be provided somewhere. The NIMBY objections do not challenge the validity of the use itself, but only its placement—hence the name "not in my backyard."

To some extent, NIMBY echoes Justice Sutherland's concern over the proverbial "pig in the parlor." NIMBY advocates generally support the underlying use, but nonetheless insist that it does not belong in their neighborhood. The ability of communities to organize against certain proposed uses raises questions of equity when the proposed use also entails negative externalities. Take, for example, an incinerator project. If the community successfully organizes against the project, the developers may choose to move locations to a community where organized opposition is less formidable and the need for jobs is more pronounced. These considerations may result in locating offending, yet important uses in low-income minority communities. Within the environmental context, commentators have argued that the tendency to place noxious uses in poorer neighborhoods implicates fundamental concerns of environmental justice. How should we apportion certain environmental burdens among our communities?

The cases in this section explore some of the limitations on the ability of communities to "pull[ ] up the drawbridge." Attempts to block certain uses have been challenged under both state and federal constitutions, with varying success. They have also been challenged on the ground that they are inconsistent with state or federal policy.

Developers who encounter community resistance have sometimes filed frivolous lawsuits against the community organizations, advocates, and individual property owners who object to their plans. Although the lawsuits often have very little chance of success, they are designed to bully and intimidate the opposition. This tactic is referred to as a "strategic lawsuit against public participation," known by the acronym "SLAPP." A number of states have enacted anti-SLAPP legislation that imposes penalties for frivolous lawsuits.

Exercise 8-16. *Village of Belle Terre v. Boraas*—Federal Law

Comprehensive zoning provides a way for local authorities to define and shape their community. As we saw from the last section, it can also allow a community to limit and restrict who can join the community. In other words, comprehensive zoning includes the ability to define community to the exclusion of certain people. In *Britton v. Town of Chester*, the court warned about communities that wanted to "build[ ] a moat around themselves and pull[ ] up the drawbridge." In this case, the dissent accuses the village of Belle Terre of attempting to "fence out those individuals whose choice of lifestyle differs from that of its current residents."

The Village of Belle Terre is located on Long Island's north shore. At the time this case was decided, there were approximately 220 homes with 700 people. The majority describes the village as a "quiet place where yards are wide and people few." Belle Terre enacted an ordinance that restricts land use to single-family dwellings. Generally, the term "single-family dwelling" refers to an architectural style, but Belle Terre also provided a definition of what constitutes a "family." As you read the case, consider what "families" would not be permitted to live in Belle Terre.

The appellees challenged the ordinance under the Equal Protection Clause of the Fourteenth Amendment to the U.S. Constitution. Pay particular attention to the standard of review employed by the majority and contrast it with the standard used by the dissent.

Village of Belle Terre v. Boraas

416 U.S. 1 (1974)

MR. JUSTICE DOUGLAS delivered the opinion of the Court. Belle Terre is a village on Long Island's north shore of about 220 homes inhabited by 700 people. Its total land area is less than one square mile. It has restricted land use to one-family dwellings excluding lodging houses, boarding houses, fraternity houses, or multiple-dwelling houses. The word "family" as used in the ordinance means, "one or more persons related by blood, adoption, or marriage, living and cooking together as a single housekeeping unit, exclusive of household servants. A number of persons but not exceeding two (2) living and cooking together as a single housekeeping unit though not related by blood, adoption, or marriage shall be deemed to constitute a family."

Appellees the Dickmans are owners of a house in the village and leased it in December 1971 for a term of 18 months to Michael Truman. Later Bruce Boraas became a colessee. Then Anne Parish moved into the house along with three others. These six are students at nearby State University at Stony Brook and none is related to the other by blood, adoption, or marriage. When the village served the Dickmans with an "Order to Remedy Violations" of the ordinance, the owners plus three tenants thereupon brought this action under 42 U.S.C. § 1983 for an injunction and a judgment declaring the ordinance unconstitutional. The District Court held the ordinance constitutional, and the Court of Appeals reversed, one judge dissenting. The case is here by appeal.

This case brings to this Court a different phase of local zoning regulations from those we have previously reviewed. *Euclid v. Ambler Realty Co.*, 272 U.S. 365, involved a zoning ordinance classifying land use in a given area into six categories. Appellee's tracts fell under three classifications: U-2, which included two-family dwellings; U-3, which included apartments, hotels, churches, schools, private clubs, hospitals, city hall and the like; and U-6, which included sewage disposal plants, incinerators, scrap storage, cemeteries, oil and gas storage and so on. Heights of buildings were prescribed for each zone; also, the size of land areas required for each kind of use was specified. The land in litigation was vacant and being held for industrial development; and evidence was introduced showing that under the restricted-use ordinance the land would be greatly reduced in value. The claim was that the landowner was being deprived of liberty and property without due process within the meaning of the Fourteenth Amendment.

The Court sustained the zoning ordinance under the police power of the State, saying that the line "which in this field separates the legitimate from the illegitimate assumption of power is not capable of precise delimitation. It varies with circumstances and conditions." *Id.*, at 387. And the Court added: "A nuisance may be merely a right thing in the wrong place,—like a pig in the parlor instead of the barnyard. If the validity of the legislative classification for zoning purposes be fairly debatable, the legislative judgment must be allowed to control." *Id.*, at 388. The Court listed as considerations bearing on the constitutionality of zoning ordinances the danger of fire or collapse of buildings, the evils of overcrowding people, and the possibility that "offensive trades, industries, and structures" might "create nuisance" to residential sections.

The main thrust of the case in the mind of the Court was in the exclusion of industries and apartments, and as respects that it commented on the desire to keep residential areas free of "disturbing noises"; "increased traffic"; the hazard of "moving and parked automobiles"; the "depriving children of the privilege of quiet and open spaces for play, enjoyed by those in more favored localities." *Id.*, at 394. The ordinance was sanctioned because the validity of the legislative classification was "fairly debatable" and therefore could not be said to be wholly arbitrary. *Id.*, at 388.

The present ordinance is challenged on several grounds: that it interferes with a person's right to travel; that it interferes with the right to migrate to and settle within a State; that it bars people who are uncongenial to the present residents; that it expresses the social preferences of the residents for groups that will be congenial to them; that social homogeneity is not a legitimate interest of government; that the restriction of those whom the neighbors do not like trenches on the newcomers' rights of privacy; that it is of no rightful concern to villagers whether the residents are married or unmarried; that the ordinance is antithetical to the Nation's experience, ideology, and self-perception as an open, egalitarian, and integrated society.

We find none of these reasons in the record before us. It is not aimed at transients. It involves no procedural disparity inflicted on some but not on others. It involves no "fundamental" right guaranteed by the Constitution, such as voting, the right of association, the right of access to the courts, or any rights of privacy. We deal with economic and social legislation where legislatures have historically drawn lines which we respect against the charge of violation of the Equal Protection Clause if the law be reasonable, not arbitrary and bears a rational relationship to a [permissible] state objective.

It is said, however, that if two unmarried people can constitute a "family," there is no reason why three or four may not. But every line drawn by a legislature leaves some out that might well have been included. That exercise of discretion, however, is a legislative, not a judicial, function.

It is said that the Belle Terre ordinance reeks with an animosity to unmarried couples who live together. There is no evidence to support it; and the provision of the ordinance bringing within the definition of a "family" two unmarried people belies the charge.

The ordinance places no ban on other forms of association, for a "family" may, so far as the ordinance is concerned, entertain whomever it likes.

The regimes of boarding houses, fraternity houses, and the like present urban problems. More people occupy a given space; more cars rather continuously pass by; more cars are parked; noise travels with crowds.

A quiet place where yards are wide, people few, and motor vehicles restricted are legitimate guidelines in a land-use project addressed to family needs. This goal is a permissible one. The police power is not confined to elimination of filth, stench, and unhealthy places. It is ample to lay out zones where family values, youth values, and the blessings of quiet seclusion and clean air make the area a sanctuary for people.

Reversed.

MR. JUSTICE MARSHALL, dissenting. This case draws into question the constitutionality of a zoning ordinance of the incorporated village of Belle Terre, New York, which prohibits groups of more than two unrelated persons, as distinguished from groups consisting of any number of persons related by blood, adoption, or marriage, from occupying a residence within the confines of the township. 1 Lessor-appellees, the two owners of a Belle Terre residence, and three unrelated student tenants challenged the ordinance on the ground that it establishes a classification between households of related and unrelated individuals, which deprives them of equal protection of the laws. In my view, the disputed classification burdens the students' fundamental rights of association and privacy guaranteed by the First and Fourteenth Amendments. Because the application of strict equal protection scrutiny is therefore required, I am at odds with my Brethren's conclusion that the ordinance may be

sustained on a showing that it bears a rational relationship to the accomplishment of legitimate governmental objectives.

The freedom of association is often inextricably entwined with the constitutionally guaranteed right of privacy. The right to "establish a home" is an essential part of the liberty guaranteed by the Fourteenth Amendment. *Meyer v. Nebraska*, 262 U.S. 390, 399 (1923); *Griswold v. Connecticut*, 381 U.S. 479, 495 (1965) (Goldberg, J., concurring). And the Constitution secures to an individual a freedom "to satisfy his intellectual and emotional needs in the privacy of his own home." *Stanley v. Georgia*, 394 U.S. 557, 565 (1969). Constitutionally protected privacy is, in Mr. Justice Brandeis' words, "as against the Government, the right to be let alone ... the right most valued by civilized man." *Olmstead v. United States*, 277 U.S. 438, 478 (1928) (dissenting opinion). The choice of household companions—of whether a person's "intellectual and emotional needs" are best met by living with family, friends, professional associates, or others—involves deeply personal considerations as to the kind and quality of intimate relationships within the home. That decision surely falls within the ambit of the right to privacy protected by the Constitution.

The instant ordinance discriminates on the basis of just such a personal lifestyle choice as to household companions. It permits any number of persons related by blood or marriage, be it two or twenty, to live in a single household, but it limits to two the number of unrelated persons bound by profession, love, friendship, religious or political affiliation, or mere economics who can occupy a single home. Belle Terre imposes upon those who deviate from the community norm in their choice of living companions significantly greater restrictions than are applied to residential groups who are related by blood or marriage, and compose the established order within the community. The village has, in effect, acted to fence out those individuals whose choice of lifestyle differs from that of its current residents.

This is not a case where the Court is being asked to nullify a township's sincere efforts to maintain its residential character by preventing the operation of rooming houses, fraternity houses, or other commercial or high-density residential uses. Unquestionably, a town is free to restrict such uses. Moreover, as a general proposition, I see no constitutional infirmity in a town's limiting the density of use in residential areas by zoning regulations which do not discriminate on the basis of constitutionally suspect criteria. This ordinance, however, limits the density of occupancy of only those homes occupied by unrelated persons. It thus reaches beyond control of the use of land or the density of population, and undertakes to regulate the way people choose to associate with each other within the privacy of their own homes.

Because I believe that this zoning ordinance creates a classification which impinges upon fundamental personal rights, it can withstand constitutional scrutiny only upon a clear showing that the burden imposed is necessary to protect a compelling and substantial governmental interest, *Shapiro v. Thompson*, 394 U.S. 618, 634 (1969). And, once it be determined that a burden has been placed upon a constitutional right, the onus of demonstrating that no less intrusive means will adequately protect the compelling state interest and that the challenged statute is sufficiently narrowly drawn, is upon the party seeking to justify the burden.

A variety of justifications have been proffered in support of the village's ordinance. It is claimed that the ordinance controls population density, prevents noise, traffic and parking problems, and preserves the rent structure of the community and its attractiveness to families. As I noted earlier, these are all legitimate and substantial interests of government. But I think it clear that the means chosen to accomplish these purposes are both overinclusive and underinclusive, and that the asserted goals could be as effectively achieved by means of an ordinance that did not discriminate on the basis of constitutionally protected choices of lifestyle. The ordinance imposes no restriction whatsoever on the number of persons who may live in a house, as long as they are related by marital or sanguinary bonds—presumably no matter how distant their relationship. Nor does the ordinance restrict the number of income earners who may contribute to rent in such a household, or the number of automobiles that may be maintained by its occupants. In that sense the ordinance is underinclusive. On the other hand, the statute restricts the number of unrelated persons who may live in a home to no more than two. It would therefore prevent three unrelated people from occupying a dwelling even if among them they had but one income and no vehicles. While an extended family of a dozen or more might live in a small bungalow, three elderly and retired persons could not occupy the large manor house next door. Thus the statute is also grossly overinclusive to accomplish its intended purposes.

There are some 220 residences in Belle Terre occupied by about 700 persons. The density is therefore just above three per household. The village is justifiably concerned with density of population and the related problems of noise, traffic, and the like. By limiting unrelated households to two persons while placing no limitation on households of related individuals, the village has embarked upon its commendable course in a constitutionally faulty vessel. I would find the challenged ordinance unconstitutional. But I would not ask the village to abandon its goal of providing quiet streets, little traffic, and a pleasant and reasonably priced environment in which families might raise their children. Rather, I would commend the village to continue to pursue those purposes but by means of more carefully drawn and even-handed legislation.

I respectfully dissent.

Exercise 8-17. *Village of Belle Terre* Revisited

1. One of the goals of comprehensive zoning is to prevent nuisance before it happens, but it is also used to build attractive and tranquil communities. As Justice Douglas explains: "The police power is not confined to elimination of filth, stench and unhealthy places."
2. The major difference between the majority and the dissent is that the dissent finds that the ordinance interferes with a fundamental right. As a result, the dissent employs the highest standard of judicial review—strict scrutiny. Can you articulate the standard of review employed by the majority?
3. Justice Marshall argued that the ordinance should only be upheld if it were "necessary to protect a compelling and substantial governmental interest" and "narrowly drawn." Justice Marshall's opinion provides a good example of a particular law or state action that is arguably both underinclusive and overly broad. You will see in the next case that sometimes a law can be so under- and over-inclusive that it fails even the rational basis standard, because the stated rationale may appear to be mere pretext.
4. In the end, Justice Douglas defers to the legislature, writing: "Every line drawn by the legislature leaves some out that might well have been included. That exercise of discretion is a legislative not judicial function."

Exercise 8-18. *Charter Township of Delta v. Dinolfo* — State Law

As we have seen in other instances, state constitutions may provide greater protection than the federal Constitution. In *Charter Township of Delta v. Dinolfo*, a very similar ordinance to the one upheld in Belle Terre is struck down because it violates the Michigan State Constitution. Consider the ways in which this case is both similar and different from *Belle Terre*.

As you read the case, ask yourself what makes a "family"? Try your hand at drafting statutory language that encompasses your definition of family.

Charter Township of Delta v. Dinolfo

419 Mich. 253 (1984)

BRICKLEY, J. This case requires us to consider the constitutionality of a township zoning ordinance which limits the occupation of single-family residences to an individual, or a group of two or more persons related by blood, marriage, or adoption, and not more than one other unrelated person. We conclude that this ordinance, which prohibits the defendants from including in their households six unrelated persons, is unreasonable and arbitrary and, accordingly, in violation of the Due Process Clause of the Michigan Constitution.

In July and September of 1977, the Sierawski and Dinolfo "families" moved into homes in plaintiff township. The defendants' homes are located in an R 3, Moderate Density Residential District, which allows for single-family dwellings, duplexes, and quadruplexes. The defendants' homes qualify only as single-family dwellings. Each household consists of a husband and wife, that couple's several children, and six unrelated single adults. All members of these households are members of The Work of Christ Community, a nonprofit and federally tax-exempt organization chartered by the State of Michigan. Each of these households functions as a family in a single housekeeping unit and members intend to reside in their respective households permanently. All of the members of these "families" have adopted their lifestyle as a means of living out the Christian commitment that they stress is an important part of their lives.

Over a year after defendants occupied these residences with their "families", plaintiff's planning department sent violation notices citing them for having more than one unrelated individual residing in their homes in violation of the plaintiff's zoning ordinance. Plaintiff's zoning ordinance limits those groups which can live in single-family dwellings to an individual, or a group of two or more persons related by blood, adoption, or marriage, and not more than one unrelated person, excluding servants. It is undisputed that the space requirements of the township building ordinance were not violated by the number of persons in each of the defendant's households. Indeed, that ordinance would allow for three more persons to live in homes the size of those owned by defendants.

Defendants jointly filed an application for a variance from the family definition section of the plaintiff's zoning ordinance, which was denied by the Zoning Board of Appeals. The minutes of the meeting at which the application was considered reflect no complaints about the defendants or the members of their households by any of their neighbors who attended that meeting. To the contrary, all present found them to be good neighbors. The variance was denied by the board because the defendants did not fall under the four general outlines for the granting of variances in the zoning ordinance.

Defendant Dinolfo then petitioned the Board of Trustees of Delta Township to overrule the decision of the Zoning Board of Appeals, and also formally presented a petition, supported by the signatures of twenty-seven neighbors, for a change in the language of the family definition section of the ordinance. Both of these efforts were unsuccessful.

The trial court ultimately ruled in favor of the plaintiff on cross-motions for summary judgment. The court relied on Village of Belle Terre v Boraas, 416 U.S. 1 (1974), to state that simply because the Legislature drew the line at one unrelated adult did not mean the ordinance was arbitrary. The court entered an order permanently enjoining defendants from occupying their residences in violation of the ordinance. The Court of Appeals affirmed, and this Court granted defendants' application for leave to appeal.

The defendants argue here, as below, that the plaintiff has no authority to define the word family and that the word "family", as it appears in the Township Rural Zoning Act, is intended to be interpreted as referring to a functional family rather than a traditional biological family. Defendants contend that they constitute functional families within that broad definition. Defendants also argue that the net effect of plaintiff's enforcement of this ordinance is to totally exclude them from the township in violation of their constitutional rights. Defendants further contend that the definition of family in the ordinance both prohibits and allows property uses in an unreasonable, arbitrary, and capricious manner in violation of the Due Process and Equal Protection Clauses of the United States and Michigan Constitutions. Finally, defendants argue that the ordinance, by interfering with their chosen lifestyle and religious needs, is an impairment of their fundamental rights of privacy, association, and free exercise of religion in violation of the United States and Michigan Constitutions.

II

In *Village of Euclid v Ambler Realty Co*, 272 U.S. 365 (1926), the landmark zoning case, the Supreme Court first upheld the constitutionality of a zoning ordinance as a valid exercise of the state's police power. The standard used was whether the regulation was "clearly arbitrary and unreasonable, having no substantial relation to the public health, safety, morals, or general welfare". The Court recognized, however, that a zoning law may be constitutional on its face, while aspects of it could be invalid as it applies to a specific property owner.

Nearly fifty years later, in *Village of Belle Terre v. Boraas*, 416 U.S. 1 (1974), the Supreme Court confronted the constitutionality of a local zoning ordinance that is in all significant respects identical to the ordinance in question here. The Village of

Belle Terre ordinance limited residential occupancy to a biological family plus no more than two unrelated persons. The case arose when the house in question was leased to eight college students. In upholding the constitutionality of the ordinance, Justice Douglas, writing for the majority, held that there were no fundamental rights involved which would require a scrutiny higher than determining if the ordinance was arbitrary. The Court found that distinguishing between a biological family and an unrelated group was not unreasonable or arbitrary under the Due Process and Equal Protection Clauses of the United States Constitution. It was argued in *Belle Terre*, as it is here, that "if two unmarried people can constitute a 'family' there is no reason why three or four may not". To that argument the Supreme Court responded "[but] every line drawn by a legislature leaves some out that might well have been included. That exercise of discretion, however, is a legislative, not a judicial, function."

We find *Belle Terre* to be clear authority for the proposition that to limit residentially zoned property to a traditional family and a number of non-related persons is permissible under the United States Constitution. Having so found, we, therefore, must conclude that plaintiff's ordinance is constitutional as a matter of federal law. We must then accept the defendants' challenge that we examine the Delta Township ordinance in light of Michigan's Constitution.

The constitutionality of zoning in Michigan is well established.

The dispute here is not between contending land uses, but about who can occupy a residential dwelling. In evaluating the relative merits and effects of mixing related and non-related persons in a single-family dwelling, planning expertise becomes more questionable and human experience and values more paramount. Thus, our task here is not to evaluate the reasonableness of the township's designation of one land use as opposed to another, but, rather, to evaluate whether the existence of the distinction made is permissible. We think the appropriate standard is that due process standard generally used to evaluate the normal use of the police power. Of course, we still presume the constitutionality of the ordinance. But, extraordinary deference given to the line drawing in traditional zoning matters is not appropriate here.

Plaintiff lists the objectives of this ordinance: preservation of traditional family values, maintenance of property values and population and density control. We cannot disagree that those are not only rational but laudable goals. Where the difficulty arises, however, is when plaintiff attempts to convince us that the classification at hand—limiting to two the number of unrelated persons who may occupy a residential dwelling together or with a biological family—is reasonably related to the achievement of those goals. It is precisely this rational relationship between the means used to achieve the legislative goals that must exist in order for this deprivation of the defendants' use of their property to pass the due process test.

Running through plaintiff's arguments is the assumption that unrelated persons will manifest a behavior pattern different from the biological family. If defendants succeed here, plaintiff fears that the next group taking advantage of the opportunity might not be of defendants' character. Plaintiff suggests that the "common bond of the group ... [might be] not the Work of Christ, but the Work of Satan".

Amicus curiae, Michigan Townships Association, is even more direct in its perception of the evils that will result if non-related persons are allowed to live as a functional family.

> The purpose of such regulations is to prohibit the influx of informal residential groups of people whose primary inclination is toward the enjoyment of a licentious style of living. While it seems apparent that defendants are not of this character, it would seem equally apparent that allowing in excess of six unrelated individuals to occupy a single-family dwelling unit would allow college fraternities, 'hippie' communes, motorcycle clubs, and assorted loosely structured groups of people associating for the purpose of enjoying a purely licentious style of living to locate at will in settled, low density residential neighborhoods and, perhaps even worse in duplexes, quadruplexes, and even in high-density apartment buildings. No somber recitations of anthropologists and sociologists are required to make one visualize the problems of noise, nuisance, vehicular traffic, and general disruption of orderly and peaceful living that could be brought about by permitting such arrangements.

We agree with amicus to the extent that the residential nature of a neighborhood is a proper subject for legislative protection. But we fail to see how plaintiff's ordinance furthers these goals. We, therefore, must part company with the United States Supreme Court. In *Belle Terre*, the Supreme Court made no attempt to suggest how a line drawn between the related and the unrelated advances these goals. It merely said that the line drawing was a "legislative, not a judicial, function". We agree that line drawing is a legislative function, but certainly there can be no argument against the well-understood rule of law that the task of deciding whether the line itself is reasonably related to the object of the line drawing is a judicial function.

Here, plaintiff attempts to have us accept its assumption that different and undesirable behavior can be expected from a functional family. Yet, we have been given not a single argument in support of such an assumption, only the assumption. Defendants, on the other hand, relying on decisions from other jurisdictions construing their own state constitutions, present a compelling argument that the means are not rationally related to the end sought.

Those states that have rejected *Belle Terre* have stressed that a line drawn near the limit of the traditional family is both over- and under-inclusive. Unrelated persons are artificially limited to as few as two, while related families may expand without limit. Under the instant ordinance, twenty male cousins could live together, motorcycles, noise, and all, while three unrelated clerics could not. A greater example of over- and under-inclusiveness we cannot imagine. The ordinance indiscriminately regulates where no regulation is needed and fails to regulate where regulation is most needed.

We know from common experience that, while the motorcycle gang argument is a threatening one, it is more a symbol, one that is not by any stretch of the imagination representative of the lifestyle of the countless people who seek residential living in something other than the biological family setting. As to the specter of a "Work of Satan" group that could slip in if defendants succeed here, we note that if this ordinance were upheld it would not keep out Ma Barker and her sons.

There has been no evidence presented nor do we know of any that unrelated persons, as such, have any less a need for the advantages of residential living or that they have as a group behavior patterns that are more opprobrious than the population at large. In the absence of such demonstration to justify this kind of classification, the ordinance can only be termed arbitrary and capricious under the Due Process Clause of the Michigan Constitution. The plight of the defendants in this case—who certainly defy the plaintiff's stereotype of the unrelated family—represents the best evidence of the perniciousness of allowing unexamined assumptions to become the basis of regulatory classification.

That government can classify, draw lines around, and support the biological family is well settled, as evidenced by our tax and inheritance laws. Our decision here is not in derogation of the cultural, economic, and moral value of the traditional family and its essential and unique role in our society, but rather is based on the fact that the exclusion of groups such as defendants from a residential neighborhood is not in any way supportive of "family values". Ironically, the enforcement of this ordinance prohibits the two defendant nuclear families from adding to their numbers in a way they choose pursuant to the highest possible motives.

The plaintiff is not, as a result of anything we say here today, without authority to regulate the behavior it finds inimical to its concept of a residential neighborhood, including a rational limitation on the numbers of persons that may occupy a dwelling. Plaintiff need not open its residential borders to transients and others whose lifestyle is not the functional equivalent of "family" life. Nor are the plaintiffs precluded from distinguishing between the biological family and a functional family when it is rational to do so, such as in limiting the number of persons who may occupy a dwelling for such valid reasons as health, fire safety, or density control.

We find that plaintiff's ordinance is capricious, arbitrary, and in violation of the Due Process Clause of the Michigan Constitution in that it limits the composition of groups in a manner that is not rationally related to the stated goals of the zoning ordinance.

Reversed.

Exercise 8-19. *Charter Township of Delta* Revisited

1. The amicus curiae was very upfront regarding its concerns regarding "hippie communes" and "motorcycle clubs." Did its brief help or hurt the Township's case?
2. Under what provision of the Michigan Constitution did the court invalidate the ordinance? What standard of review did the court apply?

Exercise 8-20. *Riverside v. Wellness Center*—Medical Marijuana

NIMBY is often directed at a particular use of property that is considered undesirable by the community, but may have high social utility and be encouraged by other laws and policies. One example of this type of use would be a group home for developmentally disabled adults. U.S. policy strongly favors housing disabled adults in family settings within the community. However, municipalities frequently place restrictions on group homes. Disputes often arise when local zoning rules undermine broader policy goals.

This case involves a medical marijuana dispensary. Legal under California law, medical marijuana dispensaries reflect a policy decision to make medical marijuana available to certain patients in need. The question presented in *Riverside v. Wellness Center* is whether communities can zone out dispensaries and thereby deny their residents access to medical marijuana. In other words, has state law effectively pre-empted the ability of localities to prohibit dispensaries from operating in their jurisdiction?

Riverside v. Wellness Center

56 Cal. 4th 729 (2013)

Baxter, J. The issue in this case is whether California's medical marijuana statutes preempt a local ban on facilities that distribute medical marijuana. We conclude they do not.

Both federal and California laws generally prohibit the use, possession, cultivation, transportation, and furnishing of marijuana. However, California statutes, the Compassionate Use Act of 1996 (CUA) and the more recent Medical Marijuana Program (MMP) have removed certain state law obstacles from the ability of qualified patients to obtain and use marijuana for legitimate medical purposes. Among other things, these statutes exempt the "collective[] or cooperative[] ... cultiva[tion]" of medical marijuana by qualified patients and their designated caregivers from prosecution or abatement under specified state criminal and nuisance laws that would otherwise prohibit those activities.

The California Constitution recognizes the authority of cities and counties to make and enforce, within their borders, "all local, police, sanitary, and other ordinances and regulations not in conflict with general laws." Cal. Const., art. XI, § 7. This inherent local police power includes broad authority to determine, for purposes of the public health, safety, and welfare, the appropriate uses of land within a local jurisdiction's borders, and preemption by state law is not lightly presumed.

In the exercise of its inherent land use power, the City of Riverside (City) has declared, by zoning ordinances, that a "[m]edical marijuana dispensary"—"[a] facility where marijuana is made available for medical purposes in accordance with" the CUA—is a prohibited use of land within the city and may be abated as a public nuisance. The City's ordinance also bans, and declares a nuisance, any use that is prohibited by federal or state law.

Invoking these provisions, the City brought a nuisance action against a facility operated by defendants. The trial court issued a preliminary injunction against the distribution of marijuana from the facility. The Court of Appeal affirmed the injunctive order. Challenging the injunction, defendants urge, as they did below, that the City's total ban on facilities that cultivate and distribute medical marijuana in compliance with the CUA and the MMP is invalid. Defendants insist the local ban is in conflict with, and thus preempted by, those state statutes.

As we will explain, we disagree. We have consistently maintained that the CUA and the MMP are but incremental steps toward freer access to medical marijuana, and the scope of these statutes is limited and circumscribed. They merely declare that the conduct they describe cannot lead to arrest or conviction, or be abated as a nuisance, as violations of enumerated provisions of the Health and Safety Code. Nothing in the CUA or the MMP expressly or impliedly limits the inherent authority of a local jurisdiction, by its own ordinances, to regulate the use of its land, including the authority to provide that facilities for the distribution of medical marijuana will not be permitted to operate within its borders. We must therefore reject defendants' preemption argument, and must affirm the judgment of the Court of Appeal.

LEGAL AND FACTUAL BACKGROUND

A. *Medical marijuana laws.*

The federal Controlled Substances Act (CSA) prohibits, except for certain research purposes, the possession, distribution, and manufacture of marijuana. The CSA finds that marijuana is a drug with "no currently accepted medical use in treatment in the United States," and there is no medical necessity exception to prosecution and conviction under the federal act.

California statutes similarly specify that, except as authorized by law, the possession, cultivation, harvesting, or processing, possession for sale, and transportation, administration, or furnishing of marijuana are state criminal violations. State law further punishes one who maintains a place for the purpose of unlawfully selling, using, or furnishing, or who knowingly makes available a place for storing, manufacturing, or distributing, certain controlled substances. The so-called "drug den" abatement law additionally provides that every place used to unlawfully sell, serve, store, keep, manufacture, or give away certain controlled substances is a nuisance that shall be enjoined, abated, and prevented, and for which damages may be recovered. In each instance, the controlled substances in question include marijuana.

However, California's voters and legislators have adopted limited exceptions to the sanctions of this state's criminal and nuisance laws in cases where marijuana is possessed, cultivated, distributed, and transported for medical purposes. In 1996, the electorate enacted the CUA. This initiative statute provides that the state law proscriptions against possession and cultivation of marijuana shall not apply to a patient, or the patient's designated primary caregiver, who possesses or cultivates marijuana for the patient's personal medical purposes upon the written or oral recommendation or approval of a physician.

In 2004, the Legislature adopted the MMP. One purpose of this statute was to "[e]nhance the access of patients and caregivers to medical marijuana through collective, cooperative cultivation projects." Accordingly, the MMP provides, among other things, that "[q]ualified patients ... and the designated primary caregivers of qualified patients..., who associate within the State of California in order collectively or cooperatively to cultivate marijuana for medical purposes, shall not solely on the basis of that fact be subject to state criminal sanctions."

The CUA and the MMP have no effect on the federal enforceability of the CSA in California. The CSA's prohibitions on the possession, distribution, or manufacture of marijuana remain fully enforceable in this jurisdiction.

B. *Riverside's ordinances.*

As noted above, the Riverside ordinances at issue (RMC) declare as a "prohibited use" within any city zoning classification (1) a "[m]edical marijuana dispensary"—defined as "[a] facility where marijuana is made available ... in accordance with" the CUA, and (2) any use prohibited by state or federal law. The RMC further provides that any condition caused or permitted to exist in violation of the ordinance is a public nuisance which may be abated by the city.

C. *The instant litigation.*

Since 2009, defendant Inland Empire Patients Health and Wellness Center, Inc. (Inland Empire), has operated a medical marijuana distribution facility in Riverside. In January 2009, the planning division of Riverside's Community Development Department notified [defendants] by letter that the definition of "medical marijuana dispensary" in Riverside's zoning ordinances "is an all-encompassing definition, referring to all three types of medical marijuana facilities, a dispensary, a collective and a cooperative," and that, as a consequence, "all three facilities are banned in the City of Riverside." In May 2010, the City filed a complaint against the [defendants] for injunctive relief to abate a public nuisance. The complaint alleged that defendants were operating a "medical marijuana distribution facility" in violation of the zoning provisions of the RMC.

DISCUSSION

A. *Principles of preemption.*

"Land use regulation in California historically has been a function of local government under the grant of police power contained in article XI, section 7 ... We have recognized that a city's or county's power to control its own land use decisions derives from this inherent police power, not from the delegation of authority by the state." *Big Creek Lumber Co. v. County of Santa Cruz* 38 Cal.4th 1139 (2006). When local government regulates in an area over which it traditionally has exercised control, such as the location of particular land uses, California courts will presume, absent a clear indication of preemptive intent from the Legislature, that such regulation is *not* preempted by state statute.

However, local legislation that conflicts with state law is void. A conflict exists if the local legislation duplicates, contradicts, or enters an area fully occupied by general law, either expressly or by legislative implication.

B. *The CUA and the MMP do not preempt Riverside's ban.*

When they adopted the CUA in 1996, the voters declared their intent "[t]o ensure that seriously ill Californians have the right to obtain and use marijuana for medical purposes" upon a physician's recommendation "[t]o ensure that patients and their primary caregivers who obtain and use marijuana for medical purposes upon the recommendation of a physician are not subject to criminal prosecution or sanction," and "[t]o encourage the federal and state governments to implement a plan to provide for the safe and affordable distribution of marijuana to all patients in medical need" of the substance.

But the operative steps the electorate took toward these goals were modest. In its substantive provisions, the CUA simply declares that (1) no physician may be punished or denied any right or privilege under state law for recommending medical marijuana to a patient, and (2) two specific state statutes prohibiting the possession and cultivation of marijuana, "shall not apply" to a patient, or the patient's designated primary caregiver, who possesses or cultivates marijuana for the patient's personal medical use upon a physician's recommendation or approval.

When it later adopted the MMP, the Legislature declared this statute was intended, among other things, to "[c]larify the scope of the application of the [CUA] and facilitate the prompt identification of qualified [medical marijuana] patients and their designated primary caregivers" in order to protect them from unnecessary arrest and prosecution for marijuana offenses, to "[p]romote uniform and consistent application of the [CUA] among the counties within the state," and to "[e]nhance the access of patients and caregivers to medical marijuana through collective, cooperative cultivation projects."

Again, however, the steps the MMP took in pursuit of these objectives were limited and specific. The MMP established a program for issuance of medical marijuana identification cards to those qualified patients and designated primary caregivers who wish to carry them, and required responsible county agencies to cooperate in this program. It provided that the holder of an identification card shall not be subject to arrest for possession, transportation, delivery, or cultivation of medical marijuana, within the amounts specified by the statute, except upon reasonable cause to believe the card is false or invalid or the holder is in violation of statute.

The MMP declared that "[q]ualified patients, persons with valid identification cards, and the designated primary caregivers of [such persons], who associate within the State of California in order collectively or cooperatively to cultivate marijuana for medical purposes, shall not *solely on the basis of that fact* be subject to *state criminal sanctions.*" However, an amendment adopted in 2010 declares that no medical marijuana "cooperative, collective, dispensary, operator, establishment, or provider," other than a licensed residential or elder medical care facility, that is "authorized by law" to possess, cultivate, or distribute medical marijuana, and that "has a storefront or mobile retail outlet which ordinarily requires a local business license," shall be located within 600 feet of a school.

We now agree, for the reasons expressed below, that the CUA and the MMP do not expressly or impliedly preempt Riverside's zoning provisions declaring a medical marijuana dispensary, as therein defined, to be a prohibited use, and a public nuisance, anywhere within the city limits. We set forth our conclusions in detail.

1. *No express preemption.*

The plain language of the CUA and the MMP is limited in scope. It grants specified persons and groups, when engaged in specified conduct, immunity from prosecution under specified state criminal and nuisance laws pertaining to marijuana. The CUA makes no mention of medical marijuana cooperatives, collectives, or dispensaries. It merely provides that state laws against the possession and cultivation of marijuana shall not apply to a qualified patient, or the patient's designated primary caregiver, who possesses or cultivates marijuana for the patient's personal medical use upon a physician's recommendation.

Though the CUA broadly states an aim to "ensure" a "right" of seriously ill persons to "obtain and use" medical marijuana as recommended by a physician, the initiative statute's actual objectives, as presented to the voters, were modest, and its substantive provisions created no broad right to use [medical] marijuana without hindrance or inconvenience. There is no basis to conclude that the CUA expressly preempts local ordinances prohibiting, as a nuisance, the use of property to cooperatively or collectively cultivate and distribute medical marijuana.

The MMP, unlike the CUA, does address, among other things, the collective or coöperative cultivation and distribution of medical marijuana. But the MMP is framed in similarly narrow and modest terms. As pertinent here, it specifies only that qualified patients, identification cardholders, and their designated primary caregivers are exempt from prosecution and conviction under enumerated state antimarijuana laws "solely" on the ground that such persons are engaged in the cooperative or collective cultivation, transportation, and distribution of medical marijuana among themselves. No provision of the MMP explicitly guarantees the availability of locations where such activities may occur, restricts the broad authority traditionally possessed by local jurisdictions to regulate zoning and land use planning within their borders, or requires local zoning and licensing laws to accommodate the cooperative or collective cultivation and distribution of medical marijuana. Hence, there is no ground to conclude that Riverside's ordinance is expressly preempted by the MMP.

2. *No implied preemption.*

The considerations discussed above also largely preclude any determination that the CUA or the MMP *impliedly* preempts Riverside's effort to "de-zone" facilities that dispense medical marijuana. At the outset, there is no duplication between the state laws, on the one hand, and Riverside's ordinance, on the other, in that the two schemes are coextensive. The CUA and the MMP "decriminalize," for state purposes, specified activities pertaining to medical marijuana, and also provide that the *state's* antidrug nuisance statute cannot be used to abate or enjoin these activities. On the other hand, the Riverside ordinance finds, for local purposes, that the use of property for certain of those activities *does* constitute a *local* nuisance.

Nor do we find an "inimical" contradiction or conflict between the state and local laws, in the sense that it is impossible simultaneously to comply with both. Neither the CUA nor the MMP *requires* the cooperative or collective cultivation and distribution of medical marijuana that Riverside's ordinance deems a prohibited use of property within the city's boundaries. Conversely, Riverside's ordinance requires no conduct that is forbidden by the state statutes. Persons who refrain from operating medical marijuana facilities in Riverside are in compliance with both the local and state enactments.

Further, there appears no attempt by the Legislature to fully occupy the field of medical marijuana regulation as a matter of statewide concern, or to partially occupy this field under circumstances indicating that further local regulation will not be tolerated. On the contrary, as discussed in detail above, the CUA and the MMP take limited steps toward recognizing marijuana as a medicine by exempting particular medical marijuana activities from state laws that would otherwise prohibit them. In furtherance of their provisions, these statutes require local agencies to do certain things, and prohibit them from doing certain others. But the statutory terms describe no comprehensive scheme or system for authorizing, controlling, or regulating the processing and distribution of marijuana for medical purposes, such that no room remains for local action.

The presumption against preemption is additionally supported by the existence of significant local interests that may vary from jurisdiction to jurisdiction. Amici curiae League of California Cities et al. point out that "California's 482 cities and 58 counties are diverse in size, population, and use." As these amici curiae observe, while several California cities and counties allow medical marijuana facilities, it may not be reasonable to expect every community to do so. [W]hile some counties and cities might consider themselves well suited to accommodating medical marijuana dispensaries, conditions in other communities might lead to the reasonable decision that such facilities within their borders, even if carefully sited, well managed, and closely monitored, would present unacceptable local risks and burdens. Under these circumstances, we cannot lightly assume the voters or the Legislature intended to impose a "one size fits all" policy, whereby each and every one of California's diverse counties and cities must allow the use of local land for such purposes.

Of course, nothing prevents future efforts by the Legislature, or by the People, to adopt a different approach. In the meantime, however, we must conclude that Riverside's ordinances are not preempted by state law.

The judgment of the Court of Appeal is affirmed.

Exercise 8-21. *Riverside* Revisited

1. Zoning can prohibit otherwise lawful uses, just as nuisance can enjoin otherwise lawful uses. Here, medical marijuana dispensaries are permitted and perhaps supported by state law, but local jurisdictions have the authority to ban them pursuant to their delegated police power. Is this an example of a "pig in a parlor"?
2. The court holds that state law does not preempt the local ordinance. It states that "nothing prevents future efforts by the Legislature, or by the People, to adopt a different approach." Accordingly, the California legislature could pass legislation that forbids a municipality from banning medical marijuana dispensaries. The court approvingly recognizes that, in the absence of state level legislation, municipalities are freed from a "one size fits all policy" and are able to follow their own values.
3. Medical marijuana dispensaries arguably have social utility, whereas the "drug dens" mentioned in the case have negative utility. Zoning laws can regulate common law nuisance, such as drug dens. It is also easier for an aggrieved neighbor to pursue a zoning violation than to file a nuisance suit.

Chapter 9

Government Takings

Introduction

The Takings Clause of the Fifth Amendment to the U.S. Constitution provides that "nor shall private property be taken for public use, without just compensation." U.S. Const., Amdt. 5. It guarantees "the security of Property," which Alexander Hamilton described to the Philadelphia Convention as one of the "great obj[ects] of Gov[ernment]." 1 *Records of the Federal Convention of 1787*, p. 302 (M. Farrand ed. 1911). Although the Takings Clause was originally a restraint on federal power, it was made applicable to the states by the Fourteenth Amendment. *Chicago Burlington and Quincy R.R. v. City of Chicago*, 166 U.S. 226 (1897). State constitutions also have takings clauses that in some instances provide greater protection than the federal Constitution.

There are two different types of government action that can constitute a taking under the Fifth Amendment. The first is a direct taking through the exercise of the power of eminent domain. An example of a direct taking would be when the government condemns private property in order to build a highway or other similar public works project. The Takings Clause requires the government to compensate the property owner and further requires that the taking must be for a "public use." The second type of taking is often referred to as an "inverse condemnation," as opposed to a "direct condemnation." In the case of an inverse condemnation, the government does not acknowledge that its action constitutes a taking and, therefore, it does not offer compensation to the property owner. Inverse condemnations can occur when the government imposes disabling land use restrictions, mandates a physical invasion of private property, or otherwise threatens a core property right.

Chapter Problem: Exercise 9-1

Your client, Frances Kulp, owns a multi-million dollar beachfront compound on the California coast. California has 1,160 miles of shoreline. By law, all California beaches are open to the public up to the mean high tide line. Under the California Coastal Access Act of 1983 (CCAA), the California Coastal Commission (CCC) is empowered to declare a public right of way through private beachfront property. Ms. Kulp has received a notice from the CCC stating that it will declare a public easement for ingress and egress across her property.

The letter states that the easement will run along the northern border of her property from the Pacific Coast Highway that parallels the shore to the dry sand beach. The easement will be 10 feet wide and will be owned by the non-profit organization Access for All (AFA). Under the terms of the easement, AFA agrees to maintain the easement and carry liability insurance.

Ms. Kulp objects strongly to allowing public access to the beach in front of her house. She suspects that the public will be rowdy and will "ruin the view" of the exclusive and unspoiled coastline. Frances was going to ignore the letter, but thought she should check with you first. When you speak with Ms. Kulp, she is outraged. She is convinced that that the action of the CCC must be unconstitutional and she goes so far as to call it "un-American." Ms. Kulp is adamant that she wants to keep the beach in front of her house off limits to the general public. Summarize your advice.

Overview of Chapter 9

In recent years, the ability of the government to appropriate private property for public purposes has become increasingly controversial. Eminent domain is now a hot topic in partisan circles, and it is frequently raised in the context of national political campaigns as an example of how government power erodes private property rights. In this Chapter, we will step back from the politically charged rhetoric surrounding government takings and study the core concepts of takings jurisprudence and read some of the most influential cases in the field. Almost all of the cases you will read will be U.S. Supreme Court decisions, which means that they are slightly longer than the cases in the other Chapters. You will learn how courts define the terms "public use" and "just compensation." You will also learn how government action can constitute a taking even when the government does not take title to the property. As you read the cases in this Chapter, consider the appropriate limits of government power and how best to allocate the burdens of citizenship.

The Chapter is divided into five subunits:

1. Direct Takings: Condemnation and the Power of Eminent Domain
2. Indirect Takings: When Does a Taking Occur?
3. Regulatory Takings: When a Regulation "Goes Too Far"
4. Exactions
5. Forfeiture Distinguished

Direct Takings: Condemnation and the Power of Eminent Domain

Eminent domain has been described as "an essential attribute of sovereignty, inherent in every independent government." *Pennsylvania Mut. Life Ins. Co. v Heiss*, 141 Ill. 35 (1892). The term eminent domain is derived from the Latin phrase for "supreme lordship"—*dominium eminens.* Grotius, the Dutch jurist, described the inherent power of eminent domain in his 1625 treatise:

> The property of subjects is under the eminent domain of the state, so that the state or he who acts for it may use and even alienate and destroy such property, not only in the case of extreme necessity, in which even private persons have a right over the property of others, but for ends of public utility, to which ends those who founded civil society must be supposed to have intended that private ends should give way. But it is to be added that when this is done the state is bound to make good the loss to those who lose their property.

The Takings Clause of the Fifth Amendment, as made applicable to the states through the Fourteenth Amendment, imposes two important restrictions on the government's inherent power of eminent domain. First, the taking must be for a "public use." Second, the government must pay the private property owner "just compensation." This Section discusses these two important limitations on government power.

The power of eminent domain allows the government to take private property for a public use. The classic example of eminent domain is when the government takes private property to build a public highway or other public project, such as a park or a school. The Takings Clause further requires that the private property owner must receive compensation for the loss of his property. The process of condemnation refers to the procedure by which title to the private property is transferred to the government. It should not be confused with when a government authority condemns a property because of unsafe conditions. In that case, the government is exercising police powers to protect public safety. It does not take title to the property. The private property owner remains responsible for remedying the defects that make the property unsafe.

Until recently, the disputes regarding eminent domain mostly centered on the requirement that the government pay the private property owner "just compensation." For example, when the township needs to widen a road and takes twelve feet of a property owner's front yard, how should the compensation be measured? Should the value represent the pro rata fair market value of the property taken to build the road? Or should the compensation reflect the diminution in value caused by the fact that the property now has a six-lane highway in its front yard? Some large public works projects have been held up for decades as property owners argued with the government over what constitutes "just compensation."

Today, much of the controversy over eminent domain centers on when the government can take private property and not simply what constitutes "just compensation." As you will see in the following cases, the U.S. Supreme Court interprets the term "public use" expansively to include "public purpose." Under this interpretation, there is no requirement that the public actually use the property in question, only that the rationale for the taking must serve a broader "public purpose." This broad interpretation provides governments with a powerful land use tool, specifically in the context of economic redevelopment.

The 2005 U.S. Supreme Court case of *Kelo v. New London* set off a firestorm of criticism when a majority of the Court approved the condemnation of an entire middle class residential community for "economic revitalization." *Kelo v. New London*, 545 U.S. 489 (2005). The Court reasserted its expansive interpretation of "public use" and rejected the property owners' argument that a heightened level of scrutiny should apply to takings cases. In the wake of *Kelo*, numerous jurisdictions passed legislation to restrict the exercise of eminent domain and strengthened protections for private property owners. Some of these laws prohibited the use of eminent domain for economic development, whereas others narrowed the definition of public use or imposed heightened levels of scrutiny. As a result, the laws in many states currently impose greater restrictions on eminent domain than the Takings Clause of the 5th Amendment.

Exercise 9-2. *Hawaii Housing Authority v. Midkiff*—Public Use

The 1954 U.S. Supreme Court decision *Berman v. Parker* approved the use of eminent domain for an economic redevelopment that was designed to eradicate urban blight even though the property would be transferred to private developers. *Berman v. Parker*, 348 U.S. 26 (1954). Thirty years later, the Court revisited the definition of "public use" set forth in *Berman* in an entirely different context. In *Hawaii Housing Authority v. Midkiff*, 467 U.S. 229 (1984), the Court considered the "public use" requirement in connection with concentrated land ownership in Hawaii. The Hawaii legislature passed a law to require large landowners to sell their property to their tenants as a means of breaking up large estates. Unlike other states, Hawaii had been settled under a form of feudalism that left the vast majority of land in the hands of only a few families. The legislature determined that this extreme concentration of ownership harmed the economy and the community.

As you read the following case, consider the following quote from Justice Chase:

> ... [A] law that takes property from A. and gives it to B: It is against all reason and justice, for a people to entrust a Legislature with such powers; and, therefore, it cannot be presumed that they have done it.

Calder v. Bull, 3 U.S. 388, 3 Dallas 386, 1 L. Ed. 648 (1798) (emphasis deleted).

How do you reconcile the decision in *Midkiff* with the prohibition on redistributing private property to another private individual?

Hawaii Housing Authority v. Midkiff

467 U.S. 229 (1984)

Justice O'Connor delivered the opinion of the Court. The Fifth Amendment of the United States Constitution provides, in pertinent part, that "private property [shall not] be taken for public use, without just compensation." These cases present the question whether the Public Use Clause of that Amendment, made applicable to the States through the Fourteenth Amendment, prohibits the State of Hawaii from taking, with just compensation, title in real property from lessors and transferring it to lessees in order to reduce the concentration of ownership of fees simple in the State. We conclude that it does not.

I

A

The Hawaiian Islands were originally settled by Polynesian immigrants from the western Pacific. These settlers developed an economy around a feudal land tenure system in which one island high chief, the ali'i nui, controlled the land and assigned it for development to certain subchiefs. The subchiefs would then reassign the land to other lower ranking chiefs, who would administer the land and govern the farmers and other tenants working it. All land was held at the will of the ali'i nui and eventually had to be returned to his trust. There was no private ownership of land.

Beginning in the early 1800's, Hawaiian leaders and American settlers repeatedly attempted to divide the lands of the kingdom among the crown, the chiefs, and the common people. These efforts proved largely unsuccessful, however, and the land remained in the hands of a few. In the mid-1960's, after extensive hearings, the Hawaii Legislature discovered that, while the State and Federal Governments owned almost 49% of the State's land, another 47% was in the hands of only 72 private landowners. The legislature further found that 18 landholders, with tracts of 21,000 acres or more, owned more than 40% of this land and that on Oahu, the most urbanized of the islands, 22 landowners owned 72.5% of the fee simple titles. The legislature concluded that concentrated land ownership was responsible for skewing the State's residential fee simple market, inflating land prices, and injuring the public tranquility and welfare.

To redress these problems, the legislature decided to compel the large landowners to break up their estates. The legislature considered requiring large landowners to sell lands which they were leasing to homeowners. However, the landowners strongly resisted this scheme, pointing out the significant federal tax liabilities they would incur. Indeed, the landowners claimed that the federal tax laws were the primary reason they previously had chosen to lease, and not sell, their lands. Therefore, to accommodate the needs of both lessors and lessees, the Hawaii Legislature enacted the Land Reform Act of 1967 (Act), Haw. Rev. Stat., ch. 516, which created a mechanism for condemning residential tracts and for transferring ownership of the condemned fees simple to existing lessees. By condemning the land in question, the Hawaii Legislature intended to make the land sales involuntary, thereby making the federal tax consequences less severe while still facilitating the redistribution of fees simple.

Under the Act's condemnation scheme, tenants living on single-family residential lots within developmental tracts at least five acres in size are entitled to ask the Hawaii Housing Authority (HHA) to condemn the property on which they live. When 25 eligible tenants, or tenants on half the lots in the tract, whichever is less, file appropriate applications, the Act authorizes HHA to hold a public hearing to determine whether acquisition by the State of all or part of the tract will "effectuate the public purposes" of the Act. § 516-22. If HHA finds that these public purposes will be served, it is authorized to designate some or all of the lots in the tract for acquisition. It then acquires, at prices set either by condemnation trial or by negotiation between lessors and lessees, the former fee owners' full "right, title, and interest" in the land.

After compensation has been set, HHA may sell the land titles to tenants who have applied for fee simple ownership. HHA is authorized to lend these tenants up to 90% of the purchase price, and it may condition final transfer on a right of first refusal for the first 10 years following sale. If HHA does not sell the lot to the tenant residing there, it may lease the lot or sell it to someone else, provided that public notice has been given. However, HHA may not sell to any one purchaser, or lease to any one tenant, more than one lot, and it may not operate for profit. In practice, funds to satisfy the condemnation awards have been supplied entirely by lessees. While the Act authorizes HHA to issue bonds and appropriate funds for acquisition, no bonds have issued and HHA has not supplied any funds for condemned lots.

B

In April 1977, HHA held a public hearing concerning the proposed acquisition of some of appellees' lands. HHA made the statutorily required finding that acquisition of appellees' lands would effectuate the public purposes of the Act. Then, in October 1978, it directed appellees to negotiate with certain lessees concerning the sale of the designated properties. Those negotiations failed, and HHA subsequently ordered appellees to submit to compulsory arbitration.

Rather than comply with the compulsory arbitration order, appellees filed suit, in February 1979, in United States District Court, asking that the Act be declared unconstitutional and that its enforcement be enjoined. The District Court found that the Act's goals were within the bounds of the State's police powers and that the means the legislature had chosen to serve those goals were not arbitrary, capricious, or selected in bad faith. The Court of Appeals for the Ninth Circuit reversed. The Court of Appeals determined that the Act could not pass the requisite judicial scrutiny of the Public Use Clause. It found that the transfers contemplated by the Act were unlike those of takings previously held to constitute "public uses" by this Court. The court further determined that the public purposes offered by the Hawaii Legislature were not deserving of judicial deference. The court concluded that the Act was simply "a naked attempt on the part of the state of Hawaii to take the private property of A and transfer it to B solely for B's private use and benefit." One judge dissented.

We now reverse.

III

A

The starting point for our analysis of the Act's constitutionality is the Court's decision in *Berman v. Parker*, 348 U.S. 26 (1954). In *Berman*, the Court held constitutional the District of Columbia Redevelopment Act of 1945. That Act provided both for the comprehensive use of the eminent domain power to redevelop slum areas and for the possible sale or lease of the condemned lands to private interests. In discussing whether the takings authorized by that Act were for a "public use," the Court stated:

> We deal, in other words, with what traditionally has been known as the police power. An attempt to define its reach or trace its outer limits is fruitless, for each case must turn on its own facts. The definition is essentially the product of legislative determinations addressed to the purposes of government, purposes neither abstractly nor historically capable of complete definition. Subject to specific constitutional limitations, when the legislature has spoken, the public interest has been declared in terms well-nigh conclusive. In such cases the legislature, not the judiciary, is the main guardian of the public needs to be served by social legislation, whether it be Congress legislating concerning the District of Columbia ... or the States legislating concerning local affairs.... This principle admits of no exception merely because the power of eminent domain is involved....

The Court explicitly recognized the breadth of the principle it was announcing, noting:

> Once the object is within the authority of Congress, the right to realize it through the exercise of eminent domain is clear. For the power of eminent domain is merely the means to the end.... Once the object is within the authority of Congress, the means by which it will be attained is also for Congress to determine. Here one of the means chosen is the use of private enterprise for redevelopment of the area. Appellants argue that this makes the project a taking from one businessman for the benefit of another businessman. But the means of executing the project are for Congress and Congress alone to determine, once the public purpose has been established.

The "public use" requirement is thus coterminous with the scope of a sovereign's police powers.

There is, of course, a role for courts to play in reviewing a legislature's judgment of what constitutes a public use, even when the eminent domain power is equated with the police power. But the Court in *Berman* made clear that it is "an extremely narrow" one. To be sure, the Court's cases have repeatedly stated that "one person's property may not be taken for the benefit of another private person without a justifying public purpose, even though compensation be paid." *Thompson v. Consolidated Gas Corp.*, 300 U.S. 55 (1937). But where the exercise of the eminent domain power is rationally related to a conceivable public purpose, the Court has never held a compensated taking to be proscribed by the Public Use Clause.

On this basis, we have no trouble concluding that the Hawaii Act is constitutional. The people of Hawaii have attempted, much as the settlers of the original 13 Colonies did, to reduce the perceived social and economic evils of a land oligopoly traceable to their monarchs. The land oligopoly has, according to the Hawaii Legislature, created artificial deterrents to the normal functioning of the State's residential land market and forced thousands of individual homeowners to lease, rather than buy, the land underneath their homes. Regulating oligopoly and the evils associated with it is a classic exercise of a State's police powers. We cannot disapprove of Hawaii's exercise of this power.

Nor can we condemn as irrational the Act's approach to correcting the land oligopoly problem. The Act presumes that when a sufficiently large number of persons declare that they are willing but unable to buy lots at fair prices the land market is malfunctioning. When such a malfunction is signalled, the Act authorizes HHA to condemn lots in the relevant tract. The Act limits the number of lots any one tenant can purchase and authorizes HHA to use public funds to ensure that the market dilution goals will be achieved. This is a comprehensive and rational approach to identifying and correcting market failure.

Of course, this Act, like any other, may not be successful in achieving its intended goals. But "whether in fact the provision will accomplish its objectives is not the question: the [constitutional requirement] is satisfied if ... the ... [state] Legislature rationally could have believed that the [Act] would promote its objective." *Western & Southern Life Ins. Co. v. State Bd. of Equalization*, 451 U.S. 648, 671-672 (1981). When the legislature's purpose is legitimate and its means are not irrational, our cases make clear that empirical debates over the wisdom of takings—no less than debates over the wisdom of other kinds of socioeconomic legislation—are not to be carried out in the federal courts. Redistribution of fees simple to correct deficiencies in the market determined by the state legislature to be attributable to land oligopoly is a rational exercise of the eminent domain power. Therefore, the Hawaii statute must pass the scrutiny of the Public Use Clause.

B

The Court of Appeals read our cases to stand for a much narrower proposition. It read our "public use" cases, especially *Berman*, as requiring that government possess and use property at some point during a taking. Since Hawaiian lessees retain possession of the property for private use throughout the condemnation process, the court found that the Act exacted takings for private use. We disagree with the Court of Appeals' analysis.

The mere fact that property taken outright by eminent domain is transferred in the first instance to private beneficiaries does not condemn that taking as having only a private purpose. The Court long ago rejected any literal requirement that condemned property be put into use for the general public. It is not essential that the entire community, nor even any considerable portion, ... directly enjoy or participate in any improvement in order [for it] to constitute a public use. As the unique way titles were held in Hawaii skewed the land market, exercise of the power of eminent domain was justified. The Act advances its purposes without the State's taking actual possession of the land. In such cases, government does not itself have to use property to legitimate the taking; it is only the taking's purpose, and not its mechanics, that must pass scrutiny under the Public Use Clause.

IV

The State of Hawaii has never denied that the Constitution forbids even a compensated taking of property when executed for no reason other than to confer a private benefit on a particular private party. A purely private taking could not withstand the scrutiny of the public use requirement; it would serve no legitimate purpose of government and would thus be void. But no purely private taking is involved in these cases. The Hawaii Legislature enacted its Land Reform Act not to benefit a particular class of identifiable individuals but to attack certain perceived evils of concentrated property ownership in Hawaii—a legitimate public purpose. Use of the condemnation power to achieve this purpose is not irrational. Since we assume for purposes of these appeals that the weighty demand of just compensation has been met, the requirements of the Fifth and Fourteenth Amendments have been satisfied. Accordingly, we reverse the judgment of the Court of Appeals, and remand these cases for further proceedings in conformity with this opinion.

It is so ordered.

JUSTICE MARSHALL took no part in the consideration or decision of these cases.

Exercise 9-3. *Hawaii Housing Authority* Revisited

1. *Midkiff* was a unanimous opinion. The Court reversed the judgment of the Ninth Circuit Court of Appeals that had invalidated the law as "a naked attempt on the part of the state of Hawaii to take the private property of A and transfer it to B solely for B's private use and benefit." Do you agree with the Supreme Court or the Court of Appeals?
2. In *Berman*, the property in question was not blighted, but it was located in a blighted area. The redevelopment plan required that all the property in the area had to be razed in order to implement the plan. In *Midkiff*, the legislation was not designed to combat blight. There were no allegations that the properties themselves were blighted or otherwise in disrepair. What public purpose did the legislation serve? How should we measure the success of the legislation?

Exercise 9-4. *Kelo v. New London* — Public Use

After Midkiff, the Supreme Court did not hear another major eminent domain case until 2005 when it decided *Kelo v. New London*. In what turned out to be a controversial decision, the Court once again affirmed that the term "public use" included a "public purpose" and did not require actual use by the public. Unlike the unanimous decision in *Midkiff*, *Kelo v. New London* was a 5 to 4 decision that included a lengthy dissent by Justice O'Connor that was joined by Chief Justice Rehnquist and Justices Scalia and Thomas. Justice Thomas also authored a dissent.

As you read the majority opinion and Justice O'Connor's dissenting opinion, pay attention to how each side characterizes the facts. Each side has a different view of what standard of review should apply to decisions to exercise eminent domain. Be sure to identify these competing standards and be prepared to discuss the potential consequences of adopting a higher or heightened standard of review in eminent domain cases.

Kelo v. New London

545 U.S. 489 (2005)

JUSTICE STEVENS delivered the opinion of the Court. In 2000, the city of New London approved a development plan that, in the words of the Supreme Court of Connecticut, was "projected to create in excess of 1,000 jobs, to increase tax and other revenues, and to revitalize an economically distressed city, including its downtown and waterfront areas." In assembling the land needed for this project, the city's development agent has purchased property from willing sellers and proposes to use the power of eminent domain to acquire the remainder of the property from unwilling owners in exchange for just compensation. The question presented is whether the city's proposed disposition of this property qualifies as a "public use" within the meaning of the Takings Clause of the Fifth Amendment to the Constitution.

I

The city of New London (hereinafter City) sits at the junction of the Thames River and the Long Island Sound in southeastern Connecticut. Decades of economic decline led a state agency in 1990 to designate the City a "distressed municipality." In 1996, the Federal Government closed the Naval Undersea Warfare Center, which had been located in the Fort Trumbull area of the City and had employed over 1,500 people. In 1998, the City's unemployment rate was nearly double that of the State, and its population of just under 24,000 residents was at its lowest since 1920.

These conditions prompted state and local officials to target New London, and particularly its Fort Trumbull area, for economic revitalization. To this end, respondent New London Development Corporation (NLDC), a private nonprofit entity established some years earlier to assist the City in planning economic development, was reactivated. In January 1998, the State authorized a $5.35 million bond issue to support the NLDC's planning activities and a $10 million bond issue toward the creation of a Fort Trumbull State Park. In February, the pharmaceutical company Pfizer Inc. announced that it would build a $300 million research facility on a site immediately adjacent to Fort Trumbull; local planners hoped that Pfizer would draw new business to the area, thereby serving as a catalyst to the area's rejuvenation. After receiving initial approval from the city council, the NLDC continued its planning activities and held a series of neighborhood meetings to educate the public about the process. In May, the city council authorized the NLDC to formally submit its plans to the relevant state agencies for review. Upon obtaining state-level approval, the NLDC finalized an integrated development plan focused on 90 acres of the Fort Trumbull area.

The Fort Trumbull area is situated on a peninsula that juts into the Thames River. The area comprises approximately 115 privately owned properties, as well as the 32 acres of land formerly occupied by the naval facility (Trumbull State Park now occupies 18 of those 32 acres). The development plan encompasses seven parcels. Parcel 1 is designated for a waterfront conference hotel at the center of a "small urban village" that will include restaurants and shopping. This parcel will also have marinas for both recreational and commercial uses. A pedestrian "riverwalk" will originate here and continue down the coast, connecting the waterfront areas of the development. Parcel 2 will be the site of approximately 80 new residences organized into an urban neighborhood and linked by public walkway to the remainder of the development, including the state park. This parcel also includes space reserved for a new U. S. Coast Guard Museum. Parcel 3, which is located immediately north of the Pfizer facility, will contain at least 90,000 square feet of research and development office space. Parcel 4A is a 2.4-acre site that will be used either to support the adjacent state park, by providing parking or retail services for visitors, or to support the nearby marina. Parcel 4B will include a renovated marina, as well as the final stretch of the riverwalk. Parcels 5, 6, and 7 will provide land for office and retail space, parking, and water-dependent commercial uses.

The NLDC intended the development plan to capitalize on the arrival of the Pfizer facility and the new commerce it was expected to attract. In addition to creating jobs, generating tax revenue, and helping to "build momentum for the revitalization of downtown New London," the plan was also designed to make the City more attractive and to create leisure and recreational opportunities on the waterfront and in the park.

The city council approved the plan in January 2000, and designated the NLDC as its development agent in charge of implementation. The city council also authorized the NLDC to purchase property or to acquire property by exercising eminent domain in the City's name. The NLDC successfully negotiated the purchase of most of the real estate in the 90-acre area, but its negotiations with petitioners failed. As a consequence, in November 2000, the NLDC initiated the condemnation proceedings that gave rise to this case.

II

Petitioner Susette Kelo has lived in the Fort Trumbull area since 1997. She has made extensive improvements to her house, which she prizes for its water view. Petitioner Wilhelmina Dery was born in her Fort Trumbull house in 1918 and has lived there her entire life. Her husband Charles (also a petitioner) has lived in the house since they married some 60 years ago. In all, the nine petitioners own 15 properties in Fort Trumbull—4 in parcel 3 of the development plan and 11 in parcel 4A. Ten of the parcels are occupied by the owner or a family member; the other five are held as investment properties. There is no allegation that any of these properties is blighted or otherwise in poor condition; rather, they were condemned only because they happen to be located in the development area.

In December 2000, petitioners brought this action in the New London Superior Court. They claimed, among other things, that the taking of their properties would violate the "public use" restriction in the Fifth Amendment. After a 7-day bench trial, the Superior Court granted a permanent restraining order prohibiting the taking of the properties located in parcel 4A (park or marina support). It, however, denied petitioners relief as to the properties located in parcel 3 (office space).

After the Superior Court ruled, both sides took appeals to the Supreme Court of Connecticut. That court held, over a dissent, that all of the City's proposed takings were valid. The three dissenting justices would have imposed a "heightened" standard of judicial review for takings justified by economic development. Although they agreed that the plan was intended to serve a valid public use, they would have found all the takings unconstitutional because the City had failed to adduce "clear and convincing evidence" that the economic benefits of the plan would in fact come to pass.

We granted certiorari to determine whether a city's decision to take property for the purpose of economic development satisfies the "public use" requirement of the Fifth Amendment.

III

Two polar propositions are perfectly clear. On the one hand, it has long been accepted that the sovereign may not take the property of *A* for the sole purpose of transferring it to another private party *B*, even though *A* is paid just compensation. On the other hand, it is equally clear that a State may transfer property from one private party to another if future "use by the public" is the purpose of the taking; the condemnation of land for a railroad with common-carrier duties is a familiar example. Neither of these propositions, however, determines the disposition of this case.

As for the first proposition, the City would no doubt be forbidden from taking petitioners' land for the purpose of conferring a private benefit on a particular private party. Nor would the City be allowed to take property under the mere pretext of a public purpose, when its actual purpose was to bestow a private benefit. The takings before us, however, would be executed pursuant to a "carefully considered" development plan. The trial judge and all the members of the Supreme Court of Connecticut agreed that there was no evidence of an illegitimate purpose in this case.

Therefore, as was true of the statute challenged in *Midkiff*, the City's development plan was not adopted "to benefit a particular class of identifiable individuals."

On the other hand, this is not a case in which the City is planning to open the condemned land—at least not in its entirety—to use by the general public. Nor will the private lessees of the land in any sense be required to operate like common carriers, making their services available to all comers. But although such a projected use would be sufficient to satisfy the public use requirement, this "Court long ago rejected any literal requirement that condemned property be put into use for the general public." Indeed, while many state courts in the mid-19th century endorsed "use by the public" as the proper definition of public use, that narrow view steadily eroded over time. Not only was the "use by the public" test difficult to administer (*e.g.*, what proportion of the public need have access to the property? at what price?), but it proved to be impractical given the diverse and always evolving needs of society. Accordingly, when this Court began applying the Fifth Amendment to the States at the close of the 19th century, it embraced the broader and more natural interpretation of public use as "public purpose." Thus, in a case upholding a mining company's use of an aerial bucket line to transport ore over property it did not own, Justice Holmes' opinion for the Court stressed "the inadequacy of use by the general public as a universal test." *Strickley v. Highland Boy Gold Mining Co.*, 200 U.S. 527, 531 (1906). We have repeatedly and consistently rejected that narrow test ever since.

The disposition of this case therefore turns on the question whether the City's development plan serves a "public purpose." Without exception, our cases have defined that concept broadly, reflecting our longstanding policy of deference to legislative judgments in this field. In *Berman v. Parker*, 348 U.S. 26 (1954), this Court upheld a redevelopment plan targeting a blighted area of Washington, D.C., in which most of the housing for the area's 5,000 inhabitants was beyond repair. Under the plan, the area would be condemned and part of it utilized for the construction of streets, schools, and other public facilities. The remainder of the land would be leased or sold to private parties for the purpose of redevelopment, including the construction of low-cost housing.

The owner of a department store located in the area challenged the condemnation, pointing out that his store was not itself blighted and arguing that the creation of a "better balanced, more attractive community" was not a valid public use. Writing for a unanimous Court, Justice Douglas refused to evaluate this claim in isolation, deferring instead to the legislative and agency judgment that the area "must be planned as a whole" for the plan to be successful. The Court explained that "community redevelopment programs need not, by force of the Constitution, be on a piecemeal basis—lot by lot, building by building." The public use underlying the taking was unequivocally affirmed:

> We do not sit to determine whether a particular housing project is or is not desirable. The concept of the public welfare is broad and inclusive.... The values it represents are spiritual as well as physical, aesthetic as well as monetary. It is within the power of the legislature to determine that the community should be beautiful as well as healthy, spacious as well as clean,

> well-balanced as well as carefully patrolled. In the present case, the Congress and its authorized agencies have made determinations that take into account a wide variety of values. It is not for us to reappraise them. If those who govern the District of Columbia decide that the Nation's Capital should be beautiful as well as sanitary, there is nothing in the *Fifth Amendment* that stands in the way.

In *Hawaii Housing Authority v. Midkiff*, 467 U.S. 229 (1984), the Court considered a Hawaii statute whereby fee title was taken from lessors and transferred to lessees (for just compensation) in order to reduce the concentration of land ownership. We unanimously upheld the statute and rejected the Ninth Circuit's view that it was "a naked attempt on the part of the state of Hawaii to take the property of A and transfer it to B solely for B's private use and benefit." Reaffirming *Berman*'s deferential approach to legislative judgments in this field, we concluded that the State's purpose of eliminating the "social and economic evils of a land oligopoly" qualified as a valid public use. Our opinion also rejected the contention that the mere fact that the State immediately transferred the properties to private individuals upon condemnation somehow diminished the public character of the taking. "[I]t is only the taking's purpose, and not its mechanics," we explained, that matters in determining public use.

Viewed as a whole, our jurisprudence has recognized that the needs of society have varied between different parts of the Nation, just as they have evolved over time in response to changed circumstances. Our earliest cases in particular embodied a strong theme of federalism, emphasizing the "great respect" that we owe to state legislatures and state courts in discerning local public needs. For more than a century, our public use jurisprudence has wisely eschewed rigid formulas and intrusive scrutiny in favor of affording legislatures broad latitude in determining what public needs justify the use of the takings power.

IV

Those who govern the City were not confronted with the need to remove blight in the Fort Trumbull area, but their determination that the area was sufficiently distressed to justify a program of economic rejuvenation is entitled to our deference. The City has carefully formulated an economic development plan that it believes will provide appreciable benefits to the community, including—but by no means limited to—new jobs and increased tax revenue. As with other exercises in urban planning and development, the City is endeavoring to coordinate a variety of commercial, residential, and recreational uses of land, with the hope that they will form a whole greater than the sum of its parts. To effectuate this plan, the City has invoked a state statute that specifically authorizes the use of eminent domain to promote economic development. Given the comprehensive character of the plan, the thorough deliberation that preceded its adoption, and the limited scope of our review, it is appropriate for us, as it was in *Berman*, to resolve the challenges of the individual owners, not on a piecemeal basis, but rather in light of the entire plan. Because that plan unquestionably serves a public purpose, the takings challenged here satisfy the public use requirement of the Fifth Amendment.

To avoid this result, petitioners urge us to adopt a new bright-line rule that economic development does not qualify as a public use. Putting aside the unpersuasive suggestion that the City's plan will provide only purely economic benefits, neither precedent nor logic supports petitioners' proposal. Promoting economic development is a traditional and long-accepted function of government. There is, moreover, no principled way of distinguishing economic development from the other public purposes that we have recognized. In our cases upholding takings that facilitated agriculture and mining, for example, we emphasized the importance of those industries to the welfare of the States in question, in *Berman,* we endorsed the purpose of transforming a blighted area into a "well-balanced" community through redevelopment, in *Midkiff,* we upheld the interest in breaking up a land oligopoly that "created artificial deterrents to the normal functioning of the State's residential land market." It would be incongruous to hold that the City's interest in the economic benefits to be derived from the development of the Fort Trumbull area has less of a public character than any of those other interests. Clearly, there is no basis for exempting economic development from our traditionally broad understanding of public purpose.

Alternatively, petitioners maintain that for takings of this kind we should require a "reasonable certainty" that the expected public benefits will actually accrue. Such a rule, however, would represent an even greater departure from our precedent. "When the legislature's purpose is legitimate and its means are not irrational, our cases make clear that empirical debates over the wisdom of takings—no less than debates over the wisdom of other kinds of socioeconomic legislation—are not to be carried out in the federal courts." *Midkiff,* 467 U.S., at 242. The disadvantages of a heightened form of review are especially pronounced in this type of case. Orderly implementation of a comprehensive redevelopment plan obviously requires that the legal rights of all interested parties be established before new construction can be commenced. A constitutional rule that required postponement of the judicial approval of every condemnation until the likelihood of success of the plan had been assured would unquestionably impose a significant impediment to the successful consummation of many such plans.

In affirming the City's authority to take petitioners' properties, we do not minimize the hardship that condemnations may entail, notwithstanding the payment of just compensation. We emphasize that nothing in our opinion precludes any State from placing further restrictions on its exercise of the takings power. Indeed, many States already impose "public use" requirements that are stricter than the federal baseline. Some of these requirements have been established as a matter of state constitutional law, while others are expressed in state eminent domain statutes that carefully limit the grounds upon which takings may be exercised. As the submissions of the parties and their *amici* make clear, the necessity and wisdom of using eminent domain to promote economic development are certainly matters of legitimate public debate. This Court's authority, however, extends only to determining whether the City's proposed condemnations are for a "public use" within the meaning of the Fifth Amendment to the Federal Constitution. Because over a century of our case law interpreting that provision dictates an affirmative answer to that question, we may not grant petitioners the relief that they seek.

The judgment of the Supreme Court of Connecticut is affirmed.

It is so ordered.

JUSTICE O'CONNOR, with whom the CHIEF JUSTICE, JUSTICE SCALIA, and JUSTICE THOMAS join, dissenting. Over two centuries ago, just after the Bill of Rights was ratified, Justice Chase wrote:

> An Act of the Legislature (for I cannot call it a law) contrary to the great first principles of the social compact, cannot be considered a rightful exercise of legislative authority.... A few instances will suffice to explain what I mean.... [A] law that takes property from A. and gives it to B: It is against all reason and justice, for a people to entrust a Legislature with such powers; and, therefore, it cannot be presumed that they have done it.

Calder v. Bull, 3 U.S. 386, 3 Dallas 386, 1 L. Ed. 648 (1798) (emphasis deleted).

Today the Court abandons this long-held, basic limitation on government power. Under the banner of economic development, all private property is now vulnerable to being taken and transferred to another private owner, so long as it might be upgraded—*i.e.*, given to an owner who will use it in a way that the legislature deems more beneficial to the public—in the process. To reason, as the Court does, that the incidental public benefits resulting from the subsequent ordinary use of private property render economic development takings "for public use" is to wash out any distinction between private and public use of property—and thereby effectively to delete the words "for public use" from the Takings Clause of the Fifth Amendment. Accordingly I respectfully dissent.

I

Petitioners are nine resident or investment owners of 15 homes in the Fort Trumbull neighborhood of New London, Connecticut. Petitioner Wilhelmina Dery, for example, lives in a house on Walbach Street that has been in her family for over 100 years. She was born in the house in 1918; her husband, petitioner Charles Dery, moved into the house when they married in 1946. Their son lives next door with his family in the house he received as a wedding gift, and joins his parents in this suit. Two petitioners keep rental properties in the neighborhood.

In February 1998, Pfizer Inc., the pharmaceuticals manufacturer, announced that it would build a global research facility near the Fort Trumbull neighborhood. Two months later, New London's city council gave initial approval for the New London Development Corporation (NLDC) to prepare the development plan at issue here. The NLDC is a private, nonprofit corporation whose mission is to assist the city council in economic development planning. It is not elected by popular vote, and its directors and employees are privately appointed. Consistent with its mandate, the NLDC generated an ambitious plan for redeveloping 90 acres of Fort Trumbull in order to "complement the facility that Pfizer was planning to build, create jobs, increase tax and other revenues, encourage public access to and use of the city's waterfront, and eventually 'build momentum' for the revitalization of the rest of the city."

Petitioners own properties in two of the plan's seven parcels—Parcel 3 and Parcel 4A. Under the plan, Parcel 3 is slated for the construction of research and office space as a market develops for such space. It will also retain the existing Italian Dramatic Club (a private cultural organization) though the homes of three plaintiffs in that parcel are to be demolished. Parcel 4A is slated, mysteriously, for "park support." At oral argument, counsel for respondents conceded the vagueness of this proposed use, and offered that the parcel might eventually be used for parking.

To save their homes, petitioners sued New London and the NLDC, to whom New London has delegated eminent domain power. Petitioners maintain that the Fifth Amendment prohibits the NLDC from condemning their properties for the sake of an economic development plan. Petitioners are not holdouts; they do not seek increased compensation, and none is opposed to new development in the area. Theirs is an objection in principle: They claim that the NLDC's proposed use for their confiscated property is not a "public" one for purposes of the Fifth Amendment. While the government may take their homes to build a road or a railroad or to eliminate a property use that harms the public, say petitioners, it cannot take their property for the private use of other owners simply because the new owners may make more productive use of the property.

II

The Fifth Amendment to the Constitution, made applicable to the States by the Fourteenth Amendment, provides that "private property [shall not] be taken for public use, without just compensation." When interpreting the Constitution, we begin with the unremarkable presumption that every word in the document has independent meaning, that no word was unnecessarily used, or needlessly added. In keeping with that presumption, we have read the Fifth Amendment's language to impose two distinct conditions on the exercise of eminent domain: the Taking must be for a 'public use' and 'just compensation' must be paid to the owner.

These two limitations serve to protect "the security of Property," which Alexander Hamilton described to the Philadelphia Convention as one of the "great obj[ects] of Gov[ernment]." 1 Records of the Federal Convention of 1787, p 302 (M. Farrand ed. 1911). Together they ensure stable property ownership by providing safeguards against excessive, unpredictable, or unfair use of the government's eminent domain power—particularly against those owners who, for whatever reasons, may be unable to protect themselves in the political process against the majority's will. While the Takings Clause presupposes that government can take private property without the owner's consent, the just compensation requirement spreads the cost of condemnations and thus "prevents the public from loading upon one individual more than his just share of the burdens of government." *Monongahela Nav. Co. v. United States,* 148 U.S. 312, 325 (1893). The public use requirement, in turn, imposes a more basic limitation, circumscribing the very scope of the eminent domain power: Government may compel an individual to forfeit her property for the *public's* use, but not for the benefit of another private person. This requirement promotes fairness as well as security.

Where is the line between "public" and "private" property use? We give considerable deference to legislatures' determinations about what governmental activities will advantage the public. But were the political branches the sole arbiters of the public-private distinction, the Public Use Clause would amount to little more than hortatory fluff. An external, judicial check on how the public use requirement is interpreted, however limited, is necessary if this constraint on government power is to retain any meaning.

This case returns us for the first time in over 20 years to the hard question of when a purportedly "public purpose" taking meets the public use requirement. It presents an issue of first impression: Are economic development takings constitutional? I would hold that they are not. We are guided by two precedents about the taking of real property by eminent domain.

The Court's holdings in *Berman* and *Midkiff* were true to the principle underlying the Public Use Clause. In both those cases, the extraordinary, precondemnation use of the targeted property inflicted affirmative harm on society—in *Berman* through blight resulting from extreme poverty and in *Midkiff* through oligopoly resulting from extreme wealth. And in both cases, the relevant legislative body had found that eliminating the existing property use was necessary to remedy the harm. Thus a public purpose was realized when the harmful use was eliminated. Because each taking *directly* achieved a public benefit, it did not matter that the property was turned over to private use. Here, in contrast, New London does not claim that Susette Kelo's and Wilhelmina Dery's well-maintained homes are the source of any social harm. Indeed, it could not so claim without adopting the absurd argument that any single-family home that might be razed to make way for an apartment building, or any church that might be replaced with a retail store, or any small business that might be more lucrative if it were instead part of a national franchise, is inherently harmful to society and thus within the government's power to condemn.

In moving away from our decisions sanctioning the condemnation of harmful property use, the Court today significantly expands the meaning of public use. It holds that the sovereign may take private property currently put to ordinary private use, and give it over for new, ordinary private use, so long as the new use is predicted to generate some secondary benefit for the public—such as increased tax revenue, more jobs, maybe even esthetic pleasure. But nearly any lawful use of real private property can be said to generate some incidental benefit to the public. Thus, if predicted (or even guaranteed) positive side effects are enough to render transfer from one private party to another constitutional, then the words "for public use" do not realistically exclude *any* takings, and thus do not exert any constraint on the eminent domain power.

The logic of today's decision is that eminent domain may only be used to upgrade—not downgrade—property. At best this makes the Public Use Clause redundant with the Due Process Clause, which already prohibits irrational government action. The Court rightfully admits, however, that the judiciary cannot get bogged down in predictive judgments about whether the public will actually be better off after a property transfer. In any event, this constraint has no realistic import. For who among us can say she already makes the most productive or attractive possible use of her property? The specter of condemnation hangs over all property. Nothing is to prevent the State from replacing any Motel 6 with a Ritz-Carlton, any home with a shopping mall, or any farm with a factory.

Finally, in a coda, the Court suggests that property owners should turn to the States, who may or may not choose to impose appropriate limits on economic development takings. This is an abdication of our responsibility. States play many important functions in our system of dual sovereignty, but compensating for our refusal to enforce properly the Federal Constitution (and a provision meant to curtail state action, no less) is not among them.

Any property may now be taken for the benefit of another private party, but the fallout from this decision will not be random. The beneficiaries are likely to be those citizens with disproportionate influence and power in the political process, including large corporations and development firms. As for the victims, the government now has license to transfer property from those with fewer resources to those with more. The Founders cannot have intended this perverse result. "[T]hat alone is a *just* government," wrote James Madison, "which *impartially* secures to every man, whatever is his *own.*" For the National Gazette, Property, (Mar. 27, 1792), reprinted in 14 Papers of James Madison 266 (R. Rutland et al. eds. 1983).

I would hold that the takings in both Parcel 3 and Parcel 4A are unconstitutional, reverse the judgment of the Supreme Court of Connecticut, and remand for further proceedings.

Exercise 9-5. *Kelo* Revisited

1. Citing concerns of federalism, the majority opinion refuses to apply a heightened degree of scrutiny and instead notes the "great respect" the Court "owes to state legislatures and state courts in discerning local public needs." The majority opinion notes that the individual states are free to provide greater protections from eminent domain than those found in the Fifth Amendment. Immediately following the decision, many states did just that. Some states mandated heightened scrutiny for eminent domain cases, and others specifically targeted economic redevelopment. Accordingly, there is currently considerable variation among the states. When practicing in this area, it is important to remember that the Takings Clause is only the starting point of your analysis. It provides the minimum level of protections that must be afforded private property owners. Many states provide greater protections.
2. The majority opinion was not without its supporters. The Mayor of New York City at the time, Mayor Michael Bloomberg, frequently spoke in favor

of a robust power of eminent domain. In a 2006, Mayor Bloomberg strongly criticized attempts to restrict eminent domain. Diane Cardwell, *Bloomberg Says Power to Seize Private Land Is Vital to* Cities, New York Times, May 3, 2006. The Mayor said, "You would never build any big thing any place in any big city in this country if you didn't have the power of eminent domain." He continued to say that some people do not "appreciate the crucial importance of eminent domain to our ability to shape our own future. They mistakenly equate it with an abuse of government power, and ignore the benefits that come to us all from responsible development of formerly blighted areas." Do you agree?

3. Petitioners asked the Court to require the City of New London to prove by a "reasonable certainty" that the intended public benefits would actually accrue. Both the majority opinion and Justice O'Connor's dissent dismissed this argument as unrealistic. As it turns out, the project itself proved unrealistic. The City spent close to $80 million to acquire the properties and demolish them, but the project never got off the ground. The developer was unable to secure financing. Pfizer closed its New London offices in 2009. Ten years after the decision, the Fort Trumbull area where Suzette Kelo's house once stood was a vacant lot.

4. In his dissent, Justice Thomas warned that low-income communities would bear the disproportionate burden of eminent domain. He wrote:

   > Allowing the government to take property solely for public purposes is bad enough, but extending the concept of public purpose to encompass any economically beneficial goal guarantees that these losses will fall disproportionately on poor communities. Those communities are not only systematically less likely to put their lands to the highest and best social use, but are also the least politically powerful.

Exercise 9-6. *J.J. Newberry Co. v. City of East Chicago* — Just Compensation

The determination of what constitutes "just compensation" has been a source of frequent controversy. The most common measure is fair market value. The classic definition of fair market value is the price that a willing buyer would pay a willing seller, both being under no compulsion to buy or sell and both being aware of all material facts. However, in some instances, property owners have argued that fair market value is not sufficient to compensate them for the loss of their property. They have argued that consequential damages should also be included in an award of just compensation. Courts have generally resisted this argument. As the U.S. Supreme Court explained in *Olson v. United States*, the property owner "is entitled to be put in as good a position pecuniarily as if his property had not been taken. He must be made whole, but is not entitled to more. It is the property, and not the cost of it, that is safeguarded by state and federal constitutions." *Olson v. United States*, 292 U.S. 246 (1934).

The determination of what compensates "just compensation" is further complicated when the property involved is less than a full fee simple interest. The following case from a state appellate court involves a claim by a tenant for just compensation. As you read the case, think back to Chapter 6 and our discussion of landlord-tenant relationships. How should we measure the value of a leasehold? Who is entitled to the benefit of the bargain? Do you think the tenant has been made whole?

J.J. Newberry Co. v. City of East Chicago

441 N.E.2d 39 (1982)

STATON, J. J.J. Newberry Company appeals a condemnation award of $760.00 plus interest for its leasehold interest in property condemned by the City of East Chicago. On appeal, Newberry raises the following issues for review:

(1) Did the trial court err in not permitting Newberry's leasehold interest to be valued by using the capitalization of income method of valuation?

(2) Did the trial court err in determining that the condemnation award for Newberry's leasehold interest and the lessor's interest could not exceed the fair market value of the property as a whole?

Affirmed.

I.
Evidence

The record reveals that Newberry and the predecessors in interest of the beneficiaries of a land trust held by the Lake County Trust Company (hereinafter "lessor") executed a 25-year written lease agreement on September 30, 1953, for a parcel of real estate and the improvements thereon located in the Indiana Harbor region of the City of East Chicago. The 1953 lease entitled Newberry to continue to operate a variety store which had existed on the premises since 1926. The lease required rental payments of a fixed monthly amount plus a percentage of the gross annual income from the business.

On December 31, 1971, a fire of unknown origin completely destroyed the building and improvements which were the subject of Newberry's lease. Under a "fire clause" in the 1953 lease, the lessor was required to reconstruct the building if the building was damaged or destroyed by fire. The lessor failed to perform its obligations under the "fire clause," and Newberry was unable to operate its retail business on the premises.

On January 4, 1973, Newberry filed a complaint against the lessor and sought either specific performance of the "fire clause," or, in the alternative, an award of compensatory damages for lost profits. A lengthy history of litigation ensued over a three-county area of northwest Indiana. The action culminated on December 16, 1980, with this Court's affirmance of the trial court's award of $116,910.33 as damages sustained by Newberry as a result of the lessor's breach of the "fire clause."

An event that affected the outcome of Newberry's action on the "fire clause" and generated the subject matter of this appeal was the condemnation of the vacant parcel of property. On June 16, 1976, the City of East Chicago exercised its power of eminent domain. As part of a project to redevelop blighted urban areas, the City of East Chicago condemned the property on which Newberry's variety store stood until the fire in 1971. The decision to condemn the property was made by the representatives of East Chicago with full knowledge of the litigation involving Newberry and the lessor for the breach of the "fire clause."

The condemnation action proceeded to trial without jury on July 26, 1979, on the issue of the amount to be awarded to Newberry and the lessor. After hearing the evidence and reviewing the trial briefs, the trial court entered the following judgment:

> It is therefore ordered that the property herein has been appropriated by eminent domain from the defendant Lake County, Trust #2081, by the plaintiff, City of East Chicago, Indiana, for and on behalf of it's [sic] Department of Redevelopment; and that such property was subject to a leasehold interest owned by J.J. Newberry.
>
> It is further ordered that said plaintiff shall pay to the defendant, Lake County Trust Company, Trust #2081, the sum of $44,240.00 for such appropriation, plus interest pursuant to I.C. 32-11-1-8 calculated from the date of possession by plaintiff;
>
> It is further ordered that said plaintiff shall pay to the defendant, J.J. Newberry, the sum of $760.00 plus interest pursuant to I.C. 32-11-1-8 calculated from the date of possession by plaintiff.
>
> Done and ordered this 19th day of May, 1980.

Newberry appealed the trial court's award of $760.00 plus interest. The lessor did not appeal its award.

II.
Capitalization of Income Method

Newberry's first assignment of error involves a challenge to the trial court's method of valuing Newberry's leasehold interest in the destroyed premises on June 16, 1976, the date of condemnation. As of that date, Newberry had an unexpired term of approximately 28 months on its lease with the lessor. Newberry contended, and the trial court properly held, that a tenant is entitled to compensation for an unexpired term of lease terminated by a condemnation action. However, the disputed issue at trial (and now on appeal) involved the method of valuing the unexpired term of Newberry's lease. Needless to say, the destruction of the building in 1971 and the subsequent five-year vacancy on the property complicated the trial court's resolution of the valuation issue.

In Conclusions of Law 7 and 8, the trial court held that Newberry's leasehold interest is to be valued as the difference between the fair market rental value of subject premises less the contract rent to be paid over the remainder of the term of the lease and that Newberry "is not entitled to lost profits as damages for the appropriation and condemnation of subject premises." Based upon the testimony of two qualified real estate appraisers who used the trial court's method of valuation, the trial court determined that Newberry's leasehold interest was worth $760.00. It is this method of valuation which Newberry challenges on appeal.

Newberry contends that the trial court committed reversible error in using the aforementioned method of valuation. Newberry posits that the trial court should have used the "capitalization of income method" of valuing a leasehold interest. Dr. Lesley Singer, an economist, testified on behalf of Newberry and stated that the capitalization of income method was the only feasible method of valuing a leasehold interest that had undergone the calamities suffered by Newberry's interest. According to Dr. Singer's computations, the capitalized value of Newberry's leasehold interest on the date of condemnation was $165,970.42. Newberry asserts that the trial court erred in not setting Newberry's condemnation award at that amount.

The capitalization of income method of valuing condemned property operates as follows:

> The income approach to valuation usually consists of arriving at an independent value of the land involved and adding to it the value of improvements arrived at by process of capitalization, i.e., converting reasonable or actual income at a reasonable rate of return (capitalization rate) into an indication of value. Land and improvements may be capitalized together in a single process.

4 Sackman, *Nichols on Eminent Domain* § 12.32(3)(c), at 12-577 (3d rev. ed. 1981).

Indiana courts permit the valuation of leasehold interests by the capitalization of income method under appropriate circumstances. However, the more traditional method of valuing a leasehold interest for condemnation purposes was enunciated by the Indiana Supreme Court:

> Generally, the measure of damages where a leasehold interest is taken under eminent domain is the fair market value of the unexpired term of the lease over and above the rent stipulated to be paid.

State v. Heslar, 257 Ind. 307 (1971). The *Heslar* method of valuation was employed by the trial court in the present case.

Upon reviewing the leading authorities on valuation of leasehold interests, this Court concludes that the trial court did not err in rejecting Newberry's request for use of the capitalization of income method. A proper application of the capitalization of income method requires that "the property is in good condition and capable of producing the income to be capitalized." 29A C.J.S. Eminent Domain § 168(2), at 724-25 (1965). Furthermore, "income cannot be capitalized to produce a residual value where the appropriated land is neither producing income nor equipped to do so...." *Id.* As such, the trial court properly rejected Newberry's alternate valuation method in light of the incendiary destruction of the building which Newberry used to produce income.

Case law from other jurisdictions support the general proposition of the law stated above. For example, in *United States v. Certain Interests in Property*, 296 F.2d 264 (4th Cir. 1961), the court held that the "very use of the capitalization-of-income method of evaluation assumes the valuation of the property as a going concern...." New York courts have reached a similar conclusion in cases wherein condemnees sought valuation under the capitalization of income method of vacant, unimproved property on which future improvements were to be constructed. The underlying reasons for the courts' holdings were that a vacant, unimproved parcel of property was not conducive to valuation under the capitalization of income method since it was the ongoing business which enhanced the value of the land.

Under the particular circumstances of the present case, the trial court properly applied the *Heslar* method of valuation. The trial court correctly concluded that the capitalization of income method was too speculative to compute the fair market value of the property, regardless of the fact that Newberry had at one time operated a business on the property as a going concern. This Court "will not disturb an award of damages in a condemnation suit where the award is within the bounds of probative evidence introduced at trial." *Indiana & Michigan Electric Co. v. Hurm* 422 N.E.2d 371 (Ind. App. 1981). The record sustains the condemnation award in the present case, and the proper method of valuing Newberry's leasehold interest was used.

III.

Undivided Fee Rule

Newberry's second challenge to the trial court's condemnation award is directed toward the trial court's Conclusion of Law 5, which provided:

> That the sum of the separate interest of each of the Defendants (Newberry and the lessor) in the subject premises cannot exceed the fair market value of subject premises as a whole.

The trial court determined that the property was worth $45,000.00 on June 16, 1976. The lessor's interest was valued at $44,240.00, and Newberry's leasehold interest was valued at $760.00. Newberry contends that the superficially appealing truism that the sum of the parts cannot exceed the whole has no application in the law of eminent domain.

Newberry cites several cases from other jurisdictions in support of the proposition that the combined value of a leasehold interest and a reversionary interest may exceed the fair market value of the property as a whole. However, this Court need look no further than the unambiguous directives of the Indiana Supreme Court which stated:

> For the purposes of condemnation proceedings, the value of all the interests or estates in a single parcel of land cannot exceed the value of the property as a whole, and that when the value of the property as a unit is paid to the various owners, or into court for them, the constitutional requirements are fully met, and the fact that the owners of the various interests may not agree as to the apportionment among themselves of the sum awarded does not concern the condemnor.

State v. Montgomery Circuit Court, 239 Ind. 337 (1959). Other Indiana appellate decisions have strictly adhered to the rule of law established in Montgomery Circuit Court. The apportionment of the condemnation award between the tenant and the lessor prescribed by the Court is commonly known as the "undivided fee rule" and has wide application in other jurisdictions.

While Newberry characterizes the above passage from Montgomery Circuit Court as mere "dicta" which should carry no precedential value, this Court will adhere to the Supreme Court's resolution of the issue as manifested in footnote one of Montgomery Circuit Court. Until the high Court indicates a deviation from the aforementioned rule of apportionment, this Court is bound to follow the "undivided fee rule."

Affirmed.

Exercise 9-7. *J.J. Newberry* Revisited

1. When the property was condemned, the lessor had 28 months remaining on the leasehold. There is no dispute that a tenant is required to be compensated for an unexpired leasehold. The question is how to calculate the amount. Be sure you can describe the difference between the method of valuation used by the trial court and the "capitalization of income method."
2. Do you think that the result would have been different if the improvements on the property had not been first destroyed by fire?
3. Newberry argued that the amount of compensation awarded to the lessor and the lessee could exceed the fair market value of the property. Can you reconcile this assertion with the notion that property is a bundle of sticks?

Indirect Takings—When Does a Taking of Property Occur?

When the government exercises its power of eminent domain, it takes title to the property in question. The direct appropriation of property then triggers the clear obligation to pay just compensation. An indirect taking or inverse condemnation occurs when the government does not take title to the property, but nonetheless damages or diminishes the property. Because the government does not acknowledge that its action constitutes a taking, it does not offer compensation to the property owner. Inverse condemnations can occur when the government imposes disabling land use restrictions, mandates a physical invasion of private property, or otherwise threatens a core property right.

In order to determine whether a taking of property has occurred, the courts employ an ad hoc balancing test. As the Court explained in *Penn Central Transportation Co., v. New York City*, 438 U.S. 104 (1978),

> In engaging in these essentially ad hoc, factual inquiries, the Court's decisions have identified several factors that have particular significance. The economic impact of the regulation on the claimant and, particularly, the extent to which the regulation has interfered with distinct investment-backed expectations are, of course, relevant considerations. So, too, is the character of the governmental action.

In addition to the ad hoc analysis, the courts have carved out several instances where a government action will be considered a per se or categorical taking of property. These instances include 1) a permanent physical invasion, 2) the deprivation of all economically viable use, and 3) the destruction of a core property right.

Exercise 9-8. *PruneYard Shopping Center v. Robbins*

Enclosed shopping malls became popular in the United States beginning in the late 1950s. Newly developed suburban areas were planned without central commercial districts. Instead, they were car-dependent "bedroom communities." The iconic "Main Street, USA" was displaced by massive shopping malls that took retail establishments, restaurants, and entertainment to otherwise residential areas and provided them all under one roof.

The decline of Main Street also reduced the venues where concerned citizens could engage in political speech and political organizing. The First Amendment protects an individual's right to set up a soapbox on a public corner and rail against the government, gather signatures, or distribute political literature. In the 1970s, a number of cases asserted that privately owned shopping malls should be subject to Free Speech guarantees because they were the functional equivalent of Main Street. To some extent, the cases were an extension of *Marsh v. Alabama*, 326 U.S. 501 (1916), where the U.S. Supreme Court held that a state trespass law could not be used to bar the distribution of religious literature on the sidewalk of a privately owned company town. The Court, however, ultimately rejected arguments to extend Free Speech protections to shopping malls. In *Lloyd Corp. v. Tanner*, 407 U.S. 551 (1972), the Court ruled that "[the] essentially private character of a store and its privately owned abutting property does not change by virtue of being large or clustered with other stores in a modern shopping center."

California took a different approach. The California Supreme Court ruled that the California state constitution protects "speech and petitioning, reasonably exercised, in shopping centers even when the centers are privately owned." *PruneYard Shopping Center v. Robbins*, 23 Cal.3d 899 (1979). In the following case, a private property owner argues that the extension of Free Speech guarantees to individuals on private property constitutes a taking of property under the Fifth Amendment and, therefore, triggers the requirement of just compensation. As you read the case, consider how the protection of Free Speech rights could be perceived as a violation of private property rights. It should remind you of similar claims that we considered in connection with the Right of Access in Chapter 3.

PruneYard Shopping Center v. Robbins

447 U.S. 74 (1980)

MR. JUSTICE REHNQUIST delivered the opinion of the Court. We postponed jurisdiction of this appeal from the Supreme Court of California to decide the important federal constitutional questions it presented. Those are whether state constitutional provisions, which permit individuals to exercise free speech and petition rights on the property of a privately owned shopping center to which the public is invited, violate the shopping center owner's property rights under the Fifth and Fourteenth Amendments.

I

Appellant PruneYard is a privately owned shopping center in the city of Campbell, California. It covers approximately 21 acres—5 devoted to parking and 16 occupied by walkways, plazas, sidewalks, and buildings that contain more than 65 specialty shops, 10 restaurants, and a movie theater. The PruneYard is open to the public for the purpose of encouraging the patronizing of its commercial establishments. It has a policy not to permit any visitor or tenant to engage in any publicly expressive activity, including the circulation of petitions, that is not directly related to its commercial purposes. This policy has been strictly enforced in a nondiscriminatory fashion. The PruneYard is owned by appellant Fred Sahadi.

Appellees are high school students who sought to solicit support for their opposition to a United Nations resolution against "Zionism." On a Saturday afternoon they set up a card table in a corner of PruneYard's central courtyard. They distributed pamphlets and asked passersby to sign petitions, which were to be sent to the President and

Members of Congress. Their activity was peaceful and orderly and so far as the record indicates was not objected to by PruneYard's patrons.

Soon after appellees had begun soliciting signatures, a security guard informed them that they would have to leave because their activity violated PruneYard regulations. The guard suggested that they move to the public sidewalk at the PruneYard's perimeter. Appellees immediately left the premises and later filed this lawsuit in the California Superior Court of Santa Clara County. They sought to enjoin appellants from denying them access to the PruneYard for the purpose of circulating their petitions.

The California Supreme Court [held] that the California Constitution protects "speech and petitioning, reasonably exercised, in shopping centers even when the centers are privately owned." It concluded that appellees were entitled to conduct their activity on PruneYard property. In rejecting appellants' contention that such a result infringed property rights protected by the Federal Constitution, the California Supreme Court observed:

> It bears repeated emphasis that we do not have under consideration the property or privacy rights of an individual homeowner or the proprietor of a modest retail establishment. As a result of advertising and the lure of a congenial environment, 25,000 persons are induced to congregate daily to take advantage of the numerous amenities offered by the [shopping center there]. A handful of additional orderly persons soliciting signatures and distributing handbills in connection therewith, under reasonable regulations adopted by defendant to assure that these activities do not interfere with normal business operations would not markedly dilute defendant's property rights.

III

Appellants first contend that *Lloyd Corp. v. Tanner*, 407 U.S. 551 (1972), prevents the State from requiring a private shopping center owner to provide access to persons exercising their state constitutional rights of free speech and petition when adequate alternative avenues of communication are available. *Lloyd* dealt with the question whether under the Federal Constitution a privately owned shopping center may prohibit the distribution of handbills on its property when the handbilling is unrelated to the shopping center's operations. The shopping center had adopted a strict policy against the distribution of handbills within the building complex and its malls, and it made no exceptions to this rule. Respondents in *Lloyd* argued that because the shopping center was open to the public, the First Amendment prevents the private owner from enforcing the handbilling restriction on shopping center premises. In rejecting this claim [w]e stated that property does not "lose its private character merely because the public is generally invited to use it for designated purposes," and that "[the] essentially private character of a store and its privately owned abutting property does not change by virtue of being large or clustered with other stores in a modern shopping center."

Our reasoning in *Lloyd*, however, does not *ex proprio vigore* limit the authority of the State to exercise its police power or its sovereign right to adopt in its own

Constitution individual liberties more expansive than those conferred by the Federal Constitution. In *Lloyd*, there was no state constitutional or statutory provision that had been construed to create rights to the use of private property by strangers, comparable to those found to exist by the California Supreme Court here. It is, of course, well established that a State in the exercise of its police power may adopt reasonable restrictions on private property so long as the restrictions do not amount to a taking without just compensation or contravene any other federal constitutional provision. *Lloyd* held that when a shopping center owner opens his private property to the public for the purpose of shopping, the First Amendment to the United States Constitution does not thereby create individual rights in expression beyond those already existing under applicable law.

IV

Appellants next contend that a right to exclude others underlies the Fifth Amendment guarantee against the taking of property without just compensation and the Fourteenth Amendment guarantee against the deprivation of property without due process of law.

It is true that one of the essential sticks in the bundle of property rights is the right to exclude others. And here there has literally been a "taking" of that right to the extent that the California Supreme Court has interpreted the State Constitution to entitle its citizens to exercise free expression and petition rights on shopping center property. But it is well established that "not every destruction or injury to property by governmental action has been held to be a 'taking' in the constitutional sense." *Armstrong v. United States*, 364 U.S. 40 (1960). Rather, the determination whether a state law unlawfully infringes a landowner's property in violation of the Taking Clause requires an examination of whether the restriction on private property "[forces] some people alone to bear public burdens which, in all fairness and justice, should be borne by the public as a whole." This examination entails inquiry into such factors as the character of the governmental action, its economic impact, and its interference with reasonable investment-backed expectations. *Kaiser Aetna v. United States*, 444 U.S. 164 (1979). When "regulation goes too far it will be recognized as a taking." *Pennsylvania Coal Co. v. Mahon*, 260 U.S. 393 (1922).

Here the requirement that appellants permit appellees to exercise state-protected rights of free expression and petition on shopping center property clearly does not amount to an unconstitutional infringement of appellants' property rights under the Taking Clause. There is nothing to suggest that preventing appellants from prohibiting this sort of activity will unreasonably impair the value or use of their property as a shopping center. The PruneYard is a large commercial complex that covers several city blocks, contains numerous separate business establishments, and is open to the public at large. The decision of the California Supreme Court makes it clear that the PruneYard may restrict expressive activity by adopting time, place, and manner regulations that will minimize any interference with its commercial functions. Appellees were orderly, and they limited their activity to the common areas of the shopping center. In these circumstances, the fact that they may have "physically invaded" appellants' property cannot be viewed as determinative.

This case is quite different from *Kaiser Aetna v. United States*, 444 U.S. 164 (1979). Kaiser Aetna was a case in which the owners of a private pond had invested substantial amounts of money in dredging the pond, developing it into an exclusive marina, and building a surrounding marina community. The marina was open only to fee-paying members, and the fees were paid in part to "maintain the privacy and security of the pond." The Federal Government sought to compel free public use of the private marina on the ground that the marina became subject to the federal navigational servitude because the owners had dredged a channel connecting it to "navigable water."

The Government's attempt to create a public right of access to the improved pond interfered with Kaiser Aetna's "reasonable investment backed expectations." We held that it went "so far beyond ordinary regulation or improvement for navigation as to amount to a taking...." *Id.* Nor as a general proposition is the United States, as opposed to the several States, possessed of residual authority that enables it to define "property" in the first instance. A State is, of course, bound by the Just Compensation Clause of the Fifth Amendment, but here appellants have failed to demonstrate that the "right to exclude others" is so essential to the use or economic value of their property that the state-authorized limitation of it amounted to a "taking."

We conclude that appellants' federally recognized property rights have [not] been infringed by the California Supreme Court's decision recognizing a right of appellees to exercise state-protected rights of expression and petition on appellants' property. The judgment of the Supreme Court of California is therefore

Affirmed.

Exercise 9-9. *PruneYard* Revisited

1. In this case, the state of California did not seize the PruneYard Shopping Center through the exercise of its eminent domain powers. Although title to the shopping center stayed in private hands, PruneYard argued that it had been denied the right to exclude in violation of the Fifth Amendment. You will recall from Chapter 3 that the right to exclude is an important stick in the bundle that is property. In many respects the right to exclude is the hallmark of private property.
2. The Court identifies three factors to determine whether a state action violates the Takings Clause: 1) the character of the government act, 2) the economic impact, and 3) the interference with reasonable backed investment expectations.
3. The decision of the California Supreme Court makes it clear that PruneYard may restrict expressive activity by adopting time, place, and manner regulations in order to minimize any interference with its commercial functions. Do you agree with the Court's conclusion that handbilling does not interfere with PruneYard's use of the property or its value?

Exercise 9-10. *Loretto v. Teleprompter Manhattan CATC Corp.*

PruneYard involved a temporary intrusion that was subject to time, place, and manner restrictions. The following case involves what the U.S. Supreme Court characterized as a "permanent physical occupation." Compare the way the Court uses the bundle of sticks metaphor in *Loretto v. Teleprompter* to how it was applied in *PruneYard*.

As you read the following case, be sure to pay attention to what the Court refers to as the ad hoc standard for determining whether a taking has occurred, thereby triggering the requirement of just compensation.

Do you agree that a permanent physical invasion—no matter how small—should constitute a taking?

Loretto v. Teleprompter Manhattan CATC Corp.

458 U.S. 419 (1982)

Justice Marshall delivered the opinion of the Court. This case presents the question whether a minor but permanent physical occupation of an owner's property authorized by government constitutes a "taking" of property for which just compensation is due under the Fifth and Fourteenth Amendments of the Constitution. New York law provides that a landlord must permit a cable television company to install its cable facilities upon his property. In this case, the cable installation occupied portions of appellant's roof and the side of her building. The New York Court of Appeals ruled that this appropriation does not amount to a taking. Because we conclude that such a physical occupation of property is a taking, we reverse.

I

Appellant Jean Loretto purchased a five-story apartment building located at 303 West 105th Street, New York City, in 1971. The previous owner had granted appellees Teleprompter Corp. and Teleprompter Manhattan CATV (collectively Teleprompter) permission to install a cable on the building and the exclusive privilege of furnishing cable television (CATV) services to the tenants. The New York Court of Appeals described the installation as follows:

> On June 1, 1970 TelePrompter installed a cable slightly less than one-half inch in diameter and of approximately 30 feet in length along the length of the building about 18 inches above the roof top, and directional taps, approximately 4 inches by 4 inches by 4 inches, on the front and rear of the roof. By June 8, 1970 the cable had been extended another 4 to 6 feet and cable had been run from the directional taps to the adjoining building at 305 West 105th Street.

Teleprompter also installed two large silver boxes along the roof cables. The cables are attached by screws or nails penetrating the masonry at approximately two-foot intervals, and other equipment is installed by bolts.

Initially, Teleprompter's roof cables did not service appellant's building. They were part of what could be described as a cable "highway" circumnavigating the city block, with service cables periodically dropped over the front or back of a building in which a tenant desired service. Crucial to such a network is the use of so-called "crossovers"—cable lines extending from one building to another in order to reach a new group of tenants. Two years after appellant purchased the building, Teleprompter connected a "noncrossover" line—i.e., one that provided CATV service to appellant's own tenants—by dropping a line to the first floor down the front of appellant's building.

Prior to 1973, Teleprompter routinely obtained authorization for its installations from property owners along the cable's route, compensating the owners at the standard rate of 5% of the gross revenues that Teleprompter realized from the particular property. To facilitate tenant access to CATV, the State of New York enacted § 828 of the Executive Law, effective January 1, 1973. Section 828 provides that a landlord may not "interfere with the installation of cable television facilities upon his property or premises," and may not demand payment from any tenant for permitting CATV, or demand payment from any CATV company "in excess of any amount which the [State Commission on Cable Television] shall, by regulation, determine to be reasonable." The landlord may, however, require the CATV company or the tenant to bear the cost of installation and to indemnify for any damage caused by the installation. Pursuant to § 828(1)(b), the State Commission has ruled that a one-time $1 payment is the normal fee to which a landlord is entitled. The Commission ruled that this nominal fee, which the Commission concluded was equivalent to what the landlord would receive if the property were condemned pursuant to New York's Transportation Corporations Law, satisfied constitutional requirements "in the absence of a special showing of greater damages attributable to the taking."

Appellant did not discover the existence of the cable until after she had purchased the building. She brought a class action against Teleprompter in 1976 on behalf of all owners of real property in the State on which Teleprompter has placed CATV components, alleging that Teleprompter's installation was a trespass and, insofar as it relied on § 828, a taking without just compensation. She requested damages and injunctive relief. Appellee City of New York, which has granted Teleprompter an exclusive franchise to provide CATV within certain areas of Manhattan, intervened. The Supreme Court, Special Term, granted summary judgment to Teleprompter and the city, upholding the constitutionality of § 828 in both crossover and noncrossover situations. The Appellate Division affirmed without opinion.

On appeal, the Court of Appeals, over dissent, upheld the statute. The court concluded that the law requires the landlord to allow both crossover and noncrossover installations but permits him to request payment from the CATV company under § 828(1)(b), at a level determined by the State Cable Commission, only for noncrossovers. The court then ruled that the law serves a legitimate police power purpose—eliminating landlord fees and conditions that inhibit the development of CATV, which has important educational and community benefits. Rejecting the argument that a physical occupation authorized by government is necessarily a taking, the court stated that the regulation does not have an excessive economic impact upon appellant when measured against her aggregate property rights, and that it does not interfere with any reasonable investment-backed expectations. Accordingly, the court held that § 828 does not work a taking of appellant's property. Chief Judge Cooke dissented, reasoning that the physical appropriation of a portion of appellant's property is a taking without regard to the balancing analysis courts ordinarily employ in evaluating whether a regulation is a taking.

In light of its holding, the Court of Appeals had no occasion to determine whether the $1 fee ordinarily awarded for a noncrossover installation was adequate compensation for the taking. Judge Gabrielli, concurring, agreed with the dissent that the law works a taking but concluded that the $1 presumptive award, together with the procedures permitting a landlord to demonstrate a greater entitlement, affords just compensation.

II

The Court of Appeals determined that § 828 serves the legitimate public purpose of "rapid development of and maximum penetration by a means of communication which has important educational and community aspects," and thus is within the State's police power. We have no reason to question that determination. It is a separate question, however, whether an otherwise valid regulation so frustrates property rights that compensation must be paid. We conclude that a permanent physical occupation authorized by government is a taking without regard to the public interests that it may serve. Our constitutional history confirms the rule, recent cases do not question it, and the purposes of the Takings Clause compel its retention.

A

The Court [has] noted that no "set formula" exist[s] to determine, in all cases, whether compensation is constitutionally due for a government restriction of property. Ordinarily, the Court must engage in "essentially ad hoc, factual inquiries." But the inquiry is not standardless. The economic impact of the regulation, especially the degree of interference with investment-backed expectations, is of particular significance. "So, too, is the character of the governmental action. A 'taking' may more readily be found when the interference with property can be characterized as a physical invasion by government, than when interference arises from some public program adjusting the benefits and burdens of economic life to promote the common good." *Penn Central Transportation Co., v. New York City*, 438 U.S. 104 (1978)

As *Penn Central* affirms, the Court has often upheld substantial regulation of an owner's use of his own property where deemed necessary to promote the public interest. At the same time, we have long considered a physical intrusion by government to be a property restriction of an unusually serious character for purposes of the Takings Clause. Our cases further establish that when the physical intrusion reaches the extreme form of a permanent physical occupation, a taking has occurred. In such a case, "the character of the government action" not only is an important factor in resolving whether the action works a taking but also is determinative.

When faced with a constitutional challenge to a permanent physical occupation of real property, this Court has invariably found a taking. As early as 1872, in *Pumpelly v. Green Bay Co.*, 13 Wall. 166, this Court held that the defendant's construction, pursuant to state authority, of a dam which permanently flooded plaintiff's property constituted a taking. A unanimous Court stated, without qualification, that "where real estate is actually invaded by superinduced additions of water, earth, sand, or other material, or by having any artificial structure placed on it, so as to effectually destroy or impair its usefulness, it is a taking, within the meaning of the Constitution." Seven years later, the Court reemphasized the importance of a physical occupation by distinguishing a regulation that merely restricted the use of private property.

Since these early cases, this Court has consistently distinguished between flooding cases involving a permanent physical occupation, on the one hand, and cases involving a more temporary invasion, or government action outside the owner's property that causes consequential damages within, on the other. A taking has always been found only in the former situation.

Although this Court's most recent cases have not addressed the precise issue before us, they have emphasized that physical invasion cases are special and have not repudiated the rule that any permanent physical occupation is a taking. The cases state or imply that a physical invasion is subject to a balancing process, but they do not suggest that a permanent physical occupation would ever be exempt from the Takings Clause. In *PruneYard Shopping Center v. Robins*, 447 U.S. 74 (1980), the Court upheld a state constitutional requirement that shopping center owners permit individuals to exercise free speech and petition rights on their property, to which they had already invited the general public. The Court emphasized that the State Constitution does not prevent the owner from restricting expressive activities by imposing reasonable time, place, and manner restrictions to minimize interference with the owner's commercial functions. Since the invasion was temporary and limited in nature, and since the owner had not exhibited an interest in excluding all persons from his property, "the fact that [the solicitors] may have 'physically invaded' [the owners'] property cannot be viewed as determinative."

In short, when the character of the governmental action is a permanent physical occupation of property, our cases uniformly have found a taking to the extent of the occupation, without regard to whether the action achieves an important public benefit or has only minimal economic impact on the owner.

B

The historical rule that a permanent physical occupation of another's property is a taking has more than tradition to commend it. Such an appropriation is perhaps the most serious form of invasion of an owner's property interests. To borrow a metaphor, the government does not simply take a single "strand" from the "bundle" of property rights: it chops through the bundle, taking a slice of every strand. Property rights in a physical thing have been described as the rights "to possess, use and dispose of it." *United States v. General Motors Corp.*, 323 U.S. 373 (1945). To the extent that the government permanently occupies physical property, it effectively destroys each of these rights. First, the owner has no right to possess the occupied space himself, and also has no power to exclude the occupier from possession and use of the space. The power to exclude has traditionally been considered one of the most treasured strands in an owner's bundle of property rights. Second, the permanent physical occupation of property forever denies the owner any power to control the use of the property; he not only cannot exclude others, but can make no nonpossessory use of the property. Although deprivation of the right to use and obtain a profit from property is not, in every case, independently sufficient to establish a taking, it is clearly relevant. Finally, even though the owner may retain the bare legal right to dispose of the occupied space by transfer or sale, the permanent occupation of that space by a stranger will ordinarily empty the right of any value, since the purchaser will also be unable to make any use of the property.

C

Teleprompter's cable installation on appellant's building constitutes a taking under the traditional test. The installation involved a direct physical attachment of plates, boxes, wires, bolts, and screws to the building, completely occupying space immediately above and upon the roof and along the building's exterior wall. In light of our analysis, we find no constitutional difference between a crossover and a noncrossover installation. The portions of the installation necessary for both crossovers and noncrossovers permanently appropriate appellant's property. Accordingly, each type of installation is a taking.

Our holding today is very narrow. We affirm the traditional rule that a permanent physical occupation of property is a taking. In such a case, the property owner entertains a historically rooted expectation of compensation, and the character of the invasion is qualitatively more intrusive than perhaps any other category of property regulation. We do not, however, question the equally substantial authority upholding a State's broad power to impose appropriate restrictions upon an owner's use of his property.

The judgment of the New York Court of Appeals is reversed, and the case is remanded for further proceedings not inconsistent with this opinion.

It is so ordered.

Exercise 9-11. *Loretto* Revisited

1. The Court noted that "[w]hen faced with a constitutional challenge to a permanent physical occupation of real property, this Court has invariably found a taking." The Court concludes that a permanent physical invasion is

a per se taking. How does this decision alter the ad hoc takings analysis enunciated by the Court in *PruneYard* and then applied in *Loretto*?

2. New York law provided an award of $1 to landlords. The nominal award was designed to represent what the landlord would have been entitled to had the property involved been condemned. Why wasn't this presumptive award sufficient?

3. The Court uses the bundle of sticks metaphor to distinguish *Loretto* from *PruneYard.* In *PruneYard*, the California law impacted one of the sticks in the bundle—the right to exclude. On the other hand, the Court in *Loretto* observed that a permanent physical occupation "does not simply take a single 'strand' from the 'bundle' of property rights: it chops through the bundle, taking a slice of every strand."

Exercise 9-12. *Babbit v. Youpee*—Core Property Right

Earlier in the course, we studied Native American land claims. The following case involves a negative consequence of the allotment policy that distributed Native American land to individual members of the tribe. Under the allotment policy, the federal government held the property in trust for the benefit for the allotee. Originally, the beneficial interest in the land descended to the allotee's heirs in accordance with the rules of intestate succession in the laws of the jurisdiction where the land is located. Congress later authorized the beneficial owners to devise their interests by will. The way the land was held led to extreme fractionalization of ownership.

In order to alleviate the situation, Congress enacted the Indian Land Consolidation Act that was designed to end fractionalization by providing that certain small property interests escheat to the state upon the death of the beneficial owner. As a result, the beneficial owner was deprived of the right to pass the interest to her heirs by devise or descent. Heirs challenged the federal law, asserting that it constituted a taking of property without just compensation. Once again, the Court applied the ad hoc balancing test to determine whether the law violated the Takings Clause of the Fifth Amendment.

The ad hoc test involves three factors: 1) the character of the government act, 2) the economic impact, and 3) the interference with reasonable backed investment expectations. As you read the following case, consider which of these three factors carries the most weight in the majority opinion and the dissenting opinion.

Babbit v. Youpee

519 U.S. 234 (1997)

JUSTICE GINSBURG delivered the opinion of the Court. In this case, we consider for a second time the constitutionality of an escheat-to-tribe provision of the Indian Land Consolidation Act (ILCA). 96 Stat. 2519, as amended, 25 U.S.C. § 2206. Specifically, we address § 207 of the ILCA, as amended in 1984. Congress enacted the original provision in 1983 to ameliorate the extreme fractionation problem attending a century-old allotment policy that yielded multiple ownership of single parcels of Indian land. Amended § 207 provides that certain small interests in Indian lands will transfer— or "escheat"—to the tribe upon the death of the owner of the interest. In *Hodel v. Irving*, 481 U.S. 704 (1987), this Court held that the original version of § 207 of the ILCA effected a taking of private property without just compensation, in violation of the Fifth Amendment to the United States Constitution. We now hold that amended § 207 does not cure the constitutional deficiency this Court identified in the original version of § 207.

I

In the late Nineteenth Century, Congress initiated an Indian land program that authorized the division of communal Indian property. Pursuant to this allotment policy, some Indian land was parcelled out to individual tribal members. Lands not allotted to individual Indians were opened to non-Indians for settlement. *See* Indian General Allotment Act of 1887, ch. 119, 24 Stat. 388. Allotted lands were held in trust by the United States or owned by the allottee subject to restrictions on alienation. On the death of the allottee, the land descended according to the laws of the State or Territory in which the land was located. In 1910, Congress also provided that allottees could devise their interests in allotted land.

The allotment policy "quickly proved disastrous for the Indians." *Irving*, 481 U.S. at 707. The program produced a dramatic decline in the amount of land in Indian hands. And as allottees passed their interests on to multiple heirs, ownership of allotments became increasingly fractionated, with some parcels held by dozens of owners. A number of factors augmented the problem: Because Indians often died without wills, many interests passed to multiple heirs, Congress' allotment Acts subjected trust lands to alienation restrictions that impeded holders of small interests from transferring those interests. The fractionation problem proliferated with each succeeding generation as multiple heirs took undivided interests in allotments.

The administrative difficulties and economic inefficiencies associated with multiple undivided ownership in allotted lands gained official attention as early as 1928. Governmental administration of these fractionated interests proved costly, and individual owners of small undivided interests could not make productive use of the land. Congress ended further allotment in 1934. But that action left the legacy in place. As most owners had more than one heir, interests in lands already allotted continued to splinter with each generation. In the 1960's, congressional studies revealed that approximately half of all allotted trust lands were held in fractionated ownership;

for over a quarter of allotted trust lands, individual allotments were held by more than six owners to a parcel.

In 1983, Congress adopted the ILCA in part to reduce fractionated ownership of allotted lands. Pub. Section 207 of the Act—the "escheat" provision—prohibited the descent or devise of small fractional interests in allotments. Instead of passing to heirs, such fractional interests would escheat to the tribe, thereby consolidating the ownership of Indian lands. Congress defined the targeted fractional interest as one that both constituted 2 percent or less of the total acreage in an allotted tract and had earned less than $100 in the preceding year. Section 207 made no provision for the payment of compensation to those who held such interests.

In *Hodel v. Irving*, this Court invalidated § 207 on the ground that it effected a taking of property without just compensation, in violation of the Fifth Amendment. The appellees in Irving were, or represented, heirs or devisees of members of the Oglala Sioux Tribe. But for § 207, the appellees would have received 41 fractional interests in allotments; under § 207, those interests would escheat to the Tribe. This Court tested the legitimacy of § 207 by considering its economic impact, its effect on investment-backed expectations, and the essential character of the measure. Turning first to the economic impact of § 207, the Court in *Irving* observed that the provision's income-generation test might fail to capture the actual economic value of the land. The Court next indicated that § 207 likely did not interfere with investment-backed expectations. Key to the decision in *Irving*, however, was the "extraordinary" character of the Government regulation. As this Court noted, § 207 amounted to the "virtual abrogation of the right to pass on a certain type of property." Such a complete abrogation of the rights of descent and devise could not be upheld.

II

In 1984, while Irving was still pending in the Court of Appeals for the Eighth Circuit, Congress amended § 207. Amended § 207 differs from the original escheat provision in three relevant respects. First, an interest is considered fractional if it both constitutes 2 percent or less of the total acreage of the parcel and "is incapable of earning $100 in any one of the five years [following the] decedent's death"—as opposed to one year before the decedent's death in the original § 207. If the interest earned less than $100 in any one of five years prior to the decedent's death, "there shall be a rebuttable presumption that such interest is incapable of earning $100 in any one of the five years following the death of the decedent." Second, in lieu of a total ban on devise and descent of fractional interests, amended § 207 permits devise of an otherwise escheatable interest to "any other owner of an undivided fractional interest in such parcel or tract" of land. Finally, tribes are authorized to override the provisions of amended § 207 through the adoption of their own codes governing the disposition of fractional interests; these codes are subject to the approval of the Secretary of the Interior. In *Irving*, "we express[ed] no opinion on the constitutionality of § 207 as amended."

Under amended § 207, the interests in this case would escheat to tribal governments. The initiating plaintiffs, respondents here, are the children and potential heirs of

William Youpee. An enrolled member of the Sioux and Assiniboine Tribes of the Fort Peck Reservation in Montana, William Youpee died testate in October 1990. His will devised to respondents, all of them enrolled tribal members, his several undivided interests in allotted trust lands on various reservations in Montana and North Dakota. These interests, as the Ninth Circuit reported, were valued together at $1,239. Each interest was devised to a single descendant. Youpee's will thus perpetuated existing fractionation, but it did not splinter ownership further by bequeathing any single fractional interest to multiple devisees.

In 1992, in a proceeding to determine the heirs to, and claims against, William Youpee's estate, an Administrative Law Judge (ALJ) in the Department of the Interior found that interests devised to each of the respondents fell within the compass of amended § 207 and should therefore escheat to the tribal governments of the Fort Peck, Standing Rock, and Devils Lake Sioux Reservations. Respondents, asserting the unconstitutionality of amended § 207, appealed the ALJ's order to the Department of the Interior Board of Indian Appeals. The Board, stating that it did not have jurisdiction to consider respondents' constitutional claim, dismissed the appeal.

Respondents then filed suit in the United States District Court for the District of Montana, naming the Secretary of the Interior as defendant, and alleging that amended § 207 of the ILCA violates the Just Compensation Clause of the Fifth Amendment. The District Court agreed with respondents and granted their request for declaratory and injunctive relief.

The Court of Appeals for the Ninth Circuit affirmed. That court carefully inspected the 1984 revisions to § 207. Hewing closely to the reasoning of this Court in *Irving*, the Ninth Circuit determined that amended § 207 did not cure the deficiencies that rendered the original provision unconstitutional. In particular, the Ninth Circuit observed that amended § 207 "continue[d] to completely abolish one of the sticks in the bundle of rights [constituting property] for a class of Indian landowners." The Ninth Circuit noted that "Congress may pursue other options to achieve consolidation of ... fractional interests," including Government purchase of the land, condemnation for a public purpose attended by payment of just compensation, or regulation to impede further fractionation. But amended § 207 could not stand, the Ninth Circuit concluded, for the provision remained "an extraordinary and impermissible regulation of Indian lands and effect[ed] an unconstitutional taking without just compensation."

On the petition of the United States, we granted certiorari and now affirm.

III

In determining whether the 1984 amendments to § 207 render the provision constitutional, we are guided by *Irving*. The United States maintains that the amendments, though enacted three years prior to the *Irving* decision, effectively anticipated the concerns expressed in the Court's opinion. As already noted, amended § 207 differs from the original in three relevant respects. These modifications, according to the United States, rescue amended § 207 from the fate of its predecessor. The Government maintains that the revisions moderate the economic impact of the provision and temper the character of the Government's regulation; the latter factor weighed most heavily against the constitutionality of the original version of § 207.

The narrow revisions Congress made to § 207, without benefit of our ruling in *Irving*, do not warrant a disposition different from the one this Court announced and explained in *Irving*. Amended § 207 permits a five-year window rather than a one-year window to assess the income-generating capacity of the interest. As the Ninth Circuit observed, however, argument that this change substantially mitigates the economic impact of § 207 "misses the point."

Amended § 207 still trains on income generated from the land, not on the value of the parcel. The Court observed in *Irving* that "even if ... the income generated by such parcels may be properly thought of as de minimis," the value of the land may not fit that description. The parcels at issue in *Irving* were valued by the Bureau of Indian Affairs at $2,700 and $1,816, amounts we found "not trivial." The value of the disputed parcels in this case is not of a different order; as the Ninth Circuit reported, the value of decedent Youpee's fractional interests was $1,239. In short, the economic impact of amended § 207 might still be palpable.

Even if the economic impact of amended § 207 is not significantly less than the impact of the original provision, the United States correctly comprehends that *Irving* rested primarily on the "extraordinary" character of the governmental regulation. *Irving* stressed that the original § 207 "amount[ed] to virtually the abrogation of the right to pass on a certain type of property—the small undivided interest—to one's heirs." The *Irving* Court further noted that the original § 207 "effectively abolish[ed] both descent and devise [of fractional interests] even when the passing of the property to the heir might result in consolidation of property." As the United States construes *Irving*, Congress cured the fatal infirmity in § 207 when it revised the section to allow transmission of fractional interests to successors who already own an interest in the allotment.

Congress' creation of an ever-so-slight class of individuals equipped to receive fractional interests by devise does not suffice, under a fair reading of Irving, to rehabilitate the measure. Amended § 207 severely restricts the right of an individual to direct the descent of his property. Allowing a decedent to leave an interest only to a current owner in the same parcel shrinks drastically the universe of possible successors. And, as the Ninth Circuit observed, the "very limited group [of permissible devisees] is unlikely to contain any lineal descendants." Moreover, amended § 207 continues to restrict devise "even in circumstances when the governmental purpose sought to be advanced, consolidation of ownership of Indian lands, does not conflict with the further descent of the property." *Irving*, 481 U.S. at 718. William Youpee's will, the United States acknowledges, bequeathed each fractional interest to one heir. Giving effect to Youpee's directive, therefore, would not further fractionate Indian land holdings.

The United States also contends that amended § 207 satisfies the Constitution's demand because it does not diminish the owner's right to use or enjoy property during his life-time, and does not affect the right to transfer property at death through non-probate means. These arguments did not persuade us in *Irving* and they are no more persuasive today. The third alteration made in amended § 207 also fails to bring the provision outside the reach of this Court's holding in Irving. Amended § 207 permits tribes to establish their own codes to govern the disposition of fractional interests; if approved by the Secretary of the Interior, these codes would govern in lieu of amended § 207. The United States does not rely on this new provision to defend the statute. Nor does it appear that the United States could do so at this time: Tribal codes governing disposition of escheatable interests have apparently not been developed.

For the reasons stated, the judgment of the Court of Appeals for the Ninth Circuit is

Affirmed.

Justice Stevens, dissenting. Section 207 of the Indian Land Consolidation Act, 25 U.S.C. § 2206, did not, in my view, effect an unconstitutional taking of William Youpee's right to make a testamentary disposition of his property. As I explained in *Hodel v. Irving*, the Federal Government, like a State, has a valid interest in removing legal impediments to the productive development of real estate. For this reason, the Court has repeatedly "upheld the power of the State to condition the retention of a property right upon the performance of an act within a limited period of time." *Texaco, Inc. v. Short*, 454 U.S. 516 (1982). I remain convinced that "Congress has ample power to require the owners of fractional interests in allotted lands to consolidate their holdings during their lifetimes or to face the risk that their interests will be deemed to be abandoned." *Hodel*, 481 U.S. at 732 (Stevens, J., concurring in judgment). The federal interest in minimizing the fractionated ownership of Indian lands—and thereby paving the way to the productive development of their property—is strong enough to justify the legislative remedy created by § 207, provided, of course, that affected owners have adequate notice of the requirements of the law and an adequate opportunity to adjust their affairs to protect against loss.

In my opinion, William Youpee did have such notice and opportunity.

Exercise 9-13. *Babbit Revisited*

1. The Court invalidates section 207 even though the law did not directly impact the beneficial owners during their lifetimes. The Court follows *Irving* and holds that section 207 constitutes a taking of property, because it abrogates the right to pass property at death, which is considered a core property right.
2. How do you reconcile the decision in *Babbitt* with the decision in *PruneYard*, where the owners of the shopping mall lost the right to exclude? Isn't the right to exclude a core property right? What is different about the character of the government action in *Babbitt*?

Regulatory Takings — When a Regulation "Goes Too Far"

Justice Holmes' majority opinion in *Pennsylvania Coal v. Mahon* is often quoted for the observation that a regulation to protect public safety sometimes "goes too far" and can violate the Takings Clause. *Pennsylvania Coal v. Mahon*, 260 U.S. 393 (1922). He wrote "[t]he general rule at least is, that while property may be regulated to a certain extent, if regulation goes too far it will be recognized as a taking." In Pennsylvania and other jurisdictions with underground natural resources, it is common for the surface rights to be owned separately from the mineral rights. We discussed this in Chapter 2 in connection with the law of natural resources.

As a result of the split of surface rights from mineral rights, a homeowner might only own the surface rights and, therefore, have no control over the disposition of coal, oil, or natural gas deposits below her property. Coal mining poses particular hazards such as the risk of subsidence and coal fires. In response to these dangers, Pennsylvania passed a law that prohibited mining if it could cause subsidence of a residential property, unless the owner of the mineral rights also owned the surface rights. Although the majority agreed that a public exigency warranted legislative action, the majority also agreed with Pennsylvania Coal that the law constituted a taking of property without just compensation. Even though the government had not directly appropriated the coal, the Court held that "to make it commercially impracticable to mine certain coal has very nearly the same effect for constitutional purposes as appropriating or destroying it."

The Court considered both the impact of the law on economic interests and reasonable investment backed expectations. Even though the government had not directly appropriated the coal, the Court held that "to make it commercially impracticable to mine certain coal has very nearly the same effect for constitutional purposes as appropriating or destroying it." The Court also noted that home owners who only held surface rights had assumed the risk and it was not fair for the law to "giv[e] them greater rights than they bought" at the expense of the holders of the mineral rights.

Since *Pennsylvania Coal*, federal, state and local laws have increasingly regulated land use for the public good. This section examines two examples of this type of regulation: historical preservation laws and environmental protections. In Chapter 8, we studied comprehensive zoning as a means to promote development and avoid nuisance before it happens. The types of regulations discussed in this section extend beyond the typical comprehensive zoning plan. They place restrictions on private property in order to further a particular public policy objective. In so doing, the cost of the policy objective is shouldered by the individual property owner. *Pennsylvania Coal* cautions that these regulations can constitute a taking of property notwithstanding their laudatory goals.

Central to a regulatory takings analysis is the question of fairness — when is it fair to ask individual property owners to bear the cost of a given policy initiative? This analysis can greatly increase the cost of public policy initiatives by requiring the payment of just compensation to property owners affected by the regulations. In many cases, increased public cost would compromise the viability of the policy. For example, a jurisdiction may want to safeguard its historic landmarks for the public good, but at what cost? The typical historic landmark legislation restricts individual landowners, imposing targeted costs on the individual properties covered by the legislation. If the restrictions are considered a taking of property that requires just compensation, then the legislation would impose diffuse costs in the form of higher taxes that would be borne by the larger community.

As you will see from the following cases, when addressing a regulatory takings claim the courts continue to apply the ad hoc balancing test applicable to indirect takings.

Exercise 9-14. *Penn Central Transportation Co., v. New York City*— Historic Preservation

The following case involves the New York City Landmarks Preservation Law and a famous dispute over the development of the iconic Grand Central Terminal, more commonly referred to as Grand Central Station. It was the first time the U.S. Supreme Court ruled on the constitutionality of historic preservation laws. If the Court had ruled in favor of Penn Central and required the payment of just compensation, it would have derailed historical preservation efforts nationwide.

Penn Central proposed to build either a 53- or a 55-story tower over Grand Central Station. The opposition to the plan among community leaders was fierce and attracted the support of Jacqueline Kennedy Onassis, who famously wrote a handwritten note to the Mayor of New York City expressing her disapproval. A plaque in Grand Central Station commemorates her efforts to save the building and quotes from her letter to the Mayor:

> Is it not cruel to let our city die by degrees, stripped of all her proud monuments, until there will be nothing left of all her history and beauty to inspire our children? If they are not inspired by the past of our city, where will they find the strength to fight for her future? Americans care about their past, but for short term gain they ignore it and tear down everything that matters. Maybe ... this is the time to take a stand, to reverse the tide, so that we won't all end up in a uniform world of steel and glass boxes.

Penn Central Transportation Co. v. New York City

438 U.S. 104 (1978)

Mr. Justice Brennan delivered the opinion of the Court. The question presented is whether a city may, as part of a comprehensive program to preserve historic landmarks and historic districts, place restrictions on the development of individual historic landmarks—in addition to those imposed by applicable zoning ordinances—without effecting a "taking" requiring the payment of "just compensation." Specifically, we must decide whether the application of New York City's Landmarks Preservation Law to the parcel of land occupied by Grand Central Terminal has "taken" its owners' property in violation of the Fifth and Fourteenth Amendments.

I

A

Over the past 50 years, all 50 States and over 500 municipalities have enacted laws to encourage or require the preservation of buildings and areas with historic or aesthetic importance. These nationwide legislative efforts have been precipitated by two concerns. The first is recognition that, in recent years, large numbers of historic structures, landmarks, and areas have been destroyed without adequate consideration of either the values represented therein or the possibility of preserving the destroyed properties for use in economically productive ways. The second is a widely shared belief that structures with special historic, cultural, or architectural significance enhance the quality of life for all. Not only do these buildings and their workmanship represent the lessons of the past and embody precious features of our heritage, they serve as examples of quality for today. New York City, responding to similar concerns and acting pursuant to a New York State enabling Act, 5 adopted its Landmarks Preservation Law in 1965. The city acted from the conviction that "the standing of [New York City] as a world-wide tourist center and world capital of business, culture and government" would be threatened if legislation were not enacted to protect historic landmarks and neighborhoods from precipitate decisions to destroy or fundamentally alter their character. The city believed that comprehensive measures to safeguard desirable features of the existing urban fabric would benefit its citizens in a variety of ways: e.g., fostering "civic pride in the beauty and noble accomplishments of the past"; protecting and enhancing "the city's attractions to tourists and visitors"; "[supporting] and [stimulating] business and industry"; "[strengthening] the lineeconomy of the city"; and promoting "the use of historic districts, landmarks, interior landmarks and scenic landmarks for the education, pleasure and welfare of the people of the city." § 205-1.0 (b).

The New York City law is typical of many urban landmark laws in that its primary method of achieving its goals is not by acquisitions of historic properties, but rather by involving public entities in land-use decisions affecting these properties and providing services, standards, controls, and incentives that will encourage preservation by private owners and users. While the law does place special restrictions on landmark properties as a necessary feature to the attainment of its larger objectives, the major theme of the law is to ensure the owners of any such properties both a "reasonable return" on their investments and maximum latitude to use their parcels for purposes not inconsistent with the preservation goals.

The primary responsibility for administering the law is vested in the Landmarks Preservation Commission (Commission), a broad based, 11-member agency assisted by a technical staff. [D]esignation as a landmark results in restrictions upon the property owner's options concerning use of the landmark site. First, the law imposes a duty upon the owner to keep the exterior features of the building "in good repair" to assure that the law's objectives not be defeated by the landmark's falling into a state of irremediable disrepair. Second, the Commission must approve in advance any proposal to alter the exterior architectural features of the landmark or to construct any exterior improvement on the landmark site, thus ensuring that decisions concerning construction on the landmark site are made with due consideration of both the public interest in the maintenance of the structure and the landowner's interest in use of the property.

In the event an owner wishes to alter a landmark site, three separate procedures are available through which administrative approval may be obtained. First, the owner may apply to the Commission for a "certificate of no effect on protected architectural features": that is, for an order approving the improvement or alteration on the ground that it will not change or affect any architectural feature of the landmark and will be in harmony therewith. Denial of the certificate is subject to judicial review.

Second, the owner may apply to the Commission for a certificate of "appropriateness." Such certificates will be granted if the Commission concludes—focusing upon aesthetic, historical, and architectural values—that the proposed construction on the landmark site would not unduly hinder the protection, enhancement, perpetuation, and use of the landmark. Again, denial of the certificate is subject to judicial review. Moreover, the owner who is denied either a certificate of no exterior effect or a certificate of appropriateness may submit an alternative or modified plan for approval. The final procedure—seeking a certificate of appropriateness on the ground of "insufficient return"—provides special mechanisms, which vary depending on whether or not the landmark enjoys a tax exemption, to ensure that designation does not cause economic hardship.

B

But this is not the only remedy available for owners of tax-exempt landmarks. As the case at bar illustrates, if an owner files suit and establishes that he is incapable of earning a "reasonable return" on the site in its present state, he can be afforded judicial relief. Similarly, where a landmark owner who enjoys a tax exemption has demonstrated that the landmark structure, as restricted, is totally inadequate for the owner's "legitimate needs," the law has been held invalid as applied to that parcel.

This case involves the application of New York City's Landmarks Preservation Law to Grand Central Terminal (Terminal). The Terminal, which is owned by the Penn Central Transportation Co. and its affiliates (Penn Central), is one of New York City's most famous buildings. Opened in 1913, it is regarded not only as providing an ingenious engineering solution to the problems presented by urban railroad stations, but also as a magnificent example of the French beaux-arts style.

The Terminal is located in midtown Manhattan. Its south facade faces 42d Street and that street's intersection with Park Avenue. At street level, the Terminal is bounded on the west by Vanderbilt Avenue, on the east by the Commodore Hotel, and on the north by the Pan-American Building. Although a 20-story office tower, to have been located above the Terminal, was part of the original design, the planned tower was never constructed. The Terminal itself is an eight-story structure which Penn Central uses as a railroad station and in which it rents space not needed for railroad purposes to a variety of commercial interests. The Terminal is one of a number of properties owned by appellant Penn Central in this area of midtown Manhattan. The others include the Barclay, Biltmore, Commodore, Roosevelt, and Waldorf-Astoria Hotels, the Pan-American Building and other office buildings along Park Avenue, and the Yale Club. At least eight of these are eligible to be recipients of development rights afforded the Terminal by virtue of landmark designation.

On August 2, 1967, following a public hearing, the Commission designated the Terminal a "landmark" and designated the "city tax block" it occupies a "landmark site." Although appellant Penn Central had opposed the designation before the Commission, it did not seek judicial review of the final designation decision.

On January 22, 1968, appellant Penn Central, to increase its income, entered into a renewable 50-year lease and sublease agreement with appellant UGP Properties, Inc. (UGP), a wholly owned subsidiary of Union General Properties, Ltd., a United Kingdom corporation. Under the terms of the agreement, UGP was to construct a multistory office building above the Terminal. UGP promised to pay Penn Central $1 million annually during construction and at least $3 million annually thereafter. The rentals would be offset in part by a loss of some $700,000 to $1 million in net rentals presently received from concessionaires displaced by the new building.

Appellants UGP and Penn Central then applied to the Commission for permission to construct an office building atop the Terminal. Two separate plans, both designed by architect Marcel Breuer and both apparently satisfying the terms of the applicable zoning ordinance, were submitted to the Commission for approval. The first, Breuer I, provided for the construction of a 55-story office building, to be cantilevered above the existing facade and to rest on the roof of the Terminal. The second, Breuer II Revised, 17 called for tearing down a portion of the Terminal that included the 42d Street facade, stripping off some of the remaining features of the Terminal's facade, and constructing a 53-story office building. After four days of hearings at which over 80 witnesses testified, the Commission denied this application as to both proposals.

[A]ppellants filed suit in New York Supreme Court, Trial Term, claiming, inter alia, that the application of the Landmarks Preservation Law had "taken" their property without just compensation in violation of the Fifth and Fourteenth Amendments. Appellants sought a declaratory judgment, injunctive relief barring the city from using the Landmarks Law to impede the construction of any structure that might otherwise lawfully be constructed on the Terminal site, and damages for the "temporary taking" that occurred between August 2, 1967, the designation date, and the date when the restrictions arising from the Landmarks Law would be lifted.

II

The issue[ ] presented by appellants [is] whether the restrictions imposed by New York City's law upon appellants' exploitation of the Terminal site effect a "taking" of appellants' property for a public use within the meaning of the Fifth Amendment, which of course is made applicable to the States through the Fourteenth Amendment.

A

Before considering appellants' specific contentions, it will be useful to review the factors that have shaped the jurisprudence of the Fifth Amendment injunction "nor shall private property be taken for public use, without just compensation." The question of what constitutes a "taking" for purposes of the Fifth Amendment has proved to be a problem of considerable difficulty. While this Court has recognized that the "Fifth Amendment's guarantee ... [is] designed to bar Government from forcing some people alone to bear public burdens which, in all fairness and justice, should be borne by the public as a whole," this Court, quite simply, has been unable to develop any "set formula" for determining when "justice and fairness" require that economic injuries caused by public action be compensated by the government, rather than remain disproportionately concentrated on a few persons. Indeed, we have frequently observed that whether a particular restriction will be rendered invalid by the government's failure to pay for any losses proximately caused by it depends largely "upon the particular circumstances [in that] case." *United States v. Central Eureka Mining Co.*, 357 U.S. 155 (1958).

In engaging in these essentially ad hoc, factual inquiries, the Court's decisions have identified several factors that have particular significance. The economic impact of the regulation on the claimant and, particularly, the extent to which the regulation has interfered with distinct investment-backed expectations are, of course, relevant considerations. So, too, is the character of the governmental action. A "taking" may more readily be found when the interference with property can be characterized as a physical invasion by government, than when interference arises from some public program adjusting the benefits and burdens of economic life to promote the common good.

[I]n instances in which a state tribunal reasonably concluded that "the health, safety, morals, or general welfare" would be promoted by prohibiting particular contemplated uses of land, this Court has upheld land-use regulations that destroyed or adversely affected recognized real property interests. Zoning laws are, of course, the classic example, which have been viewed as permissible governmental action even when prohibiting the most beneficial use of the property.

B

In contending that the New York City law has "taken" their property in violation of the Fifth and Fourteenth Amendments, appellants make a series of arguments, which, while tailored to the facts of this case, essentially urge that any substantial restriction imposed pursuant to a landmark law must be accompanied by just compensation if it is to be constitutional. Before considering these, we emphasize what is not in dispute. Because this Court has recognized, in a number of settings, that States and cities may enact land-use restrictions or controls to enhance the quality of life by preserving the character and desirable aesthetic features of a city, appellants do not contest that New York City's objective of preserving structures and areas with special historic, architectural, or cultural significance is an entirely permissible governmental goal. They also do not dispute that the restrictions imposed on its parcel are appropriate means of securing the purposes of the New York City law.

They first observe that the airspace above the Terminal is a valuable property interest. They urge that the Landmarks Law has deprived them of any gainful use of their "air rights" above the Terminal and that, irrespective of the value of the remainder of their parcel, the city has "taken" their right to this superjacent airspace, thus entitling them to "just compensation" measured by the fair market value of these air rights.

Apart from our own disagreement with appellants' characterization of the effect of the New York City law, the submission that appellants may establish a "taking" simply by showing that they have been denied the ability to exploit a property interest that they heretofore had believed was available for development is quite simply untenable. Were this the rule, this Court would have erred not only in upholding laws restricting the development of air rights, but also in approving those prohibiting both the subjacent, and the lateral development of particular parcels. "Taking" jurisprudence does not divide a single parcel into discrete segments and attempt to determine whether rights in a particular segment have been entirely abrogated. In deciding whether a particular governmental action has effected a taking, this Court focuses rather both on the character of the action and on the nature and extent of the interference with rights in the parcel as a whole—here, the city tax block designated as the "landmark site."

Secondly, appellants, focusing on the character and impact of the New York City law, argue that it effects a "taking" because its operation has significantly diminished the value of the Terminal site. Stated baldly, appellants' position appears to be that the only means of ensuring that selected owners are not singled out to endure financial hardship for no reason is to hold that any restriction imposed on individual landmarks pursuant to the New York City scheme is a "taking" requiring the payment of "just compensation." Agreement with this argument would, of course, invalidate not just New York City's law, but all comparable landmark legislation in the Nation. We find no merit in it.

It is true, as appellants emphasize, that both historic-district legislation and zoning laws regulate all properties within given physical communities whereas landmark laws apply only to selected parcels. But, contrary to appellants' suggestions, landmark laws are not like discriminatory, or "reverse spot," zoning: that is, a land-use decision which arbitrarily singles out a particular parcel for different, less favorable treatment than the neighboring ones. In contrast to discriminatory zoning, which is the antithesis of land-use control as part of some comprehensive plan, the New York City law embodies a comprehensive plan to preserve structures of historic or aesthetic interest wherever they might be found in the city, and as noted, over 400 landmarks and 31 historic districts have been designated pursuant to this plan.

C

On this record, we conclude that the application of New York City's Landmarks Law has not effected a "taking" of appellants' property. The restrictions imposed are substantially related to the promotion of the general welfare and not only permit reasonable beneficial use of the landmark site but also afford appellants opportunities further to enhance not only the Terminal site proper but also other properties.

Affirmed.

Exercise 9-15. *Penn Central* — Revisited

1. Penn Central had argued that historic preservation laws were the equivalent of spot zoning, a topic we discussed in Chapter 8. Recall that spot zoning may be unconstitutional because it arbitrarily singles out certain property for different treatment. Spot zoning contradicts the purpose of a comprehensive zoning plan and does not satisfy rational review because of its arbitrary nature. The Court in *Penn Central* responded that the distinctions made by historical preservation laws are not arbitrary, thereby affirming that historic preservation schemes are rationally related to a legitimate government purpose.
2. The Landmarks Preservation Commission did not mince words about its negative assessment of the proposed project:

   > [We have] no fixed rule against making additions to designated buildings—it all depends on how they are done.... But to balance a 55-story office tower above a flamboyant Beaux-Arts facade seems nothing more than an aesthetic joke. Quite simply, the tower would overwhelm the Terminal by its sheer mass. The "addition" would be four times as high as the existing structure and would reduce the Landmark itself to the status of a curiosity.
   >
   > Landmarks cannot be divorced from their settings—particularly when the setting is a dramatic and integral part of the original concept. The Terminal, in its setting, is a great example of urban design. Such examples are not so plentiful in New York City that we can afford to lose any of the few we have. And we must preserve them in a meaningful way—with alterations and additions of such character, scale, materials and mass as will protect, enhance and perpetuate the original design rather than overwhelm it.

3. In response to Penn Central's takings argument, the Court applied the classic ad hoc balancing test. It considered the economic impact of the regulation

on Penn Central, the extent to which the regulation has interfered with investment-backed expectations, and the character of the governmental action. The Court dismissed Penn Central's claim that it had reasonable investment-backed expectations that it would be able to build above the terminal. The Court ruled that "the submission that appellants may establish a 'taking' simply by showing that they have been denied the ability to exploit a property interest that they heretofore had believed was available for development is quite simply untenable." The Court further noted that "'[t]aking' jurisprudence does not divide a single parcel into discrete segments and attempt to determine whether rights in a particular segment have been entirely abrogated." Remember this as you read the next case and the following notes cases.

4. Penn Central was already in bankruptcy at the time of the decision. It filed for bankruptcy protection in 1970, two years after announcing the plans for the office tower. At the time, it was the largest corporate bankruptcy in the United States. Title to Grand Central Station passed to its corporate successor.

Exercise 9-16. *Lucas v. South Coastal Council*—Environmental Protection and All Economically Viable Use

In *Lucas v. South Carolina Coastal Council*, the U.S. Supreme Court set forth a categorical rule where a regulation deprived a property owner of all viable use of his land. The case was hailed as a major victory for individual property rights. It ruled that state environmental protection legislation designed to alleviate the pressing problem of beach erosion by limiting development in certain vulnerable areas constituted a taking of property without just compensation.

The decision was controversial and was thought to imperil future environmental protection laws. The following excerpts include portions of the concurring and dissenting opinions. As you read the case, keep track of the different views and objections. Which opinion do you find persuasive?

Lucas v. South Coastal Council

505 U.S. 1003 (1992)

Justice Scalia delivered the opinion of the Court. In 1986, petitioner David H. Lucas paid $ 975,000 for two residential lots on the Isle of Palms in Charleston County, South Carolina, on which he intended to build single-family homes. In 1988, however, the South Carolina Legislature enacted the Beachfront Management Act, S.C. Code Ann. § 48-39-250 *et seq.* (Supp. 1990), which had the direct effect of barring petitioner from erecting any permanent habitable structures on his two parcels. A state trial court found that this prohibition rendered Lucas's parcels "valueless." This case requires us to decide whether the Act's dramatic effect on the economic value of Lucas's lots accomplished a taking of private property under the Fifth and Fourteenth Amendments requiring the payment of "just compensation."

I

A

South Carolina's expressed interest in intensively managing development activities in the so-called "coastal zone" dates from 1977 when, in the aftermath of Congress's passage of the federal Coastal Zone Management Act of 1972, 86 Stat. 1280, as amended, 16 U.S.C. § 1451 *et seq.*, the legislature enacted a Coastal Zone Management Act of its own. In its original form, the South Carolina Act required owners of coastal zone land that qualified as a "critical area" (defined in the legislation to include beaches and immediately adjacent sand dunes) to obtain a permit from the newly created South Carolina Coastal Council (Council) (respondent here) prior to committing the land to a "use other than the use the critical area was devoted to on [September 28, 1977]."

In the late 1970's, Lucas and others began extensive residential development of the Isle of Palms, a barrier island situated eastward of the city of Charleston. Toward the close of the development cycle for one residential subdivision known as "Beachwood East," Lucas in 1986 purchased the two lots at issue in this litigation for his own account. No portion of the lots, which were located approximately 300 feet from the beach, qualified as a "critical area" under the 1977 Act; accordingly, at the time Lucas acquired these parcels, he was not legally obliged to obtain a permit from the Council in advance of any development activity. His intention with respect to the lots was to do what the owners of the immediately adjacent parcels had already done: erect single-family residences. He commissioned architectural drawings for this purpose.

The Beachfront Management Act brought Lucas's plans to an abrupt end. Under that 1988 legislation, the Council was directed to establish a "baseline" connecting the landwardmost "points of erosion ... during the past forty years" in the region of the Isle of Palms that includes Lucas's lots. In action not challenged here, the Council fixed this baseline landward of Lucas's parcels. That was significant, for under the Act construction of occupyable improvements was flatly prohibited seaward of a line drawn 20 feet landward of, and parallel to, the baseline. The Act provided no exceptions.

B

Lucas promptly filed suit in the South Carolina Court of Common Pleas, contending that the Beachfront Management Act's construction bar effected a taking of his property without just compensation. Lucas did not take issue with the validity of the Act as a lawful exercise of South Carolina's police power, but contended that the Act's complete extinguishment of his property's value entitled him to compensation regardless of whether the legislature had acted in furtherance of legitimate police power objectives. Following a bench trial, the court agreed. Among its factual determinations was the finding that "at the time Lucas purchased the two lots, both were zoned for single-family residential construction and ... there were no restrictions imposed upon such use of the property by either the State of South Carolina, the County of Charleston, or the Town of the Isle of Palms." The trial court further found that the Beachfront Management Act decreed a permanent ban on construction insofar as Lucas's lots were concerned, and that this prohibition "deprived Lucas of any reasonable economic use of the lots, ... eliminated the unrestricted right of use, and rendered them valueless." The court thus concluded that Lucas's properties had been "taken" by operation of the Act, and it ordered respondent to pay "just compensation" in the amount of $1,232,387.50.

The Supreme Court of South Carolina reversed. We granted certiorari.

II.

A.

Prior to Justice Holmes's exposition in *Pennsylvania Coal Co. v. Mahon*, 260 U.S. 393, 67 L. Ed. 322, 43 S. Ct. 158 (1922), it was generally thought that the Takings Clause reached only a "direct appropriation" of property or the functional equivalent of a "practical ouster of [the owner's] possession." Justice Holmes recognized in *Mahon*, however, that if the protection against physical appropriations of private property was to be meaningfully enforced, the government's power to redefine the range of interests included in the ownership of property was necessarily constrained by constitutional limits. If, instead, the uses of private property were subject to unbridled, uncompensated qualification under the police power, "the natural tendency of human nature [would be] to extend the qualification more and more until at last private property disappeared." These considerations gave birth in that case to the oft-cited maxim that, "while property may be regulated to a certain extent, if regulation goes too far it will be recognized as a taking."

Nevertheless, our decision in *Mahon* offered little insight into when, and under what circumstances, a given regulation would be seen as going "too far" for purposes of the Fifth Amendment. In 70-odd years of succeeding "regulatory takings" jurisprudence, we have generally eschewed any "set formula" for determining how far is too far, preferring to "engage in ... essentially ad hoc, factual inquiries." *Penn Central Transportation Co. v. New York City*, 438 U.S. 104 (1978). We have, however, described at least two discrete categories of regulatory action as compensable without case-specific inquiry into the public interest advanced in support of the restraint. The first encompasses regulations that compel the property owner to suffer a physical "invasion" of his property. In general (at least with regard to permanent invasions), no matter how minute the intrusion, and no matter how weighty the public purpose behind it, we have required compensation. For example, in *Loretto v. Teleprompter Manhattan CATV Corp.*, 458 U.S. 419 (1982), we determined that New York's law requiring landlords to allow television cable companies to emplace cable facilities in their apartment buildings constituted a taking, even though the facilities occupied at most only 1 1/2 cubic feet of the landlords' property.

The second situation in which we have found categorical treatment appropriate is where regulation denies all economically beneficial or productive use of land. As we have said on numerous occasions, the Fifth Amendment is violated when land-use regulation does not substantially advance legitimate state interests *or denies an owner economically viable use of his land.*

We have never set forth the justification for this rule. Perhaps it is simply, as Justice Brennan suggested, that total deprivation of beneficial use is, from the landowner's point of view, the equivalent of a physical appropriation. Surely, at least, in the extraordinary circumstance when *no* productive or economically beneficial use of land is permitted, it is less realistic to indulge our usual assumption that the legislature is simply "adjusting the benefits and burdens of economic life," *Penn Central Transportation Co.*, 438 U.S. at 124, in a manner that secures an "average reciprocity of advantage" to everyone concerned, *Pennsylvania Coal Co. v. Mahon*, 260 U.S. at 415.

On the other side of the balance, affirmatively supporting a compensation requirement, is the fact that regulations that leave the owner of land without economically beneficial or productive options for its use—typically, as here, by requiring land to be left substantially in its natural state—carry with them a heightened risk that private property is being pressed into some form of public service under the guise of mitigating serious public harm.

We think, in short, that there are good reasons for our frequently expressed belief that when the owner of real property has been called upon to sacrifice *all* economically beneficial uses in the name of the common good, that is, to leave his property economically idle, he has suffered a taking.

It is correct that many of our prior opinions have suggested that "harmful or noxious uses" of property may be proscribed by government regulation without the requirement of compensation. For a number of reasons, however, we think the South Carolina Supreme Court was too quick to conclude that that principle decides the present case. The "harmful or noxious uses" principle was the Court's early attempt to describe in theoretical terms why government may, consistent with the Takings Clause, affect property values by regulation without incurring an obligation to compensate—a reality we nowadays acknowledge explicitly with respect to the full scope of the State's police power.

The transition from our early focus on control of "noxious" uses to our contemporary understanding of the broad realm within which government may regulate without compensation was an easy one, since the distinction between "harm-preventing" and "benefit-conferring" regulation is often in the eye of the beholder. It is quite possible, for example, to describe in *either* fashion the ecological, economic, and esthetic concerns that inspired the South Carolina Legislature in the present case. One could say that imposing a servitude on Lucas's land is necessary in order to prevent his use of it from "harming" South Carolina's ecological resources; or, instead, in order to achieve the "benefits" of an ecological preserve. Whether one or the other of the competing characterizations will come to one's lips in a particular case depends primarily upon one's evaluation of the worth of competing uses of real estate. A given restraint will be seen as mitigating "harm" to the adjacent parcels or securing a "benefit" for them, depending upon the observer's evaluation of the relative importance of the use that the restraint favors. Whether Lucas's construction of single-family residences on his parcels should be described as bringing "harm" to South Carolina's adjacent ecological resources thus depends principally upon whether the describer believes that the State's use interest in nurturing those resources is so important that *any* competing adjacent use must yield.

When it is understood that "prevention of harmful use" was merely our early formulation of the police power justification necessary to sustain (without compensation) *any* regulatory diminution in value; and that the distinction between regulation that "prevents harmful use" and that which "confers benefits" is difficult, if not impossible, to discern on an objective, value-free basis; it becomes self-evident that noxious-use logic cannot serve as a touchstone to distinguish regulatory "takings"—which require compensation—from regulatory deprivations that do not require compensation. *A fortiori* the legislature's recitation of a noxious-use justification cannot be the basis for departing from our categorical rule that total regulatory takings must be compensated. If it were, departure would virtually always be allowed. The South Carolina Supreme Court's approach would essentially nullify *Mahon's* affirmation of limits to the noncompensable exercise of the police power. Our cases provide no support for this: None of them that employed the logic of "harmful use" prevention to sustain a regulation involved an allegation that the regulation wholly eliminated the value of the claimant's land.

When the State seeks to sustain regulation that deprives land of all economically beneficial use, we think it may resist compensation only if the logically antecedent inquiry into the nature of the owner's estate shows that the proscribed use interests were not part of his title to begin with. This accords, we think, with our "takings" jurisprudence, which has traditionally been guided by the understandings of our citizens regarding the content of, and the State's power over, the "bundle of rights" that they acquire when they obtain title to property. It seems to us that the property owner necessarily expects the uses of his property to be restricted, from time to time, by various measures newly enacted by the State in legitimate exercise of its police powers; "as long recognized, some values are enjoyed under an implied limitation and must yield to the police power." *Pennsylvania Coal Co. v. Mahon*, 260 U.S. at 413. In the case of land, however, we think the notion pressed by the Council that title is somehow held subject to the "implied limitation" that the State may subsequently eliminate all economically valuable use is inconsistent with the historical compact recorded in the Takings Clause that has become part of our constitutional culture.

Where "permanent physical occupation" of land is concerned, we have refused to allow the government to decree it anew (without compensation), no matter how weighty the asserted "public interests" involved, *Loretto v. Teleprompter Manhattan*

CATV Corp.—though we assuredly *would* permit the government to assert a permanent easement that was a pre-existing limitation upon the landowner's title. We believe similar treatment must be accorded confiscatory regulations, *i.e.*, regulations that prohibit all economically beneficial use of land: Any limitation so severe cannot be newly legislated or decreed (without compensation), but must inhere in the title itself, in the restrictions that background principles of the State's law of property and nuisance already place upon land ownership. A law or decree with such an effect must, in other words, do no more than duplicate the result that could have been achieved in the courts—by adjacent landowners (or other uniquely affected persons) under the State's law of private nuisance, or by the State under its complementary power to abate nuisances that affect the public generally, or otherwise.

On this analysis, the owner of a lakebed, for example, would not be entitled to compensation when he is denied the requisite permit to engage in a landfilling operation that would have the effect of flooding others' land. Nor the corporate owner of a nuclear generating plant, when it is directed to remove all improvements from its land upon discovery that the plant sits astride an earthquake fault. Such regulatory action may well have the effect of eliminating the land's only economically productive use, but it does not proscribe a productive use that was previously permissible under relevant property and nuisance principles. The use of these properties for what are now expressly prohibited purposes was *always* unlawful, and (subject to other constitutional limitations) it was open to the State at any point to make the implication of those background principles of nuisance and property law explicit.

It seems unlikely that common-law principles would have prevented the erection of any habitable or productive improvements on petitioner's land; they rarely support prohibition of the "essential use" of land. The question, however, is one of state law to be dealt with on remand. We emphasize that to win its case South Carolina must do more than proffer the legislature's declaration that the uses Lucas desires are inconsistent with the public interest, or the conclusory assertion that they violate a common-law maxim such as *sic utere tuo ut alienum non laedas.* As we have said, a "State, by *ipse dixit*, may not transform private property into public property without compensation...." *Webb's Fabulous Pharmacies, Inc. v. Beckwith*, 449 U.S. 155 (1980). Instead, as it would be required to do if it sought to restrain Lucas in a common-law action for public nuisance, South Carolina must identify background principles of nuisance and property law that prohibit the uses he now intends in the circumstances in which the property is presently found. Only on this showing can the State fairly claim that, in proscribing all such beneficial uses, the Beachfront Management Act is taking nothing.

The judgment is reversed, and the case is remanded for proceedings not inconsistent with this opinion.

So ordered.

Justice Kennedy, concurring in the judgment. The finding of no value must be considered under the Takings Clause by reference to the owner's reasonable, investment-backed expectations. The Takings Clause, while conferring substantial protection on property owners, does not eliminate the police power of the State to enact limitations on the use of their property. The rights conferred by the Takings Clause and the police power of the State may coexist without conflict. Property is bought and sold, investments are made, subject to the State's power to regulate. Where a taking is alleged from regulations which deprive the property of all value, the test must be whether the deprivation is contrary to reasonable, investment-backed expectations.

In my view, reasonable expectations must be understood in light of the whole of our legal tradition. The common law of nuisance is too narrow a confine for the exercise of regulatory power in a complex and interdependent society. The State should not be prevented from enacting new regulatory initiatives in response to changing conditions, and courts must consider all reasonable expectations whatever their source. The Takings Clause does not require a static body of state property law; it protects private expectations to ensure private investment. I agree with the Court that nuisance prevention accords with the most common expectations of property owners who face regulation, but I do not believe this can be the sole source of state authority to impose severe restrictions. Coastal property may present such unique concerns for a fragile land system that the State can go further in regulating its development and use than the common law of nuisance might otherwise permit.

JUSTICE BLACKMUN, dissenting. Today the Court launches a missile to kill a mouse.

The State of South Carolina prohibited petitioner Lucas from building a permanent structure on his property from 1988 to 1990. Relying on an unreviewed (and implausible) state trial court finding that this restriction left Lucas' property valueless, this Court granted review to determine whether compensation must be paid in cases where the State prohibits all economic use of real estate. According to the Court, such an occasion never has arisen in any of our prior cases, and the Court imagines that it will arise "relatively rarely" or only in "extraordinary circumstances." Almost certainly it did not happen in this case.

IV

A

This Court repeatedly has recognized the ability of government, in certain circumstances, to regulate property without compensation no matter how adverse the financial effect on the owner may be. More than a century ago, the Court explicitly upheld the right of States to prohibit uses of property injurious to public health, safety, or welfare without paying compensation: "A prohibition simply upon the use of property for purposes that are declared, by valid legislation, to be injurious to the health, morals, or safety of the community, cannot, in any just sense, be deemed a taking or an appropriation of property." *Mugler v. Kansas*, 123 U.S. at 668-669. On this basis, the Court upheld an ordinance effectively prohibiting operation of a previously lawful brewery, although the "establishments will become of no value as property." *Mugler* was only the beginning in a long line of cases. In *Powell v. Pennsylvania*, 127 U.S. 678 (1888), the Court upheld legislation prohibiting the manufacture of oleomargarine, despite the owner's allegation that "if prevented from continuing it, the value of his property employed therein would be entirely lost and he be deprived of the means of livelihood." In *Hadacheck v. Sebastian,* 239 U.S. 394 (1915), the Court upheld an ordinance prohibiting a brickyard, although the owner had made excavations on the land that prevented it from being utilized for any purpose but a brickyard. In *Miller v. Schoene,* 276 U.S. 272 (1928), the Court held that the Fifth Amendment did not require Virginia to pay compensation to the owner of cedar trees ordered destroyed to prevent a disease from spreading to nearby apple orchards. The "preferment of [the public interest] over the property interest of the individual, to the extent even of its destruction, is one of the distinguishing characteristics of every exercise of the police power which affects property."

The Court recognizes that "our prior opinions have suggested that 'harmful or noxious uses' of property may be proscribed by government regulation without the requirement of compensation," but seeks to reconcile them with its categorical rule by claiming that the Court never has upheld a regulation when the owner alleged the loss of all economic value. Even if the Court's factual premise were correct, its understanding of the Court's cases is distorted. In none of the cases did the Court suggest that the right of a State to prohibit certain activities without paying compensation turned on the availability of some residual valuable use. Instead, the cases depended on whether the government interest was sufficient to prohibit the activity, given the significant private cost.

These cases rest on the principle that the State has full power to prohibit an owner's use of property if it is harmful to the public. It would make no sense under this theory to suggest that an owner has a constitutionally protected right to harm others, if only he makes the proper showing of economic loss.

B

Even more perplexing, however, is the Court's reliance on common-law principles of nuisance in its quest for a value free takings jurisprudence. In determining what is a nuisance at common law, state courts make exactly the decision that the Court finds so troubling when made by the South Carolina General Assembly today: They determine whether the use is harmful. Common-law public and private nuisance law is simply a determination whether a particular use causes harm. (*Nuisance* is a French word which means nothing more than harm). There is nothing magical in the reasoning of judges long dead. They determined a harm in the same way as state judges and legislatures do today. If judges in the 18th and 19th centuries can distinguish a harm from a benefit, why not judges in the 20th century, and if judges can, why not legislators? There simply is no reason to believe that new interpretations of the hoary common-law nuisance doctrine will be particularly "objective" or "value free." Once one abandons the level of generality of *sic utere tuo ut alienum non laedas,* one searches in vain, I think, for anything resembling a principle in the common law of nuisance.

JUSTICE STEVENS, dissenting.

II

In its analysis of the merits, the Court starts from the premise that this Court has adopted a "categorical rule that total regulatory takings must be compensated," and then sets itself to the task of identifying the exceptional cases in which a State may be relieved of this categorical obligation. The test the Court announces is that the regulation must "do no more than duplicate the result that could have been achieved" under a State's nuisance law. Under this test the categorical rule will apply unless the regulation merely makes explicit what was otherwise an implicit limitation on the owner's property rights.

In my opinion, the Court is doubly in error. The categorical rule the Court establishes is an unsound and unwise addition to the law and the Court's formulation of the exception to that rule is too rigid and too narrow.

The Categorical Rule

As the Court recognizes, *Pennsylvania Coal Co. v. Mahon*, 260 U.S. 393(1922), provides no support for its—or, indeed, any—categorical rule. To the contrary, Justice Holmes recognized that such absolute rules ill fit the inquiry into "regulatory takings." In addition to lacking support in past decisions, the Court's new rule is wholly arbitrary. A landowner whose property is diminished in value 95% recovers nothing, while an owner whose property is diminished 100% recovers the land's full value. This highlights a fundamental weakness in the Court's analysis: its failure to explain why only the impairment of "*economically* beneficial or productive use" (emphasis added), of property is relevant in takings analysis. I should think that a regulation arbitrarily prohibiting an owner from continuing to use her property for bird watching or sunbathing might constitute a taking under some circumstances; and, conversely, that such uses are of value to the owner. Yet the Court offers no basis for its assumption that the only uses of property cognizable under the Constitution are *developmental* uses.

On the other hand, developers and investors may market specialized estates to take advantage of the Court's new rule. The smaller the estate, the more likely that a regulatory change will effect a total taking. Thus, an investor may, for example, purchase the right to build a multifamily home on a specific lot, with the result that a zoning regulation that allows only single-family homes would render the investor's property interest "valueless." In short, the categorical rule will likely have one of two effects: Either courts will alter the definition of the "denominator" in the takings "fraction," rendering the Court's categorical rule meaningless, or investors will manipulate the relevant property interests, giving the Court's rule sweeping effect. To my mind, neither of these results is desirable or appropriate, and both are distortions of our takings jurisprudence.

The Nuisance Exception

Like many bright-line rules, the categorical rule established in this case is only "categorical" for a page or two in the U.S. Reports. No sooner does the Court state that "total regulatory takings must be compensated," than it quickly establishes an exception to that rule.

The exception provides that a regulation that renders property valueless is not a taking if it prohibits uses of property that were not "previously permissible under relevant property and nuisance principles." The Court's holding today effectively freezes the State's common law, denying the legislature much of its traditional power to revise the law governing the rights and uses of property.

Arresting the development of the common law is not only a departure from our prior decisions; it is also profoundly unwise. The human condition is one of constant learning and evolution—both moral and practical. Legislatures implement that new learning; in doing so they must often revise the definition of property and the rights of property owners. Thus, when the Nation came to understand that slavery was morally wrong and mandated the emancipation of all slaves, it, in effect, redefined "property." On a lesser scale, our ongoing self-education produces similar changes in the rights of property owners: New appreciation of the significance of endangered species, the vulnerability of coastal lands, shapes our evolving understandings of property rights.

Viewed more broadly, the Court's new rule and exception conflict with the very character of our takings jurisprudence. We have frequently and consistently recognized that the definition of a taking cannot be reduced to a "set formula" and that determining whether a regulation is a taking is "essentially [an] ad hoc, factual inquiry." *Penn Central Transportation Co. v. New York City*, 438 U.S. 104 (1978). This is unavoidable, for the determination whether a law effects a taking is ultimately a matter of "fairness and justice," *Armstrong v. United States*, 364 U.S. 40 (1960), and necessarily requires a weighing of private and public interests. The rigid rules fixed by the Court today clash with this enterprise: "fairness and justice" are often disserved by categorical rules.

Exercise 9-17. *Lucas* Revisited

1. The majority decision hinged on the determination by the trial court that the property in question had been rendered "valueless." Several of the Justices took issue with this determination and were skeptical that Lucas had been deprived of all economic value. For example, Justice Blackmun argued that Lucas still enjoyed the "attributes of ownership," including the right to exclude. He also offered that Lucas could "picnic, swim, camp in a tent, or live on the property in a movable trailer." These suggestions were no doubt cold comfort to Lucas who had paid almost a million dollars for the lots, but Justice Blackmun noted that "[s]tate courts frequently have recognized that land has economic value where the only residual economic uses are recreation or camping." He also noted that Lucas could sell the property "which would have value for neighbors and for those prepared to enjoy proximity to the ocean without a house." Do you find Justice Blackmun's arguments persuasive?

2. Justice Scalia articulates a new categorical rule in the context of regulatory takings—a regulation that deprives an owner of all economically viable use of his land constitutes a taking of property without just compensation, unless the proscribed use would have been prohibited under the law of nuisance or not otherwise part of the title to the property. A number of Justices criticized the reliance on background common law principals. In his dissent, Justice Stevens warned that the majority opinion "effectively freezes the State's common law." Do you agree that incorporating common law nuisance principles will result in a static takings jurisprudence?
3. Justice Blackmun reminds us that "[t]here is nothing magical in the reasoning of judges long dead." Consider the other cases we have studied where this sentiment is expressed. Are you convinced?
4. Lucas later settled with the South Carolina Coastal Council, which agreed to pay him $1,575,000 for title to the lots, his carrying costs, and legal fees. In a startling about-face, the Council later approved the two lots for development. The Council sold the two lots with building permits for $750,000. Two large homes now stand on the lots.

Exercise 9-18. Note: Cases Post-*Lucas*

1. *Palazzo v. Rhode Island*, 533 U.S. 606 (2001). In *Palazzo*, the owner of a parcel of land constituting both wetlands and upland claimed that he suffered a per se taking because he was deprived of all economically viable use of the wetlands. The Court rejected this claim and remanded the case to state court to evaluate the claim under the *Penn Central* ad hoc analysis. The argument that a portion of the property was deprived of all economically viable use echoed the concern Justice Stevens raised in his dissent that "developers and investors may market specialized estates to take advantage of the Court's new rule." He reasoned that "[t]he smaller the estate, the more likely that a regulatory change will effect a total taking." In *Palazzo*, however, the developer had not subdivided the property. Would the result have been different if the developer had divided the property into two separately deeded properties: the upland parcel and the wetlands parcel?
2. *Tahoe-Sierra Preservation Council, Inc. v. Tahoe Regional Planning Agency (TRPA)*, 535 U.S. 302 (2002). The Tahoe Regional Planning Agency declared a moratorium on all new home construction while it considered changes to its comprehensive plan. Property owners argued that the moratorium constituted a temporary categorical taking because their property was deprived of all economically viable use. Whereas *Palazzo* involved slicing up an estate

into smaller pieces, *Tahoe* took a temporal approach to *Lucas*. The District Court had held that the moratorium constituted a categorical taking under *Lucas*, noting the moratorium did not have a termination date. Justice Stevens wrote the majority opinion. He rejected the application of *Lucas* to a temporary taking. He also noted that if all land use regulations triggered the requirement of just compensation, they would be "a luxury few governments could afford."

3. *Stop the Beach Renourishment, Inc. v. Florida Dep't of Environmental Protection*, 130 S. Ct. 2592 (2010). Two Florida counties proposed to create a public beach through the process of beach renourishment. The project would add 75 feet of dry sand to a 6.9 mile strip of eroded beachfront. The private owners of beachfront property objected to the plan, claiming that it constituted a taking of property without just compensation. The U.S. Supreme Court concluded that there was no taking, because under Florida law, the state owns the seabed in public trust and the newly created beach also belongs to the state under the doctrine of avulsion. Recall that we discussed the public trust doctrine in the context of beach access in Chapter 3.

Exactions

An exaction is a fee or dedication that a land use planning authority "exacts" from a developer in the course of the approval process. The states' purpose for an exaction is to offset the costs of development, including the impact the development will have on the surrounding community or environment. For example, a developer may dedicate streets or parks within a subdivision. In addition to the dedication of land, exactions can be in the form of fees. As we saw in *Rando v. Town of North Attleboro* in Chapter 8, developers will sometimes make monetary payments to localities to mitigate the increased costs associated with a development, such as increased traffic.

In two important cases, *Nollan v. California Coastal Comm'n*, 483 U.S. 825 (1987), and *Dolan v. City of Tigard*, 512 U.S. 374 (1994), the U.S. Supreme Court established the "nexus and proportionality" test for exactions. A land use authority is not permitted to condition the approval of a land use permit on the payment of a fee or dedication of land unless there is a "nexus" and "rough proportionality" between the government's demand and the effects of the proposed land use. These requirements are designed to strike a balance between two competing concerns that arise in the context of the permitting process. First, it is clear that development often imposes costs on the surrounding community and environment. Second, the nature of the permitting process presents the danger that land use authorities may impose extortive fees on developers. The requirement of a nexus and rough proportionality allows a locality to make itself whole while protecting the interests of developers from overreaching authorities.

Exercise 9-19. *Koontz v. St. Johns River Water Management District*

Koontz v. St. Johns River Water Management District involves a claim by a developer that a monetary exaction is excessive. The land use authority contended that the exaction was not subject to the rules set forth in *Nollan* and *Dolan* because the permit was not approved on condition that Koontz pay the exaction. Rather, the permit was denied because Koontz failed to agree to the exaction. Do you believe this is a meaningful distinction? In addition, the St. Johns Water Management District claimed that *Nollan* and *Dolan* did not apply because it was requiring a monetary exaction.

As you read the case, ask why this case is included in the Chapter on Government Takings.

Coy A. Koontz, Jr. v. St. Johns River Water Management District

133 S. Ct. 2586 (2013)

Justice Alito delivered the opinion of the Court. Our decisions in *Nollan v. California Coastal Comm'n*, 483 U.S. 825 (1987), and *Dolan v. City of Tigard*, 512 U.S. 374 (1994), provide important protection against the misuse of the power of land-use regulation. In those cases, we held that a unit of government may not condition the approval of a land-use permit on the owner's relinquishment of a portion of his property unless there is a "nexus" and "rough proportionality" between the government's demand and the effects of the proposed land use. In this case, the St. Johns River Water Management District (District) believes that it circumvented *Nollan* and *Dolan* because of the way in which it structured its handling of a permit application submitted by Coy Koontz, Sr., whose estate is represented in this Court by Coy Koontz, Jr. The District did not approve his application on the condition that he surrender an interest in his land. Instead, the District, after suggesting that he could obtain approval by signing over such an interest, denied his application because he refused to yield. The Florida Supreme Court blessed this maneuver and thus effectively interred those important decisions. Because we conclude that *Nollan* and *Dolan* cannot be evaded in this way, the Florida Supreme Court's decision must be reversed.

I

A

In 1972, petitioner purchased an undeveloped 14.9-acre tract of land on the south side of Florida State Road 50, a divided four-lane highway east of Orlando. The property is located less than 1,000 feet from that road's intersection with Florida State Road 408, a tolled expressway that is one of Orlando's major thoroughfares.

A drainage ditch runs along the property's western edge, and high-voltage power lines bisect it into northern and southern sections. The combined effect of the ditch, a 100-foot wide area kept clear for the power lines, the highways, and other construction on nearby parcels is to isolate the northern section of petitioner's property from any other undeveloped land. Although largely classified as wetlands by the State, the northern section drains well; the most significant standing water forms in ruts in an unpaved road used to access the power lines. The natural topography of the property's southern section is somewhat more diverse, with a small creek, forested uplands, and wetlands that sometimes have water as much as a foot deep. A wildlife survey found evidence of animals that often frequent developed areas: raccoons, rabbits, several species of bird, and a turtle. The record also indicates that the land may be a suitable habitat for opossums.

The same year that petitioner purchased his property, Florida enacted the Water Resources Act, which divided the State into five water management districts and authorized each district to regulate "construction that connects to, draws water from, drains water into, or is placed in or across the waters in the state." Under the Act, a landowner wishing to undertake such construction must obtain from the relevant district a Management and Storage of Surface Water (MSSW) permit, which may impose "such reasonable conditions" on the permit as are "necessary to assure" that construction will "not be harmful to the water resources of the district."

In 1984, in an effort to protect the State's rapidly diminishing wetlands, the Florida Legislature passed the Warren S. Henderson Wetlands Protection Act, which made it illegal for anyone to "dredge or fill in, on, or over surface waters" without a Wetlands Resource Management (WRM) permit. Under the Henderson Act, permit applicants are required to provide "reasonable assurance" that proposed construction on wetlands is "not contrary to the public interest," as defined by an enumerated list of criteria. Consistent with the Henderson Act, the St. Johns River Water Management District, the district with jurisdiction over petitioner's land, requires that permit applicants wishing to build on wetlands offset the resulting environmental damage by creating, enhancing, or preserving wetlands elsewhere.

Petitioner decided to develop the 3.7-acre northern section of his property, and in 1994 he applied to the District for MSSW and WRM permits. Under his proposal, petitioner would have raised the elevation of the northernmost section of his land to make it suitable for a building, graded the land from the southern edge of the building site down to the elevation of the high-voltage electrical lines, and installed a dry-bed pond for retaining and gradually releasing stormwater runoff from the building and its parking lot. To mitigate the environmental effects of his proposal, petitioner offered to foreclose any possible future development of the approximately 11-acre southern section of his land by deeding to the District a conservation easement on that portion of his property.

The District considered the 11-acre conservation easement to be inadequate, and it informed petitioner that it would approve construction only if he agreed to one of two concessions. First, the District proposed that petitioner reduce the size of his development to 1 acre and deed to the District a conservation easement on the remaining 13.9 acres. To reduce the development area, the District suggested that petitioner could eliminate the dry-bed pond from his proposal and instead install a more costly subsurface stormwater management system beneath the building site. The District also suggested that petitioner install retaining walls rather than gradually sloping the land from the building site down to the elevation of the rest of his property to the south.

In the alternative, the District told petitioner that he could proceed with the development as proposed, building on 3.7 acres and deeding a conservation easement to the government on the remainder of the property, if he also agreed to hire contractors to make improvements to District-owned land several miles away. Specifically, petitioner could pay to replace culverts on one parcel or fill in ditches on another. Either of those projects would have enhanced approximately 50 acres of District-owned wetlands. When the District asks permit applicants to fund offsite mitigation work, its policy is never to require any particular offsite project, and it did not do so here. Instead, the District said that it "would also favorably consider" alternatives to its suggested offsite mitigation projects if petitioner proposed something "equivalent."

Believing the District's demands for mitigation to be excessive in light of the environmental effects that his building proposal would have caused, petitioner filed suit in state court.

B

The Florida Circuit Court held a 2-day bench trial. After considering testimony from several experts who examined petitioner's property, the trial court found that the property's northern section had already been "seriously degraded" by extensive construction on the surrounding parcels. In light of this finding and petitioner's offer to dedicate nearly three-quarters of his land to the District, the trial court concluded that any further mitigation in the form of payment for offsite improvements to District property lacked both a nexus and rough proportionality to the environmental impact of the proposed construction. It accordingly held the District's actions unlawful under our decisions in *Nollan* and *Dolan*.

The Florida District Court affirmed, but the State Supreme Court reversed. A majority of that court distinguished *Nollan* and *Dolan* on two grounds. First, the majority thought it significant that in this case, unlike *Nollan* or *Dolan*, the District did not approve petitioner's application on the condition that he accede to the District's demands; instead, the District denied his application because he refused to make concessions. Second, the majority drew a distinction between a demand for an interest in real property (what happened in *Nollan* and *Dolan*) and a demand for money. The majority acknowledged a division of authority over whether a demand for money can give rise to a claim under *Nollan* and *Dolan*, and sided with those courts that have said it cannot. Recognizing that the majority opinion rested on a question of federal constitutional law on which the lower courts are divided, we granted the petition for a writ of certiorari, and now reverse.

II

A

We have said in a variety of contexts that the government may not deny a benefit to a person because he exercises a constitutional right. In *Perry v. Sindermann*, 408 U.S. 593 (1972), for example, we held that a public college would violate a professor's freedom of speech if it declined to renew his contract because he was an outspoken critic of the college's administration. And in *Memorial Hospital v. Maricopa County*, 415 U.S. 250 (1974), we concluded that a county impermissibly burdened the right to travel by extending healthcare benefits only to those indigent sick who had been residents of the county for at least one year. Those cases reflect an overarching principle, known as the unconstitutional conditions doctrine, that vindicates the Constitution's enumerated rights by preventing the government from coercing people into giving them up.

Nollan and *Dolan* "involve a special application" of this doctrine that protects the Fifth Amendment right to just compensation for property the government takes when owners apply for land-use permits. Our decisions in those cases reflect two realities of the permitting process. The first is that land-use permit applicants are especially vulnerable to the type of coercion that the unconstitutional conditions doctrine prohibits because the government often has broad discretion to deny a permit that is worth far more than property it would like to take. By conditioning a building permit on the owner's deeding over a public right-of-way, for example, the government can pressure an owner into voluntarily giving up property for which the Fifth Amendment would otherwise require just compensation. So long as the building permit is more valuable than any just compensation the owner could hope to receive for the right-of-way, the owner is likely to accede to the government's demand, no matter how unreasonable. Extortionate demands of this sort frustrate the Fifth Amendment right to just compensation, and the unconstitutional conditions doctrine prohibits them.

A second reality of the permitting process is that many proposed land uses threaten to impose costs on the public that dedications of property can offset. Where a building proposal would substantially increase traffic congestion, for example, officials might condition permit approval on the owner's agreement to deed over the land needed to widen a public road. Respondent argues that a similar rationale justifies the exaction at issue here: petitioner's proposed construction project, it submits, would destroy wetlands on his property, and in order to compensate for this loss, respondent demands that he enhance wetlands elsewhere. Insisting that landowners internalize the negative externalities of their conduct is a hallmark of responsible land-use policy, and we have long sustained such regulations against constitutional attack.

Nollan and *Dolan* accommodate both realities by allowing the government to condition approval of a permit on the dedication of property to the public so long as there is a "nexus" and "rough proportionality" between the property that the government demands and the social costs of the applicant's proposal. Our precedents thus enable permitting authorities to insist that applicants bear the full costs of their proposals while still forbidding the government from engaging in "out-and-out ...

extortion" that would thwart the Fifth Amendment right to just compensation. Under *Nollan* and *Dolan* the government may choose whether and how a permit applicant is required to mitigate the impacts of a proposed development, but it may not leverage its legitimate interest in mitigation to pursue governmental ends that lack an essential nexus and rough proportionality to those impacts.

B

The principles that undergird our decisions in *Nollan* and *Dolan* do not change depending on whether the government *approves* a permit on the condition that the applicant turn over property or *denies* a permit because the applicant refuses to do so. We have often concluded that denials of governmental benefits were impermissible under the unconstitutional conditions doctrine. In so holding, we have recognized that regardless of whether the government ultimately succeeds in pressuring someone into forfeiting a constitutional right, the unconstitutional conditions doctrine forbids burdening the Constitution's enumerated rights by coercively withholding benefits from those who exercise them.

A contrary rule would be especially untenable in this case because it would enable the government to evade the limitations of *Nollan* and *Dolan* simply by phrasing its demands for property as conditions precedent to permit approval. Under the Florida Supreme Court's approach, a government order stating that a permit is "approved if" the owner turns over property would be subject to *Nollan* and *Dolan*, but an identical order that uses the words "denied until" would not. Our unconstitutional conditions cases have long refused to attach significance to the distinction between conditions precedent and conditions subsequent. To do so here would effectively render *Nollan* and *Dolan* a dead letter.

The Florida Supreme Court puzzled over how the government's demand for property can violate the Takings Clause even though "no property of any kind was ever taken." but the unconstitutional conditions doctrine provides a ready answer. Extortionate demands for property in the land-use permitting context run afoul of the Takings Clause not because they take property but because they impermissibly burden the right not to have property taken without just compensation. As in other unconstitutional conditions cases in which someone refuses to cede a constitutional right in the face of coercive pressure, the impermissible denial of a governmental benefit is a constitutionally cognizable injury.

III

We turn to the Florida Supreme Court's alternative holding that petitioner's claim fails because respondent asked him to spend money rather than give up an easement on his land. A predicate for any unconstitutional conditions claim is that the government could not have constitutionally ordered the person asserting the claim to do what it attempted to pressure that person into doing. For that reason, we began our analysis in both *Nollan* and *Dolan* by observing that if the government had directly seized the easements it sought to obtain through the permitting process, it would have committed a *per se* taking. The Florida Supreme Court held that petitioner's claim fails at this first step because the subject of the exaction at issue here was money rather than a more tangible interest in real property.

We note as an initial matter that if we accepted this argument it would be very easy for land-use permitting officials to evade the limitations of *Nollan* and *Dolan*. Because the government need only provide a permit applicant with one alternative that satisfies the nexus and rough proportionality standards, a permitting authority wishing to exact an easement could simply give the owner a choice of either surrendering an easement or making a payment equal to the easement's value. Such so-called "in lieu of" fees are utterly commonplace, and they are functionally equivalent to other types of land use exactions. For that reason and those that follow, we reject respondent's argument and hold that so-called "monetary exactions" must satisfy the nexus and rough proportionality requirements of *Nollan* and *Dolan*.

A

The fulcrum this case turns on is the direct link between the government's demand and a specific parcel of real property. Because of that direct link, this case implicates the central concern of *Nollan* and *Dolan*: the risk that the government may use its substantial power and discretion in land-use permitting to pursue governmental ends that lack an essential nexus and rough proportionality to the effects of the proposed new use of the specific property at issue, thereby diminishing without justification the value of the property.

. . . .

We hold that the government's demand for property from a land-use permit applicant must satisfy the requirements of *Nollan* and *Dolan* even when the government denies the permit and even when its demand is for money. The Florida Supreme Court's judgment is reversed, and this case is remanded for further proceedings not inconsistent with this opinion.

It is so ordered.

Exercise 9-20. *Koontz* Revisited

1. The majority rejected the two-part claim of the St. Johns River Water Management District that exaction did not fall within the ambit of *Nollan* and *Dolan*. It argued that 1) the approval of the permit was not conditioned on the exaction and 2) the exaction was monetary. The majority reasoned that if these arguments were accepted, then land use authorities could easily evade the requirements of nexus and proportionality, leaving private property owners vulnerable to coercive tactics.
2. Justice Kagan authored a strong dissent (not reproduced above) that was joined by Justices Ginsburg, Breyer, and Sotomayor. She wrote that the majority opinion deprives state and local governments of the flexibility

they need to enhance their communities—to ensure environmentally sound and economically productive development. It places courts smack in the middle of the most everyday local government activity. As those consequences play out across the country, I believe the Court will rue today's decision.

Forfeiture Distinguished

Property owners generally have a right to prevent others from taking their property against their will. As discussed in this Chapter, the government can take private property for a public purpose under the power of eminent domain, but it cannot take private property merely to redistribute it to another private individual. The Takings Clause of the Fifth Amendment restricts the government's power of eminent domain to instances where the taking of private property is for a public use and the government pays just compensation.

Forfeiture is another way that the government can take property from a private individual. It does not involve the power of eminent domain and is not subject to the restrictions set forth in the Takings Clause. Private property is subject to forfeiture when it is used to facilitate a crime. The forfeiture of property (both real and personal) is based on a legal fiction that the property itself has been bad. A forfeiture proceeding is an in rem proceeding against the thing itself. For this reason, forfeiture cases bear the caption of the property interest subject to the forfeiture, such as the 2006 8th Circuit Appeals Court case *United States v. $124,700 in Currency*, 458 F.3d 822 (8th Cir. 2006).

On the state level, forfeiture has increasingly been used to address nuisance crimes such as prostitution. The U.S. Supreme Court case of *Bennis v. Michigan*, 516 U.S. 442 (1996), involved a husband who used the family car—a 1977 Pontiac stationwagon that he owned jointly with his wife—to pick up a sex worker and violate the Michigan indecency law. The car was considered forfeit as a public nuisance under Michigan state law. The wife argued that she had not consented to her husband's actions and, therefore, was entitled to one-half of the fair market value of the car. The Court ruled that an innocent owner exception was not required by the Constitution. In *Bennis*, the Court noted that the practice of forfeiture pre-dates the Constitution. Forfeiture was used a way to combat pirates that periodically terrorized the Eastern seaboard. For example, in *The Palmyra*, 25 U.S. 1 (1827), the Court sustained the seizure of a pirate ship that was operating off the cost of Charlestown. The Court reasoned that had the Framers desired to restrain the practice, they could have placed limitations on it just as they had limited the power of eminent domain under the Takings Clause of the Fifth Amendment.

Today, federal forfeiture laws have become a powerful collateral weapon in the "War on Drugs." Forfeiture was also used during Prohibition to address the sometimes flagrant violations of the Volstead Act. The following cases involve property used to facilitate the illegal use or sale of controlled substances. As you read the cases, consider why forfeiture is not a taking of property without just compensation.

Exercise 9-21. *United States v. Leasehold Interest in 121 Nostrand Avenue, Apartment 1-C*

The following case involves the application of a statutory "innocent owner" exception to the federal drug forfeiture provisions. A surge of crack cocaine use occurred in the United States from the mid-1980s to the early 1990s. It was referred to as the "crack epidemic." It devastated large urban areas, especially communities of color. The crack epidemic triggered a harsh punitive response, rather than a therapeutic or public health response. This response included enhanced penalties for crack use and other collateral consequences, such as civil forfeiture.

Civil forfeiture statutes place the burden on individual property owners to police their property or risk forfeiture. This responsibility can place property owners and family members in a difficult position.

United States v. The Leasehold Interest in 121 Nostrand Avenue, Apartment 1-C

760 F. Supp. 1015 (E.D.N.Y. 1991)

I. INTRODUCTION

The Government seeks to enforce an anti-drug forfeiture statute (21 U.S.C. § 881) against occupants of an apartment in a city-run housing project for the poor. By reducing the number of locations from which illegal narcotics are sold, the recently adopted law is expected to help alleviate the nation's drug problem and to increase the well-being and safety of occupants of public housing.

Drugs and drug-related crime are widespread in low-income housing. Dwellers in public housing need relief from the presence of drug sellers and buyers in and near their homes. Evicting drug dealers from their apartments, it is hoped, will make housing projects safer and more decent.

This case reveals some of the limitations of apartment forfeiture as a means of eliminating drugs from public housing complexes. For the poor, the shortage of livable, low-priced housing is especially acute. Tenants—and especially their minor children—who are evicted are likely to become homeless, with whatever stability their lives afforded seriously jeopardized. For reasons stated below, the owner of the defendant leasehold is entitled to retain her home. Her children, grandchildren and great-grandchildren, who look to her for shelter as the family's matriarch, may not be dispossessed because one of them has sold drugs from their apartment. That person may, however, be forced from the apartment since it was illegally used by her as a base for her own illicit drug activities. An injunction against future illegal use will be granted.

II. PROCEDURAL BACKGROUND

On May 10, 1990, the United States filed this civil forfeiture action pursuant to 21 U.S.C. §881(a)(7) against the defendant leasehold, Apartment 1-C, 121 Nostrand Avenue, Brooklyn, New York. The apartment was allegedly used to facilitate the sale or distribution of narcotics.

III. FACTS

Apartment 1-C is a small three bedroom, one bath, one kitchen and one living room unit at the Marcy public housing project in the Williamsburg section of Brooklyn. The leaseholder of record for 32 years has been Mrs. Clara Smith.

A. *Household Members*

Mrs. Clara Smith, age 51, is a great-grandmother. Most of the children, grandchildren and great-grandchildren bear the surname of Smith. She has six children. Two of her daughters, Juanita Smith, age 36, and Sylvia Smith, age 32, live in the apartment with her. Juanita Smith is a reformed heroin addict. She has a prior conviction for possession of narcotics for which she received seven days in jail. Juanita Smith's four children reside with her in the apartment. They are Chenelle Smith, age 19; Jamele Smith, age 15; Nicole Smith, age 14; and Ramel Smith, age 11. Ramel was born drug addicted; as a result, Mrs. Clara Smith has legal custody of him. Chenelle Smith has two daughters who live in the apartment; they are Fatima Smith, age 4, and Jasmine Carr, 22 months. All of Sylvia Smith's children live with her in the apartment. They are Tara Smith, age 12; Anthony Smith, age 11; Marcus Smith, age 9; Kevin Smith, age 8; Kelima Smith, age 8; and Quentay Smith, age 4. Mrs. Clara Smith also has legal custody of another three grandchildren whose mother, Pearl Smith, another of her daughters, does not live in the apartment. They are Shawn Lindsy, age 13; Shonda Lindsy, age 9; and Melissa Smith, age 23 months. All the members of the household apparently depend on public assistance for survival. The family's monthly rent of $153.00 is paid directly by the welfare department. Except for the income from drug sales, there was no evidence of other sources of funds.

The effects of poverty are especially damaging in New York City with its high cost of living and scarcity of low-income housing. The number of single-mother families in poverty grew here from approximately 170,000 to 210,000 in the period from 1979 to 1987, an increase of 23.5%. The poverty rate within these families increased from 55.1% to 62.9% during the same period. The majority of poor children now live with single mothers. In 1987 there were approximately 500,000 poor children living in families in New York City with only their mothers present. These children constituted 74.4% of all poor children in New York City.

We can take judicial notice, based upon other cases in our own court as well as information generally available in the New York community, that the incidence of drug addiction and dealing among the poorer members of society, many of them living in ghetto conditions, is greater than that of the population at large. The cheap, potent and highly addictive drug, crack, has exacerbated this problem in recent years. The incidence of AIDS, largely spread from contaminated needles used by the poor, is another terrifying surrogate statistic of the drug culture in New York City.

All of the Smith family residents of apartment 1-C were well-behaved, properly groomed and neatly-dressed while they were in the courtroom. They were noticeably subject to the control and discipline of Mrs. Smith. The evidence revealed that, on the whole, the children were far better off living with their own extended family, even in the difficult, overcrowded circumstances of Mrs. Smith's apartment, than they would be as atomized individuals in the streets, foster homes or shelters of New York. Exclusion from their apartment risks driving the eighteen Smith family residents far below a minimum standard for civilized living. Congress does not appear to have intended such a draconian result.

B. *Connection of Household to Drug Activity*

On January 31, 1990 an undercover police officer purchased two vials containing crack cocaine from a woman in apartment 1-C. The woman who sold the drugs was identified by the police as Chenelle Smith, Mrs. Smith's granddaughter.

A valid search warrant for the apartment was executed on February 14, 1990. Found in a dresser in a bedroom sometimes occupied by Clara Smith was a blue cookie canister that contained a piece of tin foil with white powder believed to be used in the manufacture of crack, a clear plastic bag filled with empty crack vials, a strainer with the white powder residue, three measuring spoons, and a razor blade. In a second bedroom, the police discovered under a bed a yellow purse containing 35 vials filled with crack. In the same bedroom, a brown paper bag with 100 empty crack vials in plastic bags and a "Gucci" handbag containing more empty crack vials were found.

Such substantial quantities of drugs and drug paraphernalia support the conclusion that the apartment was used to store drugs. It would allow an inference that there had been some packaging of crack there. Certainly there were more drugs and empty vials than would be needed for routine, personal consumption by any users in the apartment. Following the search, Clara Smith, Chenelle Smith, Juanita Smith, and Sylvia Smith were arrested and indicted. Sylvia Smith and Juanita Smith were convicted of possession of cocaine and sentenced to three years probation. Chenelle Smith was convicted of attempted sale of cocaine and sentenced to five years probation. While in the plea allocution Chenelle Smith only admitted to selling drugs in the building, the circumstances surrounding the sale lead to the conclusion that it occurred from the apartment. The charges against Mrs. Smith were dismissed. At trial the claimants conceded "that there is probable cause to believe that a sufficient nexus to render the property forfeitable exists between the defendant property and criminal activity punishable by more than one year's imprisonment."

C. *Clara Smith and the Apartment*

Mrs. Smith was almost overwhelmed by the problems of her household. Her day began early in the morning. She took care of the minor children, seeing that they were bathed, dressed and fed before being sent off to school, and trying to supervise them upon their return. She was responsible for all the cooking and cleaning. She rarely left the apartment—usually only when the food stamps arrived to do the grocery shopping for the entire family.

Because of the severe overcrowding, Mrs. Smith has been attempting to obtain a larger apartment for several years. The largest apartment in the Marcy project has four bedrooms and even it would be too small for the household. Sylvia Smith, Juanita Smith and Chenelle Smith are also trying to obtain apartments for their families. It does not appear, however, that they will be successful in the near future.

There is an overwhelming demand for low-income housing in New York City. The Housing Authority owns and operates 318 developments with 179,000 apartments and 600,000 residents. It has a zero vacancy rate. It estimates that in excess of 175,000 families are on a waiting list for housing. The families are ranked in order of priority. Individuals in overcrowded apartments are next to last in line to receive an apartment. It is estimated that, at present rates, it will take 18 years to place the families on the waiting list in public housing.

From all indications, it appears that the housing crisis is worsening. The demand for affordable housing is dramatically increasing while its availability is just as sharply decreasing. In New York City federal funding produced an average of 3,000 new apartments a year during the 1950s, 1960s and 1970s. During the entire decade of the 80s, the Housing Authority only received 1,548 new public housing units.

At one point, to relieve the cramped conditions, Mrs. Smith ordered Juanita Smith, Chenelle Smith and their children out of the apartment. They were placed in an emergency shelter. Mrs. Smith relented, however, when it became apparent that the condition of the shelters for the homeless were, in her estimation, horrendous. Compassion required that they be permitted to again join the Smith family in their lodging.

Mrs. Smith, the court finds, firmly opposed drug activities by her extended family. She did not tolerate such activities in the apartment since the well-being of the other family members would be jeopardized. She stated repeatedly that she had no knowledge of the presence of any drugs or of any illegal drug activity in her apartment. When informed by the Housing Authority of anonymous charges of drug sales from her apartment, she confronted the members of her household and satisfied herself that the allegations were not true. As a precaution, she prohibited members of the household from having guests while she was away. She also insisted that only members of her family answer the door.

IV. LAW

The civil drug forfeiture statute, 21 U.S.C. § 881 (1988), creates an *in rem* cause of action for violations of the narcotics laws. The formal defendant in this forfeiture proceeding is apartment 1-C. The statute operates on the legal fiction that "it is the property which is proceeded against, and ... held guilty and condemned as though it were conscious instead of inanimate and insentient." *United States v. United States*

Currency in the Amount of $228,536.00, 895 F.2d 908 (2d Cir. 1990). If the Government succeeds in a forfeiture proceeding, "all right, title, and interest in the property used to facilitate a drug transaction shall vest in the United States."

A. *Public Housing Forfeiture*

Forfeiture is a powerful weapon in the war on drugs. It allows the Government to "seize the profits and proceeds of illegal drug trafficking, as well as the currency and property used in connection with money laundering and drug violations."

The forfeiture provision under which the Government is proceeding provides:

> The following shall be subject to forfeiture to the United States and no property right shall exist in them:. . . .
>
> (7) All real property, including any right, title, and interest (including any leasehold interest) in the whole of any lot or tract of land and any appurtenances or improvements, which is used, or intended to be used, in any manner or part, to commit, or to facilitate the commission of, a violation of this title punishable by more than one year's imprisonment, except that no property shall be forfeited under this paragraph, to the extent of an interest of an owner, by reason of any act or omission established by that owner to have been committed or omitted without the knowledge or consent of that owner.

21 U.S.C. §881(a).

The high concentration of poverty has made public housing developments especially vulnerable to drugs and drug dealing. Low-income housing has been transformed from a place to live to "a staging area for the distribution of drugs and the violence related to drug trafficking and consumption." Frustrated in its efforts to curtail the proliferation of illegal drugs in public housing, Congress sought to create a mechanism by which tenants who violate the narcotics laws could be removed. The problems surrounding existing state and federal eviction proceedings necessitated the creation of an efficient and effective method to remove drug dealers and return the housing projects to law-abiding tenants.

D. *Probable Cause to Forfeit*

Property is subject to forfeiture upon a showing of probable cause that it was used to facilitate a narcotics crime. Probable cause in this context means that "the government must have reasonable grounds, rising above the level of mere suspicion, to believe that certain property is subject to forfeiture." In their opening statement, the claimants conceded that probable cause existed to forfeit the property.

The large number of crack vials and other drug paraphernalia in the apartment coupled with Chenelle Smith's admission in her plea allocution that she sold crack at the housing project creates probable cause to believe that the apartment was used to store or safekeep crack and possibly to package it. Having a place to package or store the crack would certainly make its sale easier. This circumstance alone is sufficient to establish the probable cause necessary to warrant forfeiture.

E. *Defenses to Forfeiture*

Once the Government establishes probable cause, the burden of proof then shifts to the claimant to the property to establish, by a preponderance of the evidence, that the use of the property was such that it is not subject to forfeiture. The claimant can meet this burden by proving "either that the property was not used unlawfully ... or that the illegal use was without the claimant's knowledge or consent."

1. Burdens of Proof

Statutory shifting of the burden of proof stacks the deck heavily in favor of the Government. It can obtain forfeiture by simply showing—by less than a preponderance of the evidence—that the property was used illegally. For a claimant to remain in her home, however, she must establish a defense to forfeiture by a preponderance of the evidence.

2. Innocent Ownership

While Congress designed the drug forfeiture statutes to be a powerful weapon in the war on drugs, it had no desire to see innocent owners lose their property. The statute allows a claimant to avoid forfeiture by establishing that she had no knowledge of narcotics activity or, if she had knowledge, that she did not consent to it. The court tentatively ruled that the innocent owner defense's lack of knowledge prong should be construed to mean lack of "willful blindness." The absence of consent prong has been construed to require a claimant to show that "he did all that reasonably could be expected to prevent the illegal activity once he learned of it." Claimant Clara Smith has successfully established both prongs of the innocent owner defense.

The civil forfeiture statute makes owners, including lessors, responsible for their property. Owners must take "basic investigatory steps" and not deliberately avoid knowledge of wrongdoing occurring on the property. In light of the enormous drug problem and the statute's intended potency, lack of knowledge should be construed to mean absence of "willful blindness." Even under the more stringent "willful blindness" standard, Clara Smith established that she lacked knowledge of drug activity in the apartment. She emphasized repeatedly that she had no knowledge of the presence of any drugs or of any illegal activity in her apartment. She also stated that she did not know of any possible illegal uses of the drug paraphernalia recovered in the search of the apartment.

When presented with anonymous charges of drug trafficking in her household, Clara Smith promptly investigated the allegations. She confronted her family members and questioned them about drug activity. She also took precautionary steps to prevent visitors from engaging in drug dealing. Her testimony is not incredible, as the Government claims. The apartment does not appear to be a "crack house" where widespread, notorious drug activity occurred. The Government only established one drug sale and the presence of hidden drug paraphernalia. The crack vials, though large in number, were not strewn through the apartment, but rather concealed from sight. Given Mrs. Smith's other burdens, she could easily have been unaware of the illegal activities. In view of her expressed antipathy to drugs, it would be reasonable to assume that her children and grandchildren would try to keep Mrs. Smith in the dark about their proscribed activities. We take judicial notice of the widespread lack of knowledge of childrens' drug activities in all kinds of families.

Since Mrs. Smith lacked knowledge of the drug activity, she has successfully established the innocent owner defense and is entitled to retain the apartment. There is no need to inquire into whether she consented to the activity since lack of consent can be presumed from her absence of knowledge. In any event, she did take reasonable steps, under the circumstances, to prevent drug activity in the apartment.

F. *Forfeiture of Other Claimants' Interests*

Since Clara Smith has successfully established the "innocent owner" defense, the Government has agreed not to proceed against the minor residents on whose behalf Clara Smith intervened. It has requested, however, that the occupancy interests of Chenelle Smith, Sylvia Smith and Juanita Smith be forfeited and an order of eviction be entered. Alternatively, the Government has requested that the court issue an injunction prohibiting the claimants and other occupants of the apartment from using it to commit or facilitate narcotics offenses.

Clara Smith's establishing the "innocent owner" defense prevents the Government from forfeiting the apartment to the extent of her interest. Here, Clara Smith is the "owner" of the leasehold. The remaining seventeen members of her family are entitled to possess, use and occupy the premises both as a consequence of her ownership and their residence. Since Chenelle Smith did sell drugs from the apartment, her independent interest in the property is subject to forfeiture. To the extent that she has any legal right to remain in the premises, that right, however defined, has been lost. Despite the demise of Chenelle Smith's property right in the apartment, her children, that is to say, the great-grandchildren of Clara Smith, retain their independent right to remain as residents and guests of their great-grandmother. This same relief is not available against Sylvia Smith or Juanita Smith. The evidence against them only establishes that they possessed crack. This is not sufficient to make their legal rights in the apartment subject to forfeiture.

Exercise 9-22. *Leasehold Interest* Revisited

1. This case represents an application of the innocent owner exception that is highly favorable to the property owner or, in this case, the leaseholder. In the context of public housing, this result is no longer possible, because Congress has clarified the law to eliminate an innocent owner exception. Despite the stated reservations of the judge, is it possible that Congress did "appear to have intended such a draconian result"?
2. The rules regulating drug-related forfeitures have been criticized on the grounds that they do not provide sufficient protection for the interests of property owners. Until 2002, the government only had to show probable

cause that the property was subject to forfeiture. The burden then shifted to the property owner to prove an affirmative defense by a preponderance of the evidence. In other words, the property owner shouldered a greater evidentiary burden than the government. Congress amended the federal forfeiture law in 2002 to increase the government's burden of proof to a preponderance of the evidence and made some changes to the innocent owner exception.

Exercise 9-23. *Rucker v. United States*

In 2000, Congress amended the law governing the leases for public housing to provide for termination of the lease on the account of "any drug-related criminal activity on or off such premises, engaged in by a public housing tenant, any member of the tenant's household, or any guest or other person under the tenant's control." 42 U.S.C. § 1437d(l)(6). *Rucker v. U.S.* involves three separate instances where a local housing authority terminated a lease because of drug use. The facts of the cases seem tailor-made for an innocent owner exception. As you read the unanimous Supreme Court decision, consider what policy considerations are in play. If you were the policy maker, would you authorize an innocent owner exception?

HUD v. Rucker

535 U.S. 125 (2002)

Rehnquist, C.J., delivered the opinion of the Court. With drug dealers "increasingly imposing a reign of terror on public and other federally assisted low-income housing tenants," Congress passed the Anti-Drug Abuse Act of 1988. The Act, as later amended, provides that each "public housing agency shall utilize leases which ... provide that any criminal activity that threatens the health, safety, or right to peaceful enjoyment of the premises by other tenants or any drug-related criminal activity on or off such premises, engaged in by a public housing tenant, any member of the tenant's household, or any guest or other person under the tenant's control, shall be cause for termination of tenancy." 42 U.S.C. § 1437d(l)(6). Petitioners say that this statute requires lease terms that allow a local public housing authority to evict a tenant when a member of the tenant's household or a guest engages in drug-related criminal activity, regardless of whether the tenant knew, or had reason to know, of that activity. Respondents say it does not. We agree with petitioners.

Respondents are four public housing tenants of the Oakland Housing Authority (OHA). Paragraph 9(m) of respondents' leases, tracking the language of § 1437d(l)(6), obligates the tenants to "assure that the tenant, any member of the household, a guest, or another person under the tenant's control, shall not engage in ... any drug-related criminal activity on or near the premises." Respondents also signed an agreement stating that the tenant "understands that if I or any member of my household or guests should violate this lease provision, my tenancy may be terminated and I may be evicted."

In late 1997 and early 1998, OHA instituted eviction proceedings in state court against respondents, alleging violations of this lease provision. The complaint alleged: (1) that the respective grandsons of respondents William Lee and Barbara Hill, both of whom were listed as residents on the leases, were caught in the apartment complex parking lot smoking marijuana; (2) that the daughter of respondent Pearlie Rucker, who resides with her and is listed on the lease as a resident, was found with cocaine and a crack cocaine pipe three blocks from Rucker's apartment; and (3) that on three instances within a 2-month period, respondent Herman Walker's caregiver and two others were found with cocaine in Walker's apartment. OHA had issued Walker notices of a lease violation on the first two occasions, before initiating the eviction action after the third violation.

United States Department of Housing and Urban Development (HUD) regulations administering § 1437d(l)(6) require lease terms authorizing evictions in these circumstances. The HUD regulations closely track the statutory language, and provide that "in deciding to evict for criminal activity, the [public housing authority] shall have discretion to consider all of the circumstances of the case...." The agency made clear that local public housing authorities' discretion to evict for drug-related activity includes those situations in which "[the] tenant did not know, could not foresee, or could not control behavior by other occupants of the unit."

After OHA initiated the eviction proceedings in state court, respondents commenced actions against HUD, OHA, and OHA's director in United States District Court. They challenged HUD's interpretation of the statute under the Administrative Procedure Act, arguing that 42 U.S.C. § 1437d(l)(6) does not require lease terms authorizing the eviction of so-called "innocent" tenants, and, in the alternative, that if it does, then the statute is unconstitutional. The District Court issued a preliminary injunction, enjoining OHA from "terminating the leases of tenants pursuant to paragraph 9(m) of the 'Tenant Lease' for drug-related criminal activity that does not occur within the tenant's apartment unit when the tenant did not know of and had no reason to know of, the drug-related criminal activity."

A panel of the Court of Appeals reversed, holding that § 1437d(l)(6) unambiguously permits the eviction of tenants who violate the lease provision, regardless of whether the tenant was personally aware of the drug activity, and that the statute is constitutional. An en banc panel of the Court of Appeals reversed and affirmed the District Court's grant of the preliminary injunction. That court held that HUD's interpretation permitting the eviction of so-called "innocent" tenants is inconsistent with Congressional intent and must be rejected under the first step of *Chevron U.S.A. Inc. v. Natural Resources Defense Council, Inc.*, 467 U.S. 837 (1984).

We granted certiorari and now reverse, holding that 42 U.S.C. § 1437d(l)(6) unambiguously requires lease terms that vest local public housing authorities with the discretion to evict tenants for the drug-related activity of household members and guests whether or not the tenant knew, or should have known, about the activity.

That this is so seems evident from the plain language of the statute. It provides that "each public housing authority shall utilize leases which ... provide that ... any drug-related criminal activity on or off such premises, engaged in by a public housing tenant, any member of the tenant's household, or any guest or other person under the tenant's control, shall be cause for termination of tenancy." 42 U.S.C. § 1437d(l)(6). The en banc Court of Appeals thought the statute did not address "the level of personal knowledge or fault that is required for eviction." Yet Congress' decision not to impose any qualification in the statute, combined with its use of the term "any" to modify "drug-related criminal activity," precludes any knowledge requirement. As we have explained, "the word 'any' has an expansive meaning, that is, one or some indiscriminately of whatever kind." Thus, *any* drug-related activity engaged in by the specified persons is grounds for termination, not just drug-related activity that the tenant knew, or should have known, about.

It is entirely reasonable to think that the Government, when seeking to transfer private property to itself in a forfeiture proceeding, should be subject to an "innocent owner defense," while it should not be when acting as a landlord in a public housing project.

[T]he en banc Court of Appeals [was not] correct in concluding that [a] plain reading of the statute leads to absurd results. The statute does not *require* the eviction of any tenant who violated the lease provision. Instead, it entrusts that decision to the local public housing authorities, who are in the best position to take account of, among other things, the degree to which the housing project suffers from "rampant drug-related or violent crime," "the seriousness of the offending action," and "the extent to which the leaseholder has ... taken all reasonable steps to prevent or mitigate the offending action." It is not "absurd" that a local housing authority may sometimes evict a tenant who had no knowledge of the drug-related activity. Such "no-fault" eviction is a common "incident of tenant responsibility under normal landlord-tenant law and practice." Strict liability maximizes deterrence and eases enforcement difficulties.

And, of course, there is an obvious reason why Congress would have permitted local public housing authorities to conduct no-fault evictions: Regardless of knowledge, a tenant who "cannot control drug crime, or other criminal activities by a household member which threaten health or safety of other residents, is a threat to other residents and the project." With drugs leading to "murders, muggings, and other forms of violence against tenants," and to the "deterioration of the physical environment that requires substantial governmental expenditures," it was reasonable for Congress to permit no-fault evictions in order to "provide public and other federally assisted low-income housing that is decent, safe, and free from illegal drugs."

We hold that "Congress has directly spoken to the precise question at issue." Accordingly, the judgment of the Court of Appeals is reversed, and the cases are remanded for further proceedings consistent with this opinion.

It is so ordered.

Exercise 9-24. *Rucker* Revisited

1. Public housing is a scarce resource. As the Court explains, the residents of public housing have a right to expect "housing that is decent, safe, and free from illegal drugs." Does that goal justify no-fault evictions?
2. The Court declined to examine the no-fault eviction provisions in public housing as a potential taking of property without compensation. Instead, the Court focuses on the provisions as part of "normal landlord-tenant law and practice." The leaseholders agreed to the provision when they signed the lease. Can you think of any argument from Contracts law that would complicate the conclusion that the leaseholders voluntarily assented to the no-fault eviction rule?

PART FIVE
Private Land Use Law: Servitudes

Chapter 10

Private Land Use Laws—Servitudes

Introduction

There are a range of different laws that regulate land use. Nuisance law is the default system that governs neighbor relationships and conflicting uses in the absence of an agreement (studied in Chapter 7). Zoning and takings laws both empower and limit the government's regulation of land use, ideally in a way that harmonizes conflicting uses and balances the interests of the public with private property ownership (addressed in Chapters 8 and 9). This chapter focuses on another component of land use planning—the law of servitudes. Servitudes law enables private agreements among owners that regulate either the way property is used by an owner or access to another's property for a specific purpose. If created in accordance with the rules, these agreements can bind the property and run with the land to successor owners.

Chapter Problems: Exercise 10-1

When you have learned the materials in this chapter, you will be prepared to analyze and evaluate how the law applies to the problems below.

Problem A

Before Owen retired, he bought a 30-acre parcel of undeveloped land in a rural area of Delvania (a fictional state). There was a lovely creek that flows across portions of the property. He always dreamed that when he had the time, he would take up fly-fishing and so he referred to the property as "Fishacres." Owen was approached several times by a developer who wanted to buy the property from him to build a residential subdivision. When the developer made Owen a very lucrative offer he felt he could not pass up, he finally agreed to sell. However, as a condition of the sale, Owen insisted on keeping 1 acre for himself. Also, still hoping to realize his dream of becoming a fly-fisherman, Owen insisted further that he retain the right to fish all along the entire length of the creek, even on the portions of the creek that flow through the 29 acres bought by the developer. There were two separate documents (executed on the same day) used to accomplish the transaction. First, there was a deed transferring (fee simple absolute) title to the 29-acre parcel to the developer. Next, the developer granted Owen the "right to fish in the creek" that flows across the 29 acres the developer now owned. The developer immediately recorded the document evidencing his ownership of Fishacres. The document evidencing the right to fish on the 29 acres transferred to the developer was never recorded. Mistrusting government officials, Owen kept that document tucked away safely under his mattress.

It took fully a year following the sale for the developer to actually start construction on the subdivision. In the meantime, Owen retired and began to fish all along the stream on any day the weather was good. If it was hot enough, or he was feeling brave enough, sometimes Owen would strip down to his boxers and swim. Often, he brought along his son Sam, also an avid fly-fisherman. The developer sold 3 lots during this pre-construction phase, and each buyer immediately recorded their interest upon sale. Before one of these buyers bought their lot, the buyer noticed Owen and Sam fishing and asked the developer about it; the developer did say: "that's ok, they have a right to do that." Sadly, Owen became ill and was unable to continue fishing. In a frenzy of estate planning just before his death, Owen transferred all his rights in Fishacres to Sam. Sam immediately recorded the documents transferring the fishing rights from his father to him. Thereafter, the developer sold the remaining lots in the subdivision.

Even 3 years after his father's death, Sam felt it was just too sad fishing without his Dad and, in fact, Sam never did fish again. Some of the other owners in the development fenced off their yards, blocking access to the portion of the creek in their yards. As it turns out, all the new development really diminished the fish population: now it is exceedingly difficult to find and catch a fish in the creek.

Sam has been approached by a prospective buyer, a fellow fisherman. Sam is seriously thinking about selling all his rights to Fishacres. He wonders whether he could sell the fishing rights separate from the land.

You represent Sam, and your discussions with him yielded the information described above. Write Sam a letter; describe and evaluate for him the issues raised and counsel Sam on how the law will likely apply to his situation.

Problem B

Olivia resides in the fictional state of Delvania and owns a lovely southwestern style house on a two acre parcel called South-acre. Like southwestern style houses generally have, the exterior of the home is covered with stucco that is painted tan and the structure is rectangular with simple straight lines and with circle shaped windows.

In Year 1, Olivia bought her home from Danielle, the developer of the 50-home community. Olivia was the fifth buyer in the development. There were no restrictions in the deed transferring South-acre from Danielle to Olivia. However, before Danielle sold any homes in the development, she duly recorded a plat that depicted the property lines for each parcel in the subdivision, as well as a common area with a large fountain and a grove of cactus trees. The community was identified as "Santa Fe East" on the plat. No other information was recorded with the plat. However, in the deeds to the first two buyers in the development, Danielle included the following language: "It is mutually agreed that every parcel in Santa Fe East shall be used for residential purposes only. Every owner is entitled to be a voting member of the homeowner association. The homeowner's association may amend the by-laws and rules of the association by a vote of 75% of the members." These provisions were also included in some of the deeds to the buyers who bought their homes after Olivia.

On New Year's Day, Year 5, Olivia became a Buddhist. She felt that communing with nature was essential to her spirituality, and she began construction of a structure about the size of a shed where she could meditate. The structure was designed to have Victorian style architecture and features, and so had a roof line with different angles and alcoves and even had a tiny wrap-around front porch. It was painted in meticulous detail with traditional Victorian colors of pink, purple, and green. It was such a contrast to the style of her home, Olivia thought the mismatch looked great.

By June Year 5, construction was nearly complete when the president of the homeowner's association approached Olivia. He advised her that the association was prepared to bring a lawsuit to stop her from continuing construction on the structure and, further, that she would have to remove it. It turns out the association adopted new rules in the month before Olivia started construction of her meditation structure. The recently adopted rules require that any new structures or modifications to existing structures must be pre-approved by the association and must be consistent with "Southwestern style" architecture. The changes to the rules were recorded after they were adopted. The new rules were adopted, because a number of structures in the development already varied from the Southwestern style, and the association members were concerned that the character and property values in the neighborhood might be quickly eroding.

This was new information to Olivia. Although she had been invited to all HOA meetings and was given a letter describing the new rules, Olivia just didn't pay attention to such mundane things. She never attended any association meetings, never voted, and never opened any letters from the HOA.

1. You represent Olivia. Describe and evaluate for Olivia the issues raised and counsel her on how the law will likely apply to her situation. Be sure to address arguments and counter-arguments.
2. Changing the facts, now assume that the rules mandating Southwestern style architecture and pre-approval of structures were in a declaration that Danielle recorded before any sales out of the properties.

Fundamentals of Servitudes and Overview of Chapter 10

Servitudes are "non-possessory" interests in land. There are two different kinds of servitudes: (1) covenants and (2) easements. A covenant is an agreement among owners that a parcel or multiple parcels of real estate will be used in a certain way. For example, owners might agree that they will use the land only for residential purposes (even if zoning law allowed non-residential uses). Such land use agreements are called either a "real covenant" or an "equitable servitude." We refer to them collectively as "covenants." What makes covenants different from a regular contract is that these agreements can (and typically do) become attached to the property and flow to whoever owns the land in the future. The promise binds the *land* and not the original parties to the agreement, once ownership is transferred. An easement is the other major kind of servitude. An easement confers specific rights of access to another's property for a particular purpose. For example, two next door neighbors might agree that one of them has a right of way to drive across the other's property to reach a public road. Like covenants, easements can also run with the land, meaning that if the property subject to an easement is transferred to a new owner, the new owner is bound by the easement. Below is an illustration of some of these core concepts.

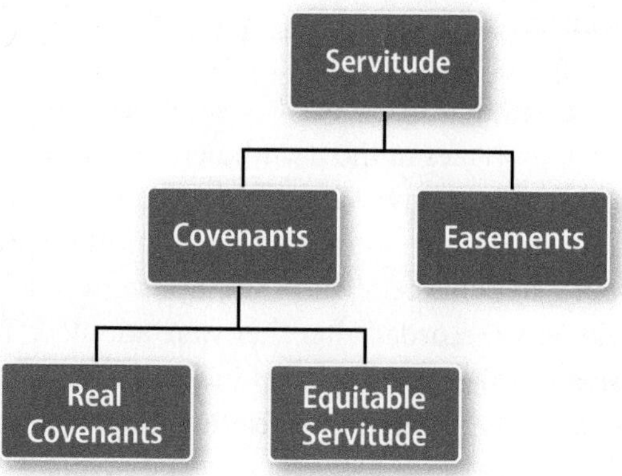

Another example is helpful in understanding how "running" servitudes operate and why they can be desirable. Imagine this happy scenario—you just bought a lovely beach-front home for a million dollars, with an amazing view of the ocean in a quiet residential neighborhood. Naturally you would like to continue to enjoy the property just the way it is now—and to maintain the property's value. Now imagine you encounter what you experience as a serious problem—your neighbor who lives on the property adjacent to yours just bought an old recreational vehicle—an orange and brown trailer circa 1970. The neighbor keeps the trailer parked in her driveway. When you look over to your right across your neighbor's property, you have that ugly old thing constantly in your view toward the ocean.

How can you resolve this conflict? You would like to limit your neighbor's use of their property so that storing an RV is not permitted. Indeed, what you really want is to make sure that *no* owner of the adjacent property can store an RV there, even when the property is transferred. What you want then is to limit use of the property itself and to have that restriction be permanent. It is possible to accomplish these goals by entering into a specialized contract with the neighbor. Provided you follow the rules for doing so, the covenant (in this example, a promise not to store an RV on the property) becomes attached to and binds the property (and once the property is transferred, no longer binds the person making the contract). Accordingly, the promise runs with the land to successor owners.

In this chapter, you will learn the rules governing these private land use agreements—for both covenants and easements. Again, an easement owner has the right to do something specific on another's land—such as a right of way. Notice an important difference between easements and covenants: easements grant rights to use *another's* property in a specific way; covenants regulate how an owner may use his or her *own* property. Further, you will see that easements typically create an affirmative right to do something, whereas covenants often are negative because they restrict use.

As you can see, there is some vocabulary you need to become familiar with. You have already been introduced to the concept of running with the land. In addition, parcels of property are sometimes referred to as dominant or servient. Let's return to our classic example of an easement, where one owner has a right of way across another's property. Review the illustration below.

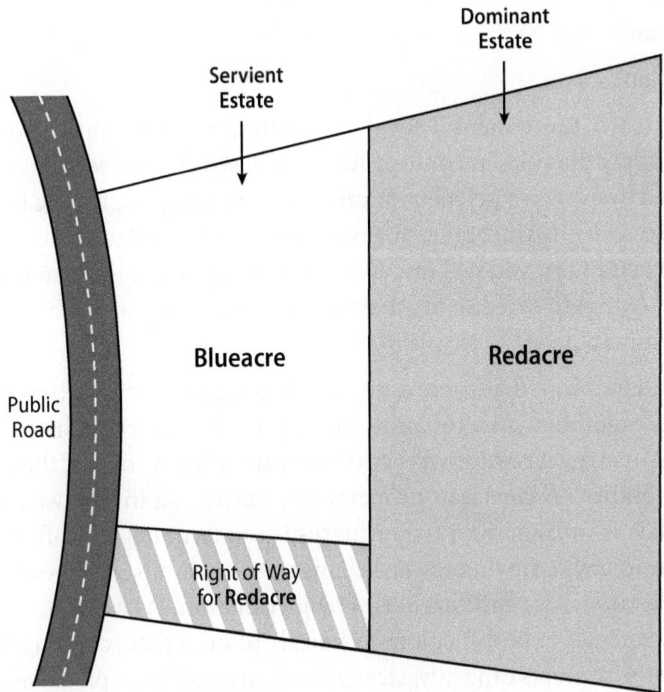

The owner of RedAcre has the right to travel across BlueAcre to access and return from the public road. RedAcre is the dominant estate and has the benefit of the easement. BlueAcre is the servient estate and is burdened by the easement. Typically, you will see the terms dominant and servient used when referring to easements and benefit/burden used in connection with running covenants.

Another set of concepts to learn is the difference between "appurtenant" versus "in gross" servitudes. If both the burden and the benefit of a servitude run with the land, then the servitude is appurtenant. The easement in the example above is appurtenant. Ownership of the benefit and burden of the easement is tied to owning the property to which the easement permanently attaches. Similarly, the benefit and burden of the covenants in the RV example given earlier are also running (or appurtenant) covenants—that flow to whoever owns the land. In contrast, an in gross servitude exists if the burden runs with the land, but the *benefit* does not attach to a piece of property. Rather, the benefit is owned by a person or an entity, just like a person might own any valuable thing, such as a stock account—having nothing to do with whether the benefited party also owns land. The benefit is an asset owned apart from land. For example, an easement to run train tracks across another's property that is owned by a railroad company is an in gross easement. Do you understand why? The benefit of being able to lay track and use it across another person's property is a valuable and useful property interest owned by the railroad. Owning the benefit does not depend on whether the railroad company also owns a nearby parcel of land. You will study the concept of running with the land more as you progress through this chapter.

This Chapter is divided into two (2) subunits.

1. Easements
2. Covenants

You will learn fundamental legal principles, review sample documents and continually apply the rules in context. As you will see, both easements and covenants can be created by express agreement or can be implied. Although there is some overlap, there are also some distinct rules for modifying and terminating easements versus covenants. In addition, you will discover that public policy can be an influential force for regulating private agreements that may go too far afield or that raise concerns about discrimination.

You should be aware that some aspects of this area of law have been critiqued and are being re-examined. As Professor Susan French, reporter for the Restatement (Third) of Property: Servitudes has said, servitudes law is "one of the most complex and archaic bodies of American property law remaining in the twentieth century." Servitudes law is in transition from the traditional model still often in place and appears to be (slowly) moving toward change. As a result, states today have a mix of old and some new laws, and this varies by jurisdiction. As a result, you might find some of the materials to be difficult or technical. To meet these challenges, this chapter breaks down the concepts explicitly, strives for clarity and offers plenty of opportunities for applied learning.

It could be that servitudes law will undergo far more dramatic changes in the future. In an effort to streamline the system, the Restatement Third (2000) proposes a merger of easements and covenants into the single category of servitudes with a uniform set of rules. This chapter will introduce you to the major reforms suggested in the Restatement. However, keep in in mind that the Restatement is a proposal for change and does not reflect the existing state of the law. We have yet to see if courts and legislatures will adopt these reforms.

Easements

Suppose you are buying a new home in a newly developing neighborhood and would like to have access to a water system where the water travels through pipes that cross multiple parcels before connecting to your home. What you need is an easement—a right to use another's property for a specific purpose—in this case, a right to have water pipes on neighboring parcels to connect to the water supply. Or, an electric or cable company might be granted an easement to lay electrical lines or coaxial cables to supply your home with these resources. Suppose further that the most convenient way for you to reach your new home from a public street is to travel across a long driveway that is owned by your neighbor. Again, you need an easement to use the driveway for ingress and egress. As you may now start to notice, easements are everywhere. Another kind of easement is a profit. A profit is 1) a right to enter another's property and 2) remove a valuable resource, such as timber or minerals or natural gas.

In the subsections that follow, you will learn about five types of easements identified in the chart below.

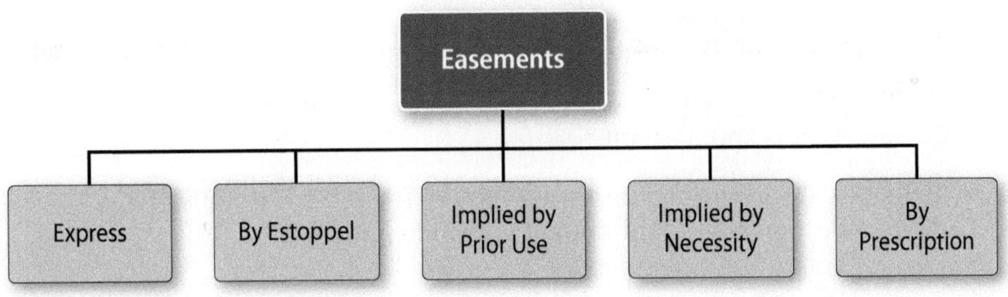

Express Written Easements

As lawyers know well, property interests should be created explicitly and clearly in a written and signed document that complies with the Statute of Frauds. You may recall from earlier chapters that the Statute of Frauds is a general rule that requires real estate transactions to be in writing to be enforceable and signed by "the party to be charged" (the person who allegedly transferred out the property interest). More specifically, the best practice for compliance with the rule is to draft:

1. A written deed;
2. that identifies the parties;

3. includes key terms describing the transaction and the property interests; and
4. is signed by the transferor and the transferee.

The Statute of Frauds is applicable in a variety of legal settings. For example, as explained in Chapter 6 on leasing property, in some states, it applies to leases that are longer than a year. You will also study the Statute of Frauds in more detail in Chapter 11 on real estate transactions. Easements are interests in land and subject to the rule. The Statute of Frauds also has some important exceptions—including the implied easements you will study soon. However, lawyers and clients would not want to rely on a claim for an unwritten easement unless there was no better option. A writing remains key for ensuring creation and enforceability of a valid easement.

Most easements are created in an express writing. Express easements can be created either by grant or reservation. By grant is most common and occurs when an owner of the property gives or sells an easement to a grantee. An easement might also be "reserved" when an owner of land transfers part of the land and retains part and then in the same transaction creates an easement in the land just transferred out. The exercise that follows gives you an example of an express easement by grant.

Exercise 10-2. Reviewing an Express Easement Deed and Evaluating Compliance with the Statute of Frauds

1. To gain some familiarity with documents regularly encountered in legal practice and to deepen your understanding of easements, carefully review the deed below.
2. Be sure to identify how the deed complies with the Statute of Frauds (it does).
3. Do both the benefit and burden of the easement run with the land? (If so, the easement is appurtenant.)
4. Easements are permanent grants unless the parties intend otherwise. Is this easement permanent—meaning it lasts indefinitely?

SAMPLE EASEMENT

GRANT OF EASEMENT FOR ACCESS TO PROPERTY

THIS AGREEMENT is effective on this 2nd day of April 2016, by and between Ned Smith (hereinafter "Grantor") and Maria Gonzales (hereinafter "Grantee").

WHEREAS, Grantor is the owner of property located at 1031 High Road, West Chester, Delaware (hereinafter "High Road"); and WHEREAS, the Grantee is the owner of property located at 919 Low Road, West Chester, Delaware (hereinafter "Low Road"); and WHEREAS, Grantee requires access over and across High Road; and WHEREAS, the parties hereto desire, by this

Agreement, to set forth the rights of ingress, egress and access over the High Road on Grantor's real estate to allow for Grantee's access to the Low Road property, all within the area more specifically depicted on Exhibit A attached hereto and legally described on Exhibit B attached hereto (the "Easement Area").

NOW, THEREFORE, for and in consideration of the mutual covenants and agreements contained herein and other good and valuable consideration, the receipt and sufficiency of which is hereby acknowledged, the parties agree as follows:

1. **Incorporation of Recitals.** The recitals set forth above are incorporated and restated herein as material terms of this Agreement.

2. **Grant of Access, Ingress, and Egress to Grantee.** The Grantor does hereby grant to Grantee, its successors and assigns, invitees, licensees, and agents a permanent, non-exclusive right of ingress and egress over and upon the Easement Area, subject to Grantee's acceptance of the obligation to maintain and keep the Easement Area in good repair and usable. The use of the term "non-exclusive" herein shall mean that the ingress, egress and access rights granted pursuant to this Agreement shall be subject to the contemporaneous and continuing right of the Grantor, its staff, patrons, licensees, and invitees to use the Easement Area for ingress, egress, and such maintenance of the Easement Area as Grantor may determine to be necessary and/or appropriate from time to time.

3. This Easement is intended to run with the lands and shall be binding upon and inure to the benefit of the parties' successors and assigns, heirs, beneficiaries and personal representatives.

IN WITNESS WHEREOF, the parties have executed or caused this agreement to be executed by their respective authorized agents, intending the same to be effective upon execution hereof by both parties hereto.

SIGNED on this 2nd day of April 2016.

GRANTOR	GRANTEE
Ned Smith	Maria Gonzales

Interpretation of Easements

To understand easements in greater depth you need to learn more about what set of features an easement can include and how to interpret easements and resolve any ambiguities. Accordingly, this subsection first addresses how to discern if an easement runs with the land and is appurtenant or in gross. Next, you will learn how to determine the scope of an easement, whether the scope has been exceeded and appropriate remedies. Last, we will explore and debate how to distinguish easements from other property interests such as a license or a lease.

Running with the Land

A central question must be answered when planning for and analyzing an easement: when do easements attach to and run with ownership of the land? This breaks into two separate issues. Does the burden of the easement run? Does the benefit of easement run with land? Recall from the overview earlier that if both the benefit and the burden of the easement run with the land, then the easement is classified as appurtenant. If the burden of an easement runs with the land, but the benefit is owned by a person or entity and is *not* tied to a piece of land—then the easement is classified as an easement in gross. As will be developed in the materials below, it is important to distinguish between these two types of easements because they produce different legal outcomes.

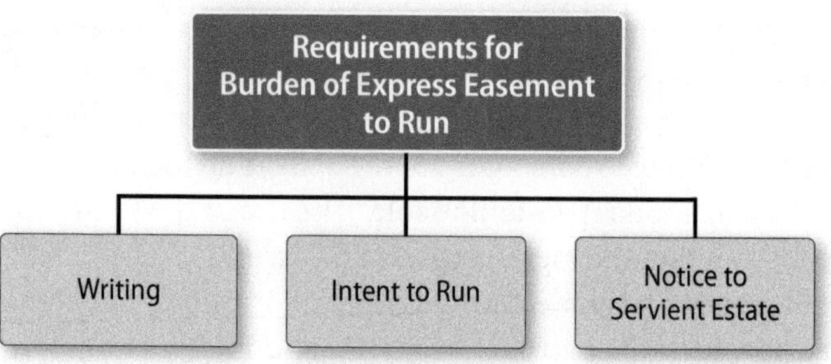

Does the burden of the easement run? There are three requirements for the burden of an express easement to attach to land and flow to subsequent owners, creating a servient estate.

1. *Writing.* There must be an original writing that memorializes the creation of an easement that complies with the Statute of Frauds. The writing need not be repeated in deed transfers to subsequent owners (although that is a good practice).

2. *Intent to Run.* An easement binds a successor owner only if it was intended to run with ownership of the land. The writing can and should specify such intent through words such as the burden of this easement "is intended to run with the land to successor owners" or "is intended to bind all heirs and assigns." If the deed is silent as to intent, then it must be ascertained. Intent can be implied by the circumstances and nature of the easement. The question to ask and answer is: is the easment most useful if it binds anyone who owns the land? For example, if an easement is for ingress and egress, then it would be useful to anyone who owns the land and likely was intended to be a part of and flow with the land. If the benefit is useful because the easment is attached to land, then the burden must also be intended to run—otherwise the purpose of the easement would be lost. Coversely, if the easement was of a personal nature such as a right to swim in a friend's pool or lake, it likely was not intended to run—it likely was intended to be limited to the parties who created it and not to flow to subsequent owners. Note, however, that this kind of personal grant for an easement is unsual.

3. *Notice to the Servient Estate Holder.* When and why should a buyer of property be burdened with an easement if she was not a party to the original agreement creating the easement? There must be notice to burden a purchaser of land with an easement. The idea is that if prospective owner knew or could have known about the easement before purchasing the land, then she is deemed to consent to it. There are three kinds of notice. Any of the three will fulfill the requirement.

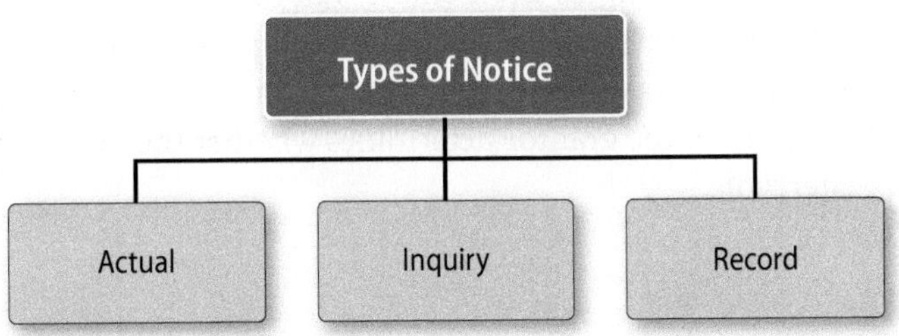

First, a buyer has *actual notice* if in fact they knew about the easement. Evidence that supports actual notice is if a buyer admits they knew or if they were told of the easement. Second, a buyer might have *inquiry notice.* This means there are visible signs of use of an easement on the servient estate, such as a road or pathway, or utility lines or poles. This physical evidence should cause a buyer to investigate and discover the easement. Buyers are charged with notice of what they should have discovered through reasonable investigation. Third, a buyer might have *record notice.* If an easement deed has been recorded properly in the appropriate registry of deeds (in the county where the property is located) and a reasonable search of the records would reveal its existence, then the buyer will be deemed to have record notice. Record notice will be imputed even if the search did not actually occur—because the easement *could* have been found. Record notice is sometimes referred to as constructive notice. Confusingly, inquiry notice is also sometimes called constructive notice. So we avoid that terminology.

Does the benefit of the easement run? There is just one legal standard that must be satisfied for the benefit of an easement to run—did the grantor intend that the benefit become a part of the grantee's land and flow to successor owners? Explicit language can be included in the deed that states whether the benefit is "intended to run with the land" or to "benefit heirs and assigns." If the deed is silent about intent, it can be inferred from the nature of the grant. Remember that the burden of an easement almost always runs. However, the benefit may run with the land, creating an appurtenant easement or, it can exist separately from the land, creating an easement in gross.

Commercial easements are typically in gross easements. For example, a cable company's right to have cables running across the property of others to provide access to cable television and the internet is an in gross easement. The burden of the easement flows with the land so that owners of the servient estate must allow the cables to remain, but the *benefit* of the easement is owned and enjoyed by the cable company as a business asset that is not tied to any land of the cable company. A key difference you will learn about more from the cases and materials that follow is that with an appurtenant easement, the easement cannot be "severed" or sold separately from the land. It must remain attached to and flow with the land. In contrast, the benefit of an in gross easement can be transferred or sold separately because it is already separate (having nothing to do with the benefitted party's land ownership). This is so as long as the benefit was intended to be transferrable. Commercial easements in gross are business assets and presumed to be transferrable. A personal easement that was intended to benefit only the grantee would not be transferrable. The intent of the grantor determines whether the benefit of an in gross easement is transferrable.

Exercise 10-3. Differentiating Appurtenant and In Gross Easements

Here are some opportunities to apply what you have just learned. In each of the following fact situations, determine if there is an appurtenant easement or an easement in gross and whether the benefit of the easement can be transferred separately from the land.

1. Mary and Frank are dear friends who live in different towns 10 miles apart. Frank is an avid runner. In a signed and duly recorded deed, Mary granted Frank personally an easement to run on the trail system she has on her 100 acre estate. Mary specifically stated in the deed that the burden of the easement is intended to run with the the land and bind future owners of her property. However, the document said nothing about the benefit. Frank owns no property and rents the apartment where he lives.
2. Leo and Paula own adjacent tracts of land in an area of the country where water is scarce. Leo has a large natural lake on his property. In a signed and duly recorded deed, Leo granted to Paula a right to withdraw water from the lake and use the water to irrigate Paula's land. Using the water for irrigation has allowed Paula to successfully grow vegetables for sale and increased the value of her land. Paula found a buyer for her land who also plans on growing crops for sale using the water from Leo's land.

Exercise 10-4. Interpreting Easements & Resolving Ambiguities—*Green v. Lupo*

In the next case you will learn more about the substantive content and interpretation of easements. You will also be introduced to some fundamental rules for resolving ambiguities in written legal documents. Specifically, you will be introduced to the Parol Evidence Rule. The rule provides that a document must be interpreted as written and no evidence outside the words of the document can be admitted as evidence unless certain exceptions are met. The rule is intended to preserve the integrity of written contacts and legal documents so that they cannot easily be contradicted by oral or other extrinsic evidence.

As you read, determine the answers to these questions:

1. What legal issues are raised in *Green*? Identify at least three.
2. How does the court resolve whether the easement is appurtenant or in gross? Be sure to identify the specific legal standards and to gather the facts that support each interpretation.
3. How does the Parol Evidence Rule apply here? What exception does the court apply that permits extrinsic evidence regarding the parties' intent?
4. Can the benefit of an easement be transferred separately from the land? As explained earlier, "severability" of the benefit depends on the kind of easement that was created. If the easement is appurtenant, the benefit cannot be severed from the land and automatically flows with the servient estate to the next owner. If the easement is in gross, the benefit is transferable by the easement holder if the grantor intended it to be. If the easement was intended to benefit only the grantee and no other person or entity, then it cannot be transferred. Which of these possibilities did the Lupos argue for? Be sure you understand why they were not successful.

Green v. Lupo

647 P.2d 51 (Wash. App. 1982)

Petrich, J. The plaintiffs, Don Green and his wife Florence, initiated this suit to specifically enforce an agreement to grant an easement. From a decree which determined that the contemplated easement was personal rather than appurtenant to their land as claimed, plaintiffs appeal. We reverse.

The issue raised on appeal is whether parol evidence is admissible to construe an easement as personal to the grantees where the easement is agreed in writing to be for ingress and egress for road and utilities purposes but the writing does not expressly characterize the easement as either personal or appurtenant. We believe that parol evidence was properly admitted here but the conclusion that the easement is personal to plaintiffs was erroneous.

The parties involved are adjoining landowners. The plaintiffs, once the owners of the entire tract, now retain several acres located south of the defendants' property. The defendants purchased their parcel (the north tract) from the plaintiffs by real estate contract. While they were still paying on that contract, the defendants requested a deed release to a small section of the north tract to allow financing for the construction of a home. The plaintiffs agreed in return for the promise of an easement along the southern 30 feet of the north tract when the defendants eventually obtained title. The express terms of the promised easement were contained in a written agreement which was executed in the form required for the conveyance of an interest in real property.

The plaintiffs' development of their land for mobile home occupancy caused tension between the landowners. Apparently some of the occupants of plaintiffs' mobile home development used the easement as a practice runway for their motorcycles. When the defendants obtained title to the north tract they refused to formally grant the easement as promised. They also placed logs along the southern boundary of the easement to restrict access from the plaintiffs' property. The plaintiffs brought this action to obtain specific performance of the promise to grant an easement and to enjoin any interference with their use of the easement.

Evidence was admitted describing a single-family cabin or residence built by or for the plaintiffs in the northeast corner of the plaintiffs' tract. It was defendants' contention, and they so testified, that the purpose of the easement was to serve the plaintiffs in their personal use and occupancy of this cabin or home. They claimed the easement was not intended to serve the plaintiffs' entire tract, part of which had been developed as a mobile home site, and which had access by other existing roads.

The trial court concluded that an easement was granted for the use and benefit of the plaintiffs alone and could not be assigned or conveyed. The court ordered the plaintiffs' use to be limited to ingress and egress for their own home or cabin and prohibited the passage of motorcycles.

It was the duty of the court in construing the instrument which created the easement to ascertain and give effect to the intention of the parties. The intention of the parties is determined by a proper construction of the language of the instrument. Where the language is unambiguous other matters may not be considered; but where the language is ambiguous the court may consider the situation of the property and of the parties, and the surrounding circumstances at the time the instrument was executed, and the practical construction of the instrument given by the parties by their conduct or admissions. Simply stated parol evidence may always be used to explain ambiguities in written instruments and to ascertain the intent of the parties.

The pivotal issue in deciding the propriety of admitting parol evidence is whether the written instrument is ambiguous. A written instrument is ambiguous when its terms are uncertain or capable of being understood as having more than one meaning.

The written instrument promised the easement specifically to the plaintiffs, to "Don Green and Florence B. Green," and described the easement as "for ingress and egress for road and utilities purpose." The designation of named individuals as dominant owners evidences an intent that the easement be personal to the named parties. The grant of an easement for ingress, egress and utilities to the owners of adjacent land is evidence of an intent that the easement benefit the grantees' adjacent land. We find that the instrument was ambiguous as to whether the easement granted was personal to the plaintiffs or appurtenant to their land. We therefore conclude that parol evidence was properly admitted.

The trial court's findings of fact are supported by competent evidence and are not assigned as error; they must be considered as verities on appeal. The court's findings do not, however, support the conclusion that the easement was personal. The court found that the easement was granted for ingress, egress, for road and utilities purposes. As we have noted, the grant of such an easement supports the conclusion that the easement was intended to be an easement appurtenant. In addition, the trial court found "the use of the easement by the plaintiff was to obtain access to the land, retained by plaintiff, for the construction and habitation by plaintiff in a cabin." This finding also supports the conclusion that the easement was intended to benefit plaintiffs' land.

The trial court's conclusion that the easement was personal to the plaintiffs was erroneous. There is a strong presumption in Washington that easements are appurtenant to some particular tract of land; personal easements, easements in gross, are not favored. An easement is not in gross when there is anything in the deed or the situation of the property which indicates that it was intended to be appurtenant to land retained or conveyed by the grantor. Viewed in this light, the court's factual findings mandate the conclusion that the easement was intended to be appurtenant to plaintiffs' property.

Easements appurtenant become part of the realty which they benefit. Unless limited by the terms of creation or transfer, appurtenant easements follow possession of the dominant estate through successive transfers. The rule applies even when the dominant estate is subdivided into parcels, with each parcel continuing to enjoy the use of the servient tenement. The terms of the easement promised do not limit its transfer. The easement promised the plaintiffs is appurtenant to their property and assignable to future owners of that property.

The defendants request that equitable limitations be imposed on any easement granted. A servient owner is entitled to impose reasonable restraints on a right of way to avoid a greater burden on the servient owner's estate than that originally contemplated in the easement grant, so long as such restraints do not unreasonably interfere with the dominant owner's use.

Testimony presented at trial showed that youngsters who now live on the dominant estate use their motorcycles on the easement in a fashion that constitutes a dangerous nuisance which was not considered when the easement was created. This evidence supports the imposition of equitable restrictions on the dominant owners' use, restrictions which will not unreasonably interfere with that use.

The trial court enjoined the use of motorcycles on the easement. There is insufficient evidence on the record to assess the impact of a complete ban on motorcycle use on the dominant estate's owners. Motorcycles are a common means of transportation. On its face, the ban appears to unreasonably interfere with the dominant owners' use of the easement. Although an equitable solution to the motorcycle problem is necessary, the trial court abused its discretion in imposing a ban on motorcycles without proper consideration of the ban's effect on the dominant owners' use of the easement.

Reversed and remanded with directions to modify the decree so as to declare the easement for ingress and egress for road and utility purposes to be appurtenant to plaintiffs' property and to devise reasonable restrictions to assure that the easement shall not be used in such a manner as to create a dangerous nuisance.

Exercise 10-5. *Green* Revisited—and Introduction to the Scope of Easements

Green is a helpful resource for learning how resolve ambiguities, how to grapple with the Parol Evidence Rule and how to identify an in gross versus an appurtenant easement. In addition, *Green* introduces you to several other issues that can arise in interpreting easements and that are studied in detail in the subsection that immediately follows.

1. Precisely what rights are included in an easement? That depends on the intent of the grantor. For example, in *Green*, did the easement include the right to use a motorcycle as a vehicle on the road?
2. Can anyone who possesses the dominant estate use the easement? If the easement is appurtenant, the answer is presumptively yes. The easement benefits the entire parcel to which it is attached. So it was not only Don and Flo who could use the right of way, but all those who possess or own a part of the dominant estate. That includes everyone who lives at the mobile home park and their guests. Do you see why?
3. Even if an easement holder is using the easement within its scope (e.g., as a right of way, by those who possess the servient estate), it is possible for an easement holder to "overuse" or overburden the easement. What was the claim for overuse in *Green?* What was the remedy?

Scope of Easements

A set of legal issues can come up in ascertaining the scope of an easement. The following is a list of recurring questions about scope that may need to be answered, depending on the fact situation. The scope of an easement is governed by the intent of the parties at the time of creation. If the scope is unclear, then the ambiguity must be resolved by evaluating the likely intent of the parties and examining the facts and circumstances and the nature of the easement. As the *Post & Beam* case (below) puts it the scope of an easement is identified based on the "intent of the parties, as drawn from the language of the deed, the circumstances existing at the time of execution, and the object and purpose to be accomplished by the easement." You will learn more about these issues in the exercises below.

1. What kind of use does the easement permit?

- For example, in *Brannon v. Boldt*, 958 So. 2d 367 (Fla. App. 2007), an easement to access the ocean across another person's property was found *not* to include hanging out, enjoying the view and partying on the servient estate.

2. What are the physical parameters of the easement?

- If the writing does not give specifics, many courts assume that the width and length of the easement at the time of the grant is the best evidence of intent.

3. Is the easement apportionable?

- In other words, who is entitled to use the easement and share the benefit of the easement with others? If the easement is appurtenant, it is presumptively apportionable, meaning the easement serves the entire parcel, including anyone who possesses any part of the dominant estate. This comes up most often when a parcel is subdivided and entitles all new lot owners to use the easement.
- With an in gross easement, the answer depends on whether the rights to the easement are "exclusive" to the grantee. For example, a right to run train tracks held by a railroad company typically would exclude the servient estate owner from doing the same in the same location of the easement.

4. Is there a "surcharge" on the servient estate?

- Is the easement being used in a way that creates an excess or unreasonable burden on the servient estate beyond what the easement allows? If the intent of the parties is unclear, the standard is to balance the interests of the servient estate against the interests of the easement holder.

Exercise 10-6(A). Case Studies Interpreting the Scope of Easements: *Shooting Point v. Wescoat; Post & Beam Equities Group v. Sunne Villages; Henley v. Continental Cablevision*

The three cases below address most of the scope issues listed above. Read each case carefully and identify the issues, the legal rules and the application of such rules, including any arguments and counter-arguments.

Shooting Point v. Wescoat

576 S.E.2d 497 (Va. 2003)

Milano Keenan, J. In this appeal, we primarily consider whether the chancellor erred in determining the location of an easement and in ruling that the proposed use of the dominant estate as a residential subdivision would not overburden the servient estate.

John W. Wescoat owns a tract of land in Northampton County (the Wescoat parcel) that is subject to a recorded easement in favor of a 176-acre tract owned by Shooting Point, L.L.C. (the Shooting Point parcel). The easement, which is 15 feet wide and 0.3 mile in length, is the only means of ingress and egress between the Shooting Point parcel and a nearby state highway. In response to a plan by Shooting Point, L.L.C. (Shooting Point) to develop its parcel into a residential subdivision, Wescoat filed a bill of complaint alleging, among other things, that Shooting Point's proposed use of its parcel would "impose an additional and unreasonable burden on the easement" over Wescoat's land.

In 1974, Wescoat's predecessors in title executed and recorded a written grant of easement establishing the right-of-way. The grant further described the right-of-way as "the only easement to provide a means of ingress and egress" from Route 622 to the Shooting Point parcel. The grant did not contain a clause limiting use of the easement. At the time the easement was established, both the servient estate and the dominant estate were used primarily for agricultural and recreational purposes.

At trial, the chancellor received evidence from expert witnesses indicating that the proposed residential subdivision would generate daily about ten vehicle trips per lot. Thus, the proposed subdivision would result in an additional 180 trips daily over the easement.

Wescoat assigns error to the chancellor's ruling that Shooting Point's use of its parcel as a residential subdivision would not overburden the servient estate. Wescoat argues that this use would create an additional burden on his property that would adversely impact his ability to use the easement. He alternatively contends that even if Shooting Point's use would only result in an increase in degree of the existing burden, that increase would have the practical effect of imposing an additional burden on the servient estate. We disagree with Wescoat's arguments.

A party alleging that a particular use of an easement is unreasonably burdensome has the burden of proving his allegation. Generally, when an easement is created by grant or reservation and the instrument creating the easement does not limit its use, the easement may be used for "any purpose to which the dominant estate may then, or in the future, reasonably be devoted." [Citation omitted.] However, this general rule is subject to the qualification that no use may be made of the easement, different from that established when the easement was created, which imposes an additional burden on the servient estate.

Applying these principles to the present case, we hold that the subdivision of the 176-acre Shooting Point parcel into 18 residential lots is a purpose to which the dominant estate may be reasonably devoted. Moreover, the record supports the chancellor's conclusion that Shooting Point's proposed use of the easement would not impose an unreasonable burden on the servient estate. Although the number of vehicles using the easement would increase substantially as a result of the proposed use, this fact demonstrates only an increase in degree of burden, not an imposition of an additional burden, on the servient estate. Like the facts underlying our decision in Hayes, the facts here do not support consideration of a further question whether an increased degree of burden could be so great as to impose an additional burden on the servient estate.

Post and Beam Equities Group, LLC v. Sunne Village Development Property Owners Association

124 A.3d 454 (Vt. 2015)

Robinson, J. This case involves a dispute between a residential subdivision property owners' association and the owner of commercial property both in and adjacent to the subdivision concerning access to property over a subdivision roadway. It also involves the conduct of the property owners' association. Defendant, Sunne Village Development Property Owners Association ("the POA"), appeals the trial court's judgment that it created a nuisance affecting the commercial landowner; the court's calculation of compensatory damages arising from the nuisance; and the court's award of punitive damages and attorney's fees. Plaintiffs, Post and Beam Equities Group, LLC, and Post and Beam of Mt. Snow, LLC (collectively "P & B"), cross-appeal, challenging the trial court's conclusion that its deeded easement over the subdivision's road does not extend to its patrons' use for access to its restaurants. We affirm with respect to the judgment for nuisance and the award of punitive damages and attorney's fees, but reverse the award of compensatory damages to P & B. In connection with the cross-appeal, we affirm the court's judgment relating to interpretation of the deeded easement.

P & B owns two adjacent parcels of property in the Town of West Dover. P & B operates two restaurants, The Last Chair and Fiddleheads, on Parcel 1. Parcel 1 also includes some space for parking. Parcel 2 consists of three lots used for parking for the restaurants on Parcel 1. The restaurant buildings are located on Parcel 1, which is bounded by Route 100 on one side and Sunne Village Lane on an adjacent side. At the time that P & B purchased Parcel 1, cars could enter the parking lot for the restaurants in two ways: from Route 100 or from Sunne Village Lane. Route 100 is a narrow, busy road, with heavy traffic during ski season, and prior to the events described below, Sunne Village Lane provided the primary access to the parking lot. Parcel 2, the parking-lot property, is bounded by Sunne Village Lane on one side, and No Name Road on an adjacent side. Parcel 2 is part of the Sunne Village Development subdivision. The three lots that make up Parcel 2 are subject to the subdivision's 1981 declaration of covenants, which provide, among other things, for a perpetual right of way and easement for lot owners over Sunne Village Lane. By virtue of its ownership of those lots, P & B is a member of the POA. Parcel 1 is not part of the subdivision.

The following schematic depicts the general relationship of the roads and parcels in question.

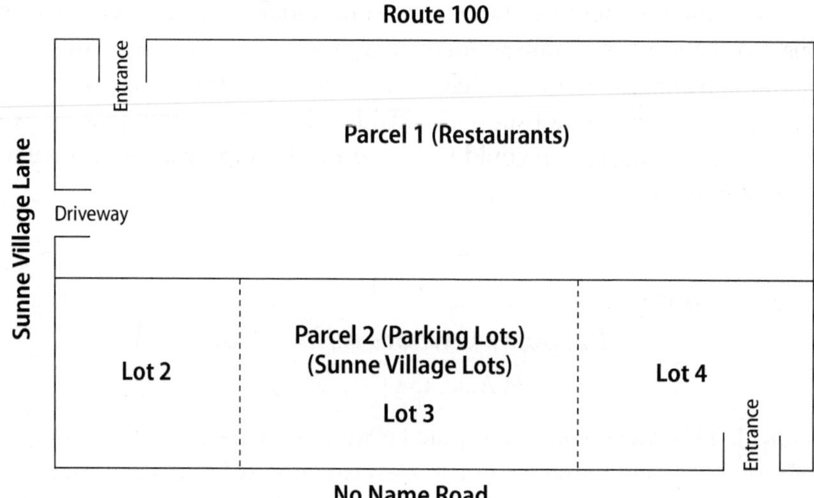

The events that gave rise to this lawsuit, as found by the trial court, are as follows. In 2010, when the POA believed that P & B had plans to close the entry onto P & B's property from Route 100 and to use the Sunne Village Lane entrance exclusively, the parties negotiated informally. In the summer of 2011, P & B and the POA reached a verbal agreement that allowed P & B to close the Route 100 entrance. The terms of the written agreement that the POA presented to P & B, however, contained terms to which P & B had never agreed. Among other things, the proposed written agreement required P & B to give up its easement over Sunne Village Lane and replace it with a revocable license. P & B refused to assent to these new terms, and reopened the Route 100 access while negotiations resumed.

In negotiations, the POA took the position that the deeded right of access for Parcel 2 was limited to residential purposes, and that P & B had no right to commercial access from Sunne Village Lane to the restaurant parking lots. Throughout this period, the POA permitted a different restaurant, Dover Joe's located directly across Sunne Village Lane from the P & B restaurants, to use an access path off Sunne Village Lane for access to its property. In the fall of 2011, after the negotiations failed, the POA placed—without notice or warning to P & B—large boulders across the Sunne Village Lane entrance to P & B's restaurants. P & B removed the boulders after consulting with the police department.

Almost one year later, in the late summer of 2012, the POA installed a guardrail in the same location, again without notice to P & B. The guardrail prevented access to P & B's property from Sunne Village Lane. The POA also put up numerous "Private Lane—Residents Only" signs on the entrance to Sunne Village Lane from Route 100. The barricades erected by the POA had a significant adverse impact on P & B's business.

Following a trial, the court ruled that the declaration of covenants granted P & B an express easement over Sunne Village Lane for the benefit of Parcel 2 (the parking-lot parcel), but not for the benefit of Parcel 1 (the restaurant parcel). The court concluded that the deeded easement for the benefit of Parcel 2 did not extend to this contemplated commercial use because such use would materially increase the burden on the servient estate. The court concluded, however, that P & B had acquired a prescriptive easement over Sunne Village Lane, including access to Parcel 1 through the area blocked by the guardrail installed by the POA. The court based its conclusion on evidence showing that the public had used the Sunne Village Lane entrance to access the restaurant property as far back as 1975.

Scope of Deeded Easement

On cross-appeal, P & B contests the trial court's conclusion that P & B's express, deeded easement allowing for the use of Sunne Village Lane to access Parcel 2 does not encompass the use contemplated here, which would overburden the easement.

The declaration of covenants establishing the express easement states:

> [T]he Subdivision Roadway ... shall be held and conveyed in common ownership among the owners of the lots within the Subdivision with each lot owner owning in fee simple an undivided 1/28th interest in said Subdivision Roadway in common with all other owners of lots within the Subdivision, provided that the ownership interest of each lot owner in the Subdivision Road shall be subject to and benefitted by a perpetual right-of-way and easement over and upon said Subdivision Road in common with the owners of other lots within the Subdivision, their respective heirs, successors, administrators, assigns, guests, and invitees....

The deed by which P & B acquired title to Parcel 2 repeats the grant of "an easement and right-of-way" to P & B and its heirs and assigns, and states that "[s]aid easement [is] to be for all normal and usual purpose of vehicular and pedestrian ingress and egress from the parcel ... to and from ... Route 100."

Because the declaration of covenants contain no language limiting the use of Sunne Village Lane or No Name Road to residential purposes, P & B argued in the trial court that it grants unrestricted use to each lot owner. The court rejected this argument, concluding that the commercial use contemplated here was beyond the intended scope of the easement. The court explained that (1) the subdivision plan laid out building lots for residential purposes; (2) the declaration of covenants referred to constructing driveways off the roadway for access to residential lots; and (3) the easement over Sunne Village Lane was for the "normal and usual purposes of vehicular and pedestrian ingress and egress." The court found that these facts indicated that the easement's intended purpose was to allow access to residential lots, and that allowing a large number of vehicles to travel onto No Name Road and P & B's parking lots "would materially increase the burden on the estate" in a way not contemplated by the easement.

On cross-appeal, P & B renews its contention that the express easement in favor of the lots on Parcel 2 allows for this commercial use. P & B emphasizes that the declaration does not contain any restriction against such use. While P & B disclaims any "present intent to utilize the No Name Road for access to the rear of the Parking Lot Property," it suggests that any future commercial use of the road would not overburden the easement, and a bar on commercial use of the road "may impede future development of the Parking Lot Property."

The interpretation of an express easement is a "question of law, which we review de novo." [Citation omitted.] In construing an express easement, as in construing a deed or declaration of covenants, "[o]ur master rule ... is that the intent of the parties governs." [Citations omitted.] If the terms of the express easement are unambiguous—that is, if reasonable people could not interpret it in different ways—then we "enforce the terms as written without resort to rules of construction or extrinsic evidence." [Citation omitted.] "If ambiguity exists, however, the interpretation of the parties' intent becomes a question of fact to be determined based on all of the evidence—not only the language of the written instrument, but also evidence concerning its subject matter, its purpose at the time it was executed, and the situation of the parties." [Citation omitted.]

Several principles guide our interpretation of express easements. First, "a dominant estate is entitled to use an easement 'in a manner that is reasonably necessary for the convenient enjoyment of the servitude.'" [Citations omitted.] Second, the easement must be used "in a manner consistent with the use contemplated at the time of its creation" and may not be used "in a way that materially increases the burden on the servient estate." [Citation omitted.] "Whether a particular use overburdens an easement ... depends on the easement's original purpose and the scope of its authorized use." [Citation omitted.] The third principle follows naturally from the other two: the "'manner, frequency, and intensity of the use [of the easement] may change over time to take advantage of developments in technology and to accommodate normal development[,] ... permit[ting] servitudes to retain their utility over time,'" *if* doing so would "'reflect[] the expectations of the parties who create servitudes of indefinite duration.'" [Citations omitted.]

In *Rowe,* we construed an easement (contained in an 1881 deed) granting the dominant estate "'the right to pass through [the servient estate] in the lane as it now is ... for all purposes whatever.'" 2006 VT 47, ¶ 3, 904 A.2d 78. We found that the use of automobiles was "consistent with the use contemplated at the time of [the easement's] creation" and would not "materially increase[] the burden on the servient estate." *Id.* ¶ 22 ("[B]ecause there was no limitation on the grantee's use of the right-of-way in the 1881 deed that created it, none should be imported merely because, over time, horses had been replaced by automobiles and cows by ATVs.").

Here, the deed in question does not contain such broad language encompassing all purposes whatsoever, but also does not expressly limit the character or volume of use. Our task is to infer the "intent of the parties, as drawn from the language of the deed, the circumstances existing at the time of execution, and the object and purpose to be accomplished by the easement." [Citation omitted.]

Although nothing in the founding documents appears to limit lots in the subdivision to residential use, the subdivision plan and the history we can glean from the record suggest that the subdivision was intended to be residential. Further, the declaration of covenants provides that each lot owner shall bear an equal percentage of the common expenses to insure and maintain the subdivision road and the common sewer system. This provision suggests an expectation that the actual use and impact of the respective lot owners would be similar. Finally, the initial deed to P & B's predecessor in title, and the subsequent deeds, state that the easement is "for all normal and usual purposes of vehicular and pedestrian ingress and egress ... to and from ... Route 100, as well as for the installation of all normal and usual utilities to serve the parcel." The burden associated with the normal and usual vehicular and pedestrian ingress and egress to a residential dwelling is far more modest than the burden associated with the operation of two busy restaurants.

P & B contends that their predecessors in title purchased the property from the developers of the subdivision for the purpose of adding to the parking for the restaurant, and that the use of the easement by P & B's predecessors in title has from the beginning always been the commercial use in place today. It is true that a year after filing the declaration of covenants, the original developer sold the three lots that make up Parcel 2 to a person who already owned and operated a restaurant on Parcel 1, and that Parcel 2 has served as a parking lot for the restaurants since that time.

We nonetheless reject P & B's argument that the easement contained in the declaration of covenants allows for a burden on the roadway easement commensurate with the operation of these restaurants. First, P & B's argument requires us to draw an inference that the original developer understood that the initial purchaser planned to use Parcel 2 as a restaurant parking lot, and that the developer believed the burden on the roadway easement associated with such use to be consistent with the declaration of covenants. There is no direct evidence on this point. Second, the transfer in question occurred more than a year after the declaration of covenants was filed, and the obligations and benefits of the covenants had attached with respect to existing lot owners. Third, and most significantly, given the trial court's findings that the disputed access to Parcel 1 was used as early as 1975, the developer could also have assumed that the initial purchaser of Parcel 2 would rely on that access for restaurant patrons parking on Parcel 2 so that the burden on subdivision roads would not be impacted by the acquisition.

For the reasons set forth above, we affirm the judgment for P & B on its nuisance claim; uphold the award of punitive damages and attorney's fees; affirm the judgment that P & B's deeded easement for access does not include access for patrons of two restaurants; and reverse the award of compensatory damages because of the lack of evidence to support the award.

Henley v. Continental Cablevision of St. Louis County, Inc.

692 S.W.2d 825 (Mo. App. 1985)

Gaertner, J. Plaintiffs, as trustees of University Park subdivision, appeal from an order dismissing their petition for failure to state a claim in an action against defendant Continental Cablevision of St. Louis County, Inc. We affirm.

The facts essential to a resolution of this matter are not in dispute. Pursuant to an indenture recorded on April 8, 1922, plaintiffs' predecessors as trustees, were expressly granted the right to construct and maintain electric, telephone and telegraphic service on or over the rear five feet of all lots in the subdivision, and to grant easements to other parties for the purposes of creating and maintaining such systems. In July, 1922 and August, 1922, respectively, the trustees conveyed an easement to Southwestern Bell Telephone Company to "construct, reconstruct, repair, operate and maintain its lines for telephone and electric light purposes" and similarly to Union Electric to "keep, operate and maintain its lines consisting of cables, manholes, wires, fixtures and appurtenances thereto." Subsequently, in 1981 and 1982, defendant exercised licenses acquired from both utilities to enter upon these easements, and erected cables, wires and conduits for the purpose of transmitting television programs.

Plaintiffs filed an action for an injunction on December 29, 1983, seeking not only to enjoin a continuing trespass and compel the removal of defendant's wires and cables, but also seeking $300,000 in damages and the reasonable value of the use of plaintiffs' property for defendant's profit based upon quantum meruit....

Both parties agree that the subject easements are easements in gross, i.e. easements which belong to the owner independently of his ownership or possession of other land, and thus lacking a dominant tenement. The dispositive issue here is whether or not these easements are exclusive and therefore apportionable by the utilities to, in this case, defendant Continental Cablevision.

We believe the very nature of the 1922 easements obtained by both utilities indicates that they were intended to be exclusive and therefore apportionable. It is well settled that where the servient owner retains the privilege of sharing the benefit conferred by the easement, it is said to be "common" or non-exclusive and therefore not subject to apportionment by the easement owner. Conversely, if the rights granted are exclusive of the servient owners' participation therein, divided utilization of the rights granted are presumptively allowable. This principle stems from the concept that one who grants to another the right to use the grantor's land in a particular manner for a specified purpose but who retains no interest in exercising a similar right himself, sustains no loss if, within the specifications expressed in the grant, the use is shared by the grantee with others. On the other hand, if the grantor intends to participate in the use or privilege granted, then his retained right may be diminished if the grantee shares his right with others. Thus, insofar as it relates to the apportionability of an easement in gross, the term "exclusive" refers to the exclusion of the owner and possessor of the servient tenement from participation in the rights granted, not to the number of different easements in and over the same land.

Here, there is no claim that plaintiffs' predecessors had at the time the easements were granted, any intention to seek authority for, or any interest whatsoever in using the five foot strips for the construction and maintenance of either an electric power system or telephone and telegraphic service. Moreover, at no time during the ensuing sixty-three years have the trustees been authorized to furnish such services by any certificate of convenience and necessity issued by the Public Service Commission pursuant to §§ 392.260 and 393.170, RSMo.1978. Accordingly, the easements granted to Southwestern Bell and Union Electric were exclusive as to the grantors thereof and therefore apportionable.

Plaintiffs also argue defendant could acquire no rights from the utilities since their easements did not mention television cables, and that the cable attachments themselves constituted an extra burden on the property. We disagree. The owner of an easement may license or authorize third persons to use its right of way for purposes not inconsistent with the principal use granted. The 1922 easements granted to Union Electric expressly provided the right of ingress and egress by Union Electric, it successors and assigns, to "add to the number of and relocate all wires, cables, conduits, manholes, adding thereto from time-to-time...." Similarly, the easement conveyed to Southwestern Bell expressly contemplated the construction and maintenance of "all poles, cables, wires, conduits, lateral pipes, anchor guys and all other fixtures and appurtenances deemed necessary at anytime by [Southwestern Bell], its successors and assigns...." It can hardly be said that the addition of a single coaxial cable to the existing poles for the purpose of transmitting television images and sound by electric impulse increases the burden on the servient tenement beyond the scope of the intended and authorized use.

The unsurprising fact that the drafters of the 1922 easements did not envision cable television does not mandate the narrow interpretation of the purposes of the conveyance of rights and privileges urged by plaintiffs. The expressed intention of the predecessors of plaintiff trustees was to obtain for the homeowners in the subdivision the benefits of electric power and telephonic communications. Scientific and technological progress over the ensuing years have added an unforeseen dimension to such contemplated benefits, the transmission by electric impulse of visual and audio communication over coaxial cable. It is an inescapable conclusion that the intention of plaintiffs' predecessors was the acquisition and continued maintenance of available means of bringing electrical power and communication into the homes of the subdivision. Clearly, it is in the public interest to use the facilities already installed for the purpose of carrying out this intention to provide the most economically feasible and least environmentally damaging vehicle for installing cable systems.

Accordingly, the judgment of the trial court dismissing plaintiffs' petition for failure to state a claim is affirmed.

Exercise 10-6(B). Lawyering Strategies & Skills

1. Addie owns a beautiful lakefront property named "LakeAcres" that is also near a spectacular mountain range. LakeAcres is used as a resort with a high end hotel where people come and play in the lake and mountains all year long. LakeAcres and the surrounding area have become a very popular tourist destination, and property values have increased enormously. Forty years ago, when the area was still rural and "undiscovered" by tourists, Addie's grandmother (who then owned LakeAcres) granted an express appurtenant easement to a neighbor, Nathan, allowing use of a half a mile stretch of a road on Lakeacres for ingress and egress so that Nathan could access his property—called TreeAcres. The easement created a link from Treeacres to a public road. Bob bought Treeacres from Nathan and has started to develop it. By the time the construction is complete, rather than the one home now on Treeacres, there will be fifty new homes. Bob is planning on using the easement to serve the homeowners in this new development and would also like to expand the width of the easement to make travel easier and safer. Addie objects. Be prepared to present arguments for and against Bob's planned used and expansion of the easement and to predict the likely outcome.
2. Assume you are a lawyer representing Post & Beam against Sunne Village. Be prepared to present arguments on behalf of your client for interpretation of the scope and meaning of the easement.
3. Assume you are a lawyer representing Sunne Village against Post & Beam. Be prepared to present arguments on behalf of your client for interpretation of the scope and meaning of the easement.
4. What would your strategies be for developing arguments if you represented the homeowners subject to the easement in *Henley*? What arguments would you make? What would you advise your client in terms of the likelihood of success?

Distinguishing Easements from Licenses and Other Property Interests

Once again, an important lawyering task that can come up is determining how to categorize a property interest. A recurring issue that is explored here is whether a property interest should be classified as an easement or something else, such as a license or a lease.

Consider parking as an example. What property right do you have to park in a lot owned by someone else? Parking could be (and often is) a license. You have seen licenses in several chapters in this text (in Chapter 6 on Landlord Tenant law and in Chapter 2 Trespass & the Right to Exclude). A license is revocable permission to access another's property. The licensee has a very limited interest in accessing the property and typically is allowed to remain or be excluded at the will of the owner. What if you have paid to park? Still, the right to park is likely to be a license—you can be excluded from the parking lot—but you may have a right to get your money back based on a breach of contract. It is possible however that a parking right is an easement. For example, if you buy an apartment that includes a parking spot (say that you paid an extra $50,000 for), you could have an easement—a permanent right to park that runs with ownership of the apartment. Another possibility is that a right to park could be a lease—consider a right to park every day for a month in exchange for a monthly fee. As you learned in Chapter 6, a lease generally includes the right to possess which is a larger property interest than an easement or a license. However, it is possible to enter into a lease for a more narrow purpose. Billboards, carts selling products at a mall and luxury boxes at a sports stadium have generated similar classification debates. The intent of the parties and the nature of the property interest drive the analysis. The next case explores these topics further.

Exercise 10-7. *Millbrook Hunt v. Smith*

Millbrook Hunt v. Smith

670 N.Y.S.2d 907 (App. Div. 1998)

The plaintiff, Millbrook Hunt, Inc. (hereinafter the Hunt), is an organization dedicated to the preservation and perpetuation of traditional fox hunting. The defendant Edgar O. Smith is the owner of a 285-acre parcel of land situated in the Town of Stanford, Dutchess County, which is subject to an agreement captioned "Lease and Easement Agreement" (hereinafter the Agreement), and which permits the Hunt to use the land for the purpose of fox hunting. The Agreement was entered into by the Hunt and Smith's predecessor in title in 1987, and was for a term of 75 years "unless terminated sooner pursuant to the terms of the Lease or pursuant to law." In 1995 Smith, who objected to hunting and who had undertaken measures to transform his property into a wildlife habitat and nature preserve, ejected members of the Hunt from his property while they were performing routine maintenance of their fox-hunting trails.

The Hunt thereafter commenced this action seeking, *inter alia*, a judgment declaring that it has an easement over Smith's property, and to permanently enjoin Smith from interfering with its use of that easement. Smith moved for summary judgment dismissing the complaint on the ground that at most the Agreement conferred a revocable license to the Hunt, which he had terminated. The Hunt cross-moved to dismiss the affirmative defenses and the counterclaims contained in Smith's answer.

The Supreme Court denied Smith's motion and granted the Hunt's cross motion, and an interlocutory judgment was entered August 20, 1996.

To determine the true character of an interest, a court must examine the nature of the right rather than the name given to it by the parties. The mere labeling of an interest as an easement does not necessarily make it an easement; it may be a license. Easements and licenses in real property are distinct in principle, though it is sometimes difficult to distinguish them. An easement implies an interest in land ordinarily created by a grant, and is permanent in nature. A license does not imply an interest in land, but is a mere personal privilege to commit some act or series of acts on the land of another without possessing any estate therein.

Here, paragraph 1 of the Agreement indicates that the Hunt leased a particular one-quarter acre parcel of land for a period of 75 years. In addition, pursuant to paragraph 6 of the Agreement, the Hunt clearly reserved an absolute right to fox hunt on the remaining parcel of land. This right was for the benefit of the Hunt and attached to it without reference to use on any particular lands. Contrary to Smith's contentions, the fact that paragraph 10 of the Agreement reserves to the grantor the "absolute right to develop his land" and the right to redirect the Hunt's trails, does not render the grant a revocable license. Although the agreement provides that the grantor may "relocate" the Hunt's improvements, or redirect their trails "in order to make such improvements to the Land," the grantor does not have the right to completely exclude the Hunt from the property. Furthermore, an essential feature of the type of easement involved herein, which distinguishes it from a license, is that the interest in the land is for some definite period. Here, the agreement specifically provides that the Hunt's right to use the parcel was for a definite period of 75 years.

It is clear that the parties sufficiently expressed their intent to reserve to the Hunt a permanent right to fox-hunt on the parcel. Thus, the Hunt has an easement in the disputed area rather than a revocable license. Smith had both actual and constructive notice of this easement prior to the date that he bought the land and is estopped from denying its existence.

Implied Easements

Up to this point you have learned about easements that are created expressly in a written document consistent with the Statute of Frauds. Next you will learn about situations when courts might recognize creation of an easement informally with no writing. These are important exceptions to the Statute of Frauds. Such easements are implied based on a number of grounds, including the presumed intent of the parties, the behavior of the parties, the situation of the properties and equity. There are four types of implied easements, depicted in the chart below. You will study the different requirements for each of them.

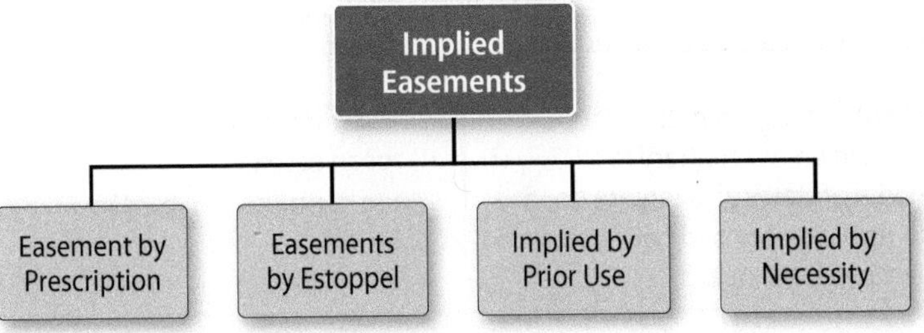

Easements by Prescription

Easements can be acquired by long-term adverse use. This is very similar to the way that title to property can be acquired through adverse possession. Both of these doctrines are studied in detail in Chapter 2 and are overviewed here more briefly. The result is the key difference between the two—a successful prescriptive easement claim confers the right to continue the use of another's property—a successful adverse possession claim confers title and the right to engage in any (lawful) use any owner might choose.

Consider this example. Adjacent neighbors Neela and Sheila do not know the true location of the boundary line dividing their properties. Neela plants a vegetable garden that she tends regularly for 15 years. At that point, Sheila has a survey done on land and discovers that Neela's garden is located across the boundary line and is situated on Sheila's property—Neela has been trespassing all this time. If Sheila brings an action for ejectment and trespass against Neela, Neela can raise the defense of adverse possession and counter-claim for "quiet title" and a declaration that she is the owner of the strip of land on which the garden sits. Alternatively, Neela could raise a defense of a prescriptive easement and rather than petitioning for ownership of the strip; she could claim she owns an easement so that she can continue to garden on Shelia's land.

To succeed, a trespasser needs to prove the elements of adverse possession or the overlapping but lesser requirements for a prescriptive easement. The table below overviews and contrasts the required elements for each claim. (The asterisks identify the elements that are different.)

Adverse Possession	Prescriptive Easement
(1) Possession Engaging in physical activities like a titled owner would ("TO")	(1) Use* Engaging in a particular and limited activity like a TO
(2) Open & Notorious Visible conduct on the land that gives notice to a reasonably diligent TO of adverse claim	(2) Same

Table continues on next page

Adverse Possession	Prescriptive Easement
(3) Adverse or Hostile (A) Without permission of the TO Presumed unless contrary facts (B) Minority of states also require good faith (mistaken) or bad faith (intentional) trespass	(3) Same Some states presume permissive use for an easement*
(4) Exclusive Possession is not shared with TO	Not required in most states*
(5) Continuous	(4) Same (generally, but check state law)
(6) For the Statutory Period Typically 10–25 years	(5) Same

Exercise 10-8. Analyzing Prescriptive Easement Claims

In the fact situations below, apply each of the required elements and determine if a prescriptive easement will succeed.

1. Aram lives in a rural area on property called DirtAcre. His neighbor, Carly, has a long paved road on her property PavedAcre that connects to a public road. For twenty years, Aram has traveled nearly every day to and from DirtAcre on a dirt road on his property and then onto the road on PavedAcre to reach a public road. He could drive an alternate route to reach a public road directly from his own property, but he prefers using the paved road because it is easier and faster. Carly recently placed a locked gate on her road to block Aram's access. Aram claims he owns an easement by prescription.
2. Here are the facts of *Zuni Tribe v Platt*, 730 F. Supp. 318 (D.C. Ariz. 1990), excerpted in Chapter 2 (Ownership and Acquisition). The Zuni Indians had been conducting a religious pilgrimage every four years for hundreds of years. The pilgrimage group consists of forty to sixty Zuni Indians and twenty to forty horses. The pilgrims walk or ride horses to travel from their reservation to a mountain with a sacred site called Kohlu/wala:wa that they believe is their place of origin, the basis for their religious life and the home of their dead. The trip is a total of 110 miles, and it takes four days for the pilgrims to travel to and return back to the reservation. If need be, the Zuni pilgrims cut or take down fences that would otherwise interfere with their customary path. The Zuni tribe asserted a right to conduct a pilgrimage across private land, including going across approximately 18-20 miles of land owned or leased by the defendant Earl Platt who objected and sought to enjoin them from coming onto his land. The Zuni tribe won. The excerpt of *Zuni* and other materials in Chapter 2 are a resource for you. Which element would you predict was the tribe's biggest obstacle?

3. A property owner lives adjacent to a golf course. For many years, golfers hit as many as five golf balls per day onto the owner's property and also come onto the property to retrieve the balls.

Easement by Estoppel

Here is an example of a case where an easement by estoppel will likely be recognized. Margo bought an undeveloped tract of land she calls HippieAcre. In order to reach her land and to build a home on it, in friendly conversation, Margo asked her neighbor Nick for permission to drive across his road on his land to access HippieAcre. Nick said, "Ok, sure." Margo has never been the type to insist on formalities so she left it at that. After about 6 months of using the road, Margo spent $3,000 to re-pave Nick's road to make travel easier. Nick noticed the paving process as it was ongoing, but never discussed it with Margo. For the next two years, Margo and her invitees continued to use Nick's road to access HippieAcre, including the construction crews who built her home. It cost Margo $200,000 to build her home. Nick then changed his mind and advised Margo that she could no longer use his road. Margo has strong claim to an easement created by estoppel.

Meaning the same thing, some courts will call this "a license made irrevocable by estoppel." Recall that a license is revocable permission to enter another's property. However, in some situations, a license is transformed into what is functionally an easement—a long term right of way or other specific use. The rationale for this is based on "equitable estoppel"—when a court concludes that given how the parties behaved, it would be unfair to do otherwise. More specifically, in assessing whether to recognize an easement by estoppel, courts will evaluate the conduct of (a) the owner of the putative servient estate and (b) the easement claimant's reliance. The claimant must demonstrate the elements below.

1. Owner Has Granted an Express or Implied License

- An owner may expressly grant acess or use rights to the easment claimant orally or in writing.
- Or, an owner may be deemed to have granted permission by inaction — by not objecting when the claimant uses the owner's property under circumstances when the owner should forsee that the claimant will rely on continued use.
- Most states do not require fraud or misprepresentation by the servient estate owner; forseeable reliance is enough.

Chart continues on next page

2. Claimant Detrimentally and Reasonably Relies on License

- Reliance (aka a change in position) usually occurs by making improvements that benefit the licensor through labor or spending money.
- Reliance might also exist when a claimant improves their own property and will be deprived of that investment if not granted an easement. (See example above.)
- Reasonableness can be debated. You could argue that reliance on an unwritten license or inaction is unreasonable or even foolish. The strongest cases are where there is clear intent to create an easement or if there is some explicit understanding. Still, even absent that, courts are empowered to exercise "equitable powers" and may well find reliance reasonable.

In the example above, these legal standards are satisfied. Nick granted Margo an oral license. He knew she was going to use the road for access and to build her home—that she would invest in reliance on continued access. Then Margo did rely on the right of way by making improvements to her own land by building her home for $200,000; by not building another road and by spending $3,000 to repave the road on the servient estate. A court could conclude this was reasonable reliance given Nick's permission and continued acquiescence to Margo's activities.

Here is another example. Neighbor Alice grants permission to neighbor Bob to use water from a well on Alice's property to supply all the water Bob needs for his home. Bob installs a pipe to carry the water from the well to his property. Alice knew of and sat by and watched the pipe installation and did not object. After construction of the pipe was complete, Alice announces she has changed her mind and revokes Bob's permission to access the water. This too presents a strong claim to an easement by estoppel. Apply the legal standards above to be sure you understand why.

Note that the rules for an easement by estoppel are consistent with the more general law of equitable estoppel that you will study in Chapter 11 on Real Estate Transactions and in other courses such as Contract law. Equitable estoppel has two core requirements 1) conduct by one party that induces 2) reasonable detrimental reliance (a change in position) by another party. You should also note that while most states recognize the doctrine—not all states do. As always, if you encounter these issues in practice, you need to be familiar with the particular law of your state.

Exercise 10-9. *Cleaver v. Cundiff*

1. As you read the next case, identify what policies are playing out. Why might it be fair and or helpful to recognize an easement by estoppel?

2. Take the time to differentiate and apply the requirements of easements by estoppel versus prescriptive easements. Sometimes claimants will assert these claims in the alternative. Think about why that might present challenges in terms of developing a cohesive strategy for litigation.
3. The last part of the case introduces you to legal protections for a "bona fide purchaser" that overlaps with the notice requirement you studied earlier for a running express easement. You will learn much more about this in Chapter 11 on Real Estate Transactions.

Cleaver v. Cundiff

203 S.W.3d 373 (2006 Tex. App.)

WRIGHT, C.J. Kenneth L. Cleaver and Cynthia Cleaver appeal from a judgment placing an easement over their land. The jury found that an easement by estoppel existed in favor of Charles Cundiff. The jury also found that the Cleavers purchased their property in good faith without knowledge of the easement. The trial court disregarded the good faith finding and entered judgment in favor of Cundiff. We affirm.

Sufficiency Standards

We will apply the following well-recognized standards to the Cleavers' challenges to the sufficiency of the evidence. In analyzing the Cleavers' no-evidence challenge, we must determine whether the evidence at trial would enable reasonable and fair-minded people to reach the verdict under review. We must review the evidence in the light most favorable to the verdict, crediting any favorable evidence if a reasonable fact-finder could and disregarding any contrary evidence unless a reasonable fact-finder could not.

Easement by Estoppel over Road 195-P

The doctrine of easement by estoppel, or estoppel *in pais,* is an exception to the statute of frauds. Under this doctrine, a landowner may be estopped from denying the existence of an easement created by "representations" upon which another has detrimentally relied. Once created, an easement by estoppel is binding upon successors in title if reliance upon the easement continues.

The supreme court has recognized that the "exact nature and extent of the doctrine ... have not been clearly defined." [Citation omitted.] Although the application of the doctrine of easement by estoppel depends upon the unique facts of each case, this equitable doctrine has been applied to circumstances such as the dedication of a street, alley, or square; a conveyance with reference to a map or plat; and expenditures by the owner of the alleged easement for improvements on the servient estate. The doctrine has also been applied to circumstances involving expenditures on the dominant estate.

In the present case, the jury was instructed that an easement by estoppel may be established by showing each of the following elements: (1) a landowner or his predecessor in interest makes a representation either by words or conduct to the adjacent landowner or his predecessor in interest that an easement exists to use the landowner's property, (2) the adjacent landowner or his predecessor in interest believes such representation to be true, and (3) the adjacent landowner or his predecessor in interest relies upon such representation. Based upon this instruction, the jury found that Cundiff had an easement by estoppel over Road 195-P from the county road across Section 172 (the Cleavers' property) to Section 171 (Cundiff's property).

The record shows that Cundiff's property is landlocked and that the only access to his property is Road 195-P from County Road 261 through Section 172 to the southern boundary of Section 171. Road 195-P was in existence when the parties acquired their respective tracts. Cundiff and his mother, now deceased, purchased Section 171 in April 2000. At that time, there were sheds, barns, a windmill, fences, and an old house on the property. Cundiff and his father spent time and money working on the house. [See map inserted below.]

Shortly after the Cleavers purchased a portion of Section 172 in August 2001, they put up a chain across the cattle guard at the intersection of Road 195–P and County Road 261 and replaced the gate between their property and Cundiff's property. At the time the Cleavers replaced the gate between the two properties, Cundiff and his father were on the Cundiff property and were locked in. Kenneth Cleaver refused to allow Cundiff's father egress through the gate and down Road 195–P, the only road out. Cundiff and his father had to drive across their rough land, take down a neighbor's fence, put the fence back, and drive through the neighbor's pasture. The Cundiffs

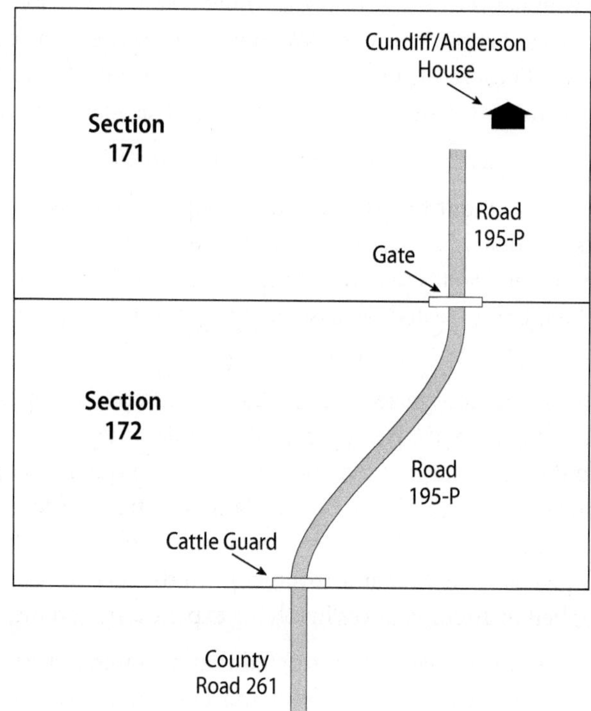

subsequently obtained temporary permission from this neighbor for ingress and egress each time they entered and left Section 171.

The Cleavers' actions clearly did not create an easement. Therefore, if one existed, it was created by Section 172's prior owners. The testimony traced Road 195-P back to the Armstrongs. Their granddaughter, Alta Jean Sawyer, testified that her grandparents were married in 1902 and built the house now located on Section 171. Sawyer testified that the road had been there for as long as she could remember and that it was the only road available to access her grandparents' house. The testimony showed that the Armstrongs maintained and bladed the road from the house down to the county road. The road was used by meter readers to read the meter at the Armstrongs' house. The Armstrongs' mailbox was at the intersection of Road 195-P and County Road 261. Sawyer lived on Section 171 and met the school bus at this intersection. Cundiff's father testified that the road served no purpose besides allowing access to the residents north of Section 172.

The Cleavers correctly argue that use alone does not create an easement by estoppel.... In this case, the evidence indicated the primary purpose of much of the road was to benefit the Armstrongs and their successors. Furthermore, the Armstrongs did not merely use the road; they maintained it. Unlike *Stallman*, there was no testimony that Section 172's owners gave anyone specific permission to use Road 195-P, which would imply the right to revoke that permission. The evidence regarding the use of Road 195-P indicates a belief that the road's use was by right.

Nothing in the record refutes this manner of use. The Cleavers purchased their land from an estate controlled by Cecil W. Brown. Brown testified that Section 172 had belonged to his family since 1927. Brown took care of the property beginning in the mid-1970s but actually went to the property only about once a year. Brown acknowledged that there were several locks on the gate between Section 171 and 172 and that he had never possessed a key to any of those locks. He testified that the road's condition had deteriorated but that in 2000 someone cut a chain over the cattle guard and cleared the road with a bulldozer. Brown put a lock in the chain, but someone knocked the post out of the cattle guard. Brown did not testify that he ever gave Cundiff permission to use the road. In fact, his testimony indicates that there was a clear difference of opinion as to Cundiff's rights.

After reviewing all of the evidence, we hold that it is both legally and factually sufficient to establish that an easement by estoppel existed over Road 195-P. From the evidence introduced, the jury could reasonably infer that Road 195-P was used from the beginning by the Armstrongs as a matter of right. The testimony does not indicate who built the road or when; however, the evidence does show that the Armstrongs had lived on Section 171 since the early 1900s, that they had used the road for as long as anyone could remember, that the road was their means of ingress and egress to the house they built on Section 171, and that they had maintained the road throughout the years. The jury could reasonably infer that the Armstrongs would not have built their house without some reliable means of access and would not have expended time and money maintaining a road over which they had no claim. The evidence regarding the conduct of the Armstrongs and the previous owners of Section 172 is sufficient to support the jury's finding that an easement by estoppel was created over Road 195-P. Because the use of Road 195-P and the reliance thereon has continued, the Cleavers are estopped to deny an easement.

Bona Fide Purchasers

The Cleavers argue that the trial court should have entered judgment in their favor based upon the jury's finding that they were good faith purchasers and that the trial court erred in disregarding that jury finding. Upon the Cleavers' specific request, the trial court included the following jury question in the jury charge: "Did Kenneth L. and Cynthia Cleaver purchase the Cleaver Property in good faith for valuable consideration and without knowledge of any outstanding claim of an easement to cross their property?" The jury answered affirmatively. The Cleavers assert that their status as good faith or bona fide purchasers precludes an easement by estoppel from being imposed against them. To be a bona fide purchaser, the purchase must be made for valuable consideration and without notice, either actual or constructive, of the adverse claim. Notice is sufficient if it would lead an ordinarily prudent man to inquire into the matter.

In this case, the road across Section 172 was obviously visible. Before purchasing the land in Section 172, Kenneth Cleaver drove around the property and down the caliche or gravel road known as Road 195-P. He observed somebody in an old, green pickup using Road 195-P to cross Section 172. He noticed that Road 195-P led to a locked gate with various locks on it and then continued on into Section 171, which belonged to someone else. The Cleavers did not contact the adjoining landowners to inquire about any rights they may have claimed to use the road. Based upon this evidence, the Cleavers could not establish that they were bona fide purchasers. Thus, the trial court did not err in disregarding the jury's answer or in refusing to enter judgment in the Cleavers' favor.

An Alternative: Constructive Trusts

It is possible to gain recognition of some rights in or against the property of another by claiming unjust enrichment and a constructive trust. As you will learn in the exercise that follows, this is an alternative claim that can be raised in circumstances that might also warrant a claim for an implied easement (or other claims).

Exercise 10-10. Developing and Evaluating Claims

A constructive trust claim was successful in *Rase v Castle Mountain Ranch, Inc.*, 631 P.2d 680 (Mont. 1981). A landowner allowed and actually encouraged non-owners to come on his land and build cabins and summer homes around his lake. After the cabins were built and used by families for decades, the landowner asked the "cabiners" to sign a license agreement for the cabins as a "formality" that would ensure the landowner continued access to the lake. Despite signed license agreements, all the parties including the landowner assumed that the cabiners would continue to have a long term right to keep the cabins around the lake and use them. When the landowner sold the property, the new owner immediately attempted to revoke the licenses and kick the cabiners off the property. The court concluded that the cabins were held in a constructive trust for the benefit of the cabiners who were entitled to continue to use the cabins for 15 more years (to recoup their investments).

What did the cabiners have to prove to succeed? A constructive trust is a remedy that is granted once unjust enrichment is proven. The claimant must prove that:

1. A benefit was conferred on the titled owner;
2. Who has knowledge of the benefit; and
3. It would be unjust under the circumstances to allow the titled owner to retain all or some of the benefits conferred.

If these legal standards are satisfied, then the court will use its equitable powers to declare the existence of a constructive trust. A trust is a vehicle for managing property, where the trustee manages the property in the trust on behalf of the beneficiaries of the trust. A constructive trust borrows from trust law and creates a legal fiction (meaning we pretend) that the titled owner is not the beneficial owner of the whole property but rather is acting like a trustee (a manager) for the benefit of the successful claimant. The result of all of this is that a court will order the titled owner to expunge (give back) the benefit to the claimant or share the benefits. Usually this means paying the claimant money, but a range of options are open to courts. In *Rase*, recognition of a constructive trust meant the owner had to allow the cabiners access to the cabins for a period of time.

1. Apply these rules to the facts in *Rase* and be prepared to argue for and against a finding of unjust enrichment/constructive trust.
2. *Rase* is also a good case for an easement by estoppel. Apply the rules to the facts to determine why. This claim apparently was not litigated in *Rase*. Recall that not all jurisdictions recognize it and a few strictly limit it.
3. Recognize that that constructive trust claims can arise in a variety of situations. For example, a constructive trust claim can arise at the break up of an unmarried couple (discussed in Chapter 4). It can arise with an improving trespasser (see Chapter 2). It is possible anytime someone invests in another's property in the absence of a formal document that clarifies the property interests. It can be used to challenge the default rule that formal title determines ownership.
4. How could the cabiners overcome the obstacle that there was a written license agreement? Recall the Parol Evidence Rule studied earlier in this chapter. When there is a document that captures the entire agreement between the

parties, the rule provides that extrinsic evidence is not permitted to contradict the terms of the document. You were introduced to an important exception to this rule in *Green v. Lupo*—when a document is ambiguous on its face. The Parol Evidence Rule is complicated and has a number of other exceptions. And it only applies to a certain set of circumstances. So the options for legal strategies on behalf of the claimants in *Rase* are to explore whether the rule is triggered at all or if the situation fits an exception. You will learn this body of law in your Contracts law course, so we do not go into the merits of these issues here

Easements Implied by Prior Use

Another easement that might be created informally without a writing is an easement implied by prior use. Suppose Peter owns a ten acre tract of land with a public road adjacent to the southern border. Peter drives back and forth on a long driveway on the south of the property to reach his home on the north part of the property. Then Peter sells the southern half of the parcel to Yolanda and nothing is said in the deed about continued use of the driveway.

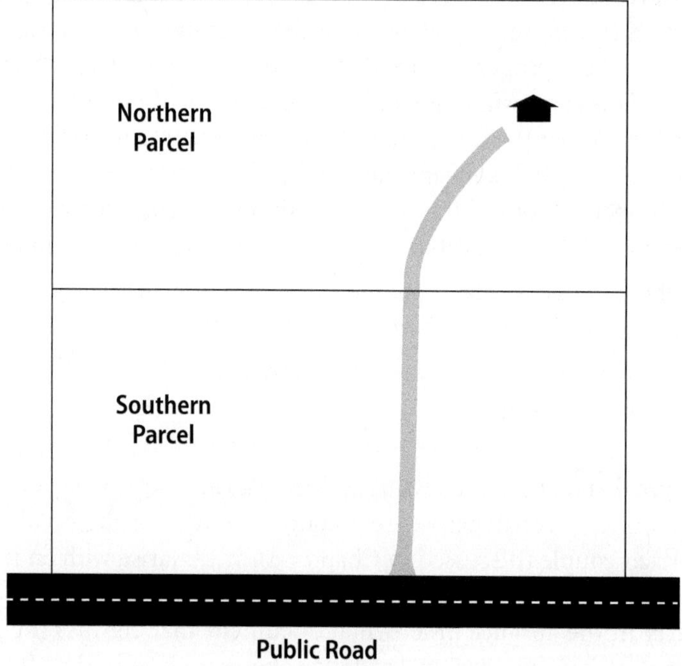

If Yolanda seeks to exclude Peter from using the driveway, Peter will nonetheless likely be entitled to use the driveway by claiming an easement implied by prior use. No doubt, the better course would have been for Peter to reserve an easement in writing at the time of the sale to Yolanda. However, even absent that, an easement can be implied if the requirements that follow are satisfied.

1. Unified Ownership Before Transfer

- Ownership of two parcels (or a large single tract of land) was vested in one person before one part was transferred to another. The facts above satisfy this.
- This is also called "common ownership."

2. Prior Use

- The owner must have used one part of the property to benefit another part in a way that is visible and continuous. In the example above, it is apparent that the road serves the northern tract.
- This use before severance is sometimes referred to as a quasi-easement. It is *as if* there was an easement. However, there can be no easement when one person owns the subject properties.

3. Reasonably Necessary Use

- This is *not* the dictionary definition of necessary you are familiar with. Instead, the term has a special meaning in this context. Courts find that a use is necessary when it is "reasonably convenient" to the dominant estate. This is a flexible concept. Easy access to a public road certainly meets the standard. Even gaining access to a lake for recreational purposes has qualified as "necessary" for an implied easment by prior use. *See Russakoff v. Scruggs*, 400 S.E.2d 529 (Va. 1991).

Cumulatively, these rules are based on an assumption that the parties to the transaction intended for the easement to be created and just did not formalize it. Are you convinced by this—is an easement probably intended in the example above? What evidence do you see to the contrary? Carefully note, however, that intent does not need to be proven and is not a specific part of the legal standards; rather, implied intent is the *basis* for the rule.

Exercise 10-11. *Thorstrom v. Thorstrom*

The next case is a helpful example that includes three distinct legal issues to work through.

1. Identify the facts that meet each element required for an easement implied by prior use, as well as any counter-facts. To do this, you will need to discern

how the different wells were used when both parcels were owned by the mother, Evelyn.

2. Why does Evelyn's writing fail to qualify as an express easement?
3. What is the scope of the easement?

Thorstrom v. Thorstrom

196 Cal. App. 4th 1406 (Cal. Ct. App. 2011)

Dondero, J. Plaintiff and intervener appeal from a judgment that granted defendants an implied easement for exclusive use of water from a well on plaintiff and intervener's property. We agree with the trial court that an implied easement exists under these facts, but further conclude that the scope of the easement granted to defendants is excessive, and reverse the judgment.

Intervener Wayne Thorstrom and defendant Alan Thorstrom are brothers. This dispute between them is focused on the right to use water from a well constructed on property owned by their mother Evelyn Sallinen, and which upon her death passed to Wayne according to trust and estate instruments.

The property owned by Evelyn before her death in February of 2003 was divided into two legal parcels situated in Fort Bragg, California: a larger parcel of 7.2 acres at 29601 Sherwood Road, on which was located the family home; and a smaller parcel of 1.37 acres at 29575 Sherwood Road, where Evelyn built a home in 1968, which she occupied with her husband Walter until her death. Wayne and his wife Arlyne have occupied the family home on the larger parcel (plaintiffs' parcel) continuously beginning in 1969. Alan moved away from the property and bought a house in Fort Bragg following his discharge from the Army in 1967. He thereafter visited his mother regularly but not frequently. After Evelyn died in 2003 Alan and his wife Linda occupied the home on the smaller parcel (defendants' parcel).

Three wells were located on Evelyn's property. A very "old hand-dug well" about 12 to 15 feet deep and pump house on plaintiffs' parcel provided good water, but would often "go dry." A well drilled on defendants' parcel in 1969 (the 1969 well) supplied Evelyn's water uses, which were exceedingly modest. Wayne and Arlyne were sometimes forced to use Evelyn's 1969 well for their source of water when their old well was dry. According to Wayne, he inspected the 1969 well pump regularly; it continued to function properly to provide Evelyn with water until her death.

In 1980, Evelyn paid for a larger well and pump placed on plaintiffs' parcel (the 1980 well), so they "would have water all the time." The housing for the 1980 well and "all the electronics" that controlled the well and pump remained on defendants' parcel, then occupied by Evelyn and Walter, to avoid additional costs associated with installation of entirely new equipment. A "faucet on the 1980 well" was connected by

Wayne to an underground hose that ran to the old well, and from there to the plumbing for plaintiffs' house. The electrical system located at Evelyn's house was used to activate the faucet and underground line to pump water from the 1980 well to the old well. No lines or pipes connected the 1980 well to the 1969 well or to defendants' parcel. After the 1980 well was installed, Evelyn continued to use the 1969 well for her water needs. Wayne and Arlyne testified that before Evelyn's death the 1980 well was exclusively used to serve plaintiffs' parcel. Evelyn told Arlyne that both the old well and the 1980 well "belonged" to plaintiffs, and the 1969 well on defendants' parcel was "Alan's well."

On September 11, 1997, Evelyn created a revocable living trust (the Trust) into which the two parcels of property were transferred. According to the Trust provisions Wayne was granted plaintiffs' 7.2–acre parcel; Alan received defendants' 1.37–acre parcel.

A will executed by Evelyn on April 9, 2000, (the Will) provided for distribution of her real property in essentially the same terms as specified in the Trust. Wayne was appointed as executor of Evelyn's estate, with Alan named as successor executor.

Evelyn also signed a rather curious handwritten document entitled "Minutes Evelyn V. Sallinen Personal Trust" (Minutes), dated "Feb 21–20001" [sic], which referred to well numbers one and two, and stated that the "water well" located on plaintiffs' parcel "shall be used for emergency purposes in the case of drought or pump break down for the home " at 29601 Sherwood Road. In the Minutes Evelyn also devised her car to Wayne and her wedding ring to Arlyne.

After Evelyn's death in February of 2003, her estate was administered through the Trust. Plaintiffs and defendants received the deeds to their respective parcels. Defendants began to occupy the house on their parcel two weeks after Evelyn's death, and, pursuant to the Trust provisions executed the required roadway and public utility easements. Arlyne testified that defendants planted various gardens, numerous trees, and a lawn on their parcel that did not exist while Evelyn was alive. To water the gardens and wash their vehicles defendants had "water going at all times."

Without plaintiffs' permission, Alan removed the faucet on the 1980 well that served plaintiffs' parcel. And over plaintiffs' objection, in 2005 defendants employed plumber David Hautala to construct a 2,500–gallon water storage tank on defendants' parcel. Defendants diverted essentially all of the water from the 1980 well to the new storage tank for use on their parcel.

Plaintiffs thereafter received only a minute and entirely inadequate quantity of "orange and really dirty" water from the 1980 well for use on their parcel. On several occasions plaintiffs attempted to have plumbers determine the reason they "weren't getting any water" from the 1980 well, but, despite a restraining order against him obtained by plaintiffs, Alan harassed and threatened plaintiffs' workers until they left. Arlyne further testified that Alan harassed her through threatening telephone calls in which he swore and screamed at her, and on one occasion by blocking a road on the property.

The Lack of Any Express Easement in Favor of Defendants.

A rather obvious premise surfaces from the facts presented here: the 1980 well is not on defendants' property; they have no right to use of the water from it absent some form of easement granting them access to the well water that originates on plaintiffs' parcel. An equally obvious second premise follows from the first: in her Trust documents and Will Evelyn distributed the 5.2–acre parcel on which the 1980 well is located to plaintiffs without granting defendants any form of express grant or reservation of an easement to use the well water from plaintiffs' parcel.

The Minutes document signed by Evelyn does not expressly grant defendants an easement to water from the 1980 well. The Minutes also fails to qualify as any form of grant deed or reservation of rights to water for the benefit of defendants' parcel. It is not notarized; it is not attested by witnesses; it does not purport to grant defendants any rights at all. Neither defendants nor their parcel is mentioned in the Minutes. At most, the Minutes is an indication of Evelyn's intent, ambiguous as it was, but clearly it neither grants defendants the right to do any acts on plaintiffs' parcel nor entitles them to the water from the 1980 well.

The Trial Court's Finding That Defendants Are Entitled to an Implied Water-Use Easement.

We move to an examination of the seminal finding by the trial court that defendants have an implied "easement for the continued and unrestricted use of water" from the 1980 well, to the exclusion of any use by plaintiffs other than for "emergency purposes." Again, we accord deference to the finding of an implied easement by the trial court, which must be upheld if supported by substantial evidence.

An "easement will be implied when, at the time of conveyance of property, the following conditions exist: 1) the owner of property conveys or transfers a portion of that property to another; 2) the owner's prior existing use of the property was of a nature that the parties must have intended or believed that the use would continue; meaning that the existing use must either have been known to the grantor and the grantee, or have been so obviously and apparently permanent that the parties should have known of the use; and 3) the easement is reasonably necessary to the use and benefit of the quasi-dominant tenement. (Citation omitted.) 'The purpose of the doctrine of implied easements is to give effect to the actual intent of the parties as shown by all the facts and circumstances.' (Citation omitted.) An easement by implication will not be found absent clear evidence that it was intended by the parties." (Citation omitted.)

Although the evidence of an implied easement in favor of defendants is again conflicting, we find that it is at least substantial. Evelyn divided her property and transferred the smaller parcel to defendants. The only source of water located on defendants' parcel was the 1969 well, which was restricted in output and, according to Alan and the expert testimony of Hautala, in disrepair or marginally functional during Evelyn's lifetime. The water pipes and electrical system associated with the 1980 well were placed on defendants' parcel, which also suggests that defendants are entitled to at least a reasonable-use easement. The evidence indicates that Evelyn constructed the 1980 well for plaintiffs' use, and thereafter made extremely limited use of the well for her own purposes. Still, we do not think Evelyn intended to transfer defendants' parcel to them without also granting them any access to the water from the 1980 well, or to make them dependent on the limited and unreliable water from the antiquated 1969 well.

Finally, defendants established that the easement is reasonably necessary for the use and benefit of their quasi-dominant tenement. The requirement that the easement must be " 'reasonably necessary to the beneficial enjoyment' of the property conveyed means no more than 'for the benefit thereof,' " and defendants were not required to prove that the easement as it existed was a strict necessity or "the only possible way" of obtaining water for their parcel. The only existing source of water located on defendants' parcel, the 1969 well, is no longer operational, so the 1980 well is vital for the supply of water to the property.

The Nature and Scope of the Implied Water-Use Easement.

We proceed to an inquiry into the appropriate extent of the implied easement. Plaintiffs claim that the trial court erred by granting defendants unrestricted use of water from the 1980 well, and relegating their water rights to specified emergency purposes. We agree with plaintiffs that no credible evidence in the record establishes an implied easement of the pervasive nature and scope granted to defendants by the trial court.

Intent is the fundamental criterion for determining the extent of a servitude. " 'Accordingly, in determining the intent of the parties as to the extent of the grantee's rights ... consideration must be given not only to the actual uses being made at the time of the severance, but also to such uses as the facts and circumstances show were within the reasonable contemplation of the parties at the time of the conveyance.' " (Citation omitted.) A correlated principle is that the use of an easement, whether created by express grant, implication, or prescription, cannot be altered to impose an unreasonable or unintended burden on the servient tenement.

We do not find, however, that defendants are restricted to the minimal historic use of the 1980 well—that is to say, the markedly austere water consumption apparently made by Evelyn during her lifetime. We perceive that Evelyn, by transferring defendants' parcel to Alan upon her death, contemplated that her minimal use of the water would be increased to reflect defendants' reasonable needs after they took possession of the property. We therefore conclude that under the facts presented plaintiffs and defendants are both entitled to reasonable residential use of the water from the 1980 well. Neither party may make excessive use of the water which unnecessarily impedes the rights of the other.

Easements Implied by Necessity

Imagine a developer owns a large tract of land that she subdivides into several parcels. You buy one of these parcels, an interior lot completely surrounded by lots owned by other people (your neighbors). The only way for you to get on and off your property is to travel across someone else's property. We refer to the parcel as "landlocked" and "surrounded by lands of strangers," because there is no direct access to a public road. At the time of the sale to you, the developer still owns a lot in the subdivision adjacent to yours. As illustrated below, in a situation like this, a court will recognize an easement implied by necessity.

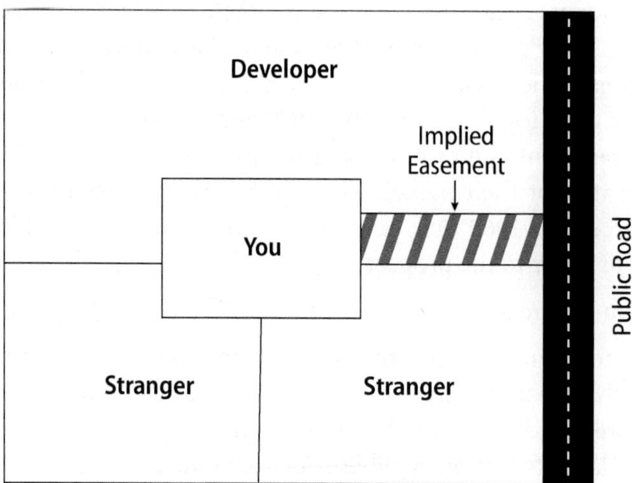

There are two elements required to make out a claim for an easement by necessity.

1. Common Ownership Before Severance

- Ownership of a large single tract of land (or two parcels) was vested in one person before a transfer out (called a severance).

2. Necessity

- At the time of severance, the property became landlocked; and
- An easement is necessary to reach a road allowing effective use of the property.

Notice that there are a couple of important differences in the requirements for an easement by necessity compared to an easement implied by prior use. First, there is no requirement of prior use of the parcel while under common ownership. Second, the definition of necessity is much stricter and more difficult to satisfy. Necessity exists only if there woud be *no effective use* of the property without an easement. In contrast, for an easement implied by prior use, necessity requres that having an easement would be "reasonably convenient." The policies underpinning the rules overlap—the doctrine assumes the parties intended to create an easement and enable access to otherwise landlocked property. This presumption arises from the circumstances. Who would buy property with no way of ingress or egress? An easement by necessity also facilitates beneficial use of land, and that is thought to contribute to societal welfare.

Exercise 10-12. *Burnham v. Kwentus*

1. Evaluate whether the requirement for a common owner is satisfied.
2. Is the definition of necessity satisfied here?
3. *Burnham* is a helpful case for putting together and thinking through all the implied easement laws you have studied so far. Consider each of the four kinds of implied easements. Which of them could be viably claimed? Which cannot be? Why?
4. As you read, determine when an easement by necessity is created and how long it lasts.

Burnham v. Kwentus

174 So. 3d 286 (Miss. Ct. App. 2015)

MAXWELL, J. For more than fifty years, Chester Burnham had crossed his neighbor's property along Ridge Road, a private road that ran from a public road to Burnham's landlocked property. Burnham's neighbor testified this access was granted out of neighborly courtesy. His family knew Burnham used the road and "in the kindness of their heart" allowed Burnham "to go through their property without question." But when Burnham's neighbor sold the family property in 2008, Burnham's new neighbors, Joseph Kwentus and Karen Richardson (collectively, Kwentus), told Burnham to stop using Ridge Road. They instead instructed him to use a newer and—in Burnham's eyes—less-passable road. Burnham sued Kwentus, claiming he owned a prescriptive easement across Ridge Road. The chancellor disagreed. And Burnham now appeals the denial of this claim.

Mississippi's property laws are clear that, if use is based on permission, express or implied, no matter how long, it can never ripen into the hostile use required for a prescriptive easement. Key to a prescriptive easement is use that is adverse to the rights of the servient-estate owner. And here the chancellor found Burnham's use of Ridge Road was not adverse but rather due to the kindness of his neighbor. Thus, we affirm the first part of her judgment, which denied Burnham's claim to a prescriptive easement.

But Burnham is not left without access to his landlocked property. The chancellor granted Burnham's alternative claim that he had an easement by necessity. This easement arose in 1937, when the bank that owned both Kwentus's property and an undivided interest in Burnham's property sold off its interest in Burnham's landlocked property. In this situation, the law assumes the common owner impliedly granted a right-of-way across its property, so the purchaser could have the needed access to his property. This type of easement is appurtenant, traveling with the land as long as the necessity still exists. Because the chancellor found Burnham was in the same need of access as his predecessors in title, we also affirm the second part of the chancellor's judgment, which granted Burnham an easement by necessity across the newer road until it connects to Ridge Road.

Background Facts

In 1937, the property that is now Kwentus's was owned by Capitol National Bank (Capitol). Capitol also owned an undivided one-third interest in the property that is now Burnham's. Capitol conveyed this one-third interest to Robert F. Young. At the time of Capitol's conveyance to Young, Burnham's property became landlocked. While Capitol had been able to access its interest in the Burnham tract because it owned the adjoining property, Young would have had to cross over Capitol's property to reach a public road. One of Young's successors in interest also acquired the remaining undivided interest in the property. So when Burnham purchased the property in 1952, he purchased the entire interest.

Following his purchase, Burnham began using Ridge Road across his neighbor's property, as it was the only way to get to his land. He used the road to access his land to hunt. And he directed his friends and hunting lessees to do the same. Burnham also used Ridge Road when harvesting timber from his property.

Burnham testified that, in the fifty-six years they were adjoining landowners, he never discussed his use of Ridge Road with his neighbor, Dr. Carl Brannan. According to Dr. Brannan, who inherited the neighboring property from his father in 1960, he and his father had known from the beginning about Burnham's use of Ridge Road. And they had "never questioned" it. Specifically, Dr. Brannan knew Burnham and those Burnham allowed to hunt on his land often parked along Ridge Road, right in front of Dr. Brannan's tenant's house. But to prevent any potential harassment of his tenant, Dr. Brannan decided not to object or ask them to stop. He instead allowed the situation to persist. While never giving Burnham "face-to-face" permission, Dr. Brannan testified he "thought [they] were being pretty gracious in the kindness of our heart to allow him to go through our property without any question about it."

Dr. Brannan sold his property to Kwentus in 2008. Sometime after, Burnham learned Kwentus had approached Burnham's hunting lessee and told him he needed to sign for permission to cross Kwentus's property. Burnham responded by filing an affidavit of adverse possession of an easement across Ridge Road. Kwentus did not outright block Burnham's access to his property, but he did ask Burnham to use a newer, less-intrusive road. Unable to work things out, Burnham sued Kwentus, claiming a prescriptive easement or, alternatively, an easement by necessity across Ridge Road.

Easement by Necessity

We begin with Kwentus's cross-appeal. He challenges the part of the chancellor's judgment granting Burnham an easement by way of necessity from the newer road over to Ridge Road. He claims the chancellor erred in concluding Burnham met the most fundamental requirement of an easement by necessity—that the necessity arose when a common owner severed a tract of land, leaving one parcel landlocked. He insists the common-owner requirement was not met because, when Burnham's property was sold, the common owner had only a one-third interest in Burnham's tract. So as Kwentus sees it, the two properties did not have a common owner. His property was owned by Capitol, he asserts, while Burnham's property was owned by Capitol and another owner.

We grant that this is not a typical easement-by-necessity case where one large tract of land is severed into smaller lots. But we do find the facts established before the chancellor support her finding of an easement by necessity.

An "easement by necessity" and an "implied easement" are the same. For more than a century, it has been "well-settled law that … when one sells interior lands surrounded in part by the other lands of the seller and in part by the lands of strangers, [an] implied grant of a way to the interior land exists over the exterior lands of the seller." *Pleas v. Thomas*, 75 Miss. 495, 500, 22 So. 820, 821 (1897). "The reasons need not be sought afar, for they are obvious at a glance." *Id.* These obvious reasons are:

> (1) The owner of the interior land could neither reach nor use his land, unless a way to it existed, or was capable of being brought into existence, the right to use, occupy, and enjoy being essential to impart value to the land; and
>
> (2) this essential right is to be sought in the grant of the seller of the interior lot, and the buyer is not to be driven to seek to acquire a way over the lands of other adjoining owners … [or] by costly and vexatious proceedings[.]

Id.

This well-settled law applies here. Capitol sold its undivided interest in an interior parcel of land that was surrounded in part by Capitol's land. When this happened, an implied grant of a right-of-way arose over Capitol's land. Young, who could not enjoy his undivided interest in the landlocked property without access, did not have to seek access over any other neighbor's property or institute any legal proceeding. Instead, the implication was that Capitol would not sell Young its interest in the landlocked property without impliedly permitting Young to cross over Capitol's property.

Further, the fact that a Young successor ended up owning not just Young's one-third interest but the entire parcel does not change this implied right. The implied easement Young was granted "is appurtenant to the dominant parcel" (i.e., the purchased landlocked property) "and travels with the land, so long as the necessity exists." *Fike v. Shelton*, 860 So.2d 1227, 1230 (Miss. Ct. App. 2003). The evidence showed Burnham is the successor to Young's interest in the landlocked property. Thus, Young's implied grant of a right-of-way traveled with Young's interest, so long as the same necessity for access continued. See *id.* The chancellor found the same necessity that arose in 1937 still exists more than three-quarters of a century later. So Burnham has an implied easement across Kwentus's property.

Exercise 10-13. *Burnham* Revisited & Applications of Implied Easements

1. Create a flow chart of the four implied easements with the requirements for each. Compare and contrast the requirements. Use this as tool to help you assess which claims are viable in *Burnham.*
2. What would the legal outcome be if a public road was built 10 years after an easement implied by necessity was created so that the land was no longer landlocked?
3. Florence owns 1000 acres of property surrounded on two sides by the ocean bay. She transferred out 100 acres to a non-profit organization which turned the land into a wildlife preserve. At the point of severance, the only way to access a public road from Florence's remaining 900-acre property was to travel across the wildlife preserve. Florence used a dirt road across the wildlife preserve for this purpose. A few years later, the non-profit organization sought to block Florence's access to the road. She claims an easement by necessity. The non-profit argues that the easement is not "necessary" because the 900 acre parcel can be reached by boat from a public boat access point a few miles away. Although it is true that the waters are navigable, neither Florence nor anyone who owned the property before her has ever accessed the property by boat. Evaluate the case and predict if an easement by necessity will be granted. For a similar case, see *Berge v. State of Vermont*, 915 A.2d 189 (2006) (finding an easement by necessity).

Beach Access & The Public Trust Doctrine

This topic is addressed in Chapter 3 Trespass and the Right to Exclude.

Limitations on Negative Easements

The easements you have studied so far have all been affirmative easements that entitle the holder the right to do something on another person's land—such as a right of way or to lay utility lines. If the goal is to restrict the way land is used, then generally, a real covenant or equitable servitude is the method for doing so. That body of law is studied later in this chapter. Easements typically are *not* used to create negative obligations. Instead, as a result of history, only a few negative easements have traditionally been recognized, and a few others have been added in modern times. Negative easements prevent an owner from engaging in certain activities on his or her own land as explained below. The first four in the list below are the traditional ones and the last three are those that have been recognized more recently.

1. **Lateral Support.** An owner cannot undermine lateral support of a neighbor's structure such as a building or wall.

2. **Water flow.** An owner cannot interfere with the flow of water in an artificial (human made) stream or canal.

3. **Blocking Air.** An owner cannot construct structures that interfere with well-defined flows of air.

4. **Blocking Light Through Windows.** An owner cannot construct structures that block light flowing through a neighbor's windows. Note that this is an exception to the general rule that there is no default right of access to sunlight across your neighbor's property.

5. **Solar Energy.** Depending on the state and statutes in place, an owner may be prohibited from constructing improvements or growing vegetation that interferes with a neighbor's access to sunlight used to supply solar energy.

6. **Conservation.** This is a common easement that is authorized by legislation in most states. These conserve land to help protect the environment by restricting development and use of the land. Usually an owner retains the land but gives away some development or use rights in the property to the government or a charitable organization who then owns the benefit of the easement. These often are set up to last in perpetuity. For example, an owner of undeveloped woodlands might give the land to a nature preservation organization and restrict the use only for hiking and enjoying the natural environment and that the land cannot be developed. There are also agricultural easements that restrict the use of the land to farming only.

7. **Historic Preservation.** Also frequently regulated by statutes, these easements prevent destruction or changes to properties that have historical importance.

Notice that negative easements function like a covenant in that they restrict the way a property can be used. However, because they are categorized as easements, the law of easements generally (or the law of a particular statute) governs their creation, interpretation and termination.

Termination

Easements can be terminated a number of different ways.

1. **Release.** An easement is terminated if the easement holder releases the easement in a writing that satisfies the Statute of Frauds.

2. **Express Terms.** Easements typically last forever, but some easements are set up to exist only for a finite term. You have already seen an example of this in *Millbrook Hunt* where the easement was for 75 years. At the end of the term, the easement terminates.

3. **Merger.** Suppose Blackacre and Whiteacre are adjacent properties and Blackacre is the servient estate. If the owner of Whiteacre purchases Blackacre, then the easement terminates by merger because the same person owns both the dominant and servient estate. It is not possible to have an easement on your own property. Note that if Blackacre is later sold again, an easement will *not* automatically be

recreated at that point. Once an easement is terminated, it remains so. Of course, a *new* easement could be created expressly or by implication. A reminder—as is explained in Chapter 5 Estates in Land—a merger similarly occurs when a present possessory estate and a future interest become owned by the same person. The estates are merged into a fee simple absolute.

4. **Abandonment.** An easement will terminate if it is abandoned by the owner of the benefit. The question is whether the easement owner intended to relinquish the interest. Abandonment can be express or implied by behavior. However, the fact that an easement holder is no longer using an easement is generally not enough alone to demonstrate abandonment. Some additional evidence of relinquishment is required beyond mere *non-use*. You will see these rules applied in our next case.

5. **Estoppel.** As you learned earlier in this chapter, there are two components to estoppel: 1) has the easement holder acted (or failed to act) in a way that 2) the servient owner relied on to their detriment? Imagine a driveway easement exists and later the dominant estate holder installs a new driveway on her own property. She advises the servient estate holder that she does not intend to use the old driveway anymore. Relying on that, the servient estate holder installs a garage on the driveway that blocks off access to the dominant estate. The easement owner will be estopped from making a claim of continued access to the old driveway.

6. **Prescription.** Suppose the owner of the servient estate installs a locked gate that blocks off access to the dominant estate holder for 30 years. The same rules apply for termination of an easement by prescription as for creating one—trespassing on the rights of the easement holder in a way that is open and notorious, hostile and continuous for the statutory period will extinguish the easement.

7. **Frustration of Purpose.** What if the circumstances change and the purpose of an easement can no longer be accomplished? Imagine an easement grants a neighbor access to water from a well—but the well permanently goes dry. In such a situation, some courts will declare the easement terminated based on frustration of purpose. As you will see, there is a similar doctrine applicable to covenants that allows for termination if conditions have changed dramatically such that there is no longer a *substantial* benefit from enforcement. The Restatement Third of Property takes the position that the changed conditions doctrine should become a single unified standard that applies to both easements and covenants. The Restatement also proposes that in such cases, easements and covenants can be modified rather than terminated if appropriate. However, these proposals are controversial and are *not* the current law in most states. The traditional view still holds—covenants can be terminated based on changed circumstances but *easements cannot* be. If a state does recognize the frustration of purpose doctrine for easements, be aware that the standard is difficult to satisfy.

Exercise 10-14. *Moody v. Allegheny Valley Land Trust*

The next case focuses on two legal issues—abandonment and scope in the context of converting rails into trails. As you read, develop legal arguments in favor of the railroad and those in favor of the owners of the servient estate.

Moody v. Allegheny Valley Land Trust

976 A.2d 484 (Pa. 2009)

GREENSPAN J. In this appeal, we hold that as long as the requirements of Section 1247(d) of the National Trails System Act are met, a railroad right-of-way is "railbanked" regardless of whether the rail operator agrees to resuscitate service. Accordingly, we affirm the Superior Court's decision below.

Railbanking is the preservation of an easement that was previously used as a rail thoroughfare by allowing interim trail use on the right-of-way, subject to revitalization of rail service at a later date, consistent with the requirements of Section 1247(d) of the National Trails System Act, 16 U.S.C. §§ 1241–1251 ("National Act").

The right-of-way, or easement, at issue here is a section of former railroad track in Armstrong County, Pennsylvania. Appellants are landowners of the servient estates. Conrail, the former holder of the contested right-of-way, obtained permission from the Interstate Commerce Commission (ICC) (now the Surface Transportation Board (STB)) to abandon rail service on the right-of-way. After receiving permission to abandon service, Conrail entered into an agreement with Appellee Armstrong County Conservancy (the Conservancy) to convey the right-of-way to an organization nominated by the Conservancy. The Conservancy nominated a rails-to-trails organization, the Allegheny Valley Land Trust (the AVLT), to receive the right-of-way. In early 1992, Conrail conveyed the right-of-way to the AVLT by quitclaim deed; the AVLT appended a Declaration of Railbanking to the quitclaim deed upon recording it. Conrail turned over responsibility for maintenance of road crossings and bridges on the right-of-way to the AVLT, the Conservancy, and Armstrong County.

In 1995, Appellants filed a complaint against Conrail and Appellees the AVLT, the Conservancy, Armstrong Rails to Trails Association, and the officers of these organizations. Appellants sought to enjoin alleged trespasses and to obtain a declaratory judgment that Conrail had abandoned the right-of-way and therefore their property was no longer subject to an easement. The Armstrong County Court of Common Pleas found that the right-of-way had been abandoned and that the servient estates were therefore no longer subject to an easement. On appeal, the Superior Court reversed, holding that evidence of cessation of rail service coinciding with transfer of the right-of-way to a "rails-to-trails" organization cannot support a determination that the property was abandoned to Appellants under state law.

We granted Appellant's petition for allowance of appeal to address: 1) whether the Superior Court erred in a) reversing the trial judge's determination that Conrail, as a matter of law, intended to abandon the easement without railbanking; and b) holding that sale of a former railroad easement to a private trail sponsor results in a railbanking and that trail use constituted continued rail use under Pennsylvania law; and 2) whether the Superior Court's holding in favor of the Appellees resulted in an unconstitutional taking of Appellants' property. The questions presented are questions of law and this Court's scope of review is therefore plenary.

With regard to abandonment of such easements, this Court has stated:

> In evaluating whether the user abandoned the property, the court must consider whether there was an intention to abandon the property interest, together with external acts by which such intention is carried into effect. In order to establish the abandonment of a right-of-way, the evidence must show that the easement holder intended to give up its right to use the easement permanently. "Such conduct must consist of some *affirmative act* on his part which renders use of the easement impossible, or of some *physical obstruction* of it by him in a manner that is inconsistent with its further enjoyment." (Citation omitted.) Mere nonuse by the railroad does not amount to abandonment.

Buffalo Township v. Jones, 571 Pa. 637, 813 A.2d 659, 664–65 (2002).

The agreement between Conrail and the AVLT provides that Conrail can provide rail service in the future. In addition, the AVLT appended a Declaration of Railbanking to the deed. With this Declaration the AVLT confirmed that it would preserve the right-of-way for future rail use while allowing interim trail use, consistent with Section 1247(d) of the National Act, which provides:

> in the case of interim use of any established railroad rights-of-way pursuant to donation, transfer, lease, sale, or otherwise in a manner consistent with [the National Act], if such interim use is subject to restoration or reconstruction for railroad purposes, such interim use shall not be treated, for purposes of any law or rule of law, as an abandonment of the use of such rights-of-way for railroad purposes.

16 U.S.C. § 1247.

Viewing the transactions in the instant case in their entirety, we hold that Conrail's sale of the right-of-way to a qualified railbanking organization like AVLT, that filed a Declaration of Railbanking at the time the deed was recorded, did not result in abandonment of the right-of-way. Conrail owned a right-of-way; it sold that right of way to an organization that a) planned to use it as a right-of-way and b) planned to hold it subject to revitalization of rail lines in accordance with the requirements of Section 1247(d) of the National Act and consistent with the railbanking requirements established in *Buffalo Township*, 813 A.2d at 670.

Pennsylvania Department of Conservation and Natural Resources, Pennsylvania Department of Transportation, and Rails-to-Trails Conservancy each emphasize the strong policy reasons supporting recognition and enforcement of railbanking. They point to the legislative concerns underlying both the National Act and the Pennsylvania's Rails to Trails Act, 32 P.S. §§5611–5622 (the State Act), which authorizes Pennsylvania's Department of Environmental Resources to develop rail-trails, and also authorizes counties and municipalities to accept title to railroad rights-of-way by quitclaim or warranty deed. Both the National and State Acts "display a strong legislative policy encouraging the preservation of railroad rights-of-way by using existing rights-of-way for interim recreational trail use." *Buffalo Township,* 813 A.2d at 667. *Amici* point out that rail transport is extremely efficient and is currently undergoing its largest development boom in more than a century. Revitalization of rail lines may well be essential to revitalizing the nation's economy in the coming years. The legislative intent of the National and State Acts expresses an interest in preserving railroad easements even where rail service is no longer active, and Section 1247(d) of the National Act places appropriate conditions on when preservation of such easements can be effective.

Appellants nonetheless argue that, by recognizing a railbanked right-of-way here, the Superior Court effected a taking of their property for which they are owed just compensation in accordance with the Takings Clause of the Fifth Amendment to the United States Constitution, and the Eminent Domain Clause of the Pennsylvania Constitution. While the United States Supreme Court has determined that it is possible for a railbanking to result in a taking, *see Preseault v. ICC,* 494 U.S. 1 (1990), the Court nonetheless upheld the National Act and stated that when determining the breadth of an easement, courts should look to state law, as "[s]tate law generally governs the disposition of reversionary interests." *Id.* In determining whether a railbanking had effected a taking in light of the United States Supreme Court's earlier decision, the Federal Circuit looked first to whether the rail operator's interest was fee simple or an easement; second, to whether the easements' terms were "limited to use for railroad purposes, or did they include future use as public recreational trails"; and third, to whether the easements had been extinguished by abandonment. *Preseault v. United States,* 100 F.3d 1525, 1533 (Fed.Cir.1996) (applying Vermont state law to hold that a particular railroad easement was not broad enough to allow subsequent trail use).

The plain language of the deed's *habendum* clause refers to the right-of-way over Appellants' land as a "Road." It is this property interest in the "Road" that Conrail conveyed to the AVLT. A road is "[a]n open, generally public way for the passage of vehicles, people, and animals," "[t]he surface of a road; a roadbed," "[a] course or path," or "a railroad." By the plain language of the deed's *habendum* clause, there is no reason to confine our understanding of the easement grant as allowing rail service, but not preservation for future rail service. Fundamentally, the deed and its *habendum* clause create an easement to allow travel through the servient estates. Subsequent holders of the easement may not transgress its boundaries, but they do not transgress the use for which it was granted when they use it for hiking and biking. Interim trail use is consistent with the terms of the easement grant.

It is also important to emphasize that simply characterizing the right-of-way in question as a "railroad right-of-way" does not so limit it, no more than characterizing a right-of-way as a driveway limits the owner of such a thing to driving on it, rather than walking or biking on it. Here, the trail is and must be maintained in rail-ready condition, and must be relinquished for rail service should the need arise. The current owners of the servient estates purchased those estates long after the easement had been granted to Conrail's predecessor railroad, and the amounts the owners paid surely reflected that fact. To limit the right-of-way's terms strictly because of the burden placed on the servient estate would needlessly degrade the easement.

The property rights of the Appellants have in no way been changed by this railbanking. No taking has occurred.

SAYLOR, J. Concurring & Dissenting. Contrary to the majority's perspective, I believe there are abundant reasons to conclude that the relevant rights-of-way were railroad rights-of-way, beginning with the identity of the parties in interest—namely, Conrail's predecessor, Allegheny Valley Rail Road Company, and landowners who were being asked to host a right-of-way for the construction of a railroad.

It is also very clear that Conrail intended to unconditionally divest itself of its own property interest in the subject rights-of-way under governing state law, and thus, to terminate the use of "said Road." Conrail obtained federal and state authorization to unconditionally abandon the rail corridor. Consistent with this authorization, it sold all of its interests by quitclaim deed; subsequently, the tracks and associated railroad equipment were dismantled and removed. In answers to requests for admissions, Conrail admitted to consummating "abandonment," according to its own understanding of the term.

The vehicle of preserving potential future rail use via indefinite, interim trail use simply did not exist at Pennsylvania common law; that is the reason for the relevant federal and state enactments. While I am sympathetic to the highly valuable efforts of Appellees to preserve our public resources, I am also cognizant of the protected interests of landowners who are faced with a substantially changed use of their land as a public recreation facility.

I have no doubt that most hikers are responsible people committed to the preservation of the environment and respect for the property of others. Nevertheless, it would be unfair to presume that all trail users are responsible and landowners will never encounter difficulties with the few who are not. I also do not support the idea that the terms of the railroad rights-of-way at issue here are broad enough to impose on Appellants such burdens as are inherent in the operation of a public recreational trail which, by its nature, invites a diverse population of visitors onto the property.

Covenants

Could your neighbors make you park in your garage instead of your driveway? Might you have control over what color your neighbor chooses to paint the outside of her house? The answer could well be yes—if there is a covenant—a land use restriction that attaches to your land and your neighbor's land that was created in accordance with the law. A covenant is a promise that becomes part of the package of property rights and runs with the land to successor owners. Unlike an easement where the holder has a right to do something specific on another's property, a covenant restricts the way a landowner uses his or her own property or creates an affirmative obligation such as paying a homeowner's association fee. Such obligations or "burdens" can be enforced by a neighbor who owns land to which the benefit attaches. Covenants allow for private land use planning and enforcement and have become quite popular.

Exercise 10-15. Document Review—Sample Covenant

To gain more exposure to covenants and how specifically they can direct an owner's behavior, carefully review the sample covenants below.

A. Owner shall be responsible for landscaping his or her Lot with trees, plant materials, ground cover, decorative rocks and/or other walkways or hardscapes to be in conformity and harmony with the external design of the Residences and the general plan established by this Declaration for the Property. All landscape plans submitted by each Owner must provide that all water drainage from downspouts shall be transported to the street through a satisfactory water collection system. Every Owner shall not later than ninety (90) days after conveyance of the Lot to Owner prepare and submit to the Architectural Committee, a landscape plan for the Lot (unless such deadline is extended). Every Owner shall landscape the front, back and side yard areas within his or her Lot in accordance with the landscape plans approved by the Architectural Committee. Every Owner shall maintain the landscaping on his or her Lot in a sightly and well-kept condition including, but not limited to, keeping the landscaping free of all weeds, trash or other debris and regularly mowing all lawns. *Fudge v. One Ford Road Community Association*, 2010 WL 2725242 (Cal. Ct. App.)

B. Commercial Use Prohibited. No part of properties shall ever be used or cause to be used or allowed or authorized in any way directly or indirectly, for any business, commercial, civil, manufacturing, mercantile, storing, vending, or other such nonresidential purposes excepting, home offices or occupations without external evidence thereof. No internal business will be allowed to infringe on Common Area. http://www.calassoc-hoa.com/Homeowners-Association/General-Information/Sample-Covenants-Conditions-Restrictions.aspx.

C. Garage Use. Garages shall be used only for the parking of motor vehicles and the enclosed storage of family effects and shall not be converted for living or recreational activities. There shall be no storage of any item in or upon a Unit except in an area not visible from the Common Area, other Units, or adjoining streets. No item of any sort may be stored by Owners, renters, lessees or residents in the Common Area. Garage doors, if any, shall remain closed at all times except

> when entering or exiting. The Board may adopt such additional rules and regulations respecting this section as from time to time seems to be in the best interest of the Owners. Garage approaches shall not be used for parking vehicles, but only for ingress and egress to garages. http://www.calassoc-hoa.com/Homeowners-Association/General-Information/Sample-Covenants-Conditions-Restrictions.aspx

Express Covenants

Covenants are frequently created as part of a common interest community ("CIC"). A CIC is created by a master plan of development typically governed by set of rules and an association of owners. A CIC might be a neighborhood of single family homes, perhaps with a commercial district, or a condominium or apartment complex. The usual structure is that owners have a fee simple interest in their residence. There may also be shared ownership of some parts of the community such as hallways and parking lots, a park or a pool. Common spaces may be owned by the community association or collectively by the owners as tenants in common (that cannot be partitioned).

Here is a typical scenario. A real estate developer owns a one-hundred acre parcel of land and subdivides the land into one acre parcels that she plans to build homes on and sell. Before the sale to the first buyer, the developer creates and records a set of rules that are intended to govern all owners in the new development. The documents also set up a homeowner's association ("HOA") where all owners are members with voting rights and from which a sub-group of homeowners will be elected to run the association (a board of directors). The HOA is empowered to interpret and enforce the existing rules and also to amend them. The governing documents in a community are usually called "Covenants Conditions and Restrictions" or CCRs. At the time of the sale to each buyer, the buyer subscribes to the recorded promises in the CCRs that then bind the buyer. Often, owners will make reciprocal promises. For example, each buyer might promise to park in the garage and not the driveway. Then each owner must comply with the promise and at the same time is the beneficiary of the same promise made by all the other owners in the neighborhood. The parcels are both burdened and benefitted by the covenant.

It is easy to see why a buyer who makes a promise to restrict land use is bound by it—it is a contract. The harder question is whether and why the next buyer of the same property should be bound by a promise an earlier owner made. Let's return to the example in the introduction of the chapter where you own an oceanfront property and are unhappy with your adjacent neighbor who parks an old ugly camper trailer on her property and within your view. One solution to this problem is that you enter into a contract with your neighbor who promises never to park an RV on her property again. However, that is not a complete solution, because what you really want is for the promise not to park an RV to bind whoever owns the adjacent property. How can you bind a future owner? Covenants are designed to do exactly that. For covenants to run, they must be created in accordance with the rules that follow. As was the case with easements, you will see that notice to the future owner is a crucial requirement. If you buy property knowing it is bound by a land use covenant, then the legal system concludes that such knowledge justifies holding you to the promise.

Covenants that run with the land are divided into two categories: 1) a real covenant and 2) an equitable servitude. As explained below, the rules for creating both kinds of covenants are overlapping with a few differences. The main difference in legal outcomes between the two is what remedies are available. If a covenant is enforceable as a real covenant "at law" then the promise can be enforced either by money damages or an injunction. If a covenant is enforceable as an equitable servitude "in equity" then the only available remedy is an injunction. These distinctions are based on traditional law and are still in place in many states. However, the modern trend in some states is for a more flexible approach where both types of remedies are available for both kinds of covenants.

To create a running covenant, you need to break the analysis into several parts. Elements one through four below must be satisfied for enforcement as an equitable servitude (by injunction). All five elements below must be satisfied for enforcement of a real covenant. Additionally, you need to consider whether the required elements are satisfied for the burden to run and then, if so, evaluate whether the requirements for the benefit to run are satisfied.

1. **Writing.** The promise must be in a writing that satisfies the Statute of Frauds. In a common interest community like the one described in the example above, the CCRs typically satisfy the writing requirement, although a reference to them in a deed to a buyer (in addition to recording them pre-sale) is clearly the best practice.

2. **Intent to Run.** The original promisor and promisee must intend that the burden and the benefit of the promise run with the land to successor owners. This intent should be expressed explicitly in the document. If not, it can be implied.

3. **Notice.** The subsequent owner must have notice of the promise for the burden to run. Notice is not required for the benefit to run. Any of the three kinds of notice is sufficient: actual notice; inquiry notice or record notice. The definitions of each are the same for covenants as those you learned in easements. Notice, too, that so far, the first three elements for a running covenant match those required for a running easement.

A buyer has *actual notice* if in fact they knew about the easement. Second, a buyer might have *inquiry notice.* Are there visible signs of the existence of a promise that a buyer should investigate? It is hard to to imagine this being the case with a negative covenant. How would a buyer be able to *see* what the current owner is *not allowed* to do? Say the restriction is that an owner cannot build a residence higher than two stories. Even if the whole neighborhood only has two-story homes, it's not obvious that the reason for that is that it is prohibited. Rather, a buyer might assume that was just the pattern of development chosen. That said, some courts have found inquiry notice when there is a uniform pattern of development. Although unusual, it is possible to reach that conclusion. Third, a buyer might have *record notice*. If the covenant has been recorded properly and a reasonable search of the record woud reveal its existence, then the buyer will be deemed to have record notice.

Differing Definitions of Record Notice. There is another layer of record notice to learn now. More layers will be added when you study real estate transactions more generally in Chapter 11.

What is the definition of record notice from "a reasonable search" of the record? Assume a developer owns a large parcel of land that is subdivided into 20 parcels. She sells one acre called FirstAcre to Buyer 1. In the deed out transferring FirstAcre to Buyer 1, Buyer 1 promises to use FirstAcre only for residential and not commercial purposes. In that same deed transferring FirstAcre out to the buyer, the *seller* (the developer) makes the same promise that she will use her remaining property (the rest of the development!) for residential purposes only. These reciprocal promises are contained in the deed for FirstAcre and only there. The deed is then recorded and becomes part of the chain of title for FirstAcre.

Next, the developer sells another acre in the development called SecondAcre to Buyer 2. However, in the deed transferring out SecondAcre, there is no mention of any restriction to residential use only burdening Buyer 2. Yet we know there was a promise made by the developer in the deed out for FirstAcre that seemingly binds all the land the developer had at the time of that first transaction and that included SecondAcre.

Does the buyer purchasing SecondAcre have notice of a promise made in a deed out to FirstAcre and that only appears in the chain of title to FirstAcre? Of course, Buyer 2 should be searching the chain of title in the record for the property he is buying—for SecondAcre. Buyer 2 is on notice for any limitations found in the official records for SecondAcre. That fits the definition of record notice you have already learned with easements and that applies here as well.

What about limitations on SecondAcre that are only discoverable in a deed out to another property? Will record notice be imputed? States differ on this. In the majority of states, the answer is yes, record notice is defined broadly and Buyer 2 should be searching not only the records for the property he is buying but also must search the records of *other* properties that the seller owned at the same time she owned SecondAcre—and that were nearby geographically. With large scale developers that could mean searching many records out to earlier buyers. Still, that is required. The reasoning for this is that buyers search records by looking under the name of the grantor and so could fairly easily look for restrictions made in earlier grants that bind the grantor's retained land. Property records are not organized by location or name of the property but rather through a grantor and grantee index. Conversely, a minority of states (a substantial number) define record notice narrowly and only impute notice for limitations on property contained in the direct chain of title to the property being purchased. To summarize, in the majority of states, Buyer 2 will be deemed to have record notice of the restriction found in the deed to FirstAcre. In a minority of states, there is no record notice and the covenant will not run to SecondAcre—Buyer 2 is free from the promise.

4. **Touch and Concern the Land.** The promise that is being attached to land must be about the way the land is used or otherwise "touch and concern" the property. This means that the promise must relate to occupancy, use, enjoyment of the property or affect its value. For example, a promise to use the property only for residential purposes satisfies the rule, because it limits the manner of use of the property. Typically, this requirement is satisfied, because covenants are designed for the very purpose of regulating land use. However, this element is sometimes controversial. For example, there used to be a debate about whether an obligation to pay a fee to an HOA was related to land use. On the one hand, paying a fee could be viewed as a personal obligation. On the other hand, the obligation is tied to and runs with the land and is a means of regulating land use. Courts today regularly find that an HOA fee touches and concerns the land.

The traditional test you just learned remains in place in many states. In modern law, the touch and concern element is also used as a tool for implementing an array of policies. One policy question raised by the test is what types of promises are sufficiently related to land use that they *should* be allowed to run with land? Consider an obligation on a buyer to belong to a gym or a pool in the neighborhood in exchange for an annual use fee. Another example—what if there is a covenant included in a property transaction that obligates an owner to buy natural gas from a particular company? These obligations seem more like a personal contract than a land use regulation. The obligation to buy fuel from a company will likely fail the touch and concern test. Yet, for the gym or the pool, it could be that such promises have an impact on property values and are part of the neighborhood scheme—and that supports an argument to the contrary.

Relatedly, the traditional approach requires that both the burden and benefit remain attached to and run with the land. Accordingly, covenants cannot bind nor be enforced by a person who does not own the property. This makes sense, since the purpose is to create a covenant tied to the property. The promise follows the property. Accordingly, once the original promisor and promiseee have transferred out the land, they no longer have any legally recognized interest in the covenant. More specifically, the benefit of a covenant cannot be held in gross. In other words, the person seeking enforcement of a covenant *must* own property to which the benefit is attached. There are some exceptions—the primary one being where an HOA seeks to enforce the benefit. This is so because even if the HOA owns no property directly, the association is comprised of members who do.

Additionally, the policy evaluation under the touch and concern test has expanded further, and the rule is now used to assess whether it is reasonable to enforce the content of the promise. Some covenants may go too far in interfering with the rights and freedoms of property owners. For example, what if your HOA prohibits religious displays for the holidays or flying the American flag? You will study this in more detail later in the chapter.

These first four elements are all that are required for enforcement of an equitable servitude.

5. **Privity of Estate.** For enforcement as a real covenant at law, both horizontal and vertical privity are required. These elements evaluate whether there is a sufficient

property relationship between the parties in connection with the promise. Horizontal privity concerns the property relationship between the parties at the time the promise is made. Vertical privity concerns the property relationship between an original owner and a successor owner.

Review the diagram below.

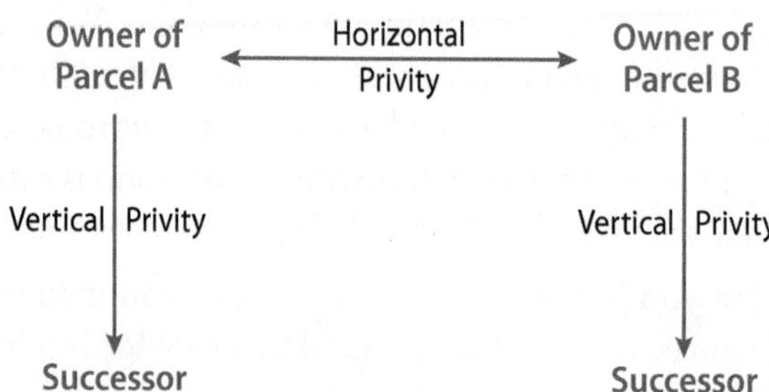

Horizontal privity can be satisfied in several different ways. At the time the covenant is created, is there a real estate transaction or other property relationship? Look for one of these relationships: (1) a transfer by one party to the other (e.g., a sale); or (2) the promisor and promise have a *mutual* interest in the same property at the same time such as a landlord tenant relationship (so the covenant is part of a lease), co-ownership or if one party owns an easement in the other's property. Some states have abandoned this requirement—so be surc to research your particular state.

Vertical privity is easier to understand and is uniformly required. Did the successor owner receive the entire property from the original parties? Since the promise and the property are bound together, vertical privity requires that the person who is burdened or benefitted by the promise own the property to which the promise is attached. This is almost always satisfied. For example, if a seller transfers a fee simple absolute to a buyer, there is vertical privity. Indeed, a fee transfer satisfies the traditional "strict vertical privity" definition which requires a complete transfer of all the interests owned by a predecessor. Many states today apply a more relaxed version of vertical privity, and as long as possession is transferred—as it is in a lease—that is enough.

Requirements	**Real Covenant**	**Equitable Servitude**
Writing	Yes	Yes
Intent to Run	Yes	Yes
Notice	Yes	Yes
Horizontal Privity	Yes	No
Vertical Privity	Yes	No
Remedy	Money Damages and/or Injunction	Injunction

Exercise 10-16. The Grateful Dead Store and *Winn Dixie v. Dolgengroup*

Apply each of the elements above for creation of running covenants to the Grateful Dead Store problem immediately below and then to *Winn Dixie.* Create a diagram of the transactions and property relationships for each.

The Grateful Dead Store

Alice owns a two-acre tract of land. She sells one acre to Bob. Included in the deed conveying Bob his parcel are reciprocal promises that Bob, Alice and their heirs and assigns will use the land for residential purposes only. The deed is duly recorded in Bob's chain of title. Alice sells her parcel to Cody. Bob sells his parcel to Diane.

Cody is a huge fan of the Grateful Dead band and an artist. He opens a small shop in his house, using up about 500 square feet of space, where he sells memorabilia with a Grateful Dead theme such as t-shirts and other clothing, earrings, dream-catchers, coffee cups and the like that he creates. Diane begins to notice that people she doesn't know and who don't appear to be from the neighborhood are coming to Cody's. She is unhappy about this "cast of characters" who are now spending time on her block. She finds out that Cody has a shop in the house and sues for an injunction and damages.

1. Assume for this question only that Bob & Alice are still the current owners of their parcels (that there was no sale to C & D) and it was Alice who opened the Grateful Dead shop. If Bob sues Alice, evaluate the claim and predict the result.
2. Assuming transfers down to successive owners as the hypothetical describes, can Diane enforce the residential only restriction against Cody as a real covenant? As an equitable servitude? What are the requirements? Are they satisfied?
3. Assuming transfers down to successive owners as the hypothetical describes, could Bob sue Cody? Could Bob sue Alice?
4. If Bob still owned his parcel (so there was no sale to Diane), and he sued Cody, what result?
5. What if Alice only leased the place to Cody, what effect does that have on your analysis?
6. What if Alice never sold anything to Bob? Instead they just agreed among themselves as stated and then each recorded the agreement with their deeds. What element is missing? What result?

Winn-Dixie Stores, Inc. v. Dolgencorp

964 So. 2d 261 (Fla. Dist. Ct. App. 2007)

Gross, J. In the circuit court, Winn-Dixie Stores, Inc. brought suit to enjoin Dolgencorp, Inc., another tenant in a shopping plaza, from selling groceries. Winn-Dixie based its suit upon a covenant in its recorded lease with the landlord giving it the exclusive right to sell groceries in the plaza. The circuit court granted summary final judgment in favor of Dolgencorp. We reverse, holding that if we view the evidence in the light most favorable to Winn-Dixie, the covenant in its lease was one running with the land that was enforceable against Dolgencorp.

Winn-Dixie operates a grocery store at the Crest Haven Shopping Plaza, where it is the anchor tenant. An anchor tenant in a shopping center is one that provides a benefit to the center and its tenants by attracting customers.

In March, 1996, the landlord and Winn-Dixie entered into a lease which granted Winn-Dixie the exclusive right to sell groceries at Crest Haven, with the exception that other stores could sell groceries, provided that they devoted no more than 500 square feet to such items. Paragraph 33 of the lease provided that all the provisions in the lease, including Winn-Dixie's grocery exclusive, were "deemed" to be covenants that ran with the land:

> This lease and all of the covenants and provisions thereof shall inure to the benefit of and be binding upon the heirs, legal representatives, successors and assigns of the parties hereto. Each provision hereof shall be deemed both a covenant and a condition and shall run with the land.

A short form of the lease, containing a legal description of the shopping plaza and the grocery exclusive, was recorded on April 23, 1996 in the public records of Palm Beach County, Florida. The recorded short form lease appears in the chain of title for the Crest Haven Shopping Plaza.

Shopping plaza exclusives similar to Winn-Dixie's are customary and standard throughout the industry, especially with regard to anchor tenants. Sophisticated tenants such as Winn-Dixie and Dolgencorp encounter exclusives in almost every shopping center in which they do business. Dolgencorp knew that Winn-Dixie stores typically operated under grocery store exclusives.

In 1998, Dolgencorp became a tenant at Crest Haven and began operating a Dollar General Store. Dolgencorp operates 7,800 Dollar General Stores in 32 states. Dolgencorp's lease contained a provision granting it the exclusive right to operate a Dollar General type of store at the shopping plaza.

Winn-Dixie learned that Dolgencorp was violating its grocery exclusive by devoting more than 500 square feet of sales area to grocery items. Winn-Dixie demanded that the landlord enforce the grocery exclusivity provision, but the landlord failed to do so. Winn-Dixie filed a complaint against the landlord and Dolgencorp seeking injunctive relief, specific performance, damages for breach of contract, and unjust enrichment.

The Grocery Exclusive in the Lease was a Real Property Covenant that Ran With the Land

Winn Dixie's grocery exclusive was a real property covenant that ran with the land and not a personal contract obligation. The distinction between the two is well established in Florida law.

We explained the difference between a covenant running with the land and a personal covenant in *Alternative Networking, Inc. v. Solid Waste Authority of Palm Beach County,* 758 So. 2d 1209, 1211 (Fla. 4th DCA 2000):

> "A personal covenant creates a personal obligation or right enforceable at law only between the original covenanting parties whereas a real covenant creates a servitude upon reality for the benefit of another parcel of land. A real covenant binds the heirs and assigns of the original covenantor, while a personal covenant does not." A covenant running with the land differs from a merely personal covenant in that the former concerns the property conveyed and the occupation and enjoyment thereof, whereas the latter covenant is collateral or is not immediately concerned with the property granted. If the performance of the covenant must touch and involve the land or some right or easement annexed and appurtenant thereto, and tends necessarily to enhance the value of the property or renders it more convenient and beneficial to the owner, it is a covenant running with the land. [Citations omitted.]

Florida courts have long enforced use restrictions in commercial leases as covenants running with the land.

[I]n *Park Avenue BBQ & Grille of Wellington, Inc. v. Coaches Corner, Inc.,* 746 So. 2d 480 (Fla. 4th DCA 1999), this court enforced a use restriction in one tenant's commercial lease against another tenant of a shopping center. There, the landlord granted a lease exclusive to a sports bar to be the only TV sports bar in the shopping center. The lease exclusive was recorded in the public records when the landlord conveyed the shopping center to a new owner. Later the shopping center leased space to a barbeque restaurant that began showing televised sporting events. The sports bar obtained an injunction against the shopping center and the restaurant enforcing its lease exclusive. On appeal, the restaurant argued that it was not bound by the sports bar exclusive because it was not in direct contractual privity with the sports bar. This court affirmed the injunction, rejecting the argument that [contractual] privity was a requirement to enforce a covenant running with the land, in light of the restaurant's actual knowledge of the restrictive covenant.

From the Florida cases, we extract the following rule: to establish a valid and enforceable covenant running with the land arising from a landlord-tenant relationship, a plaintiff must show (1) the existence of a covenant that touches and involves the land, (2) an intention that the covenant run with the land, and (3) notice of the restriction on the part of the party against whom enforcement is sought.

The grocery exclusive in this case was a covenant that "touched and involved" the land. The intent that the use restriction run with the land was expressed in paragraph 33 of the lease, which "deems" its provisions to be covenants that run with the land.

Finally, Dolgencorp had sufficient notice of the grocery exclusive so that Winn-Dixie could bring an enforcement action against it. Florida recognizes three types of notice in cases concerning covenants running with the land—constructive notice, actual notice, or implied actual notice. This record supports the conclusion that Dolgencorp had either constructive or implied actual notice of Winn-Dixie's lease exclusive.

" 'Constructive notice' has been defined as notice imputed to a person not having actual notice." (Citation omitted.) "The usual instance of constructive notice, is of course, restrictions in a recorded deed or plat. And the authorities are practically unanimous in holding that the recorded deed containing such restriction is not necessarily the immediate deed by which the instant owner takes or has taken title; it may be in an antecedent deed, even the deed from the original common grantor." (Citation omitted.)

Park Avenue BBQ is an actual notice case. The barbeque restaurant had actual knowledge of the sports bar's exclusivity provision; the restaurant's president "hand wrote language into his lease allowing [the restaurant] to televise sporting events because he was concerned about [the sports bar's] exclusivity provision." 746 So. 2d at 482. Actual or "express" notice is based on "direct information" leading to "actual knowledge of the fact in question."

Implied actual notice includes "notice inferred from the fact that the person had means of knowledge, which it was his duty to use and which he did not use." (Citation omitted.) If a person has information that would lead a reasonable man to make further inquiry for his own protection, but fails to further investigate and learn what the inquiry would reasonably have uncovered, the person "must suffer the consequence of his neglect." (Citations omitted.)

Based on this record, Dolgencorp had at least implied actual notice of the grocery exclusive when it entered into its lease. Dolgencorp was an experienced commercial tenant with 7,800 stores in 32 states, most of which are located in shopping plazas; it often sought exclusives in its own leases and secured one from Crest Haven. Dolgencorp understood that Winn-Dixie was the anchor tenant at Crest Haven. Dolgencorp was aware that anchor tenants like Winn-Dixie typically secure restrictive covenants in shopping center leases. Under these circumstances, Dolgencorp had the obligation to make further inquiry of the landlord or Winn-Dixie or to examine the shopping center's chain of title to see if Winn-Dixie had recorded its grocery exclusive. In sum, Dolgencorp had reason to know of the existence of Winn-Dixie's restrictive covenant.

Moving away from implied actual notice, the more difficult issue is whether Winn-Dixie's recording of the short form lease gave Dolgencorp constructive notice of the grocery exclusive sufficient to enforce the covenant against it. [The court finds this sufficient because the covenant was recorded.]

Implied Covenants

As the earlier discussion makes clear, express covenants are required to be in writing to be enforceable. Here you study an important exception to this rule. A covenant might be implied when 1) a developer 2) demonstrates a common plan or scheme of restrictions. The existence of the common scheme triggers the conclusion that a covenant applies uniformly in the community. Accordingly, reciprocal promises are implied among all owners.

For example, suppose a developer owned a large tract of land that she divides into 30 lots for sale. In each of the deeds transferring ownership to the first 25 buyers, the grantee promises not to use the property for commercial purposes. The developer omits such language in the sale to Buyer 26 who then opens up a convenience store. Is Buyer 26 bound by the same promise made by Buyers 1-25? Buyer 26 can put forward a legitimate defense that there is no promise in writing that binds his property. However, if Buyer 1 (or any of the earlier buyers) brings a claim for an implied covenant, many courts in this circumstance will find and enforce an equitable servitude and issue an injunction to stop the commercial use. The common scheme is the basis for implying a reciprocal promise from the *developer* not to use the property for commercial purposes at the time of the sale to Buyer 1. There is a grantee promise and an implied grantor promise. Both promises then flow to successor owners making Buyer 26 impliedly bound by the Developer's implied promise.

What evidence proves the existence a common plan or scheme? Numerous conveyances with the same or similar restrictions make for a strong claim. The percentage of properties restricted is influential as well. A common plan is more likely to be found if 95% of the neighborhood is bound by written covenants and less likely if only 50% of owners have a restriction. Other evidence to investigate that could demonstrate creation of a uniform planned community is a map or plat or voting rights among owners or an HOA. Also consider whether there are representations or advertisements by a developer about a "residential community" or common interest community. Also consider whether a subpart of a development appears to be restricted by covenants but yet another subpart or region of the development is unrestricted. Courts have been receptive to such divisions if there are differing patterns of development.

In summary, the elements that must be satisfied for recognition of an implied reciprocal covenant:

1. A common grantor (unified ownership of one tract or multiple tracts of land) and
2. A common plan or scheme.

Record Notice is *not* a separate element that needs to be proved for an implied covenant—just the two elements of a common grantor and a common scheme need to be proved.

Indeed, record notice is typically not present in circumstances that trigger an implied covenant. Recall that the general definition of record notice is that an owner is charged with notice of any covenants that could be discovered by properly searching the records—and the records must reveal a *promise was made* either by the current owner of the burdened property or by an earlier owner. (Depending on what approach a state has, you might have to search the direct chain of title or engage in a broader search of all deeds out from the grantor.) This definition is not satisfied with implied covenants. Consider the *Forster* case below. Several buyers specifically avoided making any promises against having RVs. Nor had any earlier owners of those properties made any promises against having RVs in earlier deeds. Accordingly, a record search of such properties would show them as unrestricted. Yet the doctrine of implied covenants imposes a promise when none exists of record.

However, this can get a bit slippery. You should be aware that some courts do list notice as a third requirement. When that is the case, the definition of notice applied is unique and very different than the definition of record notice you have already learned. Rather than there being a promise of record that that binds the buyer's property—implied covenants are recognized because *other properties* in the neighborhood have restrictions their deeds. To the extent courts take this view, it is applicable only in the context of implied covenants.

One foundation offered for the doctrine is consent—that the covenant reflects the demonstrated intent of the parties. Do you think that developers really intend to bind all the properties? After all, these situations arise when developers have or sell unrestricted lots. That could be done quite purposefully to maximize property values or at the request of the buyer. The next case is a good example. What then is the basis for the rule's application? Is reliance by the earlier buyers who are bound by express covenants enough? Is it justifiable?

Be aware that terminology can be confusing as this doctrine is often called an implied reciprocal negative *easement* (even though it is not an easement!) or servitude. To simplify and clarify, this text refers to the claim as an implied covenant or implied reciprocal covenant.

Exercise 10-17. *Forster v. Hall*

1. To understand the application of the doctrine, as you read this case, you will need to carefully identify which and how many of the various properties have or do not have written and recorded restrictions.
2. Analyze the elements of the claim and develop factual arguments that support the claim and that undermine it.
3. Critically evaluate the court's reasoning for recognition of an implied covenant under these facts.

Forster v. Hall

576 S.E.2d 746 (Va. 2003)

Koontz, J. In this appeal, we consider whether the chancellor correctly determined that an implied reciprocal negative easement prohibits the placement of "mobile homes" on all the lots of a residential subdivision. We further consider whether the chancellor correctly determined that certain structures that were permanently annexed to the land are not in violation of the restriction imposed by this easement.

On August 25, 1978, Goose Creek Partnership (the partnership), of which Carl Cartwright, Jr., was a member, acquired a tract of land in Tazewell County. The partnership had the land surveyed and platted as a residential subdivision to be known as "Goose Creek Estates," separating it into five contiguous sections with a total of 113 lots. The plats of sections 1, 2, and 3 of the subdivision were recorded in the land records of the County on December 29, 1978 and contained no restrictive covenants. The plats of sections 4 and 5 of the subdivision were recorded in the land records of the County on February 14, 1979 and contained only restrictions regarding approval of sewer and water systems.

Over approximately the next sixteen years, the partnership included in the vast majority of the deeds to lots in Goose Creek Estates sold to the original purchasers a restrictive covenant providing that "no mobile homes, either single or double-wide, may be parked and/or erected on the property." James S. Hall and Joyce S. Hall (the Halls) purchased Lot 3, Section 4 of Goose Creek Estates on March 9, 1994, from the partnership. The Halls' deed contained the restrictive covenant against parking or erecting mobile homes on their property.

Richard A. Forster (Forster) purchased Lot 5, Section 1 of Goose Creek Estates in March 1996 from Thomas E. Kelley and Angela A. Kelley, who had acquired the lot from the partnership in a deed that contained the restrictive covenant against parking or erecting mobile homes on the property. Forster also acquired Lot 35, Section 1 in June 1996 during the partnership's attempt to auction the remaining lots of the subdivision. Forster's deed for this lot did not contain the restriction against mobile homes, but the restriction was subsequently added by a recorded deed of correction. Similar corrective deeds were recorded for other lots conveyed pursuant to the auction.

On May 30, 1996, prior to the auction, the Halls also purchased Lot 2, Section 4 of Goose Creek Estates. At their request, the restriction against mobile homes was not included in the deed for this lot. On October 31, 1996, David Wayne McKinney and Eva Sue McKinney (the McKinneys) purchased Lot 1, Section 4 of the subdivision. At their request, the restriction against mobile homes was not included in their deed for this lot.

In 1997, the Halls permitted their son to move his "double-wide manufactured" home onto Lot 2, Section 4 in Goose Creek Estates. In 1998, the Halls also permitted their daughter to move her "double-wide manufactured" home onto this lot. The homes were placed on brick foundations. Porches were added and the tongues and wheels were removed from both homes. The Halls pay the real estate taxes on these homes.

On August 20, 1997, the McKinneys conveyed portions of their property in the subdivision by deeds of gift to their daughters, Stephanie D. Bowling and Margaret E. Brown. Bowling and Brown both moved "double-wide manufactured" homes onto their portions of Lot 1, Section 4. Each home was placed on a cinder block foundation and the tongues and wheels were removed. Bowling and Brown pay the real estate taxes on their homes.

On February 16, 1999, Forster filed a bill of complaint in the Circuit Court of Tazewell County against the Halls, the McKinneys, Bowling, and Brown (hereinafter collectively, the landowners). Forster sought a determination "that Lots 1, 2, and 3 of Section 4, Goose Creek Estates subdivisio[n], each are subject to [an implied reciprocal negative] easement that no mobile home, either single or double-wide, shall be placed on said land at any time," and that this restriction may be enforced by the owner of any lot in the subdivision. Forster requested that the chancellor enter an injunction requiring removal of the four double-wide manufactured homes from Lots 1 and 2, Section 4. The landowners filed answers denying that these particular lots were subject to the implied reciprocal negative easement asserted by Forster.

[T]he subdivision, though platted in five sections, was marketed as a single development. Cartwright testified that in a number of instances the restrictive covenant against mobile homes was not included in the deed to a particular lot at the purchaser's request. However, if no such request was made, the restriction was included in the deed to each lot as a matter of course. As a result, 105 of the 113 lots in the subdivision were conveyed by the partnership with the restrictive covenant. Cartwright explained that the purpose of the restrictive covenant was to "protect" the property of the partnership and the purchasers of individual lots from "mobile homes" and, thus, benefit the partnership and the purchasers.

We first consider whether the chancellor correctly determined that an implied reciprocal negative easement prohibiting the placement of mobile homes was created on any of the lots in Goose Creek Estates. If so, we consider whether the landowners' lots are subject to that easement even though they had expressly sought to exempt their lots from the burden of any such restriction.

An implied reciprocal negative easement arises "when a common grantor develops land for sale in lots and pursues a course of conduct which indicates an intention to follow a general scheme of development for the benefit of himself and his purchasers and, in numerous conveyances of the lots, imposes substantially uniform restrictions, conditions, and covenants relating to use of the property." (Citation omitted.) If such a scheme of development is proved, "the grantees acquire by implication an equitable right ... to enforce similar restrictions against that part of the tract retained by the grantor or subsequently sold without the restrictions to a purchaser with actual or constructive notice of the restrictions and covenants." (Citation omitted.)

Here, the record is clear that the partnership that developed Goose Creek Estates conveyed 93% of the lots in that subdivision by deeds that contained "substantially uniform restrictions, conditions, and covenants relating to use of the property." Moreover, Cartwright's testimony establishes that this general scheme of development was employed to enhance the marketability of the lots in the subdivision and was for the benefit of the partnership and the purchasers of the lots in the subdivision, such as Forster.

While it is true that the partnership, the common grantor, acquiesced in requests from a small number of purchasers to omit the restriction from their deeds, there is no evidence that this was done with the concurrence of the other lot owners. Moreover, the fact the landowners made such requests with regard to the deeds for their lots is conclusive proof that they had actual notice of the restriction in deeds to other lots in the subdivision. Thus, the landowners were at least constructively on notice that the restriction could burden the use of their lots by way of an implied reciprocal negative easement, even though the restriction was omitted from their deeds. Accordingly, we hold that the chancellor correctly determined that all the lots in Goose Creek Estates are subject to an implied restriction against parking or erecting mobile homes thereon, and that Forster is entitled to enforce that restriction.

[The court also found that the mobile homes were in violation of the covenant, and must be removed.]

Enforceability and Compliance with Public Policy

There are varying perspectives on the benefits, costs and risks of common interest communities. Are the owners experiencing a freely chosen privatopia? Or are owners being channeled into a freedom limiting private government run by neighbors that they didn't really want, nor have sufficient knowledge or bargaining power to change to protect their interests? Is this structure helpful or harmful for society? As you will discover in the materials in this subsection, these alternative views often become part of the debate over enforceability of covenants and in disputes between individual owners and the HOA. Despite the controversy, common interest communities are very popular and a growing phenomenon in the U.S. and the world.

Recall that in common interest communities, a developer can create legally recognized covenants by complying with the legal rules. Filing and recording the appropriate governing documents that includes CCRs before a sale out to the first buyer generally accomplishes that. Yet even when validly created, an owner can challenge the enforceability of a covenant on a number of grounds. First, as discussed earlier, under the traditional approach, covenants must touch and concern the land. Second, covenants will not be enforced if unreasonable. Third, some covenants are unenforceable because they undermine or violate public policy or individual rights. The Restatement (Third) of Property proposes that the touch and concern element be abolished and replaced with a policy evaluation to determine enforceability. Keep in mind that we have yet to see the extent to which this and other Restatement reforms will be adopted.

Reasonableness

Generally, a covenant will be evaluated for reasonableness by (1) weighing the burdens against the benefits of enforcement, (2) determining if the covenant is arbitrary or discriminatory and (3) considering whether the rule violates public policy. However, there are layers of the analysis that vary by state law. Most states evaluate a covenant for reasonableness in light of the covenant's impact on the entire community. A minority of states consider whether a covenant is unreasonable as applied to the owner's particular situation and use of the property.

Imagine there is a covenant that all structures in the community must be painted grey or beige. A resident paints a small shed in the back yard neon blue. However, it is unlikely anyone would notice the color of the shed because the view to back yard is enclosed by a tall opaque fence. Is the covenant reasonable generally as it applies to the entire community? Probably yes, because uniform and serene paint colors can contribute to the quality of life of the residents and positively impact property values when weighed against a modest limitation on the owner. The answer might be different with a more particularized assessment of reasonableness. Under such a standard, it could be unreasonable to insist on enforcement of the rule as it applies in this situation—one could argue there is no benefit to enforcement if no one can see the bright blue paint.

Another issue to consider is the timing of creation of the covenant. Courts are far more likely to be deferential to the community if the covenant was included in the original CCRs because all buyers had notice of the specific limitation before they purchased the property. Courts are less deferential and tend to be more demanding in assessing reasonableness when there is a post-purchase rule change or adoption of new covenants.

Rather than evaluating covenants for reasonableness, some courts in some contexts have applied a business judgment rule. This is a rule borrowed from corporate law that defers to decisions made by the board or officers of the company. It presumes that decisionmakers have acted in good faith to advance the interests of the corporation. As it applies to CICs, decisions can be challenged if they have no legitimate relationship to the welfare of the community or are arbitrary or discriminatory or exceed the scope of authority. *See, e.g.*, *Levandusky v. One Fifth Avenue Apartment Corp.*, 553 N.E.2d 1317 (N.Y. 1990).

Exercise 10-18. *Nahrstedt* and *Fountain Valley*

1. As you read *Nahrstedt*, determine which definition of reasonableness is adopted by the majority opinion. Be sure to identify who has the burden of proof.

2. Regardless of which standard applies, the majority and dissenting opinions in *Nahrstedt* disagree about whether the ban on having indoor cats is reasonable. What are the facts that support each perspective?
3. Be prepared to present arguments for and against reasonableness based on the *Fountain Valley* decision.

Nahrstedt v. Lakeside Village Condominium Association, Inc.

878 P.2d 1275 (Cal. 1994)

Kennard, J. A homeowner in a 530-unit condominium complex sued to prevent the homeowners association from enforcing a restriction against keeping cats, dogs, and other animals in the condominium development. The owner asserted that the restriction, which was contained in the project's declaration recorded by the condominium project's developer, was "unreasonable" as applied to her because she kept her three cats [named Boo Boo, Dockers & Tulip] indoors and because her cats were "noiseless" and "created no nuisance." Agreeing with the premise underlying the owner's complaint, the Court of Appeal concluded that the homeowners association could enforce the restriction only upon proof that plaintiff's cats would be likely to interfere with the right of other homeowners "to the peaceful and quiet enjoyment of their property."

Those of us who have cats or dogs can attest to their wonderful companionship and affection. Not surprisingly, studies have confirmed this effect. But the issue before us is not whether in the abstract pets can have a beneficial effect on humans. Rather, the narrow issue here is whether a pet restriction that is contained in the recorded declaration of a condominium complex is enforceable against the challenge of a homeowner. As we shall explain, the Legislature, in Civil Code section 1354, has required that courts enforce the covenants, conditions and restrictions contained in the recorded declaration of a common interest development "unless unreasonable."

Because a stable and predictable living environment is crucial to the success of condominiums and other common interest residential developments, and because recorded use restrictions are a primary means of ensuring this stability and predictability, the Legislature in section 1354 has afforded such restrictions a presumption of validity and has required of challengers that they demonstrate the restriction's "unreasonableness" by the deferential standard applicable to equitable servitudes. Under this standard established by the Legislature, enforcement of a restriction does not depend upon the conduct of a particular condominium owner. Rather, the restriction must be uniformly enforced in the condominium development to which it was intended to apply unless the plaintiff owner can show that the burdens it imposes on affected properties so substantially outweigh the benefits of the restriction that it should not be enforced against any owner. Here, the Court of Appeal did not apply this standard in deciding that plaintiff had stated a claim for declaratory relief. Accordingly, we reverse the judgment of the Court of Appeal and remand for further proceedings consistent with the views expressed in this opinion.

I

The Lakeside Village project is subject to certain covenants, conditions and restrictions (hereafter CC&R's) that were included in the developer's declaration recorded with the Los Angeles County Recorder on April 17, 1978, at the inception of the development project. Ownership of a unit includes membership in the project's homeowners association, the Lakeside Village Condominium Association (hereafter Association), the body that enforces the project's CC&R's, including the pet restriction, which provides in relevant part: "No animals (which shall mean dogs and cats), livestock, reptiles or poultry shall be kept in any unit."

In January 1988, plaintiff Natore Nahrstedt purchased a Lakeside Village condominium and moved in with her three cats. When the Association learned of the cats' presence, it demanded their removal and assessed fines against Nahrstedt for each successive month that she remained in violation of the condominium project's pet restriction.

Nahrstedt then brought this lawsuit against the Association, its officers, and two of its employees, asking the trial court to invalidate the assessments, to enjoin future assessments, to award damages for violation of her privacy when the Association "peered" into her condominium unit, to award damages for infliction of emotional distress, and to declare the pet restriction "unreasonable" as applied to indoor cats (such as hers) that are not allowed free run of the project's common areas. Nahrstedt also alleged she did not know of the pet restriction when she bought her condominium.

II

[S]ubordination of individual property rights to the collective judgment of the owners association together with restrictions on the use of real property comprise the chief attributes of owning property in a common interest development. Notwithstanding the limitations on personal autonomy that are inherent in the concept of shared ownership of residential property, common interest developments have increased in popularity in recent years, in part because they generally provide a more affordable alternative to ownership of a single-family home. One significant factor in the continued popularity of the common interest form of property ownership is the ability of homeowners to enforce restrictive CC&R's against other owners (including future purchasers) of project units.

When restrictions limiting the use of property within a common interest development satisfy the requirements of covenants running with the land or of equitable servitudes, what standard or test governs their enforceability?

In California, as we explained at the outset, our Legislature has made common interest development use restrictions contained in a project's recorded declaration "enforceable ... unless unreasonable." (§ 1354, subd. (a).) In states lacking such legislative guidance, some courts have adopted a standard under which a common interest development's recorded use restrictions will be enforced so long as they are reasonable.

In *Hidden Harbour Estates v. Basso* (Fla. Dist. Ct. App. 1981) 393 So. 2d 637, the Florida court distinguished two categories of use restrictions: use restrictions set forth in the declaration or master deed of the condominium project itself, and rules promulgated by the governing board of the condominium owners association or the board's interpretation of a rule. The latter category of use restrictions, the court said, should be subject to a "reasonableness" test, so as to "somewhat fetter the discretion of the board of directors." (*Id.* at p. 640.) Such a standard, the court explained, best assures that governing boards will "enact rules and make decisions that are reasonably related to the promotion of the health, happiness and peace of mind" of the project owners, considered collectively. (*Ibid.*)

By contrast, restrictions contained in the declaration or master deed of the condominium complex, the Florida court concluded, should not be evaluated under a "reasonableness" standard. Rather, such use restrictions are "clothed with a very strong presumption of validity" and should be upheld even if they exhibit some degree of unreasonableness. (Id. at pp. 639, 640.) Nonenforcement would be proper only if such restrictions were arbitrary or in violation of public policy or some fundamental constitutional right.

III

Under the holding we adopt today, the reasonableness or unreasonableness of a condominium use restriction that the Legislature has made subject to section 1354 is to be determined *not* by reference to facts that are specific to the objecting homeowner, but by reference to the common interest development as a whole. As we have explained, when, as here, a restriction is contained in the declaration of the common interest development and is recorded with the county recorder, the restriction is presumed to be reasonable and will be enforced uniformly against all residents of the common interest development *unless* the restriction is arbitrary, imposes burdens on the use of lands it affects that substantially outweigh the restriction's benefits to the development's residents, or violates a fundamental public policy.

Accordingly, here Nahrstedt could prevent enforcement of the Lakeside Village pet restriction by proving that the restriction is arbitrary, that it is substantially more burdensome than beneficial to the affected properties, or that it violates a fundamental public policy. For the reasons set forth below, Nahrstedt's complaint fails to adequately allege any of these three grounds of unreasonableness.

We conclude, as a matter of law, that the recorded pet restriction of the Lakeside Village condominium development prohibiting cats or dogs but allowing some other pets is not arbitrary, but is rationally related to health, sanitation and noise concerns legitimately held by residents of a high-density condominium project such as Lakeside Village, which includes 530 units in 12 separate 3-story buildings. [Domestic fish and birds are allowed.]

Nahrstedt's complaint alleges no facts that could possibly support a finding that the burden of the restriction on the affected property is so disproportionate to its benefit that the restriction is unreasonable and should not be enforced. Also, the complaint's allegations center on Nahrstedt and her cats (that she keeps them inside her condominium unit and that they do not bother her neighbors), without any reference to the effect on the condominium development as a whole, thus rendering the allegations legally insufficient to overcome section 1354's presumption of the restriction's validity.

[The court also addressed Nahrstedt's claim that the restriction violates her right to privacy under the California Constitution, and found no guarantee of the right to keep cats or dogs as household pets.]

By providing condominium homeowners with substantial assurance that their development's recorded use restrictions can be enforced, section 1354 promotes the stability and predictability so essential to the success of any common interest development. Persons who purchase homes in such a development typically submit to a variety of restrictions on the use of their property. In exchange, they obtain the security of knowing that all other homeowners in the development will be required to abide by those same restrictions. Section 1354 also protects the general expectations of condominium homeowners that they not be burdened with the litigation expense in defending case-by-case legal challenges to presumptively valid recorded use restrictions.

In this case, the pet restriction was contained in the project's declaration or governing document, which was recorded with the county recorder before any of the 530 units was sold. For many owners, the pet restriction may have been an important inducement to purchase into the development. Because the homeowners collectively have the power to repeal the pet restriction, its continued existence reflects their desire to retain it.

Plaintiff's allegations, even if true, are insufficient to show that the pet restriction's harmful effects substantially outweigh its benefits to the condominium development as a whole, that it bears no rational relationship to the purpose or function of the development, or that it violates public policy. We reverse the judgment of the Court of Appeal, and remand for further proceedings consistent with the views expressed in this opinion

Arabian, J., Dissenting. "There are two means of refuge from the misery of life: music and cats." (Albert Schweitzer) I respectfully dissent. While technical merit may commend the majority's analysis, its application to the facts presented reflects a narrow, indeed chary, view of the law that eschews the human spirit in favor of arbitrary efficiency. In my view, the resolution of this case well illustrates the conventional wisdom, and fundamental truth, of the Spanish proverb, "It is better to be a mouse in a cat's mouth than a man in a lawyer's hands."

As explained below, I find the provision known as the "pet restriction " contained in the covenants, conditions, and restrictions (CC&R's) governing the Lakeside Village project patently arbitrary and unreasonable within the meaning of Civil Code section 1354. Beyond dispute, human beings have long enjoyed an abiding and cherished association with their household animals. Given the substantial benefits derived from pet ownership, the undue burden on the use of property imposed on condominium owners who can maintain pets within the confines of their units without creating a nuisance or disturbing the quiet enjoyment of others substantially outweighs whatever meager utility the restriction may serve in the abstract. It certainly does not promote "health, happiness [or] peace of mind" commensurate with its tariff on the quality of life for those who value the companionship of animals. Worse, it contributes to the fraying of our social fabric.

What, then, is the burden at issue here? Both recorded and unrecorded history bear witness to the domestication of animals as household pets. Throughout the ages, art and literature, as well as mythology, depict humans in all walks of life and social strata with cats and dogs, illustrating their widespread acceptance in everyday life. Some religions have even incorporated them into their worship.

[T]he value of pets in daily life is a matter of common knowledge and understanding as well as extensive documentation. People of all ages, but particularly the elderly and the young, enjoy their companionship. Those who suffer from serious disease or injury and are confined to their home or bed experience a therapeutic, even spiritual, benefit from their presence. Animals provide comfort at the death of a family member or dear friend, and for the lonely can offer a reason for living when life seems to have lost its meaning. In recognition of these benefits, both Congress and the state Legislature have expressly guaranteed that elderly and handicapped persons living in public-assistance housing cannot be deprived of their pets. Not only have children and animals always been natural companions, children learn responsibility and discipline from pet ownership while developing an important sense of kindness and protection for animals. Single adults may find certain pets can afford a feeling of security. Families benefit from the experience of sharing that having a pet encourages. While pet ownership may not be a fundamental right as such, unquestionably it is an integral aspect of our daily existence, which cannot be lightly dismissed and should not suffer unwarranted intrusion into its circle of privacy.

What is gained from an uncompromising prohibition against pets that are confined to an owner's unit and create no noise, odor, or nuisance? To the extent such animals are not seen, heard, or smelled any more than if they were not kept in the first place, there is no corresponding or concomitant benefit. Pets that remain within the four corners of their owners' condominium space can have no deleterious or offensive effect on the project's common areas or any neighboring unit. Certainly, if other owners and residents are totally *unaware* of their presence, prohibiting pets does not in any respect foster the "health, happiness [or] peace of mind" of anyone except the homeowners association's board of directors, who are thereby able to promote a form of sophisticated bigotry. In light of the substantial and disproportionate burden imposed for those who must forego virtually any and all association with pets, this lack of benefit renders a categorical ban unreasonable under Civil Code section 1354.

The proffered justification is all the more spurious when measured against the terms of the pet restriction itself, which contains an exception for domestic fish and birds. A squawking bird can readily create the very kind of disturbance supposedly prevented by banning other types of pets. At the same time, many animals prohibited by the restriction, such as hamsters and the like, turtles, and small reptiles, make no sound whatsoever. Disposal of bird droppings in common trash areas poses as much of a health concern as cat litter or rabbit pellets, which likewise can be handled in a manner that avoids potential problems. Birds are also known to carry disease and provoke allergies. Neither is maintaining fish without possible risk of interfering with the quiet enjoyment of condominium neighbors. Aquarium water must be changed and disposed of in the common drainage system. Leakage from a fish tank could cause serious water damage to the owner's unit, those below, and common areas. Defendants and the majority purport such solicitude for the "health, sanitation and noise concerns" of other unit owners, but fail to explain how the possession of pets, such as plaintiff's cats, under the circumstances alleged in her complaint, jeopardizes that goal any more than the fish and birds expressly allowed by the pet restriction. This inconsistency underscores its unreasonableness and discriminatory impact.

Moreover, unlike most conduct controlled by CC&R's, the activity at issue here is strictly confined to the owner's interior space; it does not in any manner invade other units or the common areas. Owning a home of one's own has always epitomized the American dream. More than simply embodying the notion of having "one's castle," it represents the sense of freedom and self-determination emblematic of our national character. Granted, those who live in multi-unit developments cannot exercise this freedom to the same extent possible on a large estate. But owning pets that do not disturb the quiet enjoyment of others does not reasonably come within this compromise. Nevertheless, with no demonstrated or discernible benefit, the majority arbitrarily sacrifice the dream to the tyranny of the "commonality."

Fountain Valley Chateau Blanc Homeowner's Association v. Dep't of Veteran's Affairs

67 Cal. App. 4th 743 (Cal. Ct. App. 1998)

Sills, J. Like Shel Silverstein's proverbial Sarah Cynthia Sylvia Stout, the petitioner in this case, Robert S. Cunningham, would not take the garbage out. So, reminiscent of Sarah's daddy who, in the famous poem would scream and shout, Cunningham's homeowner's association did the modern equivalent. It instituted litigation. The association's theory in essence was that Cunningham's property constituted a fire hazard. Local fire authorities, however, determined that his property posed no fire hazard, either indoors or outdoors. Even so, the lawyers for the homeowner's association wrote letters demanding that he clear his bed of all papers and books, discard "outdated" clothing, and remove the papers, cardboard boxes and books from the floor area around his bed and dresser. Books that were "considered standard reading material" could, however, remain in place.

Cunningham is a senior citizen who suffers from Hodgkins' disease. The letter from the association's lawyers was, in essence, a demand backed up by threat of litigation telling him to straighten up his own bedroom. So Cunningham found a lawyer and sued the association by filing a cross-complaint for invasion of the right to privacy and breach of the homeowner's association's covenants, conditions and restrictions (commonly referred to as "CC & R's").

The association's original complaint against Cunningham was soon settled; Cunningham agreed to abide by the rules. His cross-complaint against the association, by contrast, went to trial, with the issue being the *reasonableness* of the association's conduct after the litigation started. The trial was bifurcated between liability and damage phases, and the jury found in favor of Cunningham on the liability issue. However, before the damage phase could be heard, the trial judge granted the association's new trial motion, stating he believed the association had acted reasonably. And he went on to say that he would keep on granting new trial motions as long as the jury returned liability verdicts for Cunningham. Cunningham then petitioned for a writ to set aside the new trial order, which we now grant.

Treating the new trial order as what it *really* was—a judgment notwithstanding the verdict—it cannot stand. The association's behavior, in particular the sheer presumption of telling Cunningham what sort of reading material he could keep in his own home, was easily the sort of conduct that the jury could find was unreasonable and beyond the association's rights as stated in the CC & R's. We hasten to add, however, that this is all we decide. We do *not* hold that a letter from the lawyers for a homeowner's association threatening litigation unless an adult cleans up his or her own room is necessarily actionable. That issue has not been briefed. It is enough for the moment that we merely hold that, given the actual CC & R's involved, the demands set forth in the letter were *unreasonable.*

FACTS

Robert Cunningham bought an attached home subject to the CC & R's of the Fountain Valley Chateau Blanc Homeowner's Association with the help of the Department of Veterans Affairs. The deal was structured as a traditional land sale installment contract, with the Department taking title and entering into a recorded contract with Cunningham which showed him as the real purchaser of the property.

In September 1993 a roofing contractor hired by the association complained that he could not maneuver his equipment in Cunningham's backyard due to "debris" there. That, and some previous complaints by neighbors, generated a letter from the association's lawyers demanding Cunningham not only clear his patio, but also open up the interior of his unit because there had been reports of fire hazards inside. In November 1993 Cunningham allowed association representatives to inspect his home—albeit under threat of litigation. After the inspection Cunningham removed a number of personal items from the house.

On December 9, 1993, the association returned for another inspection and decided Cunningham still had not removed enough of his belongings. That inspection generated another letter threatening litigation. Litigation came on March 14, 1994, based on alleged fire and safety hazards arising from the junk and paper stored in and about

Cunningham's home. The association named both Cunningham and the Department as defendants.

In May 1994, however, housing code and fire inspectors found no hazardous conditions on the property. Still, the association continued with the litigation. And in early February 1995, the association's attorneys wrote a lengthy letter to Cunningham detailing the inadequacies of Cunningham's housekeeping and demanding he undertake a number of actions concerning the *interior* of his home. He was told to:

—Remove paper, cardboard boxes and books from the floor area around his bed and dresser.

—Remove all boxes and papers not currently in use in the living room and dining room because they increased the risk of fire.

—Clear all objects, including cardboard boxes, from his interior stairs and stairwells to allow passage.

—Not use his downstairs bathroom for storage.

—Maintain a functioning electrical light in his downstairs bathroom.

On top of these demands, the letter contained this statement: "The Association suggests that all outdated clothing that has not been worn in the last five years be removed and/or donated to the Salvation Army or similar organization. This would allow the upstairs bathroom to be used for what [*sic*] designed for. Any other remaining clothes could be stored in a walk-in closet." The letter further told Cunningham that "[b]ooks that are currently in book shelves, and which are considered standard reading material, can remain in place." It ended by reminding him that the association's attorney fees had reached over $34,000 and were continuing.

Cunningham has Hodgkins' disease and had been, up to that point, representing himself. In February 1996, however, he found an attorney who agreed to represent him. His new attorney then obtained leave to file a cross-complaint against the association based on a variety of causes of action, including violations of the right to privacy, trespass, negligence and breach of contract, predicated on the association's use of the threat of litigation to gain entry to his home and force him to throw out various of his personal belongings. What the association had characterized as "debris" now had a name: "furniture, magazines, books, appliances, bookshelves, plants, bicycles, camping equipment and other personal items."

It Cannot Be Said That the Association Acted Reasonably as a Matter of Law

Turning then to what we must decide, we begin with the now established fact that there was no actual fire danger that a reasonable person would perceive—the relevant city departments had, after all, found no fire hazard. Further, the association did not have a good faith, albeit mistaken, belief in that danger. The jury resolved those questions against the association and, in what is really an appeal from a judgment notwithstanding the verdict, those are the operative facts.

In light of those operative facts, it is virtually impossible to say the association acted reasonably. It is true the CC & R's require "owners" to "maintain the interiors of their residential units and garages, including the interior wall, ceilings, floors and permanent fixtures and appurtenances in a clean, sanitary and attractive condition." It is also true that they provide for entry by the board "when necessary in connection with maintenance, landscaping or construction for which the board is responsible." But these sections of the CC & R's cannot reasonably be read to allow an association to dictate the amount of clutter in which a person chooses to live; one man's old piece of junk is another man's *objet d' art.* The association's rather high-handed attempt to micromanage Cunningham's personal housekeeping—telling him how he could and could not use the interior rooms of his own house—clearly crossed the line and was beyond the purview of any legitimate interest it had in preventing undesirable external effects or maintaining property values.

Particularly galling to us—and clearly to the jury as well—was the presumptuous attempt to lecture Cunningham about getting rid of his old *clothes,* the way he kept his own bedroom, and the kind of "reading material" he could have. To obtain some perspective here, we have the spectacle of a homeowner's association telling a senior citizen suffering from Hodgkin's Disease that, in effect, he could not read in his own bed! When Cunningham bought his unit, we seriously doubt that he contemplated the association would ever tell him to clean up his own bedroom like some parent nagging an errant teenager.

If it is indeed true that homeowner's associations can often function "as a second municipal government" (citation omitted), then we have a clear cut case of a "nanny state"—nanny in almost a literal sense—going too far. The association's actions flew in the face of one of the most ancient precepts of American society and Anglo-American legal culture. "A man's house is his castle" was not penned by anonymous, but by the famous jurist Sir Edward Coke in 1628. The jury could thus find that the association did not act reasonably under the circumstances (and that is all we decide).

Exercise 10-19. *Nahrstadt* and *Fountain Valley* Revisited

1. Does the reasonableness standard strike the right balance between individual interests and community interests?
2. Consider whether the lawyers representing the community in *Fountain Valley* complied with the rules of procedure below (this is a federal rule but states have similar rules) and ABA Model Rule of Conduct 3.1. Violation of the rules subjects clients and lawyers to sanctions and, potentially, disciplinary action.

Rule 11 Federal Rules of Civil Procedure

(b) REPRESENTATIONS TO THE COURT. By presenting to the court a pleading, written motion, or other paper—whether by signing, filing, submitting, or later advocating it—an attorney or unrepresented party certifies that to the best of the person's knowledge, information, and belief, formed after an inquiry reasonable under the circumstances:

(1) it is not being presented for any improper purpose, such as to harass, cause unnecessary delay, or needlessly increase the cost of litigation;

(2) the claims, defenses, and other legal contentions are warranted by existing law or by a nonfrivolous argument for extending, modifying, or reversing existing law or for establishing new law.

MRPC 3.1 Meritorious Claims and Contentions

A lawyer shall not bring or defend a proceeding, or assert or controvert an issue therein, unless there is a basis in law and fact for doing so that is not frivolous, which includes a good faith argument for an extension, modification or reversal of existing law. A lawyer for the defendant in a criminal proceeding, or the respondent in a proceeding that could result in incarceration, may nevertheless so defend the proceeding as to require that every element of the case be established.

3. What counsel might you offer a community association that is interested in heavily regulating a neighborhood?

4. Pet law has become controversial and appears to be shifting. Generally, pets are considered property—not people. However, in more recent laws, pets sometimes enjoy special protections or consideration when, for example, there is a dispute over where a dog should live if a family or couple breaks up, or if an animal has been neglected (which can be a crime). After *Nahrstedt*, effective in 2001, the legislature in California adopted the statute below.

California Civil Code § 4715
Pets within common interest developments

(a) No governing documents shall prohibit the owner of a separate interest within a common interest development from keeping at least one pet within the common interest development, subject to reasonable rules and regulations of the association. This section may not be construed to affect any other rights provided by law to an owner of a separate interest to keep a pet within the development.

What effect would this statute have if it applied to *Nahrstedt*?

5. Drawing on both cases and the body of law you have learned so far, be prepared to make closing arguments on litigation for this hypothetical. A family moves into a condominium with CCRs and an association. They move in with their dog Bear, a 150 pound Saint Bernard who is related to the famous movie dog Beethoven. The owners adore Bear and think of him as a family member. They also breed him twice a year and make significant money from

selling the puppies that are his progeny. There was no ban on pets at the time the family purchased the condo. After the family lived there for two years, by a majority vote, the condo association adopted a new rule banning pets over 25 pounds from living in the community. The basis for the new rule is to preserve quiet enjoyment of the property and property values. The family has been advised that they have to get rid of Bear. They would never do that, and they seek to challenge the covenant.

6. Would a ban on children playing in the front yard of their home be found reasonable? What about a prohibition of occupancy by a registered sex offender? *See Mulligan v. Panther Valley Property Owners Association*, 766 A.2d 1186 (N.J. Ct. App. 2001) (upholding covenant but without reaching the merits).

Restraints on Alienation

The power to transfer (alienate) property has long been of special importance in law and is afforded significant protections. It is a core aspect of individual ownership and freedom and is also understood to contribute positively to society by encouraging more widespread access to property, mitigating discrimination and facilitating market exchanges. Yet some regulation on transfers may facilitate individual ownership rights, increase property values and enable community building and planning. These competing interests are accounted for and ideally harmonized by a legal standard that prohibits "unreasonable" restraints on alienation but enforces those that are reasonable. Reasonableness is determined by balancing the costs of the restraint versus the benefits—to individuals and to society. This echoes the analysis of reasonableness you have been exploring in covenants more generally.

You see the rules and policies play out here in the context of whether a covenant that restricts leasing is enforceable. This issue is controversial, particularly when there was no restriction on leasing in the CCRs in place at the time of purchase. Although a number of states will enforce such leasing restrictions, state laws vary, and the law is still evolving. For example, compare *Wilkinson v. Chiwawa Cmts. Ass'n,* 327 P.3d 614 (Wa. 2014) (holding a new restriction on short-term rental activity invalid), with *McElveen-Hunter v. Fountain Manor Ass'n,* 386 S.E.2d 435 (N.C. App. 1989) (post-purchase restriction on leasing valid).

Exercise 10-20. *Adams v. Kimberley One Townhouse Owner's Ass'n*

Develop arguments for and against enforcement of the leasing restriction in the next case and be sure to consider whether there is adequate notice when there is a restriction adopted after an owner purchases the property.

Adams v. Kimberley One Townhouse Owner's Association, Inc.

576 S.E.2d 746 (Idaho 2015)

JONES, J. Virgil Adams appeals the district court's order granting summary judgment in favor of Kimberley One Townhouse Owner's Association, Inc. (Association). Adams purchased a townhouse, subject to a declaration of covenants, conditions, and restrictions (1980 Declaration) that did not specifically restrict an owner's ability to lease his or her unit. Subsequently, the Association amended the 1980 Declaration to provide that an owner could not rent a unit for a period of less than six months. Adams argues the amendment constitutes an invalid restraint on the free use of his land and that he did not have notice of the possibility of such a restriction under the general provision allowing "amendment" in the 1980 Declaration. We affirm.

Factual and Procedural Background

In 1980, the developer of the Kimberley One Townhouses Subdivision (Subdivision) recorded the 1980 Declaration, and the Association was formed to provide certain controls for the Subdivision. The 1980 Declaration described real property containing forty residential lots and provided that all the lots "shall be held, sold and conveyed subject to the covenants, conditions, restrictions and easements (CC & Rs) herein contained which are for the purpose of protecting the value and desirability of, and which shall run with, the real property." The 1980 Declaration defined the permitted "Use and Regulation of Uses" for the lots within the Subdivision, providing that "each lot shall be used for single family residential purposes only, on an ownership, rental or lease basis." The 1980 Declaration also contemplated the possible need for future amendments to that document by providing that the "Declaration may be amended ... by an instrument signed by not less than ninety percent (90%) of the Lot Owners."

In 2003, Adams purchased Lot 1 in the Subdivision, subject to the CC & Rs contained in the 1980 Declaration. The record does not clearly reveal who occupied Adams' unit during many of the years leading up to this case. During the pendency of this action, Adams has lived out of the country. But, it appears he lived in his Kimberley One unit from 2006 to 2007; his parents lived there in the period leading up to the short-term renting; and he began renting the unit as a vacation property in the summer of 2012, planning to use it himself during future summers.

When Adams began renting his unit as a vacation property, the short-term renters precipitated complaints from owner-occupants of other units within the Subdivision, such as renters taking produce from an owner's garden, excessive noise, and parking violations. These complaints were addressed at an Association board meeting in October 2012, the minutes from which were provided to each owner, including Adams. After receiving the meeting minutes, Adams apologized for the problems and promised to remedy the situation. However, at its next meeting the board noted that there continued to be problems with the short-term renters and decided to move forward with a proposed amendment to the CC & Rs (2013 Amendment). Adams communicated with the Association members through email to strongly oppose the amendment. His attorney attended the annual meeting on his behalf and provided comments during the discussion.

The 2013 Amendment passed by an affirmative vote of eighty-nine percent. This amendment changed the permitted use of lots within the Subdivision by providing that units may be rented "only in strict accordance with the following" conditions: (a) the owner must execute a written document with the renter; (b) the document must be approved in advance by the board; (c) advertising for the unit must be approved by the board; (d) no rentals for fewer than six months will be approved; (e) no subleasing is permitted; (f) owner must provide contact information to the board; and (g) the board has discretion to grant exceptions to these rental requirements and to create house rules for their enforcement. When Adams continued to engage in short-term renting subsequent to the 2013 Amendment, the board enacted house rules that imposed a $300 fine for each day a unit is rented in violation of the short-term lease requirements and a $100 fine for each day a unit is advertised in violation of those requirements.

Shortly after the Association notified Adams he was in violation of the 2013 Amendment, he brought a declaratory judgment action seeking to invalidate that amendment. He also sought attorney fees. The Association moved for summary judgment and Adams filed a cross-motion for summary judgment. During a hearing on both motions the district court ruled from the bench, granting the Association's motion and denying Adams' motion. The court entered judgment against Adams and awarded costs and fees to the Association. Adams timely appeals.

The district court correctly determined the validity of the 2013 Amendment.

Adams argues the rental restrictions are invalid because: (1) they do not properly reflect the intent of the parties with respect to their original agreement; (2) Adams had an unrestricted, enforceable right to rent his property under the original agreement; (3) the CC & Rs must be construed in favor of the free use of land rather than in favor of the Association; and (4) the restriction allows for arbitrary discretionary enforcement by the Association.

"Covenants that restrict the uses of land are valid and enforceable." (Citation omitted.) However, because restrictions on the free use of property are at odds with the common law right to use land for all lawful purposes, the Court will enforce such restrictions only when clearly expressed. All doubts in that regard should be "resolved in favor of the free use of land." (Citation omitted.) "Therefore, while clearly expressed restrictions will be upheld, restrictions that are not clearly expressed will be resolved in favor of the free use of land." (Citation omitted.)

This Court applies contract principles to interpret restrictive covenants. Neither party argues the 1980 Declaration or either subsequent amendment is ambiguous. Thus, we determine the intent of the parties from the language contained in that document. The provisions in question here are those relating to use of the property as a rental and to amendment of the declaration. The issue essentially boils down to whether the provision broadly allowing the "Declaration [to] be amended" authorizes the Association to restrict rental use of the property when there were previously no express restrictions on such use.

Adams' ownership of his unit is clearly subject to all the CC & Rs contained in the 1980 Declaration and he does not dispute this fact. The section of the 1980 Declaration titled "Use and Regulation of Uses," provides that "each lot shall be used for single family residential purposes only, on an ownership, rental or lease basis." Another section of the 1980 Declaration, titled "Amendment," provides that during the first thirty years of its existence, the "Declaration may be amended ... by an instrument signed by not less than ninety percent (90%) of the Lot Owners." The district court found that the amendment provision was, in substance, "a method of abrogating and modifying" the declaration. It found "amend," when given its plain and ordinary meaning, clearly included the change made to the declaration in this case. Adams argues the modification in the 2013 Amendment amounted to the *addition* of a *new* burden, which should be distinguished from the *amendment* of an *existing* burden, with the former being precluded under a general amendment provision. He argues that "amend" should be limited to smaller changes and changes to covenants and restrictions that are already addressed in the declaration.

Adams argues Idaho has not addressed the distinction between adding a new restriction to CC & Rs and amending an existing restriction, and he cites to several out-of-state cases to support his proposed distinction. Indeed, there is a split of authority among the states as to whether a new restriction on rental activity may be reasonably added under a general amendment provision, or whether a new restriction is per se unreasonable. We find Idaho's approach to CC & R amendments to be more consistent with that line of cases which do not draw a bright-line distinction between the addition of new restrictions and the modification of existing restrictions. We do, of course, agree with the *Shawver* [*v. Huckleberry Estates*, 140 Idaho 354, 365, 93 P.3d 685, 696 (2004)] Court that there is a point at which an amendment to CC & Rs will go too far, and have too adverse an effect on those bound by it, in which case the amendment would be precluded. However, the fact that a restriction was not previously addressed in the CC & Rs prior to an amendment does not automatically mean that amendment has gone too far.

The amendment in the case at hand has not reached the tipping point. *Shawver* generally suggests that parties should be bound by the terms to which they agree, including a term allowing the significant future alteration of the agreement, unless a term produces unconscionable harm. The record reflects that Adams had only been renting his unit as a vacation property for a few months when the Association began discussing an amendment. We are not faced with a situation where Adams was permitted to engage in short-term renting for ten years and then, all of a sudden, an amendment no longer permitted such use. Additionally, he is still permitted to rent his property as long as he complies with the terms of the new amendment. Even prior to the amendment, the rental activity was limited by the declaration to allow rentals or leases "for single family residential purposes only." In substance, the 2013 Amendment simply narrowed what may be considered a "single family residential purpose." That term implies a certain degree of long-term or stable occupancy of the residence, rather than it being used as a hotel as Adams had. The 2013 Amendment simply provided clarity to that term.

[A]lthough Adams purchased his home in reliance on his ability to rent it as he pleased, he is bound by the 1980 Declaration as a whole, which included the general right of the owners to amend. Adams argues the amendment deprived him of the benefit of his bargain by failing to give effect to the provision that expressly allowed him an unrestricted right to rent his unit. Adams agreed to the entire 1980 Declaration, including the amendment provision, and allowing him to now avoid compliance with that provision is inconsistent with the bargain he made.

Adams argues that to allow amendments of the type in this case creates a slippery slope that provides no protection for owners in the minority voting position. However, this disadvantage to those in minority voting position was apparent from the 1980 Declaration at the time of the original purchase. Under the 1980 Declaration, ten percent of the homeowners could be bound by an amendment they did not want if the majority had the requisite ninety percent of the vote to support the change. This fact is obvious and unambiguous on the face of the agreement, and if Adams was not willing to agree to the amendment term, he was free to walk away from the transaction.

Finally, Adams argues the 2013 Amendment is invalid because it allows arbitrary enforcement and discriminatory application. He contends the Association sought to impose the new restrictions solely on his unit. Although it was Adams' conduct that precipitated the need for the amendment, there is nothing in the language of the 2013 Amendment that could reasonably be interpreted to apply only to Adams' unit. All the rental restrictions facially apply equally to all units within the Subdivision. Adams further argues the board's discretion to grant exceptions to the rental restrictions shows that the amendment does not apply equally to all units. He argues the board provided itself with such discretion to allow it to enforce the rental restriction "solely against Appellant, Mr. Adams." However, there is nothing in the record to suggest, nor does Adams argue, that the board has engaged in any conduct amounting to discriminatory enforcement.

[W]e hold that the district court properly determined the 2013 Amendment was validly made within the scope of the plain language of the amendment provision. [The court also held that the attorney fees award to the association was appropriate.]

Discriminatory Covenants

As we have seen, some covenants are not enforceable based on public policy. The policy evaluation may be woven into an analysis of reasonableness or the touch and concern requirement. Sometimes courts address public policy explicitly, as is the case with discriminatory covenants.

Lamentably, there is a long history of racially discriminatory covenants that were in the past used to prohibit sales or leases to African Americans as well as Asian Americans, Latinos, Indians and Jews. Large numbers of parcels still have such covenants recorded in the chain of title. These covenants are clearly unenforceable today under the Federal Fair Housing Act ("FHA") which provides:

> [I]t shall be unlawful—to refuse to sell or rent after the making of a bona fide offer, or to refuse to negotiate for the sale or rental of, or otherwise make unavailable or deny, a dwelling to any person because of race, color, religion, sex, familial status [children living with parents or legal custodians and pregnant women], or national origin.

42 U.S.C. § 3604. The FHA is studied in some depth in the chapter on leasing.

A racially restrictive covenant was also struck down in *Shelly v. Kraemer*, 334 U.S. 1 (1948), a landmark civil rights case. A covenant that prohibited occupation by non-Caucasians on an entire street was found unconstitutional as a violation of the Equal Protection Clause of the Fourteenth Amendment. The Fourteenth Amendment only applies to "state action"—meaning government entities—and so does not generally reach the activities of private actors or common interest communities. However, in *Shelly*, the U.S. Supreme Court found that *judicial enforcement* of a private covenant constituted state action.

Note that this broad definition of state action has not generally been extended to covenants in other contexts, and it is not clear that it would be. Very few cases have refused to enforce a covenant on *constitutional* grounds. The application of the constitution to covenants has been quite limited, because CICs are not generally viewed as government actors. That said, it could be that if a CIC were to replace a governmental role, like policing, then a state action argument might be persuasive.

Other kinds of discriminatory covenants can be evaluated for compliance with public policy and may be found unenforceable. For example, a covenant that restricts use to "single family homes" that is interpreted to prohibit group homes for people with disabilities has been found to violate the FHA. *See Hill v. Community of Damien of Molkai*, 911 P.2d 861 (N.M. 1996). Covenants or rules that discriminate based on a particular religion would also be unenforceable under the FHA. However, neutral rules that might conflict with religious practices such as a rule not to use common spaces for worship have been upheld, because they do not make housing unavailable based on religion. *See, e.g., Savanna Club Worship Service, Inc. v. Savanna Club Homewoners Association, Inc.* 456 F. Supp. 2d 1223 (S.D. Fla. 2005).

Termination

Suppose wood shingles for roofing are required by a covenant in a CIC. Yet the HOA neglected to enforce the rules and only 5 of the first 20 houses in the CIC were built with wood shingles. Fearing that wooden shingles pose too much of a fire danger, an owner who was in the process of building the 21st home in the community requested permission by the HOA to use an alternative roofing material that is more resistant to fire. The HOA denies the request and insists on wood shingles. The owner installs a roof with alternative materials anyway and violates the covenant. The HOA seeks an injunction to enforce the covenant. (This example is derived from *Fink v. Miller*, 896 P.2d 649 (Ct. App. Utah 1995).)

Enforcement of a covenant can be challenged through a claim that it has terminated. There are a number of claims to consider. All but the last two will be familiar, as they apply to easements as well as covenants.

1. **Abandonment.** In the situation above, there is a strong claim that the covenant has been terminated by abandonment (or waiver). As with easements, abandonment requires conduct that demonstrates intent to relinquish the benefit. Tolerating violations of a covenant by other owners is grounds for this conclusion. The wood shingles case makes out this claim, because violation of the covenant was widespread and continued for a significant period of time.
2. **Estoppel.** If an owner of the dominant estate says or engages in acts that suggest the covenant will not be enforced and then the servient estate holder detrimentally relies on that, the covenant will not be enforceable. In the example given above, an estoppel claim would succeed if the HOA had granted permission to violate the covenant, and then a non-wood shingle roof was installed, and thereafter the HOA sought enforcement of the covenant.
3. **Merger.** The covenant terminates if both the dominant and servient estate are owned by one person.
4. **Release.** An covenant is terminated if the benefitted estate holder releases it in a writing that satisfies the Statute of Frauds.
5. **Express Terms.** Covenants might be set up to last only a finite period of time, such as 5 years. At the end of the term, the covenant terminates.
6. **Prescription.** Suppose the owner of the servient estate openly violates a covenant for 30 years—say by having a metal roof when only wood shingle roofs are allowed. Trespassing on the rights of the holder of the benefit like this in a way that is open and notorious, hostile and continuous for the statutory period will extinguish the covenant.
7. **Relative Hardship.** A covenant will not be enforced if the burden of the covenant is greater by a considerable magnitude than the benefit. So the hardship must be great and the benefit small for the covenant to unenforceable. One example is where neighbors had to give their consent for an owner to be able to construct a home on the parcel. The dominant estate holders refuse to give consent claiming that would keep housing density lower and prevent a decrease in value. The court found the benefits of enforcement were minimal and the harm to the servient estate holder great. *Lange v. Scofield*, 567 So. 2d 1299 (Ala. 1990). Another example is where an owner builds a home one foot over the setback line. Courts of equity traditionally have considered this doctrine when deciding whether to issue an injunction rather than damages for a breach of a covenant.
8. **Changed Conditions.** A covenant is unenforceable when 1) the conditions in a neighborhood change so substantially that 2) the benefit of the covenant can no longer be realized. Changed conditions, along with abandonment, are the most common claims for termination of covenants. You see these rules in action in the next case.

Exercise 10-21. *El Di, Inc. v. Town of Bethany Beach*

Carefully read *El Di.* If your last name begins with A through L, be prepared to take on the role as the attorney for El Di. If your last name begins with M through Z, be prepared to take on the role as the attorney for the town of Bethany Beach. Whichever role you have, consider the list above and identify which claims for termination are potentially viable, evaluate the claims and be prepared to make arguments on behalf of your client based on the law and the facts. Are there any other legal issues you would want to raise or be prepared to defend against?

El Di, Inc. v. Town of Bethany Beach

477 A.2d 1066 (Del. 1984)

Herrmann, C.J. This is an appeal from a permanent injunction granted by the Court of Chancery upon the petition of the plaintiffs, The Town of Bethany Beach, et al., prohibiting the defendant, El Di, Inc. ("El Di") from selling alcoholic beverages at Holiday House, a restaurant in Bethany Beach owned and operated by El Di.

The pertinent facts are as follows. El Di purchased the Holiday House in 1969. In December 1981, El Di filed an application with the State Alcoholic Beverage Control Commission (the "Commission") for a license to sell alcoholic beverages at the Holiday House. On April 15, 1982, finding "public need and convenience," the Commission granted the Holiday House an on-premises license. The sale of alcoholic beverages at Holiday House began within 10 days of the Commission's approval. Plaintiffs subsequently filed suit to permanently enjoin the sale of alcoholic beverages under the license.

On appeal it is undisputed that the chain of title for the Holiday House lot included restrictive covenants prohibiting both the sale of alcoholic beverages on the property and nonresidential construction. The same restriction was placed on property in Bethany Beach as early as 1900 and 1901 when the area was first under development.

As originally conceived, Bethany Beach was to be a quiet beach community. The site was selected at the end of the nineteenth-century by the Christian Missionary Society of Washington, D.C. In 1900, the Bethany Beach Improvement Company ("BBIC") was formed. The BBIC purchased lands, laid out a development and began selling lots. To insure the quiet character of the community, the BBIC placed restrictive covenants on many plots, prohibiting the sale of alcohol and restricting construction to residential cottages. Of the original 180 acre development, however, approximately 1/3 was unrestricted.

The Town of Bethany Beach was officially incorporated in 1909. The municipal limits consisted of 750 acres including the original BBIC land (hereafter the original or "old-Town"), but expanded far beyond the 180 acre BBIC development. The expanded acreage of the newly incorporated Town, combined with the unrestricted plots in the original Town, left only 15 percent of the new Town subject to the restrictive covenants.

Despite the restriction prohibiting commercial building ("no other than a dwelling or cottage shall be erected ..."), commercial development began in the 1920's on property subject to the covenants. This development included numerous inns, restaurants, drug stores, a bank, motels, a town hall, shops selling various items including food, clothing, gifts and novelties and other commercial businesses. Of the 34 commercial buildings presently within the Town limits, 29 are located in the old-Town originally developed by BBIC. Today, Bethany Beach has a permanent population of some 330 residents. In the summer months the population increases to approximately 10,000 people within the corporate limits and to some 48,000 people within a 4 mile radius. In 1952, the Town enacted a zoning ordinance which established a central commercial district designated C-1 located in the old-Town section. Holiday House is located in this district.

Since El Di purchased Holiday House in 1969, patrons have been permitted to carry their own alcoholic beverages with them into the restaurant to consume with their meals. This "brown-bagging" practice occurred at Holiday House prior to El Di's ownership and at other restaurants in the Town. El Di applied for a license to sell liquor at Holiday House in response to the increased number of customers who were engaging in "brown-bagging" and in the belief that the license would permit restaurant management to control excessive use of alcohol and use by minors. Prior to the time El Di sought a license, alcoholic beverages had been and continue to be readily available for sale at nearby licensed establishments including: one restaurant 1/2 mile outside the Town limits, 3 restaurants within a 4 mile radius of the Town, and a package store some 200-300 yards from the Holiday House.

In granting plaintiffs' motion for a permanent injunction, the Court of Chancery rejected defendant's argument that changed conditions in Bethany Beach rendered the restrictive covenants unreasonable and therefore unenforceable. The Chancery Court found that although the evidence showed a considerable growth since 1900 in both population and the number of buildings in Bethany Beach, "the basic nature of Bethany Beach as a quiet, family oriented resort has not changed." The Court also found that there had been development of commercial activity since 1900, but that this "activity is limited to a small area of Bethany Beach and consists mainly of activities for the convenience and patronage of the residents of Bethany Beach."

The Trial Court also rejected defendant's contention that plaintiffs' acquiescence and abandonment rendered the covenants unenforceable. In this connection, the Court concluded that the practice of "brown-bagging" was not a sale of alcoholic beverages and that, therefore, any failure to enforce the restriction as against the practice did not constitute abandonment or waiver of the restriction.

We find that the Trial Court erred in holding that the change of conditions was insufficient to negate the restrictive covenant. A court will not enforce a restrictive covenant where a fundamental change has occurred in the intended character of the neighborhood that renders the benefits underlying imposition of the restrictions incapable of enjoyment. Review of all the facts and circumstances convinces us that the change, since 1901, in the character of that area of the old-Town section now zoned C-1 is so substantial as to justify modification of the deed restriction. We need not determine a change in character of the entire restricted area in order to assess the continued applicability of the covenant to a portion thereof.

It is uncontradicted that one of the purposes underlying the covenant prohibiting the sale of intoxicating liquors was to maintain a quiet, residential atmosphere in the restricted area. Each of the additional covenants reinforces this objective, including the covenant restricting construction to residential dwellings. The covenants read as a whole evince an intention on the part of the grantor to maintain the residential, seaside character of the community.

But time has not left Bethany Beach the same community its grantors envisioned in 1901. The Town has changed from a church-affiliated residential community to a summer resort visited annually by thousands of tourists. Nowhere is the resultant change in character more evident than in the C-1 section of the old-Town. Plaintiffs argue that this is a relative change only and that there is sufficient evidence to support the Trial Court's findings that the residential character of the community has been maintained and that the covenants continue to benefit the other lot owners. We cannot agree.

In 1909, the 180 acre restricted old-Town section became part of a 750 acre incorporated municipality. Even prior to the Town's incorporation, the BBIC deeded out lots free of the restrictive covenants. After incorporation and partly due to the unrestricted lots deeded out by the BBIC, 85 percent of the land area within the Town was not subject to the restrictions. Significantly, nonresidential uses quickly appeared in the restricted area and today the old-Town section contains almost all of the commercial businesses within the entire Town. Moreover, these commercial uses have gone unchallenged for 82 years.

The change in conditions is also reflected in the Town's decision in 1952 to zone restricted property, including the lot on which the Holiday House is located, specifically for commercial use. Although a change in zoning is not dispositive as against a private covenant, it is additional evidence of changed community conditions.

Time has relaxed not only the strictly residential character of the area, but the pattern of alcohol use and consumption as well. The practice of "brown-bagging" has continued unchallenged for at least twenty years at commercial establishments located on restricted property in the Town. On appeal, plaintiffs rely on the Trial Court finding that the "brown-bagging," practice is irrelevant as evidence of waiver inasmuch as the practice does not involve the sale of intoxicating liquors prohibited by the covenant. We find the "brown-bagging" practice evidence of a significant change in conditions in the community since its inception at the turn of the century. Such consumption of alcohol in public places is now generally tolerated by owners of similarly restricted lots. The license issued to the Holiday House establishment permits the El Di management to better control the availability and consumption of intoxicating liquors on its premises. In view of both the ready availability of alcoholic beverages in the area surrounding the Holiday House and the long-tolerated and increasing use of "brown-bagging" enforcement of the restrictive covenant at this time would only serve to subvert the public interest in the control of the availability and consumption of alcoholic liquors.

Plaintiffs contend that the covenant prohibiting the sale of intoxicating liquors is separate from the other covenants. In the plaintiffs' view, the alcohol sale restriction serves a purpose distinct from the prohibition of nonresidential uses. Plaintiffs argue, therefore, that despite evidence of commercial uses, the alcohol sale restriction provides a substantial benefit to the other lot owners.

It is further argued that the commercial uses are restricted to a small area within the old-Town section. But significantly, the section in which Holiday House is located is entirely commercial. The business uses, the availability of alcohol in close proximity to this section, and the repeated use of "brown-bagging" in the C-1 district render the originally intended benefits of the covenants unattainable in what has become an area detached in character from the strictly residential surroundings to the west.

In view of the change in conditions in the C-1 district of Bethany Beach, we find it unreasonable and inequitable now to enforce the restrictive covenant. To permit unlimited "brown-bagging" but to prohibit licensed sales of alcoholic liquor, under the circumstances of this case, is inconsistent with any reasonable application of the restriction and contrary to public policy. We emphasize that our judgment is confined to the area of the old-Town section zoned C-1. The restrictions in the neighboring residential area are unaffected by the conclusion we reach herein.

Christie, J., with whom Moore, J., joins, dissenting: I respectfully disagree with the majority. I think the evidence supports the conclusion of the Chancellor, as finder of fact, that the basic nature of the community of Bethany Beach has not changed in such a way as to invalidate those restrictions which have continued to protect this community through the years as it has grown. Although some of the restrictions have been ignored and a portion of the community is now used for limited commercial purposes, the evidence shows that Bethany Beach remains a quiet, family-oriented resort where no liquor is sold. I think the conditions of the community are still consistent with the enforcement of a restrictive covenant forbidding the sale of intoxicating beverages.

In my opinion, the toleration of the practice of "brown bagging" does not constitute the abandonment of a longstanding restriction against the sale of alcoholic beverages. The restriction against sales has, in fact, remained intact for more than eighty years and any violations thereof have been short-lived. The fact that alcoholic beverages may be purchased right outside the town is not inconsistent with my view that the quiet-town atmosphere in this small area has not broken down, and that it can and should be preserved. Those who choose to buy land subject to the restrictions should be required to continue to abide by the restrictions.

I think the only real beneficiaries of the failure of the courts to enforce the restrictions would be those who plan to benefit commercially. I also question the propriety of the issuance of a liquor license for the sale of liquor on property which is subject to a specific restrictive covenant against such sales.

I think that restrictive covenants play a vital part in the preservation of neighborhood schemes all over the State, and that a much more complete breakdown of the neighborhood scheme should be required before a court declares that a restriction has become unenforceable.

PART SIX
Real Estate Transactions

Chapter 11

Real Estate Transactions & Finance

Introduction

Real estate transactions can have a profound impact on people's lives, on businesses and on the economy. You have probably heard the saying that owning your own home is the American dream. Home ownership can create a place for exercising freedom, privacy and a safe haven for individuals and families. Although the interests are quite different than for residential property, commercial real estate is an important tool for the operation and success of businesses. This in turn can contribute to people's livelihoods, help generate jobs and fuel the economy.

Millions of real estate transactions occur annually. Most are residential transactions that—as you will see—can include plenty of complexities. Commercial transactions such as purchasing an apartment complex, a shopping center, an office building or a farm, tend to be more complex and involved. The focus in this chapter is on residential real estate transactions. However, the same principles largely apply to both.

Lawyers take on varying roles in helping clients navigate real estate transactions. Under the large umbrella of legal problem solving, real estate lawyers communicate and counsel clients, develop strategies, negotiate terms, produce and evaluate documents such as contracts and deeds, identify and apply laws and policies, assess and mitigate risks and, if need be, resolve conflicts out of court or litigate. That said, the role of attorneys in assisting people buying homes has shifted. Although the practice varies by jurisdiction, today real estate brokers, title companies and escrow agents perform many of the functions that lawyers served say 50 years ago. Standardized forms and routines are very common. Lawyers still play a leading role in commercial transactions. For residential transactions, however, we tend to be brought in to undertake the more complicated and difficult matters and for dispute resolution in the transaction process or afterwards.

Overview of Chapter 11

This Chapter is divided into two major subparts:

1. Real Estate Transactions.
2. Real Estate Finance.

There are a host of issues that arise in real estate transactions. The chapter begins with the phases of the transaction and creation of sales contracts formally in a writing and possibly informally without one. We turn next to contract terms, their meaning and breach. Additionally, you will become educated about how to deal with two major problems a buyer might face—defects in the physical condition of the property and defects in title. How can these risks be identified and reduced? Who bears the losses? What protections and remedies might be available to the buyer? What are the seller's obligations? To develop answers, you will learn about fraud law as well as the implied warranty of habitability (for new construction). Then, after conveyancing by deed, you study title assurance through deed warrantics, the recording system and title insurance and registration. Your last subject to learn in the chapter is real estate finance law, including the core principles of mortgages, installment land contracts and other liens.

Chapter Problem: Exercise 11-1

Eddie Leporta just retained you to assist him with purchasing his first home. After you learn the materials in this chapter, you should be prepared to engage in the following lawyering tasks.

1. Counsel Eddie on what to negotiate for in the purchase and sale agreement besides the price of the home and the closing date. Identify at least three legal issues that are important for protecting Eddie's interests and what specific legal terms you would like to see included in the contract. Keep this in mind when you review the standard sales contract included in Exercise 11-2 below.
2. What kind of deed would you recommend he seek from the buyer and with what covenants?
3. Eddie does not have a good credit history and can only qualify for a traditional mortgage with a high interest rate. The seller of the property has offered to serve as the lender if Eddie is willing to enter into an installment land contract with standard terms. Eddie is not sure what he should do. Counsel Eddie on the legal advantages and disadvantages of these different financing arrangements.
4. After he signs the purchase and sales agreement but before the closing, Eddie discovered that the seller constructed the garage in violation of zoning laws that require buildings to be set back at least 15 feet from the street. The garage is set back only 5 feet. Counsel Eddie on how the law governs this problem and what his options are. What happens if he goes through with the transaction? What are risks that he faces? What advice do you have to mitigate the risks?
5. One month after the closing and moving into his new home, Eddie discovers that the pipes from the upstairs bathroom are leaking through the floor and into the first story below. Eddie's contractor opened up the floors and drywall areas where the leak was now visible (it had not been before Eddie purchased the home). The contractor is sure this has been a recurring problem, and mold is growing rampantly inside the walls and floors. It is clear that the drywall in the area of the ceiling where the leak was had been repaired before.

In the seller's disclosure statement given to Eddie when he was first considering buying the house, in response to the question "are there now or were there ever problems with water leaking in the house"—the buyer wrote in "unknown." It will cost $10,000 to remediate the mold. Is there a cause of action that Eddie can successfully bring to compensate for these losses?

Real Estate Transactions

Phases in the Transaction Process

To best understand and apply the laws in this area, it is helpful to organize the transaction into steps and phases along a timeline. There are five steps to consider: (1) before the contract; (2) contracting; (3) the executory period; (4) the closing and (5) after the closing. As we proceed though the chapter, we will key in on the executory period and the post-closing period because some different laws apply during these phases. This is illustrated below.

In the pre-contract phase, the parties are looking to sell or a buy a home. Professionally licensed real estate brokers and agents are often involved in this process—although the internet is another and growing source for finding buyers and sellers directly. The next step is to negotiate and enter into the contract. Once the parties settle on the purchase price and other basic terms, they then enter into a purchase and sale agreement. This might be drafted by an attorney. Usually, however, the parties use a standard form contract that is publicly available. The real estate agent might help fill in the blanks on this document. If that is all the agent does, it is permissible. If the agent does more, that raises a concern for unauthorized practice of law. Only licensed lawyers can practice law and not others. If the agent significantly revises the language of the contract or drafts deeds or mortgages, that line has been crossed.

In the contract the seller agrees to sell the property and the buyer agrees to buy on an agreed date in the future at the closing. The purchase price is specified along with any other terms, such as the date when possession will be transferred. The agreement also will set forth the obligations of the buyer and seller going forward and conditions that must be satisfied for the transaction to close. Another standard contract term is for the buyer to give a deposit or "earnest money" to the seller. This helps mitigate the seller's risk in taking the house off the market. However, the buyer may also be entitled to get the deposit back if certain conditions are met. If the deal falls through, refunding the deposit can be controversial. With this in mind, some parties will decide to use an escrow agent—a neutral third party—to hold the deposit and transfer it later to the party entitled to it.

Now the parties enter the executory period when the parties engage in investigations and other conduct to get ready for the closing. Typically, the transaction is contingent on: (1) inspections for defects such as faulty foundations or termites that were previously unknown; (2) on the seller getting financing on reasonable terms; and (3) on the seller's ability to provide marketable title (which you will learn about later in this chapter.) Although unusual, the agreement could also be contingent on the buyer selling another property or on the seller finding a new place to live. If all goes well, the parties proceed to the closing and complete the purchase and sale. The property is transferred or "conveyed" by a deed that may include a number of terms and warranties. Deeds are discussed in detail below.

Purchase and Sale Contract

Express Agreements

Now that you have been introduced to the basic structure of a real estate transaction, the next step is a more detailed study of specific contract terms and potential legal issues. Even though it is often "standard form," a purchase and sale agreement is quite complicated. Of course, as with any contract, lawyers need to read carefully and understand thoroughly. Consider too whether such agreements would benefit from being revised individually to adjust the rights and responsibilities of the parties to better reflect their intent or to provide more protections or a better deal for one party. Although form contracts are widely available and used frequently, be aware that they often are drafted from a seller's point of view and as such, may disadvantage buyers. As you discover more about issues of concern to buyers and sellers in this chapter, think about what terms you might add or change.

Exercise 11-2. Document Review — A Sample Purchase and Sale Agreement

PLEASE NOTE: This sample agreement is provided for educational purposes only. It is not intended to be used as an Agreement or as a complete standard form document. Form Purchase and Sale Agreements are available in most states.

SAMPLE AGREEMENT OF PURCHASE AND SALE

This PURCHASE & SALE AGREEMENT (the "Agreement") is made this ___ Day Of _____, ("Effective Date") by and between ___________ (hereafter referred to as the "Seller") and ___________ (hereafter referred to as the "Purchaser"). For good and valuable consideration, the receipt and sufficiency of which are hereby acknowledged, Seller and Purchaser agree as follows:

1. AGREEMENT TO SELL AND BUY PROPERTY. Upon and subject to the terms set forth in this Agreement, Seller agrees to sell to Purchaser and Purchaser

agrees to buy from Seller, the following real property located at __________ in the city of_________, County of__________, State of______________, the legal description of which is:______________________.

2. PURCHASE PRICE. The agreed purchase price for the property is $________ Dollars, to be paid in cash or equivalent good funds at closing. The earnest money purchaser deposit paid as described in paragraph 3 below shall be applied to the purchase price at the time of closing the sale.

3. EARNEST MONEY: $ ______ valid check or money order payable to Escrow Agent: ___________, whose address is: ____________________, will be promptly delivered to Escrow Agent no later than three (3) calendar days after the Acceptance Date. The Acceptance Date will be the date of full execution (signing) of this Agreement by all parties.

4. BUILDINGS, STRUCTURES, IMPROVEMENTS AND FIXTURES. Included in the sale as a part of the property are all improvements, buildings, structures and fixtures presently on the real estate. Fixtures include all things which are permanently attached to the property. This includes but is not limited to electrical, gas, heating, air conditioning, plumbing equipment, built-in appliances, hot water heaters, all doors and storm doors; all windows, screens, and storm windows; all window treatments (draperies, curtains, blinds, shades, etc.) and hardware, awnings, attached carpeting, radio, television antennas, all bathroom fixtures; gas logs, fireplace doors and attached screens; all security system components and controls; garage door openers and all remote controls; swimming pool and its equipment; permanently installed outdoor cooking grills; all fencing, landscaping and outdoor lighting.

Other items included in the sale:

____

Items excluded from the sale:

____

5. TITLE. At the closing Seller shall provide Purchaser marketable title to the Property, subject only to easements, zoning and restrictions of record and free and clear of all other liens and encumbrances except as otherwise stated in this Agreement. Should the title to the Property appear defective, Seller shall have ten (10) days after receipt of notice from Buyer of such defect or defects within which to remedy same at the cost of Seller. Seller shall convey title to Purchaser at the time of closing by a good and sufficient Special Warranty Deed in substantially the form attached here as Exhibit A, free and clear of all liens and encumbrances except as otherwise provided in this offer and subject to easements, zoning and restrictions of record.

6. RISK OF LOSS. The risk of loss by destruction or damage to the property by fire or otherwise prior to the closing of the sale is on Seller. If all or a substantial portion of the improvements on the property are destroyed or damaged prior to the closing and transfer of title this Agreement shall be voidable at Purchaser's option and in the event Purchaser elects to avoid this Agreement the Earnest Money deposited shall be promptly refunded.

7. LOAN CONTINGENCIES. This Agreement is contingent on Purchaser obtaining loan(s) of Purchaser's choice to finance this purchase. Purchaser must deliver to Seller no later than twenty (20) calendar days after the Acceptance Date a lender's conditional commitment letter proving that: a loan application has been made; an appraisal has been ordered; Purchaser has the necessary cash; and providing reasonable assurance of Purchaser's ability to obtain loan with rates, terms, payments and conditions acceptable to Purchaser. Failure to timely provide such commitment letter will be grounds for Seller to cancel this Agreement in which case the Earnest Money must be refunded to Purchaser.

8. APPRAISAL CONTINGENCY. This Agreement is contingent on the appraisal value equaling or exceeding the purchase price.

9. INSPECTION CONTINGENCY and TIME PERIOD: This Agreement is contingent on Purchaser's satisfaction with all property inspections and investigations. All inspections and investigations must be completed with response to Seller no later than ten (10) calendar days after the Acceptance Date. Failure to deliver to the Seller a written notice of any dissatisfaction with the results of all property inspections and investigations within the period described will be considered to be an acceptance of the Property "as is," and the Inspection Contingency will be satisfied and no longer a part of this Agreement.

10. CLOSING, EXPIRATION, & POSSESSION DATE: This offer is void if not accepted by Seller in writing on or before ______o'clock of the _____day of _________, 20____. This sale will be closed on _________ such date or this Agreement will expire on such date at 5:00 p.m. If this is not a business day, this date will be extended to the next business day. Any other change in this date must be agreed to in writing by all parties. Full possession of the entire property free of all tenants and occupants will be given to the Buyer at the time of closing, unless a different time of possession is agreed to in a separate Occupancy Agreement.

11. TIME IS OF THE ESSENCE: It is agreed that time is of the essence in this agreement. The failure to meet specified time limits will be grounds for canceling this Agreement.

12. CLOSING COSTS: Unless otherwise stated in this Agreement closing costs are to be paid as follows:

(a) Seller must pay all Seller's existing loans, liens and related costs affecting the sale of the property, Seller's settlement fees and real estate commissions.

(b) Purchaser must pay transfer taxes, deed and recording fees, transfer fees, hazard and any other required insurance, Purchaser's settlement fees, and all Purchaser's loan related or lender required expenses.

(c) The current year's property taxes, any existing tenant leases or rents, association or maintenance fees, will be prorated as of the date of closing. Taxes for prior years before date of closing must be paid by Seller at or before closing.

13. DISBURSEMENT OF EARNEST MONEY. The Earnest Money will be applied towards the purchase price at closing. If any contingencies or conditions of this Agreement are not met and the Agreement is cancelled, all Earnest Money must be refunded to Purchaser. If Seller fails to perform any obligation under this Agreement, all Earnest Money must be refunded to Purchaser.

14. DEFAULT OR BREACH: If either party fails to perform any obligation under this Agreement, the other party may do any or all of the following: (1) cancel the Agreement, (2) sue for specific performance, (3) sue for actual and compensatory damages. However, if the Purchaser fails to perform the obligations of this Agreement, Seller shall retain all deposits made under this Agreement as liquidated damages, unless Seller gives Purchaser notice otherwise within thirty days after the time Purchaser's performance was due under this Agreement.

If either party shall bring an action against the other arising out of this Agreement, the party in whose favor final judgment is entered shall be entitled to have and recover from the other party his or her reasonable attorneys' fees and other reasonable expenses incurred in connection with such action or proceeding.

15. ACCEPTANCE OF THE DEED. The acceptance of the deed by the Purchaser shall deem the terms of this Agreement fully performed and discharge every agreement and obligation included herein except for those terms that are to be performed after the delivery of the deed.

16. ENTIRE AGREEMENT. It is expressly agreed that this agreement to purchase real estate includes the entire agreement of Purchaser and Seller. This agreement shall be binding upon the heirs, personal representatives, successors and assigns of both Purchaser and Seller. This agreement shall be interpreted and enforced in accordance with the laws of the State of____________.

X____________________ Buyer Signature _________ Date & Time

X____________________ Buyer Signature _________ Date & Time

Statute of Frauds

What if two friends were talking and agreed that one would sell their home to the other who would buy it for $200,000? Then, the next day, the seller changes her mind. Can the buyer enforce the agreement? Generally, the answer is no, because real property contracts have to be in writing by virtue of the statute of frauds. However, as you will learn below, there are exceptions.

Even for property law, the statute of frauds goes way back in history. The rule is derived from the original statute of frauds enacted in England in 1677. It is intended to prevent fraud. It continues in force today in every state. Recall from your encounters with the rule in other topics, the statute of frauds is a general rule that requires real estate transactions to be in writing to be enforceable. More specifically, a real estate contract must meet these minimum requirements:

1. Be in a written contract or a memorandum;
2. Includes the essential terms of the contract—the parties, the price and a description of the real estate (enough to uniquely identify the property);
3. Signed by "the party to be charged" meaning by the person who allegedly transferred out the property interest and is resisting enforcement of a contract.

How does this rule translate into our modern technological world? What if the conversation in the example above happened through email with a signature? That likely would be enough. Electronic documents and "memos" and signatures can satisfy the statute of frauds. All states have adopted a version of the Uniform Electronic Transactions Act (UETA) that permits this or a similar law. Federal law addresses this issue to some extent as well. Known as the "E-sign Act," the Electronic Signatures in Global and National Commerce Act authorizes use of electronic signatures in transactions affecting interstate or foreign commerce. 15 U.S.C. § 7001. Emails are a form of written communication. However, emails can also be far more informal and signing feels less "ceremonial." As is true in contracting more generally, email contracts can raise the concern about whether the parties truly intended to be bound.

Implied Agreements—Part Performance and Equitable Estoppel

In the *Hickey v. Green* exercise below, you will evaluate a writing that satisfies some, but not all, of the requirements for the statute of frauds. What happens then? One possible legal outcome is that there may be no enforceable contract—like in the earlier example with the friend's oral purchase and sale agreement. Another possibility is that a fact situation might fit one of the three major exceptions to the statute of frauds:

reasonably rely

1. **Estoppel.** An oral contract may be recognized and enforced if (a) one party makes a promise (b) and another party reasonably and detrimentally relies on the promise. Estoppel is grounded in equity. The idea is if a person reasonably changed position in reliance on a promise, then it would be unfair to allow the promisor to back out. For example, if a seller and buyer agree on a sale, then the buyer sells her

own home, but then the seller changes his mind, estoppel is grounds for specific enforcement of the oral contract.

Here is how the Restatement (Second) of Contracts § 139 describes the rule in the context of a land contract:

> A promise which the promisor should reasonably expect to induce action or forbearance on the part of the promisee or a third person and which does induce the action or forbearance is enforceable notwithstanding the Statute of Frauds if injustice can be avoided only by enforcement of the promise. The remedy granted for breach is to be limited as justice requires.

This may be called promissory estoppel in your Contracts Law course.

Recall that estoppel is a general concept that applies across topics. Sometimes it has a more specific iteration in a particular context, as is true here with real estate contracts. You encounter estoppel in other legal topics in this text—easements by estoppel is a good example. Recall the most general version of estoppel: (1) one party engages in conduct that induces 2) reasonable detrimental reliance (a change in position) by another party.

Here is another example to help concretize the rules. In *Hurtubise v. McPherson,* 951 N.E.2d 994 (Mass. App. 2011), two adjacent land owners agreed to trade portions of their land so that Hurtubise could build a new storage building for his storage business on part of the land he received from McPherson. The two shook hands on the deal. Hurtubise then proceeded with his plans and built a 300-by-thirty-foot storage shed at a cost of $39,690. During the seven to eight weeks of construction, Hurtubise saw McPherson multiple times at the site. McPherson never objected to the project or its location. After construction, Hurtubise sent McPherson a detailed plan showing that the shed crossed over about 10 feet onto McPherson's land. McPherson objected, stating this was more land than he agreed to swap. He suggested a payment of $250,000 to resolve the dispute. The trial judge found that that amount grossly exceeded the value of the strip of property.

Now, apply the rules for estoppel to the case. Did Hurtubise reasonably rely to his detriment on McPherson's promise for a land swap? Be sure you understand why the answer is yes.

2. **Part Performance.** The other major exception is the part performance doctrine. An oral agreement for the sale of real property may be enforced if the buyer has detrimentally changed her position and taken steps to complete the transaction. Courts emphasize consideration of three factors—did the buyer:

a. Take possession of the property?
b. Pay all or part of the purchase price (by money or labor or other)?
c. Make improvements to the property?

If one or more of these factors is present, then a court might conclude that the contract has already been partially performed and so the promise to transfer the property should be specifically enforced. Jurisdictions vary in whether they require one, two or all three of the factors. Some require a particular combination, such as taking possession and either payment or improvements. Payment alone is usually not enough, because any losses could be replaced by money damages and so an injunction is not justified. The foundation for this approach is that if the "buyer" engaged in these ownership-like activities, there must have a contract or a promise for a transfer of real estate that the buyer relied on to their detriment.

Here is a straightforward illustration from the Restatement (Second) of Contracts § 129. "A and B make an oral agreement for the sale of Blackacre by A to B. With A's consent B takes possession of the land, pays part of the price, builds a dwelling house on the land and occupies it. Two years later, as a result of a dispute over the amount still to be paid, A repudiates the agreement. B may obtain a decree of specific performance."

The rules you just learned are core. However, the three-factor analysis fits into a broader framework structured below as a three-prong test for satisfying the part performance doctrine that can help you understand the doctrine more and encourage you to think more flexibly about it. This is important, because a challenge with these cases is whether the factfinder will be convinced that there is a contract at all.

1. Does a contract exist?
2. Is there reasonable detrimental reliance by the buyer?
3. Is specific performance required to avoid injustice (money damages are inadequate)?

First, you must evaluate the evidence of a contract. There could be an admission of the promise by the seller. That makes the existence of the contract clear and the case much easier to win. However, many cases are not so easy. There may be claims to an oral contract by the alleged buyer. But that might just beg the question. The buyer might say there was a contract and the seller might say there is not. So who is right? To resolve such conflicting claims, courts rigorously evaluate the conduct of the parties to see if the way everyone is behaving implies there was an agreement for the sale of real property. Courts are exploring whether there is an implied-in-fact contract. The three factors you just learned—possession, payment and improvements—are emphasized in the law because they are particularly strong evidence of a contract. Keep in mind, however, this is not an exhaustive list of possibilities. There may well be other evidence supporting or undermining the existence of a contract. For example, if a non-titled owner is paying the real estate taxes on the subject property, that is some evidence of a contract for sale that has been partially performed. Conversely, if the titled owner and not the putative buyer is paying the taxes, that suggests there might not be a contract. The Restatement (Second) of Contracts § 129(d) makes clear that the three hallmarks of part performance are not required when the contract is "admitted or clearly proved."

The three factors are also good evidence of the second prong of part performance—reasonable detrimental reliance by the buyer. In other words, what is the evidence that the buyer reasonably changed her position as a result of the promise? Again, consider other possible evidence supporting reliance in addition to the three factors.

Last, to use the language of the Restatement (Second) of Contracts § 129, evaluate whether "injustice can be avoided only by specific enforcement." If the situation can be remedied by payment of money damages, then an injunction forcing a transfer is not appropriate. However, a particular piece of real estate is generally viewed as unique, so money damages would not be a perfect replacement. As a result, a buyer (but not the seller) will typically be grantedan injunction.

Let's return to the *Hurtubise* case discussed earlier. Apply the three-prong test and include the three factors. Hurtubise won based on the part performance doctrine. He also could have won based on equitable estoppel. That is to be expected. Equitable estoppel focuses mostly on the buyer's detrimental reliance. Detrimental reliance is also required as one part of the part performance doctrine. If you are likely to win based on part performance, you are also likely to win based on estoppel. As you probably noticed, the doctrines are overlapping. Sometimes courts converge them or don't clearly separate them. (*Hurtubise* is a good example.) Remember though that they are separate doctrines and that equitable estoppel is a more general claim (or defense) applicable across a variety of situations.

3. Constructive Trust. As discussed elsewhere in the text, this is another cross-cutting legal claim that arises in a range of contexts. It allows a party who has invested money or labor into another's property to make a claim for unjust enrichment. It too is based in equity. A claimant must show: (1) there was benefit conferred on the titled owner; (2) knowledge of the benefit; and (3) it would be unjust under the circumstances to allow the titled owner to retain all or some of the benefits conferred. The remedy is to impose a constructive trust on the holder of the value who must expunge the benefit. Keep this possibility in mind as an alternative claim in the event that a claim for enforcement of an oral contract fails.

Exercise 11-3. *Hickey v. Green* and *Burns v. McCormick*

1. Carefully read *Hickey v. Green* and *Burns v. McCormick* to deepen your learning and apply the statute of frauds, equitable estoppel and the part performance doctrine.

2. *Burns* introduces you to a set of issues that raise important, recurring and controversial questions about how the law should treat family caregiving for elders (and others), economic opportunity losses and costs, exchanges, gifts, altruism, gender relations and sex inequality. As you discover how difficult it can be for caregivers to make successful legal claims (yes *Burns* is still good law), consider how well our current legal structures are serving individual, family and societal interests. Might the law adversely impact women? It

remains the case that even today women do far more of the unpaid carework in families than men, including child care, elder care and housework. These issues will become even more important in the years to come. Cohabitation rates have risen dramatically (and marital property default rules don't apply to this group). Elder care needs are growing tremendously, as we are in the midst of a "silver tsunami" of population aging with the proportion and number of persons of over 65 rising exponentially.

Hickey v. Green

442 N.E.2d 37 (Mass. Ct. App. 1982)

Cutter, J. Mrs. Gladys Green owns a lot (Lot S) in the Manomet section of Plymouth. In July, 1980, she advertised it for sale. On July 11 and 12, Hickey and his wife discussed with Mrs. Green purchasing Lot S and "orally agreed to a sale" for $15,000. Mrs. Green on July 12 accepted a deposit check of $500, marked by Hickey on the back, "Deposit on Lot ... Massasoit Ave. Manomet ... Subject to Variance from Town of Plymouth." Mrs. Green's brother and agent "was under the impression that a zoning variance was needed and [had] advised ... Hickey to write" the quoted language on the deposit check. It turned out, however, by July 16 that no variance would be required. Hickey had left the payee line of the deposit check blank, because of uncertainty whether Mrs. Green or her brother was to receive the check and asked "Mrs. Green to fill in the appropriate name." Mrs. Green held the check, did not fill in the payee's name, and neither cashed nor endorsed it. Hickey "stated to Mrs. Green that his intention was to sell his home and build on Mrs. Green's lot."

"Relying upon the arrangements ... with Mrs. Green," the Hickeys advertised their house on Sachem Road in newspapers on three days in July, 1980, and agreed with a purchaser for its sale and took from him a deposit check for $500 which they deposited in their own account.[3] On July 24, Mrs. Green told Hickey that she "no longer intended to sell her property to him" but had decided to sell to another for $16,000. Hickey told Mrs. Green that he had already sold his house and offered her $16,000 for Lot S. Mrs. Green refused this offer.

The Hickeys filed this complaint seeking specific performance. Mrs. Green asserts that relief is barred by the Statute of Frauds contained in G.L. c. 259, § 1. The trial judge granted specific performance. Mrs. Green has appealed.

The present rule applicable in most jurisdictions in the United States is succinctly set forth in Restatement (Second) of Contracts, § 129 (1981). The section reads, "A contract for the transfer of an interest in land may be specifically enforced notwithstanding failure to comply with the Statute of Frauds if it is established that

3. On the back of the check was noted above the Hickeys' signatures endorsing the check "Deposit on Purchase of property at Sachem Rd. and First St., Manomet, Ma. Sale price, $44,000."

the party seeking enforcement, *in reasonable reliance on the contract* and on the continuing assent of the party against whom enforcement is sought, *has so changed his position that injustice can be avoided only by specific enforcement*" (emphasis supplied).[5] The earlier Massachusetts decisions laid down somewhat strict requirements for an estoppel precluding the assertion of the Statute of Frauds. [Citations omitted.] Frequently there has been an actual change of possession and improvement of the transferred property, as well as full payment of the full purchase price, or one or more of these elements.

The present facts reveal a simple case of a proposed purchase of a residential vacant lot, where the vendor, Mrs. Green, knew that the Hickeys were planning to sell their former home (possibly to obtain funds to pay her) and build on Lot S. The Hickeys, relying on Mrs. Green's oral promise, moved rapidly to make their sale without obtaining any adequate memorandum of the terms of what appears to have been intended to be a quick cash sale of Lot S. So rapid was action by the Hickeys that, by July 21, less than ten days after giving their deposit to Mrs. Green, they had accepted a deposit check for the sale of their house, endorsed the check, and placed it in their bank account. Above their signatures endorsing the check was a memorandum probably sufficient to satisfy the Statute of Frauds. [Citations omitted.] At the very least, the Hickeys had bound themselves in a manner in which, to avoid a transfer of their own house, they might have had to engage in expensive litigation. No attorney has been shown to have been used either in the transaction between Mrs. Green and the Hickeys or in that between the Hickeys and their purchaser.

There is no denial by Mrs. Green of the oral contract between her and the Hickeys. This, under § 129 of the Restatement, is of some significance.[9] There can be no doubt

---

5. Comments *a* and *b* to § 129, read (in part):

"*a.* ... This section restates what is widely known as the 'part performance doctrine.' Part performance is not an accurate designation of such acts as taking possession and making improvements when the contract does not provide for such acts, but such acts regularly bring the doctrine into play. The doctrine is contrary to the words of the Statute of Frauds, but it was established by English courts of equity soon after the enactment of the Statute. Payment of purchase-money, without more, was once thought sufficient to justify specific enforcement, but a contrary view now prevails, since in such cases restitution is an adequate remedy.... Enforcement has ... been justified on the ground that repudiation after 'part performance' amounts to a 'virtual fraud.' A more accurate statement is that courts with equitable powers are vested by tradition with what in substance is a dispensing power based on the promisee's reliance, *a discretion to be exercised with caution* in the light of all the circumstances ... [emphasis supplied].

"*b.* ... Two distinct elements enter into the application of the rule of this Section: first, the extent to which the evidentiary function of the statutory formalities is fulfilled by the conduct of the parties; second, the reliance of the promisee, providing a compelling substantive basis for relief in addition to the expectations created by the promise."

9. Comment *d* of Restatement (Second) of Contracts, § 129, reads "*d.* ... Where specific enforcement is rested on a transfer of possession plus either part payment of the price or the making of improvements, it is commonly said that the action taken by the purchaser must be unequivocally referable to the oral agreement. But this requirement is not insisted on *if the making of the promise is admitted or is clearly proved.* The promisee *must act in reasonable reliance on the promise, before the promisor has repudiated* it, and the action must be such that the remedy of restitution is inadequate. If these requirements are

(a) that Mrs. Green made the promise on which the Hickeys so promptly relied, and also (b) she, nearly as promptly, but not promptly enough, repudiated it because she had a better opportunity. The stipulated facts require the conclusion that in equity Mrs. Green's conduct cannot be condoned. This is not a case where either party is shown to have contemplated the negotiation of a purchase and sale agreement. If a written agreement had been expected, even by only one party, or would have been natural (because of the participation by lawyers or otherwise), a different situation might have existed. It is a permissible inference from the agreed facts that the rapid sale of the Hickeys' house was both appropriate and expected. These are not circumstances where negotiations fairly can be seen as inchoate.

The case, in any event, must be remanded to the trial judge for the purpose of amending the judgment to require conveyance of Lot S by Mrs. Green only upon payment to her in cash within a stated period of the balance of the agreed price of $15,000. The trial judge, however, in her discretion and upon proper offers of proof by counsel, may reopen the record to receive, in addition to the presently stipulated facts, a stipulation or evidence concerning the present status of the Hickeys' apparent obligation to sell their house. If the circumstances have changed, it will be open to the trial judge to require of Mrs. Green, instead of specific performance, only full restitution to the Hickeys of all costs reasonably caused to them in respect of these transactions (including advertising costs, deposits, and their reasonable costs for this litigation) with interest. The case is remanded to the Superior Court Department for further action consistent with this opinion. The Hickeys are to have costs of this appeal.

Burns v. McCormick

135 N.E. 273 (N.Y. 1922)

Cardozo, J. In June, 1918, one James A. Halsey, an old man, and a widower, was living, without family or housekeeper, in his house in Hornell, New York. He told the plaintiffs, so it is said, that if they gave up their home and business in Andover, New York, and boarded and cared for him during his life, the house and lot, with its furniture and equipment, would be theirs upon his death. They did as he asked, selling out an interest in a little draying business in Andover, and boarding and tending him till he died, about five months after their coming. Neither deed nor will, nor memorandum subscribed by the promisor, exists to authenticate the promise. The plaintiffs asked specific performance. The defense is the statute of frauds.

We think the defense must be upheld. Not every act of part performance will move a court of equity, though legal remedies are inadequate, to enforce an oral agreement affecting rights in land. There must be performance 'unequivocally referable' to the agreement, performance which alone and without the aid of words of promise is unintelligible or at least extraordinary unless as an incident of ownership, assured, if

---

met, *neither taking of possession nor payment of money nor the making of improvements is essential ...*" (emphasis supplied).

not existing. 'An act which admits of explanation without reference to the alleged oral contract or a contract of the same general nature and purpose is not, in general, admitted to constitute a part performance.' (Citation omitted.)

What is done must itself supply the key to what is promised. It is not enough that what is promised may give significance to what is done. The housekeeper who abandons other prospects of establishment in life and renders service without pay upon the oral promise of her employer to give her a life estate in land must find her remedy in an action to recover the value of the service. Her conduct, separated from the promise, is not significant of ownership, either present or prospective. On the other hand, the buyer who not only pays the price, but possesses and improves his acre, may have relief in equity without producing a conveyance. His conduct is itself the symptom of a promise that a conveyance will be made.

Promise and performance fail when these standards are applied. The plaintiffs make no pretense that during the lifetime of Mr. Halsey they occupied the land as owners or under claim of present right. They did not even have possession. The possession was his; and those whom he invited to live with him were merely his servants or his guests. He might have shown them the door, and the law would not have helped them to return. Whatever rights they had were executory and future. The tokens of their title are not, then, to be discovered in acts of possession or dominion. The tokens must be found elsewhere if discoverable at all. The plaintiffs did, indeed, while occupants of the dwelling, pay the food bills for the owner as well as for themselves, and do the work of housekeepers. One who heard of such service might infer that it would be rewarded in some way. There could be no reasonable inference that it would be rewarded at some indefinite time thereafter by a conveyance of the land. The board might be given in return for lodging. The outlay might be merely an advance to be repaid in whole or part. 'Time and care' might have been bestowed 'From a vague anticipation that the affection and gratitude so created would, in the long run, insure some indefinite reward.' (Citation Omitted.) This was the more likely since there were ties of kinship between one of the plaintiffs and the owner. Even if there was to be a reward, not merely as of favor, but as of right, no one could infer, from knowledge of the service, without more, what its nature or extent would be. Mr Halsey paid the taxes. He paid also for the upkeep of the land and building. At least, there is no suggestion that the plaintiffs had undertaken to relieve him of those burdens. He was the owner while he lived. Nothing that he had accepted from the plaintiffs evinces an agreement that they were to be the owners when he died.

We hold, then, that the acts of part performance are not solely and unequivocally referable to a contract for the sale of land. Since that is so, they do not become sufficient because part of the plaintiffs' loss is without a remedy at law. At law the value of board and services will not be difficult of proof. The loss of the draying business in Andover does not permit us to disregard the statute, though it may go without requital. Inadequacy of legal remedies, without more, does not dispense with the requirement that acts, and not words, shall supply the framework of the promise. That requirement has its origin in something more than an arbitrary preference of one form over others.

It is 'intended to prevent a recurrence of the mischief' which the statute would suppress. The peril of perjury and error is latent in the spoken promise. Such, at least, is the warning of the statute, the estimate of policy that finds expression in its mandate. Equity, in assuming what is in substance a dispensing power, does not treat the statute as irrelevant, nor ignore the warning altogether. It declines to act on words, though the legal remedy is imperfect, unless the words are confirmed and illuminated by deeds. A power of dispensation, departing from the letter in supposed adherence to the spirit, involves an assumption of jurisdiction easily abused, and justified only within the limits imposed by history and precedent. The power is not exercised unless the policy of the law is saved.

In conclusion, we observe that this is not a case of fraud. No confidential relation has been abused. No inducement has been offered with the preconceived intention that it would later be ignored. The most that can be said against Mr. Halsey is that he made a promise which the law did not compel him to keep, and that afterwards he failed to keep it. We cannot even say of his failure that it was willful. He had made a will before the promise. Negligence or mere inertia may have postponed the making of another. The plaintiffs left the preservation of their agreement, if they had one, to the fallible memory of witnesses. The law exacts a writing.

Terms, Construction and Breach

You have already begun a detailed study of some typical terms of a real estate transaction by reviewing the sample contract and other materials above. Here we turn more specifically to a set of significant legal issues that can arise regarding the terms, construction and possible breach of a sale contract.

Marketable Title

Real estate sale contracts generally include an important promise that the seller will convey "marketable title" to the buyer. Many contracts provide for this expressly, but it will be implied if not addressed in the contract. This reflects that a centerpiece of the bargain is that the buyer will obtain good title to the property, meaning ownership and a set of rights that will be clear and transferable. What qualifies? The definition of marketable title is "title that is free from reasonable doubt" as to it validity. This includes not having to face risky litigation to gain title. If a reasonable buyer would pay fair market value, then title is marketable. It does not, however, require title to be perfect. You probably see the potential for ambiguity here.

If the seller cannot provide marketable title by the time of the closing, the buyer can rescind the contract and sue for breach. Note that any breach would occur during the executory phase of the transaction. Once the parties have closed on the deal and title is transferred, a buyer can no longer make this claim. As you will soon learn, there are other claims a buyer might make post-closing.

The main problems that arise are if the seller lacks ownership or if there are encumbrances against the property. If the seller does not own the title she is purporting to transfer, then title is unmarketable. For example, this defect exists if a seller has a life estate only but has promised to transfer a fee simple. Another serious problem could be that a seller does not have actually have title at all or only owns part of the subject property. For example, perhaps there was a forged deed earlier in the chain of title or a deed mistakenly describes the contours of the property. Adverse possession cases sometimes present marketable title issues. What if a seller is attempting to transfer property or a part of the property they claim to own based on adverse possession? Courts take different approaches to this. Some courts hold the view that as long as the claim is a strong one, title is marketable even though the seller does not have record title. Others find no marketable title unless there is a declaratory judgement confirming the seller's ownership. Would you feel comfortable buying property that was contingent on a successful adverse possession claim? Even so, wouldn't that change your offer price?

A claim for lack of marketable title based on an encumbrance is far more common. An encumbrance is a right or an interest in the property held by another that reduces the value of the property or restricts its use. This includes conflicting claims to title or leaseholds. It also includes non-possessory interests such as easements, covenants, mortgages or other liens. (A lien is a security interest in property that entitles the holder to force a sale of the property (foreclose) and collect the debt against the proceeds.) It is the mere existence of one of these interests that qualifies as an encumbrance. Because such interests are often present and title would otherwise then be defective, contracts regularly provide that marketable title means free of encumbrances not "of public record." Additionally, many courts find that visible encumbrances that a buyer should be aware of, like utility poles and wires, do not equate to lack of marketable title. Public laws regulating land use such as zoning laws are in a different category. The mere existence of a law is not considered an encumbrance. However, as you see in the next case, *violation* of zoning law will likely render title unmarketable.

The parties might agree on another standard governing title. Some contracts provide for insurable title—a quality of title for which a title insurance company is willing to issue a policy. Others provide for a more buyer friendly promise that title will be valid "as of record." So the title promised must be what the title records actually reflect.

Lack of marketable title must generally be distinguished from legal claims concerning the condition of the property. The promise relates to the quality of the title—to ownership rights—that the seller can convey. Defects in the physical condition of the property are regulated by different legal rules studied below.

Exercise 11-4. *Lohmeyer v. Bower*

You will see the claim of lack of marketable title (with its more old-timey name merchantability) play out in the next case. As always, be sure to read the contract terms carefully.

Lohmeyer v. Bower

227 P.2d 102 (Kans. 1951)

Parker, J.... [P]laintiff filed a petition seeking to rescind a contract in which he had agreed to purchase certain real estate on the ground title tendered by the defendants was unmerchantable. The defendants Bower and Bower, husband and wife, answered contesting plaintiff's right to rescind and by cross-petition asked specific performance of the contract.... The case was tried upon the pleadings and stipulated facts by the trial court which rendered judgment for the defendants generally and decreed specific performance of the contract. The plaintiff appeals from that judgment.

Plaintiff's petition ... avers that after execution of the agreement it came to his attention that the house on the real estate therein described had been placed there in violation of Section 5-224 of the Ordinances of the city of Emporia in that the house was located within approximately 18 inches of the north line of such lot in violation of the ordinance providing that no frame building should be erected within 3 feet of a side or rear lot line. It further avers that after execution of the agreement it came to plaintiff's knowledge the dedication of the Berkley Hills Addition requires that only a two story house should be erected on the lot described in the contract whereas the house located thereon is a one story house. It then states the violations of the city ordinance and the dedication restrictions were unknown to the plaintiff when he entered into the contract and that he would not have entered into such agreement if he had known thereof. It next alleges that after becoming aware of such violations plaintiff notified the defendants in writing thereof, demanded that he be released from his contract and that defendants refused such demand. Finally it charges that such violations made the title unmerchantable and asks that the agreement be cancelled and set aside and that all moneys paid by plaintiff under its terms be refunded.

The answer of defendants Bower and Bower admits execution of the contract and denies generally all allegations of the petition.

Pertinent provisions of the contract, entered into between the parties, essential to disposition of the issues raised by the pleadings, read:

> [The seller agrees to sell] and to convey the above described real estate to [the buyer] by Warranty Deed with an abstract of title, certified to date showing good merchantable title or an Owner's Policy of Title Insurance in the amount of the sale price, guaranteeing said title to party of the second part, free and clear of all encumbrances except special taxes subject, however, to all restrictions and easements of record applying to this property, it being understood that the first party shall have sufficient time to bring said abstract to date or obtain Report for Title Insurance and to correct any imperfections in the title if there be such imperfections....
>
> [If seller] cannot deliver title as agreed, the earnest money paid by the [buyer] shall be returned [to buyer] and this contract cancelled.

[S]ince resort to the contract makes it clear appellees agreed to convey the involved property with an abstract of title showing good merchantable title, free and clear of all encumbrances, it becomes apparent the all decisive issue presented by the pleadings and the stipulation is whether such property is subject to encumbrances or other burdens making the title unmerchantable and if so whether they are such as are excepted by the provision of the contract which reads 'subject however, to all restrictions and easements of record applying to this property.'

[Buyer] makes no complaint of the restrictions contained in the declaration forming a part of the dedication of Berkley Hills Addition nor of the ordinance restricting the building location on the lot but bases his right to rescission of the contract solely upon presently existing violations thereof....

There can be no doubt regarding what constitutes a marketable or merchantable title in this jurisdiction.

> A marketable title to real estate is one which is free from reasonable doubt, and a title is doubtful and unmarketable if it exposes the party holding it to the hazard of litigation.
>
> To render the title to real estate unmarketable, the defect of which the purchaser complains must be of a substantial character and one from which he may suffer injury. Mere immaterial defects which do not diminish in quantity, quality or value the property contracted for, constitute no ground upon which the purchaser may reject the title. Facts must be known at the time which fairly raise a reasonable doubt as to the title; a mere possibility or conjecture that such a state of facts may be developed at some future time is not sufficient. (Citations omitted)

Under the rule just stated, and in the face of facts such as are here involved, we have little difficulty in concluding that the violation of section 5-224 of the ordinances of the city of Emporia as well as the violation of the restrictions imposed by the dedication declaration so encumber the title to Lot 37 as to expose the party holding it to the hazard of litigation and make such title doubtful and unmarketable. It follows, since, as we have indicated, the appellees had contracted to convey such real estate to appellant by warranty deed with an abstract of title showing good merchantable title, free and clear of all encumbrances, that they cannot convey the title contracted for and that the trial court should have rendered judgment rescinding the contract. This, we may add is so, notwithstanding the contract provides the conveyance was to be made subject to all restrictions and easements of record, for, as we have seen, it is the violation of the restrictions imposed by both the ordinance and the dedication declaration, not the existence of those restrictions, that renders the title unmarketable.

Equitable Conversion and Risk of Loss

Imagine you just signed a contract to buy your dream home. Before the closing, a tornado destroys the house. Do you still have to buy the house? Surprisingly, the answer could be yes. An essential question to answer in negotiating the purchase agreement is who bears the risk of loss during the executory period. The default rule in many states is that this risk is on the *buyer*. That allocation is based on another doctrine called equitable conversion that treats the buyer as if she already owns the property once a contract is signed. A buyer is the equitable owner, because if the seller were to try and back out, the buyer could insist on specific performance and could force the sale by an injunction (remember real estate is considered unique, so money damages are deemed an inadequate remedy).

Buyers might be fine with the idea they equitably own the real estate, but it is counter-intuitive for the buyer to bear the risk of loss. The seller is usually the one in possession who is in a position to exercise due care for the property and often has insurance against a catastrophic loss. Following this logic, many contracts override the default rule and assign the risk of loss during the executory period to the seller. The Uniform Vendor and Purchaser Risk Act (UVRPA) § 1, 14 U.L.A. 471 (1968), adopted in 13 states places the risk on the seller—unless the buyer has taken possession. Buyers should attend to this issue, because it is an essential part of the bargain. If the buyer does bear the loss and the seller is entitled to the purchase price and to insurance proceeds, the buyer could prevent this double recovery by claiming a constructive trust based on unjust enrichment.

Equitable conversion can also drive legal outcomes with an inheritance. Assume X agrees to sells his residence to Y in a signed contract. From that point on, Y is treated as the equitable owner. If X dies before the closing, those who inherit from X now own what X owned, a property right to collect the *proceeds* from the sale—which is personal property. The right to take the real property itself is owned by Y, who then still owes the purchase price.

Exercise 11-5. *Brush Grocery Kart v. Sure Fine Market*

This case takes a position in the debate around a buyer bearing the risk of loss and signals a possible shift in the law for the future. Beyond the fair critique of the majority default rule, what is the basis for the court's allocation of the risk of loss? Identify the three approaches to allocation of risk that *Brush* highlights.

Brush Grocery Kart v. Sure Fine Market

47 P.3d 680 (Colo. 2002)

§ + l. lease

COATS J. In October 1992 Brush Grocery Kart, Inc. and Sure Fine Market, Inc. entered into a five-year "Lease with Renewal Provisions and Option to Purchase" for real property, including a building to be operated by Brush as a grocery store. Under the contract's purchase option provision, any time during the last six months of the lease,

Brush could elect to purchase the property at a price equal to the average of the appraisals of an expert designated by each party.

Shortly before expiration of the lease, Brush notified Sure Fine of its desire to purchase the property and begin the process of determining a sale price. Although each party offered an appraisal, the parties were unable to agree on a final price by the time the lease expired. Brush then vacated the premises, returned all keys to Sure Fine, and advised Sure Fine that it would discontinue its casualty insurance covering the property during the lease. Brush also filed suit, alleging that Sure Fine failed to negotiate the price term in good faith and asking for the appointment of a special master to determine the purchase price. Sure Fine agreed to the appointment of a special master and counterclaimed, alleging that Brush negotiated the price term in bad faith and was therefore the breaching party.

During litigation over the price term, the property was substantially damaged during a hail storm. With neither party carrying casualty insurance, each asserted that the other was liable for the damage. The issue was added to the litigation at a stipulated amount of $60,000. The court appointed a special master pursuant to C.R.C.P. 53 and accepted his appraised value of $375,000. The court then found that under the doctrine of equitable conversion, Brush was the equitable owner of the property and bore the risk of loss. It therefore declined to abate the purchase price or award damages to Brush for the loss.

Brush appealed the loss allocation, and the court of appeals affirmed on similar grounds. Brush petitioned for a writ of certiorari to determine the proper allocation of the risk of loss and the appropriate remedy under these circumstances.

THE RISK OF CASUALTY LOSS IN THE ABSENCE OF STATUTORY AUTHORITY

In the absence of statutory authority, the rights, powers, duties, and liabilities arising out of a contract for the sale of land have frequently been derived by reference to the theory of equitable conversion. This theory or doctrine, which has been described as a legal fiction, is based on equitable principles that permit the vendee to be considered the equitable owner of the land and debtor for the purchase money and the vendor to be regarded as a secured creditor. The changes in rights and liabilities that occur upon the making of the contract result from the equitable right to specific performance. Even with regard to third parties, the theory has been relied on to determine, for example, the devolution, upon death, of the rights and liabilities of each party with respect to the land, and to ascertain the powers of creditors of each party to reach the land in payment of their claims.

The assignment of the risk of casualty loss in the executory period of contracts for the sale of real property varies greatly throughout the jurisdictions of this country. What appears to yet be a slim majority of states, places the risk of loss on the vendee from the moment of contracting, on the rationale that once an equitable conversion takes place, the vendee must be treated as owner for all purposes. Once the vendee becomes the equitable owner, he therefore becomes responsible for the condition of the property, despite not having a present right of occupancy or control. In sharp contrast, a handful of other states reject the allocation of casualty loss risk as a consequence of the theory of equitable conversion and follow the equally rigid "Massachusetts Rule," under which the seller continues to bear the risk until actual transfer of the title, absent an express agreement to the contrary. A substantial and growing number of jurisdictions, however, base the legal consequences of no-fault casualty loss on the right to possession of the property at the time the loss occurs. This view has found expression in the Uniform Vendor and Purchaser Risk Act, and while a number of states have adopted some variation of the Uniform Act, others have arrived at a similar position through the interpretations of their courts.

This court has applied the theory of equitable conversion in limited circumstances affecting title. It has never before, however, expressly relied on the theory of equitable conversion alone as allocating the risk of casualty loss to a vendee.

Those jurisdictions that indiscriminately include the risk of casualty loss among the incidents or "attributes" of equitable ownership do so largely in reliance on ancient authority or by considering it necessary for consistent application of the theory of equitable conversion. *See Skelly Oil,* 365 S.W.2d at 592 (Stockman, J. dissenting) (quoting 4 Williston, *Contracts,* § 929, at 2607: "Only the hoary age and frequent repetition of the maxim prevents a general recognition of its absurdity."). Under virtually any accepted understanding of the theory, however, equitable conversion is not viewed as entitling the purchaser to every significant right of ownership, and particularly not the right of possession. As a matter of both logic and equity, the obligation to maintain property in its physical condition follows the right to have actual possession and control rather than a legal right to force conveyance of the property through specific performance at some future date.

The equitable conversion theory is literally stood on its head by imposing on a vendee, solely because of his right to specific performance, the risk that the vendor will be unable to specifically perform when the time comes because of an accidental casualty loss. It is counterintuitive, at the very least, that merely contracting for the sale of real property should not only relieve the vendor of his responsibility to maintain the property until execution but also impose a duty on the vendee to perform despite the intervention of a material, no-fault casualty loss preventing him from ever receiving the benefit of his bargain. Such an extension of the theory of equitable conversion to casualty loss has never been recognized by this jurisdiction, and it is neither necessary nor justified solely for the sake of consistency.

By contrast, there is substantial justification, both as a matter of law and policy, for not relieving a vendee who is entitled to possession before transfer of title ... of his duty to pay the full contract price, notwithstanding an accidental loss. In addition to having control over the property and being entitled to the benefits of its use, an equitable owner who also has the right of possession has already acquired virtually all of the rights of ownership and almost invariably will have already paid at least some portion of the contract price to exercise those rights. By expressly including in the contract for sale the right of possession, which otherwise generally accompanies transfer of title, the vendor has for all practical purposes already transferred the property as promised, and the parties have in effect expressed their joint intention that the vendee pay the purchase price as promised.

Here, Brush was clearly not in possession of the property as the equitable owner. Even if the doctrine of equitable conversion applies to the option contract between Brush and Sure Fine and could be said to have converted Brush's interest to an equitable ownership of the property at the time Brush exercised its option to purchase, neither party considered the contract for sale to entitle Brush to possession. Brush was, in fact, not in possession of the property, and the record indicates that Sure Fine considered itself to hold the right of use and occupancy and gave notice that it would consider Brush a holdover tenant if it continued to occupy the premises other than by continuing to lease the property. The casualty loss was ascertainable and in fact stipulated by the parties, and neither party challenged the district court's enforcement of the contract except with regard to its allocation of the casualty loss. Both the court of appeals and the district court therefore erred in finding that the doctrine of equitable conversion required Brush to bear the loss caused by hail damage.

Where Brush was not an equitable owner in possession at the time of the casualty loss, it was entitled to rescind its contract with Sure Fine. At least under the circumstances of this case, where Brush chose to go forward with the contract under a stipulation as to loss from the hail damage, it was also entitled to specific performance with an abatement of the purchase price equal to the casualty loss. The judgment of the court of appeals is therefore reversed and the case is remanded for further proceedings consistent with this opinion.

Remedies for Breach (Return of Deposits)

What happens if the deal falls apart because a party just changes their mind—or if a party fails to fulfill their obligations under the contract? Remedies for breach include recission, specific performance, money damages (restitution) and either return or retention of the deposit (depending on who breached). Recall that specific performance is only available when money damages are adequate. Although sparingly awarded in other areas of law, an injunction for specific performance is typically available to the buyer because real property is unique and money will not make the buyer whole. The buyer bargained for the particular home in its specific location and school district, etc. It is more difficult for a seller to meet the standard, because money damages are likely to give the seller the benefit of the bargain. This remedy could be available, however, if the seller has searched but cannot find another buyer.

How are damages measured? There may be actual damages. For example, if a buyer breaches and the seller ultimately is able to sell the property for less than the contract price, then the buyer owes the difference. However, parties often agree in advance to an amount for damages in the event of breach as a term in the contract. This is called "liquidated damages." Frequently the amount of the deposit is the amount agreed to for liquidated damages. The deposit stands in for the actual damages. Let's say the seller breaches and the actual damages are $5,000, but the deposit is $10,000. Then the buyer forfeits the deposit upon breach—and ends up paying $5,000 more than the actual damages. Conversely, if the actual damages were $15,000, then the seller is limited to the deposit amount of $10,000, and the buyer ends up paying less than the actual damages. This is a calculated risk that avoids having to determine and pursue actual damages. Courts generally will enforce such clauses if they are a modest amount such as 10% of the purchase price. Still, it is possible to challenge a liquidated damages clause. The clause will be unenforceable if deemed excessive because it functions like a penalty rather than a good faith estimate of damages. To determine this, courts compare the liquidated damages amount to the actual damages. If the contract does not speak to the issue of damages, the majority approach is to allow the seller to keep the deposit even if it is more than actual damages (mirroring liquidated damages), provided the deposit is reasonably low. A minority of states require the buyer to pay only actual damages and require the seller to refund all or some of the deposit if actual damages are lower.

Condition of the Property

The physical condition of the property is of great concern to buyers. Buyers want to make sure the property they are acquiring is in good condition or at least in as good condition as they *think* it is in and that the actual value justifies the purchase price. This is the heart of the deal from a buyer's point of view. The seller, on the other hand, often wants to be sure she is maximizing the sale price and would like to shift the risks around price and value to the buyer as much as possible.

The law in this area has changed dramatically in the last few decades. It used to be that a home buyer was at risk for bearing the losses from undiscovered physical defects in the property and every contract was basically "as is." *Caveat Emptor*—let the buyer beware—was the governing rule. Knowing full well there were problems with the property that a buyer did not know about and would have a difficult time finding, a seller could simply stay silent and let the buyer's mistaken understanding stand uncorrected. Any losses fell to the buyer. *Caveat emptor* is still the baseline law for commercial sellers and buyers. But the pendulum has swung toward more protections for residential buyers. Modern law assigns some responsibilities to homeowner sellers to disclose certain kinds of defects, who now shoulder more risk for losses in value caused by a defect. As you will see, disclosure standards vary to some extent.

Still, the obligations on most homeowners are for disclosure only and are limited. They do *not* equate to a warranty or promise of quality. The exception is for sellers who are engaged in the business of building and selling housing, who are treated like producers of commercial products. New construction homes purchased from professional developers include an implied warranty of habitability. You learn more about these laws and policies in the materials that follow.

Misrepresentation and Fraudulent Non-Disclosure

Basic fraud law applies to real estate transactions. Fraud is a false statement of material fact, that is known to be false, that is intended to induce and does induce detrimental reliance. If an owner lies about the condition of the property, there is an actionable civil tort that could also qualify as criminal fraud. Half-truths (the statement is true as far as it goes but is misleading) and concealment (hiding a defect by covering it up) are also lies that constitute fraud. This has long been the law. The relative newcomer in this arena is "fraudulent non-disclosure." A buyer can make a claim against a seller for failure to disclose when an owner has a duty to speak. In some circumstances, staying silent is the viewed as the same as lying and is fraud.

Assume an owner says to a buyer that the basement is waterproof with no water ever having come in from outside. Yet the basement has actually flooded numerous times, including the last time it rained. This is, of course, fraud. Now instead assume the seller never says anything at all about water in the basement or flooding and the buyer never asks. Is the omission of the flooding problem an actionable fraud? It could well be, but that depends on whether the seller has a legal obligation to disclose—a "duty to speak" in this kind of situation.

When and what does a seller have to disclose? The standards for fraudulent non-disclosure differ to some degree among states. There is agreement among the states for minimum obligations—sellers must disclose (1) known (2) latent (hidden) (3) defects that (4) materially affect the value or desirability of the property. A latent defect is one that is "not discoverable upon reasonable inspection." Defects qualify as material if a reasonable buyer would want to know about them. The question is would this be a factor in the decision to purchase or the price? Note that this law imposes fairly limited obligations. More than half the states have enacted statutes that go much further and require a seller to disclose any known material defects—whether they are hard to discover (latent) or obvious (patent) or somewhere in between.

Statutes also frequently require written disclosure statements. Sellers must share information with buyers about specific kinds of defects including structural defects (cracking foundations), unstable soil (is the house going to stay put?), underground storage tanks, hazardous materials, the condition of the HVAC, plumbing and electrical systems, roofing, whether licenses and inspections were obtained for renovations, housing code violations (were those stairs installed too steeply?), zoning violations and encroachments by neighbors. Owners and landlords of housing built before 1978 must disclose the presence of any known lead-based paint and provide a standard pamphlet. Residential Lead Based Paint Hazard Reduction Act, 42 U.S.C. §§4851-4856.

How far might disclosure obligations extend? Do you have to tell a potential buyer about noisy neighbors who party a lot? *See Alexander v. McNight*, 9 Cal. Rptr. 2d 453 (1992). What if there is toxic waste or pollution on a site close to the seller's property (offsite)? *See Strawn v. Canuso*, 657 A.2d 420 (N.J. 1995), superceded by N.J. Stat. §46:3C-12. What about the possibility that the property is or has been haunted by ghosts? (Remember ghosts don't exist.) *Stambovsky v. Ackley*, 572 N.Y.S.2d 672 (App.

Div. 1991). What if the home was the location of a murder-suicide? *Compare Reed v. King*, 193 Cal. Rptr. 130 (Ct. App. 1983) (yes), *with Miliken v. Jacano*, 60 A.3d 133 (Pa. Super. 2012) (no). All of these situations have been found to violate non-disclosure rules. The last few examples are known as psychological or stigma defects. In response to these types of cases, some states have stigma statutes that protect sellers. *See, e.g.*, N.Y. Real Prop. Law § 443-a (providing that a homicide, suicide, death or infection with human immunodeficiency virus is not a material defect).

You should be aware that real estate professionals are often involved with the flow of information from the seller to the buyer. Many realtor associations have a standard disclosure form (sometimes at the direction of a statute). It is standard practice for agents to ask sellers to fill these out. Buyers may expect to see them. These forms tend to ask for significantly more information than is required by law. For example, the forms often ask sellers to list any current or past problems with, say, plumbing or termites, and a host of other things. Disclosure law is concerned with *current* defects and not past problems that have *been resolved*. Pragmatically, however, these forms may cause sellers to tell all. Cumulatively then, the system results in buyers having access to a large amount of information about the condition of the property. Note that this approach protects agents and brokers as well buyers. Real estate brokers sometimes are held liable for non-disclosure of known defects or for negligent misrepresentation. This group needs to be sure not to participate in a fraud, along with lawyers and clients.

What remedies are available to a buyer for fraud? You should assume the usual civil remedies are available, including compensatory damages. Because this is a tort claim, a lawsuit can commence after the closing. If fraud is discovered before the closing, a buyer can also rescind the contract.

If a buyer wants to ensure that backing out of the contract is a straightforward option if physical conditions problems present, an inspection contingency clause is a good idea. This is a contract term that explicitly provides that the buyer has the right to inspect the property and if the results are "not satisfactory" can withdraw from the contract, with a full refund of the deposit. As you might suspect, this gives the buyer a significant amount of room to negotiate if even a small problem arises. To mitigate the risks, sellers should consider keeping the inspection and contingency period short.

Can disclosure protections be waived? Sellers seeking waivers followed quickly on the heels of widespread adoption of disclosure obligations. The law here is still evolving. A clear and specific waiver of the seller's duty to disclose that also includes explicit terms that the buyer is not relying on the seller is generally enforceable—at least in the absence of fraudulent misrepresentation. Determining the impact of an "as is" clause is more complicated and varies by state. Here is a simple example of such a clause:

> Purchaser understands that they will take the property in an "as is" condition.

What this means is that the property is being sold and transferred to the buyer with whatever problems it might have, and it implies that the seller is not making promises as to the quality of the property and is not responsible for the losses that might come from the condition of the property. Presumably, the price was reduced with this in mind. Further, "as is" clauses are interpreted to relieve sellers of their obligations to disclose patent defects and sometimes latent defects as well. So they can function as a waiver of liability for fraudulent non-disclosure. However, there are differences among the states, and also, the terms of the clause can vary. The clause can be written more narrowly so that it places the risk on the buyer regarding patent defects only—those that can be discovered, for example, by "careful visual inspection." In such a case, failure to disclose known latent (hard to discover) defects remains actionable fraud.

Another issue that has come up is whether an "as is" clause will waive claims against a seller for misrepresentations or concealment. The prevailing view is that it will not. An "as is" clause reduces or eliminates the duty to reveal defects but does not bar a claim for "positive" fraud.

Exercise 11-6. *Johnson v. Davis* and Pennsylvania Real Estate Disclosure Law—Applications and Theory

1. *Johnson* is a landmark decision in the shift from *caveat emptor* to mandatory disclosure of defects. As to you read and experience the debate, identify the reasons for and against the change and evaluate its wisdom.
2. There are two versions of fraud in *Johnson*—identify the rules for each and apply them as you consider the court's articulation.
3. What is the disclosure standard in Pennsylvania?

Johnson v. Davis

480 So. 2d 625 (Fla. 1985)

Adkins, J. In May of 1982, the Davises entered into a contract to buy for $310,000 the Johnsons' home, which at the time was three years old. The contract required a $5,000 deposit payment, an additional $26,000 deposit payment within five days and a closing by June 21, 1982. The crucial provision of the contract, for the purposes of the case at bar, is Paragraph F which provided:

> F. *Roof Inspection:* Prior to closing at Buyer's expense, Buyer shall have the right to obtain a written report from a licensed roofer stating that the roof is in a watertight condition. In the event repairs are required either to correct leaks or to replace damage to facia or soffit, seller shall pay for said repairs which shall be performed by a licensed roofing contractor.

The contract further provided for payment to the "prevailing party" of all costs and reasonable fees in any contract litigation.

Before the Davises made the additional $26,000 deposit payment, Mrs. Davis noticed some buckling and peeling plaster around the corner of a window frame in the family room and stains on the ceilings in the family room and kitchen of the home. Upon inquiring, Mrs. Davis was told by Mr. Johnson that the window had had a minor problem that had long since been corrected and that the stains were wallpaper glue and the result of ceiling beams being moved. There is disagreement among the parties as to whether Mr. Johnson also told Mrs. Davis at this time that there had never been any problems with the roof or ceilings. The Davises thereafter paid the remainder of their deposit and the Johnsons vacated the home. Several days later, following a heavy rain, Mrs. Davis entered the home and discovered water "gushing" in from around the window frame, the ceiling of the family room, the light fixtures, the glass doors, and the stove in the kitchen.

Two roofers hired by the Johnsons' broker concluded that for under $1,000 they could "fix" certain leaks in the roof and by doing so make the roof "watertight." Three roofers hired by the Davises found that the roof was inherently defective, that any repairs would be temporary because the roof was "slipping," and that only a new $15,000 roof could be "watertight."

The Davises filed a complaint alleging breach of contract, fraud and misrepresentation, and sought recission of the contract and return of their deposit. The Johnsons counterclaimed seeking the deposit as liquidated damages.

[The Court of Appeals affirmed the trial court's return of the majority of the deposit to the Davises ($26,000), and reversed the award of $5,000 to the Johnsons as well as the court's failure to award the Davises costs and fees. Accordingly, the court remanded with directions to return to the Davises the balance of their deposit and to award them costs and fees.]

The contract contemplated the possibility that the roof may not be watertight at the time of inspection and provided a remedy if it was not in such a condition. The roof inspection provision of the contract did not impose any obligation beyond the seller correcting the leaks and replacing damage to the facia or soffit. The record is devoid of any evidence that the seller refused to make needed repairs to the roof. In fact, the record reflects that the Davises' never even demanded that the areas of leakage be repaired either by way of repair or replacement. Yet the Davises insist that the Johnsons breached the contract justifying recission. We find this contention to be without merit.

We also agree with the district court's conclusions under a theory of fraud and find that the Johnsons' statements to the Davises regarding the condition of the roof constituted a fraudulent misrepresentation entitling respondents to the return of their $26,000 deposit payment. In the state of Florida, relief for a fraudulent misrepresentation may be granted only when the following elements are present: (1) a false statement concerning a material fact; (2) the representor's knowledge that the representation is false; (3) an intention that the representation induce another to act on it; and (4) consequent injury by the party acting in reliance on the representation.

The evidence adduced at trial shows that after the buyer and the seller signed the purchase and sales agreement and after receiving the $5,000 initial deposit payment the Johnsons affirmatively repeated to the Davises that there were no problems with the roof. The Johnsons subsequently received the additional $26,000 deposit payment from the Davises. The record reflects that the statement made by the Johnsons was a false representation of material fact, made with knowledge of its falsity, upon which the Davises relied to their detriment as evidenced by the $26,000 paid to the Johnsons.

The doctrine of caveat emptor does not exempt a seller from responsibility for the statements and representations which he makes to induce the buyer to act, when under the circumstances these amount to fraud in the legal sense. To be grounds for relief, the false representations need not have been made at the time of the signing of the purchase and sales agreement in order for the element of reliance to be present. The fact that the false statements as to the quality of the roof were made after the signing of the purchase and sales agreement does not excuse the seller from liability when the misrepresentations were made prior to the execution of the contract by conveyance of the property. It would be contrary to all notions of fairness and justice for this Court to place its stamp of approval on an affirmative misrepresentation by a wrongdoer just because it was made after the signing of the executory contract when all of the necessary elements for actionable fraud are present. Furthermore, the Davises' reliance on the truth of the Johnsons' representation was justified and is supported by this Court's decision in *Besett v. Basnett,* 389 So.2d 995 (1980), where we held "that a recipient may rely on the truth of a representation, even though its falsity could have been ascertained had he made an investigation, unless he knows the representation to be false or its falsity is obvious to him." *Id.* at 998.

In determining whether a seller of a home has a duty to disclose latent material defects to a buyer, the established tort law distinction between misfeasance and nonfeasance, action and inaction must carefully be analyzed. The highly individualistic philosophy of the earlier common law consistently imposed liability upon the commission of affirmative acts of harm, but shrank from converting the courts into an institution for forcing men to help one another. This distinction is deeply rooted in our case law. Liability for nonfeasance has therefore been slow to receive recognition in the evolution of tort law.

In theory, the difference between misfeasance and nonfeasance, action and inaction is quite simple and obvious; however, in practice it is not always easy to draw the line and determine whether conduct is active or passive. That is, where failure to disclose a material fact is calculated to induce a false belief, the distinction between concealment and affirmative representations is tenuous. Both proceed from the same motives and are attended with the same consequences; both are violative of the principles of fair dealing and good faith; both are calculated to produce the same result; and, in fact, both essentially have the same effect.

Still there exists in much of our case law the old tort notion that there can be no liability for nonfeasance. The courts in some jurisdictions, including Florida, hold that where the parties are dealing at arms's length and the facts lie equally open to both parties, with equal opportunity of examination, mere nondisclosure does not constitute a fraudulent concealment. The Fourth District affirmed that rule of law in

Banks v. Salina, 413 So.2d 851 (Fla. 4th DCA 1982), and found that although the sellers had sold a home without disclosing the presence of a defective roof and swimming pool of which the sellers had knowledge, "[i]n Florida, there is no duty to disclose when parties are dealing at arms length." *Id.* at 852.

These unappetizing cases are not in tune with the times and do not conform with current notions of justice, equity and fair dealing. One should not be able to stand behind the impervious shield of caveat emptor and take advantage of another's ignorance. Our courts have taken great strides since the days when the judicial emphasis was on rigid rules and ancient precedents. Modern concepts of justice and fair dealing have given our courts the opportunity and latitude to change legal precepts in order to conform to society's needs. Thus, the tendency of the more recent cases has been to restrict rather than extend the doctrine of caveat emptor. The law appears to be working toward the ultimate conclusion that full disclosure of all material facts must be made whenever elementary fair conduct demands it.

The harness placed on the doctrine of caveat emptor in a number of other jurisdictions has resulted in the seller of a home being liable for failing to disclose material defects of which he is aware. This philosophy was succinctly expressed in *Lingsch v. Savage,* 213 Cal.App.2d 729, 29 Cal.Rptr. 201 (1963):

> It is now settled in California that where the seller knows of facts materially affecting the value or desirability of the property which are known or accessible only to him and also knows that such facts are not known to or within the reach of the diligent attention and observation of the buyer, the seller is under a duty to disclose them to the buyer.

In *Posner v. Davis,* 76 Ill.App.3d 638, 32 Ill.Dec. 186, 395 N.E.2d 133 (1979), buyers brought an action alleging that the sellers of a home fraudulently concealed certain defects in the home which included a leaking roof and basement flooding. Relying on *Lingsch,* the court concluded that the sellers knew of and failed to disclose latent material defects and thus were liable for fraudulent concealment. *Id.* 32 Ill.Dec. at 190, 395 N.E.2d at 137. Numerous other jurisdictions have followed this view in formulating law involving the sale of homes. *See Flakus v. Schug,* 213 Neb. 491, 329 N.W.2d 859 (1983) (basement flooding); *Thacker v. Tyree,* 297 S.E.2d 885 (W.Va.1982) (cracked walls and foundation problems); *Maguire v. Masino,* 325 So.2d 844 (La.Ct.App.1975) (termite infestation); *Weintraub v. Krobatsch,* 64 N.J. 445, 317 A.2d 68 (1974) (roach infestation); *Cohen v. Vivian,* 141 Colo. 443, 349 P.2d 366 (1960) (soil defect).

We are of the opinion, in view of the reasoning and results in *Lingsch, Posner* and the aforementioned cases decided in other jurisdictions, that the same philosophy regarding the sale of homes should also be the law in the state of Florida. Accordingly, we hold that where the seller of a home knows of facts materially affecting the value of the property which are not readily observable and are not known to the buyer, the seller is under a duty to disclose them to the buyer. This duty is equally applicable to all forms of real property, new and used.

In the case at bar, the evidence shows that the Johnsons knew of and failed to disclose that there had been problems with the roof of the house. Mr. Johnson admitted during his testimony that the Johnsons were aware of roof problems prior to entering into the contract of sale and receiving the $5,000 deposit payment. Thus, we agree with the district court and find that the Johnsons' fraudulent concealment also entitles the Davises to the return of the $5,000 deposit payment plus interest. We further find that the Davises should be awarded costs and fees. The decision of the Third District Court of Appeal is hereby approved.

Boyd, C. J., dissenting. I respectfully but strongly dissent to the Court's expansion of the duties of sellers of real property. This ruling will give rise to a flood of litigation and will facilitate unjust outcomes in many cases. If, as a matter of public policy, the well settled law of this state on this question should be changed, the change should come from the legislature.

Homeowners who attempt to sell their houses are typically in no better position to measure the quality, value, or desirability of their houses than are the prospective purchasers with whom such owners come into contact. Based on this and related considerations, the law of Florida has long been that a seller of real property with improvements is under no duty to disclose all material facts, in the absence of a fiduciary relationship, to a buyer who has an equal opportunity to learn all material information and is not prevented by the seller from doing so.

I do not agree with the Court's belief that the distinction between nondisclosure and affirmative statement is weak or nonexistent. It is a distinction that we should take special care to emphasize and preserve. Imposition of liability for seller's nondisclosure of the condition of improvements to real property is the first step toward making the seller a guarantor of the good condition of the property. Ultimately this trend will significantly burden the alienability of property because sellers will have to worry about the possibility of catastrophic post-sale judgments for damages sought to pay for repairs. The trend will proceed somewhat as follows. At first, the cause of action will require proof of actual knowledge of the undisclosed defect on the part of the seller. But in many cases the courts will allow it to be shown by circumstantial evidence. Then a rule of constructive knowledge will develop based on the reasoning that if the seller did not know of the defect, he should have known about it before attempting to sell the property. Thus the burden of inspection will shift from the buyer to the seller. Ultimately the courts will be in the position of imposing implied warranties and guaranties on all sellers of real property.

Although as described in the majority opinion this change in the law sounds progressive, high-minded, and idealistic, it is in reality completely unnecessary. Prudent purchasers inspect property, with expert advice if necessary, before they agree to buy. Prudent lenders require inspections before agreeing to provide purchase money. Initial deposits of earnest money can be made with the agreement to purchase being conditional upon the favorable results of expert inspections. It is significant that in the present case the major portion of the purchase price was to be financed by the Johnsons who were to hold a mortgage on the property. If they had been knowingly trying to get rid of what they knew to be a defectively constructed house, it is unlikely that they would have been willing to lend $200,000 with the house in question as their only security.

Pennsylvania Statutory Disclosure Law

68 Pa. C.S.A. § 7301 *et. seq.*

§ 7301 Disclosure of Material Defects

Any seller who intends to transfer any interest in real property shall disclose to the buyer any material defects with the property known to the seller by completing all applicable items in a property disclosure statement which satisfies the requirements of section 7304 [relating to disclosure form]. A signed and dated copy of the property disclosure statement shall be delivered to the buyer in accordance with section 7305 [relating to delivery of disclosure form] prior to the signing of an agreement of transfer by the seller and buyer with respect to the property.

§ 7304. Disclosure form

(a) General rule.—A form of property disclosure statement that satisfies the requirements of this chapter shall be promulgated by the State Real Estate Commission. Nothing in this chapter shall preclude a seller from using a form of property disclosure statement that contains additional provisions that require greater specificity or that call for the disclosure of the condition or existence of other features of the property.

(b) Contents ofproperty disclosure statement.—The form of property disclosure statement promulgated by the State Real Estate Commission shall call for disclosures with respect to all of the following subjects:

(1) Seller's expertise in contracting, engineering, architecture or other areas related to the construction and conditions of the property and its improvements.

(2) When the property was last occupied by the seller.

(3) Roof.

(4) Basements and crawl spaces.

(5) Termites/wood destroying insects, dry rot and pests.

(6) Structural problems.

(7) Additions, remodeling and structural changes to the property.

(8) Water and sewage systems or service.

(9) Plumbing system.

(10) Heating and air conditioning.

(11) Electrical system.

(12) Other equipment and appliances included in the sale.

(13) Soils, drainage, boundaries and sinkholes.

(14) Presence of hazardous substances.

(15) Condominiums and other homeowners associations.

(16) Legal issues affecting title or that would interfere with use and enjoyment of the property.

(17) Condition, if known, and location of all storm water facilities, including a statement disclosing whether ongoing maintenance of the storm water facilities is the responsibility of the property owner or the responsibility of another person or entity.

§ 7307. Information subsequently rendered inaccurate

If information disclosed in accordance with this chapter is subsequently rendered inaccurate prior to final settlement as a result of any act, occurrence or agreement subsequent to the delivery of the required disclosures, the seller shall notify the buyer of the inaccuracy.

§ 7308. Affirmative duty of seller

The seller is not obligated by this chapter to make any specific investigation or inquiry in an effort to complete the property disclosure statement. In completing the property disclosure statement, the seller shall not make any representations that the seller or the agent for the seller knows or has reason to know are false, deceptive or misleading and shall not fail to disclose a known material defect.

Exercise 11-7. Lawyering Practice and Professional Conduct Hypothetical

You are a licensed attorney practicing property law. A married couple, Brad and Angie Smith, comes to consult with you. They own a residence and are about to list the property for sale through a real estate broker. About a month earlier, they received a letter from the manufacturer of the siding on their home that a portion (30%) of the siding was defective. As part of a class action lawsuit, the couple is being offered a cash settlement of $10,000 to compensate them for the defective siding—which is the replacement cost. They are wondering if they can take the settlement, not repair the siding and not disclose the problem. The Smiths feel this is justifiable because the home is 20 years old and still has the original siding and all of it has to be replaced soon anyway. They feel any buyer should know that and will probably account for old siding by reducing the offer price. Also, the real estate agent asked them to fill out an extensive disclosure form. There were some problems in the condition of the property over the many years they have lived there, including having bats living inside the roof of the house and drainage problems with the septic and sewer system. They believe that they have fixed these problems and have not heard or seen any bats for months now. The Smiths do not have a lot of money, and they want to maximize the sale price so they can buy another home. They prefer not to list past problems and are concerned a buyer might pay less or not be as attracted to the home if they knew about the bats and septic issues.

1. How you would advise your clients to proceed? Consider these questions along with your own as you evaluate the situation. What would you want to talk over more with your clients? Should they consider an as is sale? What are the risks they face? How might they be able to mitigate the risks?
2. Now assume your clients insist on taking the settlement for the siding and adamantly refuse to disclose or say anything about the siding manufacturing defect. How can they answer the question on the disclosure form that asks "are there any other problems with the house now or in the past"? What are your professional responsibilities and how will you comply with them? Consider Model Rule of Professional Conduct 1.2 (c)

   > (c) A lawyer shall not counsel a client to engage, or assist a client, in conduct that the lawyer knows is criminal or fraudulent, but a lawyer may discuss the legal consequences of any proposed course of conduct with a client and may counsel or assist a client to make a good faith effort to determine the validity, scope, meaning or application of the law.

Implied Warranty of Quality and Habitability—For New Construction

Assume you spend your life savings to buy a newly built home. A month after the real estate closing, major problems with the home develop. The plumbing and electrical systems completely malfunction and are unusable. These systems seemingly worked just fine until now. Are you the one who bears the risks of harm and financial losses from these defects? Or is the builder legally responsible for the repairs? Because this is new construction housing purchased from a builder, the builder is the one liable for the construction defects.

As you have learned, owners who sell their homes have implied disclosure duties, but they do not have an obligation to make warranties concerning the quality or condition of the property. In contrast, the law does imply a warranty for quality in sales from housing merchants to buyers of new construction homes. This is analogous to a warranty that might come with your computer or cell phone. *Caveat emptor* no longer governs in the sale of goods—and housing is viewed as such in this context. The premise is that a builder or developer who is engaged in the business of housing construction and sales makes an implied promise to the buyer that the home will be constructed properly consistent with prevailing standards for quality construction. Implicitly, that is what the parties bargained for. Beyond this, there is a policy being implemented to protect buyers by holding builders accountable to a substantial degree for the quality of the product they are producing and selling to lay consumers who do not have the expertise to evaluate the quality of the construction of the product. This is a form of consumer protection for buyers who are making a huge investment in reliance on the expertise of the developer or builder.

The warranty goes by a number of names: an implied warranty of quality, of habitability or of fitness. The specific content of the warranty varies among the states, but the basic definition is that the property was constructed in a competent and skillful, "workman-like" manner. Defects that come from faulty construction breach the warranty. New York's law is a good example:

N.Y. Gen. Bus. Law § 777-a.

> 1. Notwithstanding the provisions of section two hundred fifty-one of the real property law, a housing merchant implied warranty is implied in the contract or agreement for the sale of a new home and shall survive the passing of title. A housing merchant implied warranty shall mean that:
>
> a. one year from and after the warranty date the home will be free from defects due to a failure to have been constructed in a skillful manner;
>
> b. two years from and after the warranty date the plumbing, electrical, heating, cooling and ventilation systems of the home will be free from defects due to a failure by the builder to have installed such systems in a skillful manner; and
>
> c. six years from and after the warranty date the home will be free from material defects.

Another aspect of the law that has been evolving is whether a remote grantee can claim the benefits of the warranty. Certainly the original buyer of the home is a beneficiary because the promise is implied in the agreement. What happens if the first buyer sells to a new buyer? Increasingly, courts are extending the warranty to successor owners for a period of time (such as 2 years post-closing) both for claims of personal injuries and for economic losses.

Another legal issue is whether the warranty can be waived. The policy that supports the adoption of the warranty also supports it being non-disclaimable. On the other hand, contract terms are generally based on consent and intent, so there is an argument in favor of freedom of contract. States disagree on whether the warranty is waivable and approaches vary. This is a point of departure from the implied warranty of habitability in landlord tenant law—where the warranty cannot be waived.

The Closing and Transfer by Deed

The closing is when the real estate transaction takes place. It includes several activities: (1) the buyer pays the purchase price to the seller; (2) the seller transfers title by delivering a deed, and (3) the buyer signs any mortgage documents and the lender provides the funds (you study mortgages later in the chapter).

What is needed to effectuate a valid transfer by deed?

1. **Writing.** The deed must be in a writing that satisfies the statute of frauds.
2. **Intent.** The grantor must intend to immediately transfer ownership to the grantee.
3. **Delivery.** The grantor must deliver the deed.
4. **Acceptance.** The grantee must accept the deed.

By now you know well that real estate transfers should be in a writing that satisfies the statute of frauds. The deed, of course, is a writing. It must include the essential terms of the transaction: identify who the parties are; sufficiently identify the property with a description; state that the grantor is conveying the real property to the grantee; and be signed by the grantor. These are the basic elements. Notably, recording is *not* required for a valid transfer. It is, however, a good idea to record. You will learn the benefits of recording for "bona fide purchasers" below. Notarization is typical, and is also wise and is often required to record a deed, but it is not required for a valid transfer. Witnesses are also not required, except in a few states. Deeds might also include property restrictions such as a real covenant or an easement. We discuss the types of deeds and other promises that may be included in the deed and their effect in the section below on title assurance.

Exercise 11-8. Document Review — Sample Deed

General Warranty Deed

This General Warranty Deed, made the 4th day of April, in the year 2016, between Kim Chen, with an address at 16 Mountain Top Road, Logtown, Colorado (hereinafter referred to as "Grantor"), and Jim Patel and Chris Federico, a married couple, with an address of 619 Valley Lane, Valleytown, Colorado (hereinafter referred to collectively as "Grantee");

WITNESSETH, that in consideration of $215,000, paid by Grantee to Grantor, the receipt and sufficiency whereof is hereby acknowledged, Grantor does hereby grant and convey to Grantee, as tenants by the entirety, in and to ALL of that certain property, with the buildings and improvements thereon erected, situate, lying and being located in Logtown, County of Franklin, State of Colorado, as more particularly described as Lot 4, Franklin County Short Plat, No. 867530921, according to Plat recorded November 25, 1991, in Franklin County, Colorado.

TO HAVE AND TO HOLD the premises herein granted, the heirs or successors and assigns of the grantee forever.

Being the same premises conveyed to Grantor by deed dated October 18, 2002, recorded in Franklin County Recorder of Deeds, Book 12345, page 103.

Grantor covenants as follows:

FIRST. That Grantor is seized of the said premises in fee simple, and has good right to convey the same; SECOND. That Grantee shall quietly enjoy the said premises; THIRD. That the said premises are free from encumbrances, except for easements, rights, covenants, conditions and restrictions of record, insofar at the same may be currently in force and applicable; FOURTH. That Grantor will execute or procure any further necessary assurance of the title to said premises; FIFTH. That Grantor will forever warrant the title to said premises.

In witness whereof, Grantor has hereunto set Grantor's hand, the day and year first above written.

____

Kim Chen

State of Colorado)
) ss.
County of Franklin

On this, the 4th day of April, 2016, before me, A Notary Public, the undersigned officer, personally appeared Kim Chen, known to me (or satisfactorily proven) to be the person(s) whose name(s) is/are subscribed to the within instrument, and acknowledged that she executed the same for the purposes therein contained.

In witness whereof, I hereunto set my hand and official seals.

____

Notary Public

Has the deed been delivered? As highlighted earlier, a deed must be delivered to complete a transfer. For a typical homeowner's sale, this presents no problem, as the buyer will insist on actual delivery of a deed at the closing in exchange for the purchase money. It is transfers by gift, usually among family members, that recurrently triggers questions about whether there is a completed transfer. The questions are:

(1) Does the grantor intend to *immediately* transfer ownership or does the grantor instead intend only for a transfer at death; and

(2) Has there been effective delivery of a deed that accompanies and confirms intent?

The deed must also be accepted. This requirement is rarely controversial, because most people accept gifts and, thus, acceptance is presumed. We studied this same set of legal issues in the chapter on shared property and gifts, where you can find a more in-depth discussion. Here we focus briefly on these kinds of issues in connection with transfer by deed.

Here is a typical example. Mom, who is 80 years old, gives a signed deed to her home called Love-Acre to her son, who accepts it. As she is handing over the deed she says, "I am giving you this deed now because I want you to have Love-Acre when I die. So go put this away someplace safe and when I die, it is yours." Mom's intent here is to set up a transfer that takes effect at death, not during her lifetime. To make a transfer at death, you must comply with wills law and this likely does not (no witnesses). Even though Mom has handed Son the deed, there is no valid transfer because Mom lacks the intent to relinquish ownership during her life. In addition to failing for lack of intent, sometimes courts will say this gift fails for lack of delivery. That is because delivery is an alter ego, or a manifestation of intent. Delivery will be found if there is evidence by words or actions of intent to immediately transfer a property interest. Delivery can be effective only when it is paired with intent to transfer during life.

There is another possible outcome in the Love-Acre example. Some courts view the transaction as reserving a life estate in Mom and a remainder interest in Son. This means there was a valid gift and Mom *did* have intent during her life to immediately transfer an interest to Son—it's just that the interest was a remainder—not a fee. This might be a bit of a stretch. Then again, it might be that this is pretty much what Mom wanted but perhaps didn't know about the law of estates.

Rebuttable Presumptions. Many states have a rebuttable presumption that pushes toward a finding of delivery. The transfer of a deed or the recording of a deed often triggers such presumptions. However, as in the example above, even if a presumption is applicable, it can be rebutted with evidence of lack of intent.

Delivery to a Third Party. Another scenario that triggers similar questions is when an owner hands over a signed deed to a third party—such as a lawyer—with instructions to deliver the deed. *If* the owner intended to relinquish ownership of the gift at that time and did *not* retain the power to revoke, then the deed has been constructively delivered and the transfer is deemed complete. This is so even when the owner gives instructions to transfer at death—and can result in the life estate with a remainder conclusion. It appears that delivery to a third person is more likely to satisfy the intent and delivery requirements than giving a deed directly to a grantee. That said, attempting a transfer with either method is risky. Notably, in these types of situations, the client's goals would be better served by either writing a will or creating a trust, or both.

Title Assurance

In purchasing real property, a buyer should be concerned about exactly what package of rights they are purchasing and whether title to the property (their ownership rights) are secure against the claims and rights of others. For example, title might be burdened with easements or covenants or prior mortgages. Buyers need to think carefully about and take action to protect against the risks in a transaction that a buyer may not end up with the full set of ownership rights they are bargaining for. Title protections are crucial, because an owner isn't buying land but rather *title* to the land and to the set of property rights that go with it. This section addresses the various ways a buyer can gain title assurance at the closing and afterwards. This includes: obtaining deed covenants; taking advantage of the recording system by searching title before buying and recording the deed after; and buying title insurance or possibly registering title with the court.

As discussed earlier in this chapter, the seller's obligation to provide marketable title facilitates title assurance during the executory period. If the seller cannot provide title that is free from reasonable doubt by the time of the closing, the buyer can withdraw from agreement without penalty. At closing, the seller must perform this obligation and provide marketable title. Buyers and their lawyers need to attend closely to an important transition that occurs at the closing through the doctrine of merger. *Unless the contract or the deed says otherwise, the terms of the purchase and sale agreement are no longer enforceable post-closing.* Instead, the contract "merges" into the deed, and the deed replaces the contract. Basically, the deed is viewed as the final contract. Once closing has occurred, this means that the buyer can sue based on the deed but can no longer sue based on the original sales contract (including the promise to provide marketable title). The content of the deed then becomes crucially important in providing (or failing to provide) protections to the buyer after the sale is complete.

There are some exceptions to the merger doctrine, as well as some issues that never were governed by the contract. Grantor promises about the physical condition of the premises typically fall outside the scope of merger. Often, grantor promises concerning repairs or additional work on the house are seen as a separate contract. Or the parties might agree in the contract itself that some aspects of the sales contract *do* survive the closing. It is much better to be specific and make these kinds of things clear by including explicit language. Additionally, a buyer can bring a claim for fraud or breach of the housing merchant's warranty of quality, as these claims are actionable after the closing.

Deed Covenants

As to title assurance, after the closing, the buyer can no longer sue for breach of marketable title. Is there a claim a buyer can make if turns out that there is a limitation on ownership rights? That depends on what the deed says. There are three basic types of deeds:

1. General Warranty

- The grantor warrants and defends against any title defects regardless of whether they arose during the period of grantor's ownership or that of a predecessor owner.

2. Special Warranty

- The grantor warrants and defends against title defects that were created during her period of ownership (caused by her) but *not* by a predecessor owner.

3. Quit Claim

- The grantor makes no warranties whatsoever. The grantor simply quits and releases her claim, if any, to title.

Which one would you prefer if you are the buyer? Which would you accept? If you were the seller, what you would be willing to do? You might be wondering why anyone would ever accept a quit claim deed. If you are a buyer, you probably would not. However they can be useful in gift giving, because a donor may not want to make any warranties about the quality of the title. It is also used if there is litigation over title—part of the resolution might be for one party to agree to give up their claim.

Although there is some variation among the states, and grantors can individually tailor the covenants, general warranty deeds generally include six standard grantor covenants.

1. **Covenant of Seisin.** This is a promise that the grantor owns the property and the particular estate she is purporting to transfer. This covenant would be breached if the grantor owned a life estate and promised to convey a fee, or if a tenant in common with a fractional interest promised to convey the entire estate.

2. **Covenant of Right to Convey.** This is a promise that the grantor has the power to transfer the property. Rarely is this a problem, but it could be. For example, a life tenant may not have the power to transfer (and yes that is enforceable). The covenant would also be breached if an owner has record title but has lost some portion of ownership due to adverse possession.

3. **Covenant Against Encumbrances.** This is a promise by the grantor that there are no encumbrances against the property other than those stated in the deed. Recall that an encumbrance is any right to or interest in land that is owned or enforceable by another person or entity that reduces the value of the property or restricts its use. Mortgages, liens, easements and covenants are the typical ones that are of concern.

However, the definition is broad enough to include other things, such as a housing code violation or a zoning code violation, because the government has the power to enforce the laws against the owner. This can require major changes and expense. Note that the covenant can include exceptions. The grantor might covenant against encumbrances other than those specifically disclosed in the deed or those "of public record" (recorded). If the grantor covenants "by general warranty with no exceptions," then the existence of encumbrances will violate the covenant.

It may help to clarify the difference between the seller's promise to convey marketable title and the grantor's (seller's) covenant against encumbrances. They are designed to get to the same issue—they are protections for the buyer that title will be free of claims by third parties (encumbrances). However, the timing is different for making the claims. If the dispute over title is before the closing, then the buyer's claim is for breach of contract based on failure to provide marketable title. If there is an encumbrance that is discovered after the closing, then the buyer can sue for breach of the covenant in the deed.

4. **Covenant of Warranty—General or Special.** This is a grantor's promise to compensate the grantee if a claimant with superior title prevails. As explained above with the types of deeds, a general warranty protects against any claims that exist at the time of the closing, and a special warranty protects against claims that arose during the seller's period of ownership.

5. **Covenant of Quiet Enjoyment.** This is a grantor's promise that possession and enjoyment will not be disrupted by a superior claim. This is duplicative of the protections in a covenant of warranty.

6. **Covenant of Further Assurances.** This is a grantor's promise to take the necessary steps in the future and proactively defend against and cure any title defects. The grantor then has an obligation to act, not just to pay compensation for losses. For this reason, this covenant is rarely offered.

The first three covenants (seisin, power to convey and against encumbrances) are "present covenants" and are breached, if at all, at the time of the conveyance. The statute of limitations for breach starts to run from the closing. The last three (warranty, quiet enjoyment and further assurances) are future covenants and are breached, if at all, at the time when an event takes place that disrupts the grantee's possession. The statute of limitations runs from the time of the breach of the covenant. Notably, these covenants run with the land to remote grantees—meaning a subsequent buyer can sue for breach as well (within the statute of limitations). They provide important protections, then, not only to the current buyer, but to future owners as well.

Review the deed in Exercise 11-8 above again. Determine what kind of deed it is and what covenants are included. Some states have standardized deed covenants that may be incorporated by reference or be deemed included even though not expressly stated in the deed.

Exercise 11-9. *Feit v. Donahue*

The next case is a good opportunity to see these covenants and rules in action and to learn how several claims can fit together.

Feit v. Donahue

826 P.2d 407 (Colo. Ct. App. 1992)

Davidson, J. In this action involving the sale of a house, defendants, David J. Donahue (Donahue) and Linda L. Donahue, (sellers) appeal from the judgment entered after a bench trial in favor of plaintiffs, Glenn Richard and Penelope Larae Feit (buyers). We affirm and remand with directions.

In October 1984, the parties contracted for the sale and purchase of a home. The agreement provided, *inter alia,* that the seller was to convey merchantable title and that the property was being sold subject to building and zoning regulations. The following month, sellers conveyed the real estate to plaintiffs by warranty deed and buyers took possession of the property.

For reasons unrelated to this action, three years later buyers decided to sell the house. While they were attempting to list the property, they were notified by the City of Thornton that the certificate of occupancy issued on the house was to be revoked. The order of revocation explained that, in 1982, sellers had obtained a building permit to convert the existing garage into a family room and to build a new, detached garage. However, the zoning code required that each single-family dwelling have two enclosed off-street parking spaces, and accordingly, the building permit and certificate of occupancy had been issued conditionally upon the construction of a garage. Upon inspection in 1987, the city had ascertained that the garage had not been built. Upon receiving this notification from the city, buyers contacted sellers and requested either that sellers complete the garage or rescind the agreement. Sellers refused. Buyers were unable to obtain a variance from the zoning board and could not list or sell the house. Ultimately, the home was foreclosed.

Buyers then filed this action against sellers, seeking recovery for damages for breaches of the deed covenants of warranty, quiet enjoyment, and against encumbrances and for fraudulent concealment. At trial, the court dismissed the claims of breach of the covenants of warranty and quiet enjoyment and found against sellers on the claim of breach of the covenant against encumbrances and against Donahue only on the fraud claim.

We first address sellers' contentions of error concerning the breach of warranty against encumbrances. In its ruling, the trial court found that the fact that the city could require a subsequent purchaser to build a garage to bring the property into compliance with the zoning laws constituted a "latent burden" on the property, which "is one for which the sellers are responsible under the [deed]." Sellers argue that such zoning violation does not constitute an encumbrance within the meaning of the covenant in the deed. We agree with the trial court that here the covenant against encumbrances was breached.

Conveyances of real estate are deemed to be in fee simple unless expressly limited, and carry with them the right to immediate possession of the premises. A good title in fee simple means the legal estate in fee, free and clear of all claims, liens, and encumbrances whatsoever, "uniting all the elements constituting ownership, including right of possession and right of property." (Citation omitted.) It "imports such ownership of the land as enables the owner to exercise absolute and exclusive control of it against all others." (Citation omitted.) "[The] grantee under a warranty deed, except for matters specifically enumerated therein, should be in much the same position as [a purchaser of land with the] right to demand title which will put him in all reasonable security against loss or annoyance by litigation and will enable him not only to hold his land but to hold it in peace." (Citation omitted.)

As pertinent here, by the terms of the deed, sellers warranted the property to be free from all "liens, taxes, assessments, encumbrances and restrictions" and warranted "the quiet and peaceable possession of the grantees," and agreed to "warrant and forever defend" against any person lawfully claiming the whole or any part of the premises. Nevertheless, sellers first argue that there was no breach of the covenant against encumbrances because there was no "adverse claim of title." In light of statutory requirements for warranty deeds, conveyance of title in fee simple, and right to immediate possession, we do not view the scope of the covenant against encumbrances so restrictively.

An encumbrance within the meaning of the covenant is a right or interest in the land which diminishes the value of, but is not inconsistent with the ability to convey, fee title. It includes "any burden resting not only on the title to the real estate, but on the real estate itself which tends to lessen the value or interfere with its free enjoyment." (Citation omitted.) Thus, we have held that the existence of a lease constitutes a breach of the covenant against encumbrances. Accordingly, numerous jurisdictions have held that an existing violation of a zoning law constitutes an encumbrance. (Citations omitted.)

Here, it is undisputed that the house was sold with an existing zoning violation which eventually resulted in the revocation of the certificate allowing occupancy. The city, by ordinance, had the right to enter upon the property and physically conform the property to the zoning requirements without permission of the buyers and at their expense. Moreover, the city by court action could require buyers to build the garage. And, the undisputed evidence was that buyers unsuccessfully attempted to obtain a variance and ultimately could not even list the property for sale because it had no certificate of occupancy. Hence, at minimum, as confirmed by subsequent events, the title conveyed to buyers with the existing zoning violation was unmarketable.

Under these circumstances, we hold that the requirement which existed at the time of conveyance that a garage be built to conform to zoning laws constituted an encumbrance.

Sellers argue that, nonetheless, there could be no breach of the covenant against encumbrances because the buyers, by the language of the sales contract, agreed to purchase the property "subject to building and zoning regulations." We disagree. Preliminarily, we do not necessarily agree that a buyer who enters into a realty contract "subject to" zoning regulations is obligated to take the property "subject to" *existing* zoning violations. Regardless, by the doctrine of merger, the provisions of the contract for the sale of real estate merge at closing into the deed. Thus, here the rights of the parties are determined by the covenants in the deed rather than by the language of the contract.

We next address Donahue's argument that the trial court erred in its determination that he fraudulently concealed a material fact in the sale of the property. Specifically, Donahue contends that his failure to tell buyers about the zoning requirement was a misrepresentation of law, not fact, and thus, the trial court's finding of fraudulent concealment to the contrary was error. We disagree.

To establish a *prima facie* case of fraudulent concealment, plaintiff must prove that the defendant knowingly concealed a material fact that in equity or good conscience should have been disclosed with the intent that the plaintiff act on that concealed fact and that the plaintiff did act on the concealment resulting in damage. However, if the representation concerns law, not fact, it is an expression of opinion and is not actionable.

Contrary to Donahue's contention, the trial court did not base its finding of fraudulent concealment on Donahue's failure to disclose the applicable zoning requirement, but on his failure to tell buyers that "a two-car garage was required to be built." With record support, the trial court found that Donahue was aware from his conversations with building officials that in order to convert his original existing garage to residential space he was required to build a detached garage. Thus, to represent to buyer that there was a certificate of occupancy without disclosing that it was conditioned on the construction of a new garage was a concealment of a material fact, not a misrepresentation of law.

Recording System

A main source for title assurance is the safe-keeping of public records for instruments affecting title and related laws. This includes deed transfers, leases, mortgages, liens, easements, covenants and wills. In the U.S., land records go back as far as 1640. A purchaser should search—or have a lawyer search—the records to evaluate and render an opinion as to the state of the title. This enables buyers to find out if the seller owns the property they are about to buy and about any recorded interests in the property owned by another. Recording also gives notice to others and grants some protections for those with an interest in property such as buyers, lenders, lienholders, common interest communities and easement or covenant holders. A judgment from a lawsuit effecting title can be recorded, as can a *lis pendens*, which is notice of pending litigation before a judgment has been reached. Further, recording helps establish priority of title when there are competing claims. For example, a creditor who records a lien first will generally have priority to collect against the proceeds of a foreclosure sale over a second (junior) creditor.

Remember, recording is not required to create a valid interest. A deed that is delivered is valid *as between the grantor and grantee* and a lack of recording is not grounds for challenging that. Recording is, however, the best practice and can trigger significant legal consequences. As you will learn, the lack of recording makes it possible for *other people* to establish a superior claim to title. Special protections against unrecorded interests are provided to later buyers who qualify as *bona fide* purchasers.

Every state has a Recording Act that provides for a central registry for records—typically at the county level of government. Recording occurs when a document is submitted to this registry.

How to Search Title

You might be thinking—how hard can this be? To research title, I will type in the address of the property into a database and see what information pops up. Because land records go back before the 1700's, long before the age of computers, the public recording system you are imagining is not (yet) available. Increasingly, counties are moving to electronic record keeping and even on-line access. However, this is often only from a set point in time (say the year 2000) going forward—so only part of the records are publicly available that way. Also, the expense and risk of mistakes is often prohibitive to local governments. (Interestingly, title companies sometimes have their own private databases that they have created.) It is time to learn the old fashioned system we still have.

The records are indexed by either a grantor-grantee index or a tract index. In a tract index, each parcel is given an identification number, and looking up the records by number is straight-forward. The most common system is the grantor-grantee index organized by the names of parties. Here is how you proceed. Remember your goal is to determine what interests are recorded that impact title.

Step One—Look in the grantee index to develop a list of previous owners and thus create a chain of title.

Step Two—Look in the grantor index to see what interests were recorded during the time of ownership for each owner. You are looking for anything and everything that can affect title—such as leases, mortgages, easements, covenants, and other liens.

Let's use an example case to walk through the process.

Margo Kidder is in the process of buying her first home called Sunny-Acre and has entered into purchase and sale agreement with Jimmy Patel. *Step one*, start looking in the grantee index under the name of the seller Jimmy Patel to find a deed where he is listed as a grantee of Sunny-Acre. You start in the current year and go back in time, year by year in the record books until you find such a deed. That deed will list who the grantor was—it was Maria Lopez in 2000. Now you start looking for the name Maria Lopez going back from the year 2000 in the grantee index until you find a deed where she was a grantee in 1989 and the grantor was Owen McGuinn. You continue to go back until when the land was owned by a sovereign (the government) or follow the local practice—say 50 to 75 years. (We don't go back that far in this example.)

Now that you have a list of previous owners and times of ownership, you switch over to the grantee index and search forward in time to see what property interests were recorded during each grantor's period of ownership. You start with the grantor furthest back in time, here Owen McGuinn, to learn of any interests that attached to the property while he was the owner up until 1989 and find none. Next, you look under the name Maria Lopez and look at the records every year from 1989 to 2000 (during her period of record ownership) and find a mortgage against the property in 1991 and its release in 1999. Then you look under the name of Jimmy Patel and find an easement granted to a neighbor in 2003. Here is what we now know:

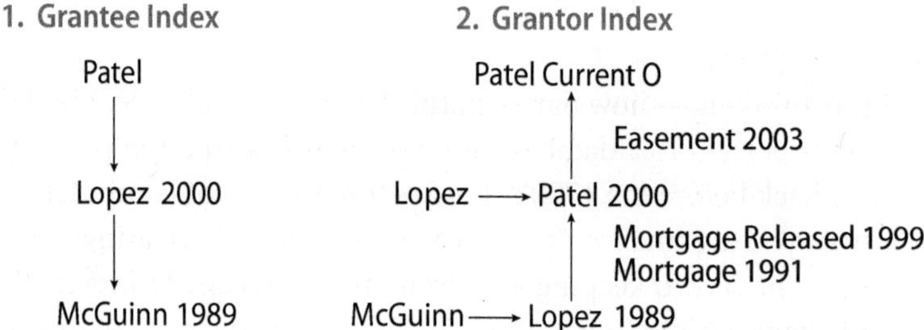

Margo should now be reasonably comfortable that she will buy good title from Jimmy. She is also going to be bound by the easement because there is record notice of it. Note that although the records provide a lot of information, they don't reveal all possible problems with title such as adverse possession claims or implied easements or covenants.

Recording Acts and Bona Fide Purchaser Protections

Now that you know more about how title searches work, you have a good foundation for learning the next body of law. In addition to creating a system of public records, the Recording Acts assign consequences for failing to record and provide protections against *unrecorded* interests for buyers who qualify as *bona fide* purchasers. If you are an owner who does not record, you are risking a later buyer gaining priority of title over your interest.

First in Time. The starting point for prioritizing competing claims is what you probably expect—the first in time to *establish an ownership interest* has priority.

Here is an example. Suppose in Year 1, Dad delivers a signed deed to Daughter with intent to transfer the interest to her immediately—so it is a completed gift. Then later, in Year 2, Dad becomes upset with Daughter and announces that he has changed his mind and is taking back the property. Dad delivers a second deed to Son. Who owns Family-Acre? Daughter is the owner and became such in Year 1. Once complete, the transfer cannot be revoked by a former owner. Dad no longer owned Family-Acre at the time he attempted to give it to Son. The first-in-time rule for ownership is the default rule for determining priority of claims. Notice in this example, the competing claimants are donees. Donees are not subsequent "buyers" covered by the rules below.

General Rules for Bona Fide Purchasers. The Recording Acts radically change the default rule in certain situations and allow a later buyer's interests to supercede the interests of the owner who was first in time *if* the earlier ownership interest was not recorded.

Here is an example. Olivia sells Purple-Acre to Abe. Abe does not record his interest—instead he puts his deed inside the mattress of his bed. Then Olivia purports to sell Purple-Acre again and delivers a deed to Ben who then promptly records the O to B deed. If Ben asserts a claim against Abe—who owns Purple-Acre? We will soon discuss the specifics and variations, but the general answer is that the Recording Acts will protect Ben's ownership of Purple-Acre and not Abe's. Ben bought the property and could not have known about Abe's ownership claim because it was not recorded (assume he did not have actual or inquiry notice either). Abe's failure to record left him vulnerable. But wait—how can Olivia effectively transfer out property to Ben that she no longer owns because she had already transferred the same property to Abe? In order to protect an innocent buyer like Ben, the Recording Acts recognize a valid transfer from Olivia to Ben. In this example, the law is choosing who, between two competing claimants, will get Purple-Acre. Because Ben is a *bona fide* purchaser and Abe could have protected himself by recording, Ben gets legal protection. Abe does have other legal claims he can assert against Olivia, such as fraud. However, our focus here in the study of Recording Acts is who has priority in title and walks away with title to Purple-Acre.

More examples. The double transfer of a fee example rarely occurs, but that is the way the rules tend to be tested on bar exams. It also clearly demonstrates the operation of the rules. Nevertheless, there are many common real world examples where a bona fide purchaser is given priority over earlier unrecorded interests. These rules apply to mortgages, easements, covenants and creditors whose interests are secured by the property. (All of these are property interests.)

Let's say an owner of Red-Acre borrows money and grants a mortgage to the lender First Bank in Year One, but First Bank does not record their security interest. In Year Two, the owner borrows more money from another lender, Second Bank, who is granted a mortgage and immediately records their interest. If Red-Acre is sold in a foreclosure and there is not enough money to pay off both mortgages, Second Bank has priority and will be paid first.

Another example—assume a right of way easement has been granted burdening Road-Acre but it is not recorded. Later, Road-Acre is sold to a new owner who does not have actual or inquiry notice of the easement. The new owner will not be bound by the easement and will be afforded priority over the easement holder who did not record. The easement can no longer be enforced. This is the same result from your earlier study of the role of record notice in easements as well as for covenants. Now, you are learning more about why and how the rules overlap with the Recording Acts.

The general rule demonstrated in the these examples is that a 1) subsequent 2) purchaser for value 3) who has no notice of the existence of an earlier conveyance 4) will prevail over a prior unrecorded interest in the same property.

Why protect bona fide purchasers? Think a minute about why the law offers protection to this group of later buyers. One reason is that it helps make buyers more confident in their purchases and that might make for a more resilient real estate market and economy.

Types of Recording Acts

Each state has its own recording statute. There are three types: race statutes; notice statutes and race-notice statutes. These variations reflect differing definitions of what a buyer has to do to qualify as a *bona fide purchaser* (BFP) who gains priority of title.

Race Statutes. This kind of statute provides that, as between an owner of a prior unrecorded interest and a subsequent purchaser, the first to record wins. This echoes a first-in-time rule, but it is not the first *owner* in time, but rather the first owner who *records* who is awarded priority. Who won the race to the recording office? If the later buyer duly records first (meaning records in a way that will give notice to a subsequent owner), that buyer's interest is given priority against a previously created interest. This is true even if the later buyer has notice about the earlier owner's interest. This "pure race" approach has fallen out of favor and only governs in North Carolina and Louisiana, and in a few other states, for mortgages.

Let's return to our basic example.

Olivia sells Purple-Acre to Abe. Abe does not record his interest.
Then Olivia purports to sell Purple-Acre again and delivers a deed to Ben.
Ben records the O to B deed.
Then Abe records the O to A deed.

Who owns Purple-Acre? In a race jurisdiction, B wins, because B recorded before A. What happens if the order of recording was switched so A records first? Then A wins. A was first to record, and B cannot qualify as a BFP.

Notice Statutes. Under this approach, a later buyer prevails over an earlier owner's unrecorded interest *if* the subsequent purchaser has no notice of the pre-existing interest. Consider whether there is record notice, inquiry notice or actual notice. The focus in applying these statutes usually centers on record notice.

Applying these rules, who has priority of title in our basic example?

Olivia sells Purple-Acre to Abe. Abe does not record his interest.
Then Olivia purports to sell Purple-Acre again and delivers a deed to Ben.
Ben records the O to B deed.
Then Abe records the O to A deed.

B wins (again), because B did not have record, actual or inquiry notice of the O to A transfer. That is it—he qualifies as a BFP. It is smart that B recorded, but it is not a requirement of a notice statute. If B did not record—he would still win. About half the states have this rule—and about half the states have a race-notice rule, studied next.

Race-Notice Statutes. These statutes define a BFP as a person who has no notice and duly records first in time. Under this approach, you ask is the later buyer innocent (without notice); and has he also won the race to record? Such a person will have priority over an earlier unrecorded interest.

Returning to our example again:

Olivia sells Purple-Acre to Abe. Abe does not record his interest.
Then Olivia purports to sell Purple-Acre again and delivers a deed to Ben.
Ben records the O to B deed.
Then Abe records the O to A deed.

Here, Ben meets the requirements of a BFP and his interests prevail over Abe's. Be sure you understand why.

Exercise 11-10. Interpreting Recording Statutes

Review each statute below and determine which is a race statute, a notice statute and a race-notice statute. These statutes provide generally for recording of documents in addition to defining BFP's, so be careful to differentiate when the statute is referring to the recording of the *earlier* buyer versus the later buyer, as in the last part of the Florida statute excerpted below.

1. No (i) conveyance of land, or (ii) contract to convey, or (iii) option to convey, or (iv) lease of land for more than three years shall be valid to pass any property interest as against lien creditors or purchasers for a valuable consideration from the donor, bargainer or lesser but from the time of registration thereof in the county where the land lies, or if the land is located in more than one county, then in each county where any portion of the land lies to be effective as to the land in that county. Unless otherwise stated either on the registered instrument or on a separate registered instrument duly executed by the party whose priority interest is adversely affected, (i) instruments registered in the office of the register of deeds shall have priority based on the order of registration as determined by the time of registration. N.C. Gen. Stat. §47-18(a).

2. No conveyance, transfer, or mortgage of real property, or of any interest therein, nor any lease for a term of 1 year or longer, shall be good and effectual in law or equity against creditors or subsequent purchasers for a valuable consideration and without notice, unless the same be recorded according to law. Fla. Stat. §695.01.

3. A conveyance of real property, when acknowledged by the person executing the same (the acknowledgment being certified as required by law), may be recorded in the office of the recording officer of the county where the property is situated. Every such conveyance not so recorded is void as against any subsequent purchaser or mortgagee in

good faith and for a valuable consideration from the same vendor, his or her heirs or devisees, of the same real property or any portion thereof whose conveyance is first duly recorded. An instrument is deemed recorded the minute it is filed for record. Wash. Rev. Code §65.08.070.

Exercise 11-11. Applying the Basic Recording Laws

Determine which party has priority of ownership of Beach-Acre. Assume each transaction follows the other in time. Assume there is no actual or inquiry notice unless the facts say otherwise. For each problem, apply a race statute, a notice statute and a race-notice statute.

1. O conveys to X, who does not record.
   O conveys to Y.
   Y records.
   X records.
2. O conveys to X, who does not record.
   O conveys to Y, who has actual notice of the earlier conveyance to X.
   Y records.
   X records.
3. O conveys to X, who does not record.
   O conveys to Y.
   X records.
   Y records.
4. O conveys to X, who does not record.
   O conveys to Y, as a gift.
   Y records.
   X records.

Complex Recording and Title Issues

There are sometimes more complex issues with the chain of title and recording to grapple with. As you will see with so called wild deeds, sometimes deeds or other documents are in the public record but cannot be readily found. This is because it is possible for a document to be recorded outside the chain of title—meaning it cannot be found by doing the required search of the record. In such a case, there is no record notice. There are other potential problems as well, such as a forged deed or one induced by fraud.

Estoppel by Deed

The following situation triggers a doctrine called estoppel by deed. Olivia expects to inherit Green-Acre from a family member. She is impatient and purports to transfer Green-Acre by giving a signed warranty deed to Zeke, even though she does not yet own Green-Acre. A month later, Olivia inherits Green-Acre and becomes the owner. "Estoppel by deed" automatically passes title from Olivia to Zeke. This comes under the umbrella of equitable estoppel that you have come across in a variety of contexts. Zeke could also sue for breach of the covenant of warranty.

Shelter Rule

Assume the following facts.

O conveys Green-Acre to X, who does not record.
O conveys to Y.
Y records.
X records.
Y conveys to Z who has actual notice about the earlier conveyance to A.

As between X and Z, who owns Green-Acre? Z wins. Can you see why? Y qualifies as a BFP under all three types of Recording Acts. The only way to protect Y's status as an owner is to accord Y the full power to transfer Green-Acre. This is so even though Z does not independently qualify as a BFP because Z has notice of X's interest. Y's BFP status shelters Z.

Wild Deeds

Here is an example of a "wild deed"—one that is in the record but cannot be found by doing a proper chain of title search.

Y conveys Wild-Acre to O. O records the deed.
O conveys Wild-Acre to A, who does not record. (A puts the deed in his mattress.)
A conveys Wild-Acre to B.
B records the A to B deed. (But the O to A deed is still in A's mattress.)
O conveys Wild-Acre to X. X records.

Does X qualify as a BFP in a claim against B? The answer is *yes* in all states. To have record notice, X would have to be able to find the A to B deed. The problem is that even though the A to B deed is sitting there in the recording office, it would not be found in a properly done chain of title search. X cannot see that B has a claim to Wild-Acre without first seeing the link between O and A. And that link does not appear in the records. Remember where the O to A deed is?

Walking through a chain of title search will help you understand how the rules operate here. Recall that the point of the search is to see who owned the property before and discover what each owner did with the property. Step One, X is buying from O and needs to search for O's name as a grantee in the grantee index. X would see that O was a grantee from Y. Then taking the names on the list of previous owners just developed (Y and O), X switches over to the grantor index and looks under Y's name going forward in time to see if there are any recorded interests against Wild-Acre during Y's period of ownership. Then, once X arrives at the deed where Y transfers to O, X starts looking under O's name and sees O is the current record owner. X has no record notice and is innocent about B's interest and, in fact, never came across the name of B (or A) in the search process.

Deeds Filed Too Late or Too Early. There are two other main situations that create a wild deed.

Some deeds are filed too late to give record notice to a subsequent buyer. This is because when you are doing a title search and are looking in the grantor index, you stop looking under a grantor's name once you find a deed transferring out the property to a new owner. Here is an example.

Y → O	O records
O → A	A does not record
O → X	X *knows* of earlier O → A conveyance
	X records
	A records [This is too late.]
X → Z	Z records

X does not qualify as a BFP in most states because he has notice. However, Z has no record notice and qualifies as a BFP against A. Z will not find A's recording, because once Z sees the O to X transfer, she will stop looking under O's name as a grantor and will look under X's name. The law does not require an owner to search for possible grantor transfers in the record *after* they are no longer record owner. The search parameters are limited. You should treat a deed recorded too late as if it were invisible (it is there but you won't find it). If A had recorded before X, then the O-A deed would have been findable. The timing really matters.

Less commonly, an owner might also record too early to give notice to a later buyer. Suppose O transfers Secret-Acre to G, but O does not own the property at that time. G immediately records. O later becomes the owner and then transfers to property to W. W is a BFP, because she is unaware of the earlier transfer and did not have to search the records of what O might have done with the property *before* O was the record owner, and no competing claims are recorded after O was the record owner. Hold on—doesn't the doctrine of estoppel by deed play out here? Yes, when O became the owner, estoppel by deed automatically transferred ownership to G. However, the record did not reflect that—so a BFP will prevail over an owner (who became an owner by estoppel by deed) who did not record after ownership accrued.

Exercise 11-12. Deeds in the Wild—*Hartig v. Stratman*

As you read the next case, identify and apply the rules. To do this, you will need to trace a chain of title search following the steps you have learned. Make a diagram of what you find in the grantee and grantor index. Determine precisely why the deed is wild and does not confer record notice.

Hartig v. Stratman

729 N.E.2d 237 (Ind. Ct. App. 2000)

SHARPNACK, C.J. This case comes to us on interlocutory appeal. Timothy Hartig appeals the trial court's order denying his motion for summary judgment. We affirm in part, reverse in part, and remand for further proceedings.

The relevant facts follow. Melvin and Louise Stratman are the owners of real property located at 2208 E. Walnut St. in Evansville, Indiana. The property next door, at 2210 E. Walnut St., is owned by Hartig. The instant dispute centers around a shared driveway that is located on both parcels of property, with the majority of the driveway being on Hartig's property.

The record of title to Hartig's property discloses that Hartig purchased the property from Sean Holmes on September 28, 1995. Holmes in turn purchased the property from John Connell on May 31, 1994. On the same day that Connell sold the property to Holmes, Connell entered into a written easement agreement with the Stratmans regarding the shared driveway. The agreement gave the Stratmans a perpetual easement over the portion of the driveway that is located upon the parcel at 2210 E. Walnut St. and gave the property owners at 2210 E. Walnut St. a perpetual easement over the portion of the driveway that is located upon the Stratman parcel. The Stratman–Connell easement agreement was recorded in the Vanderburgh County Recorder's Office on June 8, 1994, at 2:25 p.m. The deed transferring the property at 2210 E. Walnut Street from Connell to Holmes was also recorded on June 8, 1994, but it was recorded one minute earlier, at 2:24 p.m. It is undisputed that when Holmes sold the property to Hartig, he did not inform Hartig about the existence of the driveway easement agreement.

Thereafter, on February 13, 1998, the Stratmans filed a complaint alleging that Hartig was blocking the driveway and refusing to allow them to use it. The complaint further alleged that prior to Hartig's actions, "the owners of both 2208 East Walnut and 2210 East Walnut Street, used said easement under a claim of right, open, notoriously, and adverse to the interest of the adjoining owner." On February 24, 1998, the trial court granted Hartig's motion to dismiss the Stratmans' complaint pursuant to Indiana Trial Rule 12(B)(6). The Stratmans then filed an amended complaint alleging in substance that Hartig was trespassing upon their property. Then, on August 26, 1998, the Stratmans filed a "Second Paragraph of Amended Complaint," asserting the right to use the driveway by virtue of the Connell–Stratman easement agreement. Record, p. 19. Thereafter, Hartig filed a motion for summary judgment, which the trial court denied on June 29, 1999.

When reviewing the denial of a motion for summary judgment, we apply the same standard as the trial court. Therefore, summary judgment should only be granted when the designated evidentiary material demonstrates that there is no genuine issue as to any material fact and the moving party is entitled to judgment as a matter of law. We resolve any doubt as to any fact, or inference to be drawn therefrom, in favor of the nonmoving party. The party appealing the denial of a motion for summary judgment has the burden of persuading this court on appeal that the trial court's ruling was improper.

Hartig contends that he is entitled to summary judgment because the Connell–Stratman driveway easement agreement was recorded outside his chain of title and therefore not binding on him. Indiana's recording statute provides:

> "Every conveyance or mortgage of lands or of any interest therein ... shall be recorded in the recorder's office ... ; and every conveyance [or] mortgage ... shall take priority according to the time of the filing thereof, and such conveyance [or] mortgage ... shall be fraudulent and void as against any subsequent purchaser, ... or mortgagee in good faith and for a valuable consideration, having his deed [or] mortgage ... first recorded."

Ind.Code § 32-1-2-16. The purpose of this statute is to provide protection to subsequent purchasers and mortgagees. This protection is derived from the fact that a landowner will not be deemed to have constructive notice of adverse claims that appear outside the chain of title.

To determine the chain of title, the prospective purchaser must go to the recorder's office and search through the grantor index, beginning with the person who received the grant of land from the United States and continuing until the conveyance of the tract in question. The particular grantor's name is not searched thereafter.

Here, when Hartig conducted a title search of the property at 2210 E. Walnut St., he would have discovered the conveyance to Connell. Next, Hartig would have discovered the conveyance from Connell to Holmes that was recorded on June 8, 1994, at 2:24 p.m. Hartig would not have discovered the Connell-Stratford easement agreement that was recorded one minute later, however, because Connell's name would not have been searched after the conveyance to Holmes was discovered. *See id.* Therefore, the easement agreement is not within Hartig's chain of title and he cannot be deemed to have constructive notice of its existence. Accordingly, we hold that the trial court erred in denying Hartig's motion for summary judgment with respect to the issue of the driveway easement agreement.

Forgery and Fraud

Suppose A pretends to be the record owner and forges a deed purporting to transfer ownership of Forge-Acre to B. A does not own the property. B pays the purchase price and records the deed. B is unaware of the forgery, and a record search does not reveal the problem. Who prevails if O, the true owner of Forge-Acre, makes a claim to the property? O continues to be the owner because a forged deed is absolutely void and transfers no interest.

Notice that B would otherwise qualify as a BFP. (Be sure you understand why.) That does not change the result. Even a BFP will lose against the true owner with a forged deed. Why is this an exception to the usual BFP rules? A contrary rule might encourage forgeries. Also, B at least knew that there was a transaction and had some hope of discovering the forgery. The titled owner had no such information. Luckily for a grantee of a forged deed, title insurance policies (discussed below) usually protect against forgery. The grantee can also sue the forger for fraud.

The law is different when there is fraud in the inducement of a contract. Real estate transactions that are procured by fraud are voidable by the fraud victim while the property remains owned by the fraud perpetrator. However, if the fraudulently acquired property is transferred out to a BFP, the BFP will have good title. At that point the original fraud victim will not be allowed to rescind the transfer but will still be able to sue the perpetrator for fraud.

Here is an example. In *McCoy v. Love*, 382 So. 2d 647 (Fla. 1980), Mrs. Elliot, an elderly woman who could not read or write, signed a deed transferring all of her mineral rights to her land, contrary to her intent and the parties' oral agreement to transfer just some of the rights. She had repeatedly refused to transfer all her rights. Mr. Russell, the grantee, lied to her about what the deed said. Soon afterward, Russell transferred the property to a BFP. At that point, it was too late to seek cancellation of the deed against the BFP. When was the window of time when the transfer was voidable?

Deeds Out from a Common Grantor

To complete the list of deeds that may be in the record but that a "reasonable" title search would not reveal, let's circle back to the definitions of record notice you studied in detail in Chapter 10—Servitudes. You know well by now that the basic definition of record notice is that a buyer is on notice of any interests that affect the property that would be discovered in a properly done search of the chain of title. However, states have different requirements for what a buyer must do to perform a "proper" or "reasonable" search. Some states require a buyer to search only the direct chain of title for the property they are about to buy. A majority of states require a more extensive search and will impute notice to a buyer of not only the content in the records for the property he is buying but also of the content in the records of *other* properties that the seller owned at the same time she owned the subject property (and that are nearby geographically).

Assume a developer owns a parcel of land that is subdivided into 5 parcels. She sells one acre called Red-Acre to Buyer 1. In the deed transferring out Red-Acre, Buyer 1 promises never to paint the house blue, and seller makes the same promise for her retained properties (parcels 2-5). These reciprocal promises are contained in the deed for Red-Acre only. The deed is recorded. Next, the developer sells Yellow-Acre to Buyer 2. The deed transferring out Yellow-Acre makes no mention of the prohibition on painting the house blue.

Does the buyer of Yellow-Acre have notice of the promise binding Yellow-Acre but that is findable only if you search out the deed to Red-Acre that contained it? The answer depends on which approach a state has adopted. Yes, there is record notice to Buyer 2 in a majority of states. There is not in a (substantial) minortiy of states.

Marketable Title Acts

Hoping to simplify land transactions, some states (roughly 20) have marketable title acts in an effort to limit how far back a buyer must search to free the property from "ancient" or stale recorded interests. With this approach, if a person has record title for a specific period of time, usually 30 or 40 years, then any interests recorded before that can be ignored because they are no longer binding. To bind the property, earlier interests of record must be re-recorded every 30 or 40 years. Some interests are excluded from these acts, including those of a current posessor, visible easements and sometimes restrictive covenants, remainders, reversions and other future interests. This is a broad sketch of these acts and doesn't get into the details. In legal practice, you would need to become familiar with the law of your state.

Exercise 11-13. Applying Complex Recording & Title Laws

Analyze the problems that follow and predict the legal outcomes—who owns Blackacre?

1. Y → O	O records
O → M	No recording
O → P	P records
	M records
P → Z	Z records

---

2. Y → O	O records
O → A	No recording
O → X	X *knows* of earlier O → A conveyance
	A records
	X records
X → Z	Z records. Z has no actual notice.

---

3. Y → O	O records
O → A	No recording

O → X	X *knows* of earlier O → A conveyance
	X records
	A records
X → Z	Z records. Z has no actual notice.

____

4. O → Y	Y forged the deed and recorded it.
Y → Z	

____

5. Assume the same facts as 4, except O signed the deed based on fraudulent inducement.

____

6. O → R	No recording
R → S	S records R-S deed
O → T	T records

7. Consider what strategies are most effective for you learning complex materials. What has worked well for you? You may find active learning, continual application and recursion (coming back around to something several times) to be helpful. What else might you try?

Title Insurance and Registration

You can probably see why getting title insurance is wise. It is the main method for title assurance for most buyers. Most buyers purchase it. It is common practice in the U.S. for title companies to do the title searches for real estate transactions as part of the insurance process. Indeed, lenders routinely require that buyers obtain title insurance as a condition for lending the purchase money—because the lender also wants title protections, since the property is security for the loan.

Title insurance companies provide detailed information about the state of the title, drawing on the public records, including defects and encumbrances. This helps the buyer discover such issues prior to closing—and possibly get out of the deal or renegotiate. After the closing, insurance will compensate the buyer for losses that are covered within the scope of the contract—such as losing the entire property due to a forged deed. The insurance policy may also include coverage for defending title such as paying for an attorney's work and other litigation costs. However, insurance is *not* a panacea for buyers that covers all possible defects. The contracts are written to carefully *exclude* coverage against some risks. For example, some contracts exclude adverse possession or boundary dispute claims that could have been discovered through a survey or inspection—some are limited to defects that are not "of public record" like wild deeds.

Title Registration

A small number of states have a voluntary system that allows for adjudication of title by a court that results in registration or a certificate of title. This is sometimes called the "Torrens System," named after Sir Robert Torrens, who created it. Title registration is a legally binding conclusion by a court on the state of the title—who owns it and any existing limitations against it (such as a covenant). For title assurance, a buyer can simply examine the registration before the closing and then afterwards bring a deed to the register and obtain a new certificate.

Real Estate Finance

Mortgages and Deeds of Trust

Most people cannot afford to buy a home unless they borrow money to finance the purchase price. If the borrower's credit is good enough (taking into account income, assets and debts), the buyer typically can get a loan from a financial institution. A bank is willing to loan the money to be paid back with interest if: 1) it is likely that the buyer will be able to afford to make periodic payments on the loan (usually monthly); and 2) in the event the buyer defaults and fails to pay, the bank can access collateral (an asset—the house) to collect against to secure payment. Financial institutions also prefer to have priority among creditors and will record and also negotiate to create that protection. This topic is taken up in a subsection below. The buyer wants to be able to borrow money at as low a rate of interest as possible—and to pay the loan back in installments over time (as income is earned in the future). The repayment period for residential loans is traditionally quite long—15 to 30 years. Interest rates are frequently fixed, although they can be adjustable (adjustable rate mortgages—ARMs) or have a larger sum due at certain points (a balloon payment).

The most common form of real estate finance is a contract between the borrower and lender that has two parts—a note and a mortgage. The promissory note is the buyer's personal promise to repay the loan. A mortgage is a grant from the borrower to the lender of a security interest in the property that is purchased. Note that a mortgage is a property interest. The borrower is the grantor of the mortgage and so is called the mortgagor, and the lender is the mortgagee. The mortgage further grants the bank the right to foreclose on the property in the event that the mortgagor defaults on the loan. Foreclosure gives the bank the right to force a sale and collect repayment of the loan from the proceeds of sale. Mortgages also frequently include an "acceleration clause" that makes the entire loan immediately due if the buyer fails to timely pay the full amount of the monthly installments. Additionally, a mortgage agreement usually includes promises by the buyer to keep up the property (not to commit waste), to pay taxes and to maintain property insurance. These obligations protect the property and help maintain its value for both the buyer and the lender.

Another popular method for secured financing for real estate is a Deed of Trust. This includes the same note and security interest with a right of foreclosure in exchange for a loan of money as just described, except that a trustee is brought in to hold and manage title in accordance with the parties' agreement while the loan is outstanding. Title to the property is transferred by way of a deed to a trustee. If and when the loan is paid off, the trustee is obligated to transfer title to the buyer/owner. However, the arrangement is set up this way primarily to confer a power of sale in the trustee in the event of a default by the buyer so that the trustee will directly conduct a foreclosure sale. The trustee essentially is an agent of both parties and must follow the agreement about the foreclosure process. A deed of trust is a tool for creating a private management structure in the event of foreclosure. It is not intended to be, nor is it treated in law, like an ordinary trust—and the trustee does not have the usual duties.

Exercise 11-14. Document Review—Granting Clause in Deed of Trust

Review the following sample terms granting title to property to a trust by way of a deed of trust and authorizing a power of sale. The main paragraph below is a (modified) excerpt from a deed made available by the National Consumer Law Center (www.nclc.org). It is used for educational purposes only. It cannot be used for drafting; it is incomplete.

DEED OF TRUST

THIS DEED OF TRUST, made January 15, 2016, between the Trustor, Robert J. Kelly ("Trustor") and the trustee Wilmington Trust ("Trustee") and the beneficiary First Bank ("Beneficiary" or "Lender").

TRANSFER OF RIGHTS IN THE PROPERTY

This Security Instrument secures to Lender: (i) the repayment of the Loan, and all renewals, extensions and modifications of the Note; and (ii) the performance of Borrower's covenants and agreements under this Security Instrument and the Note. For this purpose, Trustor irrevocably GRANTS and CONVEYS to Trustee, in trust, with a power of sale, the following described property located in Orange County, California with the following legal description [describe and include recording information] which currently has the address of 111 Yorba Linda Way, Mendicino, California 19423.

As explained in more detail below, although many states allow a power of sale foreclosure, not all states do. Deeds of trusts then are not enforceable in states that require judicial supervision of foreclosure. Setting aside these differences, mortgages and deeds of trust are equivalents in real estate finance law.

Foreclosures

Process and Mortgagor Protections

Property owners sometimes face difficult times. What if you lose your job and cannot pay your mortgage? Sometimes lenders will be patient, but at some point, if a buyer consistently fails to pay as promised, the mortgagee can begin the foreclosure process. This section focuses on this process and an array of laws that might apply. You will see that a body of law has developed to provide some significant protections for mortgagors.

We will refer to this simple example to illustrate the concepts. Bob purchased his home several years ago for $100,000. To finance the purchase, he paid $10,000 as a down payment and borrowed $90,000 from First Bank. Bob and First Bank entered into a contract where, in exchange for a loan, Bob signed a promissory note and granted a mortgage. Bob promised to repay the loan with 5% interest in monthly installments over 30 years. Bob failed to pay his mortgage for the last 5 months. The bank is pursuing foreclosure.

Equity of Redemption (pre-foreclosure). Mortgagors like Bob who have fallen behind on their payments have a right to "redeem" the property and stop the foreclosure. This occurs by either paying the entire amount due on the loan, or in some states, just catching up with the payments by paying the past amounts due but not paid. It's a second chance, with some extra time. This right is called the equity of redemption.

This law developed in response to the old English system that greatly disadvantaged borrowers. Under the ancient law of England, a morgtagee/lender would take title to the subject property (as a defeasible fee) and also had the right of possession. The mortgagor/borrower would become the full owner only if and when the entire loan was paid off on the appointed due date. If the buyer failed to pay on that day, the lender/owner would keep title to the property; any payments that had been made; and the property value over the amount of the loan. This resulted in a windfall to lenders and left borrowers with nothing. (We will study the installment land contract which is a modern form of this arrangement but with more buyer protections.) Borrowers sought relief in courts of equity and were granted more time to pay the debt and redeem the property.

A borrower's interest came to be called the equity of redemption. This is the source of the term equity people now use commonly—equity is the amount of value an owner has in the property that exceeds the amount owed on the loan. Note that in modern law, equity belongs to the mortgagor/owner, *not* the lender. The equity of redemption continues to be strongly protected, so much so that an attempt to waive the right in a mortgage agreement is typically invalid. At some point, however, there must be a remedy for a lender with a mortgage against a borrower who fails to pay. The old system had strict foreclosure—if after having more time, the borrower did not pay the loan—then the lender would retain title free of any claims of the borrower. Strict foreclosure has been viewed as unfair and is substantially abolished in the U.S. The legal process we have now is a foreclosure sale managed either privately or by a judge, depending on the state and the terms of the contract. As you will see, there are laws that regulate the process to a significant degree.

Here is a bit more on the evolution of the law that might be helpful to your understanding of these materials. Again, drawing on the old English system, states in the U.S. adopted a title theory for mortgages that conceptualized a lender as the titled owner (title theory). Over time, many states moved to the contemporary model that views a mortgage as a lien against the property only, with the mortgagor as the titled owner (lien theory). Today, differences among states have eroded. Title theory states now view mortgages as a security interest with ownership vested in the mortgagor. Accordingly, title theory states and lien theory states are now substantively the same.

Statutory Right of Redemption (post-foreclosure). Another important right mortgagors may have is the right to redeem the property *after foreclosure*. States that have enacted a statutory right of redemption allow the defaulting borrower to buy back the property by paying the price paid at the foreclosure sale. Mortgagors are usually given six months to a year after foreclosure to exercise this right and are entitled to retain possession during this time. About half the states have enacted such statutes. It usually applies only to homes and farms.

The statutory right of redemption is designed to protect buyers in a number of ways—and in particular to encourage a sales price that is closer to fair market value (FMV). If the property is sold below market price, a borrower may be successful in finding a new lender to help finance the re-purchase because the loan amount will be less than the property value (so it's a safer loan). Of course, lenders may not be too eager to lend money to someone who has just defaulted on another mortgage. On the other hand, it is possible that the mere existence of a right of redemption will suppress the sales price. Wouldn't you pay less for a home that you might not be able to retain ownership of and that you can't possess for another 6–12 months? However, as is discussed further below, the market for foreclosure sales frequently is much more limited than the regular real estate market and often does not yield a sale price that approximates fair market value. This rule, among others, is an effort to produce a fairer process for mortgagors.

Be sure to distinguish the statutory right of redemption which allows a mortgagor to buy back the property *after* a foreclosure sale from the equity of redemption which is a right to pay off the loan or arrears *before* foreclosure to stop it from going forward.

Short Sales. You have probably heard the saying that a "property is underwater." That is when the amount owed on a mortgage is more than the value of the property. When the property is sold, the proceeds would not satisfy the mortgage. Still, a buyer who is in default of the mortgage might be better off selling the property on the regular real estate market, hoping to gain a better sales price than in a foreclosure sale and have more money to pay down the loan. In this circumstance, some banks are willing to agree to a "short sale," recognizing that the sale proceeds will be short of covering the mortgage. The bank is playing the odds too, hoping to get as much money out of the sale as possible. In a short sale, the bank agrees to release the mortgage against the property so the new owner will not have the prospect of foreclosure hovering over the transaction. This facilitates a sale and likely increases the selling price. Although the mortgage will be extinguished, that does not necessarily mean the borrower is free from the obligation to pay off the loan. The bank may still enforce the promissory note.

Can you see why it is important for the bank to agree that the mortgage will be satisfied in a short sale? If, in the regular course, the property were sold but the mortgage was not paid off and satisfied at sale, the mortgage would continue to be a cloud on title and be a priority interest against subsequent creditors. This might make it difficult for the new buyer to get a loan from a bank. Also, if the original mortgagor does not pay off the mortgage amount that is still owed, then the original mortgagee continues to have a right of foreclosure.

Foreclosure Sales. There are two basic approaches to conducting foreclosure sales: through judicial supervision or via a power of sale with the process being conducted privately by the lender or by a trustee under a deed of trust. The property goes up for sale to the public under either approach. Which method is used depends on state law and what the parties agreed to by contract. Most states allow non-judicial foreclosure. Each has pros and cons. There are important process and substantive fairness protections in a judicially supervised sale—so much so that some states require it. Yet things might move slowly and with significant expense. It is predictably faster and less expensive in a power of sale foreclosure—if a lender or trustee manages the sale. A lender sale raises concerns about self-dealing and risks less protection for buyers. The lender is, after all, an opposing party. These concerns are reduced if a disinterested trustee conducts the sale. Still, the system is private and won't come to the attention of a court unless there is litigation.

Concern forAdequacy of Sales Price. An issue that is of great concern to mortgagors and to our system of laws more generally in the foreclosure process is that it tends to yield a sale price that is below fair market value. The foreclosure market is not the same as in the regular real estate market where there are real estate agents involved in advertising the property and facilitating exposure of the property to multiple potential buyers. Instead, very few bidders typically come to the public auction. The lender frequently is a bidder and is at a significant advantage because the bank does not have to come up with cash and can instead simply offer to buy the property for the amount owed on the loan. That happens recurrently. This results in below market prices and can result in the lender who is now a buyer realizing the equity in the property, thus depriving the mortgagor.

Let's return to our example with mortgagor Bob who lost his job. Assume Bob owes $80,000 on the loan at the time of foreclosure. (To simplify, we ignore interest payments.) Assume the fair market value of property is $100,000. If that was the price paid at the foreclosure sale, then First Bank would be paid the $80,000 they are owed and Bob would keep the $20,000 in equity. If the value of Bob's property had gone up, say to $120,000, then Bob would enjoy that increase—he would have $40,000 in equity from the sale and the bank would still get repaid $80,000.

Look what happens though if the bank is the only or highest bidder at the foreclosure sale and bids the amount of the loan—$80,000. Then Bob does not get paid his equity.

The bank ends up with it. The bank could soon thereafter sell (flip) the property for at least $100,000 or perhaps $120,000 and would have an excellent profit on the set of transactions.

Declining values can also make things difficult for a mortgagor when combined with the potential suppression of the sale price in foreclosure. Assume Bob's home is underwater. The FMV is $70,000, he owes $80,000 to the bank. If the property sold for $70,000, the bank is entitled to all the proceeds and Bob would still owe the bank the additional $10,000—a deficiency. (Remember Bob promised to pay, the mortgage was just security for that and is being exhausted.) Bob also lost the $20,000 investment he put in.

Now if the bank makes a below market bid, say for $60,000, Bobs problems are exacerbated. He would now have a deficiency of $20,000 he owes personally to the bank. The bank can flip the house for $70,000 and realize the advantage of a below market purchase price.

This system raises concerns about fairness. It may well be inconsistent with the buyer's understanding and agreement in the note and mortgage—the idea being this was *not* what the mortgagor bargained for. Larger policy concerns arise as well—particularly protections for lay consumers—people buying a home and contracting with sophisticated commercial lenders. A set of foreclosure laws and process protections are designed to reduce the risks of loss to mortgagors. You have already encountered some of them. The discussion following introduces you to several more.

Deficiencies and Anti-Deficiency Statutes. Assume again that Bob is in foreclosure and that the amount he owes on the loan is more than the value of the property. The property sells for $70,000, and that amount is given to the bank at foreclosure, but Bob owed the bank $80,000. That leaves a deficiency—Bob still owes $10,000, as he promised to pay the entire loan back. If state law allows, the lender/mortgagee can get a deficiency judgment against Bob (a court order that he is obligated to pay) and seek to collect payment from Bob personally. Of course, pragmatically, this may not be all that helpful to the lender, because Bob may not have other assets or the money to pay.

Some jurisdictions have anti-deficiency statutes that prohibit lenders from obtaining deficiency judgments. So a borrower like Bob would walk away from foreclosure with no remaining liability to pay the debt. From a policy perspective, there are differing views. Prohibiting deficiency judgments incentivizes lenders to be more careful in their lending practices. On the other hand, that allows buyers to avoid contractual obligations to a significant degree.

The note and mortgage contract might also address whether the lender can collect a judgment against the borrower for a deficiency. If the parties agree that the borrower will be responsible to pay any deficiency, it is a "recourse" loan. These are enforceable only in a state that allows deficiency judgments. Conversely, the parties might agree that the lender's right to collect the debt is limited to the amount of the collateral—to the value of the property or to the proceeds from the sale of the property. That means if the sales proceeds are less than the amount owed, there is no deficiency. This is called a "non-recourse" loan. A transaction could be set up this way and is enforceable in any jurisdiction. Be sure you understand why.

Mortgagee's Duties and Gross Inadequacy of Price

Another tool is available to challenge the adequacy of a foreclosure sale price. A foreclosure sale can be set aside if the sale price is "grossly inadequate," meaning so inadequate it "shocks the conscience." Here is what the Restatement (Third) of Property § 8.3 cmt. b provides:

> "Gross inadequacy" cannot be precisely defined in terms of a specific percentage of fair market value. Generally, however, a court is warranted in invalidating a sale where the price is less than 20 percent of fair market value and, absent other foreclosure defects, is usually not warranted in invalidating a sale that yields in excess of that amount.

Exercise 11-15. *In re Krohn* and *Murphy v. Financial Development Corp.*

These next two cases demonstrate a number of the legal principles you are studying in this section. They also add some new layers. You see the general rule of "gross inadequacy" play out in *Krohn. Krohn* also addresses the issue of whether this standard applies to a trustee sale under a Deed of Trust. In *Murphy*, you will discover the obligations that mortgagees may have to ensure an adequate price. Note that *Murphy* goes further than many states do at this point in time. It reflects some reforms that critics have suggested are much needed, particularly in light of the recent mortgage crisis where many, many borrowers ended up in foreclosure and lost their homes.

1. Fill out the chart below that summarizes mortgagor protections. Think through the application of all these rules to these two cases.

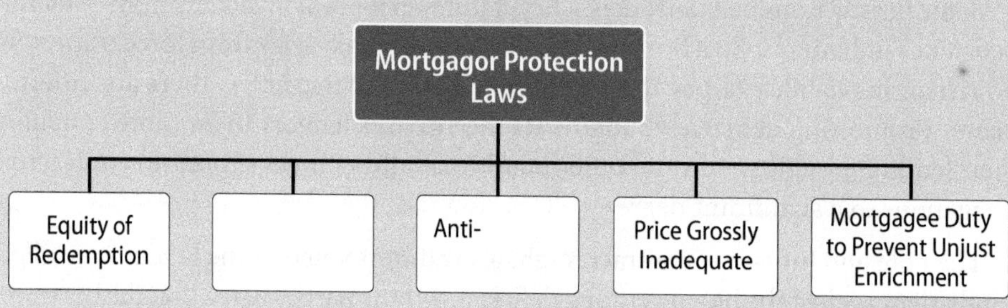

2. Consider, too, how should the system regulate the relationship between the borrower and the lender in the context of a foreclosure? What approach is best?

In re Krohn v. Sweetheart Properties

52 P.3d 774 (Ariz. 2002)

FELDMAN, J. Linda Lorraine Krohn (Krohn) filed a chapter 13 bankruptcy petition that was dismissed. Shortly after that dismissal, her home was sold to Sweetheart Properties, Ltd. (Sweetheart) at a trustee's sale conducted under authorization of a deed of trust. She filed a second bankruptcy petition seeking to have the sale of her home vacated for gross inadequacy of price. Bankruptcy Judge Redfield T. Baum certified a question of Arizona law to this court: "May a trustee's sale of real property[under a deed of trust] be set aside solely on the basis that the bid price was grossly inadequate?"

FACTS

The facts of this case were well described by Judge Baum. The following facts are relevant to our disposition and are quoted from his minute entry of March 31, 2001:

> The facts before the court are undisputed. Debtor filed this case on September 29, 2000. The debtor was in default on the payments on her home and her lender scheduled a trustee's sale. Prior to the scheduled sale, the debtor filed her first Chapter 13 case on February 27, 2000. That case was dismissed on August 28, 2000 because she had not complied with certain requirements in her Chapter 13 case. Prior to the dismissal, the lender moved for stay relief. In its motion, the lender stated that a trustee's sale "was originally scheduled for July 15, 2000 and that the Trustee's Sale was postponed and will be postponed from time to time, pending authorization from this Court that such Sale may take place." Debtor filed a response and contested the motion for stay relief.
>
> On or about September 24, 2000, the debtor receive [*sic*] a letter from her lender, which stated in part:
>
> > "The mortgage for the property in which you are living is about to be foreclosing (sometimes referred to as repossessed). We expect that ownership of the property will be transferred to ______ probably within the next 60 to 90 days."
>
> In fact, the trustee's sale was held on September 27, 2000. The amount paid at that sale was $10,304.00 by Sweetheart Properties, LTD, an Arizona corporation ("Sweetheart"). Sweetheart was a purchaser who bought in good faith and without any notice about the dealings between the debtor and her lender, including the letter described above.
>
> The debtor states that her residence is worth at least $57,500.00 and no other evidence of value has been presented to the court by the parties. The foregoing facts are compounded by the fact that debtor is disabled and resides in the residence with her two daughters.

In the present case the winning (and only) bid was slightly more than $10,000 for a property worth $57,000. Judge Baum found "the price paid is not merely inadequate but under applicable case law 'grossly' inadequate because the price was less than 20% of fair market value...." Our analysis of the question certified is informed by Judge Baum's finding that the price paid was *grossly* inadequate.

JUDICIAL FORECLOSURE

Sales in actions to foreclose mortgages are subject to judicial review for substantive fairness as well as for procedural compliance. Thus, it is well established that such sales can be overturned based on price alone. "Where a grossly inadequate price is bid, such as shocks one's conscience, an equity court may set aside the sale, thus insuring within limited bounds a modicum of protection to a party who has absolutely no control over the amount bid and this, in effect, insures that the foreclosed property is not 'given away.' (Citation omitted)

But this does not apply to bids that are merely *inadequate* when compared to the fair market value of the property. As our court of appeals has explained, the rule has a long history in this state:

> Since the case of *McCoy v. Brooks*, 9 Ariz. 157, 80 P. 365 (1905) the general rule in Arizona dealing with vacation of execution sales because of inadequate bids is that mere inadequacy of price, where the parties stand on an equal footing and there are no confidential relations between them, is not, in and of itself, sufficient to authorize vacation of the sale unless the inadequacy is so gross as to be proof of fraud or shocks the conscience of the court.

(Citations omitted.)

DEED OF TRUST AND BORROWERS PROTECTION FROM INEQUITY

Unlike their judicial foreclosure cousins that involve the court, deed of trust sales are conducted on a contract theory under the power of sale authority of the trustee. They are therefore held without the prior judicial authorization ordered in a mortgage foreclosure. "[A] power of sale is conferred upon the trustee of a trust deed under which the trust property may be sold ... after a breach or default in performance of the contract or contracts, for which the trust property is conveyed as security...." A.R.S. § 33–807(A).

The deed of trust scheme is a creature of statutes that do not contain explicit provisions for courts to set aside non-judicial sales based on the price realized at the sale, and no policy for such action has yet evolved with these sales as there has in judicial foreclosure sales.

The deed of trust provisions were added to Arizona law in 1971 following complaints by representatives of the mortgage industry that the "mortgage and foreclosure process in Arizona [was] unnecessarily time-consuming and expensive." It was said at the time that an uncontested $25,000 mortgage foreclosure could take eight months and a contested foreclosure twelve to fourteen months. The deed of trust alternative permitted lenders to bypass this time-consuming and expensive judicial foreclosure by simply using their new power of sale authority to sell the property securing a delinquent loan after complying with statutory procedural requirements. There is even a statutory presumption of procedural fairness and accuracy by the mere completion of a sale. "The trustee's deed shall raise the presumption of compliance with the requirements of ... this chapter...." A.R.S. § 33–811(B). Commenting on the two foreclosure methods, this court has said:

> A mortgage generally may be foreclosed only by filing a civil action while, under a Deed of Trust, the trustee holds a power of sale permitting him to sell the property out of court with no necessity of judicial action. *The Deed of Trust statutes thus strip borrowers of many of the protections available under a mortgage.* Therefore, lenders must strictly comply with the Deed of Trust statutes, and the statutes and Deeds of Trust must be strictly construed in favor of the borrower.

Patton v. First Federal Sav. & Loan Ass'n, 118 Ariz. 473, 477, 578 P.2d 152, 156 (1978) (emphasis added).

Aside from the issue in this case, the primary loss in protection for deed of trust borrowers lies in the absence of redemptive right because purchasers at a deed of trust sale no longer take title subject to a mortgagor's six-month right of redemption. Most observers could regard that loss of right as quite disadvantageous to the mortgagor. However, an offsetting theory holds that because there is less uncertainty as a consequence of the elimination of redemptive rights and because there is no judicial oversight, bidders can afford to offer higher prices at a deed of trust sale.

The present case is one of first impression as neither we nor our court of appeals has ever considered the particular issue of setting aside a deed of trust sale for *gross* inadequacy of price. We also note that the statutes dealing with deeds of trust are silent on that question. Moreover, as we have already discussed, we have always followed the rule that courts of equity have the power to vacate a judicial sale for gross inadequacy of price compared to fair market value even though there is no express statutory authorization to do so.

CONCLUSION

As we said earlier, if one result of our adoption of RESTATEMENT § 8.3 is that slightly higher prices prevail for sales conducted at the margin of the twenty percent yardstick, then we believe public policy is served. Accepting Sweetheart's argument and approving the sale in question would yield an inequitable and illogical result. It would protect the financial interests of defaulting mortgagors with high debt who receive credit for fair market value when creditors pursue a deficiency judgment and would neglect the financial interests of defaulting mortgagors with low debt, like Krohn, who lose all or nearly all their equity to a grossly inadequate bid price.

The rule we adopt today is consistent with our legislature's concern for debtors and its desire to respond to needs of the mortgage and home lending industry. The interests of debtors in need are protected without changing the obligations of debtors or the rights of lenders or trustees conducting valid sales, without throwing into disorder the well-established procedures for making purchases at those sales, and without creating risk for purchasers seeking bargains, albeit fair ones.

For the foregoing reasons we answer the question in the affirmative. We adopt RESTATEMENT (THIRD) OF PROPERTY: MORTGAGES § 8.3: a sale of real property under power of sale in a deed of trust may be set aside solely on the basis that the bid price was *grossly* inadequate.

Murphy v. Financial Development Corp.

495 A.2d 1245 (N.H. 1985)

DOUGLAS, J. The plaintiffs brought this action seeking to set aside the foreclosure sale of their home, or, in the alternative, money damages.

The plaintiffs purchased a house in Nashua in 1966, financing it by means of a mortgage loan. They refinanced the loan in March of 1980, executing a new promissory note and a power of sale mortgage, with Financial Development Corporation as mortgagee. The note and mortgage were later assigned to Colonial Deposit Company.

In February of 1981, the plaintiff Richard Murphy became unemployed. By September of 1981, the plaintiffs were seven months in arrears on their mortgage payments, and had also failed to pay substantial amounts in utility assessments and real estate taxes. After discussing unsuccessfully with the plaintiffs proposals for revising the payment schedule, rewriting the note, and arranging alternative financing, the lenders gave notice on October 6, 1981, of their intent to foreclose.

During the following weeks, the plaintiffs made a concerted effort to avoid foreclosure. They paid the seven months' mortgage arrearage, but failed to pay some $643.18 in costs and legal fees associated with the foreclosure proceedings. The lenders scheduled the foreclosure sale for November 10, 1981, at the site of the subject property. They complied with all of the statutory requirements for notice.

At the plaintiffs' request, the lenders agreed to postpone the sale until December 15, 1981. They advised the plaintiffs that this would entail an additional cost of $100, and that the sale would proceed unless the lenders received payment of $743.18, as well as all mortgage payments then due, by December 15. Notice of the postponement was posted on the subject property on November 10 at the originally scheduled time of the sale, and was also posted at the Nashua City Hall and Post Office. No prospective bidders were present for the scheduled sale.

In late November, the plaintiffs paid the mortgage payment which had been due in October, but made no further payments to the lenders. An attempt by the lenders to arrange new financing for the plaintiffs through a third party failed when the plaintiffs refused to agree to pay for a new appraisal of the property. Early on the morning of December 15, 1981, the plaintiffs tried to obtain a further postponement, but were advised by the lenders' attorney that it was impossible unless the costs and legal fees were paid. At the plaintiffs' request, the attorney called the president of Financial Development Corporation, who also refused to postpone the sale. Further calls by the plaintiffs to the lenders' offices were equally unavailing.

The sale proceeded as scheduled at 10:00 a.m. on December 15, at the site of the property. Although it had snowed the previous night, the weather was clear and warm at the time of the sale, and the roads were clear. The only parties present were the plaintiffs, a representative of the lenders, and an attorney, Morgan Hollis, who had been engaged to conduct the sale because the lenders' attorney, who lived in Dover, had been apprehensive about the weather the night before. The lenders' representative made the only bid at the sale. That bid of $27,000, roughly the amount owed on the mortgage, plus costs and fees, was accepted and the sale concluded.

Later that same day, Attorney Hollis encountered one of his clients, William Dube, a representative of the defendant Southern New Hampshire Home Traders, Inc. (Southern). On being informed of the sale, Mr. Dube contacted the lenders and offered to buy the property for $27,000. The lenders rejected the offer and made a counter offer of $40,000. Within two days a purchase price of $38,000 was agreed upon by Mr. Dube and the lenders and the sale was subsequently completed.

The plaintiffs commenced this action on February 5, 1982. The lenders moved to dismiss, arguing that any action was barred because the plaintiffs had failed to petition for an injunction prior to the sale. The master denied the motion. After hearing the evidence, he ruled for the plaintiffs, finding that the lenders had "failed to exercise good faith and due diligence in obtaining a fair price for the subject property at the foreclosure sale...."

The master also ruled that Southern was a bona fide purchaser for value, and thus had acquired legal title to the house. That ruling is not at issue here. He assessed monetary damages against the lenders equal to "the difference between the fair market value of the subject property on the date of the foreclosure and the price obtained at said sale." Having found the fair market value to be $54,000, he assessed damages accordingly at $27,000. He further ruled that "[t]he bad faith of the 'Lenders' warrants an award of legal fees." The lenders appealed.

The ... issue before us is whether the master erred in concluding that the lenders had failed to comply with the often-repeated rule that a mortgagee executing a power of sale is bound both by the statutory procedural requirements *and* by a duty to protect the interests of the mortgagor through the exercise of good faith and due diligence. We will not overturn a master's findings and rulings "unless they are unsupported by the evidence or are erroneous as a matter of law." (Citation omitted.)

The master found that the lenders, throughout the time prior to the sale, "did not mislead or deal unfairly with the plaintiffs." They engaged in serious efforts to avoid foreclosure through new financing, and agreed to one postponement of the sale. The basis for the master's decision was his conclusion that the lenders had failed to exercise good faith and due diligence in obtaining a fair price for the property.

This court's past decisions have not dealt consistently with the question whether the mortgagee's duty amounts to that of a fiduciary or trustee. This may be an inevitable result of the mortgagee's dual role as seller and potential buyer at the foreclosure sale, and of the conflicting interests involved. We need not label a duty, however, in order to define it. In his role as a seller, the mortgagee's duty of good faith and due diligence is essentially that of a fiduciary. Such a view is in keeping with "[t]he 'trend ... towards liberalizing the term [fiduciary] in order to prevent unjust enrichment.'" (Citations omitted.) A mortgagee, therefore, must exert every reasonable effort to obtain "a fair and reasonable price under the circumstances," even to the extent, if necessary, of adjourning the sale or of establishing "an upset price below which he will not accept any offer." (Citation omitted.)

What constitutes a fair price, or whether the mortgagee must establish an upset price, adjourn the sale, or make other reasonable efforts to assure a fair price, depends on the circumstances of each case. Inadequacy of price alone is not sufficient to demonstrate bad faith unless the price is so low as to shock the judicial conscience.

We must decide, in the present case, whether the evidence supports the finding of the master that the lenders failed to exercise good faith and due diligence in obtaining a fair price for the plaintiffs' property. We first note that "[t]he duties of good faith and due diligence are distinct.... One may be observed and not the other, and any inquiry as to their breach calls for a separate consideration of each." (Citation omitted.) In order "to constitute bad faith there must be an intentional disregard of duty or a purpose to injure." (Citation omitted.)

There is insufficient evidence in the record to support the master's finding that the lenders acted in bad faith in failing to obtain a fair price for the plaintiffs' property. The lenders complied with the statutory requirements of notice and otherwise conducted the sale in compliance with statutory provisions. The lenders postponed the sale one time and did not bid with knowledge of any immediately available subsequent purchaser. Further, there is no evidence indicating an intent on the part of the lenders to injure the mortgagor by, for example, discouraging other buyers.

There is ample evidence in the record, however, to support the master's finding that the lenders failed to exercise due diligence in obtaining a fair price. "The issue of the lack of due diligence is whether a reasonable man in the [lenders'] place would have adjourned the sale," (citation omitted) or taken other measures to receive a fair price.

In early 1980, the plaintiffs' home was appraised at $46,000. At the time of the foreclosure sale on December 15, 1981, the lenders had not had the house reappraised to take into account improvements and appreciation. The master found that a reasonable person in the place of the lenders would have realized that the plaintiffs' equity in the property was at least $19,000, the difference between the 1980 appraised value of $46,000 and the amount owed on the mortgage totaling approximately $27,000.

At the foreclosure sale, the lenders were the only bidders. The master found that their bid of $27,000 "was sufficient to cover all monies due and did not create a deficiency balance" but "did not provide for a return of any of the plaintiffs' equity."

Further, the master found that the lenders "had reason to know" that "they stood to make a substantial profit on a quick turnaround sale." On the day of the sale, the lenders offered to sell the foreclosed property to William Dube for $40,000. Within two days after the foreclosure sale, they did in fact agree to sell it to Dube for $38,000. It was not necessary for the master to find that the lenders knew of a specific potential buyer before the sale in order to show lack of good faith or due diligence as the lenders contend. The fact that the lenders offered the property for sale at a price sizably above that for which they had purchased it, only a few hours before, supports the master's finding that the lenders had reason to know, at the time of the foreclosure sale, that they could make a substantial profit on a quick turnaround sale. For this reason, they should have taken more measures to ensure receiving a higher price at the sale.

While a mortgagee may not always be required to secure a portion of the mortgagor's equity, such an obligation did exist in this case. The substantial amount of equity which the plaintiffs had in their property, the knowledge of the lenders as to the appraised value of the property, and the plaintiffs' efforts to forestall foreclosure by paying the mortgage arrearage within weeks of the sale, all support the master's conclusion that the lenders had a fiduciary duty to take more reasonable steps than they did to protect the plaintiffs' equity by attempting to obtain a fair price for the property. They could have established an appropriate upset price to assure a minimum bid. They also could have postponed the auction and advertised commercially by display advertising in order to assure that bidders other than themselves would be present.

Instead, as Theodore DiStefano, an officer of both lending institutions testified, the lenders made no attempt to obtain fair market value for the property but were concerned *only* with making themselves "whole." On the facts of this case, such disregard for the interests of the mortgagors was a breach of duty by the mortgagees.

Although the lenders *did* comply with the statutory requirements of notice of the foreclosure sale, these efforts were not sufficient in this case to demonstrate due diligence. At the time of the initially scheduled sale, the extent of the lenders' efforts to publicize the sale of the property was publication of a legal notice of the mortgagees' sale at public auction on November 10, published once a week for three weeks in the Nashua Telegraph, plus postings in public places. The lenders did not advertise, publish, or otherwise give notice to the general public of postponement of the sale to December 15, 1981, other than by posting notices at the plaintiffs' house, at the post office, and at city hall. That these efforts to advertise were ineffective is evidenced by the fact that no one, other than the lenders, appeared at the sale to bid on the property. This fact allowed the lenders to purchase the property at a minimal price and then to profit substantially in a quick turnaround sale.

We recognize a need to give guidance to a trial court which must determine whether a mortgagee who has complied with the strict letter of the statutory law has nevertheless violated his additional duties of good faith and due diligence. A finding that the mortgagee had, or should have had, knowledge of his ability to get a higher price at an adjourned sale is the most conclusive evidence of such a violation.

More generally, we are in agreement with the official Commissioners' Comment to section 3–508 of the Uniform Land Transactions Act:

> The requirement that the sale be conducted in a reasonable manner, including the advertising aspects, requires that the person conducting the sale use the ordinary methods of making buyers aware that are used when an owner is voluntarily selling his land. Thus an advertisement in the portion of a daily newspaper where these ads are placed or, in appropriate cases such as the sale of an industrial plant, a display advertisement in the financial sections of the daily newspaper may be the most reasonable method. In other cases employment of a professional real estate agent may be the more reasonable method. It is unlikely that an advertisement in a legal publication among other legal notices would qualify as a commercially reasonable method of sale advertising.

13 Uniform Laws Annotated 704 (West 1980). As discussed above, the lenders met neither of these guidelines.

While agreeing with the master that the lenders failed to exercise due diligence in this case, we find that he erred as a matterof law in awarding damages equal to "the difference between the fair market value of the subject property ... and the price obtained at [the] sale."

Such a formula may well be the appropriate measure where *bad faith* is found. In such a case, a mortgagee's conduct amounts to more than mere negligence. Damages based upon the *fair market value,* a figure in excess of a *fair* price, will more readily induce mortgagees to perform their duties properly. A "fair" price may or may not yield a figure close to fair market value; however, it will be that price arrived at as a result of due diligence by the mortgagee.

Where, as here, however, a mortgagee fails to exercise due diligence, the proper assessment of damages is the difference between a fair price for the property and the price obtained at the foreclosure sale. Accordingly, we remand to the trial court for a reassessment of damages consistent with this opinion.

Because we concluded above that there was no "bad faith or obstinate, unjust, vexatious, wanton, or oppressive conduct," on the part of the lenders, we see no reason to stray from our general rule that the prevailing litigant is not entitled to collect attorney's fees from the loser. Therefore, we reverse this part of the master's decision.

BROCK, J, dissenting [omitted].

Priority of Title at Foreclosure

Generally. As you studied earlier in the section on title assurance, the general rule is that the first in time to establish an ownership interest has priority of title. A very important exception that governs in many real estate transactions is that a *bona fide* purchaser for value will have priority over earlier unrecorded interests. To protect a property interest against claims from a BFP, an owner needs to duly record her interest. These rules are generally applicable to mortgages and other creditors with security interests in real property. A lender/mortgagee is a secured creditor, and once a mortgage is recorded, it has priority over other interests acquired and recorded later.

Here is how the priority of title system works at foreclosure if there are multiple secured creditors. Assume that there is a defaulting mortgagor named Owen and the property is sold at foreclosure. The mortgagor borrowed money to purchase the property from First Bank and granted a mortgage which was recorded immediately. Later, Owen borrowed more money and granted a mortgage to Second Bank, who immediately recorded the mortgage interest. At the time of the foreclosure sale, Owen owes $100,000 to First Bank and $50,000 to Second Bank. The sales proceeds are $120,000. What is the priority of claims among the banks? Because Second Bank took the mortgage with record notice of the first mortgage, First Bank is the senior creditor and Second Bank is junior. That means First Bank gets paid first and will be awarded $100,000 from the proceeds. Second Bank will receive the remaining amount of $20,000. If there were only $100,000 in proceeds, Second Band would receive nothing from the sale.

If allowed under state law and the loan terms, Second Bank may be able to obtain a deficiency judgment against Owen for personal liability to pay the outstanding debt of $30,000. However, the mortgage interest against the *property* will be extinguished at that point. That is because interests that are junior to the interest being foreclosed upon are terminated by the foreclosure. Interests that are senior to the interest being foreclosed will remain in force—perhaps a tax lien, for example. Another example that you may recall from the chapter on landlord-tenant law is that leases can be junior. If the lease is created after a recorded mortgage on the same property, the lease will be extinguished in a foreclosure. In contrast, if the lease is senior to the mortgage, it will survive the foreclosure

In summary:

1. Higher priority creditors get paid first.
2. Junior interests in the property are extinguished at foreclosure.

Subordination. Parties can contractually agree to change places in the priority line. A senior creditor might agree to subordinate her interest and become a junior creditor with respect to another's interest. For example, a tenant renting commercial property might agree in the lease contract that the lease is junior to any later recorded mortgage.

Super-Priority Rules for Purchase Money Mortgages. At the risk of over-simplification in a complex area of law with significant state law variation, this sub-part overviews basic principles. In limited circumstances, Purchase Money Mortgages ("PMM") are treated as "super-priority" interests—meaning the mortgage will be have better priority than would otherwise occur though the usual priority rules. The PMM can jump ahead in line. As the name implies, a PMM secures the loan given to the mortgagor to buy the property.

However, this rule is narrower than the term super-priority suggests. A PMM has priority only over mortgage claims and liens that arise: (1) out of the obligations of the buyer; (2)***prior*** to the buyer's acquisition of the property. If the buyer has secured creditors with interests that exist *before* the purchase of the property that *may reach* the property, those claims will be junior to the PMM. In some states, the PMM will enjoy this super-priority status even if the PMM is not recorded and even if the mortgagee knows about the earlier claims against title. Importantly, PMM priority can be defeated by ***subsequent*** mortgages or liens etc., by ordinary operation of the recording acts or through a subordination agreement. Of course, the holder of the PMM should record to protect the interest going forward.

Wait a minute, how can a buyer have pre-existing claims against property the buyer has yet to buy? It is possible. The main example is with a judgment lien. A judgment lien is created when a person is determined to owe money in a lawsuit and the court awards a lien to the creditor to enforce the judgment. (It is a debt collection tool.) These liens can attach not only to property the debtor currently owns but to property the debtor acquires after the lien is declared. (A judgment may be recorded in the county recording office even if the debtor owns no property.) The other situation where a PMM has super-priority is if a mortgage granted earlier by the buyer for another property includes a clause that says the mortgage applies to any after acquired property. Despite this, the PMM has priority over the earlier mortgage.

Here is an example. Olivander is buying a new home and has $10,000 as a down payment and is borrowing $90,000 for the balance of the purchase price from Town Bank. Town Bank knows Olivander is having some financial difficulties and is aware that there is a creditor with judgment lien of $25,000 against Olivander that is recorded. As part of the real estate transaction for his new home, Olivander grants a mortgage to Town Bank to secure the loan. Town Bank does not record. Olivander then borrows another $20,000, granting a mortgage to National Bank who records. Who has priority? Town Bank has priority over the judgment lien creditor (the general PMM rule), but National Bank has priority over Town Bank (the usual recording rule).

What if it is the seller who lends money to the buyer to purchase the property and is granted a mortgage to secure the loan? This is called a Vendor's PMM. A vendor's PMM also has super-priority—even over a third party PMM (lender is not the seller). If you come upon two PMMs competing for the front of the line, the Vendor PMM will probably win.

Special Rules for Mechanic's Liens. The following is an example of a situation that creates a mechanic's lien.

You decide to expand your house and build a third story master bedroom suite with a bathroom and balcony. You hire a great contactor to do the work, and she does a terrific job. Without justification, you decide to pay only half the money that you agreed to pay the contractor.

Mechanic's Liens (also called Contractor's liens) protect the contractor from non-payment in a situation like this. The contractor is entitled to a lien against the property that was improved to secure payment for the work and materials. The lien arises by operation of law and does not require consent of the property owner. Although recognized at common law, Mechanic's Liens are now primarily governed by statute. The liens have to be "perfected," usually by giving notice to the property owner and then recording the claim.

Mechanic's Liens may take priority over earlier recorded interests, because they are effective not from the date of recording but from the date that visible construction begins or is complete (the recording relates back to the time of construction). It could be that (1) work on the addition to the home begins, (2) a new buyer searches the record and finds no Mechanic's Lien and buys the property, and (3) the Mechanic's Lien is perfected and recorded. In most cases, the buyer will be bound by the lien because it has (limited) super-priority. Note however, that a Mechanic's Lien will not have priority over a PMM.

Installment Land Contracts

The installment land contract (or contract for a deed) is an alternative financing arrangement to a mortgage. Suppose S owns Red-Acre, and B agrees to buy it for $100,000. B cannot obtain a traditional mortgage and only has $5,000 for a down payment. S agrees to act as the lender. The parties agree to the terms that follow: (1) buyer makes the down payment and promises to pay the rest of the purchase price loaned by the seller in monthly installments (paying both principal and interest); (2) the buyer will take possession of the property and maintain the property (like an owner would); (3) the seller will retain title to the deed until the loan is fully repaid; (4) if the buyer defaults (even by missing one payment), the seller can cancel the contract, retake possession and keep all the payments made by the buyer. The seller's rights can be exercised without a foreclosure sale or judicial process—the buyer can be evicted since the seller still has title.

This functions like a mortgage in giving security to a seller for the loan and is set up for that purpose. However, it sidesteps the process and protections of mortgage law. It is reminiscent of the conditional fee used to secure loans in ancient English law that has been eclipsed by modern mortgage law. Why would any buyer sign up for a risky contract like this? An installment land contract may be the only financing structure available to a buyer—and it is regularly low income buyers with poor credit histories who use them, because they cannot qualify for a standard mortgage. This group of borrowers is more likely at risk for falling into default and losing the property. This is the same group of borrowers who struggled and faced foreclosure in large numbers as a result of the sub-prime mortgage market crises.

Recognizing its purpose is akin to a mortgage and the risk to buyers, the evolving modern trend is to treat an installment land contract as a mortgage and apply the mortgage laws you have been studying. More specifically, a small but growing number of states require foreclosure if the buyer defaults. That is also the position of the Restatement (Third) of Property § 3.4.

Other states are moving in a more piecemeal way and weave in some aspects of mortgage law. For example, a vendee may have a right of equitable redemption and be given another chance to pay off the loan. Additionally, a vendee may be able to make a successful claim for restitution and be awarded the difference between the total amount of the price already paid to vendor and the rental value of the property for the period of possession, plus any actual damages the seller incurred from the breach. This is similar to an owner's right to equity in the property.

That said, many states continue to enforce the land contract as it is written and allow a forfeiture of the money paid in by the buyer if there is a breach. A more traditional way to challenge the inequities that can arise from a deed contract is to make a classic contract law argument that the forfeiture clause—the term that allows to the seller to keep the property *and* all the payments that have been made—is a "penalty" and is not a fair liquidated damages clause. It will qualify as a penalty if there is a large difference between the amount paid to the seller and the rental value of the property plus actual damages. (Similar to the restitution calculation above.)

Exercise 11-16. Applying State Law Approaches

Taking the installment land contract example from above, assume B has paid the monthly installments of the principal of the loan for 15 years for a total price paid so far (ignoring interest) of $90,000 (including the down payment). B still owes $10,000 to S for the balance. Assume the property value is now $120,000. B then misses a few payments. S seeks to enforce the contract as written to repossess the property, to eject B and keep all the money paid so far as well as the property. Assume the rental value for the period of possession is $45,000.

How would B fare applying the differing state law approaches?

Index

O

P

T